Behavior Disorders in Children

Behavior Disorders in Children

SECOND EDITION

Harvey F. Clarizio
Michigan State University

George F. McCoy
Illinois State University

Thomas Y. Crowell
HARPER & ROW, PUBLISHERS
New York   Hagerstown   Philadelphia   San Francisco   London

BEHAVIOR DISORDERS IN CHILDREN, Second Edition

Copyright © 1976 by Harper & Row, Publishers, Inc.

The first edition of this book was published under the title
Behavior Disorders in School-Aged Children.

Library of Congress Cataloging in Publication Data

Clarizio, Harvey F 1934-
 Behavior disorders in children.

 First ed. published in 1970 under title: Behavior
disorders in school-aged children.
 Includes bibliographies and index.
 1. Mentally ill children—United States. 2. School
children—Health and hygiene. I. McCoy, George F.,
joint author. II. Title. [DNLM: 1. Child behavior
disorders. WS350 C591b]
RJ501.A2C57 1976   618.9′28′900973   75-37720
ISBN 0-690-00853-8

To the troubled children
whom we seek to help

Contents

Preface

The mental health problems of children are acknowledged to be a national concern. Yet few mental health professionals receive adequate training in understanding childhood disorders, and there have been few attempts in the literature to synthesize the psychological, developmental, and educational factors of variant behavior.

The purpose of writing this book was to gather and evaluate some accepted facts, principles, and theories about disturbed children and adolescents. We cast these in a developmental framework which we hope will be helpful to advanced undergraduates and beginning graduate students who are preparing to become clinical workers, special-education teachers, and, most important, regular classroom teachers. While the book is not a "how-to-do-it" manual, there are practical guides for coping with specific problems. The fundamental aim is to provide an introduction to the field of behavior disorders in children.

Primary among the changes made in the second edition are (1) the expansion of material devoted to the milder but more frequently occurring kinds of developmental problems that caregivers are apt to encounter, (2) an extensive revision of the chapter on treatment, (3) the updating of all the other chapters, (4) the inclusion of vignettes on children, (5) the inclusion of point-by-point summaries to assist students, and (6) increased readability of the book through the elimination of numerous lengthy quotes and technical tables and the addition of a glossary.

The book is organized around three major areas. Part I contains a discussion of the issues associated with normal development, together with possible outcomes. Attention is also paid to the concept of diagnosis and its current role in childhood disturbances. Finally, we consider both the incidence of emotional disturbance in youth and the factors influencing these disturbances.

Part II discusses six "types" of disorders among deviant youth, especially taking into account (1) the characteristics of various syndromes, (2) theories of etiology, and (3) various treatment programs. In keeping with the focus on school-aged youth, we have omitted certain topics customarily included in a text on the abnormal psychology of children such as habit-training problems. On the other hand, we have emphasized topics closely related to the adjustment of school-aged youth. The chapters on learning disabilities and on the socially disadvantaged are clear-cut examples of this emphasis.

Part III is concerned with intervention and prevention strategies and to this end we present some of the major approaches to therapy. Consonant with the data-oriented nature of the book, the first chapter appraises psychotherapy as a means of behavioral change and considers behavior-modification approaches, family therapy, reality therapy, and the medical use of drugs. We then discuss interventions available in the community setting. The next chapter, pertaining to classroom discipline, has been included for teachers and consultants to teachers who must cope with troublesome youth. Concluding the book is a chapter on preventive strategies.

No attempt has been made to present a consistent theoretical framework, although an eclectic sampling has been made of postulates stemming from psychoanalytic theories and/or learning theories. While we examine the contributions of biological and social forces to deviant behavior, we focus primarily on the role played by psychological factors. The most distinctive aspects of the book are, perhaps, its empirical orientation, its developmental base, and its psychoeducational emphasis.

Many people have contributed to the development of this book. We are especially grateful to Judith Worell and R. Stewart Jones for their perceptive reviews of the manuscript. We are also deeply indebted to Myrna Russell for her typing of the manuscript. Thanks are also extended to Mark Swerdlik and Robert Griffore for their careful library research.

PART I

Developmental and Diagnostic Considerations

Normality: A Developmental Perspective

In this chapter, we will deal with the confusion surrounding the concept of normality in children and try to suggest a more workable view thereof. What seems especially needed in the assessment of normality is evaluation from a developmental perspective. Such evaluation requires a consideration of normal maladjustment as well as of clinically deviant behaviors. It also requires a discussion of the stability of behavioral characteristics, especially those assumed to be abnormal. In implementing a developmental framework, we will show that all children have adjustment difficulties, but that having problems cannot necessarily be equated with pathology. We will then, in the section dealing with the controversial issue regarding the fate of deviant youth, critically examine the long-held assumption that emotional problems in children become more firmly entrenched with advancing age. Finally, following a consideration of two basic approaches to the issue of normality, a definition of normality will be cited and some guidelines stated for referral to mental-health professionals.

Normal Behavior Problems

Two points should be recognized at the outset: (1) Every parent, teacher, and clinician carries with him a set of norms and/or standards with which he evaluates the appropriateness of child behavior. (2) Over the years, certain behaviors have come to be seen as abnormal. Corresponding to these two assertions are two questions: (a) How do people acquire the norms against which they render judgmental decisions about normality or abnormality? (b) How realistically based are their judgments? In an attempt to answer these questions, we will look briefly at some of the major sources from which norms arise and then at studies that raise questions about how abnormal some behaviors are.

Parents, in addition to their life experiences, rely heavily on accessible literature that describes the mythical "average" child or perhaps confuses them with discussions of individual differences among children. Clinicians, in developing norms with which to evaluate child behavior, rely to a considerable degree on their training in psychopathology and on their clinical experiences with psychiatric populations, which may create a tendency in the beginning clinician to exaggerate the severity of many problems found in children. Teachers have been sensitized to emotional problems that children present in the classroom. Heightened teacher sensitization, stemming from college courses in education and psychology, is reflected in the fact that more children are referred to child-guidance clinics by schools than by any other agency.

Because of the current cultural propensity to be anxious about our anxieties, we may well be predisposed to overconcern about a good many minor or transient childhood problems. What may not be readily evident is the extent of problem behavior among normal children. The expanding knowledge of children indicates that "abnormal" behavior among children is plentiful. We now recognize that no child is completely free from emotional difficulties. The prevalence of problems is, in fact, so widespread that some psychologists doubt that these deviations should be regarded as abnormal. From a strictly statistical concept of normality, it is almost inadmissible to contend that such large numbers of children should be labeled as deviant. We are by no means implying that parents, teachers, and clinicians commonly overestimate the seriousness of childhood problems, or that we should dismiss problems of a developmental nature. It is our thesis, rather, that in assessing a child's behavior, we need to develop norms based on a more developmental frame of reference. Such norms can best be compiled through the study of problem behavior among fairly representative samples of children who are not pre-selected on a problem basis. The increasing focus of attention on children demands that more specific information be available regarding the significance of such behaviors so as to plan efficient and effective treatment regimens. What follows is a sampling of studies yielding information on the rates of variant behavior for children who are not regarded as problem youngsters.

Personal and School Problems

Berkeley Guidance Study. A study with which every student of child adjustment should be familiar is the Berkeley Guidance Study, beyond a doubt a landmark investigation in developmental problems of normal children (MacFarlane, Allen, & Honzik, 1954). Despite the limitations associated with longitudinal research, the Berkeley Guidance Study provides one of the best evaluative frames of reference available from a developmental standpoint. The study began in 1929 with the selection of every third child born in Berkeley, California, during an 18-month period from January 1, 1928, through June 30, 1929. The sample consisted of 252 youngsters, half of whom constituted the guidance group, and half of whom served as a control group. The present study concerns itself with the control group, whose developmental problems between the ages of 21 months and 14 years were studied through the use of open-ended interviews with mothers. The sample was admittedly biased in favor of the upper-middle-class socioeconomic population. Of the 126 subjects selected in infancy, 86 were still available for study at the age of 14. The 46 problems studied were subsumed under these categories: biological functioning and control (e.g., soiling); motor manifestations (e.g., nailbiting); social standards (e.g., lying); and personality patterns (e.g., shyness). The extensiveness of such problems is revealed in Table 1–1, which shows behavior problems manifested by one-third or more of this population at various age levels. The data contained in this chart offer us some crude norms for indicating deviant behaviors that are developmentally observed in a randomly selected group of children. Note that both sexes had an average of five or six problems at each level between 21 months and 11 years of age. From a statistical viewpoint of normality, these data do not support the contention that the average or normal child can be defined as one who has no problems.

AGE TRENDS. Basically, five developmental patterns were identified among the problems investigated. The problems, which declined with age, were (1) elimination controls (enuresis and soiling), (2) fears, (3) thumb-

Table 1–1. Behavior Problems Shown by One-Third or More of Normal Boys and Girls Aged 1¾-14 Years

Behavior		1¾	3	3½	4	5	6	7	8	9	10	11	12	13	14
Enuresis (diurnal & nocturnal)	B	+													
	G	+													
Soiling	B														
	G														
Disturbing dreams	B										+				
	G						+					+	+		
Restless sleep	B	+													
	G														
Insufficient appetite	B														
	G						+								
Food finickiness	B		+												
	G	+	+	+			+								
Excessive modesty	B														
	G														
Nailbiting	B													+	+
	G									+		+			
Thumbsucking	B														
	G	+	+												
Overactivity	B		+	+	+	+		+	+	+					
	G		+	+	+	+									
Speech	B														
	G														
Lying	B			+	+	+	+		+						
	G		+		+	+	+								
Destructiveness	B														
	G														
Overdependence	B														
	G														
Attention demanding	B														
	G														
Oversensitiveness	B			+	+	+		+	+	+	+	+	+		
	G			+	+	+	+	+	+	+	+	+	+	+	+
Physical timidity	B			+		+									
	G														
Specific fears	B		+	+	+	+	+	+	+	+		+			
	G	+	+	+	+	+	+	+	+			+			
Mood swings	B							−	−	−	+	+		+	
	G											+			
Shyness[a]	B	−	−	−	−	−	−	−							
	G											+			

Table 1–1. Continued

		Age													
		1¾	3	3½	4	5	6	7	8	9	10	11	12	13	14
Somberness	B					+									
	G						+								
Negativism	B			+		+									
	G				+										
Irritability	B														
	G														
Tempers	B	+	+	+	+	+	+	+	+	+	+	+	+	+	
	G	+	+	+	+	+	+	+				+			
Jealousy	B					+		+	+	+	+	+			
	G				+		+		+		+	+		+	
Excessive reserve[a]	B	−	−	−	−	+	+					+	+		
	G					+	+	+	+	+	+	+	+		+

[a] Data not obtained.

Source: J. MacFarlane, L. Allen, & M. Honzik. *A developmental study of the behavior problems of normal children between twenty-one months and fourteen years.* Berkeley: University of California Press, 1954. Reprinted by permission of The Regents of the University of California.

sucking, (4) destructiveness, and (5) temper outbursts. Only one problem, nailbiting, increased with age, although this too was beginning to drop off by age 14. Insufficient appetite and lying were problems that reached a peak and then subsided. Included among problems characterized by twin peaks were restless sleep, disturbing dreams, physical timidity, irritability, and demand for attention. The first elevation of these bimodal problems often occurred near the age of entrance into school, and the second elevation at the beginning of adolescence. Oversensitiveness was the sole problem unrelated to age.

SEX DIFFERENCES. Sex differences were also discovered in relation to certain problems, as shown in Table 1–2. The incidence for boys was significantly higher for such problems as overactivity, demand for attention, temper tantrums, and lying. Problems for girls more commonly centered around excessive modesty, shyness, and specific fears.

SIBLING ORDER. Another finding of interest deals with differences related to sibling order. For example, withdrawal and internalization patterns of adjustment were more common among first-born boys in contrast to more aggressive and competitive patterns of adjustment among non-first-born boys. Only two problems, thumbsucking and oversensitiveness, differentiated first-born girls from second-born girls. Interestingly, among the four sibling groups, it was the first-born girls who manifested more problems and had the most conflicting modes of adjustment.

Table 1–2.   Statistically Significant[a] Differences in the Incidence of Behavior Problems between Normal Boys and Girls Aged 1¾-13 Years

Age in Years	Boys	Girls
1¾	Diurnal enuresis Excessive emotional dependence Irritability	
3		Excessive modesty
4		Specific fears Thumbsucking
5	Temper tantrums	Thumbsucking Physical timidity
6		Food fussiness Oversensitiveness Mood swings
7	Stealing	Excessive emotional dependence Shyness Excessive reserve
8	Hyperactivity Temper tantrums Lying	Excessive modesty Excessive reserve
9	Excessive demanding of attention	Shyness Somberness
10		Excessive reserve
11	Lying Excessive demanding of attention Jealousy Competitiveness	Shyness
12	Overactivity Lying	Disturbing dreams Physical timidity
13	Overactivity Selfishness in sharing	Specific fears

[a] At the level of 5% or better.
Source: J. MacFarlane, L. Allen, & M. Honzik. *A developmental study of the behavior problems of normal children between twenty-one months and fourteen years.* Berkeley: University of California Press, 1954. Reprinted by permission of The Regents of the University of California.

The Buffalo Study.   Another study that deserves careful consideration in the examination of maladjustment among a nonpsychiatric childhood population was conducted by Lapouse and Monk (1958). These investigators conducted structured interviews with mothers of 482 randomly selected children in Buffalo between the ages of 6 and 12. The findings, as shown in Table 1–3, reinforce the findings of MacFarlane and his associates on the frequency of problems among a run-of-the-mill group of youngsters. Note that almost half of the 482 youngsters were rated as overactive or as having

Table 1–3.   The Frequency of Selected Behaviors in a Sample of Children Aged 6–12 Years as Reported by Mothers

Behavior	Percent of Children
Fears and worries, 7 or more present	43
Wetting bed within the past year	
All frequencies	17
Once a month or more	8
Nightmares	28
Temper loss	
Once a month or more	80
Twice a week or more	48
Once a day or more	11
Overactivity	49
Restlessness	30
Stuttering	4
Unusual movements, twitching or jerking (tics)	12
Biting nails	
All intensities	27
Nails bitten down (more severe)	27
Grinding teeth	14
Sucking thumb or fingers	
All frequencies	10
"Almost all the time"	2
Biting, sucking, or chewing clothing or other objects	16
Picking nose	26
Picking sores	16
Chewing or sucking lips or tongue or biting inside of mouth	11

Source: R. Lapouse & M. Monk. Fears and worries in a represenative sample of children. *Amer. Journal of Orthopsychiatry*, 1959, 29, 803–18. Copyright ©, the American Orthopsychiatric Association, Inc. Reproduced by permission.

at least 7 or more fears, according to the mothers' reports. These data would certainly suggest that such behaviors typically characterize normal development in children. Lapouse and Monk posed an interesting question: Is there an association between number of fears and worries and other so-called pathological behaviors, such as bedwetting, nightmares, and tension indicators? Surprisingly, no significant relationships were found despite the assumptions of some clinicians that fears and worries are symptomatic (or indicative) of other kinds of maladjustment.

In a later analysis, Lapouse and Monk (1964) divided the subjects according to sex, race, social class, and family size in order to disclose the relationships among these variables and the likelihood of behavioral deviations. Their findings may be summarized as follows:

1. Age was clearly the demographic factor most clearly associated with the occurrence of behavioral deviations. The prevalence of behavior deviations declined for school-age children as they grew older. In other words, the

younger children, ages 6 through 8, by far surpass the older children, ages 9 through 12, in the number of behavior deviations.

2. Boys have a higher incidence of behavior deviations than do girls. Sex differences were most pronounced with respect to management of behavior, for example, overactivity and teachers' complaints about behavior.

3. The frequency of behavior deviations was higher among black children than white children. Because of the socioeconomic differences between the two groups, it was not possible to evaluate racial differences adequately.

4. There were extremely few differences in the incidence of behavior deviations among the two white groups of different socioeconomic standings.

5. There seemed to be very little difference in the amount of deviant behavior between only children and children with siblings.

In short, younger elementary-school children, black children, and boys were, in descending order of susceptibility, the most likely to deviate from norms established on the 482 children used in the study.

The Oregon Study.   Another study that uses naturalistic observation of nonproblem children in their homes shows that the average child between the ages of 4 and 6 behaves in a way that parents consider deviant once every 3.17 minutes. Furthermore, the probability is one in four that a child will disobey any command his parents give him (Johnson, Wahl, Martin, & Johansson, 1973).

Common "Deviances" among Elementary-School Children

Of special significance to those working with school children is a study dealing solely with the prevalence of problem behavior symptoms in younger elementary-school children. This study confirmed earlier findings noting the high frequency of problem behavior symptoms in the general childhood population, the greater number of symptoms in boys, and the tendency for the number of these symptoms to decline with age (Werry & Quay, 1971). The sample in this study consisted of the entire school population in kindergarten through grade two in a Midwestern university town. Of the fifty-five examples of behavior symptomatic of disturbance studied, boys averaged 11.4 problems and girls averaged 7.6 problems.

As in the Lapouse and Monk study, the high prevalence rate of many symptoms is noted. For example, restlessness was present in 49% of boys, disruptiveness 46%, short attention span 43%, inattentiveness 43%, distractibility 48%.

One longitudinal study of 967 children in kindergarten through third grade shows that 41% of this population, which was essentially normal on socioeconomic, medical, intellectual, and school-readiness characteristics, was regarded as educationally handicapped. Special placement or services had been instituted for almost 25% of the population in this study. These findings, suggesting that schools are "oriented to a narrow band of expected pupil behavior," question the ability of present educational systems to accommodate the broad range of individual differences found within a typical school population, challenge the incidence figures of educational problems advanced by the U.S. Office of Education, and underscore the need for a diagnostic model that considers school systems as well as children (Rubin & Balow, 1971).

"Delinquent" Behavior

Additional evidence of behavior problems among normal children is forthcoming in studies on delinquency. In one study dealing with the extent of unrecorded delinquency, adolescents enrolled in institutions and in high school were asked to report anonymously whether or not they had ever engaged in any of a list of 23 acts of delinquency (Short & Nye, 1958). The most striking finding was the sweeping incidence of reported delinquency activities among the legally nondelinquent adolescents. The delinquents could be differentiated from the legally nondelinquent youth in terms of the frequency of reported delinquent acts. Yet 50% or more of the latter group reported skipping school, stealing things worth less than $2, buying or drinking alcoholic beverages, intentionally damaging property, and violating game laws. While the findings of this study should probably be tempered to some extent because of the limitations of the self-report method, the reader need only examine his own conscience relative to commission of similar acts during his high-school period to confirm the extensiveness of antisocial behavior. A certain amount of nose-thumbing is apparently not an uncommon phenomenon among adolescents in our society. Theft, property destruction, and other forms of antisocial behavior should, within limits, probably not be considered as deviant but within the boundaries of normality (Havighurst, 1966).

In sum, we are not implying that certain behaviors, such as stealing and nightmares, cannot be indicative of serious emotional disturbance in children. Also, we do not want to leave the impression that "normal maladjustments" are unimportant and therefore should be left to self-resolution. Though common, these problems are in need of alleviation since they distress both children and the adults who must deal with these disturbances. Table 1–4 is presented to assist the student in distinguishing between normal and deviant behavioral characteristics in children and their parents. Nor do we want to convey the impression that presumably normal children have as many problems as children seen at psychiatric clinics, for this is not the case (Conners, 1970). We have stressed, however, that the heightened concern about the emotional health of our youth, coupled with the sometimes faulty bases on which norms are developed, renders us somewhat prone at times to overlook a parsimonious, developmental interpretation. The magnitude of the problem might consequently be exaggerated in certain cases. For instance, in one study we are told that 58% of youngsters referred to a clinic as hyper-

Table 1–4. Development or Deviancy?

Tasks in Process

CHILD	PARENT (S)
To master greater physical prowess.	To help child's emancipation from parents.
To further establish self identity and sex role.	To reinforce self-identification and independence.
To work toward greater independence from parents.	To provide positive pattern of social and sex-role behavior.
To become aware of world-at-large.	To acclimatize child to world-at-large.
To develop peer and other relationships.	To facilitate learning, reasoning, communication, and experiencing.
To acquire learning, new skills, and a sense of industry.	To promote wholesome moral and ethical values.

Acceptable Behavioral Characteristics

General good health, greater body competence, acute sensory perception.	Ambivalent toward child's separation but encourage independence.
Pride and self-confidence; less dependence on parents.	Mixed feelings about parent-surrogates but help child to accept them.
Better impulse control.	Encourage child to participate outside the home.
Ambivalence re dependency, separation, and new experiences.	Set appropriate model of social and ethical behavior and standards.
Accepts own sex role; psychosexual expression in play and fantasy.	Take pleasure in child's developing skills and abilities.
Equates parents with peers and other adults.	Understand and cope with child's behavior.
Aware of natural world (life, death, birth, science); subjective but realistic about world.	Find other gratifications in life (activity, employment).
Competitive but well organized in play; enjoys peer interaction.	Are supportive toward child as required.
Regard for collective obedience to social laws, rules, and fair play.	
Explores environment; school and neighborhood basic to social-learning experience.	
Cognition advancing; intuitive thinking advancing to concrete operational level; responds to learning.	
Speech becomes reasoning and expressive tool; thinking still egocentric.	

Table 1–4. *Continued*

Minimal Psychopathology

CHILD
Anxiety and oversensitivity to new experiences (school, relationships, separation).

Lack of attentiveness; learning difficulties; lack of interest in learning.

Acting out; lying, stealing, temper outbursts; inappropriate social behavior.

Regressive behavior (wetting, soiling, crying, fears).

Appearance of compulsive mannerisms (tics, rituals).

Somatic illness: eating and sleeping problems, aches, pains, digestive upsets.

Fear of illness and body injury.

Difficulties and rivalry with peers, siblings, adults; constant fighting.

Destructive tendencies strong: temper tantrums.

Inability or unwillingness to do things for self.

Moodiness and withdrawal; few friends or personal relationships.

PARENT(S)
Disinclination to separate from child; or prematurely hastening separation.

Signs of despondency, apathy, hostility.

Foster fears, dependence, apprehension.

Uninterested in or rejecting of child.

Overly critical and censuring; undermine child's confidence.

Inconsistent in discipline or control; erratic in behavior.

Offer a restrictive, overly moralistic model.

Extreme Psychopathology

Extreme withdrawal, apathy, depression, grief, self-destructive tendencies.

Complete failure to learn. Speech difficulty, especially stuttering.

Extreme and uncontrollable antiscoial behavior (aggression, destruction, chronic lying, stealing, intentional cruelty to animals).

Severe obsessive-compulsive behavior (phobias, fantasies, rituals).

Inability to distinguish reality from fantasy.

Excessive sexual exhibitionism, eroticism, sexual assaults on others.

Extreme somatic illness; failure to thrive, anorexia, obesity, hypochrondriasis, abnormal menses.

Complete absence or deterioration of personal and peer relationships.

Extreme depression and withdrawal; rejection of child.

Intense hostility; aggression toward child.

Uncontrollable fears, anxieties, guilts.

Complete inability to function in family role.

Severe moralistic prohibition of child's independent strivings.

From Senn and Solnit (1968). Reprinted with permission of Lea and Febiger publishing company.

active were not judged to be so by any of the three staff members who examined them.[1] (Kenney et al., 1971). This study suggests that a sizable number of children who are referred for treatment as hyperactive do not require treatment. What might be best regarded as the exuberance of childhood was commonly viewed as pathologically hyperactive by the referral agencies. One wonders how many normally active youngsters are given medication because of "hyperactivity" or minimal brain dysfunction. As Hollister [quoted in Bendix, 1973] notes, "That a disorder (minimal brain dysfunction) usually believed to be relatively uncommon should become a major affliction of childhood is a mystifying matter."

When a "problem" such as restlessness or educational maladjustment is frequent, it is probably better to consider modifying the school setting rather than the child. Change in the situation (for example, allowing for more active participation in the case of a "restless" student), as opposed to personal change in the student, is most likely warranted.

The Stability of Deviant Behavior

What happens to youth when, because their coping abilities and defenses are not adequate to the environmental demands made upon them, deviancy results? Will the delinquent youth, for instance, become a wayward adult? What does the future hold for the schizophrenic child? for the neurotic youngster? In this section we will treat the neglected topic of stability.

We have seen that most children experience problems in the course of development and that the resolution of the difficulties in coping with environmental demands leads to differential modes of adjustment on the child's part. The question arises, however, as to whether childhood problems and maladaptive modes of behavior are transient or permanent in nature. In other words, does a child grow out of his problems with increasing age, or does he become a mentally ill adult? The answer to this question is of interest to theoreticians as well as to practitioners. Knowledge pertaining to the stability of deviant behavior furthers the theorist's understanding of both normal personality development and childhood psychopathology. Such knowledge better enables the clinician not only to predict the course and outcome of various behavior problems but also to focus treatment on the cases most in need of professional intervention.

Psychologists differ in their answers to this question of stability. Clinicians are inclined to view childhood problems as being of a chronic nature, whereas developmental psychologists view them as being of a less persistent nature. The conflicting views may be a function of the populations studied (psychiatric versus nonpsychiatric subjects), the type of research design (retrospective versus follow-up), and the number of years involved in the follow-up, as well as the status at the time of follow-up investigations (stu-

---

1. The possibility remains that the child's hyperactivity varies as the child changes settings.

dent versus adult). We will try to take these various factors into account in our discussion. We will look first at studies conducted on the children during the school years and then at research dealing with adjustment during the postschool years.

Maladjustment during the School Years

Studies Supporting Persistence. In contrast to long-term follow-up studies into adulthood, follow-up studies on behavior disorders among school children have yielded conflicting data and views on this matter of persistence.

A series of research studies carried out by a group at the University of Rochester indicates the permanence of early school maladjustment. Using a combination of procedures, these investigators identified, at the first-grade level, students with manifest or incipient problems of ineffective school functioning. Follow-up studies at the third- and seventh-grade levels yielded data indicating that pupils with early-detected dysfunction continued throughout their elementary-school years to perform more poorly in areas of educational and personal functioning (Zax & Cowen, 1972). The San Mateo study (Brownbridge & Van Fleet, 1969) identified 354 students in kindergarten through fourth grade whose maladaptive behavior placed them in the bottom 10% of all children in the school district. Evaluation three years later revealed that about one-third of these youngsters had improved spontaneously or with only minimal help. A second third consisted of youngsters whose adjustment fluctuated. The final third of the group were high-risk children from high-risk families who needed a great deal of help. Stringer and Glidwell (1967) reported that 87% of students markedly deficient in both achievement and mental health status during the early grades maintained the same status throughout elementary school. The research by Stennet (1966) likewise indicates that school maladjustment does not improve with the passage of time.

Longitudinal studies on *severe* reading disability indicate that this condition is best regarded as a relatively chronic condition requiring long-term treatment (Balow, 1965; Silberberg & Silberberg, 1969). In one intensive investigation, Elizabeth Koppitz (1971) reported that only 30 of 177 students treated for severe learning disabilities were able to return to a regular class. These youngsters did not catch up in their work and their problems did not just disappear. Almost all of the learning disability pupils who returned successfully from special class placement "lost" a year or two in the process. That is, they were placed into regular classes a year or two below their normal grade level. Koppitz notes, as have others, that there is an initial misleading spurt in achievement that arouses unwarranted optimism. Though the results of short-term studies are often dramatic, the gains made are often "washed out" in subsequent years. Finally, Koppitz' data suggest that if a student is reading at only a preprimer level by the age of 10 to 12, the chances are that this student will never get beyond a second- or third-grade reading level.

Studies Supporting Change.   On the other hand, there is an equally large and impressive body of data indicating a lack of permanence in maladaptive school behavior. Moreover, the improvement rate appears in most instances to be the same whether or not treatment is given. In the Onondaga County studies, for example, it was reported that of 515 students rated as disturbed by their teachers in 1961, only 160 (30%) were so perceived just two years later. By 1965, only 9 of the 480 children were rated as disturbed. Approximately three-fourths of the 515 students were one-shot affairs in the sense that they were designated as disturbed only once (Mental Health Research Unit, 1964, 1967). The results of the Onondaga study are consistent with those of the Buckinghamshire Child Survey (Shepherd, Oppenheim, & Mitchell, 1971). In this study, which compared a group of 50 students being treated at a child-guidance clinic with a matched group of school children not being treated, it was found that approximately two-thirds of both groups had improved over a two-year period. Similarly, Glavin (1972) reported that persistent disturbances were found in only 30% of students identified as behavior problems some four years earlier.

There is also evidence to suggest that disabled readers can overcome their problem and that remedial tutoring can have long-term effectiveness. In one study that followed-up 33 youngsters who had been given remediation at the elementary reading center, it was found that: (1) despite wide individual variations, the children as a group made considerable gains in reading during remediation; (2) the gains were persistent three years afterwards; and (3) the children were catching up with their peers (Bluestein, 1968).

At this time, it is difficult to come to any firm conclusion regarding the stability of maladaptive behavior during the school years. Because of the different methods used in identifying disturbed youngsters, in reporting of findings (e.g., percentages versus correlations), and in following up troubled youth, and because of possible variations in the quality of the intervention procedures used, much of the inconsistency reported in the above studies may be more apparent than real. At this time, let us turn our attention to the postschool adjustment of individuals who were behavior problems as children.

Postschool Adjustment

Does the child characterized by maladjustment grow up to be a mentally ill adult, or does he tend to grow out of his problems? Investigations bearing on this issue have been of two kinds, retrospective studies and follow-up studies.[2]

Retrospective Studies.   In retrospective studies, mentally ill adults are selected as subjects and their childhood histories are reconstructed through the use of case studies, inventories, and interviews with parents, teachers, and

---

2. The follow-up studies reviewed in this section are "long-term" studies; that is subjects were reevaluated after periods ranging from 5 to 30 years.

other people. Illustrative of this approach is the study by Kasanin and Veo (1932) in which school histories were obtained through teacher interviews on 54 hospitalized adult psychotics. The subjects had a mean age of 20 years and were classified into one of five categories on the basis of their earlier school histories—the fairly well adjusted, the well adjusted, the school leaders, the nobodies, and the peculiar or difficult. Of the 54 patients, 15 were the "nobodies," that is, those whom the teachers could not remember. Only 15 of the 54 patients fell into the "peculiar and difficult" category. This latter finding is rather striking since from the standpoint of rater bias, one would have expected the teacher's knowledge of the former student's hospitalized status to have influenced her recall of the deviant aspects of his earlier behavior. Thus, even though the method should have facilitated the finding of a closer relationship between child and adult disorder, only moderate evidence was found to support such a hypothesis.

Despite efforts to control rater bias among teachers, Bower and his associates (1960) found relatively similar results in their retrospective studies. While teachers in retrospect seemingly recognized the onset of schizophrenia among their former students, they did not view those who later became schizophrenic as having been emotionally sick or as having major problems. On the basis of high-school ratings, predictions would not have been accurate as to later adult pathology.

A major methodological difficulty with retrospective studies is that we do not know how many other children showed similar symptoms during the school years and yet grew up to be normal. This limitation is well exemplified in a study by Renaud and Estes (1961), who studied 100 mentally healthy adults and found that a significant proportion of them had had pathogenic childhoods. Traumatic and pathological events were so common that had the subjects been plagued with psychosomatic or neurotic disorders, background factors could easily have been identified, with the erroneous conclusions drawn that disturbed children become disturbed adults. Schofield and Balian (1959), in studying 150 normal adults, also found that nearly one-fourth of their subjects had had traumatic histories.

In one provocative and eye-opening retrospective study of the childhoods of over 400 famous twentieth-century men and women, it was found that:

1. Approximately 4 out of 5 of the later famous children loathed school.

2. Three out of 5 had serious school problems such as dissatisfaction with the curriculum; dull, irrational, or cruel teachers; students who bullied, bored, or ignored them; and school failure.

3. Three out of 4 came from homes troubled either by poverty, divorce, or parental death; by rejecting, overpossessive, aloof, or dominating parents; by physical handicaps; or by parental dissatisfaction over the children's school failures or vocational choices. In no way could these homes be considered the warm, peaceful ones recommended by mental-health specialists today (Goertzel & Goertzel, 1962). See the case studies in From Troubled Beginnings.

The reader should note that these individuals had exceptional talent and that the nonschool environment fostered learning and an intense desire to succeed. Generalization to other populations lacking in these characteristics would, therefore, be unwarranted. This study is cited to show that talented or intelligent youngsters who have difficult childhoods can sometimes achieve greatness. This study does not suggest that difficult beginnings are the main or best road to greatness. It does illustrate how the tradition of taking any kind of unpleasant fact in a person's background as causative can lead to errors in inference (Meehl, 1973).

From Troubled Beginnings

Case 1. Girl, age 16. Orphaned, willed to custody of a grandmother by mother, who was separated from alcoholic husband, now deceased. Mother rejected the homely child, who has been proven to lie and to steal sweets. Swallowed penny to attract attention at 5. Father was fond of child. Child lived in fantasy as the mistress of father's household for years. Four young uncles and aunts in household cannot be managed by the grandmother, who is widowed. Young uncle drinks; has left home without telling the grandmother his destination. Aunt, emotional over love affair, locks self in room. Grandmother resolves to be stricter with granddaughter since she fears she has failed with own children. Dresses granddaughter oddly. Refused to let her have playmates, put her in braces to keep back straight, did not send her to grade school. Aunt on paternal side of family crippled, uncle asthmatic.

Case 2. Boy, senior year secondary school. Has obtained certificate from physician stating that nervous breakdown makes it necessary for him to leave school for six months. Boy not a good all-around student; has no friends; teachers find him a problem; spoke late; father ashamed of son's lack of athletic ability; poor adjustment to school. Boy has odd mannerisms, makes up own religion, chants hymns to himself. Parents regard him as "different."

Case 3. Boy, age 6. Head large at birth. Thought to have brain fever. Three siblings died before his birth. Mother does not agree with relatives and neighbors that child is probably abnormal. Child sent to school, diagnosed as mentally ill by teacher. Mother, angry, has withdrawn child from school, says she will teach him herself.

Case 1 is identified as Eleanor Roosevelt, Case 2 as Albert Einstein, and Case 3 as Thomas Edison (Goertzel & Goertzel, 1962). These cases speak to (1) the danger of making snap decisions on the basis of superficial and incomplete evidence, and (2) the difficulties in defining mental health. Being different does not necessarily mean that one is in poor mental health.

Another serious limitation of retrospective studies involves reliance on the memories of adults who knew the subject as a child. The memories of informants are, unfortunately, most likely influenced by knowledge of the psychiatric adult status. Informants may thus selectively forget certain incidents or tend to remember the unusual. It would appear that in light of present findings and methodological limitations, retrospective studies offer at best only questionable evidence to support the notion that the maladjusted child grows up to be the maladjusted adult.

Follow-up Studies. The other major approach involves follow-up studies in which children seen by child-guidance clinics are reevaluated after a period of time has elapsed. The results of this approach vary appreciably with the criterion of mental health or illness used at the time of the follow-up. When the clinical judgment of the psychiatric interviewer is used as the criterion, the results suggest that subjects who show maladjustment as children will show maladjustment as adults. In one of the best-known follow-up studies, Robins (1966) studied 525 children who had been referred to the same St. Louis municipal clinic between 1924 and 1929. Thirty years later the adult psychiatric and social status of these subjects was compared with that of 100 control subjects. In a check of the adult psychiatric status of those subjects available for follow-up, only 20% of these former patients fell into the "no disease" category, whereas 52% of the control group were so classified. As adults, 34% of former child-guidance patients were characterized by seriously disabling symptoms, as compared to 8% of the matched group of control subjects. Differences were markedly higher in the incidence of sociopathic personalities and somewhat higher for psychotic disorders and alcoholism. There was, however, little difference between the two groups in the rate of neurotic disturbances (see Table 1–5). Such behaviors as shyness, nervousness, fears, tantrums, seclusiveness, hypersensitiveness, tics, irritability, and speech defects were not related to adult psychiatric outcomes. This finding suggests that neurotic symptoms in childhood are not predictive of adult neurosis. In fact, control-group subjects had a slightly higher rate of neurosis as adults than did the former patients. Interestingly enough, it was not withdrawn behavior that characterized the preschizophrenic group but aggressive acting-out behavior of an antisocial nature. In general, the findings of this study imply that former childhood patients, especially those who engage in seriously antisocial behavior, contribute more than their share to adult mental disorders.

Another major follow-up study, which used a more demanding criterion of mental illness, namely, admission to a mental hospital, arrived at a somewhat different conclusion (Morris, Soroker, & Burrus, 1954). The subjects were 54 childhood patients who had been classified as internal reactors at the Dallas Guidance Clinic 16 to 27 years earlier. Upon follow-up, the majority of these subjects were regarded as having achieved a satisfactory adjustment, one-third of the group was seen as marginally adjusted, and only one subject had been hospitalized. Later analysis of data obtained from this same clinic suggests, as was true in the St. Louis follow-up study, that withdrawn and

Table 1–5.   A Summary of Follow-up Studies on the Stability of Deviant Behavior

Investigator(s)	Length of Follow-up in Years	Relatively Transitory	Relatively Permanent
Robins (1966)	30	Tics; seclusiveness; nervousness; fears; tantrums hypersensitivity; speech defects.	
Morris, Soroker & Burrus (1954)	16–27	Shyness.	
Coolidge, Brodie, & Feeney (1964)	5–10	School phobia (47 of 49 returned to school).	
Hampe, Nobel, Miller, & Barrett (1973)	2	80% either symptom-free or significantly improved.	Only 7% still had a severe phobia.
Balow & Blomquist (1965)	10–15	Severely disabled readers (most learned to read at or near the average adult level).	
Levitt, Beiser, & Robertson (1959)	5	Neurotic disorders (three-fourths improved).	
Berkowitz (1955)	10	Predelinquent behavior (three-fourths had no record of delinquency).	
Robins (1966)	30	Sociopathic behavior (one-third showed moderate improvement).	Sociopathic behavior (two-thirds were unimproved).
Eisenberg (1957)	4–5	Childhood schizophrenia (one-fourth achieved a moderately good social adjustment).	Childhood schizophrenia (three-fourths either attained a marginal adjustment or required continuous institutional care).

introverted youngsters have a low probability of developing schizophrenia. Schizophrenics were found more often among the "ambiverts," the children with both antisocial and non-antisocial complaints, than among the "introverts" and "extroverts." Former child patients at the Judge Baker Clinic who later became hospitalized as schizophrenics also had histories characterized by theft, truancy, running away, and antisocial sexual activity (Nameche, Waring, & Ricks, 1964).

Conclusion

What can we conclude in the light of available evidence? It should be noted that conclusions must be tentative because there has been no study specifically designed to measure the stability of deviant behavior over time and because of the methodological shortcomings of past studies. Bearing the above limitations in mind, we can advance the following tentative conclusions:

1. It does appear that the population of disturbed children contributes more than its share to the population of adult psychiatric disability. Given the current evidence, it appears that about 3 out of 10 disturbed children will continue to have moderate to severe problems as adults.

2. While it is commonly assumed that adult behaviors and personality are established in early life experiences and while there is a body of empirical research demonstrating the stability of personality over time, there is nonetheless a real danger in overgeneralization. In fact, based on the evidence presented in this section, it appears that 70% of disturbed children (excluding psychotic and seriously delinquent youth who have gloomy prognoses) grow up to fall into the broad category of normal adults. Studies on the use of stimulant drugs (U.S. Department of Health, Education and Welfare, 1971), psychotherapy (Levitt et al., 1959), special class placement for disturbed youngsters (Morse, Cutler, & Fink, 1964), and on spontaneous remissions in untreated, nonclinic children (Shepherd et al., 1971) all report that two-thirds to three-fourths of youngsters are well or significantly improved a year or two after having been identified as having behavior problems. Even with respect to the seriously delinquent (psychopath), we are apt to be overly pessimistic in our prognostications. Robins (1966) found that more than one-third of diagnosed psychopaths showed a marked decrease in antisocial behavior in later life. Though these improved psychopaths by no means became pillars of the community, the fact that more than one-third of this group did improve noticeably challenges the notion of incorrigibility commonly associated with this diagnosis. Professional mental-health workers tend to be excessively pessimistic in their predictions of deviant behavior. That is, they overpredict later difficulties (Robins, 1972; MacFarlane, 1963).

Girl with High Problem Incidence

Case 320 was an only child. Her mother had made two unsuccessful attempts at marriage and was frustrated, immature, and unrealistic. The mother and this girl lived for the most part with the mother's parents and the mother and grandfather indulged in constant bickering. The daughter "joined in the fray" at an early age.

This girl's problems, as reported by the mother, were always more numerous than the average of the group. She was a *thumbsucker* from about 4 months, and this continued through age 9. This was followed by *nailbiting* throughout the period of the study. At 18 months she was eating when and what she liked, she was sleeping very irregularly, and was a mouth breather, which resulted in snoring. The problems that were present for 6 years or longer were:

Disturbing dreams. Reported at 3½ and 4 years and then from 8 years on. She and her mother shared a room always. Talking in sleep, calling out children's names, and screaming were reported from 9 through 15 years.

Poor appetite and food finickiness. At 6 years, she was still being fed some of her breakfast in order to get her to school; at 9 years, she was causing "a commotion" about some food at every meal; at 11 years, she demanded hot seasonings on everything. She ate candy whenever she could get it, which was very often, but ate few fruits and vegetables. Facial acne was noted from 11 years on.

Thumbsucking and nailbiting. She was wearing thumb guards at night through 7 years and sucking thumb at school at 9 years.

Destructiveness. The only 12-year-old girl in the study showing this behavior. "A devilish streak," mother called it. This was within four months of menarche and was accompanied by *mood swings* and *irritability.* The presence of this behavior through the years could easily have had its origin in the overcrowded living of the bickering three-generation household.

Attention demanding and seeking assistance. These tools were used through the first twelve years. She demanded (and received) help with feeding through the first six years and was still wanting help with dressing at 11. At 9, she insisted that she could get to sleep more easily if her grandmother rubbed her head. Some of her fears, such as of going to bed and of the dark, seemed bids for attention.

Tempers. Tempers were a family luxury indulged in by all but grandmother. Mother stated: "We all have violent tempers, all but my mother. My daughter and I fight, my father and I fight, my daughter and my father fight."

Negativism. This was a behavior pattern that the girl shared with only 12% or fewer of the girls from 8 years on.

Jealousy. This showed up when mother waited on the grandmother or when the mother became too engrossed in herself. (The mother was an inadequate narcissist.) Jealousy recurred from 4 years on.

This child was never rated as *emotionally dependent.* There was no one on whom to lean. She was never called *reserved.* She wanted friends but had none. She was consistently below the group average in mental ability as measured on tests, and there were no patterns at home of the social amenities. This resulted in floundering, unguided isolation. She went alone to movies and ate her candy, popcorn, and potato chips by herself. At 16 she was still seeking friends and stated, "None of the boys at school like me, but I can usually get a sailor."

Her peak problem load was at 8 years when she had nineteen of the thirty-six problems. At school, she had repeated first grade and was older than her classmates. Her teacher reported: "Always a commotion wherever she is; a constant silly laugh or an inane, silly grin; mouth open all the time. Has to have much supervision. Overactive, squeals and jumps around. Sings nicely and plays piano very well." At this age, 8 years, her scale score on the Stanford-Binet was at its lowest. The grandmother was sick and hospitalized. Her satisfactions and supports were almost nonexistent.

She was somewhat early in maturing. She had her adolescent growth spurt between 10½ and 11 years; the group average was at 11½. Menarche was established at 12 years, 5 months—about 4 months earlier than the group average. She was still in elementary school. Skeletal maturity was achieved at 15½ years as against the group average for girls of 16 years, 3.5 months.

In junior high school, she was in the lowest of four graded sections. One of her teachers reported: "She fails every test. She seems to accept her lack of ability." Another teacher stated: "Some of the youngsters don't care so much for her. She tries to be sociable. Could be a little cleaner and neater."

She seemed to have a fairly good relationship with her grandmother, relatively the most stable person in the household, but she had very poor ones with her mother and grandfather. There were irregular meals, irregular bedtimes, erratic personal hygiene, overcrowding, little discipline (self or otherwise). The mother seemed to operate at about the child's level in her irresponsible day-to-day living. Self-centered, exhibitionistic, critical, and carping, dreaming of yet another marriage, she was of little help to her lonely, untrained, adolescent daughter.

Our Case 320 graduated from high school at 19. She thought she was engaged the previous year but the man changed his mind. She worked for a time. The grandmother died, and the home situation worsened. She married in her early twenties. Two years later she had a baby. Later that same year, they bought a house. For the first time in her life, this girl had her own home, a family largely of her own choosing, companionship, and some security. The early history had promised much less than this.

Source: MacFarlane, J., Allen, L., and Honzik, M. A developmental study of the behavior problems of normal children between twenty-one months and fourteen years. Originally published by the University of California Press; reprinted by permission of the Regents of the University of California.

3. At present, we do not know the length of time between the onset of the problem and its disappearance. Thus, we cannot predict with any assurance how long a child's problem is likely to last. Nor can we tell with any degree of assurance which youngsters will spontaneously improve or under what circumstances. Nor do we understand why 70% do improve. Our best clue as to whether a school youngster's problems are likely to be transitory or permanent seems to be the *severity* of incapacitation and the *number* of symptoms (Robins, 1972), especially after age 6 (MacFarlane, Allen, & Honzik, 1954). The case study of the girl with high problem incidence illustrates that even the number of symptoms is by no means a sure-fire predictor.

4. In large measure, the stability of the behavior deviation depends on the nature of the problem in question as well as the child's environment. Normal problem behavior that occurs as a developmental phenomenon seems to have a very high probability of being resolved with increasing age. Clinical problems, though having a lower probability of improvement than those of a developmental nature, also seem to have a reasonably high probability of spontaneous remission. Since it is obviously misleading to speak of clinical problems as a homogeneous entity, we have in Table 1–5 categorized specific clinical problems on the basis of follow-up studies as tending to be either chronic or transitory in nature. We must not lose sight of the environment in which the individual must function as a major factor in his total adjustment. A dependent adult, for instance, may achieve an adequate adjustment if he has a supportive employer who will take time to give him the attention and direction he needs. Similarly, an individual with strong oppositional tendencies may not experience adjustment difficulties if he has a job in which he is able to work under conditions of minimal supervision and has an easygoing, submissive wife. Thus, even if personality characteristics remained perfectly constant, we could expect some change in the individual behavior as a consequence of environmental contingencies.

5. Somewhat contrary to prevailing clinical belief, it is aggressive, antisocial, acting-out behavior of a *severe* nature that is most predictive of later significant adult disturbance and most deserving of treatment efforts. In

addition to evidence cited earlier, Roff (1961) found that reliable group predictions of military adjustment could be made on the basis of earlier social adjustment in school. Children who were mean and disliked by their classmates commonly had bad-conduct records in military service. Serious delinquent behavior as reflected in a juvenile police record tends to be much more persistent than the general run of childhood disorders noted by teachers and child-guidance agencies (Robins, 1972).

6. Although two out of three unsocialized aggressive youngsters continue in their antisocial ways, it must not be assumed that the majority of young norm-violators become adult criminals. As Kvaraceus (1966) points out, it is widely agreed that much juvenile delinquency does not inevitably terminate in adult criminal activity. There appears to be a curvilinear relationship between delinquent activity and age. After reaching a peak at age 16, the "delinquency curve" begins to level off (W. Miller, quoted in Kvaraceus, 1966).

7. Shyness and withdrawn behavior tend to disappear with advancing age. At worst, these problems are less incapacitating and socially disruptive than those of the antisocial child. Moreover, there is little evidence to suggest that shyness is predictive of later schizophrenia, despite the fact that introverted behavior is often viewed as having dire consequences for mental health. There is a vast difference between the child who can relate and does not, or who wants to relate and lacks the necessary social skills, and the child who cannot relate because of a severe basic incapacity. The best evidence to date suggests that the preschizophrenic child is characterized by both antisocial behavior and serious non-antisocial symptoms (Nameche, Waring, & Ricks, 1964; Robins, 1966).

8. Neurotic symptoms (fears, hypersensitiveness, tics) often presumed to be the precursors of adult neurotic disturbances have also been found lacking in prognostic power. The findings of current empirical research challenge the long-held assumptions that adult neurotic behaviors result from disturbances in parent-child relations or from parental loss in childhood (Robins, 1966). Neurotic disorders in childhood, no matter how upsetting they may be to the child or the family, have very good long-term prognoses. With the possible exception of hysteria, adult neurosis for the most part does not have its roots in childhood disorders (Robins, 1972).

9. The probabilities of remission characterizing childhood schizophrenia and infantile autism are indeed low. These severe disabilities definitely tend to persist through time with at best only 25–30% of those so diagnosed apparently achieving reasonably adequate adjustment (Eisenberg, 1957; Quay & Werry, 1972). It does appear, however, that a psychosis manifesting itself before puberty is rarely an early form of adult schizophrenia. The psychotic child's condition does continue into adulthood where it accounts for only a small proportion of hospitalized adults (Robins, 1972).

10. Generally speaking, it is very difficult to postulate any direct causal relationship between early childhood maladjustment and later specific psychiatric disability, with the possible exception of *serious* antisocial behavior

in childhood, which does forecast problems with the law, inability to earn a living, and impaired interpersonal relations. We do know that a goodly number of disturbed children will grow up to attain a reasonably adequate adult adjustment. The truth of the matter is, however, that we still do not fully understand the role of later experiences on personality adjustment. Also, we must not overlook the possibility that some adult disturbances arise independently of childhood problems.

In our present state of knowledge, we can conclude that there is at best only mild or moderate evidence to support the notion that disturbed children turn into seriously disturbed adults. Since the less noxious childhood disorders, say, shyness, are more common than the more severe disorders, say, childhood schizophrenia, it would seem that, all in all, change appears to characterize the course of behavior deviations in children more than chronicity or stability. The conception of emotional disturbance in children as a progressively deteriorating condition is thus called into question.

Criteria of Normality

If all children have problems, what is normal behavior in children? How long must a child manifest abnormal behavior to warrant the appellation "emotionally disturbed"? What criteria are to be used in deciding what is abnormal and what is normal? How does one distinguish between the child who has problems and the child who is maladjusted? Is doing anything disapproved by the teacher to be equated with deviancy? Various approaches have been made to the definition of normality in children, although none has proven entirely satisfactory. The issue of normality in children is more than an academic question to those who must render judgments regarding the behavior of children. This question also has ethical and practical ramifications, for the child does not refer himself for treatment but is referred for treatment by the adults in his life. The child may not be in need of treatment even though his parents and teachers believe so. His referral may be simply a result of the parents' or teacher's low annoyance threshold. Shepherd, Oppenheim, & Mitchell (1966) found, for instance, that referral to a child-guidance clinic is as closely related to parental reactions (anxious, easily upset, lacking in ability to cope with children) as it is to the child's morbidity. Similarly, teachers with 3–10 years of experience tend to view undesirable acts as being more serious than do teachers with 10 years of experience (Dobson, 1967).

The Statistical Approach

One of the most commonly discussed approaches to normality employs a statistical criterion. According to this standard, normal behavior is defined as what the majority does. The more an individual is like the average, the more normal he is considered to be. For example, the average 5 year old may be found to have five nightmares a month. If so, this condition would be considered normal. We could also calculate what percentage of 5 year olds have as many as ten or as few as two nightmares a month. If a child deviated markedly from the average, he would be considered abnormal in this aspect of his behavior. Similar distributions could be established for other aspects of behavior, such as the number of fears, the frequency of truancy, the extent of aggressive attacks, for children of each sex at various age levels.

There are some rather noticeable shortcomings in this approach, however. First, the statistical concept of normality implies that what is common is normal. Smoking and excessive use of alcohol or other drugs are very common but are not regarded as desirable. Similarly, 95% of boys have masturbated by age 15 or 16, yet masturbation is not necessarily regarded as healthy by the culture at large. Second, abnormality in a statistical sense is not always unhealthy. Take the case of a very creative youngster. Genuinely creative youngsters are, by definition, not commonly found in our schools. In terms of their creative performance, they differ markedly from the average student. Are we to say that these youngsters are abnormal when their very talent may lend itself to self-actualization on their part and to benefits for society? A third problem centers around the complexity of personality. It may be possible to gather norms on certain characteristics, for example, the amount of nailbiting but it is difficult to isolate and quantify many of the subtle or more elusive characteristics of personality. Further, the statistical approach does not lend itself very readily to the study of the integrational or organizational aspects of personality formation. Still another problem exists with this approach, namely, that the norms are frequently based on clinic populations. As noted earlier in the chapter, evidence derived from epidemiological studies strongly suggests that such deviate norm groups provide misleading standards, in that many childhood behaviors, such as fears, are not as pathological as we often assume. Finally, there is the question of cut-off points. Just how many fingernails does a 7 year old have to bite to be considered abnormal? What percentage of the nailbiting population must he exceed? It is difficult to give definitive answers to such questions.

A variation or subtype of the statistical approach is the use of adjustment to social norms as the criterion of normality. Normality thus becomes defined relatively, according to a given set of cultural values, which are comprised of both laws and customs. The socialization process itself has as its aim the inculcation of social values and the development of behaviors congruent with environmental expectations. That normality be defined as adherence to social norms and abnormality as violation of these social norms is, therefore, not unexpected. Though it seems reasonable to judge deviancy by comparing behavior against social norms, that is, to take into account environmental circumstances, this approach also has its limitations. For example, to what degree does one have to be different from social norms to be judged as culturally deviant? How many times does one have to steal to be considered maladjusted? Most of us have stolen or cheated at times, but we do not consider ourselves to be delinquent. Cut-off points between the conformer and habitual norm-violator are difficult to determine and would probably have to be at least somewhat arbitrary in nature. Another difficulty occurs when a society or institution is dominated by a particular set of social-political values. Is compliance, then, a sign of normality or of personal maladjustment? Who were the maladjusted Germans—those who fought the Nazi system or those who went along with it? Also consider the lower-class youngster who rebels against school. Is he sick because of his objections to being forced into a situation in which he experiences demands and expectations he does not value, or are some of the institutions in the society irrelevant?

Children and adults can also suffer from overconformity. The problem does not seem to be resolved by a strict adherence to conformity for, eventually, conformity reaches a point beyond which normality is apt to be threatened. Compliance to the point that one's personal integrity is sacrificed is conducive neither to personal nor societal harmony. Further, as Havighurst (1966) argues, it is important that a society educate for certain forms of deviancy, for example, creative behavior. On occasion, a good adjustment demands that we rebel and express dissatisfaction with social mores and institutions. The value for the individual and for society of certain expressions of nonconformity is, unfortunately, often overlooked. Finally, we must ask whose values we are going to use in judging normality. One group in society often differs from another group in the same society with regard to what is considered normal. For example, how would ministers, teachers, social workers, doctors, cultural anthropologists, and laborers as separate groups view a child who habitually curses? In all probability, there would be widely differing views regarding the acceptability and desirability of such behavior.

The Idealistic Approach

The other major approach might be termed the idealistic approach. Whereas the statistical approach primarily describes the frequency of given behaviors, the use of the ideal criterion by definition implies evaluation of desirability. Whereas the criteria of social norms involve relativity, the ideal criterion is based on absolute standards assumed to be worthy of emulation. The statistical approach is concerned with what is, the idealistic approach is concerned with what should be. An ideal of behavior is posited for each individual, and a determination is made as to whether the individual is functioning at this level. Illustrative of this approach is Maslow's hierarchy of basic human needs. His hierarchy in ascending order lists physiological needs, safety needs, needs for affection and belongingness, esteem needs, cognitive needs such as a search for knowledge, aesthetic needs such as a longing for beauty, and self-actualization needs. When the needs at the lower levels have been met, the needs on the next step in the hierarchic structure seek satisfaction. People whose needs for self-actualization are pressing for satisfaction are seen as operating at an optimal level. According to Maslow (1954), anything that detracts from the course of self-actualization is psychopathological.

The equating of complete normality with perfection has an undeniably positive air to it, but the use of such ideal criteria is also fraught with difficulties. Ideal criteria, for one thing, have little practical meaning and, therefore, are of limited value to the clinician or educator in his decision-making process. Guidelines derived from such criteria do not aid the practitioner in deciding whether the child is normal or in need of professional help. Second, few people can ever attain the ideal; and those who do seem to qualify have human frailties and weaknesses. Finally, since ideal criteria are in terms of what ought to be, we run the risk of assuming that we *know* what the ideal attributes are and that these are supracultural in character, equally valid for child and adolescent, boy and girl, rich child and slum dweller.

Toward a Definition of Normality and Deviancy

While there is no acceptable definition of normality, there are certain ingredients that a suitable definition must include. It should take into account the child's *developmental level*, for what is regarded as normal at one age might well be viewed as abnormal at a later age—for example, physical aggressiveness or chewing on the carpet. Or poor appetite may be common among young children, while running away from home is uncommon at all ages. The child's *sex* is another factor that influences the clinician's and teacher's judgment regarding the appropriateness of behavior. For instance, passive behavior has been regarded as normal for the girl but viewed as unusual for the boy. Consideration must also be extended to a child's particular *culture* or subculture. Since judgments concerning the desirability of a specific behavior vary from one group to another and from one setting to another (e.g., neighborhood versus school) the relativity of deviancy becomes an important consideration (Havighurst, 1966). Certainly, allowances for *individuality* must be made. Also, the definition of normality must be *multidimensional* in nature; that is, it must take into account how the child functions in various representative areas of development (intellectual, social, physical). Finally, the *tolerance level* of adults in the child's life must be weighed in arriving at any judgment regarding normality and deviancy. For example, if a teacher's threshold for annoyance is low, he might seek help for behaviors that few others would view as problematic. If a teacher's tolerance is too high, then he is not likely to seek assistance for those actually in need of help.

Normality. What would the mentally healthy child look like in the school setting? Bower (1970) expects the following characteristics:

1. *Managing Symbols.* A mentally healthy child is one who is able to deal with and manage the symbols of our society. Such symbols include language symbols, mathematical symbols, sound symbols as in music, and art symbols.

Without such symbolic skill the child is virtually unable to function in school and later on in the adult society.

2. *Coping with Authority.* A mentally healthy child must be able to deal with rules, manage rapid and sometimes arbitrary changes in rules, and be able to accept penalties for breaking rules. It is highly significant that no society of adults or children can go on without goals, rules by which one reaches goals, and penalties for those who do not play by the rules. In the case of children, those who do not play by the rules are often not permitted to play. In adult society those who continually break the rules are sent to institutions which prevent them from functioning in our society. A child has little alternative but to learn how to deal with authority.

3. *Living with Peer Groups.* As part of the skill of dealing with rules one must learn how to be an individual and yet function in his peer group. The mentally healthy child has learned how to deal with the "give and take" nature of daily associations with his classmates and friends.

4. *Regulating Emotions.* The mentally healthy child is able to control and manage his emotions. This does not mean that a child must give up his feelings or inner life in order to become a mentally healthy person. The ability to control one's feelings and desires must also include the ability to loosen controls when such freedom is appropriate and desirable. It suggests freedom to be imaginative, to be spontaneous, or to be emotional when such behavior is enhancing and productive for the individual. Inhibited behavior can be just as irrational in some contexts as impulsive behavior often seems to be. A mentally healthy child needs to have access to his affective life and to be able to utilize each success appropriately. One can say that the mentally healthy individual has achieved an integrative balance between his emotional and rational capabilities.

Deviancy. The difficulty associated with the definition of deviancy is reflected in Kanner's (1962) observation that it is impossible to locate a definition of the term "emotionally disturbed children," despite the fact that this term crept into the literature sometime during the 1930s. Kanner stresses the fact that this term is too encompassing and diffuse to be of scientific value and points out that scientists generally proceed by analyzing global and nebulous concepts into more specific categories or components. One definition that is widely quoted was advanced by Bower (1961), who notes that the emotionally handicapped child has one or more of the following characteristics:

1. An unexplained inability to learn. In other words, the child's difficulty cannot be explained adequately or primarily by intellectual deficits, specific learning disabilities, or by differences in cultural or ethnic background. It should be noted that the inability to use one's intelligence efficiently as manifested by an appreciable discrepancy between actual and expected academic performance carries considerable importance as a criterion of emotional disturbance in children but not in adults. This change in adjust-

ment yardsticks might well be a major factor in explaining the instability of deviant behavior over time.

2. An inability to achieve satisfactory social relationships with children or adults. For example, the child might have difficulty following rules and in getting along with persons in authority.

3. An inability to behave at a level commensurate with one's developmental status; that is, the child operates at a less mature level, in terms of his interests and behavior, than do most youngsters his age.

4. An inability to display confidence and belief in one's self or to overcome feelings of sadness.

5. An inability to cope with stressful situations in school without developing psychosomatic reactions, such as headaches or stomachaches.

While all children may at some point in life exhibit some of the inabilities listed above, Bower argues that a child, in order to be considered emotionally handicapped, must exhibit these characteristics to a marked extent and over a prolonged period of time before the designation of "emotionally handicapped" is justified. In other words, we must also consider the frequency, intensity, and duration of the behavior in determining whether or not maladjustment exists.

Guidelines for Referral

Many parents and teachers are not sure if they should seek professional treatment for certain children. Parents, for instance, not uncommonly show up at child-guidance clinics expressing uncertainty as to whether the problem is serious enough to justify their presence at the clinic. Likewise, teachers are often in doubt about when to request the services of the school psychologist. Assuming that professional help is available, when should one refer a youngster for professional help? There are no hard-and-fast criteria whose use permits a definite answer to this issue, but Bower's definition should prove helpful in reaching a decision as to whether the child needs professional assistance. Also of value as guideposts for referral is the list of questions advanced by Mayer and Hoover (1961). If the answers to the questions that follow suggest more than the usual amount of adjustment difficulties, consideration should then be given to a search for outside consultation:

1. Is the child's behavior generally appropriate to the circumstances in which he finds himself?

2. Is the child's behavior generally in keeping with his age?

3. Are there real difficulties in the child's environment that may be blamed for his problem?

4. Has there been a radical change in the child's behavior?

5. How long has the symptom lasted?

The teacher with a problem pupil might consider three basic criteria in reaching a decision about referral. He must, first of all, ask himself if the child's social, emotional, and intellectual needs are being reasonably met within the classroom setting. If the child is unable to benefit academically or to achieve relatively satisfying interpersonal relations despite adjustments in the school program designed to promote such development, professional consultation may well be indicated.

Consideration for the rights of normal children must also be undertaken. American public education is based on group methods of instruction and has established its goals for normal pupils. Not infrequently, emotionally disturbed youngsters demand so much of the teacher's time and energy that the education of the group suffers. As any experienced educator will testify, a teacher can spend as much or more time with one emotionally disturbed pupil as he does with the rest of the class. One teacher sent a very disturbing fifth grader to the principal's office only to have him return immediately to class with a note from the principal stating that "this boy cannot learn anything here in my office." The teacher thought for a moment and then sent the boy back to the principal's office with a note reading, "True enough, but now the rest of my class (the other 28) can." When the teacher believes that the group's needs are being sacrificed for one child's needs, it is time to seek professional assistance.

The teacher must also take his own mental health into account. Behaviorally disordered youth are often quite skillful at irritating other people. They have mastered a variety of techniques and have had years of experience in antagonizing others. One kindergarten pupil so distressed his teacher that the teacher became obsessed with thoughts regarding the daily management of this child and actually dreaded coming to work. If the teacher finds that his own mental hygiene is suffering and that his teaching effectiveness is being impaired, he would do well to request an evaluation for the child so that additional therapeutic or corrective measures may be planned. The teacher should also remember that he can receive advice regarding the desirability of referral from such co-workers as the school counselor, other teachers, and the principal.

Summary

"What constitutes normality?" is best understood not as a question of fact but rather as a question of conventional definition (Scott, 1968). The definition of normality is rooted in social realities (agreements arrived at between groups of people) rather than in physical realities like the hardness of rocks or the heights of tables (Darley & Darley, 1973).

The ability to detect the abnormal depends upon knowing what is normal—that is, knowing how normal particular aspects of behavior are in various settings for boys and girls of different ages and social classes. For instance, it is helpful to know that almost 50% of preschool children and students in the primary grades are seen as overactive.

Normal development does not follow a troublefree path. For example, data from the Berkeley Guidance Study show that both boys and girls average five or six problems at any given time during the preschool and elementary-school years.

When a large proportion of children exhibit a given "problem" behavior, situational change should be given consideration as a way to alleviate the difficulty.

Many behavior problems decrease with age (fears, destructiveness, temper tantrums, enuresis, and so on), some problems peak at entrance into school and then again at adolescence, a few problems increase with age (nailbiting) or are unrelated to age (oversensitiveness).

Research findings regarding the persistence of maladjustment during the school years are mixed. Some studies suggest that problems persist and may even become more severe, while an equally impressive body of research indicates that problems clear up in a matter of two to three years. We will have to await more definite research in this area before arriving at any firm conclusion.

Follow-up studies lasting into postschool adjustment indicate that the typical, run-of-the-mill behavior disorders tend to disappear in adulthood. The fact that approximately 70% of maladjusted children appear to "outgrow" their problems can be attributed, in part, to the resiliency or developmental plasticity of youth.

Certain severe disorders (sociopathy and childhood psychosis) do show a strong tendency to persist into adulthood, but they are relatively uncommon.

Severity of incapacitation and the number of symptoms appear to be the best predictors of whether a problem will be transistory or permanent.

Defining normality is no easy matter. The two most common approaches to the definition of normality are the statistical and the idealistic models. Both models have strengths and shortcomings.

When typicality (commonness) and desirability coincide, there is no problem as to which should constitute the standard of normality, but when the desirable is not typical or the typical is not desirable, it is necessary to separate clearly the two considerations. The average is rarely valued (Scott, 1968).

Any approach to the definition of normality must include assessment of the youngster's age, sex, social class, the adult's tolerance level, and the specific setting in which the behavior occurs. Also, the assessment must be multidimensional, taking into account the intellectual, social, personal, and physical realms of development, with full allowances made for individuality.

References

Balow, B. The long-term effect of remedial reading instruction. *Reading Teacher,* 1965, **18,** 581–86.

Balow, B., & Blomquist, M. Young adults 10–15 years after severe reading disability. *Elementary School Journal,* 1965, **66,** 44–45.

Bendix, S. Drug modification of behavior: A form of chemical violence. *Journal of Clinical Psychology,* 1973, **2** (3), 17–19.

Bluestein, V. Long-term effectiveness of remediation. *Journal of School Psychology,* 1968, **VI** (2), 130–35.

Bower, E. M. *The education of emotionally handicapped children.* Sacramento: California State Department of Education, 1961.

Bower, E. M. Mental health. In R. Ebel (Ed.), *Encyclopedia of educational reearch* (4th ed.) New York: Macmillan, 1970. Pp. 811–28.

Bower, E., Shellhammer, T., Daily, J., & Bower, M. *High school students who later became schizophrenic.* Sacramento: California State Department of Education, 1960.

Brownbridge, R., & Van Fleet, P. (Eds.) *Investments in prevention: The prevention of learning and behavior problems in young children.* San Francisco: Pace I.D. Center, 1969.

Conners, C. Symptom patterns in hyperkinetic, neurotic, and normal children. *Child Development,* 1970, **41,** 667–82.

Coolidge, J., Brodie, R., & Fenney, B. A ten-year follow-up of sixty-six school phobic children. *American Journal of Orthopsychiatry,* 1964, **34,** 675–84.

Darley, J., & Darley, S. *Conformity and deviation.* Morristown, N.J.: General Learning Corp., 1973.

Dobson, R. L. The perception and treatment by teachers of the behavioral problems of elementary school children in culturally deprived and middle class neighborhoods. (Doctoral thesis, University of Oklahoma, 1966) Dissertation Abstracts 27, 1702 A-03 A, No. 6, 1967.

Eisenberg, L. The course of childhood schizophrenia. *Archives of Neurology and Psychiatry,* 1957, **78,** 69–83.

Glavin, J. Persistence of behavior disorders in children. *Exceptional Children,* 1972, 367–76.

Goertzel, V., & Goertzel, M. *Cradles of eminence,* Boston: Little, Brown, 1962.

Hampe, E., Noble, H., Miller, L., & Barrett, C. Phobic children one and two years posttreatment. *Journal of Abnormal Psychology,* 1973, **82,** 446–53.

Havighurst, R. J. Social deviancy among youth: Types and significance. In W. W. Wattenberg (Ed.), Social deviancy among youth. *Yearbook of the National Society for the Study of Education,* 1966, **65** (Part I), 59–77.

Johnson, S., Wahl, G., Martin, S., & Johansson, S. How deviant is the normal child? A behavioral analysis of the preschool child and his family. In R. Rubin, J. Brady, & J. Henderson (Eds.), *Advances in behavior therapy,* 1973, Vol. 4, 37–54.

Kanner, L. Emotionally disturbed children: A historical review. *Child Development,* 1962, **33,** 97–102.

Kasanin, J., & Veo, L. A. A study of the school adjustment of children who later in life become psychotic. *American Journal of Orthopsychiatry,* 1932, **2,** 212–30.

Kenny, T., Clemmens, R., Hudson, B., Lentz, G., Cicci, R., & Nair, R. Characteristics of children referred because of hyperactivity. *The Journal of Pediatrics,* 1971, **79** (4), 618–23.

Koppitz, E. *Children with learning disabilities: A five-year follow-up study.* New York; Grune & Stratton, 1971.

Kvaraceus, W. C. Problems of early identification and prevention of delinquency. In W. W. Wattenberg (Ed.), Social deviancy among youth. *Yearbook of the National Society for the Study of Education,* 1966, **65** (Part I), 189–220.

Lapouse, R., & Monk, M. An epidemiologic study of behavior characteristics in children. *American Journal of Public Health,* 1958, **48,** 1134–44.

Lapouse, R., & Monk, M. Fears and worries in a representative sample of children. *American Journal of Orthopsychiatry,* 1959, **29,** 803–18.

Lapouse, R., & Monk, M. Behavior deviations in a representative sample of children. *American Journal of Orthopsychiatry,* 1964, **34,** 436–46.

Levitt, E., Beiser, H., & Robertson, R. A follow-up evaluation of cases treated at a community child guidance clinic. *American Journal of Orthopsychiatry,* 1959, **29,** 337–47.

MacFarlane, J. From infancy to adulthood. *Childhood Education,* 1963, **39,** 83–89.

MacFarlane, J., Allen, L., & Honzik, M. *A developmental study of the behavior problems of normal children between twenty-one months and fourteen years.* Berkeley: University of California Press, 1954.

Maslow, A. *Motivation and personality.* New York: Harper, 1954.

Mayer, G., & Hoover, M. *When children need special help with emotional problems.* New York: Child Study Association of America, 1961. Pp. 120–22.

Meehl, P. *Psychodiagnostics.* Minneapolis: University of Minnesota Press, 1973.

Mental Health Research Unit. Onondaga County School Studies, Interim No. 1: Persistence of emotional disturbance reported among second and fourth grade children. Syracuse: N.Y. State Department of Mental Hygiene, September, 1964.

Mental Health Research Unit. Behavior patterns associated with persistent emotional disturbance of school children in regular classes of elementary grades. Syracuse: N.Y. State Department of Mental Hygiene, December, 1967.

Morris, D., Soroker, E., & Burrus, G. Follow-up studies of shy, withdrawn children: Evaluation of later adjustment. *American Journal of Orthopsychiatry,* 1954, **24,** 743–54.

Morse, W. C., Cutler, R. L., & Fink, A. H. Public school classes for the emotionally handicapped: A research analysis. Washington, D.C.: Council for Exceptional Children, 1964.

Nameche, G., Waring, M., & Ricks, D. Early indicators of outcome in schizophrenia. *Journal of Nervous and Mental Disorders,* 1964, **139,** 232–40.

Quay, H., & Werry, J. (Eds.) *Psychopathological disorders of childhood.* New York: John Wiley & Sons, 1972.

Renaud, H., & Estes, F. Life histories of one hundred normal American males: Pathogenicity of childhood. *American Journal of Orthopsychiatry,* 1961, **31,** 786–802.

Robins, L. N. *Deviant children grown up.* Baltimore: Williams & Wilkins, 1966.

Robins, L. N. Follow-up studies of behavior disorders in children. In H. C. Quay & J. S. Werry (Eds.), *Psychopathological disorders of childhood.* New York: John Wiley & Sons, 1972. Pp. 414–46.

Roff, M. Childhood social interactions and young adult bad conduct. *Journal of Abnormal Social Psychology,* 1961, **63,** 333–37.

Rubin, R., & Balow, B. Learning and behavior disorders: A longitudinal study. *Exceptional Children,* 1971, **38,** 293–40.

Schofield, W., & Balian, L. A comparative study of the personal histories of schizophrenic and nonpsychiatric patients. *Journal of Abnormal Social Psychology*, 1959, **59,** 216–25.

Scott, W. Conceptions of normality. In E. Borgatta & W. Lambert (Eds.), *Handbook of Personality Theory and Research*. Chicago: Rand McNally, 1968. Pp. 974–1006.

Senn, M., & Solnit, A. *Problems in child development*. Philadelphia: Lea & Febiger Publishing Co., 1968.

Shepherd, M., Oppenheim, A. N., & Mitchell, S. Childhood behavior disorders and the child-guidance clinic: An epidemiological study. *Journal of Child Psychology and Psychiatry*, 1966, **7,** 39–52.

Shepherd, M., Oppenheim, B., & Mitchell, S. *Childhood behavior and mental health*. New York: Grune & Stratton, 1971.

Short, J., & Nye, F. Extent of unrecorded juvenile delinquency: Tentative conclusions. *Journal of Criminal Law, Criminology and Police Science*, 1958, **49,** 296–302.

Silberberg, N., & Silberberg, M. Myths in remedial education, *Journal of Learning Disabilities*, 1969, 2 **(4),** 209–17.

Stennet, R. G. Emotional handicap in the elementary years: Phase or disease? *American Journal of Orthopsychiatry*, 1966, **36,** 444–49.

Stringer, L. A., & Glidewell, J. C. *Early detection of emotional illnesses in school children: Final report*. Clayton, Mo.: St. Louis County Health Department, 1967.

U.S. Department of Health, Education and Welfare. *Report on the conference on the use of stimulant drugs in the treatment of behaviorally disturbed young school children, 1971*. Washington, D.C.: Government Printing Office, 1971.

Werry, J., & Quay, H. The prevalence of behavior symptoms in younger elementary school children. *American Journal of Orthopsychiatry*, 1971, 41 **(1),** 136–43.

Zax, M., & Cowen, E. *Abnormal psychology*. New York: Holt, Rinehart, and Winston, 1972.

Suggested Readings

Davie, R., Butler, N., & Goldstein, H. *From birth to seven*. London, England: Longham, 1972.

Freud, A. *Normality and pathology in childhood*. New York: International Universities Press, 1965.

Goertzel, V., & Goertzel, M. *Cradles of eminence*. Boston: Little, Brown, 1962.

Roff, M. Life history research. In *Psychopathology*. Minneapolis: University of Minnesota Press, Vol. 1, 1970; Vol. 2, 1972, Vol. 3. 1974.

Scott, W. Conceptions of normality. In E. Borgatta & W. Lambert (Eds.), *Handbook of personality theory and research*. Chicago: Rand McNally, 1968. Pp. 974–1006.

2

Common Growth Problems

Successful children are secure, assertive, self-confident, reasonably independent and self-directing, consistent in meeting the expectations of others, and highly motivated to learn. Furthermore, they model their lives after an inspiring model, enjoy competing with others, show social and task responsibility, and achieve a happy balance between freedom of self-expression and the normal restrictions of school life. These personality characteristics are important for success at all levels from kindergarten through college. In fact, they are personality characteristics of the successful person even in the post-school years.

Students who fail in school are often characterized by no forward thrust and aspiration, intense fears, limited frustration tolerance, an inability to accept social behavior limits, little or no task orientation, and an avoidance of situations that might involve failure (Brenner, 1967). Briefly, students lacking in affective prerequisites experience difficulty in school with respect to its social demands and with regard to achieving traditional academic objectives.

This chapter will aid psychologists and educators in developing a fuller appreciation of the ways in which personality factors can facilitate or impair school adjustment. For each personality factor discussed, we will describe the behaviors indicative of the trait, antecedents of these behaviors, adaptive and maladaptive outcomes, and most important, management implications for teachers.

The Development of Dependency

Perhaps the most dramatic and important change that occurs during the first year of life is the advance in interpersonal relationships. It is usually assumed that the first social tie that develops—the bond between mother and infant—serves as a prototype for all later interpersonal relations. For our purpose, we will use the term of "attachment" or "dependency" to refer to this core relationship. The intense affect associated with the strong interdependence of the mother-child relationship is believed by many authorities to be the basis for most, if not all, socialization. The young child who develops a sense of trust emerges from infancy with a sense of security and is better able to deal with personal anxieties. A close relationship with the mother also facilitates moral development and proper expression of one's aggressions. In a sense, then, attachment or dependency constitutes a kind of social glue, cementing in the cornerstone of socialization processes. As Ferguson (1970) notes, "The fact that children . . . value the presence, attention, and approval of significant others, and fear their loss, has been considered a most powerful motive for conformity to the expectations of these others, for imitation and identification, for the acquisition of values, for the internalization of behavioral controls, for academic achievement, and for many other aspects of socialization."

Signs of Dependency

How does dependency manifest itself? Persistent display of the following signs is regarded as indicative of dependency. The first sign is *seeking help*. Instead of taking the initiative, the overly dependent child goes to the adult for help not only when he encounters some obstacle in attempting to perform an assignment, but even when the task is of a routine nature. Seeking assistance also shows up when the student is asked to make even small decisions by himself. He would rather lean on others than be self-sufficient. Another sign of dependency is *attention-getting* behavior. The overly dependent child habitually wants the adult to watch him or talk with him or look at something he has produced, such as a drawing. Attention-getting behavior may also take the form of whining. *Seeking physical contact* is another behavior suggestive of dependency. The very dependent child may want to sit on the parent's lap or cling to his mother tenaciously. *Physical proximity* or the desire to be close to an adult is a fourth sign of dependency. Teachers often report that extremely dependent students like to hang around the teacher's desk. *Passivity* is another characteristic commonly observed in the very dependent youngster. He may prefer to sit by himself and do nothing instead of joining classmates in a game. Finally, dependency can also be manifested in the *seeking of approval* or reassurance. The excessively dependent individual is very sensitive to what others think of him.

Some authors believe that seeking attention and wanting approval represent more mature forms of behavior than seeking physical contact or proximity do, since the former are characteristic of older children while the latter are more characteristic of younger children. Not only does the nature of the dependent response change with age, but the object of the dependency also shifts with age. As the child matures, emotional dependence on peers increases while emotional dependence on adults decreases (Heathers, 1955). A partial explanation of this shift might be attributed to the fact that older children are more socially rewarding to one another than younger, nursery-school children are (Charlesworth & Hartup, 1967).

Dependency, like the other personality characteristics discussed in this chapter, is subject to situational influence. Whether a child behaves in a dependent fashion depends in part on the particular setting (for example, how the teacher structures assignments and responds to dependent behaviors). While some children might on the basis of prior learning experience have a tendency to act in a dependent manner, whether they do or not depends on the particulars of the situation.

Most workers agree that there are two varieties of dependency—instrumental or task-oriented, and emotional or person-oriented. In instrumental dependency, the child seeks help in reaching a given goal. The student, for example, might depend on his teacher for completion of a given arithmetic assignment. He seeks help in *doing things*. In emotional dependency, the child seeks the *social responses of others*, for example, approval as a goal per se. Chronologically, instrumental dependency (the seeking of another as a means of securing assistance) apparently precedes emotional dependency (essentially affiliation or attachment). The sexes probably do not differ appreciably in term of overall dependency. Some workers believe, however, that because of cultural forces, the former has been typical of boys and the latter typical of girls. Traditional sex roles might be changing, and it will be interesting to see whether task-oriented dependency remains characteristic of males as a group and person-oriented dependency remains characteristic of females as a group.

While parents are initially very accepting of the child's total reliance on them, it is not long, particularly in our society, before the child is expected to relinquish some of his dependency and strive toward becoming a more self-reliant individual. Both sexes, although to varying degrees, are expected to become increasingly self-sufficient—to forgo some of their instrumental dependency. Yet both sexes, again to varying degrees perhaps, are expected to remain emotionally attached to or dependent on parents and friends. In light of these cultural expectations, it is hardly surprising that we learn simultaneously to depend on others and to be independent of others. We learn new ways to be helped and to help ourselves.

Roots and Consequences of Dependency

Sequence of Development.   While we cannot plot the developmental course of dependency behaviors as we can that of physical development, recent research has alerted us to a number of steps involved in the process. First, the infant develops the capacity to distinguish between himself and his external surroundings—a sense of separateness from the environment. Later in this phase, the baby may cry when held by someone other than the mother or primary caretaker. Next, the infant develops specific expectations toward the mother and shows by his behavior that he expects certain responses to his signals. Finally, a confidence relationship—a higher-level relationship involving trust—is established. He can now leave his mother and explore strange surroundings, secure in his knowledge that the mother will be there to comfort him if necessary (Yarrow, 1972).

We can describe the developmental course of dependency with reasonable accuracy, but theorists vary appreciably in their identification of factors responsible for healthy and unhealthy outcomes of dependency socialization. We will restrict our discussion to theories regarding outcomes that require attention from the classroom teacher.

Too Much Dependency.   Let us first examine the pattern of strong dependency or "overdependency," for which there are two proposed theories, both of which focus on parent attitudes. One theory, proposed by Levy (1943), suggests that *maternal overprotection* may lead to overly dependent behavior in children. In his study of 15 cases of overprotective mothers, he found their children to be passive, dependent, and submissive. Heathers (1953) likewise concluded that dependent behavior may stem from maternal overprotection. The mothers in Heathers's study not only permitted dependent behavior but also reinforced it.

Another prevalent theory views dependent behavior in children as a result of *maternal rejection.* The notion that maternal rejection results in dependent behavior in children receives considerable support from empirical research, as evidenced in Hartup's (1963) review of the literature. According to this view, the child's dependency needs are frustrated, with the result that the child, lacking sufficient support and nurturance, is unable to progress successfully through the experiences culminating in independence. Frustration of the child's requests for assistance and emotional support is quite apt to occur in our culture because of the societal emphasis on early independence training. Many parents and teachers, in their eagerness to develop independence in children, fail to recognize that dependency is a prerequisite for independence. Paradoxically, the child can become independent only after he has learned that he can depend on his parents' acceptance, approval, and support.

Stendler (1954) notes that there are two critical periods during which the preschool child might become overly dependent as a consequence of excessive frustration. The first occurs near the end of his first year of life. At this time, the child, who recognizes in a primitive fashion his dependence on the mother, begins to test out the mother to see if he can indeed rely on her. During this period, the infant is likely to experience anxiety that the child will later attempt to dissipate through excessive demands on the mother when she is available. Thus, the mother's absence during this critical period can result in overdependency. The second critical period comes between the ages of two and three when a child is expected to relinquish some of his dependency. Disturbances of a serious nature at this time such as death, separation, remarriage, or both parents' working can again arouse anxiety over his dependent relationship with the mother, thereby increasing the likelihood of excessively dependent behavior. Sears, Maccoby, and Levin (1957) reported that parents who irritably rejected their children's requests for dependency, but who eventually succumbed to such demands, produced the most dependent children. The implication is that inconsistent nurturance, whether produced by separations or erratic maternal behavior, may lead to extreme emotional dependency (Ferguson, 1970).

What becomes of the dependent child? Will he always remain dependent? The only longitudinal study on dependency underscores the importance of cultural influences on the developmental stability of this drive (Kagan & Moss, 1960). The results suggest that passive dependent behavior remains stable over time for the dependent female, but not for the dependent male. The results are interpreted in light of societal pressures for the male to become self-reliant and autonomous and for the female to be passive.

Too Little Dependency.   Not all youngsters are given the opportunity to learn dependency. As noted above, the social-learning theorist views dependency as a consequence of the mother's or caretaker's satisfying the infant's needs; that is, the mother's presence is associated with a state of comfort and well-being, while her absence is associated with anxiety. When children are deprived of a continuing relationship with a caretaker, it is difficult for the kind of learning process described above to occur. Furthermore, there is a tendency in our society for parents and teachers to overlook the importance of originally learned dependency. Youngsters who have failed to learn dependency are frequently difficult to socialize since they have not learned to desire approval from others. People interested in day care centers are particularly concerned about the child's having a close relationship with a single caretaker. For youngsters who already have a secure relationship with their mother, high-quality day care may have a beneficial effect. Even high-quality day care may hurt youngsters who are already anxious in their attachment relationship, however. The young child needs a secure relationship with the mother as a base from which to venture forth to develop competence in physical and social environments (Ainsworth, 1973).

The importance of learning dependency for the socialization process is suggested in a study by Goldfarb (1945). He compared 15 children reared in institutions with 15 children who had spent the first three years of their lives in foster homes under more normal conditions. Upon follow-up, around age 12, dramatic differences were noted between the two groups. In addition to intellectual deficits, the institutionally reared children also differed from the children in foster homes in other respects. First of all, the investigator noted the absence of a normal inhibitory pattern. The institutionally reared youngsters were characterized by hyperactivity and disorganization. They were unmanageable, and it was difficult for the adults to control the youngsters' behavior. Second, the youngsters showed what is described as affect hunger. In other words, they demanded constant affection and attention. Third, these children tended to develop very shallow emotional relationships with others despite their strong need for attention from others. Fourth, they manifested a lack of normal guilt and anxiety. Following transgressions, these youngsters would typically show no signs of remorse. This lack of anxiety was also reflected in their schoolwork, in that they could accept failure with apparently little feeling.

We do not want to leave the reader with the impression that adverse effects *inevitably* follow as a consequence of maternal separation. Whether negative consequences occur following maternal separation depends on a number of factors such as the age of the child, the stress involved in separation, the length of the separation period, the kind of care given during the separation period, and the amount of subsequent trauma in the child's life. If the infant is separated while forming a close attachment, if separation is accompanied by other stresses such as illness and followed by a prolonged stay in an impersonal, unchallenging environment, and if the child has a later history of repeated traumatic experiences, such as unsuccessful placement in a number of foster homes, he is apt to suffer severe emotional and intellectual damage. On the other hand, the negative consequences can be lessened by separating the infant before attachment develops, by reducing stress at the time of separation, by making the new surrounding warm and stimulating, and by returning the child to his mother or by finding an adequate mother substitute[1] (Wenar, 1971). Some authorities assert more

---

1. The parent-child relationship is one in which a parent, most often a mother, is involved with a child, but it is not essential that the caregiver be a parent or even a mother. What is essential is a relationship that provides specific conditions necessary for specified learnings.

strongly that *quality* day care programs (one form of maternal separation) can promote healthy development.

Action Guidelines

The following guidelines are relevant to the instruction and management of the overly dependent student.

1. Select a goal that will help him become more self-directing and less dependent on teacher support. The dependent student will frequently need guidance in acquiring such important behaviors as making decisions more independently, exploring the classroom environment, defending his own judgments and opinions, working on his own, playing alone, and leaving the teacher or parent.

2. Proceed toward your goal in a *gradual* manner. Guard against the natural tendency to make him self-reliant overnight. The case study of An Overly Dependent Child illustrates how one teacher helped a girl student to become more independent without frustrating her dependency needs.

An Overly Dependent Child

Mrs. Brown observed that when she gave Marcia arithmetic assignments requiring no more than 15 minutes to complete and stayed near her, Marcia completed the assignments quickly with few errors. But when Marcia was given assignments requiring more than 15 minutes to complete and consisting of problems equivalent in difficulty to those contained in shorter assignments, she worked only while Mrs. Brown was near her. Since Mrs. Brown did not stay near Marcia throughout the time she worked on longer assignments, the child seldom completed these and made many errors on those she did not finish.

It appears that physical proximity of the teacher was reinforcing to Marcia. In this instance, Mrs. Brown paired her presence with verbal praise to "keep up the good work, Marcia." She began by giving arithmetic assignments to Marcia that could be completed within 10 minutes. Gradually assignments were made that required more time to complete. During arithmetic seatwork, Mrs. Brown made it a point to stay near Marcia on a variable schedule of reinforcement (that is, in a way unpredictable to Marcia) and praised her for her efforts. Praise was also issued from afar in order to encourage Marcia to complete assignments. Because Mrs. Brown was observant, she was able to use those conditions that contribute to Marcia's desirable work habits (Stephens, 1970).

Note that the teacher did not simply leave the student on her own. Instead, she provided emotional support while helping Marcia to be increasingly independent of her presence. Mrs. Brown did not strengthen Marcia's dependent ways through overgratification, nor did she thwart Marcia's reliance on the teacher's presence.

3. The dependent student is likely to change his behavior on the basis of whether others approve of it or not. Because of this susceptibility to social influence, teachers can make effective use of social rewards (recognition and approval) in motivating the dependent youngster to become more mature. Doing things for himself must become more rewarding than having others do them for him if behavioral change is to occur.

4. Be sure that other students are not doing the dependent youngster's assignments for him and depriving him of valuable learning experiences.

5. Be sure that you are not reinforcing dependent behavior by your nearness, attention, and affection.

6. Be consistent in your process of systematic weaning.

Anxiety and Insecurity

Overview

The Anxious Child and the Teacher.   Teachers, while rightfully concerned with the aggressive student, are also confronted with and often perplexed by the anxious, insecure child.[2] Though less disruptive to classroom order than his aggressive counterpart, the anxious youngster can leave teachers feeling helpless in their efforts to assist him in becoming more responsive to the classroom setting. For example, the teacher cannot get Jimmy to talk in front of the group, or Sally to associate with her classmates, or Joe to overcome his fear of algebra, or Don to conquer his anxiety about tests, or Clarence to become more assertive and to defend his rights, or Audrey to stop worrying about making occasional mistakes on assignments. Behaviors such as these probably do not interfere with the performance of the class as a whole, but they do keep the afflicted individual from realizing his educational and/or social potential. The plight of anxious and withdrawn children has been aptly described by Morse and Wingo (1969, p. 395):

---

2. Many authors have distinguished between anxiety and fear by postulating that the former is a diffuse and undifferentiated apprehensive response to anticipated threat, whereas the latter is supposedly bound to a specific object or situation. In children, however, it is difficult to differentiate between these two states because the developing personality and intellectual processes do not permit the finer or sharper separations between genuine and fantasied threats that are more characteristic of the mature adult (Erikson, 1950). Further, since the experiential aspects of these two emotional responses do not appear to be appreciably different and since both terms refer to the unpleasant feeling states involving physiological reactions, the two terms will be used interchangeably for the purposes of discussion here.

All teachers will have in their classrooms children who are models of conformity yet whose behavior should be considered a problem. There are the unhappy children who have not organized themselves for productive work, the ones who feel grossly inadequate and unimportant, the quiet and withdrawn children, and the shy or fearful ones who often file quietly in and out of school and receive no more than passing consideration. Yet these children are discipline problems as much as the aggressive, noisy youngster, for they too have not yet learned the mature self-direction that will make their behavior both satisfying to themselves and acceptable to others.

Trait versus State Anxiety.   Many psychologists make a distinction between state and trait anxiety (e.g., Spielberger, 1966). State anxiety is regarded as a person's momentary or situational anxiety which varies across settings and over time. Trait anxiety, in contrast, pertains to the more stable characteristic of anxiety. True-false items similar to those used in questionnaires designed to measure anxiety are presented in Table 2–1.

Research findings suggest that anxiety is not a situation-free characteristic of the person, nor is it intrinsic to the situation alone. Anxiety reactions depend jointly on the person, the situation, and the method used to measure the anxiety (e.g., questionnaire, actual avoidance behavior, physiological arousal). These findings highlight the need to consider the individual in interaction with the situation in our attempts to predict a person's anxiety reactions.

Anxiety and Behavior

Effect on Intellectual Functioning.   In its more extreme forms, anxiety is most commonly seen in neurotic disorders, such as the rather total disorganization seen in school phobia, a condition in which the student is so fearful that he is unable to leave home and come to school. In its less extreme forms the individual feels apprehensive, ill at ease, and that some impending danger is imminent, e.g., "I just know something is going to go wrong." Overcompliance to authority, nervous habits, overreaction to criticism, pref-

Table 2–1.   Items Similar to Those used on Anxiety Scales[a]

Item	High-anxiety Response
I rarely get really tired	False
I am not a worrier	False
I cannot keep my mind focused on anything	True
I almost never blush	False
Often I cannot keep from crying	True
It's hard for me to go to school	True
Often I think I am no good	True

[a] Data from Mischel, 1971.

erence for adult company or that of younger children, withdrawal into fantasy as a means of coping with or escape from stressful situations, fear of change in one's daily routines or surroundings, and an inability to face up to stressful conditions are also common manifestations of anxiety.

Current research on anxiety reveals that, when intense, it can have undesirable effects on both intellectual and personality functioning. In terms of intellectual operations, highly anxious students tend to score lower on:

1. intelligence tests given at both the elementary- and secondary-school levels;

2. achievement tests given at both the elementary- and secondary-school levels; and

3. creativity tests.

In brief, high anxiety appears to affect adversely complex intellectual tasks such as those typically required in the classroom. Available evidence suggests that the effects of anxiety become increasingly detrimental to school achievement as the child advances through the elementary-school years. Reading achievement is affected more adversely in highly anxious students than is arithmetic achievement, perhaps because of the greater emphasis placed on reading in our culture and/or because reading is a more complex skill than arithmetic at the early grade levels (Hill & Sarason, 1966). The evidence further suggests that very anxious children might perform best in a nonthreatening, secure classroom. Classroom observations, for example, showed that highly anxious boys are less task-oriented than are low-anxiety boys. Greater insecurity is also evident in their relationships with the teacher. Curiously, anxiety seems to affect girls differently in that the highly anxious girls, in contrast to those low in anxiety, evidence less distractibility and stronger achievement motivation.

MODERATING FACTORS.   While anxiety and school performance are related, the precise effects of anxiety on school functioning depend on many variables, some having to do with the individual (for example, his level of intelligence) and some having to do with the specific classroom setting (for example, the nature of instructions given regarding an assignment). Whereas high anxiety is related to inferior school achievement among elementary-school students, this does not always appear to be the case among college students (Sarason, 1960). At the college levels, performance on complex tasks is not impaired so long as the students do not perceive the evaluation of their performance as a threat to their feelings of adequacy. By the time a student reaches college, academic tasks have lost much of their threat value, especially for high-ability students.

Whether teacher instructions are threatening or achievement-oriented, as opposed to neutral or relaxed, also seems to make for a difference in performance. When tasks are made more "testlike" and evaluative, highly anxious students tend to do less well. On the other hand, students with low anxiety tend to perform better when the evaluative features are emphasized.

The effects of anxiety also depend on the level of the task. When the task is a relatively simple one, then high anxiety facilitates performance. But when the task is a highly complex one, high anxiety tends to hinder performance. Thus, there are several factors both within the individual and within the situation that moderate the relationship between anxiety and performance. The complexity of these interactive effects makes predictions of individual behavior difficult.

Effects on Personal Functioning. Turning to the influence of high anxiety on personality and social functioning, Ruebush (1963) has noted the following:

1. High-anxiety pupils when compared to those low in anxiety are not popular with their peers.

2. High-anxiety children are more susceptible to propaganda.

3. High-anxiety children have more negative self-concepts and are more self-disparaging. Body image also seems impaired.

4. Dependency is also characteristic of high-anxiety children, though more so of boys than of girls.

5. Anxiety decreases the probability of open expression of aggression toward others but increases the probability of their having feelings of anxiety about aggressive impulses or feelings they experience.

6. Inhibitions and anxiety tend to go hand in hand as manifested behaviorally by indecisiveness, cautiousness, and rigidity.

There are three particular points that we should remember about the anxious, inhibited individual. First, fears are formed very easily in anxious students. That is, fear responses are more rapidly acquired in the highly anxious person than in his nonanxious counterpart. Secondly, fears are not only readily established in anxiety-provoking situations, but they also have a strong tendency to spread to similar situations. Anxiety facilitates generalization. For example, a fear of a particular teacher might well spread to the fear and avoidance of other teachers. A fear of one dog might well generalize to other dogs or animals. A fear learned through association with one exam might make one apprehensive about other exams. A fear of fractions might carry over to other kinds of arithmetic problems yet to be mastered. As Quay (1963) notes, "All of this means that unpleasant and fear-producing experiences are apt to have results quite beyond the immediate setting and such experience should be minimized for this type of child whenever possible."

Finally, once formed, fear reactions are difficult to eliminate. Avoidance patterns are not learned through reasoning. Thus, when in a similar or identical situation, fear more than reason dictates how a person will react. One of the major factors in the durability of avoidance behavior hinges around the fact that the phobic individual does not test his fears against reality. The person who is afraid of dogs simply stays away from them. He knows that they bite! He doesn't need to prove that again. Consequently, he never learns that most dogs do not bite under ordinary circumstances. Avoidance of dogs insures his not being bitten, thus reinforcing (rewarding) the fear. In other words, the intense anxiety prevents the student from discovering how unrealistic his fears actually are. Thus it is not surprising that fears are resistant to extinction and that the student fails to develop new ways of behaving.

Positive Effects.   While anxiety does sometimes become a crippling force, we should not regard it as necessarily undesirable, for mild to moderate anxiety can facilitate the student's social adjustment as well as serve as a spur to problem-solving and inventiveness. It is extremely difficult to improve a student's behavior when he himself is unconcerned about it. Anxiety-producing experiences should not be avoided but rather used to develop immunity to stress. By anticipating normal crises (for example, entrance into school), the teacher can help students to cope more adequately with stressful encounters. Few would quarrel with the notion that mastery of stress is a growth-inducing experience. In fact, there is a growing body of evidence suggesting the value of some noxious stimulation during the early years of life. Obviously, youngsters should not be exposed to needless anxiety-producing experiences; yet, it is equally undesirable to eliminate anxiety entirely or to reduce it to an absolute minimum, since adequate socialization requires some feelings of anxiety on the child's part. Moreover, youngsters of this generation will in all probability have to learn to live with more anxiety as adults than we do. Somewhere between the extremes, there is an optimal level of anxiety. If anxiety deviates markedly from this level in either direction, the socialization process is hindered.

How Does Anxiety Arise?

Very little empirical research has been conducted on the antecedents of anxiety. Sarason (1960) reports that mothers of high-anxiety children are quite defensive in interviews. Such evasiveness and guardedness, though in themselves clues to the personality makeup of these mothers and their manner of interacting with their children, have nonetheless hampered research on the relationship between child-rearing practices and the development of anxiety. Though research evidence concerning parental role in the production of childhood anxiety is sparse, clinical experience with anxious children and their parents has offered us some insights into its development. Cameron (1963) has discussed the following ways in which children can be given training in anxiety:

1. By having a model who is anxious, the child may become habitually apprehensive simply as a result of associations with parents and teachers.
2. Some children are taught to search out every conceivable danger in their everyday lives. We recall the case of a divorcee who was obsessed by the idea that her ex-husband would come and take her only son, as the man had once threatened. The mother alerted the son to this ever-present danger, and taught him to lock all doors at home, to keep the shades down, to stay indoors as much as possible, and to be especially careful on his way to and

from school. She also alerted her son's teachers and principal about the possibility of kidnapping so that they too might convey this concern to him. It is little wonder that this youngster became terribly tense and apprehensive.

3. Some children are used as confidants by their parents. In this role, the children are exposed prematurely to difficulties of adult adjustments such as financial burdens and marital problems. Lacking the necessary maturity to understand fully such problems as well as the ability and experience to cope with them, the children become overwhelmed and disillusioned by the uncertainties of life. Consider the boy whose mother continually tells him how bad his father is, how he does not pay the bills, how unfair he is to her, how she could have married a better man. The child's parental loyalties thus become divided, and a fundamental source of his personal security thereby undermined. Such a child is obviously vulnerable to strong feelings of personal anxiety.

Parents are not the only sources of premature exposure to life's problems. Mass media can also produce uncertainty in children by providing vicarious experiences for which they are not psychologically ready (for example, the soap operas on television).

4. Perfectionism can also make for anxious children. The parent or teacher who is never satisfied with a child's performance, who habitually tells him that he could do better, who sets standards above the child's ability level, produces a child who is self-dissatisfied and open to feelings of anxiety over his failure to live up to expectations.

5. Overpermissive parents or teachers are also likely to have highly anxious children because children need definite limits set for them in order to feel secure. Without such limits, the child is not sure of the boundaries of his behavioral freedom. Consequently, environmental predictability is lessened and uncertainty heightened.

6. Frequent or intense punishment is commonly associated with anxiety in children. Anxiety based on punishment may be reflected in concerns over bodily harm or over rejection by others. Such reactions may be particularly acute for the anxious child who has learned that not measuring up to expectations is associated with punishment of some kind (corporal punishment, ridicule, dirty looks).

7. It is important that the curriculum be sufficiently flexible in order to maximize the student's chances of success and minimize his chances of failure. When students are asked to perform assignments that are grossly inconsistent with their abilities, needs, or cultural backgrounds, they are apt to experience anxiety and fear out of self-doubt and out of an inability to please the teacher. Other policies regarding curricular practices such as grading, promotion, and grouping, if not handled intelligently, can also cause considerable anxiety among students.

8. Continuous demands for increased academic competence can also place students under greater pressure. Since educational achievement is seen as a means of maintaining international status and superiority as well as personal prestige and gain, students (especially the males) are valued

largely on how they can achieve and excel in school. Youth can respond constructively to challenge, but we must guard against their being caught up in an unremitting pressure to excel with an extreme emphasis on speed and grades (McNassor, 1967).

9. In adolescence, the search for personal direction is added to the list of anxiety sources as the teenager attempts to discover where he is going in life, what his assets and weaknesses are, and how he fits into his newly found social and biological roles.

Action Guidelines

1. Teachers should be on the alert because the student experiencing strong anxiety—particularly the bright and anxious student—is not as easily spotted by teachers as one might suspect. It should also be noted that boys are less apt to voice their anxieties than girls.

2. Teachers and parents should set realistic goals for the anxious child. Constant reminders of the disparity between the child's level of performance and the standards set for him can produce considerable anxiety. Ironically, lowering expectations to a level more commensurate with the child's development can raise the child's schoolwork by decreasing the child's anxiety.

3. The teacher can optimize the anxious child's learning by keeping the number of evaluative situations to a minimum, by providing easy tasks in which failure and criticism are unlikely, by providing personal support, and by removing time limits from tests so that there is no penalty for the often slow and cautious problem-solving approach of the anxious youngster. Allowing the anxious student a second chance on exams can also reduce his sense of threat. For example, he might be allowed to earn half credit for correcting each item he missed on an exam or project. The use of report cards with letter grades should be delayed as long as possible during the elementary-school years.

4. It is imperative that the teacher's response to inadequate performance should not convey the attitude that failure and being personally liked by the teacher are in any way related. The student's worth must be respected.

5. Recognize that teacher praise is often not a reward for the shy child, at least not initially. Such youngsters commonly have unfavorable self-concepts, and the praise given by the teacher is at odds with what others have communicated to them and with what they believe about themselves. Consequently the teacher's use of praise generates dissonance and makes the child feel uncomfortable. Where verbal approval produces unfavorable classroom behavior such as discomfort, defensiveness, unrealistic aspirations, and incredulity (the child suspects such nice words), the teacher should consider the use of tangible or activity rewards. For instance, one elementary-school student with a low self-estimate but high standards would typically tear up and discard art or written assignments whenever the teacher praised her in front of the class. This student could, however, accept points to be spent on activity rewards selected from a reward menu and nonverbal praise in the form of written comments on her assignments ("Not bad! That was a tough

assignment"). The teacher must be alert to the possibility that praise may sometimes assume partly aversive qualities. This type of ambivalent reaction should not deter the use of rewards, however. In fact, do not let this child divert you from using rewarding behavior. (Shy, withdrawn children are adept at getting others to leave them alone.)

6. The use of desensitization procedures is particularly effective in overcoming intense fears and anxieties. The logic underlying these procedures is simple and straightforward. Identify the events that evoke marked emotional discomfort, arrange the fear-producing events in a graded list proceeding from the least to the most disturbing, and associate the unpleasant events with something that elicits intense pleasure. Through repeated association with something pleasant, the feared situation eventually loses its unpleasant connotations. When the individual can relax in the face of what was once an upsetting situation, he has been desensitized.

See the story about the youngster who was afraid to speak before a group.

Fear of Speaking in Front of a Group

The use of desensitization procedures is well illustrated in the case of a girl who was afraid to speak in front of a group. Mickey was a bright sixth-grade girl who was referred to the school counselor because she became acutely anxious when asked to read aloud, give a report, or perform in any way before her peers. Though she would participate in class discussions and had warm relationships with others, she had always been unable to speak before a group, despite her desire to do so. The counselor had a conference with Mickey and explained that "learning a behavior a little at a time in a relaxed manner" can often help people do things that previously caused appreciable anxiety. Mickey met with her school counselor once a week for six weeks. During these sessions, she role-played behaviors involved in giving an oral report. Initially, she role-played getting out of her seat and coming to the front of the room. Practice in oral reading was also undertaken, but this was done initially when Mickey was still in her seat. The variety and length of activities were increased weekly. Liberal reinforcement was given for gains made—for example, "Hey, that's great!"—and progress was constantly called to her attention. She was encouraged to rehearse these behaviors, but only if she felt comfortable in doing so.

A plan of action was designed to increase her oral participation in front of her classmates gradually. Mickey was included in a social studies committee that gave weekly reports on various countries the class was studying. She did not have to participate beyond the point that made her anxious, however. Her first task consisted in standing by a large map at the front of the classroom and pointing out regions that were being discussed by other members of the committee. By and by, members of the committee, at the prompting of the teacher, increased Mickey's role by asking questions that she could readily handle—e.g., "What's the region north of Paris called?" Mickey was thanked by other members for her active participation, and she was told that she had done a fine job. Still later, the committee sat in a semicircle while Mickey gave the report, and Mickey's seat was situated so that she did not have to face the audience directly. Mickey gradually became more relaxed while giving reports in front of the class. By the end of the school year, Mickey had reached the point where she volunteered to give an oral report on class accomplishments in social studies (Hosford, 1969).

This case illustrates the combined use of gradual exposure to threatening situations, the pairing of unpleasant tasks (talking in front of the class) with something pleasant (peer and teacher approval serving as anxiety-neutralizing features), and the use of role playing or rehearsal (overlearning). School personnel were careful not to overwhelm the student by forcing her into situations in which the anxiety was unbearable, yet they were also careful to give her opportunities to confront the feared situation. Intrinsic rewards were also probably operative in that she was happy to master her difficulty.

7. Consider the use of the peer group in drawing out the anxious, shy child. Direct attention from an omniscient and omnipotent teacher often makes the anxious, withdrawn child feel more self-conscious and insecure with the result that withdrawal tendencies become even more pronounced. Select a student with whom the shy child feels somewhat comfortable and have him assist the retiring individual in becoming more outgoing and assertive. For example, the teacher might say, "Jim, I think Jerry [the withdrawn child] might like to play this game with you. Why don't you ask him?"

8. Give the anxious student opportunities to overlearn the skill(s) to bolster his confidence. We can all remember how helpful it was to prepare for anxiety-producing events (our first date, first exam in college, first job interview). Preparation can take such forms as self-rehearsal, role playing, and watching others. Guided participation in which the teacher or a peer actually takes the anxious youngster through the feared situation is a very useful technique in overcoming fears.

9. Anxious students respond well to definite, dependable, and consistent classroom routine. These students need a predictable classroom environment. Many aggressive, acting-out students are novelty seekers and thrive on frequent change in daily routines, but this is not the case with anxious and

withdrawn individuals. Novelty for them is threatening; in learning new concepts or in adjusting to new situations, they are not sure what is going to happen next, and this is upsetting. Teachers should be alert to the fact that these students require extra attention when new concepts or skills are being introduced; uncertainty and anxiety will intensify and perhaps interfere with the assimilation of these new ideas. For example, even shifting from division by one digit to division by two digits may make the anxious student nervous. A little extra instructional attention and personal support at these transition points will be worth the time invested by the teacher. Remember that a structured experience with a given kind of problem or situation reduces the anxiety associated with novelty. Gradually, the anxious student can be exposed to less structured tasks.

10. Programmed instruction also seems to hold considerable promise as a teaching technique for the frightened student. While anxiety typically interferes with the learning of complex intellectual tasks, it tends to facilitate the learning of less difficult kinds of assignments. Our task then becomes one of devising ways in which the student's anxiety enhances instead of inhibits the use of his intellectual abilities. Programmed instruction is one approach to accomplishing just this (Quay, 1963). By breaking down complex tasks into simpler sequences, we have transformed what was once a deterrent force into a facilitating one. What was once the student's disability has now become a source of strength. Programmed instruction also minimizes anxiety by insuring a high rate of success or correct answers. This helps him to develop greater self-assurance and thereby increases the probability of a more assertive approach to life. In addition to the use of programmed instruction, a greater emphasis on rote learning, which requires persistence instead of improvisation, might also be indicated because anxiety facilitates learning of a routine nature.

11. Other guidelines for treatment of the anxious, avoidant student include the following.

    a. Instruct these youngsters individually or in groups of six or fewer.

    b. Reinforce *all* emerging social behavior.

    c. Ignore occasional antisocial behavior on their part. Do not punish them for aggressive behavior unless it becomes too intense or frequent (Spaulding, 1968).

Moral Development

Following the early work of Hartshorne and May (1928–30) and the work of Piaget (1932), there was a dearth of activity and interest in moral development. In general, psychologists avoided the topic of moral development in children since psychological matters pertaining to moral development were thought to be unverifiable and inappropriate topics for psychology as a science. In so doing, psychologists neglected one of the most significant components of personality makeup. It was not until the late 1950s that there was a renewed interest in the study of moral development in children. Today, psychologists from various schools of thought recognize that moral development is essential if the child is to become socialized in the ways of his particular culture. Children in the course of development must learn to channel aggressive and hedonistic impulses, to develop self-control, and to comply to a reasonable extent with societal expectations. If they fail to do so, they and/or society will most likely suffer.

What is moral development? Psychologists have identified three major components of moral development—moral judgment, moral feeling (self-love and acceptance, self-hate and criticism), and moral conduct. No one of these three factors can be regarded as the sole criterion of moral development. Rather, moral development refers to the integration of the thinking, acting, and feeling components. We are all familiar with individuals who give good advice but who fail to follow it. Likewise we are familiar with individuals who conform (act) morally in accordance with what others say he should do but not in accordance with universal principles of justice (for example, the churchgoer who discriminates against minority groups). Finally, we all know individuals who habitually say they are sorry following their misdeeds but who succumb to temptation the next time around. Each of these three factors constitutes a necessary but not sufficient condition for promoting moral development. It is as these three aspects coalesce that genuine moral development occurs.

Roots of Moral Development

The child's moral development at birth is nonexistent. How does the child acquire self-control and set moral standards for himself? The specifics of moral development are by no means fully understood, but three broad factors have been found to play a central role in the child's development of a moral orientation—the child's cognitive level, cultural factors, and child-rearing practices.

Cognitive Factors.   Let us look first at intellectual development. Since moral behavior and knowledge both have a cognitive component, it is not surprising to see that they are influenced to some extent by the child's level of intellectual maturity.

Piaget noted the following changes in moral understanding from the preschool period to early adolescence: (1) The seriousness of an offense is judged in terms of the transgressor's intention and not in terms of the amount of physical damage done; (2) right and wrong depend upon the circumstances and not upon authoritative adults; (3) punishment should be consistent with the nature of the misdeed and serve a constructive purpose rather than being an end in itself; and (4) rules exist for social regulation and can be changed by common consent rather than being immutable.

Kohlberg's developmental scheme bears a close relationship to Piaget's work on moral development but represents a major advance both in conceptual refinement and empirical anchorage. Kohlberg postulates three levels of moral reasoning, and movement from one level to the next is regarded as an outgrowth of the child's cognitive development. The basic themes and attributes of his three levels are as follows.

1. *The Preconventional Level.* Control of conduct is external both in the sense that standards conformed to consist of pressures or commands emanating from sources outside of the individual and in that the motive is to avoid external punishment, to secure rewards, or to have favors returned.

2. *The Conventional Level.* Morality is measured in terms of performing good acts and maintaining the conventional social order or the expectations of others. Control of the individual's conduct is still external in that the rules adhered to are still those of others but now the motivation to comply with these expectations is internal.

3. *The Postconventional Level.* At the third level of moral maturity, control of conduct is now internal both in the sense that the standards conformed to come from within the individual and in that the decision to act is based on an inner process of thought and judgment concerning moral matters. There is a thrust toward autonomous moral principles which have a valid basis and application apart from the authority of the groups or individuals who espouse them and apart from the individual's personal identification with these groups or persons. Level three individuals use words like "duty" or "morally right" but in a way that implies universality, ideals, and impersonality. Expressions like "regardless of who it is" or "I would do it in spite of ostracism" are now in evidence [Kohlberg, 1975].

The major contribution of Kohlberg's work lies in the fact that it sensitizes us to the cognitive dimensions and prerequisites of a mature moral orientation (Hoffman, 1970). Others have also noted the relationship between moral development and intellectual growth. As intelligence and language develop, words, for example, come to play an increasingly important role in moral socialization. It is easier to explain expected standards and the rationale underlying them. Labels ("good," "bad") can be attached to certain misdeeds and the discrimination between what is acceptable and unacceptable is facilitated. For example, a boy might say to himself, "I am not supposed to start fights but it's all right to hit back—unless it's a girl or a crippled kid." In brief, as cognitive development proceeds, the youngster becomes capable of a deeper understanding and appreciation of moral concepts as well as a more highly developed capacity for self-evaluation and self-criticism.

Cultural Factors.   Cultural factors are also known to influence moral development. They determine, in large measure, the *contents* of conscience, that is, the standards and prohibitions the child will learn. Lower-class parents tend to place great emphasis on conformity to external cues or to authority, whereas middle-class parents emphasize internal regulation of behavior. Consistent with this differential emphasis is the finding that lower-class boys behave more aggressively and experience less guilt in the process than do middle-class boys (Mussen, Conger, & Kagan, 1969). In the lower classes, the child's parents and peer group provide different models or behaviors to be imitated from those of the middle class. The subcultural delinquent, for instance, who is a daily witness to aggression and norm violation in his neighborhood, is provided with a value system at odds with the value structure of the middle-class school.

Child-Rearing Factors.   A third factor in moral development has to do with child-rearing practices. The study by Sears and his associates (1957) found that love-oriented techniques, such as the use of praise, warmth, reasoning, and the withdrawal of love, were more effective than materialistic techniques as reflected in physical punishment and deprivation of privileges. The effectiveness of love-oriented practices probably stems from four aspects of parental behavior:

1. Warmth makes the child dependent upon adult approval and lessens his need for deviant behavior to secure attention. It is interesting to note in this connection that parents of delinquents are typically less accepting, solicitous, and affectionate in contrast to parents of nondelinquents (Glueck & Glueck, 1950).

2. The presentation of a model of self-restraint results in the imitation of socially acceptable behaviors.

3. The use of reasoning increases the child's understanding of expectations set for him and gives him additional training in making moral judgments.

4. Certain aspects relating to the timing of punishment are also important. For example, punishment administered upon the initiation of the transgression makes for the development of more effective controls than punishment administered after the misbehavior is related to the development of guilt (Becker, 1964).

Outcomes of Moral Development

Dangers Associated with Severity.   There are two dangers associated with moral development. On the one hand, individuals may be too strict with themselves; on the other hand, they may be too lenient. Both extremes can pose hardships for the individual and for society. Expecting too much and expecting too little can have equally undesirable consequences. If self-regulation is excessive, it may inhibit behaviors that are not in need of censorship. Such unnecessary restrictions reduce the child's behavioral freedom, adjustive flexibility, and personal spontaneity. The child's sense of excitement and enjoyment of life are adversely affected as is his capacity for spur-of-the-moment behavior. In the extreme, such restrictiveness can create conflicts and produce feelings of guilt, self-dissatisfaction, depression, and inhibition—symptoms commonly associated with neurosis. Though such restrictiveness can lead to the above symptomatology, it should not be automatically assumed that the neurotic youngster is necessarily any more moral than the normal youngster. What limited evidence there is suggests that the relationship between neurosis and moral development is slight. The neurotic child may be personally dissatisfied because he is not living up to what he would really like to be, but he is not necessarily self-critical because of perceived shortcomings regarding moral issues (Kohlberg, 1964). An example would be the neurotic adolescent boy whose compulsive seduction of females failed to generate in him any perceptible moral anxiety. The disturbed youth was quite concerned, however, about realizing his ideals of masculinity.

Since moral development has to do with the attainment of ideals as well as prohibitions, there is a possibility that a student who is too severe with himself will strive for standards that are difficult if not impossible to attain, thus creating excessive anxiety and frustration for himself. The reader is perhaps familiar with the student who focuses not on the nineteen problems he had correct but on the one problem he had wrong, or the student who is upset because his straight "A" average was ruined by a "B" grade. Such youngsters tend to be unduly harsh and demanding on themselves. Consequently, they are less able to enjoy life. A certain amount of striving, ambition, and self-dissatisfaction seems to be desirable, but too little self-satisfaction can become a definite handicap.

Dangers Associated with Leniency. DELINQUENCY. At the other extreme is the child whose self-regulation is inadequate. This deficiency may manifest in norm-violating behaviors such as cheating, lying, truancy, or delinquency. This youngster not uncommonly behaves as though rules were not for him. In the more severe cases of antisocial behavior, the child may not experience appropriate guilt feelings for his misbehavior. Two major investigations dealing with delinquent youth reported that both middle-class and lower-class delinquents are deficient in self-critical guilt reactions (Bandura & Walters, 1959; McCord & McCord, 1956). Similarly, Kohlberg (1964), in his study of lower-class delinquents, noticed that his subjects were functioning at an early stage of premoral judgment. He concluded that "simple developmental arrest" characterized the majority of his subjects. Lacking the self-control necessary to police their behavior, these youngsters require constant external surveillance. But external supervision is not a feasible means of handling this problem, for one cannot oversee all of the child's activity.

Redl and Wineman (1951) have described some of the ways in which delinquent youth justify their wide variety of immoral behavior. Their examples illustrate nicely the defects associated with inadequate moral development.

1. *Forgetting of intent.* Though the youngster could recall the details of the crime itself, he could not remember the original motive for performing the crime.

2. *"He did it first."* Though the action was wrong, the fact that somebody else did it served as a "legalizing" precedent.

3. *"Everybody else does the same thing anyway."* If everybody does it, then it can't be wrong, so I don't have to feel bad about doing it.

4. *"We were all in on it."* Because it was a group activity, the blame belongs to the group leader or else to no one.

5. *"But somebody else did the same thing to me before."* Because he was once a victim of a similar act, he is entitled to do the same thing to someone else without having to feel bad about it.

6. *"He had it coming to him."* The wronged party was so evil himself that he deserved what he got. Therefore, there is no need to feel guilty.

7. *"I had to do it or I would have lost face."* Here there is an attempt to justify immoral behavior on the assumption that status in a group with deviant values is more important than compliance with society's morals.

8. *"I didn't use the proceeds for myself."* If the money or goods stolen were used for honorable purposes, then there is no need to feel bad about oneself (the Robin Hood mechanism).

9. *"But I made up with him afterwards."* Befriending the victim absolves one of all responsibility for the immoral act.

10. *"He is a no-good so-and-so himself."*

11. *"They're all against me, nobody likes me, they are always picking on me."* Because he is living in the enemy's camp, all acts become justifiable.

12. *"I couldn't have gotten it any other way."* Self-absolution on the grounds that legitimate means were not open to him and/or that he was entitled to what he stole.

NONCONFORMITY.   The immature rebel or nonconformist is a self-centered, power-centered individual. The issue at stake is secondary to his defiance. His typical stance is that "nobody is going to tell me what to do." Aggravating those in authority becomes an end in itself. His primary concern is with enhancing his own power and eliminating those who threaten him. Issues are constantly confounded by his hypersensitivity.

The mature nonconformist, on the other hand, has social feelings and is interested in the common good. He can transcend self-centeredness and attend to the issues at hand. His primary concern is with combating social injustices and rebellion is his choice of technique. He does not engage in dissent for its own sake (Wenar, 1971).

Optimal Self-direction.   Ideally, the child should have an optimal amount of self-control. On the prohibitive side, he should be able to experience feelings of depression and realistic guilt as seen in self-disgust and self-criticism when he has committed a serious transgression. On the self-realization side, moral development should assist in the development of an integrated personality which can seek and achieve culturally congruent goals. The individual characterized by optimal moral development is spontaneous, natural, and free from irrational guilt. He is on good terms with himself and society and he experiences a sense of self-satisfaction when he has acted in a manner consistent with moral principle. He is constructive and ethical in his behavior. He has a high regard for others (as opposed to a "me first" orientation) and is attuned to their feelings. He has firmly established moral principles which he applies in a flexible, realistic way (Peck & Havighurst, 1960).

Unfortunately, it is difficult to achieve a mature moral orientation in our society since cultural pressures often discourage the individual from thinking through matters of a moral nature for himself. On the one hand, moral development may be stunted because of the emphasis on material gains and success regardless of how they are achieved. On the other hand, one is taught not to question moral authority but to accept it with humility. Another factor that has hindered the development of a mature moral outlook is society's emphasis upon the prohibitive side of moral development. Increased emphasis upon the positive side of moral development which concerns itself with self-actualization, feelings of self-acceptance, and altruistic behavior is sorely needed. Fortunately, psychologists are now moving in that direction.

Action Guidelines

Discussion of the implications of moral development can be conveniently divided into three parts—the cognitive, behavioral, and affective aspects of morality. The cognitive implications pertain to the child's making of moral judgments about the correctness of choice in various situations involving moral conflict. The behavioral aspect deals with the student's ability to resist temptation or to perform altruistic acts. The affective implications involve the emotional reactions (for example, self-disgust) following transgression.

Moral Judgment.   One of the major implications has to do with the stimulation of moral judgment. The development of character requires more than preaching or conventional moralizing by teachers and parents. Indeed, preaching and exhortation are probably the least effective. "To be more than Mickey Mouse, a teacher's moralizings must be cognitively novel and challenging to the child, and they must be related to matters of obvious, real importance and seriousness" (Kohlberg, 1969). This does not mean that the moral matters discussed need be only ones of immediate and real life issues. Any issue can be of potential value as long as the conflict situations are challenging and capable of generating serious, lengthy debate. The pat little stories in school readers depicting the inevitable triumph of virtue or everyone as really nice will not advance moral development. Only the discussion of interesting and difficult moral conflicts can lend to a dissatisfaction with one's current level of moral understanding and stimulate moral judgment (for example, discussion of drugs, abortion, busing). Too often teachers dwell upon trivial classroom rules that have no moral meaning outside of the classroom.

In order to disturb the student's equilibrium careful consideration must be given to the match between the teacher's level of moral explanation and the youngster's stage of moral development. Conventional moral training has not had much impact on students' moral judgments because it has disregarded this problem of developmental match. It has usually involved a set of adult moral clichés that are meaningless to the child because they are either too abstract or too patronizing, talking down to the student. A series of studies (Turiel, 1969) suggests that the communicating of moral messages should be aimed at a level one stage above the student's current stage and secondarily at the child's own level. If the level of explanation too far exceeds the child's level of understanding—that is, by two or more stages—he will be unable to show any appreciable understanding of the moralizing. While children can comprehend moral communications beneath their level of understanding, they do not seem to *accept* it as readily as if it is slightly in advance of their level but still comprehensible. It is perhaps worse to err by being at too low a level because the child loses respect for the message (Kohlberg, 1969). Nobody enjoys being talked down to. The teacher must begin by listening to the student's level of moral judgment and then involve him in dialogue at the next stage of moral development. Further, the teacher must become concerned with the child's moral judgments as well as the child's conformity to the teacher's behavior or judgments.

Moral Conduct.   It is also essential that school authorities exemplify the kinds of moral behavior they want to develop in their students. Teachers must practice what they preach or run the risk that their practices will counteract their moral verbalizations. Because a teacher's authority protects him from social feedback from his students, a teacher can slip into the habit of exemplifying bad manners, bullying, or even mild sadism without realizing it. To teach justice requires just schools. To teach altruistic behavior requires observation of charitable acts. If we preach the importance of accepting others, we must refrain from treating others as inferiors. The potency of an altruistic model is demonstrated, for instance, in one study showing that elementary-school pupils were more likely to donate highly valued gift certificates to children of a fictitious orphanage if they had seen an adult do so (Rosenhan & White, 1967). Remember that we teach by example, and that a teacher must be fully aware of the example he is setting. The first step for anyone who has to take responsibility for the moral education of children should be to examine the morality of his own conduct toward them (Wright, 1971).

In addition to the use of suitable models, the schools can foster moral conduct through consistent use of punishments and rewards. Various studies suggest, for example, that the ability to resist temptation is related to the timing, frequency, consistency, intensity, and rationality associated with the use of punishment. More will be said about the role played by reward, punishment, and modeling as means of modifying behavior in the chapter on classroom discipline. Suffice at this point to note that care must be taken to see that rewards and punishments are associated with the moral behaviors that we wish to strengthen or weaken respectively. It is quite possible for a school to encourage excessive compliance, lying, snobbery, and expediency and to discourage truthfulness, altruism, and integrity without intending to do so.

Moral Affect.   The perfectionistic child who has been taught to require unusually high standards of himself must be helped to achieve with less effort and concern. There are various ways in which tension can be reduced. When assigning a theme, the teacher can specify that spelling must be correct but that punctuation will not be graded on that particular task. The use of speed tests should be curtailed. Shorter assignments should be given so that the perfectionistic student can succeed without extraordinary effort. If several quizzes or exams are given, the practice of dropping the two lowest scores in arriving at a grade is a special comfort to the perfectionistic student. Parents should also be helped to see that overconcern hinders rather than helps performance (Verville, 1967).

An Overly Conscientious Student

The following case illustrates how one teacher worked with a student who had excessively high standards. Jim, a 9-year-old fourth grader, was a "model student." He was responsive to teacher demands and extremely meticulous in carrying out assignments. His perfectionistic tendencies were readily evident. If he completed a math assignment with 95% accuracy, he focused on the 5% that he got wrong. If a theme didn't turn out the way he wanted it, he would tear it up in disgust, become angry, and be on the verge of tears. In short, Jim became very self-punitive when he felt that there were shortcomings in his performance.

After discussing Jim with the school psychologist, the teacher launched a multipronged attack on the problem. Jim's comment that his teacher never made mistakes and that he shouldn't either led her to believe that she had been providing Jim with a perfectionist model to live up to. She realized that she had also been inadvertently rewarding Jim's perfectionistic tendencies by praising him when he got "100" and by withholding praise when his paper was less than perfect. She knew he could be a good student and she expected him to be just that. Now she had to change her tactics somewhat. She still wanted him to be a competent student, but he had to learn that the world doesn't always fall apart because of human errors.

One of the first things she did was to stop rewarding his flawless performances and to begin rewarding him for just good performance—e.g., she would write on his paper, "Jim, that was a tough assignment and you did a good job on it." In brief, she tried to ignore "undesirable" behavior, namely, perfectionist behavior, and to strengthen desirable behavior, namely, "good performances."

Another thing she did was to discuss some historically well-known people, carefully pointing out their strong points but also noting that all of them failed at something in their lives. It was noted, for instance, that even the brilliant Einstein admitted confirming only one in a thousand of his ideas. Later, she asked the students to think about an incident which in some ways might be comparable to those discussed earlier. Jim was a little bit shaken after hearing how many people had events in their lives not go as planned. Then the teacher pointed out how she had "goofed" in her first year of teaching but how the occurrence of such errors had actually made her a better teacher and person today.

Another technique involved playing "stump the teacher." This game was used as a reward on Fridays when the class had worked hard. Students were free to ask any question on any subject. Jim's teacher, though competent, could not, of course, answer all of the questions addressed to her. Jim and the rest of the class would laugh when she did not know the answer and she would laugh with them, thereby showing that she could be less than perfect and yet self-accepting. The message implicit in these modeling incidents was that "I don't know everything but yet I am an adequate and worthwhile person both in my own eyes and the eyes of others."[3]

The teacher also taught Jim the difference between "good mistakes" and "poor mistakes." The former entail use of the correct process even though execution of the process leaves something to be desired. Through this technique, Jim was able to become more accepting of certain types of mistakes. Once he had learned to be more accepting of "good mistakes," he was encouraged to become more accepting of the poor mistakes too.

The parents were also well aware of the stress and strain associated with their son's perfectionist ways and were eager to do whatever they could. In a conference with the parents, the teacher explained some of the strategies that she had used in school and encouraged them to carry these over to the home. The father, a journalist, could point out, for instance, that he had to rewrite almost every article he published despite his years of experience and training. Yet he was still respected as a person of talent. Such experiences were to be related in a casual, nonobvious way so that Jim would not get the impression that others were just trying to make him feel good following a "failure" experience. By the end of the school year, Jim no longer tore up papers in disgust. Though he still set high standards for himself, he seemed more self-accepting and reported that he could live with himself more easily now.

---

3. Ideally, in a good classroom, questions the answers to which the teacher would not know would often be raised.

We have discussed the overly conscientious student. How about the student who has the opposite problem. For the student with too little guilt, the school must provide a well-controlled, highly structured classroom environment which will permit the management and realignment of unacceptable conduct. Since self-control is not well developed in this child, greater reliance has to be made on external controls or supervision. The learning experience should be structured so that it consistently strengthens those behaviors the school is trying to promote and weakens those behaviors that the school hopes to extinguish. This student needs a reality rub-in, that is, the teacher must unapologetically let him know what the standards are and what he will get for compliance with them. He must come to know in a very personal way that there are rewarding alternatives to his way of coping with the world.

While external control is necessary initially, the uncontrolled child must eventually learn to set a desirable standard and to reinforce himself for reaching it or to criticize himself constructively for not reaching it. As the capacity for self-reinforcement and self-criticism develops, there is less need for external consequences. Standards of performance for self-control are conveyed through (a) direct reinforcement (one reinforces himself consistent with the way that others have directly rewarded him), (b) observation of others (the self-rewarding and self-critical remarks made by a model are acquired by and applied to observers), and (c) social control (self-reinforcement and self-criticism reflect the standards of those encountered in daily contacts—for example, the peer group). The shift from external to internal control must be a gradual one, however (Kazdin, 1975).

Aggression

Aggressive behavior is very common in children. Sears and his associates (1957) reported that almost all mothers had to handle instances of intense aggression directed against the parents by the preschool child. Moreover, teachers frequently find aggressive students difficult customers to manage, especially in the case of male students who tend to express their aggressiveness in direct, physical, and nonconforming ways. Childhood aggression is so common as to be thought almost universal. Yet if the child is to become a socialized adult, he must relinquish a certain amount of his aggression or learn new modes of expressing it. Again, there are dangers involved in the socialization process. Socialization of aggressive behavior must not be so harsh as to inhibit its expression severely, for aggression is necessary for a successful adjustment both in childhood and in later life. Without the healthy derivates of aggression—assertiveness, competitiveness, and self-confidence—the child is placed at a distinct disadvantage in coping with the demands of life, for it is not the meek or submissive who inherit the earth in our success-oriented culture. Rather, in our society as in many others, training in and encouragement of assertiveness, exploitiveness, and striving for achievement represent particularly important aspects of the socialization process, traditionally for males and increasingly for females. Training in aggression is necessary not only for fulfillment of one's economic role, but for other aspects of psychosocial functioning as well. Unless children are responsive to socialization pressures in this area, societal punishment of either an overt or a covert nature is likely to be their fate.

A certain amount of aggression is a sign of a robust and well-balanced personality. We consider it both normal and desirable for the child to defend his rights and to fight back if the situation warrants. The child should not be made to feel dissatisfied with himself or fearful in exercising his right to justified anger. On the other hand, aggressiveness cannot be allowed a free rein, for such a license too can have an equally undesirable socialization consequence. The aggressive child is not at peace with himself or with his peer group. Since aggressive attacks elicit aggressive responses, it is not surprising to find that the hostile, acting-out child is unpopular (Winder & Rau, 1962).

Learning theorists recognize that a desire to harm others is only one of the factors that can give rise to aggressive acts. In the case of instrumental aggression, aggressive behavior serves purposes other than injurious, destructive ends. The youngster's temper tantrum may, for example, bring the teacher's attention and enable him to get his own way and secure some material gain. It is not always an easy matter to distinguish between instrumental and hostile aggression (Hartup, 1974). The student who engages in name calling may be seeking the teacher's attention as well as wanting to hurt the feelings of his victims. A given behavior can serve more than one end.

Theories of Aggression

Theories of aggression vary in the extent to which they stress biological as compared to psychological factors, such as learning and experience. Early psychoanalytic theorists such as Freud assumed that the child is born with an aggressive drive but the ways in which it is expressed are learned. Later, ethologists such as Lorenz favored a modified instinct view, in which aggressive responses are seen as innate responses to particular stimulus patterns. We will examine a rather different modification of the instinct position, in the form of the "frustration-aggression" hypothesis, as well as theoretical positions that emphasize learning experiences as determinants of aggressive behavior.

Probably the most widely known theoretical explanation of aggressive behavior is the frustration-aggression hypothesis. According to this view, aggression is a highly probable response to a frustrating situation. Where one encounters aggressive behavior, one can assume that it has been initiated by frustration. There is some evidence to support this assumption. One study found that aggressive male pupils had fathers who severely punished aggression in the home (Eron, Banta, Walder, & Laulicht, 1961). In comparing a group of delinquents with nondelinquents, Glueck and Glueck (1950) reported a higher use of physical punishment and lower use of reasoning among parents of delinquents. The existence of a family milieu characterized by punitiveness, threat, and profound parental rejection was found to be one major factor among familiar correlates of aggression in male children observed in another study (McCord, McCord, & Howard, 1961). Thus, various investigators have consistently reported that in some manner the punishment of aggression, which frustrates the child, is related to heightened aggressiveness in the child. The authors view this finding as supporting the position that aggressive behavior is learned as a consequence of early childhood interactions within the family setting. It has become increasingly evident, however, that the frustration-aggression hypothesis cannot account for all aggressive behavior. This theory has proved too simple and too sweeping. Many research studies have revealed an increase in aggression following frustration, but some have found that sometimes there is a decrease and sometimes there is no change in aggression. Frustration is a facilitative but not a necessary condition for aggression. Frustration is only one—and not necessarily the most important—factor affecting the expression of aggression (Bandura, 1973). Recent evidence leads us to a second theory, which centers around the concepts of modeling and reinforcement, cognition and situational factors.

Various authorities have emphasized the role of *imitation* in the acquisition and maintenance of aggressive behavior in children. According to social learning theory, exposure to aggressive models should lead to aggressive behavior on the part of the child. This view is reasonably well substantiated by several experimental studies showing that increases in aggression follow exposure to aggressive models even though the subject may not have been frustrated. In keeping with this theory, lower-class children manifest more overt physical aggression than do middle-class children, presumably because the lower-class model is typically more overtly aggressive. McCord, McCord, and Zola (1959) noted that boys who had deviant parental models were more apt to engage in antisocial activities. In brief, both laboratory and real-life field studies generally buttress the notion that imitation plays an important role in the genesis and maintenance of aggressive behavior. Aware of this modeling influence, authorities have again become concerned about the effects of viewing violence on mass media.

Reinforcement also plays a large role in the expression of aggression. If a child finds that he can get to the head of the lunch line by bullying or that he enjoys hurting others' feelings, he is likely to continue in his aggressive ways if unchecked by others. *Situational factors* can also control the expression of aggressive acts. Aggressive behavior varies with the social setting (for example, ghetto sidewalk, church, algebra classroom, school gymnasium, or nightclub), the targets (for example, weaker peer, policeman, teacher, or clergyman), and the role held by the would-be aggressor (for example, football player, salesman, teacher, or detective). Social learning theory does not question the existence of motivated behavior but rather whether such behavior is explained by ascribing it to the action of aggressive drives.

Cognitive factors also play a prominent role in explaining how aggressive behavior is acquired, provoked, and maintained. Man's higher thought processes provide him with some power of self-direction. People can anticipate consequences without having to enact various alternatives to problem situations. They can reinterpret the behavior or intention of others—e.g., "He didn't mean to do it." They can become aware of what is reinforced in various settings. They can learn by watching, remembering, and mentally rehearsing how others handled difficult situations. Situational determinants, prevailing conditions of reinforcement, and cognitive influences all interact to determine aggressive behavior.

Adjustment Outcomes

Too Little Aggressiveness. Some youngsters are submissive to the extent that they seemingly invite others to take advantage of them. Because of their passivity, these children are victimized, exploited, or disregarded. They are often rejected by their peers, who find little or nothing in them worthy of respect or of interest. During the elementary-school years their passivity leads to timidity in social situations, avoidance of sports, and withdrawal from peer groups (Kagan & Moss, 1962). These children have difficulty asserting their legitimate rights and often harbor strong feelings of resentment rather than seeking redress for justified grievances. Instead of responding aggressively to attack, they experience feelings of fear, self-deprecation, or embarrassment. Life must indeed be strained for those who cannot stand up for their rights.

Uncontrolled Aggression. Whereas the combination of parental restrictiveness and hostility not uncommonly produces seemingly neurotic problems in children, the combination of parental permissiveness and hostility is commonly found in cases of maximal aggression and delinquency (Becker, 1964). In other words, the highest level of aggressive behavior occurs when the child is persistently subjected to conditions that promote feelings of hostility in him, and that at the same time fail to impose limits on his acting-out behavior when he expresses his hostility.

Although still widely accepted, the catharsis theory of reducing overt aggression, which emphasizes the tension-releasing features of emotional release, has received surprisingly little empirical support (Berkowitz, 1973; Bandura, 1973). According to this view, the release of aggressive behavior should produce a diminution of such behavior; that is, aggressive behavior should extinguish itself if allowed unrestricted expression. In actuality, it appears that a permissive approach to the treatment of acting-out behavior in children achieves the opposite effect. In a permissive atmosphere, the child is less fearful of punishment and his inhibitions decrease. Cathartic release may be appropriate for withdrawn youngsters, but its use with excessively aggressive children certainly seems contraindicated. Encouraging the aggressive child to "get it off his chest" or "have it out" has three unfortunate consequences. This method (1) reinforces the child's belief that aggressive overreactiveness is expected, "normal," and approved; (2) reinforces the expectation that whenever angry feelings occur, he will need to act them out;

(3) provides an unsuitable model for classmates, thereby increasing the likelihood that the problem will spread (Good & Brophy, 1973). Violence begets more violence. Aggression leads ultimately to more aggression.

Passive Aggression.   Another undesirable outcome occurs in the case of the student who develops a preference for passive-aggressive modes of coping with hostility toward authority figures such as teachers and parents. According to psychodynamic interpretation, the passive-aggressive child commonly sees teachers and parents as unjust and tyrannical and himself as being badly used by those in control. Because of harsh, repressive tactics on the part of parents in early life, this child comes to fear retaliation for any direct expression of negative feelings toward authority figures. Thus, in contrast to the child who engages in open aggression through such behaviors as hitting, grabbing, pulling, and destroying, the passive-aggressive individual learns to release his anger through more veiled maneuvers. Thus, for example, angry outbursts give way to stubbornness, sullenness, and pouting; and productive accomplishment valued by authority figures gives way to dawdling, procrastination, inefficiency, and obstructionism in the classroom. Poor academic performance together with conformity to the letter of the law but not its spirit serves as an aggressive act against those who try to dominate him. The student resists teacher authority by *habitually* bringing the wrong book to class, forgetting assignments at home, losing his place when reciting, needlessly sharpening pencils when he should be working, forgetting to write assignments down, studying the wrong material for the exam, overlooking certain parts of the lesson, or interrupting his work to go to the bathroom. Such children want freedom and resent being told what to do or having demands made of them. Yet they cling to dependency. To teachers, they seem lazy, unsociable, irresponsible, and critical of others while being overly sensitive to criticism by others.

Action Guidelines

How should aggressive behavior in children be handled? Very permissive handling of outbursts leads to increased aggressive activities on the child's part. If the teacher and other significant adults in the child's life are both permissive and punitive, the child is apt to become even more highly aggressive, and perhaps even delinquent. And if the teacher is restrictive and punitive, the probability that the child will become socially withdrawn and intrapunitive is increased. So neither overly strict nor overly permissive treatment seems to be the desirable way of coping with this kind of behavior. The following guidelines are offered:

1. It is sometimes possible to reduce or eliminate aggressive behavior by ignoring it while at the same time paying attention to and rewarding other behaviors incompatible with aggression (such as sharing). In one study, we are told how a 2-year-old child's tantrums were successfully eliminated merely by ignoring the screaming (Williams, 1959). In a more ambitious

experiment involving 27 nursery-school boys, their teachers were able to decrease violent behavior by ignoring aggressiveness while reinforcing acceptable behavior (Brown & Elliott, 1965). A note of caution is in order, however, regarding the use of this technique. While one can render verbal attacks, annoying actions, and oppositional behavior ineffective simply by not responding to them, a tough aggressor can often get what he wants by physical force regardless of the interest shown by his victims (Bandura, 1973). Ignoring is not feasible in cases in which aggressive behavior is injurious, is likely to spread, or seriously infringes upon the rights of the teacher or fellow students. There is also the realistic danger that the teacher's failure to act may be interpreted as a sign of approval or as an absence of concern for his aggressive acts.

2. In those instances wherein ignoring is not the method of choice, the teacher must let the disorderly student know that his overly aggressive behavior will not be tolerated. The student must know that this behavior is out of bounds and that anger does not justify personal assault or destructiveness. Reasonable rules must be enforced.

3. Firm, narrow, and clear-cut limits must be set. A no-nonsense, I-mean-business approach must be adopted and a specific routine should be followed.

4. To the extent that it is possible, do not leave this student unsupervised. Because of his poor self-control external surveillance is necessary.

5. Minimize encounters with the aggression-evoking situations or individuals. For example, if two boys often fight when they are together, it would be wise to change seating arrangements and make sure they do not work on projects together.

6. Try to instruct him in a small group of six or less. Or assign him to a work station in the classroom where he can work alone.

7. Hostile behavior must be stopped, but through techniques other than physical force if at all possible. The generation of additional frustration and anger must be avoided or minimized in the management process. Punitiveness and firmness are not the same.

8. Punishment of aggressive behavior might have to be used at times. In these instances, the unacceptable aggressive behavior (name calling, pushing, destroying, talking loudly, criticizing, manipulating, bossing, etc.) should result immediately in the student's being socially isolated.

9. The teacher can help promote better control in the student by setting an example of self-control. The teacher who explodes when things go wrong hardly provides a model worthy of emulation. But the teacher who remains calm and rational when frustrated does teach self-control by example.

10. The reasons underlying the rules prohibiting certain forms of aggressive acts should be explained to the troublesome student. If the explanations are geared to the student's level of understanding, the standards for conduct become more meaningful and less arbitrary or authoritarian. Youngsters are less apt to be resentful when they can see that the teacher had no aggressive intent in thwarting them.

11. A teacher-student relationship characterized by warmth and per-

sonal interest also reduces the likelihood of deviant behavior. Students are less apt to offend someone about whom they care.

12. The acting-out student must be taught that such behavior is inappropriate under certain circumstances but acceptable at other times and places. He must learn *when* and *where* to be aggressive. Pushing and shouting is unacceptable in the classroom and on the lunch line but appropriate in football games and tug-of-war matches. The objective of socialization is not to squelch aggressiveness but to direct its expression along acceptable lines.

13. The use of educational contracts is helpful. In the case of the passive-aggressive student, the use of contracting enables the teacher (a) to set broad limits, (b) to give the student a voice in terms of assignments and the rate at which they are to be accomplished, providing many choices in terms of the conditions and circumstances of work undertaken, (c) not to supervise closely but to be watchful enough to reward cooperative and productive behavior by granting increased freedom, privileges, or tangible rewards (personal approval is to be avoided), (d) to ignore delay and resistance (if this behavior continues for 3 to 4 weeks after initiating this treatment program, it should be punished through isolation. Remember, however to reinforce productive behavior), and (e) to avoid direct commands and confrontations (Spaulding, 1968).

14. In the case of submissive youngsters, assertion training is needed. These youngsters have to learn how to complain about unfair treatment, to respond to unfair criticism, to question or refuse unreasonable demands, to make rightful claims to their goods, to defend their viewpoints, to fight back when challenged, and in other ways to defend their rights. The techniques of positive reinforcement, modeling, and desensitization that are discussed in chapter 12 on classroom management are all helpful in cases of this nature.

Achievement Motivation

The notion of personal competence has assumed a central status in recent years among many mental-health professionals. The concept of competence is to some extent replacing that of contentment as a yardstick of mental health. The ability to handle the stresses and strains associated with one's roles in life is assuming greater significance as an index of one's mental health than is psychic freedom from anxiety. To be considered competent in our culture, an individual must be able to sustain himself in coping with the demands of reality. In the case of the child, the demands of reality in large measure center around the demands of our educational system, for school is the child's main job and success in this training is regarded as a necessary if not sufficient condition for effective functioning as an adult. In our society, youth must achieve, and to do this they need some degree of achievement motivation.

What is achievement motivation? Stated most simply, it is the child's desire or attempt to do something well. He may want to perfect a skill such as jumping rope, running a mile faster, or performing a task more efficiently.

The child comes to judge his own performance in terms of certain standards of excellence. In addition, he comes to experience pleasant feelings when he achieves these standards and unpleasant feelings when he fails to measure up.

Achievement motivation is by no means homogeneous in nature. Ausubel and Sullivan (1970) identify three components. First of all, there is the *cognitive* component, which has to do with acquiring knowledge and solving problems for its own sake. The reward is intrinsic to the task. The second and dominant component involves enhancement of one's *self-esteem*. School achievement becomes a means to prestige and recognition. This dimension of achievement motivation may become very pronounced among students who do not have a deep conviction of personal worth. Because this person does not have a feeling of intrinsic self-worth, he continually earns self-esteem through accomplishment. A fear of loss of self-esteem resulting from failure can often be a principal ingredient in his achievement orientation. Whereas failure may be disappointing to a child bolstered by a sense of personal worth, it is not devastating because achievement is still peripheral to his self-esteem. Failure, on the other hand, can be catastrophic to the child who has little sense of personal worth, for he has no reserve of self-esteem to fall back on. Finally, there is the *affiliative* component in which approval is sought through achievement. In other words, achievement enables one to meet others' expectations and leads to acceptance by them. Accomplishment of this kind does not lead to status or prestige, nor is it for knowledge's sake. Rather it is to guarantee continued acceptance by those important to the person. This aspect of motivation is probably very important in early childhood when parental acceptance is important. Later, females apparently continue to seek external social approval to a greater extent than do males.

What characteristics differentiate the individual with high achievement motivation from those with low achievement motivation? A review of the research (Atkinson, 1965; Atkinson & Feather, 1966; Heckhausen, 1968; McClelland, 1965a) on this topic indicates that the student with high achievement motivation is characterized as follows:

1. He is concerned with the excellence of his performance.

2. He is confident of succeeding. Associated with his history of success is a trust in his own abilities rather than in luck or fate.

3. He is able to set realistic goals. That is, his level of aspiration is appropriate to the tasks he undertakes.

4. He is willing to take moderate or calculated risks. His desire to achieve is strongest when the chance for success is about 50–50. That is, he likes challenging but attainable goals. The student with a strong need to achieve will avoid activities involving extreme risk or very minimal risk.

5. He is able to delay gratification. His extended future time perspective enables him to curb his impulses and to give up what he wants at the moment. He would rather have a ten-cent chocolate bar next week than a one-cent tootsie-pop today.

6. The individual with a high need to achieve makes efficient use of his

time and energy. This economical expenditure of effort facilitates his productivity.

7. Though there has so far been no connection established between achievement motivation and the degree to which one feels responsible for his own achievement-related activities, theoretically one would expect that those with high achievement motivation would feel highly responsible for their successes and their failures whereas those with low achievement motivation (or fear of failure) would be more defensive and attribute outcomes to sources outside themselves.

How Does Achievement Motivation Develop?

Certainly, children are not born with standards of excellence. When and how does the desire to achieve arise? There appears to be no research that has investigated the age or conditions surrounding the emergence of achievement behavior. We do know, however, that individual differences in achievement motivation exist as early as age 4 or 5. Students in the primary grades also differ from one another with respect to the degree and area of achievement motivation. Crandall (1961) found, for instance, that some pupils spent more time and worked more intensely on intellectual pursuits, while others concentrated on artistic or mechanical pursuits. The desire for excellence in achievement not only arises early, but also tends to persist into adulthood. In one major longitudinal study (Moss & Kagan, 1961), it was reported that intellectual and recognition strivings were stable from childhood (grades 1 through 4) to young adulthood. Moreover, such strivings were equally stable for both sexes. Heckhausen (1968) has postulated a critical period for the development of achievement motivation occurring around age 4 or 5.

It would seem that parental interaction is a crucial determinant of achievement motivation in the young child. What parental behaviors are associated with the development of intellectual striving in young children? The pioneering study in this area was conducted by Winterbottom (1958), who reported that mothers of boys rated high in achievement motivation expected self-reliant behavior relatively early and gave a freer rein to the child's spontaneous desire to be independent. In addition, these mothers directly reinforced independent behavior when it occurred. Moss and Kagan (1961) also noted that maternal "pushing" of the developmental timetable was a moderately successful predictor of intellectual competence in adulthood. Bandura and Kupers (1964) demonstrated that preschoolers, merely by observing the achievement behavior of others, may develop similar standards of excellence. It appears that high levels of parental involvement provide a basis for achievement motivation, although the impact of parental attitudes and child-rearing practices on achievement motivation will vary with the sex of the parent and child and the kind of achievement motivation. As Singer and Singer (1969) comment:

The parents of boys with a high need to achieve are themselves models of people who frequently engage in achievement behaviors. They set goals of excellence for their children and reward them for progress toward those goals and punish them for failure to make progress. They allow a choice of routes to excellence but do not reward lack of effort, and certainly punish failure. How to accomplish a task may be up to the boy, but he must accomplish it somehow. It is not surprising, therefore, that, for the sons of such parents, reaching standards of excellence acquires emotional value which helps to motivate them to succeed.

A female child is most apt to develop achievement behavior and independence when her parents are moderately warm, moderately to highly permissive, and when they encourage achievement efforts. Parental warmth is more often associated with male's than with female's achievement orientations. Also, males seem to fare better with slightly less permissiveness than females.

While some studies on socialization indicate that the child-rearing practices conducive to feminine sex typing are often antagonistic to those conducive to achievement-oriented behavior (Stein & Bailey, 1973), research in the area of avoidance of success is new and findings are not consistent. Indeed, the most authoritative work available indicates that the sexes are quite similar with respect to those aspects of achievement motivation for which evidence is available. They show similar degrees of task persistence. There is no evidence that one sex works more than the other because of intrinsic interest in a task rather than for social approval. In fact, boys have to be challenged by appeals to ego or competition motivation to bring their achievement imagery up to that of girls (Maccoby & Jacklin, 1974). It is not until the years following completion of formal schooling that female achievement drops off so sharply. Whether this decline is brought about by the measured decrease in self-confidence, or the belief that they are now less able to control the events in their lives, or by characteristics of the post-school world (for example, the demands of domestic life), is by no means clear at this time.

Adjustment Outcomes

Too Much Pressure.   What happens when the student has too much achievement motivation? Are the schools and parents of today pressuring students too much? One way of attempting to answer this question is to examine the personality characteristics of achieving students. Virginia Crandall (1967), an active researcher in this area, had the following to say:

> It would appear . . . that achieving children, in contrast to peers who perform less well, do not need to depend upon adults but are somewhat compliant and conforming to their demands and accept and incorporate adults' high evaluations of the importance of achievement. They are also able to work without being immediately rewarded for their efforts, show initiative, self-reliance, and emotional control. While achieving children of preschool

and early elementary age are somewhat aggressive and competitive, their social relationships are generally good. Achievement, however, seems to be exacting in its toll. By later elementary school or junior high age, aggression and competition have become accentuated, relationships with siblings, peers, and adults show some disruption, and the children are less creative, more anxious, and less able to resist the temptation to cheat. Research on high school students . . . indicates that these attributes become increasingly pronounced at later ages. Does this mean that the effort to achieve "produces" the less desirable personality attributes? Or does it mean that only if children have acquired such a personality constellation will they then be able to achieve in our highly competitive, post-Sputnik educational system? Cause and effect relations cannot be determined from these data, but it is obvious that our "education for excellence" is accompanied by certain psychological costs.

Findings such as these most naturally raise questions about the impact on students' emotional well-being of the knowledge explosion and the emphasis on academic excellence. Debate will most likely continue as to whether academic competition is beneficial or detrimental to later adult coping. Some of the questions that require further investigation have been formulated by Rogers (1969): What goals should we have adolescents seek to achieve? Do some individuals suffer because of a too persistent need to achieve? Is achievement stress a factor in the high incidence of teenage schizophrenia? Are we apt to develop students who achieve out of a fear of failure?

The current stress on achievement is perhaps having its most severe impact at the preschool level. It seems especially fashionable today for a parent to have a preschooler who can read. The parents rarely ask if such instruction could be accomplished more readily at a later age. Nor can they verbalize the potential advantages to the child able to read early. Yet, this precocity is something middle-class and upper-middle-class mothers value. The authors are not opposed to early instruction or academic competency in students. We do want to point out, however, that the intense parental involvement that helps to form the basis for achievement motivation also entails some undesirable attitudes and behaviors—rejection, hypercriticism, hostility, and demands for accomplishment beyond individual readiness—which could do more harm than good. Though there might well be dangers associated with too great an emphasis on the child's doing well, it is likely, given our achievement-oriented society, that we will have little choice other than to prepare students to cope with increasing demands for accomplishment.

Too Little Motivation.   So far we have discussed the dangers associated with too much press for achievement. What is the child like who possesses too little achievement motivation and low levels of accomplishment? A partial answer to this question is provided in Gallagher's (1964) portrait of the underachiever:

1. The underachieving child grows up in, or belongs to, a cultural

group which does not value education, independence, or individual achievement.

2. He has poor parental relationships, in which the parents, especially the father, either show limited interest in academic matters or try to put undue pressure on their children to succeed.

3. The child, unable to obtain satisfaction from parental contacts, seeks out his peer group for satisfying human relationships. Since he searches for others of the same interests as himself, he will often find himself allied with other rebellious and angry children.

4. These children will be faced by teachers and other school officials who ask them to meet standards of behavior which are not possible for them, and who treat these children, in many ways, as their parents do. The children thus place the teachers and the school in the same authority category as parents and reject them and their program.

5. The school, in its attempt to deal with these nonconforming and angry children, is likely to take more strict and repressive measures which will turn the children even more emphatically against the school.

Further, Douvan and Adelson (1958) have pointed out that upwardly mobile boys are characterized by effective, autonomous ego functioning; downwardly mobile adolescents, by demoralization. What are the effects of such demoralization? Among urban ghetto youth, Smith (1968) notes that deviant behavior may result as a consequence of the feelings of powerlessness and hopelessness associated with their incompetence:

> Some antisocial behavior, deviant from the point of view of the environing and superordinate society, may in part be directed toward alternative modes of competence that remain available and indeed become normative in the ghetto subculture when legitimate channels of effectance are closed off. The combative prowess of the gang leader and member, virtuosity in aggressive "mother talk," audacity in sexual exploits, and competence in the risky skills of the hustler belong under this heading, though these directions of activity obviously also yield extrinsic rewards. The larger society will regard these directions of activity as bad, but those who plan and direct rehabilitation programs will do well to remember that for many slum youth, all of their resources of competence motivation get channeled in these deviant directions. A lot of self is invested in them.

Thus, even among antisocial individuals, who not uncommonly convey the impression of being happy-go-lucky and carefree, we note a serious and intent desire to become competent and achieve recognition from others.

As with other aspects of socialization, it appears that too much or too little training can produce adjustment difficulties. We do not want to produce either extreme—those who are obsessed with achievement or those who are inclined to follow the pleasure principle. Some spend too much time in "becoming," others too much time in just "being." We must strive to develop those capable of productive accomplishment without minimizing their capacities for creative leisure. A balance among work, love, and play is the ideal.

Action Guidelines

1. *Expectancy of Success.* One implication has to do with the notion that success experiences will always strengthen the student's tendency to engage in the same task later on. This generalization is commonly referred to as the law of effect and must be qualified by noting that the student whose motive to succeed is greater than his fear of failure will be likely to engage in the same task if he was successful at a task that he perceived as *difficult.* If in his eyes the task was easy or of intermediate difficulty, he would probably prefer to engage in a slightly more difficult or challenging task. Bright, highly motivated students became bored with long periods of uninterrupted success. For these students, the tasks must be truly challenging. Success becomes genuinely rewarding then. For capable students with high achievement motivation, the teacher should provide harder and more challenging assignments following success—tasks that offer a 25–50% expectancy of success. Bear in mind, however, that there is often a fine line of distinction between a truly challenging task and an overwhelming one.

In the case of children with a low need to achieve and a high fear of failure, the law of effect will hold only if the task is perceived as easy. For those with low motivation to achieve, the teacher should offer similar assignments or perhaps gradually increase the difficulty level to keep their motivation at an optimal level (see Table 2–2).

2. *Persistence after Continual Failure.* A student with a strong need to be successful is more apt to persist following failure at a task that he initially believed to be easy than following failure at one he initially believed to be *extremely* difficult. On the other hand, the student with a low need to achieve and with a dominant need to avoid failure, will be much more persistent following failure at a task that he initially believed to be very difficult than following failure at one he believed to be very easy. Because no one can blame him for failing at a difficult task, he experiences little anxiety and consequently feels free to try the hard task again. Failure at a quite easy task does, however, generate considerable anxiety and discourages the student with low achievement needs from further efforts. In such instances, teacher

Table 2–2. Expectancy of Success and Achievement Motivation

	Task Perceived as	
Student with	*Easy*	*Difficult*
High achievement motivation	Will raise his level of aspiration and seek a more difficult task	Will not be inclined to engage in the same activity
Low achievement motivation	Will not be inclined to repeat the task	Will strengthen his tendency to engage in the same activity

support and encouragement are needed if mastery of these tasks (for example, reading skills) are essential to the student's development. On the other hand, the student with a strong desire to achieve can probably be left to work on his own as he will be motivated to accomplish the task. Regarding failure following difficult tasks, the teacher must prevent the student with low achievement motivation from "beating his head against the wall" and provide the student with a high need to achieve with easier but more challenging assignments (see Table 2–3). Provided that the failure experiences are not too frequent or overwhelming, they can be helpful in that they help to develop persistence motivation.

3. *Using Moderate Levels of Motivation.* Although the advantages of achievement motivation in school success are evident, too much achievement motivation may create problems for a student. How much is too much depends on the complexity of the task, the amount of pressure applied by the teacher, the tolerance level of the student, the student's capabilities, and the incentive offered for successful completion of a task. Achievement motivation that is too intense could cause one to overreact to additional "pressure" for achievement in ways that disrupt both achievement and social relations. Strong motivation, especially when associated with anxiety, tends to be better for relatively easy assignments but not for difficult tasks. As a general rule, moderate levels of motivation will result in the greatest efficiency in learning. Increase motivation gradually and be prepared to stop if there are signs of disruption such as overexcitement, aggression, freezing, or an inability to give more than stereotyped, unthinking responses. One's response to external pressure is affected by other aspects of his personality also. Withdrawing children, for example, tend to be more "inner motivated," than extroverts; hence they are more easily overstimulated by external pressures, such as those associated with threats or competition. The same is true for persons who are characteristically apprehensive or anxious. Withdrawing and "high anxious"

Table 2-3.   Continual Failure and Achievement Motivation

	Task Initially Perceived as	
Student with	*Very Easy*	*Very Difficult*
High achievement motivation	Will persist; can probably accomplish task by self	Will not persist as he prefers tasks of intermediate difficulty; should be given more challenging (easier) assignments
Low achievement motivation	Will not persist; will need teacher's guidance and support if mastery of assignment is essential	Will persist; must be persuaded to work on easier assignment

students tend to respond well to moderate motivation, reassurance, a calm demeanor, and considerable freedom. Outgoing and "low anxious" students, on the other hand, may need external rewards, exhortation, rivalry, or other forms of pressure.

A special word of caution is needed with respect to emotionally unstable and slow children. The tolerance of the emotionally disturbed child for strong external motivation may be lower than that of the normal child. At the same time the disturbed child is less capable than most children of performing well under stress. The child who is severely limited in what he can do is easily threatened and, hence, also easily disturbed by strong motivation. Moderate levels of motivation are especially recommended for both the disturbed child and the slow learner.

4. *Increasing the Probability of Success.* Since the student's expectation of success is related to his motivation to achieve, one way to increase achievement motivation is to increase the student's probability of success. This can be accomplished through various strategies, such as breaking the assigned task down into subunits that the student can handle more easily, providing additional help in skill training, and consulting with the teacher about the student's abilities, interests, and needs.

5. *Training in Achievement.* A quite different yet complementary approach to increasing achievement motivation emphasizes changing the personality characteristics that underly achievement-oriented behaviors. McClelland (1965a, 1965b) believes that a high need for achievement in students and adults can be best accomplished through a training program designed to produce attitude and personality change. Such a program should have the following characteristics:

a. It must create strong positive expectations that the person can, will, and should become more achievement oriented. Using "prestige suggestion," the program calls upon high-status individuals to express their beliefs and the evidence for the possibility and desirability of change.

b. The participants learn about the concept of achievement motivation and its importance in becoming successful.

c. The program must demonstrate that the change sought is consistent with the demands of reality and the individual's own makeup and cultural values.

d. It must get the trainee to commit himself to accomplish realistic, practical, and specific goals as a consequence of his new motive to achieve.

e. It must have the trainee record his progress toward the goals to which he is committed.

f. It must provide an atmosphere wherein the individual feels warmly yet honestly accepted and respected as a person capable of directing his future.

Programs such as McClelland's are designed to produce persons with a new understanding of achievement motivation that will lead them to take moderate risks, to face the challenge of moderately difficult tasks, to set realistic goals, to have confidence in their ability to handle specific problems, to seek feedback on their performance, and to defer gratification. In brief, they are expected to learn a high need for achievement and to behave like high achievers.

What are the results? McClelland's review (1972) describes some quite dramatic gains in the achievement of students in grades 8 and 10, as measured by tests and grades. More out-of-school achievement-related activities such as earning money, career planning, and competing in games are also reported after achievement training. Another interesting finding is that similar changes in students have been observed following training in achievement for teachers. Although experimentation with achievement motivation programs has been reported at all grade levels, the present training programs seem best suited to the junior high years and above.

When interpreting the results of training designed to improve achievement motivation, McClelland (1972, p. 145) cautions that what has been demonstrated is improved *learning* and effective *instruction*. While a change in achievement motivation may be *inferred* from performance, it is not proved. The results might in fact be attributed to a change in one's expectation of success, rather than an increase in any basic need for success.

6. *Making the Incentive More Worthwhile.* One can also increase the desire to achieve by increasing the attractiveness of a specific goal. One first-grade teacher made excellent use of a Mickey Mouse watch as a reward in "reaching" Tom, who refused to go near his math worksheet. The teacher recognized his fascination with her Mickey Mouse watch. She struck a bargain with him. If he would let her help him with his arithmetic for ten minutes, then he could wear the watch for five minutes. Given this "foot in the door," it was not too long before Tom began to develop an interest and skill in math (Clarizio, 1976).

7. *Capitalizing on Social Motives.* The preadolescent school years are ones in which the peer group takes on additional meaning for the student. As Sullivan (1953) notes, this is the "juvenile era" during which time the preadolescent acquires a "chum" and special friends of the same sex. Group acceptance and exclusion become important concerns. Any consideration of enhancing the students' desire to achieve should accordingly consider the peer group and its sanctions. The desire for social approval, the need for belongingness, and the urge to conform to group norms all offer powerful motives for achievement which the teacher can tap. To capitalize upon the constructive potential inherent in these social motives, various authorities have advocated the use of strategies such as scholastic competition between schools (music and drama contests, industrial arts and science fairs, debate teams, and intellectual games) (Coleman, 1968), the use of teams within the classroom for purposes of mutual aid as well as competition, the active involvement of older students of the same sex both as individuals and groups in the education of younger students (Bronfenbrenner, 1970), and the widespread use of group recognition and approval for accomplishment. We must shift to a greater degree from interpersonal competition with its conflict-producing

effects to intergroup competition, in which group rewards reinforce achievement. Motivation can be sharply changed by using informed peer group rewards to reinforce the arms of education.

8. *Providing Models of Achievement.* Providing students with models of achievement can result in increased motivation and achievement. Teachers themselves can serve as examples of individuals who are concerned with the excellence of performance in their own lives. Teachers can provide such examples by relating stories about personal accomplishment and through their classroom behavior. For a teacher to serve effectively as a model, however, it is important that students have a positive relationship with the teacher. Pep talks and stories about the high achievement behavior of other adults and students can be a useful procedure.

9. *Eliminating Sexual Discrimination. The plight of boys.* One of the male's unhappy incidental learnings is that he and the school do not get along very well. He discovers that he must function in a way that is opposed to his more aggressive life style. The school with its emphasis on neatness, good manners, and docility clearly places the boy at a disadvantage. Boys quickly learn that they are naughtier than girls and that they have trouble competing with girls for good grades. Boys constitute two-thirds of all grade repeaters in the elementary-school years. While the majority of boys eventually overcome their initial school difficulties and achieve well in school, we must remember that a large percentage never graduate from high school. Ways in which the schools can help the male student include ridding the school of unnecessary rituals, needless regimentation, overemphasis on form rather than substance (Brophy & Good, 1974), the changing of curriculum and teaching strategies so that they hold more appeal, and, perhaps most important, changing the definition of a good student so that there is less emphasis on passivity, conformity, and inactivity. The hiring of more male teachers at the elementary-school level would appear not to help, for sex of the teacher does not seem to be a crucial variable in a boy's adjustment to school (Brophy & Good, 1974).

The plight of girls. Although girls fare better than boys during the elementary-school years by applying careful, cautious work habits, they too suffer from sex typing (Sadker & Sadker, 1972). Schools reinforce neatness, conformity, and docility while they discourage active curiosity, analytical problem solving, and a competitive achievement orientation. Reading texts portray girls as helping with the housework, baking cookies, and babysitting for their brothers. The message of female inferiority also manifests itself in texts of America's history. There is much to read about male heroes such as George Washington, Ben Franklin, Paul Revere. But, aside from Betsy Ross, there is little about female characters to fill youngsters with respect and admiration. Recorded history is replete with material about our founding fathers but has almost nothing about our founding mothers. Female subservience is again modeled for girls as they watch the female teachers take orders from principals, about 80% of whom are males.

Elementary school teaches girls about keeping their place. Fortunately,

Table 2–4. Common Growth Problems

Personality Factor	Behavioral Manifestations	Antecedents	Adaptive Outcomes	Maladaptive Outcomes	Action Guidelines
Dependency	Commonly seeks assistance, approval, physical proximity or contact, and recognition; low tolerance for ambiguity, whining.	Overpermissiveness; maternal overprotection; maternal rejection; punishment.	Sense of trust, responsiveness to social reinforcers, warmth toward others.	Dependent passivity; submissiveness; inadequacy; mistrust.	Guide student toward greater independence gradually; make ample use of personal approval in rewarding gains made; be careful not to overindulge or to frustrate dependency needs; do not allow others to do things for him.
Moral Development	Expresses remorse; resists temptation; is able to make moral judgments; is capable of self-evaluation; engages in altruistic behavior.	Perfectionism; unrealistic expectations; love-oriented techniques.	Realistic emotional reactions to transgression; adaptive, productive conformity; wholesome expression of basic desires; a sense of self-satisfaction; concern for others.	Chronic sense of failure, or fear; low self-esteem; ability to enjoy life and spur of the moment behavior adversely affected; inadequate self-regulation (fighting, overly self-critical).	Foster moral judgment by gearing moral explanations slightly above the student's level of moral development; use rewards, punishments, and personal example to promote moral behavior; assist perfectionistic student to achieve less emotional strain; provide a reality rub-in for those deficient in character development.
Anxiety and Insecurity	Physiological changes (e.g. heart rate, respiratory rate; motor behaviors—tremors, jumpiness, fidgeting), verbal reports	Apprehensive model; direct training; premature exposure to adult problems; perfectionism; overpermissiveness.	Facilitation of social and intellectual performance if not severe.	Severe conflicts; generalized behavioral constrictions (avoidance or escape from social or competitive situations; lack of enthusiasm; fearfulness; low tol-	Use desensitization procedures; consider programmed instruction for anxious child with a learning problem; provide opportunities for overlearning; provide a structured classroom atmosphere; realize that personal approval might be embarrassing to the shy student;

Characteristic	Description	Contributing factors	Related traits	Possible problems	Suggestions for teachers
	about feelings of apprehension, embarrassment and worry; marked sensitivity to criticism; easily discouraged.			erance for error; indecisiveness; undue caution), impaired, higher-level cognitive functioning.	consider using the peer group in drawing out the shy student.
Aggressiveness	Fights others physically or verbally; tries to hurt others; is cruel, disruptive, and unruly; is uncooperative and unproductive; is submissive; pouts and procrastinates.	Repeated severe punishment; indulgence; direct reinforcement; aggressive parental models.	Self-assertiveness; competitiveness.	Acting-out hostile behavior; delinquency; anxious compliance; concern about aggressive acts and feelings; neurotic-like problems; inability to defend rights.	Ignore if feasible; let student know that hostile behavior will not be permitted; set firm and clear-cut limits; stop aggressive behavior but avoid being hostile; provide an example of self-control: explain the rationale for various rules; develop a personal interest in the offender; point out when and where aggression is allowable; use contracts especially with passive-aggressive behaviors; provide practice in assertion for the submissive child.
Achievement motivation and achievement	Strives to excel; has high standards; is confident; sets realistic goals; delays gratification; uses time and energy efficiently; is willing to take moderate risks.	High levels of parental involvement.	Striving and productive accomplishment; delay of gratification; curiosity about environment; persistence; satisfaction with accomplishments.	Demoralization, sense of powerlessness and hopelessness; obsession with achievement.	Recognize that students with high and low achievement motivation react differently with respect to their expectancy of success and persistence after extended failure experiences; provide programs designed to modify the personality characteristics related to achievement; capitalize on social motives; strive for moderate levels of motivation; provide models of achievement motivation.

there is now considerable concern about sexist practices and about equality of opportunity. Hopefully, the day will soon arrive when females will no longer have to feel guilty or fear social rejection over achievement-oriented behavior. School personnel can help by actively combating the stereotype of the passive, helpless female, by reinforcing girls for assertiveness, by encouraging open discussion of career planning, by promoting competitive athletics for girls, by discussing textbook stereotypes of females, and by bringing in or visiting prestigious, high-achieving females. Society can ill afford the loss of female talent. Even more important, females should not be robbed of their initiative and self-respect. Although much is being done in the fairer treatment of females in textbooks for elementary school and the use techniques for confronting sex-role stereotypes, much remains to be done.

Guidelines for each of the problems discussed in this chapter are presented in Table 2–4. There, in briefer form, the reader will find the behavior manifestations, antecedents, outcomes, and guidelines.

Summary

The school must consider personality factors in the students' makeup if it is to accomplish its traditional academic objectives to the fullest and is to assist youth in realizing their intellectual, social, and personal potentials.

Socialization techniques that are either too severe or too lax are apt to interfere with adequate resolution of common developmental problems.

Proper socialization practices, on the other hand, lead to feelings of self-worth and self-realization.

Excessive dependency manifests itself in behaviors such as seeking physical contact, seeking to be near others, seeking attention, seeking praise and approval, and resisting separation.

Instrumental dependence refers to the seeking of help in doing things. Emotional dependence refers to the seeking of personal attachment or nurturant attention from other people.

Dependent behavior is more likely to remain stable over the years for females than for males. This pattern of stability may change, however, as sex roles continue to change.

Desirable outcomes of the socialization of dependency needs include the development of a sense of trust as well as responsiveness to various forms of social approval. In this sense, dependency is a prerequisite for most future socialization. Undesirable outcomes include submissiveness, passivity, a sense of inadequacy, whinyness, and standoffishness.

Teachers must encourage independent behavior without frustrating or overindulging the student's dependency needs.

Conscience refers to the internalization of "do's and don'ts" which regulate moral judgment, conduct, and emotion.

The specifics of moral development are far from being fully understood; but it is clear that cognitive, child-rearing, and cultural factors play an important role in character development.

The student with an overly strict conscience is prone to feelings of guilt and low self-esteem. Because this student sets excessively high standards for himself, school can become drudgery as he tries to live up to his expectations.

The student with too lax a conscience may well encounter difficulty because of unacceptable rule-breaking antics.

An optimal level of character development allows for self-realization at both the societal and personal levels.

A sound program of character education will address itself to the cognitive, behavioral, and affective aspects of moral development.

Nervous habits as well as feelings of inadequacy are commonly associated with anxiety.

A moderate amount of anxiety is healthy in that it promotes social and intellectual performance.

Anxiety that is either too high or too low appears to impair both intellectual and social performance.

For the highly anxious students, fears form easily, spread readily, and are difficult to extinguish.

The use of desensitization procedures, programmed instruction, overlearning, and a structured classroom are among the strategies beneficial to the management and instruction of the anxious, insecure student. Remember that the effects of anxiety on performance depend in part upon factors under the teacher's control, such as task difficulty, type of instruction, and evaluation procedures.

A reasonable amount of aggression is a sign of a healthy individual.

The combination of frustration, hostile models, and a permissive atmosphere is most conducive to the development of aggressive individuals.

In coping with the acting-out student, the teacher must set firm and clear-cut limits, avoid being punitive, provide a structured classroom setting, offer an example of self-control, and explain the reasons for classroom regulations.

To be considered competent in our society a student must achieve in school.

Achievement motivation is the individual's desire to do something well.

The student with high achievement motivation is characterized by a sense of confidence, realistic goal setting, moderate risk taking, delay of gratification, efficient use of time and energy, and presumably a sense of self-responsibility.

Achievement motivation can develop very early in life and some authorities have gone so far as to postulate a critical period.

Sound educational practice takes into account the student's expectancy of success, the impact of continual failure, the need for moderate levels of motivation, modifications in the learning environment to increase the student's probability of success, programs designed to modify personality characteristics related to achievement, the desirability of more worthwhile incentives, the potential inherent in social motivations, the provision of suitable models of achievement, and consideration of sex typing as it relates to achievement.

References

Ainsworth, M. The development of infant-mother attachment. In B. Caldwell and H. Ricciuti (Eds.), *Child Development Research*, Vol. 3, pp. 1–95. Chicago: University of Chicago Press, 1973.

Atkinson, J. W. Some general implications of conceptual developments in the study of achievement-oriented behavior. In M. R. Jones (Ed.), *Human motivation: a symposium*. Lincoln: University of Nebraska Press, 1965.

Atkinson, J. W., & Feather, N. T. *A Theory of achievement motivation*. New York: Wiley, 1966.

Ausubel, D., & Sullivan, E. *Theory and problems of child development*. New York: Grune & Stratton, 1970.

Bandura, A. *Aggression: a social learning analysis*. Englewood Cliffs, N.J.: Prentice-Hall, 1973.

Bandura, A., & Kupers, C. J. Transmission of patterns of self-reinforcement through modeling. *Journal of Abnormal and Social Psychology*, 1964, **69,** 1–9.

Bandura, A., & Walters, R. H. *Adolescent aggression*. New York: Ronald Press, 1959.

Becker, W. C. Consequences of different kinds of parental discipline. In M. L. Hoffman & L. W. Hoffman (Eds.), *Review of child development research*. Vol. 1, New York: Russell Sage Foundation, 1964, pp. 169–208.

Berkowitz, L. Control of aggression. In B. Caldwell & H. Ricciuti (Eds.) *Child development research*, Vol. 3, pp. 95–140. Chicago: University of Chicago Press, 1973.

Brenner, A. *Readiness for school and today's pressures*. The Inter-Institutional Seminar in Child Development, 1967, p. 1.

Bronfenbrenner, U. *Two worlds of childhood U.S. and U.S.S.R.*, New York: Russell Sage Foundation, 1970.

Brophy, J., & Good, T. *Teacher-student relationships.* New York: Holt, Rinehart and Winston, 1974.

Brown, P., & Elliott, R. Control of aggression in a nursery school class. *Journal of Experimental Child Psychology*, 1965, **2**, 103–7.

Cameron, N. *Personality development and psychopathology.* Boston: Houghton Mifflin, 1963.

Charlesworth, R., & Hartup, W. W. Positive social reinforcement in the nursery school peer group. *Child Development*, 1967, **38**, 993–1002.

Clarizio, H. *Toward positive classroom discipline.* (2nd ed.) New York: Wiley, 1976.

Coleman, J. Academic achievement and the structure of competition, socialization, and schools. *Harvard Educational Review*, 1968, Cambridge, Mass.

Crandall, V. *Parents as identification models and reinforcers of children's achievement behavior.* Progress Report, NIMH Grant M-2238. Washington, D.C.: Government Printing Office, 1961.

Crandall, V. C. Achievement behavior in young children. In W. W. Hartup & N. L. Smothergill (Eds.), *The young child.* Washington, D.C.: National Association for the Education of Young Children, 1967, pp. 165–85.

Douvan, E., & Adelson, J. The psychodynamics of social mobility in adolescent boys. *Journal of Abnormal and Social Psychology*, 1958, **56**, 31–34.

Erikson, E. H. *Childhood and society.* (Rev. ed.) New York: Norton, 1968. (Orig. pub. 1950)

Eron, L., Banta, T., Walder, L., & Laulicht, J. Comparison of data obtained from fathers and mothers on childrearing practices and their relations to child aggression. *Child Development*, 1961, **32**, 457–72.

Ferguson, L. *Personality development.* Belmont, California: Brooks/Cole Publishing Co., 1970.

Gallagher, J. *Teaching the gifted child.* Boston: Allyn & Bacon, 1964.

Glueck, S., & Glueck, E. *Unraveling juvenile delinquency.* Cambridge: Harvard University Press, 1950.

Goldfarb, W. Psychological deprivation in infancy and subsequent adjustment. *American Journal of Orthopsychiatry*, 1945, **15**, 247–55.

Good, T., & Brophy, J. *Looking in classrooms.* New York: Harper & Row, 1973.

Hartshorne, H., & May, M. A. *Studies in the nature of character.* Vol. 1, *Studies in deceit*; Vol. II, *Studies in self-control*; Vol. III, *Studies in the organization of character.* New York: Macmillan, 1928–1930.

Hartup, W. W. Dependency and independence. In H. Stevenson (Ed.), Child psychology. *Yearbook of the National Society for the Study of Education*, 1963, **62**, Part I, pp. 333–63.

Hartup, W. Aggression in childhood developmental perspectives. *American Psychologist*, 1974, **29**, 336–41.

Heathers, G. Emotional dependence and independence in a physical threat situation. *Child Development*, 1953, **24**, 169–79.

Heathers, G. Emotional dependence and independence in nursery school play. *Journal of Genetic Psychology*, 1955, **87**, 37–57.

Heckhausen, H. Achievement motive research: Current problems and some contributions towards a general theory of motivation. In W. J. Arnold (Ed.), *Nebraska symposium on motivation*, 1968. Lincoln: University of Nebraska Press, 1968.

Hill, K. R., & Sarason, S. B. The relation of test anxiety and defensiveness to test and school performance over the elementary-school years: a further longitudinal study. *Monographs of the Society for Research on Child Development,* 1966, **31** (2).

Hoffman, M. L. Moral development. In P. Mussen (Ed.), *Carmichael's Manual of Child Psychology.* New York: Wiley, 1970, pp. 261–360.

Hosford, R. Overcoming fear of speaking in a group. In Krumboltz J., & Thorensen, C. (Eds.), *Behavioral counseling cases and techniques.* New York: Holt, Rinehart, and Winston, 1969.

Kagan, J., & Moss, H. A. The stability of passive and dependent behavior from childhood through adulthood. *Child Development,* 1960, **31,** 577–91.

Kagan, J., & Moss, H. A. *Birth to maturity.* New York: Wiley, 1962.

Kazdin, A. *Behavior modification in applied settings.* Homewood, Ill.: Dorsey Press, 1975.

Kohlberg, L. Development of moral character and moral ideology. In M. L. Hoffman & L. W. Hoffman (Eds.), *Review of child development research.* Vol. I. New York: Russell Sage Foundation, 1964, pp. 383–432.

Kohlberg, L. The moral atmosphere of the school, 1969. Paper delivered at Association for supervision and curriculum development. Washington, D.C.: January 9, 1969.

Kohlberg, L. The cognitive-developmental approach to moral education. *Phi Delta Kappan,* 1975, **61,** 670–77

Levy, D. *Maternal overprotection.* New York: Columbia University Press, 1943.

McClelland, D. C. Achievement motivation can be developed. *Harvard Business Review,* November–December, 1965.

McClelland, D. C. Toward a theory of motive acquisition. *American Psychologist,* 1965, **20,** 321–34 (2).

McClelland, D. What is the effect of achievement motivation training in the schools? *Teachers College Record,* December 1972, Vol. 74, No. 2.

Maccoby, E., & Jacklin, C. *The psychology of sex differences.* Stanford, California: Stanford University Press, 1974.

McCord, W., & McCord, J. *Psychopathy and delinquency.* New York: Grune & Stratton, 1956.

McCord, W., McCord, J., & Howard, A. Familial correlates of aggression in non-delinquent children. *Journal of Abnormal and Social Psychology,* 1961, **62,** 79–93.

McCord, W., McCord, J., & Zola, I. *Origins of crime: a new evaluation of the Cambridge-Somerville youth study.* New York: Columbia University Press, 1959.

McNassor, D. This frantic pace in education. *Childhood Education,* 1967, **44,** 148–54.

Mischel, W. *Introduction to personality.* New York: Holt, Rinehart, and Winston, 1971.

Morse, W., and Wingo, M. *Psychology and teaching.* Glenview, Ill.: Scott, Foresman, 1969.

Moss, H. A., & Kagan, J. Stability of achievement and recognition-seeking behaviors from early childhood through adulthood. *Journal of Abnormal and Social Psychology,* 1961, **62,** 504–13.

Mussen, P. H., Conger, J. J., & Kagan, J. *Child development and personality* (3rd ed.) New York: Harper & Row, 1969.

Peck, R. F., & Havighurst, R. J. *The psychology of character development.* New York: Wiley, 1960.

Piaget, J. *The moral judgment of the child.* Glencoe, Ill.: Free Press, 1948. (Orig. pub. 1932)

Quay, H. Some basic considerations in the education of emotionally disturbed children. *Exceptional Children,* September, 1963, Vol. 30, No. 1, pp. 27–31.

Redl, F., & Wineman, D. *Children who hate.* New York: Free Press, 1951, pp. 145–56.

Rogers, D. *Issues in adolescent psychology.* New York: Appleton-Century-Crofts, 1969.

Rosenhan, D., & White, G. M. Observation and rehearsal as determinants of prosocial behavior. *Journal of Personality and Social Psychology,* 1967, **5,** 424–31.

Ruebush, B. K. Anxiety. In H. Stevenson (Ed.), Child psychology. *Yearbook of the National Society for the Study of Education,* 1963, **62,** Part I, pp. 460–516.

Sadker, M., & Sadker, D. Sexual discrimination in the elementary school. *The National Elementary Principal,* Vol. LII (2), 1972.

Sarason, S. B. *Anxiety in elementary school children.* New York: Wiley, 1960.

Sears, R., Maccoby, E., & Levin, H. *Patterns of child rearing.* New York: Row, Peterson, 1957.

Singer, R., & Singer, A. *Psychological development in children.* Philadelphia: W. B. Saunders, 1969.

Smith, M. B. Competence and socialization. In J. A. Clausen (Ed.), *Socialization and society.* Boston: Little, Brown, 1968, pp. 270–320.

Spaulding, R. L. *Classroom behavior analysis and treatment.* San Jose, Calif.: San Jose State College, 1968.

Spielberger, C. *Anxiety and behavior.* New York: Academic Press, 1966.

Stein, A., & Bailey, M. The socialization of achievement orientations in females. *Psychological Bulletin,* 1973, **80,** No. 5, pp. 345–66.

Stendler, C. B. Possible causes of overdependency in young children. *Child Development,* 1954, **25,** pp. 125–46.

Stephens, T. M. *Directive teaching of children with learning and behavioral handicaps.* Columbus, Ohio. Charles Merrill, 1970.

Sullivan, H. *The interpersonal theory of psychiatry.* New York: Norton, 1953.

Turiel, E. Developmental processes in the child's moral thinking. In Paul H. Mussen, J. Langer, & M. Covington (Eds.), *Trends and issues in developmental psychology.* New York: Holt, Rinehart, and Winston, 1969, pp. 93–133.

Verville, E. *Behavior problems of children.* Philadelphia: W. B. Saunders, 1967.

Wenar, C. *Personality development from infancy to adulthood.* Geneva, Ill.: Houghton Mifflin, 1971.

Williams, C. The elimination of tantrum behavior by extinction procedures. *Journal of Abnormal and Social Psychology,* 1959, **59,** 269.

Winder, C., & Rau, L. Parental attitudes associated with social deviance in pre-adolescent boys. *Journal of Abnormal and Social Psychology,* 1962, **64,** 418–24.

Winterbottom, M. The relation of need for achievement in learning experiences in independence and mastery. In J. Atkinson (Ed.), *Motives in fantasy, action and society.* Princeton, N.J.; Van Nostrand, 1958, pp. 453–78.

Wright, D. *The psychology of moral behavior.* Baltimore: Penguin Books, 1971.

Yarrow, L. J. Attachment and dependency: a developmental perspective. In J. Gewirtz, (Ed.), *Attachment and dependency.* New York: Wiley, 1972, pp. 81–96.

Suggested Readings

Bandura, A. *Aggression: a social learning analysis.* Englewood Cliffs, N.J.: Prentice-Hall, 1973.

Fischer, W. *Theories of anxiety.* New York: Harper & Row, 1971.

Gewirtz, J. (Ed.) *Attachment and dependency.* Washington, D.C.: Winston, 1972.

Havighurst, R. *Developmental tasks and education.* (3rd ed.) New York: McKay, 1972.

McClelland, D. What is the effect of achievement motivation training? *Teachers College Record*, 1972, **74,** 2, 129–45.

Maccoby, E., & Jacklin, C. *The psychology of sex differences.* Stanford, Calif.: Stanford University Press, 1974.

Wright, D. *The psychology of moral behavior.* Baltimore: Penguin Books, 1971.

3

Diagnosis and Incidence of Maladjustment

Certain specific problems involved in the evaluation of children's behavior, such as the vast prevalence of childhood problems, the nonpersistence of many developmental problems, the inappropriateness of many measuring instruments for children, and so forth, have been discussed in the first two chapters. The present chapter focuses on the generic concept of diagnosis and its applicability to behavior disorders in children. We mention the typical classification schemes of children's behavior disorders and four of the most recent efforts in classification. Finally, we discuss the topic of incidence and take notice of major variables related to the frequency of maladjustment in childhood.

The Concept of Diagnosis

The concept and the term *diagnosis* come from the field of medicine. Etymologically, the term derives from the Greek and means "thorough knowledge." As used in medicine, diagnosis involves determination of the nature and circumstances of disease. More specifically, diagnosis permits the distinguishing of one disease from another by establishing mutually exclusive categories of illness. Diagnosis is based on a conception of disease as a condition or process that is characterized by (1) a common specific etiology, (2) a common set of observable signs and symptoms, (3) a known course, and (4) a known outcome that, through specific interventions, can be altered. This line of reasoning has proven a reasonably fruitful one for medicine.

Reasoning analogously, psychologists and psychiatrists have carried over the concept of diagnosis to the study of behavioral disturbances. After all, both medicine and psychology were concerned with phenomena labeled as "illnesses." Hence, it seemed reasonable that the "medical model" would have a beneficial effect in the resolution of behavioral disturbances. No one seriously questioned whether physical and psychological problems were in actuality alike. Currently, however, several psychiatrists and psychologists are questioning the validity of the analogy, and basic differences between physical and psychological disturbances are now becoming increasingly evident.

As London (1964) notes,

> Insofar as he is concerned with the diagnosis and treatment of illness, the modern psychotherapist has grown up in the tradition of medicine. But the nature of the ailments he deals with and the way he treats them set him apart from the physician and in some ways make him function much like a clergyman. He deals with sickness of the soul, as it were, which cannot be cultured in a laboratory, seen through a microscope, or cured by injection. And his methods have little of the concreteness or obvious empiricism of the physician's—he carries no needle, administers no pill, wraps no bandages. He cures by talking and listening. The infections he seeks to expose and destroy are neither bacterial nor viral—they are ideas, memories of experiences, painful and untoward emotions that debilitate the individual and prevent him from functioning effectively and happily.

In a similar vein, Smith (1968) questions why medicine rather than religion or education should provide the framework for helping troubled individuals to cope with their problems. He notes that mental illness is more than a personal faltering. The social systems on which the individual depends—family, church, school, job, friendship—have also failed to sustain him. Thus the task is not to cure an ailment inside his skin but to strengthen him to the point where he can function once again in daily life. To accomplish this, one must help the social systems function in ways that promote the well-being and effectiveness of individuals who take part in them.

These differences have certain ramifications with respect to the applicability of the concept of diagnosis to children's disorders. The nature of these differences renders it more difficult for a diagnosis to accomplish its traditional objectives—namely, to achieve reliable assignment to a given category on the basis of observable symptoms, to provide some reference to etiology, to offer a differential prognosis, and to suggest treatment procedures. We shall now consider how effectively psychiatric diagnostic categories meet the criteria characteristic of an adequate classification scheme.

Agreeing on What the Problem Is

First of all, the clinician should be able to make reliable judgments as to diagnostic categories. In other words, different clinicians should agree on the classification of a given patient. Unfortunately, most diagnostic systems have not satisfied the criterion of reliable classification. Regrettably, it is not uncommon for children to receive different diagnoses as they move from clinic to clinic. Thus, the child who has difficulty in school is labeled aphasic in a speech clinic, a passive-aggressive personality at the child-guidance center, and a reading-disability case at the psychoeducational clinic. The diagnosis a child receives is often a function of the clearinghouse through which he is routed. Even articulate proponents of the medical model recognize that diagnoses exist more in the mind of the diagnostician than in the behavior of the diagnosed (Ey, 1963). Indeed, a clinical judgment may reveal as much or more about the clinician than it reveals about the child (Kessel & Shepherd, 1962). Clinicians have long decried the inadequacy of the American Psychiatric Association's *Diagnostic and Statistical Manual of Mental Disorders* (1952, 1968), the classification scheme that has been applied to children's disorders since the initiation in 1954 of reporting by psychiatric clinics nationwide. Many adult disorders, clinicians complain, are rarely found in children, and most childhood disorders must be squeezed into a very small number of categories. In short, the most commonly used classification system today fails to take into consideration the differences between child and adult disorders. Anna Freud (1965) points out that symptoms in children do not necessarily assume the same significance they do for the adult patient.

In addition to the clinicians' complaints, there is ample research evidence to substantiate the shortcomings of this classification system. The most extensive data available indicate that of children seen at more than 1,200 psychiatric clinics, 32% were undiagnosed and another 40% were labeled simply as "transient personality disorders" without further differentiation

(Rosen, Bahn, & Kramer, 1964). Assignment to a diagnostic category thereby conveys little in the way of accurate information about the symptomatology of a child. Other available data indicate that 8 out of 10 child patients seen in outpatient clinics apparently do not receive a detailed diagnosis (Redick, 1973). Inadequacies inherent in the classification system, difficulties involved in the examination of children, and a reluctance to pin certain diagnostic labels on children (for example, childhood schizophrenia) probably all contribute to this rather unfortunate state of affairs. The unreliability of psychiatric diagnosis with adult patients is notorious, and there is little reason to suspect that reliability is any higher with children. Moreover, factor-analytic studies of behavior ratings of children in public schools do not support the present diagnostic classification system. For example, studies by Peterson (1961) and by Quay and Quay (1965) found that there are two major dimensions, conduct disorder and personality disorder, which account for the majority of the variance among behaviorally disordered children in need of clinical services.

Stuart (1970) has identified four factors that contribute to the low reliability associated with diagnostic inquiry.

1. The first source of error centers around the individual characteristics of the clinician. Because different psychologists have differing expectations, they ask different questions and therefore elicit different behaviors or reports from the child, parent, and teacher. In addition to sampling different characteristics of behavior, diagnosticians are likely to interpret behavior in accordance with their own theoretical biases. "Human error" also enters the picture in the form of loose reasoning and inaccurate observation. Meehl (1973) notes that there is a tendency to see the clinical case conference as having the delightful free-associative features of a psychoanalytic hour or group therapy session.[1]

2. Another source of unreliability centers around individual characteristics of the child. Because clinical judgment is an interpersonal process, it is only natural that characteristics of the child contribute to this outcome. For example, client characteristics such as one's socioeconomic status, race, nationality, style of dress, manner of speaking, and attitude toward being tested may all be influential in determining, sometimes erroneously so, conclusions drawn about the child. Many characteristics of the child may contribute to favorable or unfavorable judgments made about him despite the fact that a number of these have no direct bearing upon the formal decisions to be made.

3. Stuart contends that the logic underlying the category system is faulty. For instance, great disagreement exists about the definition of some of the general categories such as "schizophrenia." Moreover the categories

---

1. For a scholarly analysis of the low intellectual level characterizing the diagnostic process, we highly recommend Paul Meehl's (1973) article "Why I Don't Attend Case Conferences."

are deductively derived from assumptions rather than inductively derived from direct observation of given conditions. Also, it is commonly assumed that when one pattern of behavior is observed that the presence of other patterns can be inferred. It is also assumed that the categories are mutually exclusive. Yet most individuals fitted into a diganostic entity do not possess all the characteristics posited for it. Consequently, a typical "sociopath," minimally brain-injured child, or learning disability case is much harder to find than textbook descriptions of these and other diagnostic designations would suggest. For instance, while hyperactivity has been singled out for special attention as a characteristic of children with minimal brain dysfunction, only 20% of schoolchildren so classified will display noticeable hyperactivity—a characteristic that varies with the situation (McIntosh & Dunn, 1973). It is not too farfetched to envision two members of the same category who have no symptoms in common (Draguns & Phillips, 1971).

4. A final factor contributing to low agreement has to do with the context in which the judgments are made. Many studies indicate that diagnosis represents an interaction between the situation, the diagnostician, and the child (Moos & Clemes, 1967). Altogether too frequently diagnoses are made of problems in an isolated setting that is not representative of the setting in which the problem is occurring. For instance, a child who behaves aggressively in a group setting may be a perfect gentleman in a one-to-one setting.

Finding Causes

Many workers feel that the nature of etiology differs significantly between the two types of disturbances. Unlike physical illnesses, psychological disturbances typically do not have a specific etiological agent. Rather, psychosocial problems are rooted in multiple causes, a fact that forces one to deal with information on more than the physical level. In addition to genetic and constitutional factors, consideration must be given to the interaction between psychological and social forces. Some classifications attempt to assign disorders to such broad etiological groups as organic or functional. The question arises, however, as to how successful this endeavor can be since the etiology is commonly inferred from the symptomatology. After all, if the diagnosis is based on symptoms that cannot be reliably classified, how can inferences as to etiology based on such observations be any more reliable? Furthermore, when and if we do eventually reach the stage at which our judgments permit reliable assignment to various categories, we are still forced to assume that homogeneous behaviors mean homogeneous determinants (Patterson, 1964). Many clinicians suggest that this is not the case. As White and Watt (1973) point out:

> Because symptoms are surface phenomena their logical classification corresponds scarcely at all to the logic of the underlying disorders. It is a good deal like classifying books according to the material and color of their bindings rather than by what is discussed inside. It is necessary in every case to

go behind the symptoms if we are to understand the nature of a patient's trouble. In addition, symptoms do not fit together, even on the surface, in such a way as to provide an intelligible classification.

On the other hand, Jenkins (1953) argues that if discrete classes of disorders exist, they should be characterized by discrete symptom clusters. This assumption cannot be tested, however, until we have reliability of judgment.

Predicting Outcomes

Whereas physical illnesses follow basically the same course and have a known outcome, mental disturbances do not. Anna Freud (1965) points out that it is virtually impossible to distinguish between harmless, temporary disturbances and dangerous, permanent regressions in children. We have at present no sure means of telling which disorders are transitory and simply by-products of developmental strains and which are predictive of later serious problems. We cannot assume, for example, that childhood neuroses are the forerunners of adult neuroses. Also, spontaneous cures are not at all uncommon in children. To further complicate matters, neither symptom formation, intensity of suffering, nor degree of impairment in functioning is a dependable predictor as to course or outcome among behavior disorders in children. Thus, there are wide differences in course and outcome among children within the same diagnostic category.

Following a most careful review regarding the predictability of adult mental health from childhood behavior, Kohlberg, La Crosse, and Ricks (1972) had the following to say: "Put bluntly, there is no research evidence yet available indicating that clinical analysis of the child's emotional status or dynamics leads to any more effective prognosis of adult mental health or illness than could be achieved by the man on the street who believes psychosis is hereditary and that criminality is the result of bad homes and neighborhoods in the common-sense meaning of that concept." In brief, there is no satisfactory evidence that current classification systems enable us to predict course or outcome of most behavior disorders.

Factors in Erroneous Forecasts. BETTER THAN PREDICTED. Psychologists tend to be overly pessimistic in their forecasts. MacFarlane (1963) for example, noted that close to 50% of youngsters in the Berkeley Guidance Study turned out to be more stable and effective adults than any of the psychologists predicted. Why is it that people often do better than we predict? As MacFarlane examined the case histories of these individuals, she uncovered a number of factors that seem to have led to erroneous predictive judgments.

1. The troublesome and pathogenic aspects of development were overweighted and the stabilizing, growth-inducing factors were underweighted. Because much of personality theory has been derived from work with pathological groups, we tend to be oversensitized to current dilemmas and undersensitized to maturity-enhancing aspects.

2. We unquestionably tend to overestimate the durability of adjustment patterns. It appears that no matter how well entrenched behavior patterns may be, they are dropped or modified if they are no longer effective to achieve desired ends in new situations. This relearning does not occur without wear and tear or without erratic behavior. But nonetheless, relearning does take place.

3. Becoming mature frequently requires that one live through the pains and confusions of maturing experiences. What were often regarded as traumatic and debilitating experiences by psychologists were regarded by the subjects as forcing them to clarify goals and to achieve a new sense of direction in life. Many of these painful experiences forced people to ask themselves what they wanted out of life. (The authors recall the case of a black acquaintance who had been ready "to quit everything and everybody"—his wife, his children, his job, and his close friends. He said that he finally realized that he could not go on that way. He knew that withdrawing from people and situations he found frustrating was self-defeating and was quickly becoming a life style. He took stock of himself, laid realistic plans, and took concrete steps to achieve them. Today, he is a successful school principal.)

4. Many subjects were not able to function effectively until later in life when they were given an opportunity to fulfill a responsible role that gave them a sense of worth.

5. There was also a failure to realize that long, continuous patterns would be modified or converted into almost the opposite characteristics. For instance, nearly all of the dependent boys picked for wives girls who were lacking in confidence, thereby giving themselves a role as the proud male protector and provider of support. Likewise, many of the socially inept compensatingly became supersalesmen requiring social skills.

6. Some subjects seemed to be "late bloomers" or "slow jellers" who took a long time and a change of situation away from their community and family to work through early confusions or inhibitions. In addition to the factors noted above by MacFarlane, there are three others that deserve mention.

7. Undoubtedly, some of the erroneous predictions can be attributed to the differential standards of adjustment for children and adults. In the case of children, the ability to master academic tasks constitutes a primary yardstick for normality. In the case of adults, however, this ability no longer looms large as a basic criterion of adjustment. Life or living becomes the test. Now, the basic yardstick is one's vocational and social adequacy. If the adult can adapt reasonably well to his surroundings, he is apt to be seen as normal. In brief, academic competencies are stressed in childhood, whereas social and vocational competencies are emphasized in adulthood. Because the relationship between these two sets of competencies is not as close as we might suspect (Kohlberg et al., 1972), predictions will often be in error.

8. The adult has much greater choice in selecting suitable or psychologically comfortable surroundings than does the child. The adult can change his spouse, his job, his boss, his friends, and his community. The child, however, cannot change his home, his teacher, his school, or his neighborhood.

Thus, the adult is freer than the child to choose a setting compatible with his style of life. In a sense, he can select his own norm group, while for the child there is essentially only one set of norms.

9. Youngsters are much more durable than is often believed. It is becoming increasingly apparent that children are able to bounce back from emotional insult. The notion of permanent psychological damage resulting from a traumatic episode is overdrawn. Children for whatever reasons are quite resilient and we have underestimated the "toughness" of children in our forecasts.

Three Youngsters Who Turned Out Better Than Predicted

A marginal student who was a social isolate and a self-centered, unhappy boy is now the manager of a large construction firm. He states that his major satisfaction on the job is "feeding graded doses of increasing responsibility and difficulty in assigned jobs to the work staff and watching them grow in confidence as their competencies increase."

Another—a large, awkward, early-maturing girl who labored under the weight of her size and shyness and felt that she was a great disappointment to her mother—worked hard for her "B" average to win approval and was a pedestrian, uninteresting child and adolescent. She had periods of depression when she could see no point to living. Then, as a junior in college, she got excited over what she was learning (not just in grades to please her mother) and went on to get an advanced degree and to teach in college. Now she has taken time out to have and raise her children. Again we see an understanding, compassionate person, and one full of zest for living, married to an interesting, merry, and intelligent man she met in graduate school. "Life is now very good— but it took so very, very long to be comfortable and happy."

One who defied our predictions at age 30 accurately described himself during the years previous to graduation from high school as "a listless oddball." His average IQ through year 18 was around 100. He was held over three times in elementary school, finally graduated from high school at age 21 without college recommendations. He left the community, made up high school deficiencies, and now is a highly talented architect, "living out a normal childhood through my children," is active in his community, and "life is exciting and satisfying." Obviously his tested IQ's up through age 18 were no measure of his true ability, although they corresponded with his grades.

WORSE THAN PREDICTED.   MacFarlane found that 20% of subjects failed to do as well as predicted. Although these subjects showed great promise up to age 18 on the basis of high ability or talents (artistic and athletic) and/or easy, successful family and social relationships, they did not live up to their potential, or showed a strained dissatisfaction with their lives, or far less depth and substantiality of character than expected. The early successful athletes, the early good-looking and conspicuously socially successful girls were among the major examples of those not living up to their early promise. MacFarlane comments:

> Later life has not brought them the excessive approval poured on them by their peers, teachers and parents, themselves in need of identifying with success. Extravagant success came when they were too young to take it with a grain of salt, when too much of their energy went into maintaining their image; and life subsequently had not so indulged them. The measure of success at one age is frequently not the measure of success at a later age. Too much success, if not really earned, can be a millstone.

Factors in Accurate Forecasts.   Slightly less than one-third of subjects turned out as predicted in MacFarlane's study. These more accurate predictions came for those who early were overcontrolled, constricted compulsive individuals. Their patterns of behaving had become so entrenched that they became largely autonomous and presented a hard shell that may have protected them from environmental insult but at the same time kept them from being open to many kinds of learning experiences. Predictions were also accurate for two other groups—the mentally retarded and those subjected to extremely inconsistent discipline (e.g., indulgence then harsh criticism). The majority of compulsive adult drinkers came out of this last group. More will be said about the topic of prediction in chapter 13 on prevention.

Prescribing Treatment

The real advantage of a classification system is that it suggests the treatment of choice. Again, however, there is an absence of evidence to indicate that present diagnostic systems enable us to make a direct correspondence between specific treatments and specific disabilities. As London (1972, p. 915) notes, "Etiology and treatment have no logical connection. Anxiety, for example, may be the result of prior experience, but can be alleviated chemically; or it may be aroused by essentially chemical circumstances (like fatigue plus mild arousal to danger) but can be smoothed physically or verbally."

In practice, the type of therapy one receives depends primarily on the orientation of the therapist and only secondarily on the child's diagnostic classification. Patterson (1959) notes that the choice of therapy is more contingent upon the training, experiences, and preferences of the therapist than upon the diagnosis. Rosenthal (1962) recalls psychotherapy being referred to as an unidentified process for unspecified problems with unpredictable outcomes. In many instances, it seems that the services offered to patients are determined more by clinic policies than by the patient's needs (that is, by the severity of his disorder). Thus, in children's clinics, children presenting psychotic disorders are less apt to be treated than are children presenting neurotic disorders (Bahn, Chandler, & Eisenberg, 1962). As we will see later in this chapter, the greater services afforded whites as opposed to nonwhites clearly suggest that factors related to the child's prognosis play a more important role than do diagnostic needs in determining the availability of clinic service.

Brain-damaged, Retarded, or Autistic

At the age of four Noah is neither toilet-trained nor does he feed himself. He seldom speaks expressively, rarely employs his less-than-a-dozen-word vocabulary. His attention span in a new toy is a matter of split seconds, television engages him only for an odd moment occasionally, he is never interested in other children for very long. His main activities are lint-catching, thread pulling, blanket-sucking, spontaneous giggling, inexplicable crying, eye-squinting, wall-hugging, circle-walking, bed-bouncing, jumping, rocking, door-closing, and incoherent babbling addressed to his finger-flexing right hand. But two years ago, Noah spoke in complete sentences, had a vocabulary of well over 150 words, sang the verses of his favorite songs, identified the objects and animals in his picture books, was all but toilet-trained, and practically ate by himself.

What's the matter with Noah? For the longest time it seemed to depend upon what diagnosis we were willing to shop around for. We'd been told he was mentally retarded; emotionally disturbed; autistic; schizophrenic; possibly brain-damaged; or that he was suffering from a combination of these conditions. But we finally discovered that the diagnosis didn't seem to matter; it was all so sadly academic. The medical profession was merely playing nomenclature and classification games at our expense. For though we live in one of the richest states in the nation, there was no single viable treatment immediately available for Noah, no matter what category he could eventually be assigned to. (Greenfeld, 1973, pp. 3–5.)

Therapists will sometimes state that certain forms of therapy are suitable for certain groups of children, but the criterion for such statements is a subjective one, not an objective one based on empirical evidence. As London (1964) writes,

> Now if this plentitude of treatments involved much variety of techniques to apply to different persons under different circumstances by different specialists, there would be no embarrassment of therapeutic riches here, just as there is not within the many specialties of medicine or law or engineering. But this is not the case, and psychotherapeutic "systems" (or "orientations," as they are often glibly called) speak more to epithets than entities, and more to the perspectives and labels of their founders than to the facts of human behavior. One hardly goes to a psychoanalyst to be cured of anxiety and a nondirective therapist to be treated for homosexuality, as he might to a cardiologist for one condition and a radiologist for another. Nor does the same doctor use Freudian therapy for psychogenic ulcers and Rogerian treatment for functional headaches, as a physician might use medicine for one ailment and surgery for another. On the contrary, being a certain kind of psychotherapist has little bearing on treating a certain kind of problem, but refers rather to the likelihood of treating all problems from the vantage of a certain system. And its champion may see his system either as implying something more grand than mere technique, so that he feels no need for technical precision, or alternately as positing a technique comprehensive enough to apply in general rather than particular, so he feels no diagnostic limit on the ailments it can treat.

Draguns and Phillips (1971) also note that "the treatment options at the disposal of the diagnostician are just not numerous or differentiated enough to enable him to do justice to the variety and number of subcategories. One must conclude that diagnosis is the more useful the less ambitious it is."

At our present stage of development, we do not know what kind of therapy is best for what disorder. Furthermore, we cannot test the assumption that differential treatment programs can be developed for different classes of behavior disorders until a reliable classification system is established.

The basic difficulties discussed above have served to underscore the discrepancies existing between the concepts of physical and mental disorders and have prompted mental-health specialists to wonder if it is appropriate to speak of both under the rubric of "illnesses." (See Table 3–1.) Current thought regarding this semantic error is aptly expressed in the following statement by Adams (1964):

> Failure to clarify these distinctions has had unfortunate consequences. Efforts toward understanding and effective alleviation have long been hampered by the semantic confusion which results when the word illness is used to denote both physical disease entities and maladaptive patterns of interpersonal behavior. This ambiguous usage has perpetrated the glib fallacy that mental and physical illnesses are the same thing. It has interfered with the understanding of fundamental psychological phenomena and made for an ineffectual and often harmful approach to some of the most serious recurring problems in human relationship.

Szasz (1960) who continues to be one of the most articulate critics of the medical model, contends that "mental illness" is a myth, pointing out that a

Table 3–1.   Contrasts between the Medical and the Psychosocial Models of Illness

	Medical Illnesses	*Psychosocial Illnesses*
Cause(s)	Can usually be isolated and identified; tend to be specific, tangible, and singular.	Difficult to isolate and identify; tend to be less definite, less tangible, and multiple.
Classification	Moderate agreement as to what constitutes a given illness.	Diagnostic categories often convey little meaningful information; tend to be unreliable.
Prognosis	Outcome is generally known and predictable for those with same diagnosis.	Outcome is often uncertain and unpredictable; varies considerably within a given diagnostic category.
Treatment	Tends to be specific for specific illnesses.	Not precisely formulated nor based primarily on the diagnosis.

person's troubles cannot be explained as a disease of the nervous system. He feels that man's troubles are best viewed as "problems of living." He charges that "mental illness can only be regarded as a metaphor." For him, mental illness is a harmful myth. How can there be an illness of something that doesn't exist? As the traditional model has come under close critical attacks based on both empirical and logical grounds, many prefer to speak of "failures of human adaptation" (Draguns & Phillips, 1971) than to speak in terms of "mental illness" in either the literal or metaphorical sense. Other critics have used such phrases as "the paralysis of analysis" and "hardening of the categories" to accentuate the potential dangers associated with diagnostic classifications used in conjunction with the medical model. Over seventy years of biological, biochemical, and genetic research have isolated few diseases responsible for behavior disorders in either children or adults. As valuable as certain advances have been (for example, phenylketonuria—PKU), they have hardly dented the bulk of disturbed children. Moreover, expansion of the mental illness concept has the medical model straining at the seams. The traditional model even when used metaphorically has come to be seen as an inadequate and incomplete guide to the problems of today's children. Advocates of community mental health charge that what is needed is a catalogue of real-life social, educational, and eventually occupational assets and liabilities across various settings and over time rather than placement in a diagnostic category. Proponents of behavior modification also contend that the information contained in the diagnostic formulation is of little or no use to them. In light of continued challenge to its adequacy and applicability, the persistence of the medical model is remarkable. At this time, it appears that the "medical model is alive though not well" (Draguns & Phillips, 1971, p. 14).

Conclusion

There are two schools of thought regarding diagnosis. One contends that the concept of diagnosis is of little value and should be discarded because of its limitations. The other school, while recognizing the limitations inherent in current classification systems, nevertheless believes that some form of taxonomy (one aspect of diagnosis) is necessary. This school concurs with Ausubel (1958), who notes that classification is needed to make possible generalization, concept formation, and investigation of relationships between important variables impinging upon the phenomena encompassed within the discipline.

Scientists cannot work effectively unless they have some scheme for ordering the array of facts or observations they encounter. This is why there is—and will remain—classification.

The first stage in any theory consists in the classifying of data. Despite imperfections in present schemes, they nevertheless represent the best means available for prediction (Hunt, 1948). Although current classifications are lacking in clarity, abandonment of them would lead only to greater chaos. How can we compare the differential effectiveness of various therapies for certain types of patients if we have no classification system? How can we communicate effectively with one another? How can any hypothesis be developed and then subjected to a crucial test? How can any general laws ever be formulated? Without classification, we can have no science. It should be noted that classification merely implies that all cases within a given category have certain similarities, not that they are identical. Classification need not, therefore, preclude further description of individual differences in personality within a given category. The classification we develop must, however, avoid the pitfalls of the medical model by allowing for varied approaches to treatment. As noted earlier, biological, psychological, and sociological factors all interact in the development of maladaptive behavior. The current trend is to stress the role of psychosocial factors in our conceptual schemes, with attention being addressed to the reality conditions, such as family and community factors, which adversely influence the behavior of children. The notion of learning thus becomes a central one in the explanation and treatment of behavior disorders in children.

Although the presently used classification systems are highly imperfect in conception, application, and consequence, the student working with children having behavioral disturbances should be conversant with the present diagnostic categories because they are shorthand guides to much of the knowledge that has been accumulated over the years regarding these youngsters.

Classification Schemes

Having briefly explored the concept of diagnosis, let us turn to a discussion of recent classification schemes which have been applied to children. A review of the literature reveals more than two dozen attempts at formal classifications of the totality of behavior problems occurring during childhood and adolescence. As the Committee on Child Psychiatry (1966) notes:

> These schemes are based upon strictly descriptive or phenomenological points of view in relation to behavior; currently popular concepts of etiology, ranging from somatic origins to psychogenesis; chronological or developmental perspectives; considerations regarding total versus partial personality reactions, parent-child relationships and family interactions; the degree of treatability; or more commonly a combination of several of these conceptional viewpoints.

The Psychiatric Descriptive Approach

In 1966, the Committee on Child Psychiatry devised a proposed classification of childhood behavior disorders which retained many of the important aspects of the standard nomenclature and at the same time introduced modifications necessary for more adequate classification of deviant behaviors in children. Since this recent conceptual framework does allow for greater differentiation between adult and childhood disorders and since it maintains many features of the widely applied standard nomenclature, it will be discussed at length.

While recognizing the importance that genetic and dynamic factors should play in classification, the Committee on Child Psychiatry believes that it is only the clinical-descriptive aspect of classification that lends itself to study at our present state of knowledge. In keeping with this view, the following ten clinical descriptive categories were proposed: (1) healthy responses, (2) reactive disorders, (3) developmental disorders, (4) psychoneurotic disorders, (5) personality disorders, (6) psychotic disorders, (7) psychophysiological disorders, (8) brain syndromes, (9) mental retardation, and (10) other disorders. This list represents an approximate hierarchical arrangement from wholesome responses to more severe psychogenic disturbances to somatogenic disturbances.

1. *Healthy Responses.* The inclusion of the category "healthy responses" represents the first time that such a category has been included in any system. Its inclusion was designed to overcome the tendency of clinicians to overestimate the seriousness of relatively minor problems or to diagnose in the absence of disease. Although reliable and valid indexes of robustness remain to be delineated, attempts at positive assessment can be undertaken through the use of criteria for specific areas of development. Thus, standards are considered for intellectual functioning (for example, reality-testing ability, inquisitiveness); social functioning (for example, ability to empathize with peers, satisfactory balance in dependence-independence strivings); emotional functioning (for example, frustration power, general mood); and personal and adaptive functioning (for example, flexibility drive toward mastery). Developmental crises of a limited duration arising from a child's efforts to master developmental tasks (for example, the identity crisis in adolescence)

are also included in this category. Note that the concept of stage-appropriateness of behavior thus becomes a basic consideration in evaluating the healthiness of behavior.

2. *Reactive Disorders.* This term has replaced the term "transient situational personality disorders" found in the standard nomenclature and emphasizes the fact that certain maladaptive behavior is a reaction to a given external situation. For example, one girl became aggressive and failed to complete assignments in school upon hospitalization of her mother with cancer. She feared that she would have to assume major responsibility in caring for the four younger siblings and the house. Also, there were no other relatives in the immediate area to whom she could turn for help and she felt all alone in this situation. In such cases, deviant behavior reflects a conscious incompatibility between the child's impulses-emotions and the social situation. Such situations as excessive academic pressures, parental loss, hospitalization, and so forth are illustrative of events capable of producing a reactive disorder, which can assume many forms (acting-out behavior, withdrawal, depression). Reactive disorders do not constitute an age-bound phenomenon, but they do occur more frequently in young children, whose fluidity of personality organization lessens the possibility for the development of internalized conflicts.

3. *Developmental Deviations.* Developmental deviations constitute another new category which is designed to permit classification of certain deviations heretofore unclassifiable. Disorders so classified extend beyond what is regarded as a developmental variation within the normal range. To diagnose such a disorder, the clinician must have a detailed knowledge of what constitutes normal "abnormal" behavior, which would ordinarily be grouped under "developmental crises." Developmental deviations are sometimes phasic, disappearing with time or parental guidance. In any event, such deviations are not regarded as inevitably of a chronic or permanent nature. Hereditary, constitutional, and maturational factors presumably play a major role in the production of such deviations, although consideration is also given to psychosocial factors in their initiation, maintenance, and alleviation. In the grouping of such disorders, consideration is given to how much of the child's functioning is impaired. Thus, one subcategory, "Deviation in Maturation of Patterns," refers to generalized, widespread delays as well as to precocities or unevenness in developmental patterns. A second subcategory deals with the deviations in specific dimensions of development and accordingly includes disturbances in such particular part functions as motor development, sensory development, speech development, cognitive functioning, social development, psychosexual development, affective development, and integrative development.

4. *Psychoneurotic Disorders.* Disorders in children deriving from unconscious, intrapsychic conflicts are subsumed under this class. Such disorders are viewed as stemming from repression of basic drives, such as aggression and sex. Though their origins date back to the preschool years, neuroses usually do not manifest themselves until the early school-age years, when a

certain level of personality development has been achieved. Being unconscious and unverbalized, they tend to have a self-perpetuating character. Even at that, however, the prognosis seems favorable with or without professional treatment. The symptoms resulting from partial repression of the conflict may take various forms. The category of psychoneurotic disorders is therefore subdivided on this basis into the anxiety type, phobic type, conversion type, obsessive-compulsive type, and depressive type.

5. *Personality Disorders.* The term "personality disorders" has been retained although the subcategories differ from those used in the standard nomenclature. The term refers to those deeply ingrained personality traits that are in harmony with the child's ego. As such, they are not generally a a source of anxiety for the child. Although not clearly manifested until the early school ages, they presumably date back to the early childhood conflicts centering about the management of impulses toward aggression, dependency, autonomy, and sexual differentiation. These disorders may run the gamut from positively organized compulsive traits regarded as assets, at one extreme, to destructively organized personality traits that flagrantly clash with social mores, at the other extreme. The following personality traits are subsumed under this disorder: compulsive personality, oppositional personality, overly inhibited personality, overly independent personality, isolated personality, mistrustful personality, tension-discharge disorders (antisocial personality), sociosyntonic personality disorders (subcultural delinquent), and sexual deviations.

6. *Psychotic Disorders.* Psychotic disorders in childhood are seen as severe disturbances in ego functioning which impair, for example, the child's capacity for adequate thought, speech, emotional responsiveness, and self-identity. The behavioral manifestations, not surprisingly, vary with the child's developmental level. This category is therefore subdivided into psychoses of infancy and early childhood, psychoses of later childhood, and psychoses of adolescence.

7. *Psychophysiological Disorders.* This term applies to physiological disturbances in which psychological factors together with predisposing biological factors and present precipitating events are operative in varying etiological degrees. Affected by such disorders are the organ systems regulated by the involuntary nervous system. It appears that almost any such organ system can be so afflicted, and such ubiquity is reflected in the classification system. Illustrative of psychophysiological disorders are such subcategories as disorders of the skin, respiration, gastrointestinal tract, cardiovascular system, and nervous system. Whenever a more total or primary personality diagnosis (for example, psychoneurosis) seems indicated, it should be employed. In fact, multiple classification (for example, psychoneurotic and psychophysiologic skin disorder) is recommended in categorizing psychophysiological disorders exhibiting end-organ responses.

8. *Brain Syndromes.* These disturbances arise from diffuse impairment of the brain tissue and typically interfere with intellectual operations, such as memory, judgment, and discrimination, as well as with emotional stability

and impulse control. The prospects for rehabilitation seem more favorable in the case of children than adults. Since cerebral insults adversely influence the emerging functions and those functions not yet developed, it is difficult to correlate the severity of intellectual functioning with the severity of actual tissue damage. The two subcategories, "Acute Brain Syndrome" and "Chronic Brain Syndrome," reflect the degree of reversibility, not the onset or duration of the illness or the damage to the central nervous system. As is true of psychophysiological disorders and mental retardation, multiple classification is recommended if warranted.

9. *Mental Retardation.* This category is subdivided on the basis of presumed etiology. The three subcategories thus include the biological group, the environmental group, and the intermediate group in which both the biological and environmental agents are operative. The degree of intellectual impairment—mild, moderate, or severe—is also to be included in the diagnosis.

10. *Other Disorders.* This classification is reserved for disorders uncovered in the future or for future differentiation of currently known disorders.

Another new feature of childhood classification systems is the development of a symptom list. Although the standard nomenclature has such a list, it is not geared to childhood disorders as such. The use of this list should enable the clinician to provide a more detailed description in recording a specific symptom associated, either individually or in clusters, with different disorders at a given age or developmental period. This listing, which is to be used in conjunction with the descriptive categories, should also prove helpful especially where a given case does not fit neatly under one class. Moreover, use of this list could establish a basis for later follow-up of specific patterns that occur during development or treatment.

The classification system proposed by the Committee on Child Psychiatry undoubtedly allows for a more refined differentiation between adult and childhood disorders, thereby affording the clinician a more realistic diagnostic system in which to operate. Yet, the authors cannot help but feel that this proposed system will not allow for reliable assignment except perhaps to broad categories. Use of the standard nomenclature with adults, after which the proposed classification is modeled, has not resulted in satisfactory psychiatric diagnosis, and there seems to be little reason to believe that use of the proposed classification will yield a more reliable system of classification when applied to children's disorders. The use of psychoanalytic terminology with its vague and ill-defined meanings (e.g., partial repression of conflict) will do little to promote a reliable and valid classification system. Nor will the use of overlapping categories based on varying criteria—organic, learned, motivational—help any in that regard.

The Empirical Approach

An alternative approach to psychodynamic or conceptual attempts at classification is the empirical approach. Though more limited in number, empirical classification approaches which search for few and more general dimensions (the irreducible common denominators) of maladjustment are receiving increasing attention.

Dissatisfied with traditional approaches to classification, some psychologists have advocated an empirical approach which, in contrast to the conceptual approach, not only uses a minimum of assumptions and concepts regarding personality development and behavioral disorders, but renders dimensions of disturbed behavior more explicit and operational. Whereas the psychiatric approach relies upon such measures as case histories, interviews, and projective techniques in its approach to classification, the empiricists rely more on behavioral descriptions, validated scales, and checklists. The statistical techniques employed in this approach permit independent confirmation of dimensions or categories derived from clinical observation. Thus, greater credence is lent to a classification system if clinicians and factor theorists are able to derive similar dimensions of categories despite their having used very divergent methods.

Quay (1965), in discussing the structure of children's behavior disorders, notes that behavior disorders are most profitably viewed as dimensions, along which all children range, rather than types of disease entities. A disturbed child, according to this view, is one whose behavior falls at the extreme of one or more of these dimensions. Quay notes that dimensions should satisfy four internal criteria: They should be (1) as mutually exclusive as possible, (2) as objective as possible, (3) specifically demonstrable as a cluster, and (4) derived from more than one kind of data. The dimensions should also be related to meaningful external criteria tied to etiology, behavioral correlates, and appropriate differential treatment. Current research evidence based on factor analysis of case-record data, behavior ratings, or personality questionnaires obtained on populations from public schools, child-guidance clinics, and correctional institutions can be consistently reduced to four dimensions or syndromes: (1) the unsocialized aggressive or conduct disorder; (2) the overinhibited neurotic or personality disorder; (3) a socialized or subcultural conduct disorder; and (4) the inadequacy-immaturity disorder. Symptoms associated with the conduct disorders include restlessness, distractibility, laziness in school, irresponsibility, disobedience, hyperactivity, and impertinence. Behavioral manifestations characteristic of the personality disorders include self-consciousness, feelings of inferiority, daydreaming, distractibility, shyness, and lethargy. Behaviors typical of the inadequacy-immaturity dimension include hyperactivity, impertinence, short attention span, distractibility, feelings of inferiority, and self-consciousness (Quay & Quay, 1965). Note that there is some overlapping of symptoms among the three dimensions. Distractibility, for instance, is common to all these dimensions. Thus, in rendering a decision as to which category a child belongs, the clinician or teacher should consider the general list of symptoms rather than relying solely on a single, specific symptom.

Since these are dimensions rather than types, the practicing clinician must deal with values from these dimensions in diagnosing each case. At this time, the data relating these syndromes to meaningful outside criteria (for example, personality questionnaires, parent and teacher ratings) remain meager, although the evidence indicates that there are differential correlates of these behavioral dimensions and that these are consistent with what one would expect.

This approach is tempting in its elegant simplicity but critics continue to wonder if maladaptive behavior in children can be reduced to so few categories. One wonders why learning difficulties do not show up as a dimension, particularly in those studies where school populations have been used. Moreover, as O'Leary (1972) notes, the approach does not allow one to conclude that a particular behavior can be modified by a particular treatment. For instance, while lying, swearing, and stealing are all included in the conduct problem dimension, it is possible that a given treatment may influence only one of these behaviors with any consistent effectiveness. Yet a change in the score on the conduct-problem dimension does not indicate which of these behaviors was changed by the treatment procedures. Finally, we must remember that the dimensions are not dimensions of child behavior but dimensions of adult reports of child behavior. The ratings obtained in various studies may tell us more about the teacher's or parent's perceptions than about the child's actual behavior. To achieve a more useful model, it will be necessary to maintain a focus on objectively observable behavior while spelling out the conditions under which this behavior is observed (Ross, 1974). Whether because of limitations inherent in this approach or because of the dynamic bias of American psychologists, the empirical approach has barely influenced clinical practice with children, and is limited primarily to research.

Though some psychologists may view the empirical approach as doing away with concepts central to advancing the understanding of personality development and psychopathology, the tough-minded clinician would welcome to an area characterized by subjectivity what appears to be a more reliable and objective procedure for the determination of underlying syndromes or dimensions of disturbed behavior. As Quay (1972) notes,

> The statistical approach clearly disposes of two fundamental weaknesses characterizing the psychiatric, clinical approach. First it provides empirical evidence that the dimension exists as observable constellations of behavior. Second, the objective nature of most of the constituent behaviors permits reliable judgments regarding the extent to which a child shows a given dimension.

Behavioral Analysis

Whereas many of the psychodynamic systems lead one to pursue hypothetical internal determinants of abnormal behavior (for example, Oedipal conflicts), behavioral approaches contend that deviant behavior constitutes "a learned response pattern that often can be directly modified by manipulating the stimulus variables of which both the mediating and terminal behavior are a function" (Bandura, 1968). In other words, once maladaptive behaviors are modified, it is unnecessary to deal with the underlying cause. Whereas many systems focus primarily on the characteristics of persons (for example, passive-aggressive personality), the behavioral analysis approach to taxonomy stresses the *interaction* between the individual's responses and stimulus situations.

There are four major phases in behavior analysis.[2] The first step consists of identifying the target behaviors that are to be modified. Quite often there will be one target behavior that we want to discourage (for example, staring out the window) and one target behavior we want to encourage (for example, listening to the teacher when instructions are given). The target behavior should be stated in a way so that the behavior would be recognizable to any observer.

In the second step, attention is focused on what is called the A,B,Cs—the antecedents of the behavior, the behavior itself, and the consequences attached to the behavior. The antecedents used in this type of analysis consist of factors in the immediate situation which happen before the desired or undesired behavior (e.g., the example of other students). The behavior simply refers to what the student does (e.g., pays attention, fights). The analysis of consequences accruing to the behavior provides clues as to why the behavior occurs by noticing what happens afterward (e.g., student gets his own way by fighting). Some of the more common classroom antecedents and consequences are listed in Table 3–2.

Among the questions that the behavior analyst might typically ask regarding antecedents are these:

> At what time of the school day does the problem occur?
> In what subject matter does the problem occur?
> What degree of accuracy is demanded for a given assignment?
> By whom does the child sit when he misbehaves?
> What is the size of the group when the student misbehaves?

Table 3–2.   Common Classroom Antecedents and Consequences

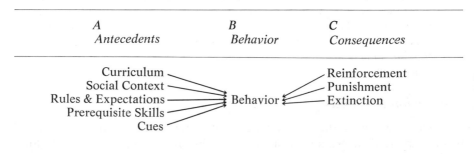

A *Antecedents*	*B* *Behavior*	*C* *Consequences*
Curriculum Social Context Rules & Expectations Prerequisite Skills Cues	Behavior	Reinforcement Punishment Extinction

---

2. For a fuller discussion of these four steps, see pages 497–498.

Are classroom rules definable, reasonable, and enforceable?
Does the student have the academic skills to do his assignment?
Does the student have the social skills necessary to make friends?
Is the student aware that something pleasant will happen once he accomplishes his target behavior?

Among the questions asked regarding consequences are these:

How does the teacher respond to the student's undesired behavior? desired behavior?
How do the other students react?
How does the child himself respond to the outcomes of his behavior?

The third step involves selection of a strategy for modifying behavior. The school counselor will frequently use a combination of such techniques as positive reinforcement, modeling, punishment, extinction in attempting to change behavior.

Finally, the results of program changes are plotted so that the psychologist, teacher, student, and other involved parties, such as the building principal, probation officer, or parents, can determine whether the strategies being used are effective or not. (See Table 3–3.)

In addition to holding promise for a more reliable and valid classification scheme, behavioral analysis has the following advantages (Stuart, 1970):

1. It uses everyday language (without its ambiguity).

2. It offers specific statements regarding the individual (as opposed to general statements regarding a category of individuals).

3. It takes situational factors into account rather than assuming that the child possesses certain traits (for example, aggressiveness) that express themselves in all settings.

4. It focuses as much or more on the development of acceptable and positive behaviors as it does on undesired behaviors.

5. It is parsimonious in that it includes only such information as is necessary for decision making. (Many diagnostic systems entail the collection of considerable information that is never used.)

The Psychoeducational Approach[3]

Adopting a social-competency model, Bower (1970) has classified the mental-health problems of children into five levels. In this model, one is not concerned with the student's anxiety or intrapsychic discomfort but with his inability to handle his anxiety constructively in a school setting. In short, the emphasis is on the student's ability to cope, not on his personal contentment. The five levels, or categories, which might be more accurately construed as a

---

3. Hewitt's model (see pages 370–373) also represents an educationally oriented diagnostic system.

Table 3–3. Behavioral Analysis of Aggressive Behavior in a First Grader

Before the Misbehavior	Undesired Behavior	After the Misbehavior
Games of low organization at recess	Kicks others	Is sent home; "babysitter" lets him watch TV and do what he wants
Eating lunch	Throws various objects	Gets own way from peers
Being in hallways	Bullies others	Teacher and/or principal talks with him
Parents curse and fight with each other	Swears	Peers report him
Parents tell him to fight (e.g., "If somebody hits you, you hit him back ten times harder")	Hits others	Parents give him a pat on the back for attacking others
Certain classmates ask him to fight their battles		Peers cheer him on when he beats up students they do not like

Before the Acceptable Behavior	Acceptable Behavior	After the Acceptable Behavior
Structured playground games	Gets along o.k. with others	Classmates accept him into games and do not avoid him
Adult leader present	Follows rules of game and gets along with peers	Gets peer recognition for his leadership role; parents agree to pay him 25¢ for each "good" day he has; teacher tells him within earshot of class what a good job he did recording behavior; teacher also sends home a "Happy Gram" on good days; principal praises him for his leadership abilities
In charge of recording and reporting "nice" behavior engaged in by self and others on the playground	Takes turns, helps others, shares, doesn't hurt others	

continuum indicating the degree of handicap or social incompetency, are as follows:

Group 1. Those pupils who manifest the ordinary, everyday problems.

Group 2. Those pupils who manifest beginning or minor problems in learning and behavior which exceed normal expectations.

Group 3. Pupils who manifest marked and recurrent difficulties in learning and behavior.

Group 4. Pupils who manifest severe problems in learning and behavior.

Group 5. Pupils who manifest such severe problems that they cannot be maintained in a public-school setting.

For each level, Bower has indicated the most pertinent and beneficial type of school program. An obvious advantage of this system is its facilitation of the psychoeducational decision-making process for deviant youth. For Group 5 youngsters, educational provisions suggested for consideration include a 24-hour residential program, a day-care school program, or home-bound instruction or teaching norms. Children falling into Group 4 can probably still derive some benefit from school attendance if provided with special-class placement. If these youngsters prove unable to maintain some positive contact with the school setting, then placement in a day-school arrangement becomes a possibility. For Group 3 pupils, who are often hanging by their educational bootstraps, educational provisions center around remedial group work, individual tutoring, or mental health consultation with their teachers. For Group 2 youngsters, the school's role involves early identification in the form of screening programs and early treatment, such as parent-counseling programming. For Group 1 students, the school's job is to provide a wide variety of ego-building experiences. A curriculum broad and flexible enough to encompass individual differences in interest, ability, and cultural background can go far in laying a sound base for a mental-health program.

Labeling: Pros and Cons

In recent years there has been an increasing concern regarding the potentially harmful effects of labels and the stigma attached to them. In large degree, the disproportionate number of blacks and Chicanos in special school programs has led to charges that these programs are dumping grounds for problem children from minority groups. The following negative aspects associated with labels and their stigma have received common mention in the literature:

1. Placing a label on an individual may prejudice the response of teachers, peers, family, and society. A vicious circle is thereby established in which behavioral disturbance leads to diagnosis which in turn leads to greater behavioral distress.

2. Labeling creates a new level of fear, fear not of the real condition but of the condition which is implied—often incorrectly—by some exotic term (Menninger, 1963)—for example, "minimal brain dysfunction."

3. Labels emphasize negative characteristics, whereas education and treatment programs should focus on the positive characteristics. A deficit-oriented approach does not produce an appreciation of the child's assets that can provide the focal point for affirmative programming.

4. A given label refers to only a small part of the child's behavior. Consider the case of the "six-hour" retarded child who does poorly in school but who functions satisfactorily the remaining hours of the day in the home and community environment (Hobbs, 1975).

5. Labels lead to a neglect of individual differences and obscure the

services needed to meet the child's particular strengths and weaknesses. Many public school systems still lack the variety and flexibility of services needed to provide in a significant manner for individual differences. School systems must move beyond the "two-box" theory of education (i.e., the dichotomy between regular and special education) and institute a variety of arrangements to improve children labeled "exceptional" (Hobbs, 1975).

6. There is the dangerous possibility of a self-fulfilling prophecy as a result of change in others' expectations for the child.

7. Labeling lowers the child's expectations of himself.

8. Labeling lowers the child's self-esteem.

9. Labeling can lead to placement in special programs which often results in exclusion rather than remediation. Children become "warehoused" instead of treated. Sadly, society too often relocates problem youth instead of treating them.

10. Because labeling is often an unreliable and invalid process, it can expose children unnecessarily to the dangers sometimes associated with treatment (for instance, the example set by other emotionally disturbed or delinquent children, the absence of normal models, rejection by normal peers, decreased access to growth-inducing opportunities, self-perception as deviant, increased law violation following apprehension, exclusion from certain employment opportunities, perception as objects of fear and distrust, victims of blaming and scapegoating). Whether we are referring to short-term or long-term effects, labeling can hurt more than it helps.

11. Labeling implies that the problem is within the child. Using the child as the basic unit for describing, classifying, and programming leaves much important information unaccounted for and unattended to. Family, school, and community influences must be weighed (Hobbs, 1975).

12. Diagnostic systems discourage a sensitivity to change in the child's condition. Problems frequently are not fixed or immutable.

Although the practice of labeling has been roundly attacked, it is not without its ardent supporters. Mentioned in defense of labeling practices are the following:

1. Labeling has made it possible for society to identify major social problems and to marshal vast resources of money, facilities, and talent to attack problems. Without labeling, literally millions of youngsters would never have had any special attention to their needs (Gallagher, 1972). Kolstoe (1972) notes that labeling has the positive effect of allowing society to press for solutions to problems. (Ironically perhaps, those most inclined to speak about the evils of labeling are often among the most eager to seek the funds resulting from identification of children in need.) For better or for worse, funding comes around the categories.

2. Special programs do not produce cleavage between the special child and peers. The cleavage already exists. A sense of difference develops long before any special class placement (Meyers, Sundstrom, & Yoshida, 1974).

3. Although special programs may not be more effective than regular

school programs with respect to the three Rs, they have been successful in helping to promote employability and self-management in the postschool years (Kolstoe, 1972).

4. The notion of a self-fulling prophecy has not been substantiated by subsequent research. Nor have the "negative" effects associated with labeling been proven (Kolstoe, 1972).

5. If special programs geared to fit the abilities and needs of youth are charged with being ineffective, how can general education programs provide the necessary services? If general educators were adequate to the task to begin with, special programs would not have arisen.

Labeling is a complex phenomenon that has variable consequences. There is no simple predictable consequence of labeling for a given youngster. Instead, there is a range of potential outcomes. Research findings are not clear. Most of the data available have failed to separate the effects of labeling from other significant factors, such as the child's prelabeling experiences, postlabeling experiences, and the impact of the condition itself. Moreover, the data available are problematic for reasons related to sampling biases, the use of questionable instruments to assess self-concept, and a failure to consider the child's perception of the label. A search for generalized labeling effects will probably not prove enlightening. Rather, there is a need for definitive research that attempts to specify which youth are most susceptible to labeling effects given certain situational and developmental circumstances (Hobbs, 1975). At this time, the labeling phenomenon has not been well demonstrated.

Because labels are demanded by those agencies responsible for maintaining statistics and by those responsible for funding categorical programs, labeling will most likely continue despite its limitations and unwanted consequences (Imhoff, 1973). As diagnoses focus more upon the development of competencies and less upon pathologies and as individual differences are accommodated adequately within the setting of a regular class, children may not need to bear the burden of stigmatic labels. We will then be able to retain the benefits of classifying children while diminishing the negative consequences of such labeling.

Problems in Evaluating Children's Behavior

1. *Limited Language of Children.* In addition to the problems that apply generally to the entire field of diagnosis, there are specific problems encountered in the evaluation of children's behavior. Children, especially those of preschool age, typically are very limited both in language facility and in vocabulary. Yet personality-measuring instruments are highly language-oriented. They may require actual skill in reading and interpretation of printed material. In any event, they rely heavily upon the comprehension of oral language by which directions and instructions for making a response are given to the children. In part because of their language limitation, chil-

dren are often reported by research investigators as being negative and un-cooperative. It seems likely that they simply do not understand what has been asked of them and what is expected of them.

2. *Limited Experiences of Children.* Children also have had limited practice in reporting their own feelings and wishes. This may in part be a function of their limited facility with language, but it is also probably associated with their simply being inexperienced and thus not being certain of what their feelings and intentions are. A child, for example, may be able to report accurately that he likes something or doesn't like it, but he may be puzzled as to whether he likes something strongly, moderately, very little, or sometimes. He may be totally at a loss when asked to report feelings such as loyalty.

3. *Impact of Sex Differences.* There is growing evidence that there are differential developmental rates, with girls maturing more rapidly than boys. These differences are probably at an optimum at about the time a child ordinarily enters school and continue into early adolescence. There are few measuring scales, however, that present separate normative data for boys and girls throughout this age period. Initially, these differences were thought to be most pronounced with respect to motor responses. Recent evidence suggests that the differences are much more general and probably involve intellectual functioning and other types of performance as well.

4. *Relative Instability of Children's Personalities.* Another source of specific problems is that the child is undergoing constant and sometimes rapid developmental growth and change. Failure to take this factor into consideration could result in the erroneous crediting of maturational changes to experimental manipulation efforts. Maturationally induced changes in performance can manifest themselves suddenly within the individual and may be easily masked if the child's performance is represented by the "average" of his group.

5. *Negativism.* While many youngsters are a pleasure to work with, not all youngsters who have the skills to comply are accommodating. The child who has the ability but refuses to cooperate disturbs many teachers. His typical response is "No, I don't want to do that" (Kicklighter, 1966). This kind of response is especially likely from the negative youngster who is given alternatives, e.g., "Would you like to finish drawing your picture?" A firm attitude, specific directions, and the elimination of alternatives can all be of value when assessing a negative child.

6. *Shyness.* Every professional will encounter a shy child from time to time. Some shy youngsters' behavior stems from being badly frightened. On other occasions, the youngster may simply have never learned the skills necessary to participate in the assessment procedures. Then again, some shy children have learned the necessary skills but have not been adequately reinforced for using them. Regardless of the cause, shyness, (for example, unwillingness or inability to say much, failure to put forth reasonable effort to answer questions) can seriously interfere with evaluation of children's behavior.

7. *Hyperactivity.* One of the most difficult youngsters to evaluate is the

extremely hyperactive or distractible child. This youngster may walk around the room, throw objects (some of which may belong to the psychologist), focus on various things in the room, or climb under the desk. Because of the child's inattentiveness, it is difficult to know if one has a valid measure of the child's typical or maximum performance. Holding the youngster gently, shortening tasks, minimizing distractions, providing occasional breaks, and redirecting his attention to the task often prove helpful, but it is never an easy matter to know if an accurate evaluation has been made.

Incidence

It is difficult to determine with any degree of accuracy the incidence of emotional disturbance in children since estimates of maladjustment will vary with the definition of disturbance used, the agencies sampled (school, child-guidance clinic, juvenile court, resident hospital), and the identification methods employed (referrals to professional specialists, rating scales, self-report inventories, and sociograms). Illustrative of some of the above difficulties are the following findings:

1. If mild disturbances are included in the definition of emotional disturbance, the incidence figures may run as high as 1 in every 3 elementary-school pupils (Rogers, 1942).

2. Schoolteachers are apt to overlook the emotionally disturbed but bright hard-working pupil who is doing well in class (Sarason, Lighthall, Davidson, Waite, & Ruebush, 1960).

3. On the other hand, schoolteachers may be more inclined to see maladjustment in lower-class children than in middle-class pupils (Eisenberg, 1960).

4. Rating scales tend to be more valid for boys than for girls, whereas self-report inventories seem to be more valid for girls than for boys (Ullmann, 1952).

5. Incidence figures based on admission to resident hospitals or out-patient clinics are not likely representative of the prevalence of mental disorders because of the many selective factors that determine admission.

6. Court statistics on delinquency must also be interpreted cautiously, in that the quoted figures are affected not only by the types of cases and ages of children over which the juvenile courts in different regions or states have jurisdiction but also by the number and scope of other social agencies available in the community. The great amount of unrecorded delinquency must also not be overlooked.

Bearing in mind these limitations, let us review some of the available statistics in order to gain a rough perspective as to the scope of maladjustment in children.

One of the most wide-ranging studies of public-school youngsters, which was carried out by Bower (1969) in California, indicates that at least 3 youngsters in the average classroom (10% of students) are sufficiently upset as to warrant the label emotionally handicapped. White and Harris (1961), after carefully reviewing six major studies on the incidence of serious maladjustment in public-school children, arrived at a "working estimate" of 4 to 7%. These rates were based on studies conducted between 1927 and 1958 and relied primarily on teachers' judgments. The most recent and thorough review of incidence studies on maladjustment in elementary-school pupils is contained in a report prepared for the Joint Commission on the Mental Health of Children by Glidewell and Swallow (1968). Their data, which are based on 27 studies reported between 1925 and 1967, indicate that 30% of the elementary-school youth show at least mild adjustment problems, 10% are in need of professional clinical assistance, and 4% would be referred to clinical facilities if such services were available (see Appendix). As might be expected, rates based on admissions to outpatient psychiatric clinics yield a somewhat lower rate. Eisenberg (1960) estimates this rate to be approximately 1% of the childhood population.

Crime statistics for 1972 indicate that there were over one million juvenile delinquents handled by juvenile courts in the United States. In terms of percentages 2.9% of all children in the country between the ages of 7 and 17 were seen in juvenile courts during that year (U.S. Department of Health, Education and Welfare, 1972). If traffic offenses are included, another 312,000 cases, or an additional 1% of the child population in the 7–17 age range, were processed by the juvenile courts. Though it is generally conceded that delinquency has increased over the past decade, there has been much discussion as to whether emotional disturbance is more common today than it was some years ago.

Whether the incidence of childhood disturbance in the United States is on the rise or not is a difficult question to answer since the statistics pertaining to this matter do not lend themselves to unequivocal interpretations. It may well be, however, that the increase in cases seen by child-guidance clinics reflects a heightened concern over childhood disorders rather than an actual increase in such problems. Schofield (1965) suggests that although man through the ages has always experienced anxiety and dealt with stress, current societal attitudes toward man's problems have caused him to "feel anxious about his anxiety." In fact, Glazer (1955), in his analysis of data pertaining to rates of mental disorders in Massachusetts some 100 years ago, contends that the rate of psychosis among the hospitalized population has not changed appreciably except for geriatric populations. Regardless of whether or not mental illness is on the increase, we do know that emotional disturbance in children is not randomly distributed throughout the childhood population. Rather, it is commonly associated with certain variables, the discussion of which follows.

Factors Related to Incidence

Age and Sex.   That the variables of age and sex are consistently related to both outpatient and inpatient treatment of children has been well established. We know, for example, that referral rates to psychiatric clinics are most commonly highest during the preadolescent and middle-adolescent periods.[4] Thus, Gilbert (1957), in his study of four metropolitan clinics, found that problems occurred most frequently in children aged 6 to 10. Figures based on national records of psychiatric clinics indicate the highest incidence of occurrence in ages 10 to 14 (Redick, 1973). Bower (1961), in studying a public-school population, similarly noted that the highest percentage of emotionally handicapped pupils are in the elementary and junior-high grades, with the lowest percentage of emotionally handicapped children in the early primary grades and later high-school years. In addition, Morse, Cutler, and Fink (1964) reported that approximately two-thirds of classes for emotionally disturbed children in the public schools are at the later elementary and junior-high levels.

We also know that overt pathology in children is largely a male phenomenon. Gilbert (1957), for example, in his study of 2,500 consecutive cases seen at four metropolitan clinics, found that boys outnumbered girls nearly 4 to 1 with respect to aggressive acting-out behavior problems and approximately 3 to 1 for academic difficulties. Contrary to popular belief, he found that the boys even outnumbered the girls with respect to passive-withdrawn behaviors. His data, in fact, revealed a sex differential for every major referral problem. The number of both inpatients and outpatients likewise indicates a higher rate of disturbance for boys (Redick, 1973). A large-scale investigation of public-school classes for emotionally disturbed children also revealed a sex ratio of more than 5 to 1 (Morse et al., 1964). Juvenile-court records indicate that more than four times as many boys as girls are referred for delinquent behavior (U.S. Children's Bureau, 1963).

Another interesting finding pertaining to the variables of age and sex is the sex ratio after adolescence (Rosen et al., 1964). The rate for clinic termination per 100,000 population for males was 276.5 for patients under 18 years of age in contrast to only 186.5 per 100,000 for male patients 18 years of age or over. In other words, the rate for males dropped approximately one-third after late adolescence. Whereas the rate for males decreased gradually in late adolescence and adulthood, the rate for females increased during these periods. The clinic termination rate per 100,000 for females under 18 years of age was 144.5, in contrast to 176.9 per 100,000 for patients 18 years of age and over. This represents an increase of 22%. With the decrease in disorders for males and the increase in disorders for females, the sex ratios eventually equalize in adulthood. Data based on patients in resident hospi-

---

4. Glidewell and Swallow (1968) report that age differences per se in the prevalence of *clinical* maladjustment are not great. Data from the Nobles County study also indicate that emotional problems are unrelated to age (Anderson, Harris, Werner, & Gallistel, 1959). It might well be that *clinical* maladjustment becomes more difficult for adults to cope with during the preadolescent and adolescent years. Further, teachers and parents are inclined to give the young child a chance to rally and "to grow out of this stage" before seeking professional help. Both of these factors may, in part, account for the higher rate of referrals during the preadolescent and adolescent years of development.

tals likewise show an equalization of rates following adolescence (U.S. Department of Health, Education and Welfare, 1965).

Another curious finding is the greater number of children (especially boys) receiving treatment in comparison to the number of adults receiving treatment. One reason for this differential rate probably has to do with the fact that children are brought to the clinic by others, whereas adults are more likely to bring themselves. The adult might not recognize that he has a problem, or if he does, he may not wish to change himself. These options are not open to the child. If his problem bothers someone else, he is apt to be referred to the clinic even if he is not motivated to modify his attitudes and behavior. Another explanatory factor probably can be sought in clinic admission policies, which may be based on the assumption that early detection of emotional problems results in a favorable response to treatment. The higher childhood rates may also reflect the concern on the part of parents and teachers for the mental health of their children and pupils (Schofield, 1965). Finally, those subscribing to a genetic theory of primary causality for mental illness might attribute the higher incidence of mental disorders in children to "weak protoplasm" which breaks down early in life.

Major Disorders.   Clinic admission rates vary not only with respect to the age and sex of the patient but also with respect to the type of psychiatric disorders. Gilbert in 1957 studied the data based on 2,500 consecutive cases seen at two metropolitan education clinics and at two metropolitan community clinics. The current emphasis placed on learning disabilities in our society is reflected in the fact that academic difficulties constituted the most frequent referral complaint in the school clinics, followed by mental retardation and aggressive, antisocial behavior. Among the community clinics, aggressive, antisocial behavior was the most frequent referral problem, followed in descending order by anxious behavior, withdrawn behavior, and academic difficulty. Problems of a sexual nature were the least common referred to either type of clinic. These data, in general, suggest that somewhat different types of cases are referred to the different types of clearinghouses available. For example, cases of learning disability and mental retardation tend to be more commonly referred to educational clinics.

The most comprehensive data on type of disorder as it relates to incidence come from the national reporting program on outpatient psychiatric clinics (Rosen et al., 1964). The data contained in Figure 3–1 pertain to both major and detailed diagnostic categories and are based on clinic termination rates. While the data are presented in the form of termination rates, they nonetheless provide an accurate estimate of admission rates because of the limited clinic stay for the majority of patients. The major findings of this study can be summarized as follows:

1. During the first decade of life, central nervous system deficits were relatively high but then declined, with prenatal factors constituting the most common disease entity associated with the brain syndromes in children. During the school years, however, mental deficiencies without organic basis

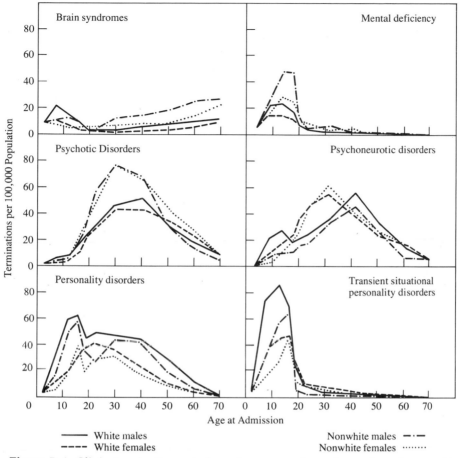

Figure 3–1. Clinic termination rate by color, age, and sex for each major psychiatric disorder, 1961, data for 579 of 682 clinics in 25 states. (*Source*: B. M. Rosen, A. K. Bahn, & M. Kramer. Demographic and diagnostic characteristics of psychiatric clinic outpatients in the U.S.A., 1961. *American Journal of Orthopsychiatry*, 1964, **34**, 455–68. Copyright © the American Orthopsychiatric Association. Reproduced by permission.)

were higher than the brain syndromes. After age 18 the rates for mental deficiency dropped to a low level—a finding consistent with follow-up studies of the mentally retarded which suggest that certain signs of mental retardation are more evident in academic situations than in nonacademic adulthood situations. Severely retarded children seen at the clinics were more commonly aged 5 to 9, whereas both mildly and moderately retarded youngsters were most apt to be 10 to 14 years of age.

2. Psychotic disorders were relatively infrequent prior to adolescence, according to these data; however, the rates rose sharply in adolescence. Interestingly, the rates for childhood schizophrenia were about 8 or 9 per

100,000 for boys and about 3 per 100,000 for girls at ages 5 through 14. A chronic, undifferentiated type of schizophrenia is the most commonly identified psychosis during the adolescent years.

3. The psychoneurotic rate increased somewhat earlier than the psychotic rate, with a slightly more steady rate for females than males. Anxiety reaction was the predominant neurosis for both sexes, although depressive reactions increased for girls during adolescence.

4. Personality disorders constituted the second most frequent diagnosis for children over 5. Among the personality disorders, the passive-aggressive personality was predominant.

5. Transient situational personality disorders were the most common reported diagnostic category until age 18, at which time the rate dropped abruptly.

6. Psychophysiological disorders constituted the least frequent diagnosis rendered, accounting for only slightly more than 1% of cases with a diagnosed disorder. Perhaps the youngsters suffering from psychosomatic illnesses are more commonly treated by a pediatrician or a general practitioner in a regular medical setting.

These data are interesting but probably should not be accepted at face value. Because of the inadequacies associated with psychiatric diagnoses, noted earlier, it is difficult to state with certitude the types of psychiatric problems with which children of a given age range are afflicted. In interpreting these data, the reader would do well to remember the reluctance to "label" children as well as the inadequacies associated with psychiatric diagnoses.

Intelligence and Deviancy.   Kohlberg and his associates (1972) note that the IQ test is the best childhood test for predicting adult adjustment but this finding is more testimony to the inadequacy of personality tests than it is to the predictive power of IQ. In qualifying the crude assertion regarding the association between intelligence and adjustment, they note that: (1) It is difficult to separate parental socioeconomic status and child's IQ. (2) Bright children as compared to average children or average children as compared to dull children are almost as likely to show the most extreme forms of adult adjustment (e.g., suicide, psychosis, serious criminal behavior). (3) Even with respect to less extreme behavior, moderate or high IQ is not a guarantee against later poor adjustment. Low IQ, however, may be a "guarantee" against later high adjustment. (4) The relation between IQ and adjustment is not fixed throughout the life cycle. For example, a bright youngster reaches a given level of maturity faster than a slower-learning child, but at a later age there may be no difference between the two children on a given characteristic such as moral development. Also greater mental maturity brings problems as well as solves them. Because brighter youngsters often face developmental tasks at an earlier age they sometimes look more disturbed than their duller counterparts. MacFarlane's data indicate that bright preschoolers had slightly more problems than average children. During the elementary years the bright children had fewer problems than average children. With the coming of adolescence, however, the advantage of the bright children dropped noticeably, presumably because they were again facing problems later faced by average youth.

Educational Maladjustment.   There is considerable evidence to show that educational maladjustment is associated with personal maladjustment in school-age children. Burke and Simons (1965), using a questionnaire technique with institutionalized delinquents, reported that more than 90% of the sample had records of truancy and poor school adjustment, nearly three-fourths had failed two or more grades, more than 75% had left school at or before the legal age of 16, two-thirds were reading below the sixth-grade level, and 60% had IQ scores in the average range. A large-scale investigation of public-school classes for emotionally disturbed children of normal intellectual ability revealed that a significant degree of academic retardation accompanied the emotional maladjustment characteristic of this population (Morse et al., 1964). Evidence of the relationship between academic and emotional disturbance was also forthcoming from Gilbert's (1957) findings that academic difficulty constituted a very frequent reason for referral to metropolitan community clinics. Data on hospitalized emotionally disturbed pupils indicated that female students were 1 year retarded and male students 2 years retarded in reading and arithmetic achievement when mental age was used as the expectancy criterion (Motto & Lathan, 1966).

Not uncommonly, it is very difficult to distinguish between educational maladjustment and personal maladjustment in school-age youth. The finding of a close relationship between the two is not unexpected since accomplishment in school-related activities constitutes perhaps the major developmental task of youth in our society. Hence, if something interferes with the achievement of a reasonable mastery of this developmental task, it is difficult to conceive that such failure would not adversely influence other aspects of the child's personal adjustment. By definition, developmental tasks are interrelated, so that success or failure in one task tends to increase the likelihood of success or failure in others. We are not by any means equating educational and personal maladjustment. It is obvious that broader and more nonacademic criteria must be considered or applied in arriving at a definition of emotional disturbance in children. We are, however, stressing the notion that adjustment to schoolwork must exercise a pervasive influence on the child's mental health. Figure 3–2 provides a schematic representation of various possible cause-effect relationships. Academic failure, whether cause or effect or related to a host of other variables, does offer us one yardstick for pupil unhappiness and teacher frustration. Furthermore, improvement in adaptation and school performance go hand in hand (Morse et al., 1964).

Typical findings illustrating the relationship between educational and personal maladjustment are those of Bedoian (1954), who reported that overage children receive significantly lower scores upon sociometric testing than do pupils who are underage or at-age for their grade level. To gain a fuller

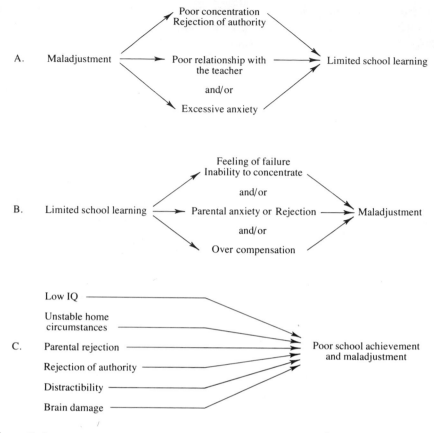

Figure 3–2

appreciation of the potential impact school can have on personality formation, the reader has only to reflect on Miller's (1936) estimate that a pupil
will spend approximately 12,000 hours in a classroom setting during the
course of his 12 years of schooling. One can imagine the number of positive
and negative social reinforcers a child receives over such an extended period
of time. If the psychology of learning has taught us anything, it is that over-
learned activities become a part of us, for better or for worse.

Socioeconomic Status and Race.   Mental-health specialists are becoming
increasingly aware of and concerned about the role played by social and
cultural factors in childhood psychopathology. Clinic termination rates based
on data for 579 of 682 clinics in 25 states indicate that nonwhite rates are
higher during most of adolescence and adulthood, although lower in early
childhood (ages 3 to 11) except for mental deficiency. Moreover, nonwhites
tend to be seen for disorders with the greatest impairment (brain syndromes,
psychotic ditsurbances) in contrast to whites (Rosen et al., 1964). Data
based on a broader coverage of psychiatric facilities, such as hospitals, pri-

vate practitioners, and emergency departments, similarly reflect these racial differences (Gardner, Miles, & Bahn, 1963). State-hospital admission rates likewise show considerably higher incidence for nonwhites than for whites (Pugh & MacMahon, 1962). Racial differences at the elementary-school level have not been carefully studied, although problems of classroom management do tend to be more common in the black slum school (Glidewell & Swallow, 1968).

The higher incidence of behavior disorders in blacks than in whites can be attributed to the debilitating influence of such factors as prejudice, discrimination, segregation, an unstable and matriarchal family structure, restricted educational and vocational opportunities, and a deeply rooted negative self-image (Ausubel & Ausubel, 1963). According to Douglass (1959), externalization of frustrations resulting from such conditions has resulted in a juvenile-delinquency rate in blacks that surpasses that of whites by at least 2 to 1. Not surprisingly, suppressed feelings of aggression (Karon, 1958) and a high level of anxiety (Palermo, 1959) have been identified as salient features of black maladjustment. Though the need for mental-health services appears to be greater for blacks than for whites, clients from impoverished backgrounds have a relatively shorter length of clinic stay (Bahn, Chandler, & Eisenberg, 1962). As noted earlier in the chapter, psychiatric services are not necessarily correlated with the needs of the clientele.

When socioeconomic status, irrespective of race, is examined, the picture remains basically unchanged. Bower (1961), in his California study, reported a higher incidence of disturbed children among certain occupational groups. The group whose fathers' occupations were categorized as "service" or "semiskilled" produced more than twice as many emotionally handicapped pupils as would be anticipated on the basis of their percentage of the state's total population. Fathers in the "unskilled" occupation category also produced more than their share of emotionally disturbed children. Pupils of fathers who were employed in professional or managerial positions, on the other hand, produced far fewer emotionally disturbed children than was expected. In another study (McDermott, Harrison, Schrager, & Wilson, 1965), psychiatric evaluation of 263 children of blue-collar workers indicated a significantly higher incidence of personality and borderline states among children in the "unskilled" group than in the "skilled" group. Further, there were noticeable differences in school performance in favor of the "skilled" group. Yet, somewhat paradoxically, referrals to clinics for professional treatment nonetheless were made relatively later for the unskilled group. Additional evidence regarding the influence of socioeconomic variables on mental health is found in Hollingshead and Redlich's (1958) classical study which reported families of unskilled laborers and semiskilled factory workers contributing almost twice their expected share of both disturbed boys and girls for the age group 15 years and under. Conversely, families occupying positions of high social prestige contributed only their expected share of disturbed boys and none at all to their expected share of disturbed girls. In sum, such studies indicate that maladjustment in children

is not randomly distributed throughout the social classes. On the contrary, teachers tend to view maladjustment as more prevalent in the lower strata of society. It should be noted, however, that the findings relative to social-class differences are not as consistent and clear-cut as those associated with sex.

As was noted earlier, clinic services appear to be inversely related to the needs of the patients; that is, those patients or groups of patients who need the services most are least apt to get them, while treatment is extended to those who are thought to have a higher improvement rate. Although there is no deliberate policy designed to limit acceptance of the less-advantaged classes (who tend to have the most severe prognoses for treatment), there is considerable evidence to suggest the culture-bound nature of our treatment agencies (Schneiderman, 1965). The notion that social-class status is correlated with acceptance or rejection for psychiatric treatment is given support in a study completed by the Family Service Association of America, showing that a client from the lower classes has only a 30% chance of continuing service in contrast to a 60% chance for middle-class clients. It was also discovered that termination of service by the social worker as opposed to termination by the client himself increases sharply as the social class decreases (Cloward, 1963). Data gathered on public, tax-supported agencies yield essentially similar results. Applying for psychiatric service is apparently like applying for a loan. If you can demonstrate that you really don't need the money, you can get it. On the other hand, if you demonstrate that you really do need it, you are considered a poor risk and you do not get it. Analogously speaking, if the client can demonstrate that he has a stable family, reasonable ego strength, a capacity for insight, adequate verbal facility, and so on, he can get treatment. On the other hand, if he is lacking in these, he is regarded as not ready for treatment and therefore cannot get help. Further, there is evidence to suggest that the mere addition of services per se will not change this state of affairs (Rudolph & Cumming, 1962). It was found, for example, that the higher the status of the community agency, the more rigid or fixed it becomes in technique and in the problems it considers suitable for treatment. Also, the more highly trained the staff, the more efficient they become at rejecting clients who are not yet ready for service. The study concluded that the role of the agency workers is defined not so much in terms of the needs to be met as in terms of the special skill of the workers. Evidence thus suggests that the more professional services improve, the more they are geared to a middle-class clientele.

Therapist-centered problems in working with the poor and uneducated do not justify decisions not to treat. Several recent findings regarding the treatment of low-income patients are apropos (Lorion, 1974). (1) Although a patient's socioeconomic status is an important correlate of acceptance for and duration of individual treatment, it is not predictive of treatment outcome. (2) The earlier belief on the part of therapists that low-income applicants necessarily hold more negative attitudes toward treatment than middle- or upper-income applicants is unsupported by more recent objective findings.

(3) Some form of patient preparation given early in treatment and designed to develop accurate expectations regarding therapy merits further considera- tion. Pretreatment preparation may help by making therapy less mysterious and more comfortable for low-income clients. (4) Consideration should also be given to modifying treatment procedures so that they more closely approx- imate the patient's expectations. Behavioral approaches, short-term treatment, crisis intervention, and walk-in services may permit the practitioner to treat the needs of poor people more flexibly. (5) While we have become increas- ingly aware of the mental health needs of the lower socioeconomic segments of our society, we need to pursue additional research and practice on training-supervisory problems if we are to expand our competencies to treat those vast numbers who are now being neglected.

Summary

Traditionally a diagnosis is supposed to yield agreement as to what the problem is, to tell how the child got that way, to forecast where the student is headed, and to make clear what we can do for him.

Controversy continues as to whether a medical or a psychosocial diagnostic model is more appropriate for dealing with behavior disorders in children. There continue to be two schools of thought on this subject.

The psychiatric descriptive approach advanced by the Committee on Child Psychiatry might well become the system most widely used in the ordering of behavioral disturbances in children. Despite the vast improvement over the previous adult psychiatric nomenclature, this approach with its overlapping categories and ill-defined psychoanalytic terminology will probably not provide us with a reliable and valid classification system.

The empirical approach with its reliance upon behavioral descriptions and validated checklists seeks to identify the irreducible factors or dimensions that underlie behavior disturbances. While this approach attempts to introduce objectivity into a field characterized by subjectivity, it has unfortunately had minimal impact on everyday clinical practice.

Behavioral analysis consists of four steps: selection of a target behavior; identification of factors occurring immediately prior to and immediately after the target behavior; selection of such strategies as positive reinforcement, extinction, modeling, and punishment; and the recording of results. Because of its many advantages (use of everyday language, specific prescriptions, allowance for situation influence, focus on positive behavior, parsimonious collection of information), this approach has been achieving increased acceptance and recognition. Behavioral analysis is not intended to lead to assignment of the child to a diagnostic category. Instead, it should serve as a basis for making decisions about specific therapeutic interventions.

The psychoeducational approach, as advanced by Bower, divides children into five levels based on the degree of incompetency. This model will undoubtedly hold appeal to those who provide help within the school setting.

The use of labeling has been objected to on the grounds that it prejudices the responses of significant others, it heightens fears, emphasizes negative aspects of a child's behavior, refers only to a small portion of the child's functioning, lowers self-esteem and expectation, can result in exclusion rather than help, implies that the problem resides primarily or solely in the child, and can sometimes expose children unnecessarily to the dangers associated with the helping process.

The defenders of labeling practices point out that without labeling, much of the assistance given to maladjusted youngsters would not have been forthcoming. Advocates of labeling also state that the damage attributed to labeling has not been clearly and consistently substantiated by research.

The view was expressed that labeling practices will continue. As special and regular class programs merge in the schools and as more positive aspects of the child's behavior are focused upon, labels may lose much of their stigma.

Special problems involved in the assessment of children's behavior include the limited language and experiences of children, the influence of sex differences, the relative instability of children's personalities, negativism, shyness, and distractibility.

Approximately one in every ten public-school children has moderate to severe adjustment problems. If one uses the criterion of mild adjustment problems, the prevalence rates jump to three in every ten students.

Behavioral disturbance is not a randomly distributed phenomenon; rather prevalence figures vary with a host of factors.

Referral rates to clinics are highest during the preadolescent and adolescent years. This finding may be due more to referral policies (e.g., the tendency to wait and let the child grow out of his problems) than to differential rates of disturbance at various ages. In fact, there is evidence to suggest that the incidence of behavioral disturbance is unrelated to age.

Information on sex differences in maladjustment indicates an approximate sex ratio of 3 boys to 1 girl. Thus, 15% of boys and only 5% of girls have moderate to severe problems of adjustment. It is interesting to note that this sex ratio begins to change following adolescence.

Reactive disorders and learning disabilities constitute the most common diagnoses given troubled youth.

Although being bright is generally an advantage with respect to one's adjustment, the relationship between high intelligence and adjustment varies with age.

There is a close relationship between educational maladjustment and personal maladjustment, although the two are not synonymous concepts. Cause-effect relationships have not been clearly established.

References

Adams, H. Mental illness or interpersonal behavior. *American Psychologist,* 1964, 19, 191–97.

American Psychiatric Association. *Diagnostic and statistical manual of mental disorders.* Washington, D.C.: Mental Hospital Services, 1952, 1968.

Ausubel, D. *Theory and problems of child development.* New York: Grune & Stratton, 1958.

Ausubel, D., & Ausubel, P. Ego development among segregated Negro children. In A. H. Passow (Ed.), *Education in depressed areas.* New York: Teachers College Press, 1963, pp. 109–41.

Bahn, A., Chandler, C. A., & Eisenberg, L. Diagnostic characteristics related to services in psychiatric clinics for children. *Milbank Memorial Fund Quarterly* 1962, **15,** 289–318.

Bandura, A. A social learning interpretation of psychological dysfunctions. In P. London & D. Rosenhan (Eds.), *Foundations of abnormal psychology.* New York: Holt, Rinehart, and Winston, 1968, pp. 293–344.

Bedoian, U. H. Social acceptability and social rejection of underage, at-age, and overage pupils in the sixth grade. *Journal of Educational Research,* 1954, **47,** 513–20.

Bower, E. *The education of emotionally handicapped children.* Sacramento, Calif.: California State Department of Education, 1961.

Bower, E. M. *The early identification of emotionally handicapped children in school.* (2nd ed.) Springfield, Ill.: Thomas, 1969.

Bower, E. M. Mental health. In R. Ebel (Ed.), *Encyclopedia of educational research.* (4th ed.) New York: Macmillan, 1970, pp. 811–28.

Burke, N. S., & Simons, A. E. Factors which precipitate dropouts and delinquency. *Federal Probation,* 1965, **29,** 28–32.

Cloward, R. Social class and private social agencies. *Proceedings of the Annual Meeting of Council on Social Work Education,* Boston, 1963.

Committee on Child Psychiatry. *Psychopathological disorders in childhood: theoretical considerations and a proposed classification.* New York: Group for the Advancement of Psychiatry, 1966.

Douglass, J. H. The extent and characteristics of juvenile delinquency in the United States. *Journal of Negro Education,* 1959, **28,** 214–29.

Draguns, J., & Phillips, L. *Psychiatric classification and diagnosis: an overview and critique.* New York: General Learning Press, 1971.

Eisenberg, L. *Emotionally disturbed children and youth: children and youth in the 1960's.* Survey of papers prepared for 1960 White House Golden Anniversary Conference on Children and Youth. Washington, D.C.: Government Printing Office, 1960.

Ey, H. Esquise d'un conception organo-dynamique de la structure de la nosographic et de l'ethropathologenic des maladies mentales. In H. Gruhle, R. Jung, W. Mayer-Gross, & M. Muller (Eds.), Psychiatric der Gegenwart, Vol. 1/2, Berlin: Springer 1963, pp. 720–62.

Freud, A. *Normality and pathology in childhood.* New York: International Universities Press, 1965.

Gallagher, J. The special education contract for mildly handicapped children. *Exceptional Children*, 1972, **38**, 527–35.

Gardner, E. H., Miles, H. C., & Bahn, A. K. A cumulative survey of psychiatric experience in a community: report of the first year's experience. *Archives of General Psychiatry*, 1963, **9**, 369–78.

Gilbert, G. M. A survey of "referral problems" in metropolitan child guidance centers. *Journal of Clinical Psychology*, 1957, **13**, 37–42.

Glazer, N. Trends in mental disorder. In A. M. Rose (Ed.), *Mental health and mental disorder.* New York: Norton, 1955, pp. 117–22.

Glidewell, J., & Swallow, C. *The prevalence of maladjustment in elementary schools.* Chicago: University of Chicago Press, 1968.

Greenfield, J. *A child called Noah.* New York: Paperback Library, 1973.

Hobbs, N., *The Futures of Children,* San Francisco: Jossey Bass, 1975.

Hollingshead, A. B., & Redlich, F. C. *Social class and mental illness: a community study.* New York: Wiley, 1958.

Hunt, W. A., Diagnosis and non-directive theory, *Journal of Clinical Psychology*, 1948, **4**, 232–36.

Imhoff, K. Legal and educational consequences of the intelligence testing movement: handicapped & minority group children. *School Psychology Newsletter*, 1973, **28**, 1:4.

Jenkins, R. Symptomatology and dynamics in diagnosis: a medical perspective. *Journal of Clinical Psychology,* 1953, **9**, 149–150.

Karon, B. P. *The Negro personality.* New York: Springer, 1958.

Kessel, N., & Shepherd, M. Neurosis in hospital and general practice. *Journal of Mental Science*, 1962, **108**, 159–66.

Kicklighter, R. Problems in the psychological evaluation of children. *Psychology in the Schools*, 1966, **3** (2), 164–67.

Kohlberg, L., LaCrosse, J., & Ricks, D. The predictability of adult mental health from childhood behavior. In B. Wolman (Ed.), *Manual of child psychopathology,* New York: McGraw-Hill, 1972.

Kolstoe, O. Programs for the mildly retarded: a reply to the critics. *Exceptional Children*, 1972, **39**, 1,: 51–56.

London, P. *The modes and morals of psychotherapy.* New York: Holt, Rinehart and Winston, 1964.

London, P. The end of ideology in behavior modification. *American Psychologist*, 1972, **27**, 913–20.

Lorion, R. Patient and therapist variables in the treatment of low-income patients. *Psychologic Bulletin* 1974, **81**, 344–54.

MacFarlane, J. From infancy to adulthood. *Childhood Education*, 1963, 39, 336–42.

McDermott, J., Harrison, S., Schrager, J., & Wilson, P. Social class and mental illness in children: observation of blue-collar families. *American Journal of Orthopsychiatry*, 1965, **35**, 500–08.

McIntosh, D., & Dunn, L. Children with specific learning disabilities. In L. Dunn (Ed.), *Exceptional children in the schools.* New York: Holt, Rinehart, and Winston, 1973.

Meehl, P. *Psychodiagnostics.* Minneapolis: University of Minnesota Press, 1973.

Menninger, K. *The vital balance.* New York: Viking, 1963.

Meyers, C., Sundstrom, P., & Yoshida, The school psychologist and assessment in special education. School Psychology Monograph 1974, **2**(1) 3–57.

Miller, E. Classification of the disorders of childhood. In Sir Humphrey Rolleston (Ed.), *British encyclopedia of medical practice.* London: Butterworth, 1936.

Moos, R., & Clemes, S. Multivariate study of the patient-therapist system. *Journal of Consulting Psychology,* 1967, **31,** 119–30.

Morse, W. C., Cutler, R. L., & Fink, A. H. *Public school classes for the emotionally handicapped: a research analysis.* Washington, D.C.: Council for Exceptional Children, 1964.

Motto, J. J., & Lathan, L. An analysis of children's educational achievement and related variables in a state psychiatric hospital. *Exceptional Children,* 1966, **32,** 619–23.

O'Leary, K. The assessment of psychopathology in children. In H. Quay & J. Werry (Eds.), *Psychopathological disorders of childhood.* New York: Wiley, 1972.

Palermo, D. S. Racial comparisons and additional normative data on the children's manifest anxiety scale. *Child Development,* 1959, **30,** 53–57.

Patterson, C. H. *Counseling and psychotherapy: theory and practice.* New York: Harper, 1959.

Patterson, G. R. An empirical approach to the classification of disturbed children. *Journal of Clinical Psychology,* 1964, **20,** 326–37.

Peterson, D. Behavior problems of middle childhood. *Journal of Consulting Psychology,* 1961, **25,** 205–9.

Pugh, T. F., & MacMahon, B. *Epidemiologic findings in United States mental hospital data.* Boston: Little, Brown, 1962.

Quay, H. The structure of children's behavior disorders. Paper read at colloquia at the University of Minnesota, 1965.

Quay, H., & Quay, L. Behavior problems in early adolescence. *Child Development,* 1965, **36,** 215–20.

Quay, H. Patterns of aggression, withdrawal and immaturity. In H. Quay & J. Werry (Eds.), *Psychopathological disorders of childhood.* New York: Wiley, 1972.

Redick, R. Utilization of psychiatric facilities by persons under 18 years of age. United States, 1971. Statistical Note 90. Department of Health, Education and Welfare, 1973.

Rogers, C. R. The criteria used in a study of mental health problems. *Educational Research Bulletin,* Ohio State University, 1942, **81,** 29–40.

Rosen, B. M., Bahn, A. K., & Kramer, M. Demographic and diagnostic characteristics of psychiatric clinic outpatients in the U.S.A., 1961. *American Journal of Orthopsychiatry,* 1964, **34,** 455–68.

Rosenthal, D. Book reviews. *Psychiatry,* 1962, **61,** 377–80.

Ross, A. *Psychological disorders of childhood.* New York: McGraw-Hill, 1974.

Rudolph, C., & Cumming, J. Where are additional psychiatric services most needed? *Social Work,* 1962, **7,** 15–20.

Sarason, S. B. Lighthall, F. F., Davidson, K. S., Waite, R. R., & Ruebush, B. K. *Anxiety in elementary school children.* New York: Wiley, 1960.

Schneiderman, L. Social class diagnosis and treatment. *American Journal of Orthopsychiatry*, 1965, **35,** 99–105.

Schofield, W. *Psychotherapy: the purchase of friendship*. Englewood Cliffs, N.J.: Prentice-Hall, 1965.

Smith, M. B. The revolution in mental health care—a bold new approach? *Transaction*, 1968, **5,** 19–23.

Stuart, R. *Trick or treatment*—how and when psychotherapy fails. Urbana, Ill.: Research Press, 1970.

Szasz, T. The myth of mental illness. *American Psychologist*, 1960, **15,** 113–18.

Ullmann, C. A. Mental health screening of school children. *Public Health Report*, 1952, **67,** 1219–23.

U.S. Department of Health, Education and Welfare. *Juvenile court statistics*, 1971. Washington, D.C. Government Printing Office, 1972.

White, M. A., & Harris, M. *The school psychologist*. New York: Harper, 1961.

White, R., & Watt, N. *The abnormal personality*. (4th ed.) New York: Ronald Press, 1973.

Suggested Readings

Committee on Child Psychiatry. *Psychopathological disorders in childhood: theoretical considerations and a proposed classification*. New York: Group for the Advancement of Psychiatry, 1966.

Dreger, R. Behavior classification project. *Journal of Abnormal Psychology*, 1973, **1,** 1, 88–120.

Glidewell, J., & Swallow, C. *The prevalence of maladjustment in elementary schools*. Chicago: University of Chicago Press, 1968.

Hobbs, N. *The futures of children*. San Francisco: Jossey-Bass, 1975.

Kohlberg, L., La Crosse, J., & Ricks, D. The predictability of adult mental health from childhood behavior. In B. Wolman (Ed.), *Handbook of child psychopathology*. New York: McGraw-Hill, 1972.

Meehl, P. *Psychodiagnostics*. Minneapolis: University of Minnesota Press, 1973.

Stuart, R. *Trick or treatment—how and when psychotherapy fails*. Urbana, Illinois: Research Press, 1970.

Behavior Disorders in Children

4

Childhood Compulsive, Obsessive, and Phobic Reactions

Adjustment difficulties with a core of compulsive, obsessive, and phobic behaviors have been the objects of extensive study by behavioral scientists and practitioners. These behaviors are prominent in the group of conditions termed psychoneurotic disorders, believed by some workers to have origins in childhood. Fears, rituals, and repetitive acts are obvious and common behaviors that can be observed in children developmentally. Because of the apparent close relationship with anxiety, psychoneurotic reactions can be easily replicated in the laboratory. The relative ease with which communication can be established with psychoneurotic persons and the seemingly favorable results elicited by a variety of treatment methods undoubtedly served to encourage and reinforce their investigation. Strangely, psychoneuroses have enjoyed a popular acceptance that has reached a point of investing the appellation "neurotic" with something of the aura of a status symbol.

Many of the initial beliefs about psychoneurotic reactions have had to be altered or discarded, but continuing exploration of what are more popularly referred to as "neuroses" has generated explanations about such puzzling aspects of behavior as why a person may enjoy being a self-made invalid. Situated somewhere between the severe disorders, as represented by the psychoses, and the "normal" personality, the psychoneuroses have bridged a crucial gap. From this intermediate position, links between the normal and the pathological have sometimes been easier to identify, a factor that may have provided support for the concentration of study on normal personality development rather than on pathological conditions. An understanding of the ways in which the normal individual attempts to deal with stress and of how response patterns can be acquired and perpetuated has added greatly to the clinician's skill in evaluating all behaviors.

This chapter reviews current concepts and points of view about neuroses as they are encountered in children and adolescents. We examine types of stresses, techniques for coping with stress, diagnostic problems, and the necessity for the cooperative involvement of several professional specialties in the management of childhood psychoneuroses.

Definitions

The literature of behavior disorders contains a generous number of formulations describing psychoneuroses. The differences in definition are relatively minor and pertain largely to the relative importance assigned to hereditary, experiential, and psychodevelopmental influences in contributing to the origins of the disorder. Descriptions of psychoneuroses have centered about two major theoretical orientations, the psychonanalytic and the behavioristic. According to the psychoanalytic point of view, neuroses are regarded as the manifestation of a conflict between the major personality components, designated as the id, ego, and superego. The press of sexual, aggressive, and guilt feelings can become the origin for neurotic conflicts. The ego, acting in its function as mediator, is taxed to maintain a balance between the id and superego. Impairment is a consequence of the necessity to divert excessive amounts of energy to counter these feelings, which threaten the psychological integrity by upsetting the equilibrium between the personality components. The symptomatology of the neurosis mirrors the ego's attempt to resolve the conflicting psychic forces and thus lower the uncomfortably high degree of tension to a more tolerable level. Kessler (1972), discussing the psycho-analytic approach, has stated that neurotic disorders take many forms, but all have these common features: (1) the child is anxious and is aware that he feels anxious, (2) the child suffers more than do the persons in his sur-roundings, and (3) the stress of the neurosis is directed primarily on the self rather than against others. A brief example may serve to illustrate this con-ception. A pupil felt a powerful resentment against a teacher who constantly criticized his efforts in mastering writing. The strength of the pupil's fear that he might strike the teacher was second only to his anxious concern for having such unacceptable thoughts. Resolution of the conflicting feelings found expression in a sudden paralysis of the arm that might be used to strike the teacher.

From a behavioristic or learning-theory perspective, a high level of anxiety is also deemed essential for the formation of a psychoneurotic reaction. Since anxiety can be aroused by any situation in which self-esteem is jeopardized, the source is of minor importance. The anxiety and its arousal come to be associated with a stimulus representative of some real and intense emotional experience (darkness of a closet or time-out room, a tall teacher, fear of a speeding train, smell of a hospital, failure in math, confines of a small room). What is crucial is that the level of anxiety is uncomfortably high and must be lowered to more endurable ranges. The child seeks to avoid this unpleas-antness by the use of avoidance or escape behaviors. Initially, techniques for coping with the anxiety may be selected on the basis of chance availability or personal preferences, but they are retained on the basis of success in reducing, eliminating, or avoiding the discomforting anxiety level. Thus, by processes of conditioning, generalization, and reinforcement, a complex set of associations is formed between the arousing stimulus and the behaviors used to cope with the anxiety. The perception of the threat and the methods used for combating the stress are highly individualized but follow standard learning principles, especially as exemplified by conditioning. The methods are maintained on the basis of immediate short-term success and become habitual response patterns. To the extent that these behaviors are situation-ally inappropriate, the child may be regarding as evidencing "neurotic" behaviors. From a long-range perspective, the ways for meeting the stress situation are maladaptive and constitute the basis for an impairment in the individual's functional capacity.

Wolpe (1958), representing the behavioristic approach to neuroses, de-scribed these conditions as requisite for a psychoneurotic disorder: (1) high anxiety level, (2) absence of direct assault or damage to the nervous system by chemical or physical agents, and (3) a persistent pattern of responses inappropriate for the situation. The story of Mary's disorder may clarify the behavioristic conception of psychoneurosis.

Mary, a Girl with a Psychoneurotic Disorder

A shy girl, Mary, was seldom successful because others answered before she was ready to respond. As the number of failures increased, Mary began to doubt her ability to succeed in any situation. As she became less assertive, she failed even more frequently. Mary felt helpless and feared to do anything. On seeing her listlessness and apathy, people commented that she must be ill. Gradually the girl withdrew from participation in all new events, offering the excuse of not feeling well. Although Mary secretly longed for success in competition with others, the meager satisfactions garnered from playing the role of an invalid were sufficient to bar her from actively applying her abilities to gain usual achievements.

There is general agreement that a psychoneurotic reaction entails extreme anxiety associated with ineffectiveness in meeting life demands. The impairment tends to be more readily observable in one large life area, such as adjustment to work, friendships, school, or physical health. Inadequate functioning persists in the face of evidence of adequate intellectual ability, good physical health, and normal family and home background. A disproportionate amount of personal resources must be directed to coping with high anxiety levels. Behavior reveals an inconsistent mixture of rigidity, an overlay of immediacy, and a declining efficiency. Complaints of personal unhappiness, inability to function, and nagging discomfort are common to this cyclic pattern of intense anxiety and compensatory efforts to reduce the anxiety to a more tolerable level.

Sources of Data on Incidence

Estimates of the prevalence of psychoneuroses vary considerably. The early clinicans treating emotional disturbances apparently saw a disproportionate number of neurotic disorders. Signs and symptoms characteristic of a psychoneurotic reaction may have been misjudged when observed as isolated behaviors. Children with psychoneurotic disorders may have complaints of being ill which bring them to a pediatrician. When a careful examination turns up no somatic dysfunctions, the child may be advised that his health is good and be dismissed. These are some of the practices which can introduce exaggerations in estimates of the frequency of a behavior disorder. Although data reporting on the incidence of any behavior disorder present many problems of interpretation as was discussed in Chapter 3, these data provide the best available source for suggesting the prevalence of a condition.

1. *Outpatient Clinics.* A report presented by Rosen, Bahn, & Kramer (1964) enumerates persons given terminal outpatient service at community mental-health clinics in 1961. Children (persons under 18 years of age) made up 54% of the approximately 350,000 patients reported. Of the total number of children seen, 1 in 10 was diagnosed as psychoneurotic. In the psychoneurotic category, the number of boys was only slightly higher than the number of girls. The incidence rates followed interesting age-trend patterns, however. Boys showed a peak prevalence in the age range from 9 to 14 years, whereas the peak prevalence for girls was in the 14- to 16-year range. The number of boys in the psychoneurotic category at age 10 years was twice that for girls. The incidence rates became equal at about age 14, and by age 20 the picture was reversed, with female outnumbering male psychoneurotics by 2 to 1.

2. *Hospitalized Inpatients.* The report compiled by Rosen and his colleagues (1964) enumerates similar data for approximately 270,000 persons admitted to a state, county, or private mental hospital in 1962 with no prior history of hospitalization (first admissions). In these statistics, persons under 15 years of age are classed as children. The data indicate that approximately 1 in 13 children was diagnosed as psychoneurotic. The incidence ratio for psychoneuroses indicated by inpatient data (1 in 13) is not much lower than that for outpatient data (1 in 10). This figure is surprising when it is considered that hospitalization for children is regarded as a drastic measure to be taken only as a last resort. Nevertheless, the many factors influencing the data as reported make it inadvisable to generalize or to offer much interpretation of suggested statistical patterns.

3. *Schools.* Data that might be the most helpful for planning programs to alleviate psychoneuroses, detailed analyses of school populations, have been least available. This fact is unquestionably related to the uncertainty that schools have felt about the entire matter of responsibility for the treatment of behavior disorders. The popular procedure has been to refer these children to facilities outside the school agencies for care and treatment. The few scattered studies reporting on incidences of psychoneuroses in school populations often do so in gross ways that may raise more questions than they answer. In a study of children seen at a community child-guidance clinic, for example, Kurlander & Colodny (1965) reported that from 25 to 50% of the children were suffering from psychoneuroses. In a survey of the characteristics of public-school pupils in special classes for the socially and emotionally maladjusted, Morse, Cutler, & Fink (1964) concluded that 60% of the children in these classes were psychoneurotic. There were approximately 3 boys for every 2 girls in the student group studied. One study carried out in a public-school system carefully assessed the prevalence of the psychoneurotic reaction "school phobia." In this study, Leton (1962) stated that

the incidence of school phobia was 3 per 1,000 pupils in the primary grades but increased to 1 per 100 students by high school. Pointing out that most mild and moderate cases may go undetected, he estimated that less than half of the cases of school phobia may actually be diagnosed. The peak of incidence occurs in pupils aged 6 to 10. Leton randomly selected 12 pupils for detailed study as representative of the disorder. It is interesting that in this group of 7 girls and 5 boys, only one pupil came from the lower sociocultural level, three from the upper, and the other eight from the middle.

Much of the confusion encountered in interpreting incidence data stems from biases inherent in the "rules" for making a diagnosis at given treatment agencies. Clinics providing only outpatient services, for example, tend to favor diagnoses emphasizing situational and temporary conditions (for example, reactive disorders). This emphasis on the immediate may mask chronic elements, a feature essential for making a diagnosis of psychoneurosis. Many children may never be identified because the stress of psychoneurotic disorders tends to be turned more to the self rather than being acted out on other persons. Another difficulty is the significance of certain behaviors (fears, nail-biting, night terrors, and enuresis) that contribute to the diagnosis. These behaviors are also developmentally normal for some ages, and the context in which they are interpreted may spuriously inflate or deflate the reports of incidence of neuroses. The probabalities are that such reports are underestimates.

Nevertheless, such data as are available must be taken as a start in planning the alleviation of psychoneurotic disorders. The data indicate that, although not the most frequent, psychoneurotic disorders are one of the major behavior problems seen in children. The relationship between incidence rates and sociocultural levels is not clear and needs additional study.

Characteristics

Although the accompanying behavioral responses vary from one to another individual, the problem common to all psychoneurotic disorders is that of handling the distressingly high level of anxiety. The behaviors have the object of preventing the buildup of additional anxiety and serving as the release for anxiety already present. Constitutional, personal, and social factors contribute to the choice of ways for handling anxiety, which takes the form of extreme responses in the following areas:

1. *Motor Characteristics.* Deviations in motor responses are among the most commonly observed of psychoneurotic symptoms. The expressions often are of an active nature and include episodes of running, floor pacing, restlessness, hand wringing, temper outbursts, and tearing or throwing objects. Passive activities seem to be effective in releasing anxiety for some persons. Thus immobile freezing and loss of muscle tone and control (as in fainting or paralysis) are also encountered. Motor responses may take on a persistent

quality, such as the repetitious washing of hands or walking so as to avoid cracks in the sidewalk. These repeated acts are termed compulsions. In still other instances, the motor activity may have a pronounced ceremonial quality. Preoccupations with seeing that books are stacked in exact alignment, clothes are hanging in a fixed arrangement, shoes are placed in a precise row, or a rigid carrying out of stereotyped patterns of going to bed are examples of such ritualistic motor activities. Yet another variety of motor reactions entails the rhythmic contracting of small or specific muscles, frequently facial muscles; such muscle twitches are known as tics.

2. *Somatic Characteristics.* Many psychoneurotic symptoms are of a somatic nature, so that there is difficulty in differentiating them from actual physical illnesses. Sometimes these physical complaints are of a vague and general nature, such as not feeling well (malaise), loss of pain sensitivity (anesthesia), loss of appetite (anorexia), feeling dizzy (vertigo), or inability to sleep (insomnia). Other somatic complaints are of a specific nature and include headaches, irregularities in breathing, variations in heartbeat, regurgitation of food, constipation, and loss of vision or hearing. A particularly interesting somatic complaint frequently encountered is that of choking and inability to swallow (globus hystericus). Symptoms in the form of somatic complaints are readily accepted as valid excuses and even secure a certain amount of attention and sympathy for the individual.

3. *Intellectual Disturbances.* The impairing consequences of high anxiety levels are plainly evident in lowered scores obtained on a variety of psychological measuring scales (intelligence, achievement, creativity). Certain characteristics seen in psychoneuroses can be regarded as breakdowns in intellectual functions. The more common of these symptoms have obsessive-compulsive qualities. The repetitious counting of otherwise unimportant objects (lights on the ceiling, telephone poles, tiles in the floor, steps in a stairway) and persisting thoughts, songs, or sayings are examples. There may be a ritualistic absorption with magic and counteractions to avoid the "bad-luck" of breaking a mirror or having a black cat cross one's path. More spectacular but less frequently observed intellectual dysfunctions are brief memory lapses (amnesias); longer periods of losses are known as fugues. Intellectual dysfunctions that are more difficult to detect entail rigid and inflexible types of thinking.

4. *Emotional Deviations.* In addition to the basic overlay of anxiety, depression and unhappiness, social withdrawal, and sensitivity are common emotional reactions associated with neuroses. Inhibition and excessive control of impulses, seen as prominent features in some types of neurotic adjustments, result in a sober and overly serious emotional tone. Other neurotic individuals can become excitedly "charged-up" for brief periods of time, but emotional outbursts of anger and spells of uncontrollable laughing or crying are more typically observed. With these emotional episodes, the person may appear distraught and apprehensive.

5. *Language Characteristics.* Distortions in speech are not commonly observed with neuroses. Some speech pathologists have attempted to relate

such a speech impairment as stuttering to a psychoneurotic reaction, but the connection has not thus far been convincingly demonstrated. The voice volume is often low for persons with a neurosis, giving a kind of weak voice. There are also episodes of the other extreme, with shouting and ranting, usually in conjunction with hypermotor activity. Although rarely encountered, undoubtedly the most dramatic language disability is that of a sudden loss of speech (aphasia). The recovery of customary speech facility is usually spontaneous.

6. *Social Characteristics.* Perhaps more than for any other behavior disorder, behaviors symptomatic of psychoneurotic reactions are distinguished by a social relevance. Pacing the floor, restlessness, and episodes of intense grief or joy are all normal reactions. Keeping one's belongings in some orderly arrangement, being neat, and knowing the correct date and time are realistic expectations made of the responsible person. The fear and avoidance of certain objects or situations are taken as indications of intelligence and of the capacity to profit from experience. The paniclike fears of specific situations (closed-in places, high places, elevators) observed as part of some neurotic syndromes and technically referred to as phobias may, at least when first acquired, have had some of these same survival qualities.

Classification

All of these symptoms are seen in varying combinations and degrees. Continued efforts to deal with the anxiety, combined with influences from constitutional and social factors, typically lead to the development of rather durable organizations of responses. As the neurosis persists, a particular characteristic (amnesia, restless motor hyperactivity, profuse sweating, and so on) may come to stand out in the pattern. But many times, and especially in the case of children, the symptoms are in a mixed group. These varied possibilities for handling the stress of a neurosis form the basis for diagnostic classification in one of several psychoneurotic reaction types:

1. *Anxiety Type.* In this disorder, manifest anxiety as an intense feeling of apprehension or impending catastrophe is the predominant feature. There is a minimum of other motor, somatic, or language symptoms, and the acute anxiety may be related to any obvious aspects of the environment, such as the simple announcement "Now we are going to study arithmetic." The anxiety level may subside as suddenly and inexplicably as it appeared. This type of neurotic reaction may be difficult to identify in children because of the cyclical changes in anxiety level and the scarcity of other symptoms.

2. *Phobic Type.* In this neurotic reaction, a situation, object, or event seen by a child as threatening provokes intense anxiety. The relationship between the original and the manifestly feared object or situation can become distorted or displaced, but it is still possible to trace the connection. For example, a child may fear being separated from his parents, but he claims to fear

going to school. The fear of attending school is designed to serve the purpose of remaining at home with the parents.

3. *Conversion Type.* In this reaction, the emphasis in resolving discomforting anxiety follows a pattern of focusing on a disturbance involving structures and organ systems. Paralyses, tics, blindness, deafness, choking, or more vague conditions of malaise and weakness designate this type of neurosis. It is not purely a chance matter that the symptom typically has possibilities for secondary gains for the individual. That is, not only is the child with a "paralyzed" arm not required to write his lessons, but in addition he is generally given solicitous attention by his teacher and classmates.

4. *Obsessive-Compulsive Type.* The disorders of this type represent an attempt to counteract the arousal of anxiety by deliberate thoughts (obsessions) or acts (compulsions). The overt behavior may be the opposite of the threatening impulse. Constant washing of the hands, for example, may be a cover-up for a desire to be messy. The thoughts and acts are carried out even when they are admittedly unreasonable or inappropriate, and the child may in fact actively resist any effort to interfere with or block the behavior.

5. *Mixed Type.* This kind of "catch-all" category allows for classification of psychoneurotic reactions that do not clearly meet criteria for inclusion in one of the other types. It is also useful for psychoneurotic reactions in which a combination of several major symptoms is identifiable, as is often the case with children.

Differential Diagnostic Considerations

The diagnosis of a neurosis properly begins when the teacher or parent finds himself unable to cope with the child's behavior. The diagnostic study is continued when the child is referred for the services of guidance counselor, social worker, physician, or psychologist. These services may be available from regular members of the school staff, or the child may be directed to some community source for service (mental-health clinic, pediatrician, psychiatrist, family service agency, psychologist). Steps in diagnosing a psychoneurotic disorder must be adjusted for the response capability of the child. Conceptual ability, language facility, skill in reporting feelings, accuracy in labeling environmental components, preferred modes for self-expression, and proficiency in communication methods will influence the decisions. The final choice may be dictated by the professional orientation of the specialist serving the child. Some professionals prefer to collect data from interviews with parents, some rely heavily on interpretation of test scores, others are trained to collect information from interviews or observations in "free-play" sessions with the child. Psychological measuring scales ("tests") for assessing psychoneurotic tendencies are available and can be useful with children age 10 years or older (Children's Manifest Anxiety Scale, Coopersmith Measure of Self-Esteem). Check lists measuring children's fears are available for both parental use (e.g., Louisville Behavior Check List, Miller, Barrett, Hampe, &

Noble, 1971) and teacher use (e.g., School Behavior Check List, Miller, 1972). Physiological measures of childhood anxieties seem to hold promise but have for the moment little clinical use (Miller, Barrett, & Hampe, 1974). Frequent reports of psychoneurotic disorders, usually in the form of a phobic reaction, occurring in children of less than 5 years of age can be found in the literature, but many professional workers take issue with these reports. Kessler (1972), for example, believes it unlikely for a psychoneurotic reaction to exist in very young children because a certain level of intellectual and social maturity is required. She points out that minimum degrees of the combination of ability to experience anxiety, feel guilt, and exercise the rudiments of "logic" that she believes are basic for a neurosis are not attained until the age of 6 or 7 years.

The wide range of behaviors that are observed in psychoneurotic reactions makes it necessary to compare these symptoms with those seen in other behavior disorders. Final diagnosis may be safely arrived at only after consultative collaboration that brings together observations of the teacher, interviews obtained from parents, appraisal by a physician, a home study carried out by a social worker, and examination by a psychologist. It is of utmost importance that the data for diagnostic consideration eliminate the possibility of a real physical illness. The pattern of high level of anxiety directed into familiar social outlets lends a reality orientation and social relevance to neurotic reactions and provides a sharp distinction from the disoriented and bizarre behaviors of a psychosis. Functioning efficiency is temporarily reduced by a neurosis and can result in below-average performance similar to that seen in mental subnormality. The functioning of the mentally subnormal person remains consistently below par, whereas that of the psychoneurotic fluctuates inconsistently from above to below par. As was remarked earlier, psychoneurotic disorders are not generally seen in preschool-aged children, who apparently lack the required intellectual and social development. Neuroses grow out of the common process of development and personality acquisition, however, and they are easily confused with normal reactions and response patterns.

Reactive Disorders

There are many events (sickness, accidental injuries, death of a parent or sibling, disappointment from a significant failure) that can be expected to precipitate an intense emotional reaction. Such reactions may be especially pronounced in adolescents who are experiencing one of life's traumas (death of a parent or relative) for the first time. The role of environmental factors in these disorders is evident in the diagnostic category preferred by some workers, "transient situational reaction." The intensity of the response will vary according to the child's developmental stage and his adaptive resources for coping with the situation. Reactive disorders differ from psychoneurotic reactions by being of intense but short duration. They usually show a spontaneous recovery. These characteristics are generally sufficiently unique to avoid confusion with psychoneurotic disorders, even though the symptomatic behaviors may be temporarily similar. Reactive disorders may be more frequently confused with developmental deviations.

Developmental Deviations

The diagnostic category of "developmental deviations" is provided to accommodate behavioral responses that are variations of normal maturational patterns. The importance of referring to developmental norms for interpreting supposed adjustment difficulties has been considered in Chapter 1. Accumulating data provide ample evidence that thumbsucking fears, enuresis, temper tantrums, and the like follow developmental patterns that are unique for any one individual. Even though there are normative tendencies, the integration and achievement of these behaviors vary as to time and occurrence, sequence, and degree. They are not ordinarily accompanied by anxiety, and the developmental pattern is normal for the person in the sense that progression is evident, but at a pace consistent for the individual child. The actual deviation, which may be in the direction of acceleration (precocity), delay (retardation), or mixed (uneven) quality, can include disruptions in motor, sensory, speech, cognitive, social, psychosexual, or emotional attainment.

Personality Disorders

The most difficult diagnostic problem is that of differentiating personality disorders from psychoneuroses. Even an experienced clinician finds the distinction is not easily made. The similarity of the overt behavior associated with the two conditions may have contributed to earlier impressions that psychoneurotic disorders are highly prevalent and that they are resistant to change.

Personality disorders are conditions in which the personality has become organized about a dominant trend, such as compulsivity, dependency, isolation, or opposition. Passive-aggressive personality, compulsive personality, and schizoid personality are some examples. The predominating trait is so deeply ingrained in the personality makeup that it identifies the prevalent reaction pattern of the individual—is "characteristic" for the person. This situation is reflected in the term "character disorders," preferred by some clinicians to designate personality disorders. As is also true for psychoneurotic disorders, personality disorders are not identifiable until the middle school-age period, even though they may have origins in problems and conflicts encountered in infancy or early childhood. A certain amount of stability and development of personality is necessary before this type of reaction can take place. As the organization assumes more structure, there is the impression of chronicity of the character trait, and personality disorders become highly resistant to change by usual treatment methods. Although ordinarily only mildly incapacitating, over time and in the face of repeated failures to resolve stresses satisfactorily, another possibility comes into the picture.

Such chronic failure, with associated cumulative threat to the individual's security, can provide the nucleus for the development of a typical psychoneurotic disorder.

When compared to that of psychoneurotic disorders, the level of anxiety associated with personality disorders is minimal. Reactions to stress are moderate and not regarded as clinically pathological. The consequences of personality disorders are usually limited to impairment of interpersonal relations, where they may contribute to the child's being regarded as a nuisance, as immature, or as just hard to get along with. The incidence of personality disorders is very high, but only a small number of such persons are seen in treatment centers. They are, in many ways, only slight exaggerations of normal traits.

Etiological Considerations

There is general agreement that anxiety plays an essential role in the development of a neurosis. In a summary of theoretical, experimental, and clinical data pertaining to anxiety, Maher (1966) discussed three ways in which anxiety may influence performance:

1. Anxiety may function as a fundamental distress reaction that occurs automatically in any situation threatening survival of the individual, including his value system (self-concept).

2. Anxiety may be a condition of overarousal brought on by a prolonged exposure to intense stimulation which results in disabling the capacity to inhibit any subsequent stimulation.

3. Anxiety may function as a conditioned fear response made to stimuli which in the past were associated with pain or punishment.

Anxiety and behaviors that closely resemble those observed in psychoneurotic disorders can easily be demonstrated in experimental conditions of the laboratory where these phenomena have been extensively investigated. In the comprehensive review of his laboratory studies on anxiety and the associated neuroticlike behaviors induced, Wolpe (1958) outlined two major conditions capable of generating the anxiety and subsequent behaviors referred to as "experimental neuroses":

1. Situations of ambivalent stimulation (those in which opposing responses are simultaneously elicited, forcing the subject to make an exceedingly fine choice):
   a. presenting difficult discriminations (such as might take place in training for cursive writing when the child who has learned a response to "n" and "m" must now respond differently to "*n*" and "*m*");
   b. increasing the delay before reinforcing a conditioned response (when the subject is used to receiving a shock two seconds after

being shown a circle, the time for giving the shock is progressively increased);

   c. rapid alternation of stimuli that elicit opposing responses (when the subject has learned to respond differently to a circle and to a square, and now the two stimuli are flashed almost simultaneously).

2. Situations presenting noxious stimulation (those in which pain or discomfort is produced):

   a. introducing a clash between excitation and inhibition (when running to the playground, the child is caught and made to return to his seat to clean up his desk);

   b. interrupting a pleasurable activity (when the child is scolded for being messy while enjoying making objects with molding clay);

   c. use of painful stimuli alone (banging a piano or loud ringing of a bell to make children stop talking).

These laboratory situations and the behaviors elicited are remarkably similar to reactions seen in psychoneurotic disorders and the conditions that gave rise to the disorders.

A clearer picture of how anxiety may operate is suggested by studies of reactions to stress. Two types of stress are to be considered. Brief acute stress, popularly designated as "traumatic," is typically experienced in intense emergency situations. By contrast, moderate or mild stress, termed "chronic," is experienced over a prolonged period of time. Possibly because the impact of acute stress is dramatic and obvious, parents and educators have tended to be more concerned with alleviating the consequences of traumatic stress. Relatively little attention, however, has been paid to problems posed by demands of chronic stress. Research by Davis (1956) indicated that different adjustment processes are called upon to handle acute and chronic stresses. Data gained from studies of men in combat during the Korean War showed that recovery to normal physiological functioning after chronic stress required twice as much time as did recovery from acute stress.

In a follow-up investigation, Funkenstein, King, & Drolette (1957) observed reactions of college undergraduates to an acute stress situation (memorizing a story under conditions of delayed auditory feedback, unannounced time limits, and electric shock) and to a chronic stress situation extending over two years (solving computational problems under conditions of razzing, criticism, announced time pressure, and frustration). Enormous individual differences in subjects' ability to cope with acute and chronic stress were found. But groups of variables differentially related to ability to cope with the two types of stress were also identified. Perceptions of parents, concepts of self, and fantasies were found to be related to the capacity to deal with acute stress but not related to the ability to deal with chronic stress. Variables related to the ability to master chronic stress but unrelated to the capacity to cope with acute stress included interpersonal relationships, assessment of reality, and integration of personality.

It is generally agreed that the factors related to chronic stress are acquired in a later developmental period, whereas the first set of variables is associated with earlier childhood experiences. In view of the observation that neuroses seem to require an extended time to develop, the capacity to cope with chronic stress may be a crucial factor in neurosis formation. Thus experiences of anxiety are essential, but the type of stress and the capacity for dealing with anxiety may be more important in influencing individual outcomes. A variety of factors—preferred individual adjustment techniques, underlying expectations, and acceptable patterns of behavior for males and females—may differentially favor particular adjustment mechanisms. Parsons (1942), for example, sees socialization experiences as normally favoring obsessive-impulse characteristics for males whereas support is given to hysterical traits as being typical of females.

It is possible to outline two general types of adjustment, each potentially neurotogenic, which may be used in resolving anxiety. The intent is to illustrate modes or styles for coping rather than actual discharge outlets, which can be variable. In one pattern, the child may be very cognizant of the dynamics of his conflicting situation. There is no doubt that he is unwanted and unappreciated by his parents. The low regard by the parents is contradicted by esteem and recognition in which he is held by other persons. He wants to believe in himself, to be wanted and liked by other people, yet the persistent influences of his parents' attitudes cast a shadow, clouding the entire issue. He is painfully aware of his searching questions as to his own adequacy and personal worth. He becomes urgently concerned about his competency and acceptance by all other persons. He begins to take measures to "tighten up the ship" and insure that he will remain in charge. He invests energy and resources into monitoring, hoping to keep in control of things by carefully sorting out the good and pushing away the bad things other persons say about him. Relationships become agonizingly clear and center about the child's sensitive fear of being unable to remain his own master. Isolation, withdrawal, structured control, and ever-increasing use of suppression are essential to keeping the lid screwed down tightly. The tighter the lid is held, the more energy that must be given to holding the lid down. All new experiences, and possible chances for making a more satisfactory adjustment, must be avoided. The child can't afford to make a false move or the castle will tumble.

In another possibility, the child may also be aware of anxiety, but the awareness is qualitatively different. His concern is not so much for the source of the anxiety as for the obvious fact that the high level of anxiety impairs his effectiveness and he fears that this will mean loss of face. His conflict then becomes one of being "anxious about being anxious" and he feels pressured to get rid of the anxiety as quickly as possible. Just as the source of the original anxiety was not too important, so the child is not too selective about how to discharge the anxiety; any way will do. There may be little reliance on repression, and no concern for the long-term effectiveness of the various outlets. Immediate satisfaction, prospects for secondary gain, and simple availability influence the choice of release methods. Total capacity for evaluation is more impaired in this situation than in the conflict described in the preceding paragraph. Consequently, there may be more extreme behaviors and more external indications of tumultuous personality disorganization. The methods chosen for release of tension are frequently so immature as to result in greater loss of face, more desperation, and more anxiety. Genuine insight is difficult, even impossible, for these children.

Psychological Factors

The outlines sketched are very general, but it is hoped that this will serve to make the reader more aware of the obvious: There is no one explanation that can adequately account for the origins of all psychoneurotic disorders. Recognizing this principle may aid in understanding why so many theoretical explanations of the etiology of neuroses are to be found. In this section, we will review briefly the contributions made by psychoanalytic theorists, learning theorists, and cognitive developmental theorists.

The Freudian View of Childhood Origin.   Freud (1949) was convinced that the neurotic disorders he saw in adults had origins in unsatisfactorily resolved childhood conflicts. He provided a classical description of neurosis ensuing from the person's fear that primitive id instincts, especially those of sex and aggression, would overpower the ego. The personality organization would thus be upset and disorganized. Although id impulses constituted the primary source of threat, conflict and resulting disturbance of the personality balance would also occur when excessive guilt from the superego menaced the ego. In either situation, the ego was faced with having to take steps to defend the personality. The protective measures taken entailed a symbolic representation of the unresolved conflict, or, put in other terms, the symptoms were expressions of the perceived threat.

Freud's followers have made many additions to his original concepts. Most of the extensions have been in the nature of allowing greater importance for the influence of socialization. Such accounts have been developed by Karen Horney, Harry Stack Sullivan, and more recently Robert White.

Horney (1937) was primarily concerned with adjustment as the establishing of socially and personally acceptable relationships with other persons. She described three basic approaches for relating to persons as compliance, aggression, and detachment. When any one of these approaches came to be relied on excessively, the conditions for a neurotic conflict were set in operation.

In his interpersonal theories, Sullivan (1953) believed that the nature of the child's relationships with other persons was the basis for conflicts. When the child experienced warm and satisfying relationships, he gained a feeling of personal security and adequacy. Where these satisfactions were not comfortable or satisfying, the child was inclined to feel insecure and to have a chronic level of anxiety.

White (1964) recognizes two sources of stress in childhood that can set the stage for neurotic conflict: sudden, intense trauma (being in an accident) or chronic threat (years of never being able to please parents). Either of these threats can leave an impairment, a condition White compares with the residual motor deficit of the cerebral-palsied child. Such a neurotogenic deficit typically is one involving aggression, dependency, or rejection. The child must establish a protective organization to compensate for the deficit. His entire range of responses becomes oriented toward concealment of the defect. In order to maintain this protective organization, the child makes excessive efforts. These overdriven strivings are identifiable on the basis of three criteria:

1. *Indiscriminateness.* A given response is made all the time—the child who always seeks approval.
2. *Insatiability.* The child is never satisfied no matter how great the reward; given one gold star, he wants two, and so on.
3. *Overreaction.* An increase to an excessive level of frustration, aggression, or desperation.

By this time the neurosis is well defined, and White believes that the overdriven strivings constitute the basis for maintaining the neurotic disorder and its essential trait of chronicity.

Learning Theory. Laboratory explorations of anxiety have clarified many phenomena seen in association with psychoneurotic reactions. Dollard & Miller (1950) found that anxiety does function as a potent drive, facilitating the acquisitions of responses and having properties of generalization. Clinicians had long been puzzled by the apparently maladaptive responses of neurotics, such as the child who is "too ill" to attend a party but complains that he has no friends. Reactions of this type, referred to as the neurotic paradox, were shown by Mowrer (1950) to be retained on the basis of having immediate reward value, which seemed to outweigh the eventual consequences of punishment and discomfort.

Continued study indicated that any response could serve to release anxiety and be sufficiently rewarding to become a durable reaction. Thus reaction patterns that had previously seemed irrelevant and illogical were understandable as anxiety-reducing conditioned responses. The difficulty encountered in the laboratory in extinguishing these rewarding responses also suggested a basis for the clinically observed characteristics of chronicity and resistance to change associated with neuroses. The pupil who becomes highly worried about how well he will do on an examination may find the worry reinforced whether he does poorly or well. A situation is then set for his becoming a "worry bird" in response to each new demand.

Kurt Lewin's (1935) investigations have provided a productive frame of reference for understanding how anxiety is generated by everyday activities. We are constantly faced with having to make choices between two sets of relationships, or goals. Sometimes the choice is a very easy one, but other times it can be difficult. The situation may be an attractive one which holds pleasant rewards, or it may be a negative one which holds unpleasant consequences. Different degrees of conflict may arise from decisions made in resolving four kinds of situations:

1. *Approach-Approach.* In this case, a decision is made between two pleasant alternatives, such as when a child is asked to choose between a cookie and a piece of candy.

2. *Approach-Avoidance.* Here the decision entails selecting a pleasant or an unpleasant outcome. A youngster may want to make the football team but at the same time be reluctant to give up the time required for practices.

3. *Avoidance-Avoidance.* In this set of affairs, the child finds it necessary to decide between two objectives, both unpleasant. He must choose whether to complete a disliked homework assignment or to face a parent angered by the fact that the homework is not completed.

4. *Double Approach-Avoidance.* This type of conflict is possibly best understood as a complex approach-avoidance situation. Rather than holding only approach or avoidance attractions, the two goals have both approach and avoidance qualities. A common example is found in considering possibilities of doing well or doing poorly on an exam. Other persons have suggested "double bind" to refer to these cases where whatever response is made has both positive and negative consequences.

It is believed that resolutions of approach-approach situations are the least likely to have unfavorable consequences, since the outcome in either case is pleasant. Although sometimes presenting clear alternatives and relatively simple choices, approach-avoidance situations can demand exceedingly fine discriminations that delay solution and introduce a state of suspended tension. There are moderate possibilities for a chronic stress state and subsequent maladjustment. Avoidance-avoidance and double approach-avoidance circumstances are regarded as having the greatest potency for fostering pathological behavior. Not only is a high degree of anxiety aroused by the prospect of punishment for whatever response is made, but there is a built-in feature of chronicity as the individual may seek to avoid making any decision and the conflict hangs unresolved.

Consistent with their belief that the important sources of conflict are inherent in socialization processes, Dollard & Miller (1950) and Sears (1951) have described ways in which acculturization demands associated with training in eating, toileting, cleanliness, sex role, competition, and handling are replete with such stress situations.

As will be seen later in this chapter and in the chapters on therapy and classroom management, there has arisen a group of learning theorists known as behavior therapists who deal strictly with behavior change. In practice, behavior therapists deal rather directly with the symptoms or surface behavior of the disturbed child. For them, a neurosis consists only of neurotic behavior. There is no attempt to invoke or treat underlying "causes." Behavior-modification workers use basic laboratory concepts and techniques as reward, modeling, extinction, and desensitization. Consider phobias as one type of neurotic reaction. Phobias may be learned through association with a fear-producing state of affairs and then generalized to a range of stimuli similar to the original obnoxious stimulus (an event, situation, or person). If the original conditioning situation is repeated (for example, continued failure in school) or is of high intensity, the conditioned phobia will persist without obvious reinforcement. In other cases, phobias may be acquired and maintained through obvious kinds of modeling influences and reinforcement. Parents and other important persons in the child's life may teach children to fear such things as separation, school, dogs, and the dark by selectively attending and rewarding avoidant behaviors. In such cases, the parents and others reinforce phobic behavior by responding with affection, impatience, reassurance, cautious approaches, and permission to avoid the anxiety-producing stimulus.

Cognitive Developmental Theory.   Cognitive developmental theory derives most recently from the work of the famous Swiss psychologist Jean Piaget. While there is no developmental theory emanating from Piaget's writings that bears directly on neurotic reactions in children, his works do have potential for helping us to understand at least some seemingly neurotic behaviors in children. Consider the case of phobic reactions. One consistent finding is that certain phobias are more prevalent at some ages than at others (see Table 4–1) and that phobias in children tend to disappear much more rapidly than in adults.

Cognitive developmental theory stresses the notion that the child is not merely a passive receiver who directly takes on the adult's view of the world. This theory also places importance upon the child's cognitive understandings in his adaptation to his surroundings. These two basic tenets may help to explain why phobias occur at certain ages. For example, before a child can develop a phobia about being separated from his mother, he must

Table 4–1. Developmental Fears at Different Age Levels[a]

Age	Fears
0–6 Months	Loud noises, loss of support
6–9 Months	Strangers
1st Year	Separation, injury, toilet
2nd Year	Imaginary creatures, death, robbers
3rd Year	Dogs, being alone
4th Year	Dark
6–12 Years	School, injury, natural events, social
13–18 Years	Injury, social
19+ Years	Injury, natural events, sexual

[a] From Miller, Barrett, & Hampe, 1974.

develop the notion of object-permanence, namely, that his mother exists when she is out of his sight. Prior to the time that the child is intellectually mature enough to develop this notion, out-of-sight seems to mean out-of-mind. Thus, the child may be intellectually incapable of developing this particular phobia until he understands that his mother continues to exist despite the fact that she is out of his visual or auditory field. Likewise, because the preschool child attributes life to inanimate objects, he may become fearful and cry when the head comes off his stuffed toy. Or the 12 year old whose central nervous system has matured to an adult level is now at a stage when school phobias are a more serious problem.

In brief, cognitive developmental theory alerts us to the distinct possibility that (1) the child's stage of mental development plays an important part in how a child perceives a situation and how he reacts emotionally to it at a given point in time; (2) child phobias may be actually quite different phenomenon from adult phobias, even though there is behavioral similarity, and (3) that far from being pathological, child phobias may be a normal aspect of development, if not a necessary and desirable one (Miller et al., 1974).

Parent-Child Relations.   Research investigations have regarded parent-child relationships as having a prime influence on the origins of neurotic behavior. The study of parent-child relationships correctly recognized the importance of early experiences and the crucial role of initial contacts with significant adult persons in contributing to behavior. There were errors, however, in classifying parent-child relationships as pure types, when most often they are mixtures. It would in fact be highly unusual for a child to be exposed exclusively to rejection or to acceptance, for example. In his experiences, the child ordinarily encounters a variety of relationships (as overindulgence from parents, acceptance from teacher, domination from scoutmaster, and so on). An even more crucial question is how much "rejection" is necessary to convince a child that he is worthless and inadequate.

It is easy to see how a clinician may assume that children in a tense, tumultuous, discordant home will have many frustrations but few satisfactions. One can picture a child in such a situation using any method in the struggle to maintain himself. Extremely maladaptive reactions to excessive aggression, servile dependency, or helpless immaturity could be successful in the battle to maintain himself. Any identification with parents would likely favor the acquisition of additional socially inadequate behaviors. Behavior disorders, including neuroses, could thus be inferred as concomitants of lack of warmth, unsatisfying parent-child relationships, and inferior identification models.

Although an interesting hypothesis, the evidence simply does not support a direct correlation between parent-child relationships and consequent behavior disorder. Robins (1966) found that parental rejection or parental deprivation is not a reliable predictor of adult adjustment. Leton (1962) identified sibling rivalry as frequently as parent-child conflicts in the background of his group of school-phobic children. Bronfenbrenner (1967) believes the parental influence is supplanted by that of the peer group by the time the child is 9 years old, long before the peak in incidence of neuroses. After reviewing the studies investigating the relationship between parent-child patterns and behavior problems, Frank (1965) concluded that there was no obvious consistent connection between the two areas.

If there is a relationship between parent-child interaction and behavior disorder, it is likely of a subtle and indirect nature; for example, the parent may exact a driving achievement orientation on the part of the child as the price for acceptance. Parents undoubtedly influence such crucial personality variables as the child's value system, the type of punishment to be avoided, the kinds of rewards to be expected, the degree of persistence at a task. The child may acquire the maladaptive value system of parents who reject him just because there is no other value system available for incorporation. It is not easy to demonstrate the pathological outcome when a frustrated mother encourages her son to be antisocial as a way of guaranteeing his masculinity.

Hetherington & Martin (1972) touch on some of the methodological problems encountered in studying the relationships between patterns of family interaction and the pathology found in children. Most studies have focused on mothers, but only mothers of neurotic children have been interviewed. Data from families where children are free of pathology have not been routinely collected. Focus on the mother's influence in personality formation has a certain plausibility because psychoanalytic theory emphasizes the role of the mother in maternal caretaking functions, and learning theorists have stressed the importance of the mother as the source of the child's first social relationships. Although the points seem logical at first glance, much of the initial mother-child relationship does seem to center about caretaking, an activity that tends to be routinized and is generally adequate for satisfying the basic biogenic wants of the infant. More casual relationships, periods of free play and reciprocal entertainment, such as are likely to be shared with the father, may actually bear greater resemblance to later social interactions. Recent investigations have attempted to collect data from the observed interactions among entire family groups as a way of correcting the biases inherent in asking parents to fill out check lists or to respond to questions sampling parent-child interactions. The same tendency to behave in stereotyped ways seems to be manifest in these group observation situations and apparently for the same reasons; conscious of being observed, the family group endeavors "to make a good impression."

Constitutional Factors

There have been relatively few studies of the relationship of constitutional factors to neurosis. In an investigation of the incidence of neuroses in twins, Shields and Slater (1961) found concordance rates of 53% for monozygotic (MZ, same egg) twins and 25% for dizygotic (DZ, different eggs) twins. Gottesman (1963) studied 34 pairs of MZ and 34 pairs of DZ twins in an attempt to identify neurotic personality traits of high concordance. He concluded that neurotic patterns with hysterical or hypochondriacal themes had little or no genetic basis, whereas those with anxiety, depression, or obsessional features had a substantial genetic component.

There has been a surge of interest in studying the role of hereditary factors in behavior disorders on a less direct level. These investigations try to identify constitutional tendencies, potentials, or traits. Some of the more successful studies of this type have been conducted by Eysenck and Prell (1951), who found evidence for a heritable tendency for neuroticism. Eysenck has also found that level of anxiety follows familial lines. Based on observations begun in infancy and continued into the middle-childhood period, Thomas, Chess, and Birch (1968) have identified constitutional levels of autonomic activity and response patterns that are unique and relatively stable for a specific individual. No single trait acting alone accounted for a given child's development pattern. Aggregations of traits and clusters of reaction tendencies, groups of factors that in combination form temperament, play a significant role in the origin and development of the child's adjustment patterns. Children with temperaments characterized by excessively high or low activity, irregularity, withdrawal in response to new stimuli, inflexibility, high intensity, persistence, and distractibility were prone to develop behavior disorders. Clarifying the meaning of their findings, Thomas, Chess, and Birch emphasize that temperament cannot be used as the sole explanation for any given behavior disorder. The demonstrated constitutional individuality, however, makes it necessary to recognize that the same overtures and responses made by persons interacting with the child and the same objective features of the environment will have differential functional consequences, depending on the temperamental style of the child. An approach that considers the interaction of constitutional, environmental, and learning forces specifically acting on each child is needed to account for any behavioral reaction. Information from such indirect investigations must be interpreted as to its relevance for psychoneuroses; for example, if a high level of anxiety facilitates the learning of neurotic behavior, then a significant constitutional basis for psychoneuroses is suggested. In fact, one of the investigators' key conclusions challenges the role attributed to anxiety in producing neurotic symptoms in children. They believe that anxiety is a consequence rather than a cause of symptom formation. This interpretation is given further support by the fact that successful removal of symptoms has positive consequences for the child's functioning and has not resulted in the appearance of overt anxiety or substitute symptoms. While not denying the basic assumptions of unconscious influences, childhood sexuality, or the meaningfulness of free association or other analytic techniques, the investigators do suggest that the factors considered by Freudians to *cause* childhood neuroses may in fact be *effects* or may have other nonetiological significance. That is, anxiety may follow rather than precede the development of neurotic symptoms in young children.

Even more subtle are the possibilities for an interplay between the child's inherent abilities or predispositions and the environmental forces that shape these potentials into his own unique personality organization. The outcome may be a healthy or an unhealthy one. In this connection, Fries and Woolf (1953) carried out an ingenious study that explored the differential impact on personality development occurring when a physically active child is born to parents who cherish peace and quiet rather than to parents who are physically energetic and athletic. In the first instance, the stage is set for chronic conflict.

Although there is evidence indicating a constitutional influence in the development of psychoneurotic disorders, the inability to account for all neuroses on a constitutional basis justifies the contention that other factors also make a contribution.

Sociocultural Factors

Clinicians have implied that psychoneurotic reactions are related to sociocultural background, maintaining that essential neurotogenic conditions are more prevalent in some sociocultural strata. Borderline status, where the person is about to move upward or downward to another sociocultural level, is said to be an especially vulnerable position. It is probable that persons in such positions are subject to greater uncertainty, may feel greater pressure to achieve, and have less of the usual support tendered a well-established member of a sociocultural group, but it is also apparent that many persons are successful in making this transition. There is the possibility that persons on one or another sociocultural level are subject to greater stresses of one type or another, yet no one is free from all stresses. There may be factors in the life styles associated with membership in a particular sociocultural level that differentially favor a psychoneurotic reaction. If so, it seems likely that there is greater tolerance of deviant behavior extended members of the lower sociocultural groups who are almost expected to do less but enjoy it more. Poverty, excessive use of alcohol, broken homes, physical aggression, and family conflicts, features alleged to be more prevalent among lower sociocultural groups, were found by Frank (1965) to be inadequate for accounting for the sources of conflicts in the backgrounds of psychoneurotics. The question of relationship between sociocultural factors and psychoneurotic disorders is clouded by the presumption that persons from high sociocultural groups would be more likely to seek treatment. Persons in lower sociocultural groups, less able to afford treatment, would not be identified for inclusion in study groups.

In the light of the presumed importance of sociocultural factors in contributing to neuroses, there is a surprising lack of data showing incidence broken down by sociocultural levels, especially data for children. In a timely follow-up study of persons with behavior problems, Robins (1966) included a group of 50 psychoneurotics. Of the patients in this group, 31 (62%) came from blue-collar homes, 10 (20%) came from homes in which the family head was dependent or chronically unemployed, and 9 (18%) came from white-collar homes.

A report presented by Proctor (1958) deals with a group of 191 continuous, serially selected patients seen at the Child Psychiatric Unit, School of Medicine, University of North Carolina. Of the 191 cases, 25 (13%) were diagnosed as having hysterical psychoneurotic disorders. Proctor explained what he regarded as a disproportionately high number of such cases as a reflection of sociocultural forces acting upon the population served by the clinic. He described the area as having predominantly rural inhabitants with low educational and economic levels. The ratio of boys to girls in this neurotic group was about equal. By contrast there were nearly twice as many boys as girls in the other 166 cases.

Treatment and Prognosis

The correction of an impairment has the objective of improving performance, of increasing capacity for getting the job done. Completing a task can be considered in terms of two variables, effectiveness and efficiency. To be completed, a task must be finished to a certain minimum level of acceptance (effectiveness), and the completion must be attained with the expenditure of a minimum amount of energy (efficiency). For example, assume a task of correctly spelling a list of 25 words dictated by a teacher. A pupil with fingers so severely deformed as to make it impossible for him to write out even one word is not effective at this task. The pupil may be rendered effective by training him to use a specially modified typewriter. Another pupil having intact sensory-motor abilities may break his pencil, become nauseated and have to stop to rest, complain of being unable to see his paper, have to go to the bathroom, need to start all over again, make numerous erasures, stop working to listen to the sound of a distant siren, and thus require hours to finish a job other pupils complete in 15 minutes. The dawdling, disrupting pupil gets the job done (is effective), but his performance is unacceptable because he is markedly inefficient.

Invoking the distinction of efficiency as contrasted to effectiveness is a useful step in planning the treatment of a psychoneurotic disorder. In the neurotic reaction, energies are displaced from usual life functions and directed into nonadaptive (inefficient) types of activities. It follows that the impairment is an interference with the smooth functioning of a potential that is otherwise intact. There is a breakdown in personal efficiency. As a generality, treatment is focused on measures for improving articulation and promoting integration of the existing personality components, thus restoring normal efficiency. Because the psychoneuroses are sometimes regarded as only other manifestations of physical illnesses and other times looked on as purely psychological phenomena, such uncertainty has influenced efforts to correct these disorders. The variety of situations and factors that have been considered as contributing to the development of psychoneuroses is reflected in a corresponding variety of treatment procedures. The choice of treatment invoked has probably been most closely related to the background and orientation of the particular therapist, but falls into one of the following areas.

Medical Approaches

Physicians, who are probably the therapist group most frequently called upon to deal with neuroses, tend to treat psychoneuroses as they would any other illness. Accordingly, recognized medications of a tranquilizing consequence have been used to calm active distress symptoms, and those of a stimulating nature have been given to pep up and revitalize the depressed and melancholic. In conjunction with the medication, the actively distressed patient may be advised to get more rest; the depressed patient, to arrange a program of experiences with potential for generating new interests. Treatment by a physician generally entails a minimum of contacts with either the child or the parents.

Psychotherapeutic Approaches

Consistent with the differing definitions and etiological concepts of neurosis, the application of psychotherapy to the treatment of neuroses has followed two theoretical orientations: the psychoanalytic approach and the learning-theory (behavioral) approach. (These are discussed in greater detail in Chapter 10.) From a psychoanalytic approach, therapy sessions have concentrated upon searching out the hidden internal conflict that is considered to be the cause of the trouble. Once the conflict has been identified, the child is helped to understand the relationship between his neurotic behavior and the conflict. More effective ways for resolving the conflict may be given the child, or a more equitable balance among the id, ego, and superego personality components may be attempted. The latter may involve releasing repressed id impulses or strengthening the existing ego. Correction entails direct work with the child, and in many instances follow-up sessions with the parents, who are viewed as having a significant influence upon the maladjustment problem.

Other psychotherapeutic approaches pay less attention to the possible influences of hidden conflicts and concentrate on changing behavior by direct application of learning principles. Evaluation of the problem first identifies the factors that are rewarding the undesired behavior and then looks for evidence of residual responses that will meet with greater social approval. These desired responses are then systematically rewarded. When appropriate responses are not found, they may be trained by using the child's existing skills. The parents are generally equally involved since their importance as givers of rewards and as reinforcers of the new patterns of behavior is recognized. In some instance, successes have been reported when only the parents are worked with in this framework of supplying cues and rewards for reinforcing new behaviors.

Some therapists report success in neutralizing neurotic reactions by a brief series of intensive training sessions, a technique termed desensitization. This method seems to work especially well where phobic reactions are prominent in the disorder, and entails the use of conditioning to pair the uncomfortable fear with pleasant emotional feelings.

Treating a Phobic Behavior through Desensitization

An 8-year-old girl whose prior school adjustment had been normal suddenly became seized with severe panic on having to go to art class. When the upset began to last for longer periods and threatened to disrupt her attendance at school, she was referred to the school psychologist. Prior to seeing the girl, the psychologist conferred with the pediatrician who served the family. The pediatrician was familiar with the girl, indicating she was frequently brought to his office. The pediatrician reported that the girl's physical health was good. He added that he had observed she was unusually neat in her dress and overly serious. The psychologist carried out an examination of the child, eliciting a picture of preoccupation with cleanliness and a marked fear of getting dirty. In art class, the children were working on projects making large pictures and designs with water paints. Although they wore smocks, the enthusiasm for painting resulted in some splashing of paint. The girl was panic-stricken by the few small drops of paint that sometimes landed on her fresh clean dress or shoes. Her terror became so intense as to lead to complete disruption of her ability to function. After a conference with the parents, the psychologist arranged to see the girl in a playroom during the art period. The girl enjoyed playing a game of "keep-away" using a large rubber ball. When the girl had become highly excited and involved in the play, the ball was bounced in a pan of water soiled with paint. Play continued even though some of the dirty water splashed on the psychologist and the girl. At the end of the session, the girl was matter-of-factly shown how to perform temporary "clean-up," to suffice until she could change her dress at home after school. During the fifth session, the girl bounced the ball in the pan of paint-soiled water and seemed to enjoy this as though it were all part of the game. The sessions were terminated after the seventh one, and follow-up queries with her teachers indicated "no problem" for the remainder of the school year.

Features of psychotherapy approaches are presented in detail in Chapter 10, and an extensive discussion of behavior-modification strategies is to be found in Chapter 12.

The evaluation of effectiveness in treating psychoneuroses suggests the same outcomes described in Chapter 3. Generally speaking, about two-thirds of the cases are improved, and about one-third or one-fourth of the cases are unimproved. These outcomes remain amazingly constant irrespective of the type of treatment applied and, in fact, even when no specific treatment is made available. Hence it is reasonable to expect that from two-thirds to three-fourths of children referred for treatment of a psychoneurosis will be benefited.

At this time there are no data to indicate that psychoanalysis can cure or ameliorate neurotic conditions in children. The only direct test of the efficacy of child analysis showed no clear evidence for the superiority of child analysis over weekly therapy (Heinicke, 1969). While there has been only one published, controlled study of the effects of psychoanalysis on neurotic children (Heinicke, 1969), there have been several evaluative studies on behavior-modification procedures. Table 4–2 provides a sampling of the various behavior-modification techniques that have been used to treat a variety of seemingly neurotic behaviors in children. The new behavior therapies hold promise, but firm evidence of therapeutic efficacy is not clear at this time.

As yet, the data reporting on treatment outcomes do not suggest which cases are likely to benefit and which are not. Carr (1974) reported that training in decision making brought improvement in some compulsive reactions that had been resistant to other therapeutic approaches. There is insufficient information for indicating whether work with the child, with the parents, or some combination of methods will prove most effective. More specific data are needed, especially in view of the common necessity for

⌐ **Table 4–2.   Controlled Studies Using Behavior-Modification Techniques on Seemingly Neurotic Behaviors** ⌐

Study	*Problem*	*Technique*
Barabasz, 1973	Test anxiety in elementary-school students	Group desensitization
Miller, Barrett, Hampe, & Noble, 1972	Phobic children	Desensitization
Gardner, 1967	Hysterical symptoms in a 10-year-old girl	Extinction (removal of parental attention)
Eysenck & Rachman, 1965	Compulsive behavior	Satiation
Bandura, 1969	Animal phobias	Modeling
Clement, Roberts, & Lantz, 1970	Shyness, withdrawn behavior in elementary-school boys	Positive reinforcement

delaying the treatment program until medical evaluations have been completed and in consideration of the fact that neurotic reactions seem to show improvement, at least for a time, in response to even benign treatment. Fears and phobias in children under 10 years of age arise and dissipate rapidly, and there is some evidence to suggest that this process is hastened with therapy (Bandura et al., 1967). There is little information on the outcomes of phobias among adolescents, but the long-term prognosis of adolescent phobias appears quite good. Phobias in adults are much more intractable, with only 20 to 30% showing full recovery (Miller et al., 1974). Recently, an increase in psychoneurotic depressive reactions has been noted. An excellent discussion of this condition is presented by Friedman and Doyal (1974). Whether the trend is permanent or transitory remains to be observed.

Supplementary discussions of treatment outcomes are presented in Chapter 10, where attention is particularly focused on findings obtained by Levitt. A detailed outline of the course of treatment, including treatment methods and outcomes, is also given at the conclusion of the following discussion of a typical childhood psychoneurotic reaction, school phobia.

Example: School Phobia

School phobia is a term that has appeared frequently in the last decade in literature dealing with children and their problems. Technically designated as "childhood psychoneurotic disorder, phobic type, evidenced by chronic anxiety reactions toward school and related facilities," the more popular short title "school phobia" refers to a neurotic reaction in which the classroom, school building, teacher, janitor, classmates, school bus, cafeteria, principal, or other specific aspects of the school become extremely fear-arousing for the child. Since it is one of the more frequently encountered types of psychoneurotic reactions observed in children, we have selected it for detailed illustration.

Incidence.   In the comprehensive investigation carried out by Leton, identifiable school phobia was found to occur at a rate of 3 per 1,000 pupils. An additional 7 in 1,000 pupils also had school phobia, but in a mild or moderate form which was therefore less easily identifiable. As a group, children with psychoneurotic reactions have been found to have average academic achievement, at least for the initial few years. This holds true for children with school phobia, despite the tumultuous and erratic surface behavior (Leton, 1962; Coolidge, Brodie, & Feeney, 1964). School phobia is one of the few behavior disturbances more frequently observed in girls than in boys. This differential requires the inclusion of cases from the secondary-grade levels, however, where girls begin to contribute heavily to the incidence rate.

A disproportionately greater number of children with school phobia appear to come from higher socioeconomic levels (Leton, 1962; Levison, 1962). This may be an outgrowth of the fact that families at the higher socioeconomic level as a rule have fewer children. The mothers would thus have more time to become involved in the reciprocally dependent relationship with the child which is frequently observed in school phobia. It is also to be considered that costly treatment would be more available to children from such families, with consequent greater likelihood of identification of neuroses in this group.

Two Types of School Phobia Reactions. Work with school-phobic children has led to the identification of two subgroups of this disorder. According to Miller, Barrett, and Hampe (1974), distinctly recognizable characteristics and differential implications for treatment are associated with the two types. The major characteristics are summarized in Table 4–3, Characteristics of Types I and II School Phobics. Stressing that not all the relationships between behaviors are understood, the presence of 6 of the 9 characteristics is sufficient for classification as Type I or Type II. Children with the Type I disorder tend to be younger, have more cooperative parents, and make a comparatively rapid response to intervention, even though the onset of their disorder may be of an acute nature. In contrast, children with Type II school phobia are likely to be older, have less cooperative parents, and respond slowly to even intensive treatment, such as hospitalization.

Onset and Course. School phobia is characterized by an acute panic state and an aversion to being in school. As observed by the teacher, the onset seems to be sudden. On closer study, it is usually found that the condition has been slowly developing for a year or more. At first there may be

Table 4–3. Characteristics of Types I and II School Phobics[a]

Type I	*Type II*
1. The present illness is the first episode.	1. Second, third, or fourth episode.
2. Monday onset, following an illness the previous Thursday or Friday.	2. Monday onset following minor illness not a prevalent antecedent.
3. An acute onset.	3. Incipient onset.
4. Expressed concern about death.	4. Death theme not present.
5. Mother's physical health in question; actually ill or child thinks so.	5. Health of mother not an issue.
6. Good communication between parents.	6. Poor communication between parents.
7. Mother and father well adjusted in most areas.	7. Mother shows neurotic behavior; father, a character disorder.
8. Father competitive with mother in household management.	8. Father shows little interest in household or children.
9. Parents achieve understanding of dynamics easily.	9. Parents very difficult to work with.

[a] From Miller, Barrett, & Hampe, 1974.

reluctance to attend school, voiced dislike for school, or recurrent questioning, "Why do I have to go to school all the time?" The first real indication of a neurotic problem may be suggested by the appearance of complaints of somatic nature. Parents who are not much impressed with verbal gripes and grumblings are often spurred to action by their child's claims of having a headache or a stomachache. Fainting or vomiting can easily support the child's contention of illness.

Some parents of school-phobic children seem to have a callous indifference toward their children. In this case the child is often driven to greater and greater excess display and demonstration in order to gain even a flicker of attention. Unfortunately, parents become absorbed in the pattern of excess reactions. Other parents of school-phobic children have just the opposite relationship. They are overly sensitive to the child's expressions. Not only do they overrespond, but they preempt. It is their anticipation tendency that may be the most damaging to the child since it denies him all say-so in his affairs. Overreactive parents are quick to put the child to bed when he says he has a headache; they read to him, entertain him. They call the physician and insist that he immediately see the child. They call the teacher and raise questions as to why the teacher has been so demanding and lacking in understanding of their child, who is now sick. They walk with him to and from school or drive him in the warm car.

The onset of the school-phobic reaction is often triggered by specific happenings associated with school. The child may receive a low score on a test, be severely ridiculed by classmates, be scolded for not having completed an assignment, or be the victim of a physical beating by other pupils. These events also play right into the hands of the domineering or oversolicitous parent, who feels compelled to protect, to somehow make up for and replace something essential. (At the deepest level, such parents may feel their competency as parents is at issue.) As relevant historical details are uncovered, however, it is clear that such a child has a deep and well-defined fear for his security and adequacy. Generally he has no friends. He seems to feel more safe if he remains inside the house. He refuses to walk to and from school with his classmates and waits to be escorted or chauffeured by his parents or older siblings. While waiting to be picked up at school he may request to be near the teacher or principal.

With the onset of acute symptoms, the child becomes visibly more apprehensive. If questioned as to why he does not want to go to school, he may offer a story of a wild animal roaming near the school, his fear that the school might burn down, or his concern that there may be a terrible explosion at school. When reassured about these fears, others of equally doubtful plausibility arise: endless expressions of fear the food in the cafeteria will make him ill, the janitor doesn't like him, or a gang of pupils plans to waylay him. The fear often begins with some localized aspect of the school, but quickly generalizes. In a short time, bringing the child even close to the school can be sufficient to bring on nausea, vomiting, blind running, loss of sphincter control, or active resistance in the form of crying, biting, kicking, holding breath, or fainting. Outbursts of crying and temper tantrums are common. The child actively resists being kept at school, especially if he has been away for a week or two. When the child is permitted to remain at home, these more acute symptoms subside, giving rise to a false sense that recovery has been effected. Of greater long-term consequence, however, is the subtle reinforcement of those same acute symptoms which a return to the home can accomplish. This factor makes the treatment of school phobia a matter demanding carefully coordinated management.

In some respects it is unfortunate that the label "school phobia" has come to be extensively applied to this condition since it is something of an incorrect depiction of the problem. The term implies a behavior disorder limited to a marked fear of school. On investigation, school is found to be only one of a number of fears such children have. These children tend to fear many "familiar" and all new situations (attending a movie, watching a ball game, going to the store, going to Sunday school). To be more exact, they are panicked by any situation in which they are alone and away from their parents. As Leton (1962) and White (1964) point out, it just happens that school is a major common demand for all children. Attendance at school is legally compulsory. When the child does not attend school, this fact is invariably called to his parents' attention. But no official is likely to check on whether or not the child attended a movie or ball game.

Studies of the etiology of school phobia make it increasingly apparent that separation from the parent figures prominently in this behavior disorder. The child is struggling to cope with the problem of weaning himself from his parents. A certain amount of independence is a real developmental task that children in our society must attain in order to make the initial school adjustment satisfactorily. It may be that the rigors of coping with this developmental task contribute to the peak of incidence of neuroses, which is seen at about grade 4 or 5.

It has also been pointed out that the relationship with the mother seems to be more critical than that with the father. Studies by Leton (1962), Levison (1962), White (1964), and Coolidge and his associates (1964) have identified a conspicuous reciprocal relationship in which the child is very dependent upon the mother. The mother nurtures the child's dependency on her as gratification for her own need to be important and needed. Such mothers are very susceptible to the child's apparent upset condition, fears, and failures, which they tend to interpret as tangible evidence of their child's need for mothering. The parents' actions are more understandable as efforts to cover up their personal inadequacies rather than as realistic attempts to help the child. The parent may assume the role of an intervening bulwark, protecting the child from what the parent may claim are actions by school officials and clinicians to mistreat or be mean to the child.

Treatment Outline. The treatment of school phobia has become a matter of increasing concern. Various treatment procedures have been advocated, including removal of the child from school, control by medication, some type of psychotherapy, or a form of behavior modification such as desensitization. There is a growing recognition that prolonged treatments, such as psychoanalysis or psychotherapy, generally are not necessary. As Kelly (1973) points out in a review of theories and treatment, most cases of school phobia can be treated effectively by a variety of short-term techniques. The general treatment strategy should follow these steps:

1. The child should have immediate attention. The longer the problem exists without intervention, the more chronic and resistant to treatment it becomes.

2. The child should be given a thorough physical examination by the family physician. This step is necessary to settle once and for all any questions of physical health which are an integral aspect of the symptoms.

3. Persons carrying out the treatment must be assured that the child is tough and won't "fall apart" as they impose treatment demands on him.

4. The parents must be involved in the treatment program and given specific functions to carry out. The parent should not be made to feel guilty. The parent must be reassured as to the toughness and resiliency of the child.

5. Medications, as prescribed by a physician, can be a significant source of support for alleviating many of the acute symptoms and thus helping to keep the child in school.

6. The child should be kept in school and any relevant modifications of his school program should be considered. The child must have potent support for his attending school.

What seems critical to the effective treatment of school phobia is placing the child back in the school with a minimum of delay. For each day, for each hour, that the child is permitted to remain outside of school, there seems to be a proportional increase in the severity of symptoms and the level of panic regarding return to school. Such a course of events is a characteristic feature common to psychoneurotic reactions. If the child maintains that he is afraid of school to the point that he cannot go to school, he is likely to behave in a way that justifies his complaint. If his simple complaint that he is afraid of school does not work, then he may do other things to "prove" that he is really sick. Thus nausea, vomiting, diarrhea, stomachaches, or headaches can be anticipated as the child is kept in school. It is recommended, however, that the child attend school, even though there may be an increase in the severity of symptoms for a few days. The increase in intensity of symptoms can be planned for in the knowledge that the child is resilient and will not be traumatized or bear permanent injury from having to be in school. Everyone must firmly believe that the child can adjust to school and that the problem is to find out what modifications and changes are needed to enable the adjustment to be made.

It is important to include the parents in the treatment regimen from the beginning. Ideally, the parent should be given specific assignments which are obviously part of the treatment procedures. One of the first contributions that the parent makes is to secure a complete physical examination for the child. The pediatrician may see fit to prescribe medications that render the child less anxious and more tractable. Care should be exercised to prevent the parents from feeling they are at fault, for parents of school-phobic children often have problems of guilt or question their adequacy as parents. The school social worker, nurse, or other person working with the parent must convey reassurances that the child can, with assistance, make a satisfactory adjustment to school. Showing the parent samples of the child's satisfactory work at school can be especially meaningful support for the parents.

Most of all, the child himself needs to have reassurance and support for the times that he is at school. It must be repeatedly communicated to the child that he can and will overcome his fear, and that everything is being done to accomplish that end. In some instances, a slight reduction of the child's school day might be considered. Such giving-in to the child should be avoided as a routine measure, however, since this can obviously play into the child's symptoms. An approach more recommended entails adjustment of the pupil's school program. Beneficial results can come from school tasks that provide guaranteed success experience. Carefully planned assignments should enable the pupil to receive support and encouragement from his teacher and classmates. Praise for real successes and recognition for efforts in attending school will soon act to alleviate the condition.

The behavior-modification approach is illustrated in Garvey & Hegrenes' report (1966), which used desensitization (or counterconditioning) to eliminate a boy's fear of school. (See the case study of A School-Phobic Child.)

A School-Phobic Child

Jimmy had been treated for six months in a traditional psychotherapeutic situation. Treatment was stopped when school was closed for the summer. After summer Jimmy was still unable to attend school. A desensitization procedure was then started. Having obtained the cooperation of the school, the therapist worked with Jimmy for 20 to 40 minutes every day. The therapist used the following steps:

1. Sitting in the car in front of the school.
2. Getting out of the car and approaching the curb.
3. Going to the sidewalk.
4. Going to the bottom of the steps of the school.
5. Going to the top of the steps.
6. Going to the door.
7. Entering the school.
8. Approaching the classroom.

    9. Entering the classroom.
    10. Being present in the classroom with the teacher.
    11. Being present in the classroom with the teacher and one or
two classmates.
    12. Being present in the classroom with a full class.

These steps were carried out over a period of 20 consecutive days.
At the end of that time, Jimmy resumed his normal school routine
with no return of the symptom during a two-year follow-up period.
The authors explain that:

> since Jimmy and the therapist had a good relationship, the presence of
> the therapist may be considered as a relatively strong stimulus evoking
> a positive affective response in the patient. As a consequence, because
> there was reduced anxiety in the presence of the fear stimulus, instead
> of an avoidance response, Jimmy was able to make an approach re-
> sponse which was reinforced by the therapist with strong praise.

It was felt that if the child had been forced into the classroom, the
therapist might have acquired a negative stimulus value. Garvey and
Hegrenes think that their method requires less time but that their results
are just as effective as those of the methods of traditional psychoanalysis.

Prognosis.   In a follow-up study conducted by Coolidge et al., (1964),
a group of 66 children were restudied in 1963 after having been diagnosed
as "school phobic" during the period between 1953 and 1958. Of the 66,
10 could not be located, and 7 were eliminated because they were found to
have more pervasive disorders such as epilepsy. The remaining 49 subjects
had a median age of 16 years (median age was 7 years at the time of the
original diagnosis). For 2 of the 49 subjects, there was insufficient information to assess, but the other 47 were evaluated as to current emotional
adjustment appropriate to their age. Thirteen subjects (3 boys, 10 girls)
were found to be making satisfactory adjustments and were rated as
"normal" adolescents. Twenty subjects (7 boys, 13 girls) showed definite
limitations in their adjustments which could still be regarded as neurotic.
Fourteen subjects (9 boys, 5 girls) were found to be having serious adjustment problems, ranging from severe character disorders to frank psychoses.
These children had all but given up trying, had indefinable goals, and were
struggling to simply "stay in the boat." Although errors in original diagnoses
are apparent in these outcomes, a more important consideration for the welfare of children generally is the indication that the children were experiencing critical adjustment problems and desperately needed assistance. The
findings offer compelling support for the advisability of active intervention
rather than waiting to see if the child will outgrow his adjustment problems.
    Psychoneurotic reactions respond to a variety of treatment procedures,

including medications, rest, formal psychotherapy, and behavior-modification techniques. The treatment regimen requires the collective contributions of clinicians, teachers, and parents. There will be crises and stormy points, but there is reason to expect that any one of several methods will work. Although data on recovery are sporadic and incomplete, the outcome for school phobia seems especially favorable. If "returned to school" is taken as the criterion, meaning that the child soon was able to resume usual school participation and to continue normal school attendance during the 5-10 year period of follow-up observations, then from 71 to 94% of the school-phobia cases reviewed met this criterion. The improvement rate seems unrelated to the type of treatment, or, in fact, to whether any treatment was received.

Robin's (1966) findings suggest that a preponderance of antisocial symptoms (aggression, sexual deviancy) indicates a poor prognosis. Data from Coolidge et al. (1964) caution that boys are less likely to rise above their neurotic problems than are girls. Both studies indicate that low academic achievement and borderline sociocultural status are associated with a poor prognosis.

Summary

A psychoneurotic disorder is characterized by impaired efficiency while basic potential remains intact.

High levels of anxiety are often associated with psychoneurotic reactions.

Anxiety ensuing from a chronic moderate conflict may have greater predictive significance than that generated by a single traumatic event.

Behaviors that develop into a neurotic syndrome typically have immediate success for the individual but are ineffectual in the long term.

Interest in psychoneurotic behaviors has encouraged extensive experimental study in the laboratory seeking to clarify the role of reinforcement, constitutional influences, and extinction in their maintenance and management.

Psychoneurotic reactions seem to require some time to develop and are not ordinarily identifiable until a child is about 8 or 9 years old.

Psychoneurotic disorders can be confused with personality disorders, transient situational disorders, reactive disorders, and various physical illnesses.

Initially, psychoneurotic conditions are observed with greater frequency in boys, but by adolescence, the picture is reversed.

Making a definitive diagnosis of a neurosis entails close cooperation between teachers, social workers, physicians, and psychologists.

A variety of approaches have been found successful in treating psychoneuroses.

Treatment outcomes are less likely to be favorable when antisocial symptoms, chronicity, low academic achievement, and borderline socioeconomic background are involved.

Follow-up studies indicate that the common adult neuroses for the most part do not begin in childhood. Indeed, many of the symptoms for which youngsters are commonly referred to mental-health specialists—tics, fears, oversensitiveness, shyness, nervousness, irritability, insomnia—occur as often in children who later have normal adult adjustments as they do in those who became neurotic.

References

Barabasz, A. Group desensitization of test anxiety in elementary school. *Journal of Psychology*, 1973, **83**, 295–301.

Bandura, A. *Principles of behavior modification.* New York: Holt, Rinehart and Winston, 1969.

Bronfenbrenner, U. The split-level American family. *Saturday Review*, 1967, **50**, 60–66.

Carr, A. T. Compulsive neurosis: a review of the literature. *Psychological Bulletin*, 1974, **81**, 311–18.

Clement, P., Roberts, P., & Lantz, C. Social models and token reinforcement in the treatment of shy, withdrawn boys. Proceedings, 78th Annual Convention, American Psychological Association, 1970.

Coolidge, J. L., Brodie, R. D., & Feeney, B. A ten-year follow-up study of sixty-six school-phobic children. *American Journal of Orthopsychiatry*, 1964, **34**, 673–84.

Davis, S. W. Stress in combat. *Scientific American*, 1956, **194**, 31–35.

Dollard, J., & Miller, N. E. *Personality and psychotherapy.* New York: McGraw-Hill, 1950.

Eysenck, H. J., & Prell, D. B. The inheritance of neuroticism: an experience study. *Journal of Mental Sciences*, 1951, **97**, 441–65.

Eysenck, H., & Rachman, S. *The causes and cures of neurosis.* San Diego: R. R. Knapp, 1965.

Frank, G. H. The role of the family in the development of psychopathology. *Psychological Bulletin*, 1965, **64**, 191–205.

Freud, S. *An outline of psychoanalysis.* New York: Norton, 1949.

Friedman, R. J., & Doyal, G. T. Depression in children: some observations for the school psychologist. *Psychology in the Schools,* 1974, **11**, 19–23.

Fries, M., & Woolf, P. Some hypotheses on the role of the congenital activity type in personality development. In R. S. Eissler, A. Freud, H. Hartmann, & M. Kris (Eds.), *The psychoanalytic study of the child*, Vol. 8, New York: International Universities Press, 1953, pp. 48–62.

Funkenstein, D. H., King, S. H., & Drolette, M. E. *Mastery of stress*. Cambridge: Harvard University Press, 1957.

Gardner, J. Behavior therapy treatment approach to psychogenic seizure case. *Journal of Consulting Psychology*, 1967, **31**, 209–12.

Garvey, W., & Hegrenes, J. Desensitization techniques in the treatment of school phobia. *American Journal of Orthopsychiatry*, 1966, **36**, 147–52.

Gottesman, I. I. Heritability of personality: a demonstration. *Psychological Monographs*, 1963, **77**, (9).

Heinicke, C. Frequency of psychotherapeutic session as a factor affecting outcome: analysis of clinical ratings and test results. *Journal of Abnormal Psychology*, 1969, **74**, 553–60.

Hetherington, E. M., & Martin, B. Family interaction and psychopathology in children. In H. C. Quay & J. S. Werry (Eds.), *Psychopathological disorders of childhood*. New York: Wiley, 1972, pp. 30–82.

Horney, K. *The neurotic personality of our time*. New York: Norton, 1937.

Kelly, E. W., Jr. School phobia: a review of theory and treatment. *Psychology in the Schools*, 1973, 33–41.

Kessler, J. W. Neurosis in childhood. In B. J. Wolman (Ed.), *Manual of child psychopathology*. New York: McGraw-Hill, 1972, pp. 387–435.

Kurlander, L. F., & Colodny, D. "Pseudoneurosis" in the neurologically handicapped child. *American Journal of Orthopsychiatry*, 1965, **35**, 733–38.

Leton, D. A. Assessment of school phobia. *Mental Hygiene*, 1962, **46**, 256–64.

Levison, B. Understanding the child with school phobia. *Exceptional Children*, 1962, **28**, 393–98.

Lewin, K. A. *Dynamic theory of personality*. New York: McGraw-Hill, 1935.

Maher, B. A. *Principles of psychopathology*. New York: McGraw-Hill, 1966.

Miller, L. School Behavior Check List: an inventory for deviant behavior for elementary school children. *Journal of Consulting and Clinical Psychology* 1972, **38**, 134–44.

Miller, L., Barrett, C., & Hampe, E. Phobias of childhood in a prescientific era. In A. Davids (Ed.), *Child Personality & Psychopathology*. New York: Wiley, 1974, pp. 89–134.

Miller, L., Barrett, C., Hampe, E., & Noble, R. Revised anxiety scales for the Louisville Behavior Check List. *Psychology Reports*, 1971, **29**, 503–11.

Miller, L., Barrett, C., Hampe, E., & Noble, R. Comparison of reciprocal inhibition, psychotherapy, and waiting list control for phobic children. *Journal of Abnormal Psychology*, 1972, **79**, 269–79.

Morse, W. C., Cutler, R. L., & Fink, A. H. *Public school classes for the emotionally handicapped: a research analysis*. Washington, D.C.: Council for Exceptional Children, 1964.

Mowrer, O. H. *Learning theory and personality dynamics*. New York: Ronald Press, 1950.

Parsons, T. Age and sex in the social structure of the United States. *American Sociological Review*, 1942, **7**, 604–16.

Proctor, J. T. Hysteria in childhood. *American Journal of Orthopsychiatry*, 1958, **28**, 394–406.

Robins, L. N. *Deviant children grown up*. Baltimore: Williams & Wilkins, 1966.

Rosen, B. M., Bahn, A. K., & Kramer, M. Demographic and diagnostic characteristics of psychiatric clinic outpatients in the U.S.A., 1961. *American Journal of Orthopsychiatry*, 1964, **34,** 455–68.

Sears, R. R. A theoretical framework for personality and social behavior. *American Psychologist*, 1951, **6,** 476–83.

Shields, J., & Slater, E. Heredity and psychological abnormality. In H. J. Eysenck (Ed.), *Handbook of abnormal psychology*. New York: Basic Books, 1961, pp. 298–343.

Sullivan, H. S. *The interpersonal theory of psychiatry*. New York: Norton, 1953.

Thomas, A., Chess, S., & Birch, H. G. *Temperament and behavior disorders in children*. New York: New York University Press, 1968.

White, R. W. *The abnormal personality*. (3rd ed.) New York: Ronald Press, 1964.

Wolpe, J. *Psychotherapy by reciprocal inhibition*. Stanford: Stanford University Press, 1958.

Suggested Readings

Adams, P. L. *Obsessive children*. New York: Penguin Books, 1973.

Berkowitz, P. H., & Rothman, E. R. *The disturbed child*. New York: New York University Press, 1960.

Lazarus, R. L., *Psychological stress and the coping process*. New York: McGraw-Hill, 1966.

Quay, H. C., & Werry, J. S. *Psychopathological disorders of childhood*. New York: Wiley, 1972.

Wolpe, J., & Lazarus, A. A. *Behavior therapy techniques*. Oxford: Pergamon Press, 1966.

Learning Disabilities

This chapter looks at several types of disabilities whose importance stems from the fact that they impair the capacity to profit from new experiences. Identifiable as discrete deficits, attitudes, or ways for processing stimulation, these disabilities are distinguished as precise conditions in contrast to the more general impairments observed in cultural deprivation or mental retardation, for example. These specific deficits, as well as presenting barriers to the acquisition of new knowledge or skills, may become the focal points for compounded adjustment difficulties, often with a prominent emotional overlay.

The treatment of learning disabilities rightly demands the interested concern of many specialists because of the associated complexities in performance and because of the large number of children who are involved. Specific learning disabilities frequently are manifested as degrees of academic nonachievement and undoubtedly contribute significantly to the large number of children—estimated by Kessler (1966) to be three-fourths of pupils of elementary-school age—referred for individual study and treatment because of poor school achievement.

Specific learning disabilities are usually uncovered by means of a case study assessing the child's intellectual ability, emotional development, social maturity, and experiential background. When the information from such diagnostic studies is evaluated in depth, there has frequently been an inability to ascribe the disability in functioning to any one specific cause.

A Boy with a Specific Auditory-Visual Association Learning Disability

As a young child, Larry accomplished early developmental tasks such as sitting alone, walking, feeding himself, and talking, within the normal range of time. At first his parents were modestly proud but not greatly concerned about Larry's developmental accomplishments. As he became older, however, they grew to be concerned about the possibility of injuries and began to fear that Larry might injure himself. Acting in accordance with social expectancies that they be good parents, they began to restrict Larry's participation in those activities they regarded as holding chances for injury.

The parents' anxious concern about his ability to cope successfully with new situations was recognized by Larry, who then began to doubt himself. Larry became more sensitive to his inadequacies and sought to avoid any new demands because he was not sure whether or not he could be successful. Since he was reluctant to try, he gave only casual attention to new situations and new objects. He could see nothing to be gained from looking carefully or listening intently. In fact, Larry much preferred to shut out such information because it only seemed to be another situation in which he might fail. The indifference and unconcern resulted in his not developing his ability to remember, organize, and relate visual and auditory stimuli. When Larry entered first grade, he learned the letters of the alphabet but he could not recognize words made of combinations of these same letters. He could not consistently associate the correct sound with a letter.

Larry's anxious concern increased as he failed while his classmates were successful. Specific auditory and visual memory deficits placed him at a distinct disadvantage in learning to read. He failed more frequently. His failures gave his parents more reason to think that Larry was basically inadequate. Finding substantiation for believing that Larry was inadequate, the parents then began to react to him in terms of expected failure. Larry responded to his parents' expectations of failure by more confusion, anxiety, and inability to remember. In this way a mutually reinforcing pattern of anxious inability to remember, failure, and resulting heightened level of anxiety with associated impairment of memory became established and influenced Larry's effectiveness in dealing with other tasks.

A clearer picture of the interrelationships among factors that contribute to success in meeting any demand has been gained from work with children who have specific learning disabilities. At first glance the prospects for intervention into such an apparently self-reinforcing and cyclical pattern of behavior seem formidable. These same qualities of mutual reciprocity and interrelatedness, however, have served as the basis for treatment programs directed toward the correction of specific learning disabilities, as will be seen elsewhere in this chapter.

Definitions

Even though there is currently a widespread interest in the child with specific learning disabilities, this type of disordered functioning is not a new concept. Persons concerned with adjustment failures in the past have recognized these same problems, as is all too evident from a review of the work describing past attempts to correct disabilities encountered in children. Some of the terms to be found include aphasic (impaired use or understanding of speech), brain-injured, dyslexia (difficulty in reading), interjacent, educationally retarded, emotional blocking, word-blind, underachiever, and idiot savant.

An examination of the variety of terms reflects an interest in these problems on the part of persons trained in such fields as general medicine, neurology, psychiatry, education, and psychology. In the general field of clinical work, there has usually been an abundance of diagnostic labels, but frequently a paucity of appropriate treatment procedures. Whether it is called classification, description, labeling, or diagnosis, proper identification of a problem is the essential first step in correcting the difficulty. Many deficits are not visible directly and must be inferred on the basis of impaired functioning so that diagnosis entails examining the individual's performance. Thus specific learning disabilities have been identified on the basis of observed inability to learn or progress at the expected rate in a well-controlled training situation. What is meant by this type of disorder may be clarified by the consideration of some examples of learning disabilities.

Characteristic Dysfunctions

1. *Visual Disabilities.*   Frequent mention is made of visual (spatial) difficulties in which there is an inability to differentiate figure from background, to recognize reversal or inversion of letters and forms, and/or to perceive forms with visual consistency in the face of measured "normal" visual acuity. For example, the child may be able to recognize squares when they are presented by themselves, but unable to perceive them when presented against a distracting background. Or the child may have a weakness in discriminating two letters or words which look alike such as "p" and "q," "b" and "d" or "on" and "no" or "left" and "felt." The problem of visual constancy may show up when the child is given a picture of a two- or three-dimensional object and asked to find the same object in a field of different objects elsewhere on the page.

2. *Motor Disabilities.*   Another commonly encountered area of deficit involves motor disabilities, such as the inability to write or reproduce figures accurately, awkward and gross motor coordination, and/or clumsiness and ineptness in performing fine motor skills. Parents and teachers may describe the child as "having two left feet," as having unusually poor handwriting, as being picked last when baseball teams are "choosing up" sides, as being unable to ride a bicycle until age 9 or 10, and as having had difficulty in learning to button buttons, tie shoelaces, and cut with scissors. Note, however, that some learning disabled youngsters have histories of advanced motor coordination and of always having been good at athletics (Wender, 1971).

3. *Language Disabilities.*   Certain language disorders are also cited as examples of specific learning disabilities. These include conditions ranging from mutism, omission or substitution of sounds and words, to confusion of tenses and acceptable syntax arrangements. Possibly closely related to these language disorders is another group of specific disabilities that are classed as communication deficits and include such problems as the inability to acquire usual competency in reading, to achieve in arithmetic, and/or to spell correctly.

4. *Auditory Disabilities.*   Included in the group of auditory disabilities is the inability to discriminate sounds when these are presented as isolated elements, such as the sounds of syllables which make up a word. Audiological examination with an audiometer shows that hearing as thus assessed is "normal." Yet, the child may not be able to discriminate the short vowel sound in "pin" and "pen," or to break the word "dog" into its individual

component sounds, or discriminate between nonphonemic sound elements such as loudness or pitch. More frequently, auditory deficits are seen as the inability to repeat more than five or six words in a sentence, a group of "nonsense" words, or a series of digits.

While it may be reasonable to assume a child who has weaknesses in auditory skills involving sound blending, memory, discrimination, and auditory-visual integration may be unable to read, this is not necessarily the case. Moreover, it appears that a large percentage of children who perform adequately on tests of auditory perception experience difficulty in learning to read and that an equally large percentage who score poorly on these same tests have *no* problem in reading (Hammill & Larsen, 1974a).

5. *Hyperactivity.* No symptom has perhaps received more attention than that of hyperactivity, a term which refers to a child's restlessness, inattentiveness, distractibility, excitability, disciplinary difficulty, and lack of frustration tolerance. These children will often be characterized by parents and teachers as nervous, constantly fidgeting, "into everything," walking around the classroom, and bothering other students. Motoric hyperactivity is often accompanied by verbal hyperactivity.

Hyperactivity can be associated with learning disability, but should not be taken as conclusive since: (1) Objective attempts to document a gross increase in motor activity have yielded inconclusive findings. In part, this may be due to the use of different devices to measure gross motor activity. And, in part, this may be due to the fact that hyperactive youngsters only appear more active because of a lack of goal-directed activity (Wender, 1971). (2) Only about 20% of children classified as learning disabled or brain injured will show noticeable hyperactivity (Keough, 1971; Werry & Sprague, 1969), but over half of these youngsters are given drugs to make them behave better. (3) Furthermore, whether a child shows hyperactive behavior also depends partly on the setting, with higher levels of activity being exhibited in structured situations (Tarver & Hallahan, 1974). (4) A few learning-disabled children are actually listless. (5) These children tend to outgrow their hyperactivity as they reach adolescence. (6) Children are commonly judged hyperactive, a reflection of their greater general activity level.

In brief, all learning disabled children are not hyperactive just as all hyperactive children are not learning disabled. In fact, some researchers have gone so far as to state that the learning disabled and the hyperactive constitute relatively distinct clinical groups (Campbell, 1975). Using a purely behavioral definition of hyperactivity, various investigators report that only a small percentage (less than 15%) of children studied had a definite history of brain injury and that hyperactive children did not have histories of difficult delivery and similar events more often than control subjects (Stewart et al., 1974).

6. *Emotional Disabilities.* A large number of specific learning disabilities may be recognized on the basis of an emotional condition that impairs effective functioning. In this category are disruptions associated with such char-

acteristics as impulsivity, destructiveness, daydreaming, aggressiveness, emotional lability, negativism, and uncooperativeness. It is of interest to note that this group of disabilities encompasses a range of traits extending from active assertion to the opposite extreme of passive withdrawal.

7. *Social Disabilities.* A little-understood and probably frequently unrecognized group of learning impairments may be classed together because they seem to represent deficits in organizing or relating to social surroundings. It is possible that misperceptions of social relationships figure prominently in this group of disabilities, which is also comprised of more easily identified disabilities such as erratic judgment, irresponsibility, nonparticipation, and irritability. Sociometric study of peer relationships indicates that normal children readily assign negative attributes to learning disabled children (Bryan, 1974b).

8. *Cognitive Disabilities.* Many authorities regard normal intelligence as a characteristic of learning disabled children and regard any findings to the contrary as reflecting misdiagnosis. Yet several studies indicate that learning disabled children have lower IQs (Stewart et al., 1974). One investigator reports that about 25% of children seen at the Gesell Clinic had IQs in the mentally retarded range (Ames, 1968). Bryan's research supports this finding (1974a). This finding raises a number of questions. Is learning disability sometimes just another term for mental retardation? Or as many critics contend is the learning-disability label a middle-class nicety while lower-class children showing the same behavior are likely to be labeled mentally retarded (Hobbs, 1975)? Or are learning disabled youth with lower IQs the ones who are most often referred for help? Do adults tend to overestimate the IQs of hyperactive children because of their energy, curiosity, and alertness (Stewart et al., 1974)? These questions remain for future research to answer.

9. *Combinations of Disabilities.* Not infrequently, deficits are observed which involve several areas of functioning, with the result that the learning disability is referred to as visual-motor, social-emotional, or language-communicative. There are several possibilities for such combinations based on discrepancies revealed by the evaluation of various kinds of responses or behaviors varying as to level of complexity. Sometimes the functional interrelatedness of two or more major systems contributing to a particular performance is reflected in the use of the term association disability (visual-motor association, auditory-language association, auditory-visual association). Other workers recognize the basic interaction of several systems in producing behavior but believe that deficiencies in one area may be of primary importance, whereas deficits in another related area are of secondary importance (primary motor incoordination with secondary irresponsibility and secondary social-learning disability, for example).

In summary, many children will show the above characteristics but it is not clear to what extent children must exhibit them in order to be labeled as learning disabled. It also is clear that further research is needed before any causative role can be assigned to these characteristics. The definition with associated characteristics must receive firmer support and be more precisely defined if they are to have greater utility.

Differential Diagnostic Considerations

Overview of Assessment Procedures. The assessment of learning disabilities follows the same plan and relies on the same procedures as are involved in seeking to identify the sources of any difficulty limiting a child's functioning effectiveness. The diagnostic process is a judgmental one, based on the critical scrutiny of four major areas: physical health, developmental history, comparisons of capacity and achievement, and family and home situation. The diagnostician explores these areas until he feels that he has sufficient information for making a decision.

In collecting information, some specialists make use of laboratory tests, X-rays, and electrical measures of performance. Other specialists rely more on the question-and-answer probing of the interview. Possibly the most important source of data is observation as the child functions in varied situations. Observation is frequently made in the controlled conditions for administration of a standardized measuring scale, or by asking the child to remember a series of words or digits. Although gained in less formal conditions, taking note of the child's participation in play groups, his manner of fitting in with his classmates, even the way he walks, sits, and waits in the examiner's office, supplies valuable information.

Ideally, a diagnostic study should answer all questions posed by the adjustment difficulty, ranging from the cause and nature of the disability to suggested treatment and prognosis. In practice, it is seldom that any specialist covers all the major areas of investigation in detail. His evaluation will rely heavily upon the findings elicited by the particular set of techniques in which the specialist has been trained. For example, the physician (pediatrician, neurologist) will depend predominantly on findings concerning physical health and developmental history. The educator will be advised by information obtained from comparisons of capacity and achievement and from the family and home situation. The social worker is primarily interested in surveying the developmental history and the family and home situation. The psychologist will count mostly on data supplied by comparisons of capacity and achievement and from developmental-history materials. Experience in dealing with behavior disorders, which tend to be vague and more uncertain than most somatic disabilities, has shown that effectiveness in treatment demands the collaboration of all these specialists. A complete picture of the disorder is formed only by having available information elicited from each of the four major areas outlined below (with sample coverage) :

1. Physical Health
   a. General physical health (stamina, fatigue, regularity of functions, complaints of pain or discomfort).

  b. Review of systems (survey of functioning of sensory, digestive, skeletal, motor, and endocrine systems).

  c. Neurological examination (balance, coordination, reflexes, responsiveness to pain and pressure stimuli).

  d. Prior illnesses (age of onset, severity, type, incapacitation).

  e. Accidents and injuries (age, nature, associated deficits, treatment).

  f. Possible significant hereditary influences.

 2. Developmental History

  a. Accomplishment of developmental tasks (age of sitting, standing, walking, talking, completion of toilet training).

  b. Language acquisition (making speech sounds, vocabulary, ease of speaking and understanding).

  c. Growth of interests (activities enjoyed, activities disliked, passive versus active participation).

  d. Emotional controls (intensity of emotions, appropriateness, stability).

  e. Adjustment to school (favored subjects, disliked subjects, educational goals).

 3. Comparisons of Capacity and Achievement (focus is on school adjustment for school-age children)

  a. Indices of general capacity (intelligence, aptitudes, language).

  b. Measures of general achievement (attainment in reading, writing, arithmetic).

  c. Measures of specific abilities (memory, dexterity, listening, eye-hand coordination).

  d. Speech fluency (enunciation, inflection, articulation, smoothness of expression).

  e. Personality organization (goals, motivation, reality orientation, self-evaluation).

  f. Capacity for independent work (distractibility, remembering instructions, understanding directions).

  g. Progression in school (age of entrance, failures, achievements).

 4. Family and Home Situation

  a. Parent-child relationships (acceptance-rejection, permissive-controlling, consistency, mutuality).

  b. Socialization (place in family group, friends, relations to neighborhood and community, conformity).

  c. Adequacy of home and neighborhood (intactness, recreational facilities, sources of stimulation, ease of getting about).

  d. Prevailing models and value standards (personal responsibility, type of gratification encouraged, release outlets available, social standards).

Assessment of Specific Disabilities.   In practice, a specific learning disability is identified on the basis of findings gained in a series of assessments that contrast potential with performance. The first phase (Level I) consists of establishing whether or not there is a real discrepancy between capacity and attainment, thus establishing a deviation that might be the manifestation of a specific learning disability. Indices of general capacity, usually expressed as mental age, chronological age, achievement age, learning age, vocabulary age, or motor age, are obtained. General level of functioning is ascertained according to performance on measures of educational achievement, motor coordination, language comprehension and usage. The actual level of performance is compared with the expected level of performance as suggested by the MA (mental age), CA (chronological age), or other appropriate normative scores. A learning disability is regarded as probable when there is a significant discrepancy between the measures of capacity and performance.

The second phase (Level II) of the assessment turns to a more detailed investigation and description of the learning disability. Preliminary study (first phase) may show that a child has, for example, a test age of 8 years on a scale measuring general intellectual capacity, but scores only at the level of the average child of 6 years on a measure of language comprehension and usage. Subsequent study would attempt to account for the discrepancy by evaluating abilities that contribute to language acquisition and use.

Standardized as well as informal analytic measuring techniques may be utilized in this second phase of the diagnostic study. The child may prove to have normal auditory acuity, but have an inability to remember or fuse sounds into the patterns that make up words. Another line of investigation would center about assessment of the speech and vocal processes as indicated by an articulation measure, or by a test such as the Illinois Test of Psycholinguistic Abilities (ITPA). A profile of ITPA scores obtained from a 7-year-old boy is shown in Table 5–1. This second phase would be pursued until the deficits and strengths in abilities associated with the impaired performance are sufficiently identified to suggest an appropriate approach to the correction of the disability.

The tendency to have expanded diagnostic categories for classifying specific learning disabilities reflects the fact that a deficit may influence more than one type of functioning. The child with a visual perceptual disability may encounter difficulty in reading and in walking and become irritable because of these failures. The problem of identifying a learning disability is rendered difficult, however, by the awareness that the blind learn to read and to walk. It is advisable to keep in mind that there is a hierarchy of relationships between abilities and performance.

The child who has difficulty in remembering letters in a fixed sequence, such as would provide a consistent clue for the visual recognition of words, can be expected to have low performance in reading. This expectation would be especially justified if his training in reading emphasizes an approach placing a high demand on visualization abilities. The same child may find that his visual memory-sequencing deficit results in his having some difficulty in playing baseball. The difficulty in baseball will probably not be as marked as it is in reading since baseball playing requires mainly motor-ability responses that are indirectly based on visual clues. A careful evaluation of the

**Table 5-1.   Profile of Psycholinguistic Ages for a Child with a
Visual Channel Disability**

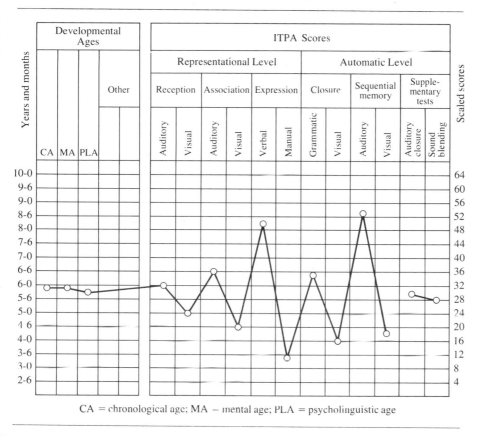

CA = chronological age; MA — mental age; PLA = psycholinguistic age

child's capacity to respond orally to problems presented to him verbally may
show that he has no difficulty with these types of tasks since the performance
required of him does not even indirectly involve visual memory-sequencing
ability. Some samples of a specific learning disability are shown in Figure 5-1.

Differentiation from Other Disorders.   Efforts to delineate learning disabilities as separate from another type of impaired functioning are evident
in descriptive diagnostic classifications such as "academic retardation without mental retardation." The problems observed in the child with a specific
learning disability should not be attributable to such global conditions as
ataxia, blindness, deafness, mental retardation, or social-emotional disorder.
It is necessary to differentiate a specific learning disability from conditions
that sometimes manifest a closely similar set of characteristics, including
achievement discrepancies.

SOCIAL AND EMOTIONAL MALADJUSTMENT.   Social and emotional
adjustment difficulties are frequently observed in association with other diffi-

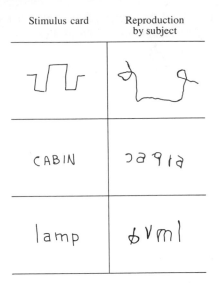

Figure 5–1. Drawings made by an eight-year-old boy of normal intellectual ability. (From the authors' files.)

culties, initially to a mild degree. For example, Bryan (1974b) found that learning disabled children, particularly white females, were rated as significantly less attractive and more rejected than the normal children studied. Later, these problems may become more severe and can be confused with primary social-emotional adjustment difficulties. A study carried out by Schroeder (1965) investigated the reading and arithmetic achievement of elementary-school pupils who had been diagnosed as falling into one of these five categories: psychosomatic, aggressive, having school difficulties, school-phobic, and neurotic-psychotic. Schroeder concluded that the wide ranges and variations in achievement observed did not support the classification of all the pupils into one large category such as "emotionally disturbed." A similar study of emotionally disturbed children of elementary-school age referred to the Child Psychiatry Service of the State University of Iowa was conducted by Stone & Rowley (1964). They found that only 52% of their sample ($N =$ 116) had lower than expected deviations, where 29% had higher than expected deviations when achievement in reading and arithmetic was compared to mental age. In addition to these differences in academic achievement, the degree of emotional disturbance and disorganization observed in the socially or emotionally maladjusted pupil is much greater than that observed in the child with specific learning disabilities. In contrast, Davie, Butler, & Goldstein (1972) found 4 out of 10 "backward readers" in their impressive study were "maladjusted." They concluded that for their subjects, maladjustment was a cause or an accompaniment of the reading disability rather than the result of the reading problem.

ORGANIC DYSFUNCTION.   It has also been found that not all children with brain damage have specific learning difficulties, even when the condition is so obvious as to lead to a classification of epilepsy (Maher, 1966). The mentally retarded present a rather uniform and general retardation in achievement which is, however, consistent with indices of their general capacity, such as mental age. Although the child with a specific learning disability presents characteristics that allow for a differential diagnosis from brain damage, emotionally disturbed, or mentally retarded, some children within these same groups are found to have specific learning disabilities that may or may not be associated with their other disorders.

DEVELOPMENTAL DISABILITIES. Systematic efforts to deal with a large group of deficits, mainly associated with some form of organic trauma, have been organized under programs for the "developmentally disabled." The choice of the terms "developmental" and "disabilities" makes it possible to confuse these conditions with specific learning disabilities which many authorities also recognize as having pronounced developmental aspect. Programs for the developmentally disabled appeared from an administrative reorganization that intended to combine services offered for the neurologically impaired (cerebral palsied, epileptic) and mentally retarded. It is additionally specified that these conditions must originate before age 18 years, be expected to continue as a permanent handicap, and present a major impairment that prevents the individual afflicted from participating in ordinarily available social, economic, and recreational opportunities. Some persons identified as having these more general conditions may be found also to have the circumscribed deficits designated as specific learning disabilities, although at the present the two conditions are not known to be inherently related.

Incidence and Distribution

Reports of the incidence of learning disabilities must be interpreted in the light of several problems encountered in any attempt to quantify these difficulties. Perhaps the most prevalent problem rests in the lack of agreement among the various professions as to just what constitutes a specific learning disability. Earlier in this chapter, we provided a list of terms encountered in the literature pertaining to learning disabilities. Each of these terms can be seen to have slightly different implications as to the manifestation of the disability, its origins, and its possible treatment. The persistence of these varied labels reflects the many points of differences about learning disabilities. Sometimes the differences are slight and technical, but in other instances they are considerable.

As might be expected, these differences in what constitutes a learning disability must be considered in reports of the frequency of learning disabilities, since incidence depends on definition. It follows that those persons who accept the more general categories (as, for example, "underachiever") in classifying learning disabilities will report a higher number of cases identified than will be reported by those persons who favor a more restrictive and narrow definition of the problem ("dyschronometria"—difficulty in telling time).

Hobbs (1975) reported that 700,000 children in the United States have specific learning disabilities. Bateman (1964), in her review of developments in the field of learning disabilities, suggests that from 5 to 10% of the general school population may have learning disabilities that are identifiable as reading problems and that deficits in other academic areas also occur but with less frequency. Myklebust & Johnson (1962), who provide for a large number of disabilities grouped under the general category of dyslexia, state that "at least five percent of school children have some type of psychoneurological learning disorder." In one study based on 1,056 consecutive children referred to a major mental health center, it was found that 77% were diagnosed as having minimal brain dysfunction, a label frequently given to learning disabled youth (Gross & Wilson, 1974). Bakwin (1949) notes that from 2 to 3% is frequently cited for the incidence of cerebral damage, and Bender (1956) has suggested a frequency of about 1% for the number of children who would be classified as brain-injured.

Hagin (1973) collected 306 papers dealing with reading disabilities from the "grass roots" literature of education and psychology from January 1956 to June 1972. She placed each paper into one of three intervention models:

1. *Pathology Model.* Learning disability is a manifestation of pathology in the child or his psychological environment (comparable to our psychoneurological and psychodynamic approaches).

2. *Educational Mis-match Model.* Failure to learn is the result of a mismatch between materials of instruction and the child's current developmental level of capacity for learning (comparable to our psychoeducational approach).

3. *Reading Process Model.* Failures to learn are related to faulty relationships between reading and perceptual, language and cognitive skills (also comparable to our psychoeducational approach).

When the percentage of papers for each intervention model that appeared in the various time periods was computed (shown in Figure 5–2), a pattern emerged that indicated a tendency for these models to equalize the frequency of activity. The steady decline in the pathology category was balanced by an increase in the other two areas. Hagin suggests the pattern indicates increasing recognition and acceptance of the Educational Mis-match and Reading Process approaches as well as the tendency for professional workers to attack learning disabilities cooperatively.

There is a paucity of reports in which entire populations have been exhaustively studied by any of the existing diagnostic criteria, and most of the information used for making estimates of the incidence of learning disabilities has been gained from such restricted population groups as children referred to child-study clinics, remedial-reading clinics, psychiatric hospitals, or school psychologists. Incidence figures vary with the orientation of the reporting agency.

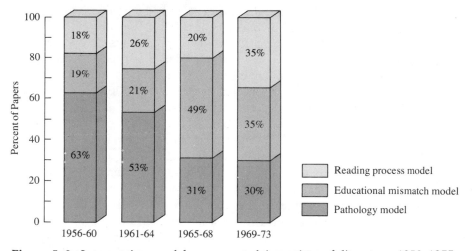

Figure 5–2. Intervention models represented in review of literature 1956–1973. (*Source*: R. Hagin. Models of intervention with learning disabilities; ephemeral and otherwise. *School Psychology Monograph*, 1973, **1**, 1–25. Published by the Division of School Psychology, American Psychological Association.)

Detailed investigations of carefully selected samples would do much to clarify the exact incidence of learning disabilities, which probably falls somewhere in the range suggested by Bateman (1964), a frequency of from 5 to 10% of schoolchildren. One such attempt was reported by Burks (1960), who evaluated all pupils (524) in an elementary public school (kindergarten through eighth grade) with a rating scale designed to identify the hyperkinetic child. It was found that 8% (42) of the children showed a large number of the diagnostic criteria from a moderate to a severe degree. The National Committee on Dyslexia and Related Reading Disorders (1969), arrived at an incidence rate of 15% and Kline & Lee (1972) report a number of cross-cultural studies citing incidence rates ranging from 6 to 16%, with boys from 6 to 10 times more frequently identified than girls.

Factors Influencing Reported Incidence

1. *Sex.* Although estimates of the incidence of learning disabilities vary considerably, there is rather general agreement among all investigators that the condition is more commonly observed in males than in females. Myklebust & Johnson (1962) report that dyslexia "occurs at least five times more frequently in males than in females." This proportion seems to be remarkably consistent with, and even overshadows, some of the differences found in the definitions of what characterizes a learning disability. In the group of "minimal brain dysfunction" children studied by Gross and Wilson (1974), boys outnumbered girls by a ratio of 3.6 to 1. These findings have sometimes been used to support the claim for some sex-linked genetic factor influencing the disabilities, but it can be interpreted with equal plausibility as supporting

the impact of socialization upon development and functioning. Studies such as those carried out by Maccoby and Jacklin (1974) and Brophy and Good (1974) have examined the impact of socialization demands on children.

2. *Socioeconomic Status.* Reports of the incidence of specific learning disabilities in relation to socioeconomic status are difficult to interpret. On the one hand, investigations such as reported by Eisenberg (1962) and Pasamanick and Knobloch (1966) indicate a higher frequency of all problems as a consequence of a "deprivation syndrome" affecting all persons in lower socioeconomic levels. Other authorities point to a greater frequency of specific learning disabilities being diagnosed in higher socioeconomic children because their parents are more likely to be able to afford the costly diagnostic and treatment services that are required to identify such deficits.

3. *Age.* The obvious influence that specific learning disabilities can have on school adjustment has resulted in more information being available about schoolchildren than about any other age group. Regardless of the explanations, not the least pervasive of which centers about the contribution of maturation to learning disabilities, the picture indicates clearly that there is a peaking of the incidence of learning disabilities at about the second or third grade. There is then a progressive decline in the incidence with each successively higher grade level. The frequency may approximate as much as 20% at the peak point and then diminish to approximately 2 or 3% in the advanced high-school grades (Burks, 1960; McCarthy & Kirk, 1963). A portion of the reduced incidence in the higher grade levels is undoubtedly accounted for by the dropping-out of pupils who have become discouraged with the school failures they experience because of their specific learning disabilities.

4. *Assessment Techniques.* Previous mention was made of the difficulties in diagnosing learning disabilities because of different persons' viewpoints as to what constitutes a learning disorder. Closely related to this factor is the nature of the instruments and techniques used to assess human performance. The evaluation of children is an arduous task rendered more laborious by the limited language facility of the young child. Emphasis upon verbal responses and communicative ability is inherent in most psychoeducational measuring devices. Often there is no suitable standardized measuring instrument for eliciting a specific type of functioning in detail (such as auditory blending and sequencing, or visual memory), and the examiner must invent his own techniques. At best this individualistic procedure may yield qualitative information that is difficult to communicate precisely to other interested professionals.

5. *The Diagnostic Team.* Much confusion also rests in the prevailing system of diagnosis on the basis of evaluation by a "team" of specialists. Each such specialist tends to consider the child only from the vantage of his particular training, and in fact may exercise great care to avoid impinging upon the "area" covered by another member of the team. In practical situations the theoretical advantages of the "diagnostic team" are often unable to rise above the built-in walls that delimit the various disciplines. There is a lack

of necessary interdisciplinary communication and understanding as to who is to bear the primary diagnostic and treatment responsibility.

6. *Lack of Follow-up Reports.* The uncertainty as to who is the responsible person contributes to another problem, namely, the lack of adequate follow-up study for many children who have been seen for diagnostic evaluation. Such follow-up observation is essential to the perfection of appropriate treatment procedures. Follow-up could, for example, give some indication as to which children have specific deficits as distinct from those children who are only evidencing delayed developmental or maturational patterns.

The Major Theoretical Approaches

When the teacher observes that a pupil is consistently unable to keep up with classroom assignments, she may refer the child for study by other specialists on the school staff. The referral request includes a brief account of the difficulty, such as "unable to progress in arithmetic even though his work in all other areas is average" or "does average work in reading and other subjects but consistently fails in spelling, where he cannot differentiate such words as *lake* and *like*." The problem often centers about a marked lack of attainment in a particular area in the face of average achievement in other areas and indications of at least average intellectual ability. Frequently, the difficulty is a lack of progress in acquiring reading skills.

The several child specialists on the school staff (often psychologist, social worker, nurse) will carry out an evaluation of the pupil's capacity for doing schoolwork. They will assess and consider his personality, learning abilities, social development, and physical health. In addition to the measures of his present performance, the staff will compile a historical account of his past adjustment and development. Inabilities to be successful with particular tasks and previous failures in the developmental sequence will be carefully noted. In a case conference, information obtained by these several specialists will be shared and added to by the teacher's impressions. From the case-conference discussion will evolve a picture of the pupil's capacity for learning, his strengths and his deficits. The complete description will indicate the pupil's potential for achieving and will identify the factors limiting his ability to perform. The proceedings of a case conference in one school are paraphrased here:

> The school nurse, in reporting the pupil's physical health and development, indicated frequent illnesses of the upper respiratory system, ear infections, and associated high temperatures. The pupil had received prompt medical attention for these illnesses and was even hospitalized twice. He was regarded as having good health. The social worker's account of the home and family relationships described a family group in which there was a limited amount of verbal interchange to the point that the pupil's pattern of delayed speech acquisition was not a matter for concern on the part of the parents. The psychologist pointed out that the pupil was of better than

average intellectual ability; however, the many doubts about his ability made it difficult for the pupil to make full use of his intellectual ability. The psychologist raised the question of whether the pupil was deliberately performing at a level much below his real capacity for attainment.

In expanding upon the pupil's difficulty in spelling, the teacher brought out that the pupil had previously attended school in another city, where there was more emphasis upon training visual skills and less attention given to drills or other practice in auditory abilities. The teacher stated that the pupil was one of the worst readers in her class and seemed to be having increasing difficulty in this area. She wondered if his poor reading skills had not led the other children in the class to think of him as being inadequate in other activities. He was usually among the last chosen for team games.

In later phases of the case-conference discussion, it was recognized that performance in spelling emerges from the integration of various abilities (attending, hearing, writing), which in turn originate from the action of several organ systems (skeletal muscle, auditory, central nervous system). An injury or defect in any one of these organic components can be expected to result in impaired performance.

Performance is also influenced by the nature of the pupil's personality organization, which must take into account deficits as well as assets and then formulate defenses or compensations to maintain his individual psychological integrity. At still another level, functioning is modified by factors within the situation itself. The task of spelling words correctly and the approval of the teacher and classmates constitute a particular set of expectations and consequences that require specific abilities and reactions. Organic injury, psychological makeup, and environmental demands may thus be involved in this pupil's inability to spell.

The concepts of interaction and interrelatedness are central to understanding the problems of specific learning disabilities. They also make it necessary to consider several approaches in establishing the type of learning disability, its etiology, and its treatment: the psychoneurological approach, the psychodynamic, and the psychoeducational. It will be noted that the three approaches contrasted have certain commonalities and areas of overlap (see Table 5–2).

The Psychoneurological Approach

Characteristics.   From the psychoneurological approach, recognition of the child with specific learning disabilities is made on the basis of the presence of general behavioral characteristics and specific functional deficits. A list of these characteristics as suggested by Strother (1963) includes:

1. General Personality Characteristics
   a. Hyperactivity (restlessness, aimless activity, random movements).
   b. Distractibility (uncontrollably drawn to all new stimuli).
   c. Impulsiveness (spontaneous and compelling inclination to respond).

Table 5–2. A Summary of the Psychoneurological, Psychodynamic, and Psychoeducational Approaches to Learning Disabilities

Theoretical Approach	Etiological Factors	Diagnostic Procedures	Treatment Methods	Diagnostic Terminologies
Psycho-neurological	Trauma, injury, or damage to central nervous system.	Neurological examination, EEG findings, case history.	Depressant drugs, stimulant drugs, surgical intervention, physical therapy, corrective devices, developmental training.	Alexia, aphasia, dyslexia, agraphia, strephosymbolia, dyscalculia, brain injury, autistic, minimal brain dysfunction, hyperkinetic, word-blindness, dyspraxia, agnosia, dysjunctive, achronometria.
Psycho-dynamic	Impaired parent-child relationships, conflicting social values, excessive failure, inadequate early stimulation, deficits in ability, inadequate self-concept, maladaptive habits and attitudes.	Projective techniques, measures of general and specific abilities, case history, interview, observation, measures of achievement, interpretation of physical-health data.	Psychotherapy with parent and/or child, environmental intervention, educational remediation.	Passive-aggressive personality, oral character, anxious personality, emotional block, insecurity, immaturity, delayed developmental sequence, reading disability, motor incoordination, mild social and emotional maladjustment, inattentiveness, poor self-concept, inadequate control of emotional impulses, inadequate experiential background.
Psycho-educational	Etiology of minimal consideration; some mention of the correlates or factors that appear to be associated with the disability.	Case history, observation, measures of achievement, performance in specific situations requiring particular skills, consideration of measures of general abilities, review of physical-health data.	Compensatory training, corrective remediation.	Perceptual handicap, educational disabilities of auditory or visual perception, perceptual speed and tracking, visual or auditory discrimination, selective capacity to attend, skill in auditory and visual fusion, auditory-visual association, visual and auditory memory, kinesthetic sensitivity, laterality, language temporal sequencing, eye-hand coordination, spatial orientation, educationally retarded.

    d. Emotional instability (sudden mood changes, exaggerated and inappropriate emotional responses).
2. Specific Disabilities
    a. Perceptual disorders (errors in form discrimination, form constancy, spatial orientation).
    b. Motor disorders (incoordination, awkwardness, clumsiness).
    c. Language disorders (errors in processing auditory components of speech, inability to associate words with objects, confusion as to time and sequential patterns).
    d. Concept-formation and reasoning disorders (inability to grasp concepts, inability to make associations between ideas, faulty judgment of relevance of associations made).

It must be pointed out that the list presented by Strother is very comprehensive and seeks to incorporate a variety of conditions into a more comprehensive categorization. Groupings such as dyslexia (difficulty in reading), aphasia (inability to use or understand speech), hyperkinesthesis (increased muscular movement), and agraphia (inability to write) often proved to have limited value in the practical problem of treating these same conditions. It is generally recognized that no one child will likely exhibit all of the characteristics, although a child showing several of these characteristics would be considered as falling into the classification. The absence of a fixed pattern of behaviors and deficits manifested by all children with specific learning disabilities has been the source of no small amount of the confusion in dealing with this type of disorder. Not only does the combination of these characteristics observed in any child vary, but there is a wide range for the same characteristic when observed in different children.

Perhaps the most obvious of these characteristics, and certainly the one most distressing to parents and teachers, centers about the continual and intense motor activity exhibited by such children. The combination of hyperactivity, distractibility, and impulsivity is so pronounced that these children have been referred to as "motor-driven." The inappropriate emotional control and resulting lability are also prominently observed characteristics. Although the personality characteristics are gross and rather easily recognized, the specific disabilities are considerably more difficult to detect. These specific disabilities, which may be slighted or overlooked in a usual evaluation such as neurological examination, may, nevertheless, exert a profound influence on the child's development and performance.

Etiological Considerations. Although adherents of the psychoneurological approach to specific learning disabilities accept a variety of characteristics as constituting the syndrome, these impairments are taken as evidence of injury or damage to the central nervous system. Initially the treatment of learning disabilities was relegated to physicians, who naturally attempted to understand these problems from the framework of their particular training. The central nervous system was regarded as the center for regulating and coordinating all functioning. It was believed that, in the course of development, the central nervous system becomes organized into many specialized areas, directive centers for particular activities and responses. Information on the location of these specialized areas led to the preparation of "maps," with coded numbers referring to designated centers. One such brain map, prepared by McIntosh and Dunn (1973), is shown in Figure 5–3.

Any effort to review the extensive research findings pertaining to brain functioning would lead to discussions beyond the scope of this chapter. Although a controversial issue, some evidence, largely obtained from studies carried out on adults, can be interpreted as lending general support to a localization of function theory as illustrated in Figure 5–3.

The psychoneurological approach has given much importance to etiologies, possibly reflecting the influence of the training undergone by physicians. The field of medicine has had great success in dealing with the identified causes of disorders. The emphasis on anatomical-physiological factors has led to a

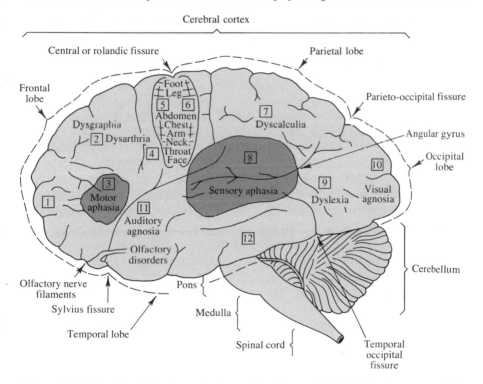

Figure 5–3. Exterior right, lateral view of the human brain indicating some of the established and hypothetical functions and dysfunctions of the various areas of the cerebral cortex. Key: 1. Thought association, reasoning, and idea generation; 2. written expression; 3. Broca's speech-expression area; 4. voice and articulation control; 5. voluntary-movement expression; 6. body-surface sensations; 7. arithmetic understanding; 8. Wernicke's speech-understanding area; 9. reading recognition and comprehension; 10. visual sensations; 11. auditory sensations; 12. information organization, interpretation, and storage. From McIntosh and Dunn (1973).

consideration of such factors as heredity, diseases, and accidents, as these may result in injury or damage to the central nervous system. In discussing factors resulting in brain damage, Bakwin (1949) and Walker (1974) listed diseases and infections, tumors, anoxia, metabolic disturbances, toxins, fevers, and injuries as being of primary etiological significance. Damage from anoxia is probably the most frequently encountered.

Assessment Procedures.   Despite the acceptance of brain injury as being responsible for impaired functioning, assessment procedures used in the psychoneurological approach are not pointed to the direct examination of the brain. The present development of assessment techniques does not make it possible to conduct a detailed scrutiny of the intactness of the human brain. Instead, the diagnosis is arrived at on the basis of interpretations drawn from observed functioning, with inferences as to the mediating role of the central nervous system (Peters, Davis, Goolsby, & Clements, 1973).

Indications of the intactness of the central nervous system are suggested by walking a line with the eyes closed (balance), inserting marbles on a board with cutouts (dexterity), touching finger to nose (accuracy), reactions to heat, cold, pain, light, strong odors, sounds, and touch (sensitivity). The electroencephalograph (EEG) provides a record of the electrical activity of the brain as tasks of varying degrees of complexity are performed (rest, reading, solving abstract problems). X-ray pictures of the brain, placed in sharper detail by injections of air into cerebral passageways, may provide evidence of blocked passages or tumors.

The findings may be supplemented by other measures. Motor-visual coordination is revealed in writing and copying figures. Visualization effectiveness is evident in the discrimination of forms or by reading. Auditory abilities are ascertained by audiometric examination or by repetition of words and sentences. A careful appraisal of speech facility may be revealing of specific deficits. In some instances, the influence of drugs or medication on these functions may be of importance in establishing an impairment. It is interesting in practice that the psychologist is often inclined to pay heed to neurological findings, whereas the neurologist is prone to consider psychological assessment findings.

The making of a diagnosis of specific learning disability, now frequently referred to as "minimal brain dysfunction," following the deliberations of a task force on terminology and identification (Clements, 1966), also entails differentiation from other conditions of neurological impairment. The distinction is usually made on the basis of the rather generalized impairment associated with mental retardation, cerebral palsy, encephalitis, psychosis, cultural deprivation, and such, in contrast to the more limited impairment observed in specific learning disabilities. The ultimate diagnostic choice may depend upon information provided by a detailed developmental and clinical history.

Treatment Approaches.   In the past, treatment of specific learning disabilities was largely relegated to the physician. The specific disabilities encountered were mostly seen in adult clients, as consequences of some injury. Initially, the medical concern was for describing, classifying, and seeking neuroanatomical correlates for the specific deficits observed (Bateman, 1964). There was little attempt at correction, especially in the presently accepted techniques of retraining, prior to the work of Orton (1925), a physician. Orton's interest in education may have inadvertently contributed to some of the confusion that prevails concerning who is responsible for the treatment of specific learning disabilities. Attempts to dodge a charge by other professionals has added to physicians being caught in a kind of "buck-passing" situation regarding treatment of these disorders, which are puzzling to everyone.

Certain corrective procedures for remedying defects of the visual, auditory, motor, and central nervous systems can be performed only by a physician. These include surgery, the administration of medications, and in some instances the fitting of hearing aids and corrective lenses. Advances in medical treatment have been extensive. Drugs are available for selectively increasing a child's attentiveness by reducing his reaction to stimuli or by making him more responsive to stimuli. Making a diagnosis has been facilitated by more refined electrical apparatus such as the electroencephalograph. Progress in refining and standardizing the neurological examination is being carried out by Reitan (1975), who has been credited with success in pinpointing cerebral focal points of malfunctioning.

Even so, there are instances in which surgical or medical procedures cannot be used in treatment. For example, careful neurological examination may reveal that a child has a deep and centrally located cerebral lesion. Surgical correction may be contraindicated, and there may be no medication that will act selectively on the lesion. The child must learn to live with and in spite of his defect. Treatment in such cases becomes largely a matter of medications that facilitate education and training (refer to pp. 420–428). Physicians are presently apt to be concerned with the possibility of correcting the disability by some training program. They generally do not become so directly involved in the amelioration by education as did Orton, but may cooperate with teachers or other educators in developing a total corrective program. The pediatrician is likely to consider a referral to a psychologist or to a psychoeducational clinic known to have developed extensive developmental training programs for correcting specific disabilities.

The Psychodynamic Approach

Characteristics. A second major approach to understanding specific learning disabilities places emphasis on psychological as opposed to organic dysfunction. The psychodynamic framework focuses on the individual arrangement of energies, skills, and abilities as these become organized by experience. Of particular importance is the capacity for handling emotions and for achieving new learning. From the psychodynamic view, specific learning disabilities are seen as any impairment that might prevent learning. Consideration is directed to the processes for coping with demands and to pressures associated with the demands. Characteristics of concern in the psychodynamic approach to the identification of specific learning disabilities can be grouped under six major categories:

1. Emotional (negativism, inattentiveness, anxiety, self-depreciating passive aggressiveness, depression, dependency).
2. Social-impulsive (immature, poor peer acceptance, antisocial-compensating, hostile).
3. Sensory (hyperresponsive, visually incompetent, tone-deaf, insensitive).
4. Physical (uncoordinated, clumsy, awkward, malaise, disoriented).
5. Communication (stammering, inarticulate, sparse vocabulary, uncomprehending).
6. Performance discrepancy (underachieving, poorly motivated, nonreader).

Actually, the characteristics acknowledged by proponents of the psychodynamic approach do not differ greatly from those recognized in the psychoneurological approach, as Mesinger (1965) pointed out. There is an expansion to encompass environmental demands and attitudinal factors in the categories of "academic" and "social." In this way, the child's reaction or "adjustment" to his deficit is given weight equal to that of the particular deficit itself. This may have important implications in formulating a treatment program. One of the most profound features of emotional influences upon behavior is the possibility of a self-perpetuating circular reaction such as failure-aggression-failure or anxiety-failure-anxiety.

As was true for the psychoneurological approach, there is no specific set of characteristics forming a "specific learning disability syndrome" within the psychodynamic framework. Possibly because of the broader framework in which the child's functioning is evaluated from the psychodynamic approach, the child with specific learning disabilities is more likely to show multiple deficits involving three or more of the major groups of characteristics from all six areas because of the interrelatedness of performance made by the same person.

Teachers are more likely to be aware of characteristics within the "academic" and "emotional" categories, whereas parents may be more concerned about those of the "emotional" and "communication" categories. Characteristics in the "sensory" and "physical" categories are perhaps the most frequently overlooked by teachers and parents, especially since the detection of these impairments may require special equipment and training.

Etiological Considerations. The psychodynamic approach places primary concern on the modification and development of the individual as a result of his individual experiences. It holds that emotions, as the motivational sources for maintaining and sustaining performance, play a crucial role in learning (Berlyne, 1964). Unchanneled energy results in an uncontrollable overflow which disrupts performance. Too little energy leads to insufficient involvement and failure to learn. In other instances, energy expended may find no satisfaction and attach itself to inappropriate objects or tasks, with consequent perseveration or fixation.

Emotions evolve out of experiences, especially those of success and failure. The most important experiences for humans are social learnings incurred in contacts with other persons. Social learning, a major field of study in its own right, places emphasis on the social possibilities for rewards and the channeling of emotions (frustration, aggression, anxiety) into socially acceptable outlets. A personal directional-integration center (self-concept) develops from individual experiences of success and failure. Concurrently, concern must be given to the acquisition of consensually agreed cues and meanings (attitudes) which serve as the basis for interpreting all situations and events.

Just as it is not possible to be exact in pinpointing brain damage, so are emotions and experiences impossible to present in tangible forms. In the light of this difficulty, the assumed influence of emotions is implied by stating that the impaired performance, which is demonstrable, is associated with one or another emotional feeling. These somewhat abstract relationships may be made more comprehensible by a synopsis of examples of psychodynamic factors that Weisskopf (1951), Weiner (1971), and Asbury (1974) found to be associated with specific learning disabilities in children referred to school psychologists for study. These factors are briefly described below:

1. *Conscious Refusal to Learn.* A boy feels real hostility toward his parents and other adults. He readily expresses his dislike for all adult persons, including teachers, who he claims try to "use" him. His rejection of adults has so generalized that he refuses to do anything he associates with being adult, such as reading. A girl has strong loyalties to her parents, who have only limited educational attainment. They do not value educational achievement, and she feels that applying herself at school would be inconsistent with the wishes of her parents and might even alienate her from them.

2. *Overt Hostility.* A girl has intense feelings of resentment. She is hypercritical and has a continual chip on her shoulder. Her anger spills over at the slightest provocation. She sees only the possibilities for battle in any situation, and it is impossible for her to enter into and profit from the usual classroom learning relationships.

3. *Negative Conditioning.* A negative emotional response (fear, anger, dislike, failure) to a particular task (reading) may be acquired out of previous associations. Reading, having been presented with someone or something already feared or disliked, becomes capable by itself of producing these negative emotional reactions. A child's first-grade teacher would walk around the room rapping knuckles with a ruler. The teacher placed great stress on reading. The child's panicky reactions to this teacher continued in response to reading lessons from other teachers in later years.

4. *Displacement of Feelings.* This process involves the transfer of feelings

originally aroused by some object or person to a similar object or situation. A child is extremely jealous of a favored brother who excels in reading. The resentment is transferred to the act of reading, which is the sibling's strong point. A variation of this impairment is seen in the case of the child whose parent is an avid reader. The child is unable to express his hostility toward the parent in an open or direct fashion, but feels free to dislike the reading which is so important to the parent. Displaced hostility is seldom recognized by either the parent or the child.

5. *Resistance to Pressures.* Our culture has been repeatedly cited for its undue emphasis on achievement. Rendered overanxious by his sparse food intake, a child's mother begins forcibly to cram food into the child, and is surprised that the child capitalizes on the possibility for asserting his rights by even stronger refusal of foods. Similarly, the overambitious parent pushing for intellectual attainment runs the risk of resistance that may take the form of lack of interest in reading.

6. *Clinging to Dependency Status.* The overprotected and babied child may, consciously or unconsciously, choose to preserve his infantile status and secure attention through being helpless. Such children may reject everything associated with growing up, including the self-reliance evidenced by being able to talk well or being successful in school. The arrival of younger siblings may accentuate this pattern on the part of an older child, who can interpret being sent to school as an attempt to get him out of the house so that his mother can give all her attention to the new baby.

7. *Limited Persistence.* This factor is operative in the child who launches into a task but meets with some initial difficulty. He quickly becomes discouraged and stops trying. As a rule, such children come to school with marked feelings of inferiority and uncertainty. Their home life has not provided them with security and self-confidence. The parents may have been hypercritical, rejecting, or plagued with self-doubts. These children seem predisposed to failure and are easily convinced that they are stupid, readily accepting an inferior status.

8. *Fear of Success.* For some children, almost any successful form of self-expression may stir up feelings of intense anxiety and distress related to unacceptable fears of being destructive or hostile. Success in reading may symbolize entering into an adult activity and therefore competing with a parent. Such competition, in turn, may imply the possibility of dreadful forms of retaliation. The child may seek safety in self-destruction and passivity. This type of reaction, involving deep-seated unconscious conflicts, tends to be highly resistant to all remedial help.

9. *Extreme Distractibility or Restlessness.* When tension builds up to a level exceeding the usual capacity for control, the child may seek ways to lower the tension so as to feel more comfortable. Release in motor activity is often chosen. The child is unable to sit still, does not remember directions given him, and falls behind in learning. The realization that he has failed leads to discouragement and heightens the level of tension. The child becomes unable to direct his attention selectively and is helplessly impelled to react to

all objects, persons, and situations. The ensuing disruption and disorganization make it impossible for him to persist at a task except under the most
controlled conditions.

10. *Absorption in a Private World.* A child may become so absorbed in
his own thoughts that he can give only intermittent attention to his real surroundings. Memorizing the complicated rules and logical formats of mathematics requires much more effort and gives much less satisfaction than does
the preoccupation with daydreams. The reverie may entail the excitement of
hitting a home run, scoring a winning touchdown, finding romantic adven-
ture; or it may be concerned with morbid fantasies of burning cities and
destroying whole races of people. In either instance, the child's abilities are
diverted from opportunities for real praise and recognition gained from being
successful with a task.

11. *Exaggerated Emotional Responses to Instructional Material.* Instructional materials are selected to have meaning for the learner. Stories are
about people, families, and friends. They tell of incidents, happenings, and
situations. The meanings given such content will vary according to the needs
and experiences of the child. The sudden surge of emotional feelings experienced by a child from a broken home as he reads a story dealing with happy
family life may obscure any new learning presented by the story.

12. *Suppression and Constriction.* Some children are faced with having to
cope with unacceptable feelings of destruction, guilt, or hatred. They may
seek to handle these impulses by denial, compartmentalization, and noninvolvement. The rigid controls established over these emotional feelings and
the effort required to keep up a constant guard exact a considerable reduction
in the capacity for any new learning. The total inhibition manifests itself in
such impairments as the unwillingness to express ideas, the inability to recite
or answer questions, and the deliberate tuning-out of any new information.

Assessment Procedures.   It should be apparent by now that a wide
range of behaviors is encompassed in the classification "specific learning disability." It may well be that variability of behavior is the one incontestable
characteristic consistently associated with this disorder. The psychodynamic
concept of learning disabilities as impairments influenced by many different
factors gives compelling support to the total evaluation of the child's potential for intellectual, emotional, and social performance. The detailed assessment will include an examination, observation, and study of the child.
Generally this threefold task can be adequately carried out by a psychologist,
but provision should also be made for psychiatric, neurological, audiological,
speech, or social-worker consultation if indicated. Examinations by other
specialists, such as an ophthalmologist or otologist may be suggested by evidence of visual or auditory defects. A developmental history and account of
the child's family life and home background can serve as an important source
for the interpretation of identified deficits in performance.

Measures of potential for achievement are compared with measures of
actual attainment. Mental age or test age from the Stanford-Binet Intelligence

Scale or the Wechsler Intelligence Scales may be used as the basis for predicting a certain level of attainment on an achievement test. If some of the achievement scores (reading, arithmetic, vocabulary) do not fall within the expected range, a specific learning disability is suspected. The low-performance area is investigated in greater detail. Frequently, the discrepancy is between expected and actual attainment in reading.

From the psychodynamic point of view, it is also necessary to differentiate consistent nonachievement in limited and particular areas from the more general lack of achievement seen with mental retardation or with speech and hearing disabilities and from the inconsistent achievement typical of the severely emotionally disturbed. To make such a differential diagnosis, information obtained from the psychologist must be carefully interpreted in the light of findings presented in a case history of physical health and family relationships and in reports of examinations carried out by other specialists.

Suggestions of factors contributing to the learning disability are sought in the nature of the child's social and emotional adjustment. The assessment of social and emotional development comprises the unique contribution of the psychologist. In carrying out the personality evaluation, the psychologist makes extensive use of specific measures and observations. Favored measuring devices include projective and paper-and-pencil self-report tests of personality. On the basis of responses to a series of inkblot pictures, the Rorschach test supplies information regarding such important personality characteristics as aggression, fantasy, introversion, emotional controls, intellectual efficiency, and general approach to a task. Material elicted by ambiguous pictures (for example, the School Apperception Test), sentence-completion techniques, drawings, and diagnostic play sessions provides clues as to the person's needs, sources of satisfaction, reactions to success or failure, currently perceived pressure of demands, and individual attitudes and value systems.

More specific information regarding particular attitudes, values, and demands is suggested by paper-and-pencil measures, such as sentence-completion tests, Sixteen Factor Personality Inventory, or an adjustment inventory. The general social acceptability of the individual's personality makeup is indicated by other paper-and-pencil scales and inventories such as the Coopersmith Self-esteem Inventory or the Childrens' Manifest Anxiety Scale. There are many other personality measures and assessment techniques. It must be cautioned that giving meaning to data gained from these measures is a highly skilled matter and demands extensive training and practice.

The interpretation of material from personality tests in fact frequently requires the consideration of other impressions. Thus the psychologist finds it necessary to observe the child's reactions in a variety of situations: the unstructured setting of the playroom and the more formal organization of the classroom. The importance of precisely identifying attitudes and feelings that may contribute to specific learning disabilities often makes it appropriate for the psychologist to supplement his entire battery of objective measures by carrying out a detailed interview with the child.

Ideally, the psychologist should be able to complete his evaluation of specific learning disabilities by a detailed assessment of basic motor, visual, and auditory skills. Such information, generally provided by a diagnostic reading test or one of several special scales (Bender Visual Motor Designs Test, Wepman Auditory Discrimination Scale, Frostig Perceptual Development Rating Scale), would be of great value in planning a remedial program for correcting the disability. Some psychologists working in the school are competent to do this type of assessment, but unfortunately the majority of psychologists have not had such training.

Treatment Approaches.   The treatment of specific learning disabilities by psychotherapy is only a particular application of techniques that are extensively discussed in Chapter 10 of this text. Common sources of psychopathology and resulting impaired functioning associated with specific learning disability are inadequate parent-child relationships and consequent heightened aggression or dependency, self-perceptions of inadequacy and inferiority, excessive levels of anxiety and concern about failure, and confusion resulting from unsuccessful experiences in coping with tasks encountered in the past. Breakdowns in communication and family dynamics may also be factors to be considered in treatment plans (Peck & Stackhouse, 1973).

Psychologists, psychiatrists, social workers, and counselors have attempted to correct these conditions and the associated impaired performance by a variety of methods. The techniques applied have tended to be of the more conventional types, such as regularly scheduled counseling interviews, play therapy, psychoanalysis, and group-therapy sessions. Some therapists prefer to see only the parent; others see only the child. In another arrangement, both the parent and the child are worked with but in separate sessions. A recent development entails the entire family participating in a therapy session as a unit.

Innovations in the psychodynamic approach are being explored. One such change finds the trained psychotherapist serving as a consultant and directing a nonformally trained therapist (such as the classroom teacher), who actually carries out the therapy. Psychologists, especially those working in the schools, have been particularly inclined to recommend the treatment of learning disabilities by remedial educational methods.

Wider application of the less conventional forms of psychotherapy has been urged by Cohn (1964) and by Bower (1966). They point out that since specific causes of learning disabilities are generally not known, treatment must necessarily be nonspecific. An approach that emphasizes support and assistance for the child to grow and develop in ways consistent with his intact abilities is more promising than one that insists on the child giving up self-respect and security to correct his disabilities by conventional psychotherapy procedures.

The Psychoeducational Approach

Characteristics.   Relatively new but growing in acceptance is the psychoeducational approach to specific learning disabilities. Perhaps the most comprehensive list of deficits indicative of a specific learning disability from this point of view is that presented by Bateman (1964). The list organizes the skills and abilities maximally called upon in ordinary classroom learning into four main groups:

1. Sensory Skills
   a. Auditory and visual perception.
   b. Visual and auditory discrimination.
   c. Auditory and visual fusion.
   d. Visual and auditory memory.
   e. Kinesthetic sensitivity.
2. Motor Skills
   a. Eye-hand coordination.
   b. Laterality.
   c. Perceptual speed and tracking.
3. Language Skills
   a. Temporal sequencing.
   b. Verbal facility.
   c. Language comprehension.
4. Association Skills
   a. Selective capacity for attending.
   b. Auditory-visual association.
   c. Spatial orientation.

It is of interest that these characteristics have evolved primarily from the observation and comment of educators, those professional persons most involved in dealing with specific learning disabilities. There is less emphasis on "personality" traits such as hyperactivity, negativism, distractibility, or impulsiveness, which are apparently of greater significance to adherents of the psychoneurological and psychodynamic approaches. The diffcrences in emphasis may be a reflection of the teacher's interest in identifying what skills the child does have for learning rather than those he does not have.

Another difference is the specificity with which the learning disability is described. This feature contrasts especially with the rather general classifications, such as "emotional instability" or "motor incoordination," which have a major position in other lists of learning disability characteristics. These disabilities are so explicit as to make it unlikely that they would be recognized by parents or other professional persons (physicians, psychologists) without a considerable familiarity with classroom learning activities.

Etiological Considerations.   There is a common belief that "diagnosis" consists of a search for the cause of a disability. Diagnosis, in such a limited sense, reflects the medical model and its concern for specific etiologies. The psychoeducational differs most from other approaches in that there is a minimal interest in the cause of a disability. Etiology is presumed to be related to an essential experience that has somehow been missed, and diagnosis is to be understood as a detailed description of a disability. Reliance is placed on being able to identify and describe behavioral deficits sufficiently and then to prescribe appropriate correction by direct training or by compensatingly drawing upon other skills and abilities. A psychoeducational diagnostic statement such as "reading disability associated with auditory memory deficit" implies that there is a correlational rather than a causal relationship between the reading problem and the auditory defect. As Bateman (1964) has stated, "The very fact that we cannot exchange parents or repair damaged brains has led to the present-day concern of many with behavioral and symptomatic rather than pathological or etiological factors."

The most substantial support for the position of the psychoeducational approach comes from studies of learning. It has been repeatedly demonstrated that performance can be shaped or altered, a task can be successfully completed, without detailed knowledge of the learner's nervous system or his remote prior experiences. Although from a practical point of view there is little attention given to original causes, suggestions as to the causes may be implied in correlates included in the description of the disability. It is assumed that somewhere there has been inadequate opportunity for learning. It may be noted, for example, that the child who has an inability to maintain correct verb tenses has limited language stimulation in his home, or poor auditory discrimination, or temporal confusion.

Pragmatically, the deemphasis on usual etiological considerations has been reinforced by the observation that successful educational treatment of a disability seems to be unrelated to its supposed cause. The remedial teacher has about equal success with those children who have hostile uncooperative attitudes toward reading, who have minimal brain dysfunction, or who have visual sequencing deficits. Even the most exhaustive diagnostic study frequently produces only implicit etiological factors, which can seldom be verified. The teacher is still faced with the problem of having to provide learning experiences with which the child can be successful. Etiological correlates are deemed useful only insofar as they contribute to the planning of appropriate educational experiences.

Assessment Procedures. The identification of a specific learning disability with the psychoeducational approach entails obtaining evidence of specific lack of attainment in view of other indications of normal general ability in intelligence, vision, hearing, and locomotion. Even though the focus is on the current functioning capacity rather than on an extensive history of the nature of the previous adjustment, mental retardation, severe social or emotional disorder, and major physical handicaps (orthopedic, blind, deaf) must be ruled out. This is not to deny that some children in some of these categories (mentally retarded, emotionally disturbed, blind, and so on) may have specific learning disabilities. Rather the concern is for making the most effective educational placement.

Specific learning disabilities are identified on the basis of interpretations made of the child's functioning as observed in a variety of performance situations. The diagnostic study is directed to providing an educationally useful description of the disability. It is often carried out by a psychologist or a remedial educational specialist. The assessment must frequently make use of nonstandardized or informal techniques and procedures.

Standardized measuring scales developed for normal groups are seldom suitable for the evaluation of children with specific learning disabilities. For example, a child with a suspected learning disability may be shown, one at a time, a series of words of varying complexity. He is allowed to look at each word for a fixed time and then asked to write the word from memory. He may be asked to tell what was said as the examiner sounds out the phonic elements of words (m-e, t-o-p). The interpretation of performance elicited by such techniques places considerable demand upon the ingenuity and experience of the diagnostician. Fortunately, the number of standardized psychoeducational measuring scales suitable for this detailed assessment is increasing, although they tend to be limited to the evaluation of skills required for reading. Those currently available include the Illinois Test of Psycholinguistic Abilities, Frostig Developmental Test of Visual Perception, Kephart Perceptual Rating Scale, Parson's Language Scale, Minnesota Percepto-Diagnostic Test (Fuller & Laird, 1969), and Wepman Auditory Discrimination Scale.

When assessed from the psychoeducational point of view, the child with a specific learning disability is likely to be described in educationally relevant terms. The disability is described in terms of impairments to achievement in basic areas of academic attainment such as writing, arithmetic, reading, remembering, listening, and communicating. This tendency represents a significant step in recognizing the potential the school holds with respect to the correction of specific learning disabilities.

Treatment Approaches. Although not a new approach to the correction of learning disabilities, the psychoeducational method of treatment has gained increased acceptance. The application of educational training has been underscored by practioners who believe in the positive role of experience in the development of abilities. Advances and improvements in other aspects of society are analogously to be observed in the educational system. More reliable psychoeducational measuring devices, the addition of other professional specialists in support of the classroom teacher, and the development of many ingenious methods and materials for instruction have extended the school's capability for dealing with all problems. To further this effort, preventive oriented programs have been developed for the early identification of specific learning disabilities as discussed in Chapter 13.

The psychoeducational approach includes diagnostic study, treatment, and follow-up evaluation of the pupil. Specialists trained in fields other than education, such as nurses, speech therapists, social workers, counselors, psychologists, and physicians may assume significant roles in the diagnosis and evaluation. The actual treatment is provided in the main by such educational specialists as special remedial teachers and regular classroom teachers. Speech therapists, social workers, and psychologists may participate in lesser degrees.

The special teacher is likely to work with a pupil on a one-to-one basis, or with very small groups homogeneously placed on the basis of common educational disabilities, presenting a sequence of experiences that have been individually planned for the pupils. Some major areas of concentration advocated by specialists in the field are:

1. Motor Development (Barsch, 1967; Kephart, 1971).
2. Perceptual Training (Frostig, Lefever, & Whittlesey, 1961; Wepman, 1960; Getman, Kane, Halgren, & McKee, 1968).
3. Language Training (Dunn & Smith, 1966; Minskoff, Wiseman, & Minskoff, 1972).
4. Concept Formation by Motor-Perceptual-Language Integration (Strauss & Lehtiner, 1947; Gellner, 1959; Epps, McCannon, & Simmons, 1958).
5. Reading Skill (Bond & Tinker, 1973; Harris, 1970).
6. Stimulus Control (Bender, 1956; Strauss & Lehtiner, 1947).

Some workers attempt to correct a disability by direct training of the deficit; others prefer to present a task in a way that is consistent with the identified strengths of the pupil. Yet another technique entails strengthening deficits by associating them with stronger abilities. The actual training experiences presented to any one pupil are geared to the pupil's particular learning disabilities and assets and are therefore individual and unique. There is no research evidence at this time to indicate the superiority of any one method. Several sets of general guidelines are available for planning an educational treatment program. Those suggested by remedial-reading specialists (Bond & Tinker, 1973; Harris, 1970) are perhaps the most detailed. Others warranting consideration, although in some instances less specific, have been proposed by Frostig, Lefever, & Whittlesey (1961), Hewett & Forness (1974), Kephart (1971), Whelan & Haring (1966).

Critical Evaluation of Approaches

The major approaches to the treatment of specific learning disabilities have been outlined according to the etiology emphasized. Since all three are widely used, a critical appraisal of each approach can serve to clarify the inherent limitations and applicability. They will be contrasted from the standpoint of evidence supporting the rationale, principal inadequacies, and general effectiveness for correcting learning disabilities.

The Psychoneurological Approach

Rationale and Supporting Evidence.   When the problem of brain damage and resulting behavioral deficits is examined, the key question is the relationship between performance and neuroanatomical structure. The psychoneurological approach assumes that behavioral functions are carried out under the direction of localized cerebral centers. It is generally accepted that the brain does indeed carry out coordinating and directive activities. Unfortunately, even when a deficit is identified, it is not possible to verify actual brain injury. The data from which localization of function is assumed are sparse and mostly obtained from adults. Inferences following injuries, postmortem investigations, observation of electrical stimulation, the effects of drugs, and examination of infrahuman animals are the principal sources of information about the brain.

Although the available data may be interpreted as suggesting a general localization of cerebral function, the picture is by no means consistent. The assessment procedures are as yet gross, and relatively little specific information regarding brain functions has been discovered. The amount of damage and the child's developmental status at the time of injury may be more important than the locus of the injury. Complex types of performance may be more impaired by any injury than are simple automatic types of performance (Teuber, Battersby, & Bender, 1951). Maher (1966) observed that a cerebral injury might result in temporary losses that disappear after a time, or that disabilities might suddenly appear long after an injury was incurred. The situation is well summarized by Eisenberg's comment, "Thus, knowledge of the relation between nervous structure and function, however useful it may be, cannot suffice for an understanding of the problems of the brain-damaged child" (Eisenberg, 1957, p. 74).

Major Inadequacies.   Numerous studies indicate that information collected in the psychoneurological assessment tends to be unreliable. Concern for making a diagnosis and ascertaining the cause of the disability, typical of the psychoneurological approach, does result in labeling the condition. But diagnoses expressed in such ambiguous terms as dyslexia, aphasia, or agraphia have limited utility, even in communication with other medical specialists who may respond with equally nonspecific treatment, including indiscriminate use of medications. In practice, then, adherents of the psychoneurological approach have inconsistently followed an eclectic approach of a behavioral emphasis focusing on psychoeducational management. Illustrative of the difficulty is Cohn's (1964) discussion of the tendency to explain learning disabilities as "minimal brain damage." Cohn (1964) cited three reasons contraindicating such a position:

1. The signs and symptoms are only qualitative indicators.
2. Minimal clinical signs have not been neuropathologically demonstrated to be related to minimal brain pathology.
3. The type of clinical signs elicited has been found to depend on the basic philosophy of the examining neurologist.

Cohn, who has had extensive experience and follow-up observation of schoolchildren with neurological damage, believes that, to be useful, neurological evaluation should identify those sensory and motor channels that can be used in learning.

General Effectiveness.   The psychoneurological approach has only limited efficacy. The mere labeling of a condition is, in itself, of no real therapeutic value. To be useful, the diagnosis must suggest treatment procedures. Frequently, no medications, surgical interventions, or corrective prostheses are implied by diagnoses of learning disabilities made by the neurologist. As a group, physicians have generally been slow to appreciate the possible corrective benefit of special training to correct a disability. Even when special training is considered, there may be no way to coordinate this treatment. The cost of treatment suggested by neurological evaluation varies from moderate to so expensive as to be prohibitive for most families.

Even otherwise highly competent and well-trained neurologists may consider only gross performance in making an evaluation. It is a rare neurologist, for example, who is trained to assess in detail the child's capacity for learning to read. When effective, treatment prescribed in the psychoneurological approach can result in dramatic improvement which tends to be permanent. When ineffectual, it is likely to be lengthy, expensive, and entail certain discomfort and risk for the patient.

The Psychodynamic Approach

Rationale and Supporting Evidence.   The psychodynamic approach to specific learning disabilities holds that any impairment in functioning mirrors impairments in the individual's experience. Although deficiencies in the number and quality of objects and situations to which an individual is exposed are recognized, particular significance is given to deficits in relationships with other people. Experiences that are so intense as to be overwhelming, experiences that have inadequate or inappropriate consequences, or no experience may all lead to deficits. These deficiencies in experience are difficult to identify, and their influence on behavior is not easy to demonstrate. Existing psychological measuring devices have a marked inability to differentiate low achievement associated with brain injury from low achievement due to social and emotional maladjustment or to mental retardation (Yates, 1954; Klebanoff, Singer, & Wilensky, 1964). Factors identified as contributing to a disability are thus vague and not readily verifiable. The same experience may facilitate or impair performance. A child deprived of the rewards associated with a comfortable, happy home may either work harder or give up.

Major Inadequacies.   Adherents of the psychodynamic approach are likely to waste many hours in an exacting diagnostic study that only identifies possible causes. When identified, these are, moreover, historical and cannot be directly changed. McWilliams (1965) has described the psychodynamic approach to diagnosis as more a matter of ruling out rather than of finding etiological factors. Lack of an adequate personality theory and the interrelatedness of performance and ability contribute to superficial and circular explanations of disabilities. Some of the ineffectiveness of this approach is illustrated in a study of the value of psychiatric consultation with teachers regarding the referral of students with specific learning disabilities. Case findings were made available to teachers for only 40% of the students referred, and in less than half of these the findings were not considered by the teachers to be of any assistance in their work with children (Nichol, 1974).

Deficits are frequently pictured as resulting from multiple causes. Although Bond & Tinker (1973) believe that emotional maladjustments tend to be consequences of deficit-induced failures, they admit also that failures in performance may result in emotional maladjustment. This same entangling of maladjustment and reading disabilities was found by Davie, Butler & Goldstein (1972). It is puzzling to find that treating either the disability or the emotional problem leads to improvement in performance. Treatment of the emotional aspects of a disability seems to take longer to show improvement in performance than does direct treatment of the disability, possibly because remediation will ordinarily provide more immediate and tangible success experiences.

General Effectiveness. The psychodynamic approach is regarded as being moderately successful in correcting specific learning disabilities. Despite comprehensive diagnostic study and extensive use of measuring devices, evaluations of the efficacy of treatment give somewhat confusing results. The outcome is about equally effective when the child is seen alone, when only the parent is seen, or when both parent and child are seen. The same is true whether play therapy, psychoanalysis, or counseling is used. Follow-up evaluation of therapeutic outcomes is complicated by the lack of precise statements of causal factors and because the influence of the causal factors is difficult to prove or disprove.

The detailed psychodynamic evaluation is time-consuming and can be relatively expensive. It tends to provide a picture emphasizing the individual's deficits and may thus be threatening and undermining to the child. The psychodynamic approach can contribute to the fragmentation approach, cautioned against by Bower (1966). The child can be confused by treatment given by a team of specialists who communicate minimally among themselves when no one assumes responsibility for coordinating the treatment program. On the other hand, psychodynamic evaluations are couched in general traits, such as negativistic, inattentive, or hyperactive. These are moderately useful educationally and serve to communicate meaningfully even though they do not suggest much in the way of specific corrective training.

The Psychoeducational Approach

Rationale and Supporting Evidence. The psychoeducational approach seems at first blush to be highly pragmatic. If it has a rationale, it is the belief that each child must be provided with opportunities to promote the maximum development of his abilities. The realities of life are such that each person must acquire ways of meeting the demands and expectations society makes. Success with one type of task is likely to be followed by success in dealing with another type of task. That capacity for learning and performing can be improved with training is suggested by studies investigating effects of early stimulation and deprivation on future performance.

Training is the chief concern of the school. There has been an implicit acceptance of the impossibility of redoing the child's past experiences and a commitment to working with the pupil as he is. This view has led to the recognition that each pupil brings assets and deficits for new learning experiences. Although much of the educational training is provided in a group organization, there has been an increasing awareness of the necessity for matching individuality of capacity with individuality of instruction. This trend has made it more important to carry out an educational diagnosis that identifies in detail the pupil's potential for education. To some extent, the psychoeducational approach may be said to emphasize learning abilities rather than learning disabilities.

Major Inadequacies. Some of the inadequacies associated with the psychoeducational approach to specific learning disabilities can be attributed to past reluctance to become more actively involved in providing training. The potential of education has been more acknowledged than made use of. Educational offerings, presented in the curriculum, have been very general and geared to the majority two-thirds of pupils. Necessary diversification from formal academic instruction to include motor development, perceptual training, concept formation, and stimulus control has created organizational problems. Sometimes there is no administrative supervisor who can pull these varied activities into a coordinated sequence. Follow-up of pupils who are provided with these services is often lacking.

Related to the organizational difficulties associated with providing educational programs for specific learning disabilities are problems related to personnel for staffing such programs. Effective educational treatment requires specially trained teachers who must have support and assistance from psychologists, physicians, nurses, social workers, and guidance counselors. Of practical importance is the availability of assessment and remedial materials that are sufficiently specific for identifying and correcting particular disabilities. The lack of organized coordination, properly trained staff, and adequate assessment and instructional materials may contribute to the overlooking of critical factors of a medical or home and family nature. Although probably infrequent, when they exist such factors should have appropriate correction in order to facilitate the educational treatment.

General Effectiveness. Although not free of all problems, the psychoeducational approach promises a highly favorable way for correcting specific learning disabilities. It has the advantage of being only a particular extension of educational activities already established. Thus it can minimize a pupil's impression of being singled out or embarrassingly put on the spot. The pupil is better able to see the direct benefit of his treatment, and improvement in his performance can bring immediate rewards from many sources—classmates, teachers, and parents.

Increasing assuredness on the part of the school as to its effectiveness in correcting learning disabilities can only enhance the psychoeducational approach. The cost of remedial programs is much less expensive than psychoneurological or psychodynamic treatment programs. The educational diagnoses of specific learning disabilities, expressed as visual-memory deficit, auditory-discrimination disability, and such, are readily translated into educational programs. Better administrative organization, refinement of diagnostic techniques, a greater number of specially trained teachers, and earlier intervention will make the psychoeducational approach even more telling.

Outcomes of Psychoeducationally Oriented Treatment

One of the most comprehensive long-term study of pupils with specific learning disabilities is reported by Koppitz (1971), and details outcomes for a group of 177 children as observed over a 5-year period. The children were served in special classes by a large cooperative special education program in New York, which included thirteen rural, suburban, and small-town community school districts, a total school population of approximately 50,000 pupils. As might be anticipated in consideration of the diagnostic difficulties in identifying specific learning disabilities and in view of the possibility for specific learning disabilities to exist concurrently with other impairing conditions, the number of children with uncomplicated learning disabilities in the group is questionable. For example, 26 were hospitalized for psychiatric treatment, another 38 dropped out (withdrew, moved, transferred to other programs), while 27 were essentially educationally mentally retarded. After 5 years, 42 pupils had been returned to regular classes and 71 remained in special classes. It is possible that only 63 of the original group (177 pupils) for which complete follow-up information was reported were "pure" specific learning-disabilities cases.

The presence of these diagnostic difficulties tends to add to rather than to detract from the importance of the study, which should be examined in detail by everyone concerned with specific learning disabilities. Dr. Koppitz draws a number of conclusions from her experience, the most profound of which centers about the fact that a sizable group (about 40%) of the pupils studied made little academic achievement gains after the first 3 years of being provided the best known services. For this "unimproved" group, it is stressed that new and alternative instructional methods (audio and video taping, demonstration models), different from traditional techniques anchored in mastery of reading, writing, and arithmetic, must be found in order to enable these disabled pupils to learn in the classroom. Whereas other studies have also not been highly encouraging with regard to the outcomes of educationally oriented intervention with learning disabled children (Serwer, Shapiro, & Shapiro, 1973; Silverberg, Iversen, & Goins, 1973; Hammill & Larsen, 1974; Eaves & Crichton, 1974–75), most practitioners continue to stress the need for instruction tailored to the child's specific educational strengths and weaknesses. Whether the disquieting findings are due to (a) the severity of the problem in the populations studied, (b) the invalidity of diagnostic measures used, (c) the inadequacy inherent in the remediation effort, or (d) the possibility that the disabilities treated are either untrainable or highly resistant to training is not clear at this time (Hammill & Larsen, 1974).

Future Trends

It seems that interest in the alleviation of specific learning disabilities will increase. The coming together of various specialists dealing with these problems will improve communication and promote an exchange of ideas. New understanding of relationships, more acceptance of responsibility by schools, and successes with existing methods will encourage the continuation of these same procedures. Advances will be made in all areas for dealing with specific learning disabilities. New medications, surgical methods, and therapeutic techniques will be developed, but the greatest progress is anticipated in education. Educational programs, supported by psychoneurological and psychodynamic advances, bid to become the major treatment procedures.

As operated by the schools, educational programs will provide for systematic identification by group screening of pupils. Treatment results will be regularly evaluated by routine follow-up of pupils served. Teachers especially trained for correcting specific learning disabilities will draw on particular techniques and measuring scales. Applications of procedures adapted from behavior-modification findings and measurement devices, such as the Illinois Test of Psycholinguistic Abilities and the Frostig Developmental Test of Visual Perception, already show considerable promise. Diagnosis and treatment will be closely integrated, with treatment being initiated at a much earlier time, perhaps eventually on a preventative basis in the form of intensive preschool readiness training. The key to making these developments possible rests in the formulation of an acceptable organizational plan that will supply necessary administrative control for the educational management of specific learning disabilities.

There are indications that some of these trends are becoming actualities. Agreements reached by a joint committee from the United States Office of Education and the Council for Exceptional Children assigned greater responsibility for the treatment of children with specific learning disabilities to the schools. Following the work of the committee, there has been a noticeable increase in the number of such programs in the schools.

Summary

Specific learning disabilities are manifest as particular impairments in performance. The disability persists in the presence of indications of average or better general ability.

Examples are inabilities to remember, to make visual or auditory differentiations, to follow usual patterns for sequential arrangement of words in a sentence, to keep the orientation of geometric figures, to carry out a series of arithmetical operations, or to copy letters in the spatially correct form.

Generally limited to a single area (motor, visual, auditory, emotional), they may take the form of deficits in integrating two major areas, such as visual-motor association or auditory-motor association disabilities.

Learning disabilities must be differentiated from mental retardation, social and emotional maladjustment, and language, hearing, or visual defects. A specific learning disability is a limited deficit.

Typically seen as a reading problem in school-aged children, the impairment in performance has accompanying feelings of failure and frustration that can contribute to or speed up the development of a more severe behavior disorder.

Learning disabilities reach a peak incidence in the primary grades and are much more prevalent in boys than in girls.

Although constitutional defects, emotional blockings, and faulty training experiences are frequently cited as having etiological significance, the actual causes of specific learning disabilities are not agreed upon.

Because of the uncertain origins, the evaluation of specific learning disabilities requires extensive diagnostic exploration and the compilation of findings made by physicians, audiologists, social workers, nurses, teachers, and psychologists.

The correction of specific learning disabilities has important consequences for rendering the individual more adequate and effectively able to profit from new learning opportunities. Medical procedures, parental support, and individual counseling are often part of treatment approaches.

Remedial education is being increasingly used as a correctional procedure.

The possibility for correction by educational training has served to focus attention on the early identification of specific learning disabilities and on the development of efficient group preventive methods.

Long-term follow-up studies indicate that a sizable group of pupils are not appreciably helped by conventional educational treatment methods.

References

Ames, L. A low intelligence quotient often not recognized as the chief cause of many learning difficulties. *Journal of Learning Disabilities*, 1968, **1**, 45–58.
Asbury, C. A. Selected factors influencing over and under achievement in young school age children. *Review of Educational Research*, 1974, **44**, 409–28.

Bakwin, H. Cerebral damage and behavior damage in children. *Journal of Pediatrics*, 1949, **34**, 371.

Bakwin, H., & Bakwin, R. M. *Behavior disorders in children*, 4th ed. Philadelphia, Pa.: Saunders, 1972.

Barsch, R. *Achieving perceptual-motor efficiency*. Seattle: Special Child, 1967.

Bateman, B. Learning disabilities—yesterday, today and tomorrow. *Exceptional Children*, 1964, **31**, 167–78.

Bender, L. *Psychopathology of children with organic brain disorders*. Springfield, Ill.: Thomas, 1956.

Berlyne, D. Emotional aspects of learning. *Annual Review of Psychology*, 1964, **15**, 115–42.

Bond, G. F., & Tinker, M. A. *Reading difficulties: their diagnosis and correction*. New York: Appleton-Century-Crofts, 1973.

Bower, E. M. The psychologist in the schools. Paper read at meeting of Illinois Psychological Association, Chicago, October, 1966.

Brophy, J., & Good, T. *Teacher-student relationships*. New York: Holt, Rinehart, and Winston, 1974.

Bryan, T. H. Learning disabilities: A new stereotype. *Journal of Learning Disabilities*. 1974a, **7**, 304–9.

Bryan, T. H. Peer popularity of learning disabled children. *Journal of Learning Disabilities*, 1974b, **7**, 10–31.

Bryan, T. H., & Bryan, J. H. *Understanding learning disabilities*. Port Washington, N.Y.: Alfred Publishing Company, 1975.

Burks, H. F. The hyperkinetic child. *Exceptional Children*, 1960, **27**, 18–26.

Campbell, S. B. Mother-child interaction: A comparison of hyperactive, learning disabled, and normal boys. *American Journal of Orthopsychiatry*, 1975, **45**, 51–74.

Clements, S. D. *Minimal brain dysfunction in children*. Washington, D.C.: National Institute of Neurological Diseases and Blindness, 1966.

Cohn, R. The neurological study of children with learning disabilities. *Exceptional Children*, 1964, **31**, 179–86.

Davie, R., Butler, N., & Goldstein, H. *From birth to seven*. London, England: Longman, 1972.

Dunn, L., & Smith, J. *Peabody language development kits*. Circle Pines, Minn.: American Guidance Services, 1966.

Eaves, L. C., & Crichton, J. U. A five-year follow-up of children with minimal brain dysfunction. *Academic Therapy*, 1974–75, **10**, 173–79.

Eisenberg, L. Psychiatric implications of brain damage in children. *Psychiatric Quarterly*, 1957, **31**, 72–92.

Eisenberg, L. The sins of the fathers: urban decay and social pathology. *American Journal of Orthopsychiatry*, 1962, **32**, 5–17.

Epps, H. O., McCannon, G., & Simmons, Q. D. *Teaching devices for children with impaired learning: a study of the brain-injured child from research project fifty at the Columbus State School*. Columbus: Ohio School for Retarded Children, 1958.

Frostig, M., Lefever, D. W., & Whittlesey, J. R. B. A developmental test of visual perception for evaluating normal and neurologically handicapped children. *Perceptual and Motor Skills*, 1961, **12**, 383–94.

Fuller, G., & Laird, J. Minnesota Percepto-Diagnostc Test. *Journal of Clinical Psychology*, Monograph Supplement No. 16, 1969, Vol. 39.

Gellner, L. *A neurophysiological concept of mental retardation and its educational implications.* Chicago: J. Lewinson Research Foundation, 1959.

Getman, G. N., Kane, E. R., Halgren, M. R., & McKee, G. W. *Developing learning readiness.* Manchester, Missouri: McGraw-Hill Webster Division, 1968.

Gross, M., & Wilson, W. *Minimal brain dysfunction.* New York: Bruner Mazel, 1974.

Hagin, R. Models of intervention with learning disabilities; ephemeral and otherwise. *School Psychologist Monograph*, 1973, **1**, 1–25.

Hammill, D., & Larsen, S. The relationship of selected auditory perceptual skills and reading ability. *Journal of Learning Disabilities*, 1974, **7**, 429–35.

Harris, A. J. *How to increase reading ability.* 5th ed. New York: David McKay, 1970.

Hewett, F. M., & Forness, S. R. *Education of exceptional learners.* Boston: Allyn & Bacon, 1974.

Hobbs, N. *The futures of children.* San Francisco: Jossey-Bass, 1975.

Keough, B. Hyperactivity and learning disorders: Review and speculation. *Exceptional Children*, 1971, **38**, 101–9.

Kephart, N. C. *The slow learner in the classroom*, 2nd ed., Columbus, Ohio: Merrill, 1971.

Kessler, J. W. *Psychopathology of childhood.* Englewood Cliffs, N.J.: Prentice-Hall, 1966.

Klebanoff, S. G., Singer, J. L., & Wilensky, H. Psychological sequences of brain lesion and ablations. *Psychological Bulletin*, 1954, **51**, 1–41.

Kline, C. L., & Lee, N. A. transcultural study of dyslexia. *Journal of Special Education*, 1972, **6**, 9–26.

Koppitz, E. M. *Children with learning disabilities.* New York: Grune & Stratton, 1971.

McCarthy, J., & Kirk, S. *Illinois test of psycholinguistic abilities.* Institute for Research on Exceptional Children, University of Illinois, 1963.

Maccoby, E., & Jacklin, C. *The psychology of sex differences.* Stanford, Calif.: Stanford University Press, 1974.

McIntosh, D., & Dunn, L. Children with specific learning disabilities. In L. Dunn (Ed.), *Exceptional children in the schools.* New York: Holt, Rinehart, and Winston, 1973.

McWilliams, B. J. The language-handicapped child and education. *Exceptional Children*, 1965, **32**, 221–28.

Maher, B. A. *Principles of psychopathology.* New York: McGraw-Hill, 1966.

Mesinger, J. F. Emotionally disturbed and brain-injured children—should we mix them? *Exceptional Children*, 1965, **32**, 237–38.

Minskoff, E., Wiseman, D., & Minskoff, G. *The MWM program for development of language abilities.* Ridgefield, N.J.: Educational Performance Associates, 1972.

Myklebust, H. R., & Johnson, D. Dyslexia in children. *Exceptional Children*, 1962, **29**, 14–25.

Nichol, H. Children with learning disabilities referred to psychiatrists: A follow-up study. *Journal of Learning Disabilities*, 1974, **7**, 64–68.

Orton, S. T. "Word blindness" in school children. *Archives of Neurology and Psychiatry*, 1925, **14**, 581–615.

Pasamanick, B., & Knobloch, H. Retrospective studies on the epidemiology of reproductive causality: Old and new. *Merrill-Palmer Quarterly of Behavior and Development,* 1966, **12,** 7–23.

Peck, B. D., & Stackhouse, T. W. Reading problems and family dynamics. *Journal of Learning Disabilities,* 1973, **6,** 43–48.

Peters, J. E., Davis, J. S., Goolsby, C. M., & Clements, S. D. *Physicians handbook for screening for minimal brain dysfunction.* New York: CIBA Medical Horizons, 1973.

Reading disorders in the United States. Report of the Secretary's National Advisory Committee on Dyslexia and Related Reading Disorders. Washington, D.C.: U.S. Department of Health, Education and Welfare, 1969.

Reitan, R. Assessment of brain-behavior relationships. In P. McReynolds (Ed.), *Advances in psychological assessment.* San Francisco: Jossey-Bass, 1975, pp. 186–224.

Schroeder, L. B. A study of the relationships between five categories of emotional disturbance and reading and arithmetic achievement. *Exceptional Children,* 1965, **32,** 111–12.

Serwer, B. L., & Shapiro, B. J., & Shapiro, P. P. The comparative effectiveness of four methods of instruction on the achievement of children with specific learning disabilities. *Journal of Special Education,* 1973, **7.**

Silverberg, N. E., Iversen, I. A., & Goins, J. T. Which remedial reading method works best? *Journal of Learning Disabilities,* 1973, **6,** 547–55.

Stewart, M., Palkes, H., Miller, R., Young, C., & Welner, Z. Intellectual ability and school achievement of hyperactive children, their classmates, and their siblings. In D. Richs & M. Roff (Eds.), *Life history research in psychopathology,* Vol. 3. Minneapolis: University of Minnesota Press, 1974.

Stone, B. F., & Rowley, V. N. Educational disability in emotionally disturbed children. *Exceptional Children,* 1964, **30,** 423–26.

Strauss, A. A., & Lehtiner, L. E. *Psychopathology and education of the brain-injured child.* Vol. I. New York: Grune & Stratton, 1947.

Strother, C. R. *Discovering, evaluating, programming for the neurologically handicapped child with special attention to the child with minimal brain damage.* Chicago: National Society for Crippled Children and Adults, 1963.

Tarver, S. G., & Hallahan, D. P. Attention deficits in children with learning disabilities: A review. *Journal of Learning Disabilities,* 1974, **7,** 560–68.

Teuber, H. L., Battersby, W. S., & Bender, M. B. The performance of complex visual tasks after cerebral lesions. *Journal of Nervous and Mental Disorders,* 1951, **114,** 413–29.

Walker, S. Drugging the American child. *Psychology Today,* 1974, **7,** 43–48.

Weiner, I. Psychodynamic aspects of learning disability: The passive-aggressive underachiever. *Journal of School Psychology,* 1971, **9,** 246–51.

Weisskopf, E. Intellectual malfunctioning and personality. *Journal of Abnormal and Social Psychology,* 1951, **46,** 410–23.

Wender, P. *Minimal brain dysfunction in children.* New York: Wiley, 1971.

Wepman, J. M. Auditory discrimination, speech, and reading. *Elementary School Journal,* 1960, **9,** 325–33.

Werry, J., & Sprague, R. Hyperactivity. In C. Costello (Ed.), *Symptoms of psychopathology.* New York: Wiley, 1969.

Whelan, R. J., & Haring, N. E. Modification and maintenance of behavior through systematic application of consequences. *Exceptional Children,* 1966, **32,** 281–90.

Yates, A. J. The validity of some psychological tests of brain damage. *Psychological Bulletin*, 1954, **51**, 359–79.

Suggested Readings

Bryan, T. H., & Bryan, J. H. *Understanding learning disabilities.* Port Washington, N.Y.: Alfred Publishing Company, 1975.

Gardner, R. *MBD: The family book about minimal brain dysfunction.* New York: Aronson, 1973.

Hammill, D. D., & Bartel, N. R. *Educational perspectives in learning disabilities.* New York: Wiley, 1974.

Johnson, D. J., & Myklebust, H. P. *Learning disabilities.* New York: Grune & Stratton, 1967.

Lerner, J. W. *Children with learning disabilities: Theories, diagnosis, and teaching strategies.* New York: Houghton-Mifflin, 1971.

Mann, P., & Suiter, P. *Handbook in diagnostic teaching: A learning disabilities approach.* Boston, Mass.: Allyn & Bacon, 1974.

Potter, T. C., & Rae, G. *Informal reading diagnosis.* Englewood-Cliffs, N.J.: Prentice-Hall, 1974.

Mental
Subnormality

Mental subnormality is not a uniform condition. Rather it is one characterized by heterogeneity and variation. Work with the mentally subnormal has contributed significantly to the understanding of all behavior deviations. The condition of mental subnormality is one of the oldest concerns for those who deal with adjustment difficulties. Descriptions of individuals slow to comprehend who required multiple attempts in order to acquire only borderline coping skills are to be found in all cultural groups. In years past, these simple persons were often victimized and sometimes dealt with inhumanely by other members of society. Benefactors who sought to intercede and assist these unfortunate individuals initiated trends that paved the way for assisting many persons with behavioral adjustment difficulties. Attempts to intervene by approaches offering nothing more than patience and understanding were ultimately sufficiently successful to contradict former explanations of deviant behavior as the work of demons and evil spirits.

It became apparent that some disorders had obvious constitutional components whereas others seemed to have been acquired. Subnormal mentality was found conjointly with organic defects in some instances, but not in others. Cataloging these observations marked the beginnings of classification systems to encompass all behavior problems. Continued refinement of descriptions of mental retardation established this condition as one peculiar to developmental processes rather than a regressive reaction to adult pressures. This realization provided a basis for viewing children's adjustment difficulties in a different perspective from the pathological conditions of adults.

Overshadowing the question of organic or functional etiology was a rather consistent subpar performance in meeting many everyday life demands, the difficulty showing most clearly in the face of academic demands. This characteristic provided an avenue for developing techniques of identifying the mentally subnormal on the basis of quality of performance in selected situations. The fledgling movement of psychoeducational measurement, which had floundered for many years, was given powerful support by the success of Alfred Binet's measuring scale. Scores from the Binet scale could be used successfully to identify those children whose less-than-average intellectual potential rendered them unable to profit from the usual classroom curriculum. Assessment of intellectual ability continues to be a significant step in identifying mental subnormality.

Physicians were frequently in charge of the management of the mentally subnormal. As might be expected, their concerns focused on the role of constitutional factors. Organic defects identified as having etiological significance in some mentally subnormal persons, such as the blocked cerebral circulation associated with hydrocephaly, were sometimes correctable by surgery. Impaired organic functions, such as the thyroid deficiency condition of cretinism, could sometimes be restored by medication. These findings served to stimulate a continual quest for medical intervention procedures that could be applied to correct behavior deviations. Current lines of interest include studies of the part played by malnutrition and the role of genetic factors in contributing to mental subnormality.

In addition to the medical intervention approaches, interest centered about efforts to control mental subnormality by manipulating the environment. The assumption that mental subnormality is the consequence of inadequate acquisition of necessary experiences suggested two main lines of correction. One approach, illustrated by the classic work of Itard and Sequin, was based on the possibility that there had been a total lack of exposure to most ordinary experiences. A program of intense stimulation was then provided for the individual. The essential role of stimulation in developing capacity for coping is today well accepted and has been extended to form the base of programs for the culturally disadvantaged, as will be seen in the next chapter.

Marty, a Boy Who Is Mentally Retarded

It was a beautiful warm spring day and Marty, a 10-year-old boy, was busily participating in one of his favorite family projects, washing the car. Marty's dad had given Marty the special job of cleaning the auto's wheels, pointing out that Marty was willing to take the time to scrub all the ridges carefully and get the dirt from all the cracks. Hearing his dad say that he was the best, better than his older sister and his younger sister and brother, made Marty feel especially good. Although Marty tried very hard, more so than others it seemed, still he often wound up being less successful than even his younger brother and sister. This was embarrassing to him, and he used to get angry and cry. School was a place where Marty found a lot of things he was unable to do. Despite the fact that he was just as big as other boys and girls in class, he could not read or write his name like the other kids. Sometimes Marty was glad that the teacher did not call on him, but other times he wanted desperately to participate in discussions. If he could just be sure of the things they were talking about. . . . All in all, it seemed much safer to be quiet and try to look busy. Recently, Marty had been attending a new class where there were fewer pupils. Marty still did not really like school and found it difficult to believe his new teacher was really interested in him. His new teacher was in many ways different from his former teachers, and Marty had it over his pesky younger brother now because he had a man teacher, *Mr.* Allen. One day Marty told Mr. Allen that he was not like other teachers, and Mr. Allen started talking, telling Marty that lots of people were different in the way they do things. Marty guessed that the thing he liked best about Mr. Allen was the way he never seemed to be in a hurry. When Marty had trouble doing something, Mr. Allen could help Marty find another way to do it or find some other important job to do. This whole business about arithmetic, for instance, seemed a lot easier since Mr. Allen took the class on a weekend camping trip where the kids had to count out and divide the food and camping equipment. Kids in the other classes didn't think that going on a camping trip was "dumb" or something just for "retards." Marty rewashed a spot on one of the wheels. His dad smiled and nodded approval. Marty thought that someday he might drive a car, maybe even a big bulldozer like his dad. If he could just get through school . . . if he could always have Mr. Allen as his teacher. . . .

A second line of intervention rests on the possibility that the mentally subnormal person encounters adjustment difficulties because of specific experiential deficits. Support for this contention is gained from observations that the mentally subnormal do not do well in certain situations but may be successful in other situations. They may, for example, fail in the face of highly academic demands in the usual school situation but perform satisfactorily in some occupational settings. This approach to correcting adjustment problems capitalizes on identifying the "success-possible situation" and then providing the necessary specific training that will be demanded of the individual. Originated by Goddard at the Vineland Training School, this method is the core of most public-school educational programs for the mentally subnormal.

Conceptions of Mental Subnormality

The core concept of mental subnormality has been that of reduced intellectual ability, less than average mental capacity. The social adjustment difficulties of the mentally subnormal are presumed to be in some way related to their attenuated intellectual powers. The existence of terms such as idiot, feeble-minded, mental deficiency, handicapped, retarded, illustrates the frequent change in names, but the basic concept has remained the same.

The variety of terms encountered raises questions as to their meaning, interchangeability, and applicability. Their existence also suggests that mental subnormality is a condition encompassing a wide range of characteristics capable of being dealt with from a number of perspectives. A look at the program for the American Association for Mental Defiency, a professional organization of persons working with the mentally subnormal, reveals that physicians, social workers, nurses, educators, and psychologists are actively represented. Each of their disciplines has tended to approach the condition of mental subnormality in a particular way, generating concepts, terms, and assumptions useful to their professional orientation. The major approaches have been outlined by MacMillan & Jones (1972):

> *Medical.* Used extensively by physicians, the medical approach has had a wide influence. Focusing on pathology and pathological symptoms, it is especially applicable to the severely subnormal who usually have genetic anomolies, metabolic disorders, or structural damage of the central nervous system. A bi-polar orientation (one is either normal or subnormal), it is less appropriate for the borderline moderately or mildly subnormal who tend to be differentiated on the basis of behavioral rather than pathological symptoms.
>
> *Social-system.* Applied to sociological analyses, this conception of mental subnormality emphasizes the appropriateness of role performance. Status is assigned on the basis of this performance. Persons who appear to cope with demands adequately are regarded as "normal." Failure to fulfill a given role adequately results in reassignment to another status or role

where the person can function more effectively. Mentally subnormal persons then are ones who have been reclassified downward, assigned to less demanding roles in situations where they can function with more success. This loose classification system provides an explanation for some puzzling enigmas, such as the marked variations in the number of persons classed as mentally subnormal in preschool, school, and postschool age periods. It fails to supply the specificity which many persons believe is necessary in order to establish effective prevention and correction procedures for the problem.

Statistical. Popular with educators and psychologists, this approach defines "normal" on the basis of position in a distribution of scores or measures of a specified attribute. Extremes in either a high or low direction are abnormal. If the characteristic measured is of minor social importance, there is little consequence in being at the extreme positions. When the characteristic is highly valued, as is so for intelligence, then value judgments are assigned to persons whose scores fall at extreme positions. The ease with which measurements can be made and the tendency to assign value judgments constitute the advantage and disadvantage of this approach. A low score from a scale measuring intellectual ability can be readily obtained and just as easily equated with values inherent in "bad" or "pathological," despite the fact that no such inference is made by the statistical model itself.

Classifications

Complete description, identification, and record of the course of a behavioral problem is necessary in order to understand and correct a condition. Conflicting with this objectivity are deeply humane considerations. Placing a person in a particular classification may be requisite for obtaining help for the alleviation of the condition, but once a diagnosis has been made, the label tends to stay even though the condition is corrected or is no longer of particular consequence. Mental subnormality can be of special importance in planning educational objectives, but is of little consequence in many vocational choices. In such cases, the stability of a classification is called into question and the possible negative effects must be balanced against the possible favorable outcomes for a given individual.

Single-Group Classifications

The discussion of definitions of mental subnormality has emphasized the presence of less than average intellectual ability, but it is failure to cope with adjustment demands that results in the individual's being identified for study and classification. Individuals were usually not referred for help until they had become enmeshed in a maze of severe adjustment difficulties. Too frequently, "treatment" terminates with diagnostic appraisal. Diagnosticians had little opportunity for continued contacts with persons classed as mentally subnormal and could not predict what optimal adjustments a mentally subnormal person might attain in situations where expectations were reduced.

Diagnostic techniques were gross and unrefined, relying heavily upon results from scales measuring intellectual ability, usually given in the form of a single global score.

It was presumed that all persons with low IQ's experienced chronic adjustment difficulties. There were only limited recommendations that might be offered, such as institutional or special-school placement. The diagnostic appraisal suggested a common predicament of adjustment failures for the mentally subnormal because the individual had less intellectual ability than the situation demanded. It was sufficient to establish that the person had a diminished capacity for meeting demands.

This state of affairs encouraged professional workers to deal with mental subnormality as a general condition. The orientation of the clinician was a manifestation of his particular training. Physicians, accustomed to identifying dysfunctions having physiological or anatomical origins, viewed the problem as a defect of the nervous system and used the term "mental deficiency." Psychologists, trained to evaluate the effectiveness of performance, saw the mentally subnormal as having limited intellectual capacity for meeting many life demands and used the term "mentally handicapped." For the educator, who saw the mentally subnormal child as being slower than average in school progress, the term "mentally retarded" was preferred. Even though all clinicians were aware that the condition existed in varying degrees, not much attention was given to the degree of impairment since the limited choices available for treatment made a qualitative evaluation adequate. The classification terminologies and levels of impairment used in the United States are contrasted in Table 6–1.

The initial terms used to designate degrees of incompetency (idiot, imbecile, moron) have been replaced with severe, moderate, mild, or custodial, trainable, educable. Diagnostic study is carried out by a physician, psychologist, or educator, frequently in collaboration. The diagnostic assessment culminates in the mentally subnormal person's being classified according to the terminology used by the diagnostician's professional discipline.

Table 6–1. **Classification Terms and Levels of Impairment for Mental Subnormality Used by the Medical, Psychological, and Educational Disciplines**

	Medical	*Psychological*	*Educational*	*Associated IQ Range (Approx.)*
Generic term	Mentally deficient	Mentally handicapped	Mentally retarded	
Degree of incapacitation	Mild	Mild	Educable	55–80
	Moderate	Moderate	Trainable	35–55
	Severe	Dependent	Custodial	Below 35

Proposed Two-Group Classification

Continued work with the mentally subnormal generated information that has forced the expansion of the concept to accommodate definable types or subgroups. Differentiating the various kinds of subnormality can order the etiological factors in a clearer perspective and help to indicate which corrective-remedial procedures are likely to be successful for the condition. Sarason & Gladwin (1959), as a result of years of working with and observing the mentally subnormal, came to the conclusion that the field was too heterogeneous to be represented by a single common denominator. They were impressed by observed differences between the subnormal intellectual ability that was a consequence of injury or defect of the central nervous system and that which resulted from cultural-familial forces. Accumulating evidence supports the practice of recognizing two types of mental subnormality which have a small cluster of overlapping characteristics but a larger number of differentiating characteristics.

The necessity for recognizing two types of mental subnormality has a strong advocate in Zigler (1966, 1967). He has presented an impressive case for differentiating one type of mental subnormality as the outcome of a predominantly organic defect. Another type is the consequence of the interaction of familial with psychosocial factors. Even though there are as yet no reliable diagnostic methods for classifying a mentally subnormal person as being of one or the other type, the distinction can conveniently be made on the basis of the individual's history. The identification of specific organic deficits and pathology is largely an unresolved area. The differentiation is useful in present programming and is promising for the future since a complete understanding of etiologies is the only way the condition may eventually be prevented.

Although in practice the terms "mentally deficient" and "mentally retarded," depending upon the practitioner's orientation, are used to refer to all mentally subaverage persons, it is possible in discussion to speak separately of the two types of subnormality. There is, moreover, a certain benefit in maintaining the distinction, for it adds to the understanding of the condition of mental subnormality. Accordingly, this presentation will follow closely the differentiation as outlined by Zigler (1967). The terms "mentally handicapped" and "mental subnormality" will be used in the more general sense, as suggested by Sarason, to include both types or all cases.

Characteristics of the Mentally Deficient (Organic). There are relatively few traits common to all individuals of less than average intelligence. Other than a small cluster centering about comparable scores on measures of intelligence, the picture is confusing. Zigler has suggested that a part of the disagreement can be attributed to the failure to recognize the two types of mental handicap and what he believes to be rather distinctly associated characteristics.

Pointing out that the term "mentally deficient" itself stresses the salient characteristic of this group, that of a physiological or anatomical defect,

Zigler has listed several other distinctive traits. These include a tendency to have a lower degree of measurable intellectual ability (IQ of less than 50) and a high frequency of other physical disabilities including sensory and motor defects. The mentally deficient are inclined to have poorer general health, markedly less stamina, and to appear disjunctive. Their very limited intellectual potential appears to become even more reduced when observed over a long period of time. Poor motor coordination, speech problems, and general frailty predispose the majority of them to a dependent status. Contributing to a generally less favorable outcome for this group is the fact that there are as yet few specific medications or surgical procedures for correcting organic defects of the central nervous system, even when these defects can be identified.

Characteristics of the Mentally Retarded (Familial). Zigler (1966) points out that the chief characteristic of this group is also aptly conveyed by the term "retardation." By way of illustration, he draws upon the analogy of a person who has tuberculosis but may in many situations not be incapacitated. Contending that the mentally retarded may well constitute the lower end of a normal continuum of intellectual ability as represented by a distribution of IQ scores, Zigler holds that the mentally retarded is the larger of the two groups of mentally handicapped. Generally speaking, the mentally retarded include those persons with an IQ from about 50 to 75, although there is some overlap in IQ of the two groups, as is shown in Figure 6-1.

Persons in the mentally retarded group, approximately 75% of all mentally subnormal persons, are very comparable to the average person from

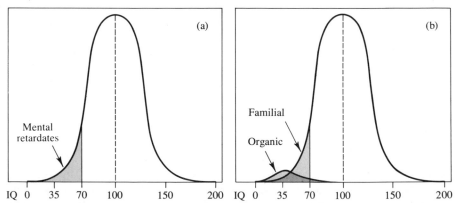

Figure 6–1. (a) Conventional representation of the distribution of intelligence. (b) Distribution of intelligence as represented in the two-group approach. (*Source:* E. Zigler. Familial mental retardation: a continuing dilemma. *Science,* 1967, **155,** 292–98. Copyright 1967 by the American Association for the Advancement of Science.)

whom they differ mostly in degree. Their impairment shows itself most clearly in specific situations demanding a high degree of ability to deal with the abstract. They tend to have good physical health, fair motor coordination, and in general attain an adequate degree of personality integration even though they take longer to realize their potential. Although less persistent, less self-confident, and more dependent, the expectation of eventual self-sufficiency and independent adjustment is justified for these "late bloomers." The mentally retarded, also referred to as the "familial" retarded, and by Sarason as the "garden variety" retarded, as a group make the most promising responses to habilitation programs.

Creating a definition of mental retardation acceptable to all persons who work with the mentally subnormal has been a difficult task. The varied background of professional workers, the necessity for evaluation in different social situations, and the fact that several factors can contribute to mental subnormality have added to the problem. As a way of overcoming some of these differences, representatives from concerned groups have gotten together from time to time and agreed upon a common definition. These conferences have been sanctioned by the American Association for Mental Deficiency (AAMD), and the most recent definition states: "Mental retardation refers to significantly subaverage general intellectual functioning existing concurrently with deficits in adaptive behavior, and manifested during the developmental period" (Grossman, 1973).

As presented in this definition, "mental retardation" refers to behavioral performance, while having no stipulations for etiology or prognosis. The definition requires that intellectual ability and adaptive behavior be considered with equal weight in making a diagnosis. Only persons with demonstrable deficits in both areas are to be classed as mentally retarded.

Intellectual level is to be assessed according to performance on standardized measuring scales, and only those scores two or more standard deviations below the mean are acceptable as "significantly subaverage" (IQs less than 68 for the Binet and 70 for the Wechsler scales). The "developmental period" is specified as the time from birth to age 18 years.

Adaptive behavior, defined as the degree of effectiveness with which the person meets standards for personal independence and social responsibility for his age and cultural group, is the most difficult criterion to ascertain. Impairment in adaptive behavior is evaluated according to a specially constructed scale, the AAMD Adaptive Behavior Domains scale, sampling areas of maturation, learning, and social adjustment. Maturation is understood as the rate of attainment in such sensorimotor skills as sitting, walking, and talking. Learning is interpreted as achievement in the acquisition of academic skills. Social adjustment refers to competency in such aspects of living as personal self-reliance and independence, gainful employment, and the ability to conform to social demands and standards of the community. Behavioral levels are related to age, and result in the evaluated person's being placed in a behavior category of mild, moderate, severe, or profound. The behavioral categories correspond to similar levels of intellectual capacity. Samples of the intellectual and behavioral levels used in classification are shown in Table 6–2.

The definition is commendable in that it seeks to make classification contingent upon several factors, rather than relying on a single characteristic (as,

Table 6–2.   Intellectual and   Behavioral Levels Used in Classification of Mental Retardation[a]

Age and Level Indicated	Illustrations of Highest Level of Adaptive Behavior Functioning
3 years: Mild 6 years: Moderate 9 years: Severe 12 years and above: Profound	*Independent functioning*: Feeds self with spoon (cereals, soft foods) with considerable spilling or messiness; drinks unassisted; can pull off clothing and put on some (socks, underclothes, boxer pants, dress); tries to help with bath or hand washing but still needs considerable help; indicates toilet accident and may indicate toilet need. *Physical*: May climb up and down stairs but not alternating feet; may run and jump; may balance briefly on one foot; can pass ball to others; transfers objects; may do simple form-board puzzles without aid. *Communication*: May speak in two or three word sentences (Daddy go work); name simple common objects (boy, car, ice cream, hat); understands simple directions (put the shoe on your foot, sit here, get your coat); knows people by name. (If nonverbal, may use many gestures to convey needs or other information.) *Social*: May interact with others in simple play activities, usually with only one or two others unless guided into group activity; has preference for some persons over others.

IQ Ranges for Three Frequently Used Intelligence Tests

	Obtained Intelligence Quotient	
Levels	Stanford-Binet and Cattell (s.d. 16)	Wechsler Scales (s.d. 15)
Mild	68–52	69–55
Moderate	51–36	54–40
Severe	35–20	39–25 (Extrapolated)
Profound	19 and below	24 and below (Extrapolated)

[a] From Grossman (1973).

for example, IQ). Requirements of irreversibility and specific etiology, prominent in previous definitions, have been dropped from the new criteria. Possibly the most important aspect of the definition is the fact that a group with diverse training and backgrounds can come to agreement about a complex condition.

Identification

A basic concern for the practitioner is often that of correctly identifying a disorder, since this then suggests the path to be followed in the subsequent management of the condition, including probable response to treatment. In view of the lack of certainty associated with most behavior disorders, there is always a certain amount of controversy as to diagnosis. These exchanges of opinion generally advance the state of knowledge about the condition even though they are sometimes heated. Undoubtedly, the greatest difficulty presented by the AAMD definition is that of ascertaining an impairment in adaptive behavior even though there is general agreement that this is the variable that most often brings the individual to the attention of a professional worker. Impairment in adaptive behavior is contingent upon what demands are made of the individual. Failure in adaptive behavior is characteristic of all behavior disorders. Behavior that is satisfactory (adaptive) in one situation may be unsatisfactory (maladaptive) in another situation, so that even the notion of "adaptive behavior" is itself a loose concept, not easily measured. Measures of intellectual ability, in contrast, can be readily obtained. This has resulted in measures of intellectual ability being given what some contend to be exclusive consideration in the diagnosis of mental subnormality. Clausen (1972) is an advocate for diagnosis of mental subnormality exclusively on the basis of scores from measures of intelligence, arguing that all the other characteristics of mental subnormality are reflected in these scores. There is a certain convenience in accepting an IQ as the explanation of behavior, thus reducing a complex problem to a simple (and measurable) statement. A brief consideration of the enormous differences to be found in persons having the same IQ and the fact that there are no specific behaviors exclusively associated with specific IQs leads back to the same dilemma. The only justifiable position is one that recognizes mental subnormality as a complex condition, the identification of which demands detailed and extensive study, preferably by a team representing various professional specialties

Several methods are followed in arriving at a diagnosis of mental subnormality. They have in common the collection of samples of behavior. The amount and type of data collected is guided by the objective that a diagnosis should present alternatives or suggestions for dealing with the condition. As Leland (1972) has stated it, the ideal diagnosis would identify individuals who are similar in certain aspects of adaptive capability and who are amenable to modification by a given treatment program. Each of the several major approaches used in identifying the mentally subnormal person has advantages as well as limitations. None is free from error. The orientation of the clinician, the purposes of the classification, and the stage of refinement of diagnostic techniques are only a few of the factors influencing identification. In practice, specialists working with the mentally subnormal typically emphasize one or another approach, but most of them consult information collected from several sources before making a final diagnosis. A developmental history, scores from intelligence scales, and school-achievement results are suggested as minimally essential data. Understandably, most specialists defer making a final diagnosis of mental retardation in other than the most severe cases until the child has been observed for several years.

Familial and Developmental History

A carefully compiled account of the individual's development is one of the major aids used in diagnosis. Physicians are particularly likely to rely on this method, which begins by reviewing the adequacy of the adjustment made by parents, siblings, and other near relatives. A majority of the mentally subnormal have close relatives who also are subaverage, and this evidence of familial tendencies can be revealed only in a carefully obtained history. The exploration next considers possible sources of trauma from illnesses and injuries the child may have incurred. Rounding out the history taking is a detailed review of the developmental attainments of the individual.

The mentally subnormal consistently lag in age of sitting up, feeding self, walking, dressing self, talking, and toilet training. They are slower in all anatomical, physiological, motor, and social functions, so that the pattern indicated by the history may clearly justify a diagnosis of mental subnormality. The "defect" type of mental handicap is probably most readily identified by a history. Making a diagnosis from a history of developmental slowness can become difficult because other conditions, such as motor, sensory, or emotional disabilities, can also lead to lags in accomplishment. This makes it necessary to give importance to the consistency of the retardation and to agreement with other findings.

Measures of Intellectual Ability

Scores from scales assessing intellectual ability are the single most frequently used criteria for rendering a diagnosis of mental subnormality. The field of psychoeducational measurement was given great impetus by Alfred Binet's success in identifying young children who could not be expected to do well in school because they had less than average learning ability. Mental subnormality was the first behavioral impairment for which a psychological diagnosis was acceptable. Assessing intelligence continues to be a favored method for diagnosis by psychologists and educators, who may be inclined to rely too heavily on the IQ. A number of scales measuring intellectual ability have been developed. Even though scales with high verbal content have proved to be the most dependable predictors of school achievement, most measuring scales offer a balance of verbal and nonverbal tasks.

Guilford (1967) has pointed out that scales measuring "intelligence" sample only a restricted range of mental processes, and are not measures of general intelligence. Scores from intelligence tests will predict outcomes in certain situations with higher accuracy than for other situations. But the individual's perception of a given situation, his attitudes about himself, and the effects he produces on other persons are also variables making important contributions to capacity. Most measures of general intelligence do not specifically assess these later variables which are crucial in influencing outcomes when total learning capacity is applied to a situation. Scores from intelligence scales may predict very well how a person does with the academic tasks of school but give poor predictions of social and vocational adjustments. Intelligence scores are, and doubtless will continue to be, given wide acceptance in diagnosing mental subnormality. This practice persists in spite of the well-known unreliability of such scores in predicting specific adjustment outcomes and in the face of increasing awareness of cultural (language, attitudes, values) influences on most measures of intelligence. The practitioner with years of experience in working with the mentally subnormal is well aware of the pitfalls inherent in too much reliance on the IQ and withholds making a definitive diagnosis until other relevant data are available.

Social Competence

Historically, the mentally subnormal have been identified on the basis of being unable to finish school, keep a job, stay out of jail, or provide for a family. No one would deny that there are many persons among the unemployed, school dropouts, convicted law violators, and similar groups of socially incompetent who prove to be mentally subnormal. Such data have been generated by frequent psychosocial investigations and are easy to come by. It is strange that the suggestion of equating social incompetence and mental subnormality, as implied by such studies, persists in the face of refutation of the contention, which is inherent in the very same investigations. No study has found that all jobless, all law violators, or all persons of any socially incompetent group are mentally subnormal. Most persons included in such socially deviant groups are in fact of average or above-average intellectual ability. The condition known as "sociopathic personality disturbance" is a particularly relevant example illustrating this point.

There is some justification for expecting a greater percentage of mentally subnormal persons to encounter failure in meeting social demands. Skill in meeting social expectations is apparently largely the outcome of acquisitions gained in being acculturated. Behaviors acquired in the socialization process, such as inappropriate language, poor maintenance of clothing, lack of general cleanliness, are frequently the focus for corrective efforts and in this sense can be considered the reversible aspects of subnormality. Caution must be taken to guard against these learned traits being accepted as specific to mental subnormality. Definition of subnormality should be based on the stable characteristics. Social learning frequently deals with values and attitudes, intangibles that may be elusive for the mentally subnormal. Society holds a number of possibilities for acceptable adjustment, and it is unlikely that any one person is in fact equally competent in all areas. The mentally subnormal person can be expected to be less proficient in academic skills because of the high degree of abstraction involved. But the pioneering work of Goddard offers ample evidence for showing that most mentally subnormal persons have sufficient abilities for making an adequate nonacademic adjustment. Rosen (1967) has been actively engaged in this same objective by correcting deficiencies in the existing educational and institutional programs. Too often, sheltered institutional life has promoted tendencies for dependency and denied realistic opportunities for the mentally subnormal.

The criterion of social competency must then be carefully weighed in arriving at a classification of mental handicap. It is difficult to list generalized behaviors that are specific to mental subnormality. Identification seems to be more a matter of examining specific behaviors evidenced in specific situations making specified social demands. Zigler (1966) has pointed out that a greater frequency of mentally subnormal persons are in lower socioeconomic groups and acquire values and behavior patterns typical of these groups. These values and standards may be the critical factor in meeting demands of a predominantly middle-class society. Social competency is, unquestionably, a relevant criterion for identifying the mentally subnormal. In practice, this ability is difficult to evaluate. What constitutes a good parent, a steady worker, a respectable citizen, and so on cannot be easily measured. Social maturity is attained at different rates and in different degrees. It should be considered in classifying a person as mentally subnormal, but its significance must be decided only in the light of other information.

Personality Factors

The survival of efforts to identify the mentally subnormal on the basis of distinctive personality traits is possibly best explained as another indication of a wish to reduce behavior to simple units that can be easily quantified. The major personality traits proposed for inclusion in the mentally subnormal configuration have been referred to in the discussion of characteristics of the mentally handicapped. Those most frequently cited include perseveration, dependency, a preference for dealing with the concrete and tangible, slowness and limited ability to deal with the abstract. Slight variations in the phrasing of these qualities are to be encountered in literature dealing with mental subnormality, but the emphasis is about the same.

In part, the search for a typical personality associated with mental subnormality has been given some impetus by refinements in procedures for assessing personality. Advancements in the field of projective techniques have contributed to this line of interest. However great the convenience and interest, to date no personality pattern has been discovered that is exclusively associated with mental subnormality. Continued investigation of the problem has in fact produced an increasing amount of evidence contraindicating such a contention. For example, a study carried out by Zigler and Butterfield (1968) suggests that the dependency is a consequence of the docile adjustment demanded by institutionalization. After investigating the social adjustment of mentally subnormal children in public schools, Lapp (1957) concluded that the low social acceptance common for such children was not related to any identifiable personality trait. The low acceptance was simply a realistic reflection of the fact that the mentally subnormal had very little to contribute to an academically oriented group. In short, identification of mental subnormality on the basis of a purported characteristic personality is at once the most hazardous and the least substantiated procedure.

Performance in Learning

A difference in the ability to learn a task is the most consistently observed quality of the mentally subnormal. An excellent summary of studies contrasting the learning ability of persons with less than average intelligence and those of average intelligence is presented by Lipman (1963). As a result, the mentally subnormal take longer to learn a task, reach a peak performance at a lower attainment level, and seem to retain less. There are considerable individual differences, so that explanations of these differences must take into account the degree of mental subnormality and individual variations in relevant personality traits. In his detailed analysis of performance in various situations and with varied tasks, Maher (1966) emphasizes the influence of previous experiences, the nature of the task, and the procedures used to measure learning as contributing to the generally poor performance of the mentally handicapped.

Irrespective of what factors may be influencing the outcomes, the mentally subnormal are identifiable on the basis of performance in learning. The distinction becomes more obvious when the task is a complex one and involves the making of abstractions. Although the mentally subnormal are identifiable on the basis of characteristics revealed in learning a task, the special situations in which this feature becomes apparent are not generally available for use by the clinical diagnostician. Diagnosis from such minutely analyzed performance is more cumbersome and requires more time than most practitioners are willing to invest.

Differential Diagnostic Problems

Emotional Maladjustment.   Perhaps the most common problem in diagnosis is encountered in evaluating low performance that is the result of impairment associated with an emotional disorder. Unless skillfully managed, most preschool children will be inhibited and upset by the diagnostic process. The examiner is a stranger who makes specific demands to be carried out in fixed time limits. These temporary emotional reactions are generally easily managed, but chronic emotional disorders present greater difficulties. Emotional disorders are frequent in children and are often sufficiently severe to markedly limit the child's efficiency in coping with a task. The differentiation can be facilitated by keeping in mind that erratically uneven performance, disturbances of affect, and bizarre behaviors typically accompany emotional disturbance. In contrast, the performance of the mentally subnormal is uniformly below average, affect remains congruous, and behaviors are appropriate. The performance of the mentally subnormal is consistent and suitable but quantitatively less than average.

Language Disorders.   Another major diagnostic problem centers about the differentiation of language disorders from mental subnormality. The magnitude of this problem can be appreciated when it is considered that auditory impairments and associated language difficulties make up one of the three most frequently encountered areas of impairment found in children. Psychoeducational measuring scales routinely used in the diagnostic study of children tend to have high verbal content. The child with a language disability is thus penalized in this situation and may perform much below average, suggesting mental subnormality. The question of a hearing loss can be resolved only by competent audiometric evaluation, which should be routinely included in all diagnostic evaluations of children. Where a hearing loss is identified, classification as mentally subnormal should be deferred. The developmental history will often show that the language-disabled child has a rate of attainment in other areas (sensory-motor, social) in the normal range. The developmental accomplishment of the mentally subnormal child falls below that of the average. The performance of the language-impaired child, although below average in situations demanding language facility, rises to the average range in situations where minimal language facility is required. The functioning of the mentally subnormal child is consistently low in verbal and nonverbal situations.

Cultural Difference.   Persons working with the mentally subnormal have long been aware of the entangling of cultural variables with traits of mental subnormality. The widespread concern for the educational problems of the culturally different child has provided information for separating these conditions. The diagnostician must take steps to differentiate substandard school performance resulting from a low value for school achievement as contrasted to performance ensuing from a lesser intellectual potential. Lack of interest in an activity can be merely an extension of the child's life style as well as the consequence of inadequate intellectual capacity for sustaining the interest. Scales assessing intelligence tend to be highly verbal, even many so-called nonverbal and "culture-fair" scales. There is general recognition that persons from lower socioeconomic, rural, and bilingual backgrounds are at a disadvantage in situations making even modest demands for language facility and comprehension. On the other hand, a study carried out by Bartel, Bryen, & Keehn (1973) found that 50% of children classed as trainably mentally retarded were unable to comprehend the concept of "same-different" even though they had measured mental ages of 5 years and higher. Items using a same-different response paradigm are frequently on scales included in a diagnostic battery. Limited social opportunities, different motivational patterns, and sparse economic resources, factors often related to socioeconomic levels, can depress scores on scales measuring intelligence. Efforts to correct these difficulties by developing many separate scales have not proven very helpful in practice. Consider, for example, the infinite variety of dialects to be found in areas where Spanish is the major language. Removal of highly biased items from measuring scales is desirable, but clinicians must extend their skills to include an understanding of cultural differences. Flexibility in the interpretation of scores on existing scales and a detailed assessment that considers extensive supporting data may be a better answer to the problem than developing special scales for special groups. Relevant diagnostic clues will be found in sorting discrepancies that can be explained by cultural differences from those that are consistent with a lesser intellectual ability.

Concern for Adequate Classification.   The increasing number of services available for children has resulted in a proportionately greater number of children being seen for diagnostic study. Classification is frequently the first step required in order to qualify the child for the service. This chain of circumstances has created a number of reasons for concern about the diagnostic procedures. The category in which a child is grouped as a consequence of the diagnostic study, however well intentioned, tends to become a permanent attachment. It is often placed in a child's record, becoming a label that serves to distinguish him in all situations, even those where the diagnostic category may have no real significance. Thus an employer, seeing "mentally handicapped" on the report of a prospective employee, may prejudicially terminate any further consideration of such an individual. In other instances, a classification of mental subnormality may have been made on the basis of incomplete data, such as test scores without consideration of developmental history or family background information. Possibly the most frequently recurring error leading to a questionable diagnosis of mental subnormality involves accepting test scores obtained from young children. The rapid expansion of early school programs has resulted in more frequent diagnostic study of the young child, even though assessment of such children is known to be of limited reliability. The issues and alternatives are not simple and will not be easily resolved. Funding for special programs for specific groups of children is usually contingent upon the child's being identified and declared eligible for that program. Albeit more accurate and reliable, individual study of children takes more time, costs more, and may turn up fewer numbers of qualified children than does a group screening type of diagnostic study. Individual study carried out by a less than fully trained and experienced professional worker (paraprofessional, professional aide) tends to place reliance on a single procedure, carefully administered, but omitting the consideration of crucial supporting data. Another problem is the typically limited kinds of programs available for a child who needs some type of special help. When a carefully carried out diagnostic study has correctly identified the child's deficit, there may not be a program providing just that specific treatment. There is a temptation to slant the recommendations so as to qualify the child for placement in any program where there is a low teacher-pupil ratio, since the teacher in such a class can generally be counted upon to work with the child's deficit area. Another factor relevant to the classification of children is the provision for regular follow-up study and review of the original diagnosis made of the child. Pressured by heavy caseloads, educational diagnosticians have struggled to maintain quality diagnostic services, including regular follow-up evaluations of children they serve. The amount of error uncovered by these reevaluations is difficult to state because of the lack of available data. The authors' experience in the schools suggests that such errors may be as high as 15% of early school-aged children, dropping rapidly as the child advances in school. It is readily apparent that the classification of children is a serious and complex matter that can have as a consequence the child's not receiving needed treatment, being denied chances for essential growth experiences, or being molded in the fashion dictated by an incorrect label. The concern has reached such a point that the U. S. Department of Health, Education and Welfare has assumed an active role in coordinating the work of a Special Project, an Advisory Committee, and an Interagency Task Force, all studying different aspects of educational practices in diagnosing children. The Project on the Classification of Exceptional Children, headed by Dr.Nicholas Hobbs, has announced three objectives:

1. to increase public awareness of the problems associated with the classification and labeling of children;

2. to provide a rationale and practical suggestions for public policy as expressed in legislation and administrative regulations and guidelines; and

3. to improve professional practice of educators, psychologists, physicians, lawyers, social workers, and others responsible for the well-being of exceptional children.

Materials developed by the project have been published and are available to professionals working with children (Hobbs, 1975).

In general, the differential diagnostic questions can be resolved on the basis of the consistently below-average performance that typifies the mentally handicapped child. Total evaluation of all aspects of the child is the only safeguard for bringing to light deficits that may impair performance in specific situations. In some instances, mental subnormality may be found in combination with other disabilities. Making a diagnostic choice in such cases may be dictated by what is most likely to facilitate the child's getting the necessary treatment. In other instances, there may be "reasonable doubts" that make it inadvisable to make a specific diagnostic choice. In such situations, it is best to mention the possible classifications suggested and to defer a final category until supplementary information is obtained from long and close observation of the child.

Incidence

At this point it may be apparent to the reader that the number of mentally subnormal persons will vary according to the diagnostic characteristics being followed and the method of identification. An accounting of the mentally subnormal is made difficult by the lack of agreement among clinicians as to what constitutes mental subnormality.

Illustrative of the difficulties to be encountered in a search to identify the mentally subnormal is the following incident shared by the authors. While engaged in a research project studying the incorporation of on-the-job training experiences into a high-school program for mentally handicapped pupils, it became apparent that classroom teachers were not referring for individual psychological evaluation all potentially eligible pupils. A preliminary group screening had given some indication of the number of pupils with below-average intellectual ability. This situation was announced to the teachers in a group meeting, and teachers were scheduled for individual conferences in which the referral criteria were reviewed. In the individual conferences, each teacher acknowledged that there were pupils meeting the criteria who had not been referred. Several of the teachers even admitted that the nonreferred pupils (who were not by accident almost entirely girls) were "probably" mentally handicapped. The teachers justified not referring these pupils on the basis of their being "good" girls, that is, compliant and "clean." Boys not referred were described as cooperative and "willing to try as best they can." In this rather typical public-school system, our rather comprehensive survey indicated that about 6% of the approximately 10,000 pupils were mentally handicapped. Allowance should be made for the concern for educational classification. Only about two-thirds of the total mentally handicapped group in this school system were in special classes.

An incidence rate of 3% of the general population is frequently cited as designating the portion of mentally subnormal. This figure evolved from surveys made many years ago and was probably based on estimates gained from experiences with the more severe cases and extreme degrees of social maladjustment. Nevertheless, various explanations, including genetic ones, have been offered to substantiate this figure, which was cited as recently as 1965, by the President's Panel on Mental Retardation.

Although a few specialists believe that 3% is too high an incidence figure, others believe the figure too conservative. Approximately 2% of the general population have IQs in the range specified by the AAMD criteria as warranting additional study and possible classification as mentally retarded (two standard deviations below the mean). School systems commonly use a higher IQ (75 or 80) as a screening criterion for possible classification as educably mentally handicapped, a figure that would include from 7% to 10% of the school population.

The actual incidence of mental subnormality is and may well remain an unknown since it is unlikely that the entire population of the United States will ever be assessed. Even if such a massive undertaking were carried out, it might only serve to illustrate what is already apparent—that the frequency of mentally subnormal persons varies according to many sets of factors. When the preschool-age group is considered, the incidence is lowest. There is a sharp and sudden rise in incidence with the start of school, another peak at about the age persons ordinarily graduate from high school and take a job, and another peak occurring with aging. In general, more males than females are identified at all levels as being mentally subnormal.

Whatever the actual frequency of mentally subnormal persons may be, these variations in incidence are of interest in themselves. They suggest very clearly that mental subnormality is a complex condition not identifiable by any one single criterion. It is apparent that social inadequacy is an important criterion for identifying mental subnormality. This raises a question as to just what is implied by mental subnormality—a lower than average intellectual potential or a demonstrated social incompetency? Clarification of this question might help to explain why mental subnormality is more prevalent in the lower socioeconomic groups. Greater understanding of the nature of mental subnormality is essential to the development of effective countermeasures for correction of the condition.

Etiological Considerations

Realization that identifying the causes of mental subnormality was the only approach that might lead to the prevention of the condition undoubtedly spurred efforts to identify its precursors. Establishing causal relationships has not been an easy task. Mental subnormality, especially the mild and moderate cases (which are the more numerous), is sometimes not identified until the child is of beginning school age or older. Reconstruction of the relevant past events and circumstances is problematic. There is general acknowledgment of the relevance of such factors as genetics, the central nervous system, dependence on stimulation for development of cell tissue potentials, and nutritional process. Specifics regarding the ways in which learning ability is impaired and reduced by aberrations in these processes remain largely unknown and inconclusive. Many agents and conditions that result in organic damage frequently found associated with mental deficiency have been specifically identified. Mental retardation seems to be the outcome of factors that are less specific and not easily identifiable. In some instances the processes seem to be reversible, but in other cases they override any efforts for control. In some cases the origins of mental subnormality appear to involve complex interrelationships between the individual and his surroundings. It is almost axiomatic that traumas incurred early in development have widespread and general consequences, whereas traumas incurred at later stages tend to produce specific and limited effects. In reviewing the following groups of etiological factors, it is advisable to recognize the interactions between these variables, a situation so common that it seldom can be stated that any single agent or condition is the cause. Jervis (1968) summarized his review of etiological factors by stating that approximately one-fourth of the mentally subnormal appear to have alterations of genetic materials; one-fourth have a history of infections, toxins, and physical traumas; while the remaining one-half show no obvious etiological factor.

Organic Factors

Constitutional factors are frequently the first sources to be considered as causes of mental subnormality. They appear to have a special prominence in the mental deficiency type of subnormality. Organic factors that may result in mental deficiency can be arranged in four subgroups (which can be reviewed in greater detail in *Psychological problems in mental deficiency,* by S. B. Sarason and J. Doris, 1969) :

1. *Hereditary.* This group includes known genetic factors and aberrations such as amaurotic idiocy, trisomy 21 (mongolism), phenylketonuria, and galactosemia.
2. *Prenatal.* Of significance in this group are traumas, nutritional deficiency, anoxia, infections (virus, rubella), blood incompatibilities (Rh reactions), irradiation, and toxins.
3. *Natal.* Prematurity, asphyxia, and traumas are important factors in this group.
4. *Postnatal.* Toxins, neurotropic infections (virus, encephalitis, meningitis, chicken pox, mumps, scarlet fever), fevers, and, rarely, traumas are included in this group. Dietary deficiencies should also be considered.

Because many of the consequences of these internal or organic etiological factors occur before birth, it is not possible to give reliable estimates of the relative contribution attributable to each factor. Collectively, they account for about 25% of the total group of mentally subnormal.

Nutritional Factors

Efforts to improve living standards have in recent years focused much attention on nutrition. Sweeping statements have been made as to the debilitating effects of dietary deficiencies stunting the developmental potential of entire populations. Support for these claims of inferior physical and mental outcomes is sometimes secured by dramatic photographs or charts contrasting average daily consumption of particular foods for persons in selected geographic areas or regions of a country. Dietary intakes deficient in minimum daily required amounts of total food intake or in specified classes of foods are suspect. Reduced amounts of vitamins, proteins, or essential minerals are most often cited as precedents for comparably reduced mental growth. The pronouncement twenty years ago that injections of the nutrient glutamic acid would shortly "cure" all mental subnormality is an example of the disappointment wrought by "simple explanations and easy solutions." At the present state of knowledge, unique characteristics of mental subnormality are not readily captured in a photograph. The widespread and prolonged undernourishment experienced by large populations during World War II was not accompanied by an increase in the amount of mental subnormality. To date, the most convincing evidence regarding negative consequences of dietary deficiencies comes from laboratory studies of infrahuman animals. In these laboratory investigations, undernourishment incurred early in development seems to be especially conducive to inferior functioning adults. Complicating the extrapolation of the findings to humans is the fact that those persons who might have dietary deficiencies as a part of their general living standard are also subject to other varieties of deprivation, some of which are also thought to result in mental subnormality. In a review of studies of malnutrition and mental deficiency, Kaplan (1972) points out that a conclusive study has yet to be carried out with humans. Citing the difficulties in parceling out effects of fluctuations in ordinary eating habits, individual variations in digestive processing of foods, and the impact of psychosocial stresses often found in association with malnutrition, he concludes that it is impossible to make a definitive statement unequivocally linking mental retardation and malnutrition.

Cultural Factors

Features of the home, life style, community, and economic resources surrounding the person have been implicated as determinants of some types of subnormality. Although vaguely defined and of unknown number, these variables are thought to contribute prominently to mental retardation. Absence of intellectually stimulating materials, unstable family organization, inappropriate language, lack of models to provide approved work habits, poverty-restricted educational experiences, and the demeaning and devaluing stresses associated with limited opportunities are some of the more frequently advanced explanations. Gaps in current knowledge make it impossible to say which, if any, of these antecedents contribute to the intellectual status of a given child. Laboratory investigations of the effects of restricted experiences have, however, suggested three mechanisms by which these factors may be transmitted:

1. *Deprivation.* This explanation is based on a continual absence of materials, objects, persons, and situations with which the child might interact. Normal growth potential is not realized.

2. *Cumulative deficits.* A prevailing lack of attention from parents, poor role models, or insufficient provision of specific experiences at sensitive developmental stages is central to this explanation. These insufficiencies force the child to have to play "catch-up" and jeopardize his benefiting from normally encountered developmental opportunities.

3. *Chronic stress of frustration and failure.* The key factor in this concept is the succession of defeats the individual incurs in attempting to cope with demands for which he is unprepared and the constant thwarting and restric-

tion of alternatives. Reaction to these situations eventually forces the child to adopt low aspirations and to make minimal effort in the face of anticipated defeat.

Management Considerations

Plans for ameliorating mental subnormality are more likely to succeed when constructed about the concept of effectiveness rather than that of efficiency. Situations requiring discrete, stable, routine, mechanistic, accurate, and repetitious responses are typical of those in which the mentally subnormal do best. The diversity of conditions contributing to mental subnormality makes it mandatory to think in terms of an equivalent number of treatment measures. Mental handicap is a prevalent and persistent condition, second only to emotional disorders in terms of human resources lost to society. Advances in technology, particularly in the field of medical science, and the growing cultural gap between the advantaged and disadvantaged groups of our society could add materially to what is already a sizable social problem.

Medical Perspectives

The field of medical science has made many significant contributions to dealing with problems of mental subnormality. At present, medical treatment is probably most indicated for the defect group. Surgical techniques have been perfected for correcting hydrocephaly. Mysteries of the developmental arrests induced by metabolic dysfunctions of cretinism, galactosemia, and phenylketonuria have been unraveled. Recently a serum has been developed to counteract the devastating effects of the Rh-negative blood-incompatibility reaction. The marauding consequences of measles, scarlet fever, small pox, and polio have been practically eliminated by the development of specific vaccines.

Less heralded, but possibly of far greater long-term benefit, are the reductions in the incidence of mental handicap which will drive from continual improvement in general medical care. The number of mothers given prenatal care, children born in hospitals, and children routinely provided pediatric services increases with each passing year. Although a part of the consequences from these same advances is an increase in the number of defective children who will survive, the benefits far outweigh the disadvantages. A comprehensive program for the management of mental subnormality will always require medications, surgical intervention, and ongoing research investigations from medical specialists.

Institutional Programs

Formerly regarded as centers for the protective isolation of the mentally handicapped, institutions specializing in the care of these individuals have recently been undergoing many changes. New objectives have been incorporated into intensive treatment programs. As an initial step, residents are put through a detailed diagnostic evaluation, in which physical health status, sensory-motor systems, personality traits, and social skills are reviewed in addition to intellectual ability. Interestingly, such detailed scrutiny frequently turns up a picture of an individual with low but adequate intellectual ability. His adjustment potential is reduced by one or more areas of impairment, with emotional and sensory-motor difficulties being the more commonly identified.

Back-up programs for rendering the individual more suitable for independent adjustment outside the institution concentrate on correction of these secondary deficits by means of a coordinated educational program. In addition to training in basic academics, the educational program must make provisions for the acquisition of competency in selecting clothes, using public transportation, managing money, finding a job, and related social skills and habits. Rosen (1967) has been instrumental in establishing a model program of this type at the Elwyn Institute in Media, Pennsylvania.

Not all mentally subnormal persons can be made capable of independent life adjustment by such programs, and there may always be a certain population of severe cases requiring permanent custodial care. At no time, however, have a majority of mentally subnormal persons been institutionalized. Institutionalization is more likely to be a consideration in the management of mentally defective individuals and for persons with multiple disabilities, one of which is less than average intellectual ability. Success in placing qualified residents into real-life situations may require initial supervision by specialists on the staff of the training institution, or an arrangement such as halfway houses.

Public-School Programs

Management of subnormal mentality by an educational approach is based on providing training and experiences geared to a slower rate of maturation. The educational approach is then usually more appropriate for the mentally retarded, the uncompounded "garden variety" child whose difficulties appear to be consequences of a slower than average rate of attainment. That such persons are suitable for education in the special programs of the public schools is indicated by educational designations of "educable mentally handicapped," "educable mentally retarded," and "slow learner." They have IQ scores ranging from about 50 to 75 and are usually identified on the basis of inability to do work assigned in regular classes. They are referred to qualified school staff members for individual psychoeducational evaluation as a first step in planning an appropriate educational program.

Although the children may spend most of the day in regular classrooms, the program will probably include some time in a special class, especially while they are attending elementary school.

Public-school special classes for the educable mentally retarded are usually about half the size of regular classes and have a teacher trained in the educational problems of the retarded. Assignments are made on the basis of mental age so as to avoid excessive failures inherent in too high demands. Basic skill in reading, arithmetic, and writing is mastered to about the fourth-grade level by most pupils in these special classes by the time they are 14 or 15 years old. Subsequent school experiences then shift to social and vocational skills, with the pupils spending about half the day in selected job-training situations. "Graduation" can be any time the pupil gives satisfactory evidence of being able to function independently on the job, usually around the chronological age of 19.

Although most pupils in public-school programs are of the "educable" category, a smaller number are classed as "trainable." They have less total potential and obtain IQ scores ranging from about 35 to 50. Trainable mentally handicapped persons are not generally regarded as being capable of self-sufficient social and vocational adjustment. They seldom acquire even minimal skill in the basic academic areas. Special classes for this group emphasize training in self-care, personal safety, and basic household tasks. It is conceded that many of this group ultimately will require the protection of institutional placement, a step increasingly considered as the person reaches age 16 years and older. Actual outcome and final placement vary according to the demands of the surrounding community and the possibilities for continued protective supervision such as a community-sheltered workshop.

The number of special programs for the educable mentally retarded in the public schools increased rapidly, perhaps spurred on by claims of considerable success in aiding the mentally retarded. Typical of the findings are these summarized from the investigations of Carriker (1957), Porter & Milazzo (1958), Goldstein (1964), and Reynolds & Stunkard (1960):

1. Approximately 80% of graduates become economically self-supporting.

2. Commonly held jobs are of a service nature but some are semiskilled.

3. About 80% marry and maintain a family.

4. There is a higher crime rate compared to persons of normal intelligence, but the violations are of a minor nature (misdemeanors).

The picture is not entirely favorable, however, and many crucial issues as to the place of special classes must be regarded as not definitively answered. Some important studies questioning the effectiveness of special-class placement are those carried out by Cassidy & Stanton (1959), Mullen & Itkin (1961), and Goldstein, Jordan, & Moss (1962). The investigations compared mentally retarded pupils in special classes with those in regular classes and came up with these interesting findings:

1. Pupils in regular classes did as well or better academically than those in special classes.

2. Pupils in regular classes had a higher self-esteem.

3. Pupils in special classes had a more favorable sociometric standing.

There are factors associated with special-class placement that may offer some explanation for these outcomes. As Dunn (1968) has pointed out, special classes are too often dumping grounds for a ragtag of social misfits. The labeling of the child and the special class create a basis for social stigma and isolation. Even when the child is truly mentally retarded, he is not identified for placement until his troubles in the regular classroom become so pronounced as to bring attention to his plight. The curricular offerings in many special classes may have the same unappealing academic emphasis, albeit presented at a slower rate. In view of these possible limitations, it seems advisable to defer making a final evaluation of the efficacy of special classes.

Concerns have also been expressed that children classed as mentally retarded and placed in special classes are isolated from major life activities. Special class placement can become a barrier limiting chances for friendships and restricting participation in potentially stimulating sociocultural activities. In recognition of these penalizing potentials in addition to the negative impact of labeling (Jones, 1972), some school systems have made intensive efforts to return children from special to regular classes. Unless carefully managed, the wholesale return of retarded children to regular classes, sometimes referred to as "mainstreaming," can have seriously damaging consequences for the child. In the first place, the retarded child's limitations are most obvious in the ordinary classroom. Exposure to these high-demand situations can lead to increased social and academic failure, shattering self-esteem and reducing ability to profit from any learning opportunity. The positive and negative consequences must be carefully considered before making the decision to place the child in a regular or a special class. Necessary supportive services (consultation, resource rooms), regular observation of progress, systematic evaluation of capacity, and continuing diversification of school curricular offerings are needed to assure adequate educational opportunity for the mentally retarded. Unless these are included in the program, there is no reason to believe that mere placement in a regular class will in any way guarantee a more favorable end result for the mentally retarded pupil. However, when appropriately implemented, mainstreaming can be a vital experience for promoting maximum individual development.

Behavioral Approaches

Structured programs for producing specific behavior changes, popularly known as "behavior modification," have proven especially suitable for the mentally retarded. Replacement of disruptive with constructive group participation behaviors (a difficult but necessary task for younger children) is accomplished more readily under a behavior modification program. The same program elements can be applied for mastery of numbers, letters, and reading skills once the "readiness" training has been completed (Thompson & Grabowski, 1972). In high schools, behavior modification techniques have made it possible to implement the kinds of training (neatness in grooming, punctuality, dependability, looking busy on the job) that may be of the greatest advantage to the mentally retarded in postschool situations. The severely retarded, formerly given custodial care in institutions, now actively participate in programs in which undesirable responses of a destructive or aggressive nature are extinguished and acquisition of self-care and basic language skills is achieved (Neisworth & Smith, 1973). The application of behavior modification techniques is extensively discussed on pp. 496–51.

Rehabilitation Provisions

A plan that leads to placement of the mentally subnormal in a desirable situation is the most successful management of the condition. One way this objective can be accomplished is to create a situation to accommodate the person. This approach makes minimal effort to alter the mentally subnormal person, who is assumed to have known characteristics of a relatively immutable nature. Care must be exercised in designing such situations to guard against their becoming too artificial and removed from prevailing social trends; otherwise they may serve only to further limit and restrict.

In one sense, custodial institutions may be thought of as a situation created for those of severely limited intellectual ability. Placement in a custodial institution should be a last resort. An intermediate step is placement in a sheltered workshop. In some ways, the sheltered workshop is an extension of conditions prevailing in ordinary institutions. In neither situation is the person entirely self-sufficient and on his own. Cost of care may be reduced by the sheltered-workshop arrangement, and a degree of continuing community participation is possible for the mentally subnormal person. Adverse consequences are frequently aroused by such public-supported industries competing with private enterprise. All factors considered, sheltered workshops can probably make the most substantial contribution as temporary placements. As an example, essential training for later real-life demands may be most effectively carried out in a sheltered workshop where job conditions are simulated.

The most promising approach, and the really strong point of all rehabilitation planning, entails the shaping of the individual to fit carefully selected existing situations. Situations of particular relevance in this effort are jobs where the person can earn an adequate living. The federal and state vocational rehabilitation programs have enjoyed huge successes in placing all types of handicapped persons, including the mentally subnormal, in jobs where they can be self-supporting.

In making a placement, vocational-rehabilitation counselors marshal all facilities and services that can improve the employability of the person, including medical, surgical, psychological, educative, and training services. The individual is carefully assessed to identify his strengths and skills. Placement is made from the counselor's knowledge of the current job market and of the personality characteristics of the prospective employer. Success in placing the mentally subnormal has undoubtedly been enhanced by the educational emphasis on training for relevant social skills and personality traits. A tendency to be slow and a little dull is easily overlooked if the individual is clean, neat, polite, and dependable.

Impact on the Family

Treatment should focus on direct assistance to the subnormal child, but there has been a growing realization of the necessity for treatment encompassing the entire family. This movement may be just an open acceptance of what has been the practice rather than an innovation in treatment. Several books aimed at helping parents who have a subnormal child are in existence. Grossman (1972) has recently carried out an extensive investigation of the social and psychological reactions siblings, parents, and friends have to a retarded child. The presence of a mentally subnormal child poses various demands for a family. Such children often require more than ordinary amounts of costly medical care, including surgery, medications, and special therapy. Costs of placement in a special institution or hiring someone to watch the child add to the expense. The more the child is incapacitated, the more demands are imposed upon the family. Families with limited financial resources are hard pressed to care for a severely retarded child. Money that might ordinarily be used for pleasurable or enjoyable activities must be diverted to purchase services for the child. Time members of the family might have for their own recreation or personal pursuits has to be given to watching over the retarded child. Parents must spend a disproportionate amount of time with him.

Financial pressures are not the only sources of stress. Members of the family are subject to penetrating and embarrassing questions from friends and associates. They may be sharply criticized by casual observers of their public management of the child. Taking time to respond to questions and queries poses added demands. The stresses are less stringent when the child's potential approaches the normal range of abilities. In these cases, the pressures on siblings can still be great, for the normal siblings are frequently assigned to supervise the less able child. The normal siblings are also faced with having to explain and interpret a retarded sibling's behavior, or even his very reason for being, to comrades and acquaintances.

Formulating measures to counter these pressures may be the most important aspect of management. Backlash in the form of rejection because of the resentment and confusion associated with these pressures can have a devastating effect on the mentally subnormal child. Favorable results of other treatment procedures can be minimized by unsettled family and home conditions. The specific steps that are required to maintain a balance must be planned on the basis of an appraisal of each family situation. There are few generalities that can serve as absolute guidelines, but these observations may be of some assistance:

1. The amount of pressure is frequently directly related to the severity of the impairment.

2. The stresses are inversely related to the economic resources of the family.

3. Normal females, mother and sisters, compared to normal males, are recipients of a disproportionate amount of the demands for care imposed by a mentally subnormal child.

4. Some of the most valuable resources are found in parent groups where these exist in the community.

Again, no one approach holds the entire answer to the management of the mentally handicapped. The mentally retarded are more likely to be regarded as essentially suitable for eventual job placement than are the mentally defective. Vocationally oriented rehabilitation services are working in close cooperation with education programs in public schools and institutions. Cooperation can be expected to increase in the future since this avenue provides what may be the ideal treatment program.

Prevention

To some extent, prevention can be an aspect of the management and treatment of mental subnormality. From this perspective, the fields of medicine and education assume importance. Although improvements in medicine may lead to a slight rise in the number of mentally deficient, there are promising advances available for controlling many subtypes of mental deficiency. These include genetic counseling, therapeutic abortions, continued elimination of defect-producing illnesses, compulsory tests for phenylketonuria, galactosemia, and Rh compatibility, and increased knowledge of the body's use of nutritional materials.

Many exciting possibilities are to be expected for extension of educative procedures. Although the complex interactions that ensue developmentally between individual capacity and the environment are far from being adequately understood, the earlier belief that mental retardation is essentially an unchangeable condition is no longer tenable. An impressive array of hard data suggests that measured intellectual ability can be increased by controlled experiences systematically presented at critical periods of development. Studies carried out in orphanages and institutions for children have come to be referred to as "deprivation" studies. They show very clearly the importance of adequate stimulation maximizing the development of intellectual potential.

A frequently cited deprivation study was carried out by Kirk (1958). At the start of the study, children 3 to 6 years old with IQ scores ranging from 45 to 80 were put into four groups. Two groups lived with their families in a community. Two groups were studied in an institution for the mentally subnormal. The 28 children in one community group and the 15 children in one institutional group attended a special preschool program for three years, while no special treatment was given the control groups. Assessment of intellectual ability at the end of the three-year period indicated that the

43 subjects provided with school experiences had significantly higher IQ scores, with individual gains of from 10 to 30 points. Of the 15 children in the institutional group, 6 now had IQ scores high enough to qualify them for adoption outside the institution.

The Kirk (1958) study has evoked considerable disagreement as to how the gains in IQ might be explained. Some reviewers have been impressed with the fact that 13 of the 43 subjects showed no gain in IQ after three years of schooling. Others have questioned the reliability of IQ scores obtained on 3-, 4-, and 5-year-old children and raised queries as to the adequacy of the family and home backgrounds of the subjects. Some knowledgeable persons feel that the efficacy of education for dealing with mental subnormality is still an unknown quantity. Dunn (1968) has openly urged a hard look at the present practices of placing mentally retarded children in special classes. He claims that socially and emotionally maladjusted problem children are hidden away in special classes intended for the mentally handicapped.

Prospects for the "educability" of intelligence continue to stimulate creative research investigations. One such project attracting attention is the Milwaukee Project, directed by Dr. Rick Heber (Heber, Garber, Harrington, Hoffman, & Farber, 1972). In this study an experimental and a control group of low SES black children whose mothers all had IQs of less than 80 were studied over a five-year period. Children were identified at age 3 months and were judged free of discernible neurological and physical defects. The 20 children in the experimental group regularly attended a day school. There was one teacher for each child with the teacher-pupil ratio slowly changing until by age 5 years three teachers were provided for a room of six or eight children. Mothers of children in the experimental group attended classes in nutrition and home management. It is claimed that the curriculum of the school did not differ from any usual nursery school with the exception of the high percentage of teacher time available for each child. Children in the control group remained in their usual home surroundings except for regular visits to the project center for scheduled assessment. No special assistance was provided mothers of the children in the control group. Assessments made in May 1972 revealed that the 16 children still in the experimental group had a mean IQ of 126 (range 100 to 140). Children in the control group had a mean IQ of 94 (range 65 to 105). Dr. Heber has taken a very cautious position regarding his preliminary data, citing the small number of children involved, the unreliability of measures made of young children, and the lack of long-term data.

Studies reporting gains in IQ as a result of increased stimulation or intensive experiences have been criticized from many quarters. Some have questioned the real importance of gains of 10 or 15 IQ points when the person is still markedly below average in intellectual ability. These critics may have a point, since an IQ in itself offers very little from which to make a prediction. Other critics, impressed with the fact that there appear to be limits in the extent to which IQ gains can be attained, have suggested that intellectual ability itself is not changed by the early training. They explain the apparent gain as accruing from the child's acquisition of other habits and skills (attending, remembering, wanting to please) which enable him to make maximum effective use of his potential.

Let us hope that the critics have correctly analyzed the problem and that the chief influence of early education is made by instilling more efficient personality traits and social skills. If so, this opens a potent possibility for dealing with mental retardation since the adjustment failures of the mentally retarded appear to be more related to deficits in social skills than in intellectual potential.

Aside from these practical applications of medical and educational techniques, the prevention of mental subnormality touches on obscure sociocultural variables. It is apparent that programs of population control must eventually include population limitation. Population limitation may have as a corollary provisions for population selection based on more accurate genetic counseling information. Another possibility is that living will become an increasingly demanding matter for all individuals, for they will have to cope with technological conditions of growing complexity. In order to accommodate persons of limited ability, artificial situations may have to be created that present demands commensurate with their limitations. This would be especially likely if subsequent study over the next few years indicates that intelligence level cannot be raised beyond a certain point by any educational program.

As Telford & Sawrey (1967) have so cogently pointed out, the more we succeed in efforts to render all persons uniform in ability, the more otherwise small differences become significant. At the present state of progress, capacity seems to be the outcome of many inherent abilities. Some of these abilities are favored by one procedure; others are enhanced by yet another set of conditions. We must conclude that there is at present no one approach, no one program, sufficient for dealing with the problem of mental subnormality. Continued investigation of the many inconsistencies is necessary to resolve the problems found in connection with mental subnormality.

Summary

The condition of mental subnormality refers to impairment associated with having less than average intellectual ability.

The impairment is most obvious in the mastery of a new situation, especially one involving abstract or symbolic learning.

Mentally subnormal persons tend to be predisposed to a greater number of failures and thus may be more susceptible to social and emotional problems.

A number of factors seem to have potential for contributing to mental subnormality, a fact evident in the number of terms used to designate the condition.

Mental subnormality exists in varying degrees of severity and seems to be the outcome of interaction between constitutional and environmental factors.

Mental subnormality can be difficult to differentiate from emotional and language disorders.

A diagnosis of mental subnormality can be made only after considering intellectual ability, social competence, and cultural indices.

Estimates of the incidence of mental subnormality vary about a figure of 3% of the general population.

Conditions of mental subnormality respond favorably to a number of treatment efforts, but intensive educational-social-vocational training seems to be the most promising.

Work with the mentally subnormal has stimulated research and treatment programs that have added to understanding and correction of all behavior adjustment difficulties.

References

Bartel, N. R., Bryen, D., & Keehn, S. Language comprehension in the moderately retarded child. *Exceptional Children*, 1973, **39**, 375–83.

Carriker, W. R. A comparison of postschool adjustments of regular and special class retarded individuals served in Lincoln and Omaha. *Nebraska Public Schools Project* No. 146. Washington, D.C.: U.S. Office of Education, 1957.

Cassidy, V. N., & Stanton, J. E. *An investigation of factors involved in the educational placement of mentally retarded children: a study of differences between children in special and regular classes in Ohio.* Columbus, Ohio: Ohio State University Press, 1959.

Clausen, J. Quo vadis, AAMD? *Journal of Special Education*, 1972, **6**, 51–60.

Dunn, L. M. Special education for the mildly mentally retarded—is much of it justifiable? *Exceptional Children*, 1968, **35**, 5–22.

Goldstein, H. Social and occupational adjustment. In H. A. Stevens & R. Heber (Eds.), *Mental retardation: a review of research.* Chicago: University of Chicago Press, 1964, pp. 214–58.

Goldstein, H., Jordan, L., & Moss, J. W. *Early school development of low IQ children: study of special class placement.* Urbana, Ill.: Research Institute for Exceptional Children, 1962.

Grossman, F. K. *Brothers and sisters of retarded children.* Syracuse, N.Y.: Syracuse University Press, 1972.

Grossman, H. J. *Manual on terminology and classification in mental retardation.* Washington, D.C.: American Association on Mental Retardation, 1973.

Guilford, J. P. *The nature of human intelligence.* New York: McGraw-Hill, 1967.

Heber, R., Garber, H., Harrington, S., Hoffman, C., & Farber, C. *Rehabilita-*

tion of families at risk for mental retardation—Progress Report, 1972. Rehabilitation Research and Training Center in Mental Retardation, University of Wisconsin, Madison, Wisconsin.

Hobbs, N. *Issues in the classification of children.* Vols. I and II. San Francisco: Jossey-Bass, 1975.

Jervis, G. A. Remarks on etiological factors of mental retardation. In B. W. Richards (Ed.), *Proceedings of the first congress of the international association for the scientific study of mental deficiency.* Reigate, England: Michael Johnson, 1968.

Jones, R. L. Labels and stigma in special education. *Exceptional Children,* 1972, **38,** 553–64.

Kaplan, B. J. Malnutrition and mental deficiency. *Psychological Bulletin,* 1972, **78,** 321–34.

Kirk, S. A. *Early education of the mentally retarded.* Urbana, Ill.: University of Illinois Press, 1958.

Lapp, E. A. A study of the social adjustment of slow-learning children who were assigned part-time to regular classes. *American Journal of Mental Deficiency,* 1957, **62,** 254–62.

Leland, H. Mental retardation and adaptive behavior. *Journal of Special Education,* 1972, **6,** 71–80.

Lipman, R. S. Learning: verbal, perceptual-motor, and classical conditioning. In N. R. Ellis (Ed.), *Handbook of mental deficiency.* New York: McGraw-Hill, 1963, pp. 391–423.

MacMillan, D. L., & Jones, R. L. Lions in search of more Christians. *Journal of Special Education,* 1972, **6,** 81–91.

Maher, B. A. *Principles of psychopathology.* New York: McGraw-Hill, 1966.

Mullen, F. A., & Itkin, W. The value of special classes for the mentally handicapped. *Chicago School Journal,* 1961, **42,** 353–67.

Neisworth, J. T., & Smith, R. M. *Modifying retarded behavior.* Boston, Mass.: Houghton Mifflin, 1973.

Porter, R. B., & Milazzo, T. C. A comparison of mentally retarded adults. *Exceptional Children,* 1958, **24,** 410–12.

Reynolds, M. C., & Stunkard, C. L. A comparative study of day class vs. institutionalized educable retardates. *Cooperative Research Project.* No. 192. Minneapolis: University of Minnesota Press, 1960.

Rosen, M. Rehabilitation, research, and follow-up within the institutional setting. *Mental Retardation,* 1967, **9,** 24–41.

Sarason, S. B., & Doris, J. *Psychological problems in mental deficiency.* (4th ed.) New York: Harper & Row, 1969.

Telford, C. W., & Sawrey, J. M. *The exceptional individual: psychological and educational aspects.* Englewood Cliffs, N.J.: Prentice-Hall, 1967.

Thompson, T., & Grabowski, J. *Behavior modification of the mentally retarded.* New York: Oxford University Press, 1972.

Zigler, E. Mental retardation: current issues and approaches. In M. L. Hoffman & L. W. Hoffman (Eds.), *Review of child development research.* Vol. II. New York: Russell Sage Foundation, 1966, pp. 107–68.

Zigler, E. Familial mental retardation: a continuing dilemma. *Science,* 1967, **155,** 292–98.

Zigler, E., & Butterfield, E. C. Motivational aspects of changes in IQ test performance of culturally deprived nursery school children. *Child Development,* 1968, **39,** 1–49.

Suggested Readings

Adams, M. *Mental retardation and its social dimensions.* New York: Columbia University Press, 1971.

Grossman, H. R. (Ed.). *Manual of terminology and classification in mental retardation.* Washington, D.C.: American Association on Mental Retardation, 1973.

Kirman, B. *The mentally handicapped child.* New York: Taplinger, 1974.

Lambert, N. M., Wilcox, M. R., & Gleason, W. P. *Assessment manual for the diagnosis of educable mentally handicapped pupils.* New York: Grune & Stratton, 1974.

Neisworth, J., & Smith, R. *Modifying retarded behavior.* Boston, Mass.: Houghton Mifflin, 1973.

Sarason, S. B., & Doris, J. *Psychological problems in mental deficiency.* (4th ed.) New York: Harper & Row, 1969.

The
Culturally
Different

This chapter deals with persons who are regarded as having adjustment problems because their way of living runs counter to what may be arbitrarily designated as the main current of the stream of life. As with all the adjustment problems we have reviewed in this text on behavior disorders, those of the culturally different child are "new" only for those very recently come upon the scene. The problem has been around for as long as societies have advanced to a point where there are layers of organization, customarily referred to as "classes" or "subcultures." Although our presentation is concerned with the problem of the culturally different in the United States, the problem is a universal one, to be found all over the world.

Manny, a Culturally Different Boy

Manuel, or Manny as he preferred to be called (he would even accept the "Man" that some of the bigger kids used in addressing him), walked slowly along the street trying not to step in puddles made by the melting snow. It was bad enough that the wind cut through his jacket, but having wet cold feet was the worst. Manny hated the snow and half disbelieved his father's stories that it never snowed in the Philippine Islands where he had grown up. Lots of things his father said never happened anyway, like his always saying that he would take the family on a vacation. Manny wondered if all their family could even squeeze into the car at the same time. At least Manny's father stayed with them and didn't leave like lots of the other fathers where he lived. Manny remembered that he was supposed to see that his brothers and sisters also stayed out of the puddles and arrived at school on time. Just to make sure, he shouted out for them to be more careful or he would hang one on them. He wondered why he had so many brothers and sisters who always needed watching or something done for them. Manny hadn't had time to eat all of his breakfast and now he remembered there was no lunch money today as was often true on Friday and sometimes even on Thursday. Manny's father worked hard on a truck that cleaned the city streets and he had another job loading boxes down at the market besides that. Saturday nights and Sundays, there was plenty of money, but it seemed to be all gone soon. Manny thought he should get a job himself. Sometimes he worked at the market loading boxes, too. School took up so much of his time, and lots of times he just couldn't understand his teacher. She talked so fast and said so many big words he'd never heard. She thought everyone liked school and couldn't believe that Manny didn't remember something she had shown him how to do last week or sometime. At least, she didn't ask Manny why his hair was so straight, or why he had lost his pencil again, or why he was in another fight. Having a job would probably be a lot better than school . . . maybe he could even start smoking cigarettes . . .

Solutions proposed for dealing with the culturally different mirror the enormous complexity of correcting the problem. Some situations may warrant the revolutionary approach of creating basic changes in the structure of society by redistributing wealth, organizing the poor and giving them a sense of belonging, and changing leadership hierarchies. The major line of attack dictated by social planners in the United States has followed a more evolutionary plan of trying to incorporate the subculture of the lower class into the culture of the middle class.

In recent years much has been said about the culturally different and their problems. A bleak picture of otherwise able persons soaking up welfare benefits, persons uneducable and therefore unrehabilitatable, excessively large families whose children will contribute little more than to increase the number of criminals, dope addicts, and prostitutes, and the frank outbreaks of destructive waves of rioting—all makes dramatic reading. But how prevalent is such behavior? And is it, as often seems the case in news-media presentations, invariably associated with, or for that matter even attributable to, the culturally different? Even the brief mention of these happenings raises a host of issues which must be resolved in one manner or another since they center about a schism that if not healed poses a sizable threat to our total society.

The problem of the culturally different who are variously referred to as "culturally deprived," "educationally deprived," "socially disadvantaged," as well as "disadvantaged" or "deprived," is one with many facets. Dealing with the adjustment problems encompassed may properly demand multiple approaches and solutions. Not the least of the difficulties encountered are ethical ones, such as the extent to which one segment of a social order is justified in imposing its will on another. It is impossible to discuss the situation meaningfully without considering the social and cultural framework in which the problem manifests itself. Our discussion reviews this frequently neglected framework before proceeding to a description of the more salient characteristics of the difficulties and concluding with an evaluation of some of the more educationally oriented proposals for remediation.

Identification

Information relating to the culturally different has poured forth in the past few years as this area has assumed its turn for consideration as a major social problem. Unfortunately, much of what has found its way to the public has been of a shocking, extreme, and flamboyant nature. Such exaggerations may serve the purpose of capturing the attention of the audience, but they have fostered many misconceptions about the culturally different. Let there be no doubt about it: the culturally different are persons assimilated in and acculturated to a legitimate subculture. Members of this subculture are not necessarily intent upon breaking all the laws, burning the existing social order to the ground, spitefully destroying the educational system, furiously acting out a chronic hatred for all organizations, or chaotically consorting in the slums of major cities.

⌈Anthropologists designate values, attitudes about life, customs, traditions, and patterns of living as the most important aspects of culture. Cultures evolve over long periods of time and are themselves enduring. ⌉Each culture provides its members with a design for living in the form of suggested solutions for common life problems. The members of the culture have available the distillate from previous efforts to cope with life problems.⌉ Regardless of the fact that these prescriptions for meeting life demands may seem inept or ineffectual, judged from the frame of reference of another culture, compelling testimonial as to their effectiveness, at least for the members of the cultural group concerned, is found in the durability of the culture over time. A culture that offers no rewards or benefits to its members simply does not long exist.⌉ Realization of this principle is essential to understanding the culturally different and holds the only hope of an approach for changing the behavior of the group. Looked at from this perspective, as an effort to cope with one's surroundings, the allegations of ineffectiveness, failure, hostile counterreaction, or being the product of scapegoating must be rejected as explanations of the problem. Attention can then be turned away from fruitless rationalizations of the negative factors to the less dramatic but potentially more constructive factors that govern the behavior.

Contrast with Social and Emotional Maladjustment

⌈In one sense, the culturally different are socially maladjusted. This statement holds true if the condition of being out of step with the predominant social code is taken as a gross criterion. Most experts in the behavioral sciences, however, recognize the generality of such a criterion and its inadequacy for dealing with this problem.⌉ Social maladjustment is more properly a social deviancy, a reaction built upon frankly antisocial tendencies. Such patterns of adjustment—which range from mild lying, irresponsibility, disobedience, and shiftlessness through sexual deviancy and a disruptive disregard for others' property to the more severe acts of theft and fraud—are usually seen as single dominant traits of the personality organization. Social deviancy as nonconformity is to be found in varying degrees among the members of any culture, family, or social class.

The culturally different must also be delineated from the emotionally maladjusted.⌉ It may be true that some of the culturally different are also emotionally maladjusted, but this is not a characteristic of all the culturally different.⌉ Emotional maladjustment is a personal problem—the inability of the individual to attain a personally effective and satisfying organization, meshing his abilities with the demands of his particular culture. Emotionally maladjusted persons are generally chronically unhappy and are severely limited psychologically in the extent to which they can participate in their culture. In more extreme cases, the incapacitation reaches degrees of total breakdown. Emotional maladjustment is likely to respond to intervention by psychotherapy, medications, and rest. Acute episodes of emotional maladjustment often show a clear connection to specific events of an emotionally traumatic nature, such as the death of a loved person, the failure to gain a desired goal, or a harrowing experience.

The culturally different person, in contrast, has problems only in the context of comparison with another culture. Evaluation in the setting of his own social group reveals no difficulties. The problems arise when he is weighed according to the standards of another and foreign culture. As Cloward & Ohlin (1960) summarized the problem, the so-called culturally different are, more correctly, caught up in a cultural conflict. A comparison of values and standards that prevail in "middle-class" and "lower-class" cultures points up the differences that are at the root of the conflict.

Differences in Class Values

In order to understand the problem clearly, it is constantly necessary to keep in mind that a culture is an organization of techniques, procedures, and ways for making an adaptation to conditions. The organization is, moreover, effective, in that it provides solutions to life problems and rewards its members. If it is not effective, it does not long endure. This simple principle, well known to cultural anthropologists, is often obscured by the prevalent use of the terms "middle class" and "lower class." These terms were introduced in early studies by social scientists to designate a position in society based on relative acquisition of materials, education, and income even though these researchers were more interested in studying such nonmaterial aspects as the attitudes, beliefs, and values of the individuals. It is illuminating that the classification system was, from the first, set up so that "lower class" had a negative "lesser than" connotation. The names have stuck with us, and other than perhaps Lewis's suggested phrase "culture of poverty," no less biased labels have been proposed. It is to be expected that behavioral scientists, who come predominantly from the middle class, are likely to defend and justify their origins. At this stage of the game, our concern is not to provide a new or more "objective" framework; the problem remains the same regardless of the terms in which it may be couched. Use of "middle class" and "lower class" is a choice made for convenience in communication.

The core of middle-class culture is achievement. All resources are organized for production. Participants in the system receive an abundance of material gains—houses, cars, refrigerators, clothing, dishwashers. The niceties of such affluence are comforting, but the actual cost of these gains is seldom objectively reckoned. There are in fact built into the system safeguards for preventing too careful an accounting, for the credit ledger is never closed. Things are always going to be better, greater gains are to be expected. All the person has to do is work and keep on working. If he is not getting the benefits, material rewards, it is because he is not working hard enough. A member of the middle class can easily persuade himself to participate in long-range programs and can be counted on to deliver his bit with reliance and punctuality. He skeptically rejects luck and fast success in favor of deliberation, control, and guaranteed small gain. The middle-class person, then, has his eye on the future. He is concerned with developing abstract intellectual skills for thinking and planning. He must live a carefully planned life pattern with calculated moves toward anticipated "improvement." Immediate rewards available today are inconsequential and are to be forestalled in exchange for a glorious tomorrow. The middle-class person is altruistic in a distant way, mostly by paying others to deal with those struggling at a lower level. To stay on his narrow, achievement-oriented path, he must know where he has been but especially where he is going. Priding himself on being responsible, he is intolerant of those who do not have a shoulder to the wheel of "progress."

By contrast, members of the lower-class culture are more likely to be "enjoyers" rather than "doers." Believing that no one person or group can really beat the system (so why fight it?), the lower-class person's orientation is current and directed to the here and now. It makes no difference how much or how hard you may work, events are largely prearranged. Some days you are lucky; other times, unlucky. A dollar in the pocket will buy many pleasures. But in the bank—who knows if the bank will burn down or be robbed and the dollar lost for all time? Best to spend it while you can; tomorrow you may be dead. This transitory orientation accounts for many significant personality features of the lower-class person, who is spontaneous and impulsive in loving and in fighting. His belief in a kind of magic makes him adventuresome and ever ready to "travel on," where he may find new friends or greater fortunes. He is mistrustful of anyone who approaches him on the grounds of doing something today for a reward promised two weeks or a month from now. Makers of such offers are only scheming to take advantage of someone, to trick him into doing a few days' work—for who can be sure what tomorrow will bring? He is aware of the plentiful supply of everything and sees nothing wrong with "borrowing" food or money from someone who has more than anyone really needs for a day. After all, doesn't he generously share his lucky fortunes with everyone? Not only does he share freely his "wealth," but he also tolerantly extends to other persons his own low aspirations. He has no great ambitions, no accumulations of unnecessary objects, and sees no reason for others to have them either. Anyone who is ambitious and strives to acquire property is really creating a situation for bad luck. Such persons should be viewed with suspicion. The choice between having a television set or a bathroom is really no problem; one can find many places for toileting.

To sum up, the "culturally different" child is going to encounter adjustment difficulties if he is expected to adopt a set of values, beliefs, and mores different from what he has acquired. When evaluated according to the standards of his particular cultural group, he is very well adjusted. Teachers trained to work with the middle-class child may be puzzled by behaviors that reflect differences between the values of the lower-class and middle-class cultures. Major differences in the values of lower-class and middle-class persons in the United States are listed in Table 7–1.

The incorporation of lower-class values into the personality organization of members of the lower class forms a basis for behaviors that differ from the values and standard of the majority middle class. Members of the lower class are said to be culturally disadvantaged to varying degrees as they are caught up in a cultural conflict.

Incidence

Making a count of the precise number of persons who can be designated as culturally different is a staggering task. As has been pointed out, the criteria for evaluation consist of values and ideals that are abstract and elusively resistant to quantification. There are no handy measuring scales that can be brought into service to carry out such a survey. It has been necessary to rely on extensive observations carried out in detailed field studies by cultural anthropologists and sociologists. These field studies have suggested certain indices that are rather sensitive indicators of class membership. Possibly because the lower class is a minority of the total population, it is often thought that the culturally different can be identified as members of minority groups. Thus, American Indians, Spanish-Americans, Chinese-Americans, and blacks suggest themselves as the culturally different. A large percentage of these groups may be culturally different, but a sizable percentage of each group is not. The majority of the culturally different are native-born whites. The culturally different cannot be identified on the basis of residence in big-city slums, the Appalachian hill country, or the rural areas of the South, although many of the persons in these areas are culturally different. Migrant workers, the unemployed, and the poor are groups that also contribute substantially, but not exclusively, to the number of culturally different.

Number of years of school completed (less than 10), occupation (labor-

Table 7–1.   A Comparison between Lower-Class and Middle-Class Values

Lower Class	Middle Class
Present time orientation	Future time orientation
Preference for concrete and tangible	Preference for abstract
Adventurousness and spontaneity	Responsibleness and control
Acceptance of "fate" without worry	Use of intellect to plan and think
Immediacy of gratification	Delay of gratification
Emphasis on physical activity and sensual, with tolerance for violence	Emphasis on beauty, altruism, and perfection
Indulgence and low aspiration	Criticalness and high aspiration

ers, semiskilled, farm workers), and total annual income (less than $5,000) are generally accepted as providing a composite index for designating the culturally different. Depending upon the weight given the several indices, from one-fourth to one-third of the total population of the United States may be classed as culturally different. Of interest to child-welfare specialists is the fact that culturally different families tend to be large, with a result that from one-third to two-fifths of all children may be in the culturally different group (Witmer, 1964).

Characteristics

Common Misconceptions

Descriptions of the culturally different, although plentiful in number, are frequently found to be sparse in presenting a realistic picture. The tendency to relegate the culturally different to an unfavorable condition is perhaps best understood as an example of the general tendency to defend and protect one's own reference group by minimizing all other groups. By ways of accomplishing this goal, generous use is made of the defense mechanisms of social psychology. Stereotyping, exaggeration, overgeneralization, and repetition are relied upon to create an unfavorable impression. These defense mechanisms often have a certain amount of half-truth, which is exploited to give a basis for credibility. More than merely "nasty habits," social defense mechanisms act to obscure the individuals who make up the group and to perpetuate themselves by increasing the gap between groups. If accepted, they provide a bleak, hopeless, and immutable picture. Therefore it is essential to examine some of the more grossly erroneous attributes leveled at the culturally different.

1. *Social-Depravity Traits.* It is frequently alleged that the culturally different are criminals, dope addicts, engaged in illicit enterprises (prostitution, stolen property), alcoholics, family deserters, and all on relief. The allegations are surprisingly persistent in the light of the extreme improbability associated with each of these contentions. A major theme in Lewis's accounts of the life activities of the culturally different is a marked dislike and fear of jails. This attitude is rivaled only by their contempt for criminals and sexual deviates who take refuge in the comparatively disorganized living conditions of metropolitan areas where many culturally different live. Family arrangements are loose, but may actually be closer to arrangements in other cultural groups where children are regarded as community property and all adults are "father" and "mother." It is surprising to find that many of the culturally different spurn any form of welfare assistance, other than perhaps medical services, for simple reasons of not wanting to bother with the stack of papers to be filled out or because of a basic suspicion of all nosey outsiders. It takes only a minute to compute that the absolute number of criminals, dope addicts, and such is smaller than the total number of culturally different. The majority of poor people are law abiding and hard working.

2. *Ethnic Traits.* Another group of demeaning qualities is based to a large extent on traits supposedly basic to particular racial groups. Blacks, Indians, Spanish-Americans, Chinese, and other members of distinctly recognizable racial groups are blanketed with charges of being unattractive, unclean, sensual, menial, and shiftless. This discrimination and prejudice has the added support of distortions associated with the fact that many members of such ethnic groups are culturally different. They are belied by the fact that members of each of these ethnic groups can be found in all cultural classes.

3. *Personality Traits.* A cluster of unfavorable characteristics is often directed indiscriminately to the culturally different by otherwise well-informed persons. The charges seem to be attempts to account for what is interpreted as inferiority, incompetency, and inadequacy. Possibly suggested by the poverty, dearth of material acquisions, and generally lesser attainment of the culturally different, these unfavorable traits include conceptions of being intellectually dull, having inferior physical and mental health, an inaptitude for schooling, irresponsibility, and dependency. But when any one of these ascribed traits is objectively investigated, about as many negative as positive cases are discovered. For example, St. John (1975) found that there are no appreciable racial differences in self-esteem between blacks and whites.

Controversial Conceptions

The student who embarks on a review of reports on almost any subject will usually find that he doesn't have to look very far before he encounters differing opinions about what seems to be the same topic. These variations in observations of a problem are related to many factors, including personal biases, theoretical background of the research investigator, and the complexity of forces influencing the phenomenon. When these factors are considered, it is not surprising that there are many conflicting traits ascribed to the culturally different. Some of these are rather easy to explain (purported non-verbalness), but others defy any consistent explanation (patriarchal versus matriarchal orientation, attitude toward school). Knowing that these traits are controversial may keep the issues open so that needed follow-up investigations will be carried out and eventually indicate the way the pieces of the puzzle may be fitted together.

Intellectual Ability. The plethora of scales for measuring "intelligence" and academic achievement has probably made it all too convenient for such devices to be used in behavioral research. The findings are rather consistent in placing the culturally different at a less favorable position on such scales. More specifically, groups of culturally different are reported as having scores from 10 to 15 points below the IQ scores obtained by groups from the middle class. A typical example of these studies is that reported by Bloom (1964), who has drawn together a wide array of studies. There seems very little reason to question the picture of lower scores on measures of intelligence associated with lower-class status, even though there are consistent findings of occasional high IQ scores among such groups. Our concern is for the interpretations that are given to such data.

In view of the uncertainty as to just what the widely used intelligence and achievement scales are really measuring, it is very surprising that the culturally different do as well as they do. It has been suggested that existing intelligence and achievement tests are highly loaded in favor of middle-class cultural values. Accordingly, the scores obtained from such tests should predict success in coping with middle-class cultural demands and in the achievement of middle-class scholastic objectives. This the tests seem to do adequately. Whether this kind of success alone constitutes "intelligence" or is only one manifestation of intelligence is quite another matter. As was seen from the discussion of the mentally subnormal, variables included in the IQ are only a portion of factors involved in adjustment. Correlations between IQ and any given outcome (job success, effectiveness of adjustment, school success) seldom range as high as $r = +.70$. They generally are more of the size of $+.35$. Even in the rare instance of a $+.70$ value, such a correlation indicates that common factors account for less than one-half the performance in the two situations. More than one-half the factors contributing to the relationship would not be accounted for by IQ. Depending on the sizes of the groups compared, smaller correlation coefficients and small IQ differences may be statistically significant. When it comes to predictions about individual outcomes, the IQ is seldom contraindicative for any plan. The range in IQ scores in any one group of individuals frequently exceeds the difference between two groups.

To say the culturally different are less intelligent is one thing; to say they are lacking in certain test-taking habits is another, and to say they are less "middle-class" is still another.

Verbal and Language Skills.   A deficit in the areas of language and verbal proficiency is so frequently cited as to be automatically accepted by many persons dealing with the culturally different. When the findings gathered by dozens of studies are considered, there is irrefutable evidence that the culturally disadvantaged as a group have a limited vocabulary and are less able to deal with the kinds of language items that make up the prevailing scales for assessing these functions. Our intention is not of arguing these findings, which speak for themselves.

The crux of the matter is just what all these measures may mean. Language is an integral aspect of culture. The position has been taken that we are dealing with a conflict of cultures. It should not be surprising, then, that members of two different cultures are found to have differences in language. When the data reporting the difficulty the culturally different have with middle-class language are analyzed in a cultural context, some interesting patterns are discernible. Such analyses have been made by Bernstein (1960) and Riessman (1962). Bernstein carried out a comprehensive study of the total language patterns and contrasted "formal" and public" language as used in communication. Formal language is characterized by following certain technical arrangements and prescribed structures; it is thus rigid and syntactical. These qualities of formal language are what the culturally different person finds perplexing.

Riessman (1962) has made a compelling case for the culturally different having great language facility and fluency, but the language is that of their culture. This observation is readily verifiable in the behavior of the culturally different. Their language is colorful, flexible, and richly descriptive. Riessman suggests that much innovation and creativeness in communication originates with the culturally different. Greater use of nonverbal methods in communication are also made by the culturally different who may freely and spontaneously combine hand clapping, body swaying, and singing to express their feelings.

Continuing study of language patterns indicates that Bernstein's notions of "formal" and "public" communication styles may not adequately explain all the observations. Some linguists are questioning the reported "primitive" language ascribed to black children. Data collected by Labov, Cohen, Robbins, & Lewis (1968) on blacks in Harlem show that the syntactic structures of black speech and standard English are basically the same. Cross-cultural studies also indicate that scattered groups do not differ much in the fundamentals of language. A "difference" hypothesis seems to be more tenable than one based on "deficits."

Family Structure. A consideration of the family arrangements of the culturally different entails a look into one of the more jumbled aspects of this cultural group. Information on family relationships has suffered from efforts to squeeze the picture to fit the frame of recognized psychoanalytic explanations of pathology and from what appear to be ethnically related influences among some of the more numerous subgroups of the culturally disadvantaged.

One of the major points of controversy centers about a prevailing pattern of dominant influence by adult females (matriarchal) as opposed to adult males (patriarchal). Lewis (1966), who has collected extensive cross-cultural data, insists that the pattern is one of matriarchy. Riessman (1962), who has made extensive analyses of the lower-class culture in the United States, is equally convinced that a pattern of patriarchy is typical, except for the black group. Several investigators have attached considerable importance to the consequences of the absence of biological fathers from the home and subsequent devastating effects for the development of male children. An excellent review of these studies is presented by Herzog & Sudia (1968). They conclude that the importance of these findings has been exaggerated and overgeneralized and that the existing data do not permit a decisive answer on the consequences of father absence. They suggest that what may be needed to provide illumination of the problem is the direct study of children in fatherless homes, rather than the present inferential approach of attempting to isolate an elusive "single factor" from what are obviously multiple and interacting factors.

The pattern of compulsive masculinity (machismo) has been cited as a reaction to excessive female domination, but this may be erroneous labeling of behaviors which are of a physical, motor, and tangible orientation. The females in the lower class may daily carry out physical feats of lifting, carrying, and fighting that exceed the physical exertions of the most active middle-class male. When the matter of who is the figure of authority, the decision maker, is considered, there is growing question as to how much of this responsibility is assumed by the middle-class male, and many sociologists have long ago conceded that the females dominate the middle-class family.

Another controversial point hinges about "extended" and "nuclear" family units. In the extended family, all adult females (sisters, aunts, mother, grandmothers) fill roles as "mothers" and all adult males are "fathers" (brothers, uncles, father, grandfathers). The extended family can include a large number of persons. The nuclear family is limited to parent (or parents) and their children, ordinarily a smaller number of persons. The nuclear family can be said to be more structured and definitive with clearer lines of interactions and relationships that permit the members to know just where they are. But contacts and alternatives are fewer, and a chronic atmosphere of tension from which there is little escape can develop when there are conflicts between members of this small group.

There are many positive claims that can be made for the extended family unit, which is presumed to be more prevalent with the culturally different. Children in such families can be expected to profit from multiple identification models without having to be concerned with pleasing only one particular person. Attaining help and status as an adult should be an easier matter, and sibling rivalry may be reduced, to name a few possible benefits. Negative consequences for the child in the extended family are related to possible inconsistencies and limited attention because parents are frequently occupied with one or another crisis situation rather than spending time with children. Early independence in self-help is emphasized, with children depending on each other much of the time. Parental attention is secured by creating crises that compete with those already confronting the parent. This may have important implications for later adjustment at school. Regardless of the presence or absence of the real father or mother, children grow up as recognizable males and females.

Zigler (1973b) believes the extended family unit has generally declined in frequency, being supplanted by the nuclear family. He is concerned that this change, coupled with what he sees as a tendency for all adults to reject the parenting role, has serious implications for child care. Zigler sees an urgent need for nationwide training for all adults in order to assure that children will have adequate parental care.

Physical and Motor Skills. The culturally different are typically depicted as having a preference for the physical and concrete, which finds expression in motor activities. For a long time, it was considered more appropriate to assess the intellectual ability of the culturally different with tasks that demanded skill in motor manipulation and visual-motor coordination. It was expected that the culturally different would be more adequate in dealing with motor-manipulation items, such as the assembly of cut-out puzzles and the arrangement of blocks to copy geometric patterns. It was recommended that the culturally different have chances to play in games and to work with tools as a way of fostering appreciation for school. Another line of support for the contention of great motor skill has been that of citing the high percentage of black members of athletic teams. This feature has become so widespread that some black leaders have objected to the continued participation of black athletes on the grounds that it is a special case of Uncle Tomism.

The concern of this discussion is to explore the many facets of this reputed physical-motor attribute, for which we find some supporting and some dissenting opinions. In his monumental study of social-class patterns and practices, Davis (1948) noted a lower-class preference for physical activities as releases for emotional feelings of all kinds. Members of this group fought, used physical punishment, and engaged in all types of physical activities and contests more than did members of other cultural groups. Miller & Swanson (1960) have verified and expanded on what they term the "motoric orientation" of the culturally different. This characteristic can be observed in a predilection for dealing with objects—handling them and juggling them. Such behaviors are sometimes referred to as a propensity for "thinking with one's hands." The motoric orientation is credited with accounting for the heavy use of gestures in communication, the physical rather than verbal expression of violence and affection, a marked interest in competitive sports, and an admiration for feats of strength and endurance.

Despite the claims for a high degree of agility and motor skill, there are puzzling gaps that call into question the generality of this assertion. Granted that many culturally different persons have achieved success in boxing, football, baseball, and basketball, a smaller number have gained recognition as violinists, artists, or dancers. In the preschool programs there seems to be as much need for presenting experiences that will develop motor-coordination skills of the culturally different as for language stimulation. Some social scientists have suggested that the concern for physical prowess is an expression of compulsive masculinity to defend against total domination by females in a matrifocal culture. Yet other social scientists have emphasized the fact that the culturally different live in a world where physical activities predominate. They often carry water, chop wood, have fewer labor-saving gadgets, and must typically use their hands in their work. There have been discoveries of possible constitutional factors that suggest a greater potential for physical and motor skills, at least for those culturally different who are black. This evidence consists of differences in the bones and musculature of the legs and in the observed accelerated motor development of Uganda infants in Africa (Gerber, 1958). These infants accomplish developmental motor tasks of controlling the head movements, sitting alone, grasping, and walking alone in less than half the time required by white Occidental infants. Regardless of what the causative factors may be, a true picture of motor-skill potential and development is essential for effective educational planning. Potential skills in the physical and motor areas can provide solid assets for acculturation.

Attitudes toward Education. The culturally different are often credited with having attitudes of not wanting to do much to help themselves get ahead. The rejection of education particularly is said to be widespread. Excessive dropout rates and a disproportionate number of persons in the lower school-achievement range are taken as expressions of a dislike for education on the part of the lower class. The opportunity to add to their educational attainment by attendance in night-school programs, frequently made easily available to the culturally different, has been received less than enthusiastically. The attitude is difficult to understand in view of the constant emphasis on "better education—better pay" and in the light of the actual opening up of better vocational opportunities as discrimination practices subside. Adding to the confusion is the well-known tendency for members of the lower class to give "lip service" to values and objectives of the middle class while acting according to the standards and values of the lower class.

Recent studies have produced findings challenging the belief that the culturally different dislike, or are even uninterested in, getting an education. Riessman (1962) collected responses from lower-class adults to an open-ended question, "What do you miss most in life that you would want your children to have?" More than half the respondents answered, "Education." The answer was given more frequently by black than by white persons in the study group. This response takes on an added importance when it is remembered that open-ended questions do not provide any choices or selections for answers but require the respondent to furnish his own answer. Even more unexpected are data reported by Durkin (1961), who found that 55% of a group of children identified on the basis of being able to read on entrance to school came from lower socioeconomic families. Teaching a child to read demands consistent and concerted effort on the part of the older members of the family. In some areas, notably St. Louis, interest and follow-through have been generated among lower-class parents at least sufficient for getting children started in school and in preschool programs.

Yet the patterns of dropping out and low achievement continue and demand clarification. It seems likely that lower-class families are at least favorably disposed to getting their children started in school. Data gathered by Lewis (1966) suggests that what is from the start a tenuous venture may ultimately be undone by the cumulative effects of being unable to keep up with more academically oriented classmates. Not only are the culturally different less interested in dealing with the school curricula, which are increasingly of an abstract and intangible nature, but they are less likely to have suitable clothing, books, pencils, lunch money, and the like. They give up, often retaining a belief that they will return someday. No small part of the matter of dropouts may rest with school curricula themselves. School curricula have remained amazingly inflexible and unchanged. There is a distinct narrowing to more and more of an academic orientation with each higher grade level. Not only do such academic tasks have little that appeals to the culturally different, but they demand a lot of effort. It would in many ways be more strange if all pupils remained in such a thwarting situation indefinitely.

When all is considered, the controversy as to attitudes and responses toward education may not be such a dilemma. Children from the lower classes like to learn, and they do learn. Riessman (1962) has provided a succinct resolution of the apparent inconsistency. He maintains that "education" must be differentiated from "what schools offer." The school program is only one kind of educational experience, requiring particular talents and offering specific rewards. If the schools really intend to provide universal education, they must greatly diversify the experiences and the rewards available so as to reach the members of all social classes. As matters presently stand, lower-class children may be at their greatest disadvantage in the school.

Educationally Relevant Characteristics

Whatever the picture with regard to characteristics of the culturally different, experiences and events that occur prior to entrance into school are of paramount interest to the educator. It is these early experiences that develop the skills, goals, and rewards the child brings to school. The general process of development, in which learning occurs out of the interaction between the child and his surroundings, is the same for all children. The children themselves may be very similar at the start, but different surroundings, rewards, and coping skills foster comparably different personality organizations which must be approached in appropriate modes and channels if development is to continue.

Home Conditions. The importance of home-family influence in determining educational outcomes was cited by Coleman (1966). Lower-class families tend to be large, with children appearing in rapid succession. The parents have only marginal acquisitions of skills and attributes highly valued by the middle class. The situation then does not facilitate the instilling of middle-class values. Under ordinary conditions, the parents are strapped in coping with the routine operation of the family. There are endless dishes to be washed, clothes to be washed and ironed, food to be prepared, beds to be made. Life for both parents has been described as a never-ending cycle of crises which begin anew with each day. Thus engaged, parents may have little time to give to any child. In many homes the potential parental time available for children is further reduced by parental absence due to death, desertion, divorce, or diversion.

As a consequence, children in such situations have minimal chances for talk and discussion with their parents. They become independent at early ages and may learn more from and depend more on older siblings and peers than on adults. Punishment may never be administered in many instances, because time simply runs out. More commonly, punishment is delayed and/or given in a physical form that is not easily related to the undesired behavior. Left to figure things out for himself, the child may decide that he should develop greater skills for avoiding detection or that he should try to change his "bad luck" to "good" in some magical way. Operating only with his own resources, his curiosity may not be directed into useful channels. He may take an object apart, destroying it by dismanteling, with no regard for trying to figure out how it "works." Parents often have little time to deal with the children as individuals. The child has little choice for obtaining needed attention other than to generate a crisis situation greater than the one currently absorbing the parent's concern. The child may also learn very early that he must grab his share of everything quickly while he can because what is gone is gone.

It is difficult to calculate the consequences of not being read to because there are too many diapers to be changed as a part of getting everyone bedded down. The never-ceasing demands on the parent's energies must undoubtedly result in many similar situations where honest intentions go astray. The impact of countless broken promises of trips to the zoo, going to the movies, or getting a new toy can easily be a feeling of suspicion, mistrust, and a reaffirmation for the immediate and tangible. Learning to be "good" or to work hard for future reward has little chance under such conditions. Along with these diminished opportunities for listening, remembering, and persisting there may be other deficits in chances to manipulate books, pictures, paper and pencil, and other materials that will be encountered in the classroom. The parent may have a minimum of these same skills to share with the child or to serve as a resource for assisting the child to gain proficiency in them.

Social Learning. Throughout this text, the importance of social learning as a contributor to the understanding of adjustment difficulties has been emphasized. The principle is a particularly useful one when applied to the problems of the culturally different, for there are three major acquisitions that have important implications for education.

1. Home and family arrangements are such that lower-class children early weld into a cohesive group. Needs for contacts of all sorts, approval, recognition, and support are satisfied by this group affiliation. Intrusive efforts by outsiders, including adults, are warded off as being not needed. In a similar way, any efforts that may cost group membership are to be avoided. The safest course of action is not to be too ambitious and to be careful not to achieve too much. A violation of either of these standards would jeopardize group status. Moreover, gains made by an individual would be attained at a cost of making others appear incompetent or bad, and no one intentionally wants to hurt his best friends.

2. A second feature of the learning of the culturally different child grows out of his greater reliance on tangible units of experience. Specifics can be handled and are "for real." Possibly because he can be the victim of many broken promises of good things to come that never materialize, or possibly because of an inherent predisposition for specific rewards, the culturally disadvantaged child has a definite orientation for dealing with the concrete. He has little capacity for accepting criticism and making corrections just to get praise in the future. It is difficult for him to comprehend the difference between the "Й" that he makes and the "N" the teacher holds

out as the model. He may see no important difference between a picture of a bear and that of a guinea pig. He finds it difficult to learn something by reading about it and is wary of those who seek to goad him with promises that he knows well may never materialize.

3. A third major tendency of significance is the culturally different child's expectancy of concrete rewards. A pat on the head, a stick of gum, or a small stamp in the form of a rocketship is acceptable as a reward. Being told he is a good citizen, a good worker, or a good scholar elicits little other than confusion. He has had long experience with withholding of rewards and is not bothered by the experience. In the same way, he is not concerned (guilty) that he has behaved badly because he cheated. Exhortations to be nice, to work hard, or to be a good sport are ineffective as techniques for increasing his output. His tendency to be self-reliant minimizes any inclination for accepting criticism of his work in a positive sense. Optimal performance is more likely to be in evidence when specific responses are provided in the form of definite and concrete rewards immediately given.

Educational Difficulties.   By this time it should be clear that the culturally different child has objectives, responses, and expectations different from those observed in the middle-class child. There are rewards, reinforcement patterns, and methods of approach that can be advantageously manipulated in controlling and influencing his learning. More correctly, the culturally different child is confronted with a situation of cultures in conflict. Lindgren (1972) has provided an excellent picture of the ways in which the culturally different child has difficulty at school.

1. The culturally different child is unfamiliar with the roles that govern classroom organization. He appears impulsive, interruptive, and inattentive.

2. The culturally different child is less able to learn from someone *telling* him how to do something or how things are. He prefers a demonstration and direct participation.

3. The culturally different child is less likely to look to adults (teachers) as persons who will help him.

4. The culturally different child prefers frequent changes in what he is doing and doesn't remember directions or instructions well.

5. The culturally different child has trouble grasping the formality and correctness of syntax.

6. The culturally different child finds it difficult to make abstract associations; shown a group of pictures and asked which one is good to eat, he may give a verbal response of something far removed from any of the objects pictured.

7. The culturally different child is casual and finds it difficult to make specific differentiations necessary to identify the dirtiest, prettiest, and so on.

8. The culturally different child may have a rather narrow range of experiences, so that he is uncertain as to whether an animal is a lion, cow, or buffalo or whether an eating place is a restaurant, cafeteria, or cafe.

Etiological Considerations

Offering explanations to account for the adjustment problems of the culturally different may seem at first glance a redundant effort. This may be especially so since our presentation has emphasized the notion of a basic cultural conflict rather than a deficit in the strict sense. "Culture" is a system made up of many factors that serves as an organization of patterns by which individuals come to experience their surroundings. Cultural disadvantage might then be expected to originate from defect or impairment in the organization of patterns of living, as these are experienced, in the individual's potentials for absorbing this experience, and in the unique personal organization the individual acquires as a result of his cultural experiences.

Cultural Deprivation Factors

Many behavioral scientists have attempted to present the problems of the culturally different in the frame of reference of deprivation. Impressed with the manifest lack of material objects, the minimal housing and dietary conditions, and the generally narrow experiences typical of the lower classes, the approach has been that of equating these shortages with a total lack of all experiences. To a large extent, these investigators have found additional support for the interpretation of experiential deficit in the large number of so-called sensory-deprivation studies. It has been conclusively established that the withholding of visual, motor, or other stimulation in infancy has devastating consequences for the adult animal. Such results are demonstrable only where there is complete denial of stimulation, whereas only small amounts of stimulation are adequate for the development of a normal capacity to deal with experiences. There is a suggestion that any depression in stimulation has a correlated reduction of capacity for the adult individual. Evidence for the latter contention comes from comparisons of persons in usual family situations as compared with persons placed in foster homes and in institutions.

The data are open to other interpretations, however, since constitutional factors are usually not controlled and there is considerable doubt about the permanent irreversibility of the consequences of limited experiences on later development. In either case, it is difficult to make a convincing argument that the early years of the culturally different are missing in any kind of experience. The differences, where identifiable, are more qualitative than quantitative. There is every reason to believe the culturally different have as much visual, kinesthetic, auditory, and other stimulation as does the middle-class child. In fact, the noisy, active surroundings of the lower class can be said to hold more stimulation than does the quiet and controlled atmosphere of the middle-class home.

What is different about the experiences is a basic one involving acculturation in two different cultures. The members of each of the two contrasting cultures successfully incorporate the language, customs, mores, values, objectives, and coping techniques of their own culture. Differences in the attributes of the two cultures form the root of conflict and adjustment problems when an individual attempts to live in a culture other than the one native to him. A core of values emphasizing responsible planning, attainment by continuous education, competitive acquisition of material possessions, and future time orientation can be expected to have associated behavior that differs markedly from that elicited by belief in luck, doubt about the future, taking immediate pleasures, and tolerant indulgence. If the two sets of values did not hold enough disparities, sufficient discrepancies to form the basis for a struggle would be found in membership and allegiance choices by any one individual in the larger society made up of several major subcultures. In many respects, a clash is built into such a society. The impossibility of saying which of the opposing sets of values is the better intensifies the expectation of contention and disagreement.

Constitutional Factors

The integrity and durability of a culture boils down to success in supplying workable solutions and acceptable rewards for dealing with life's problems. In solving a problem, the individual must rely on patterns of skills, talents, and energies within his behavioral-response potential. These are potentials packaged in a genetic container. The capacity for experiencing rewards is also genetically stipulated. It is consistent with observations of behavior to conceptualize a pattern of a particular genetic potential finding a suitable environment, developing and maintaining itself, and thus perpetuating the entire relationship. While it is obvious that individuals, whatever their culture, develop within the limits set by genetic endowment, contrary to Jensen's (1968) impressive data indicating that hereditary factors may have a dominant role, there are other reasons to believe that social class membership is determined mainly by the circumstances of life (Jencks, 1972).

There appear to be somewhat more subtle constitutional forces that can influence social-class membership. Relevant for this contention are findings discovered in research directed by Pasamanick. Reporting on data collected in association with events during pregnancy and child-health outcomes, Pasamanick and Knobloch (1961) were able to show connections between abnormalities during pregnancy or at birth and later impairments in the child. Mothers who have poor diets, are fatigued or harassed, have any type of illness, or receive less than minimal prenatal medical care gave birth to children who showed a higher incidence of defects and deficiencies of all types. These significant events in pregnancy are commonly observed in lower-class mothers and could be one factor contributing to the kind of marginality of potential which sometimes seems to typify members of the lower class.

Nutritional Factors

Malnutrition and hunger have been extensively studied following information that damage to the nervous system and impaired school performance can result from inadequate diets. Although often controversially received, reports such as "Hunger, U.S.A." have presented a startling picture with these highlights:

1. One-fifth of United States' households have "poor" diets.

2. Of low-income-level households, 36% subsist on "poor" diets.

3. There are 256 counties in the United States that should be declared hunger areas.

4. The worst nutritional conditions are found among migrant farm workers and on certain American Indian reservations.

5. Existing governmental food programs are deplorably insufficient.

6. Even in areas where there is no "hunger," as many as 10 million U.S. citizens are malnourished.

There is little doubt that physical and mental development, more than half of which occurs during the first two years of life, can be grossly influenced by inadequate nutrition and lack of quality prenatal care. Disadvantaged children are particularly susceptible, but the situation is a complex one not likely to be resolved by simplistic solutions such as enriched diets or a "good breakfast" program. The extent and severity of the consequences of malnutrition and inadequate prenatal care for physical and mental development should be given high priority in future research studies.

Ego-Development Factors

It is possible that processes by which the individual acquires a perception of himself are the most significant source of problems encountered by the culturally different. An excellent review of patterns by which lower-class children develop self-concept has been presented by Ausubel & Ausubel (1963). The acquisition of an integrated set of values, attitudes, aspirations, and satisfactions centering about the self, designated as ego development, encompasses constitutional and cultural factors. This is sufficient to ascribe primary importance to this developmental process in and of itself. Turning to a more specific consideration of ego acquisition, there appear to be particular steps that have special reference to the subsequent adjustment of lower-class members. These have to do with the consequences of parent-child relationships, the opportunities for acquiring status, the types of approved behaviors, and the kinds of achievement motivation sanctioned.

Previous reference has been made to the small amount of interaction between parent and child in the lower-class family. Parents are busy coping with many crisis situations, are drawn to various diversions, hold limited resources for meeting any demand, or are simply exhausted. The net result is that the child has difficulty in effecting a necessary satellizing with the parent. He is denied an important source of positive self-esteem, and the fleeting encounters with parents are likely to be ones of harsh punishment. The multiplicity of parents he must obey and please can make for confusion in identification or deny practice in learning how to please some authority person. For boys, there may be special problems of living in a female-dominated world. The lower-class child thus can be uncertain of his identity, ambivalent about authority, and can find it difficult to subjugate himself to the control of an adult whom he tends not to trust.

Opportunities to acquire status are also limited for the lower-class child. Within his immediate family, he finds that status is uncertain and difficult to come by. Many matters poorly understood by the child seem to absorb the parents' attention, and he is forced to be excessively resourceful in gaining their interest. Even if he is able to identify with his family, he quickly learns that they are demeaned and degraded for no apparent reason. In some instances, his efforts to gain respect may encounter the added rebuff of discrimination and segregation practices as a response to situations he cannot change. Only the peer group seems to hold a place for him where there is some semblance of recognition, and to this haven he turns. In making the move, he carries with him feelings of frustration, bitterness, and counter-rejection.

Each culture tends to sanction certain types of behaviors. This is one of the distinguishing features of a culture, and it involves the types of opportunities for behaving, the kinds of demands confronting the person, and the rewards available. Parents and authority persons in control of the culture are likely to promote their own standards and values and to feel threatened by any deviations. They are inclined to disapprove of excessive ambition and to reward an acceptance of one's "place in life." They actually have a minimum of resources, moreover, for the real support of ventures into the business and professional world. The child soon learns not to ask for much. Early manifestations of independence are encouraged. At least, the child's "getting out of the parent's hair" also gets the parents out of the child's hair. The outcome is one favoring a facade of compliance and subjugation while taking covert urges of a hostile nature to the peer group for expression.

A final important ego-development process is the acquisition of motivational components. Prospects for the culturally disadvantaged person incorporating a pattern of high achievement are bleak. From the first, important persons seem to care very little about what he does. So long as he is not bothersome to them, his parents are not likely to inquire or check up on what he has been doing. Casting about, he sees his own kind getting very little of the material benefits of life even though they may work very hard. Contacts with the middle-class culture may serve to sharpen rather than to invite ways to change this disparity. Attendance at school all too frequently proves to be anything but his cup of tea and may only enhance a nucleus of doubt as to his competence, even when he tries very hard to please. The final blow can come when he is fed up and leaves school to test the vocational world. There he finds more doors closed than opened. Little choice remains but to succumb to low aspirations although high attainments may be verbalized in the "right" places.

Treatment Programs

Efforts to deal with the problems of the culturally different have been as numerous as are the manifestations of the difficulties. Physical and mental health services, dietary and housing improvements, recreational and cultural opportunities, and vocational and educational offerings are among the major approaches. Each of these lines of assistance has particular possibilities and each has shown a degree of success. While acknowledging that all these services are essential in dealing with the problem, our discussion gives greater exposition to programs with an educational orientation. The choice is not dictated by a belief that an educational approach is the only solution to the problem, although this contention can be defended. It must not be overlooked that there are unique and real contributions, for example, from the fields of medicine and community planning, in addition to the important functions these services may have in reinforcing and maintaining changes affected by an educational program. The emphasis on educational programs in this discussion is simply a reflection of the basic educational orientation of the text, the belief that all treatment programs for children are most effective when integrated, and the recognition that the school can and should be the most appropriate coordinating center.

Approaches to the Problem

The book *Families of the Slums,* edited by S. Minuchin (1967), is an excellent cross section of materials showing the intensive effort witnessed during the decade 1960–1970 to assist many of the culturally different. The careful reader will find much new light to illuminate obscure corners and ambiguous notions about these families. It is pointed out that programs have been organized about several major conceptions, each of which has certain justifications and a group of adherents who can marshal some evidence in support of its position. These approaches will be briefly examined.

⌐*Nothing Can Be Done.*   This position views the problem as being of such overwhelming magnitude as to crush and overrun all efforts for correction. While conceding that the difficulty is actually hopeless, token efforts and piecemeal programs, halfheartedly presented, are thus sanctioned. Accountability and evaluation of program outcomes are never considered since defeat is a foregone assumption.

The acceptance of such a position does have the possibility for getting us off the hook. It is quickly evident that the difficulties associated with cultural difference are in fact exceedingly complex and defy organization into a neat four-square package. To say that attitudes cannot be changed, so save your money may solve the immediate aspects of the problem, but from a long-range consideration this may ultimately prove to be the most costly of all omissions. Initial studies of the life patterns of members of the several socioeconomic levels in the United States found lower-class families were indulgent and permissive toward their children in contrast to middle-class parents who were inclined to be strict and demanding in dealing with children. Less than twenty years later, these patterns had reversed themselves (Mnookin, 1973). Planning for bringing about attitudinal change is enormously challenging, but apparently it does happen. It may not be easy to implement such changes, but much more study seems warranted before the matter can be accepted as impossible.

The Fault Is in the System.   This is the explanation frequently preferred by well-meaning professionals who are struck with the fact that the culturally different are often at the bottom of the pile, having less money, limited education, inferior jobs, etc. According to this interpretation, the culturally different are to be expected to engage in antisocial and irresponsible behaviors in retaliation for the supposed frustration and denial they experience. When interpreted by a zealous social scientist, this explanation can appear highly convincing. When the culturally different are considered in their entirety, however, a normal range of intact and organized families, abilities, interests, incomes, and law-abiding records is found (Minuchin, 1967).

There are, nevertheless, some subtle quirks in the system that bear added study. Much of the middle-class life style is organized for production of material things. There is an emphasis on having the best one, the latest model, the newest gadget, the biggest. Material possessions are, of course, purchased by the individual's work, so work hard and you can buy a lot. It follows that the harder you work, the more you can buy. And the more everyone buys, the more everyone can buy. Persons caught up in such a system are enmeshed in a more vicious and destructive slavery system than has been imagined. It demands that everyone be a consumer because the more consumers, the more everyone can be a consumer.

A conflict ensues when any individual or group of individuals take a position of being unwilling to commit themselves to a life of consuming. Are such persons indolent or stupid because they purchase only a rocking chair and a radio for about one-hundredth of the cost of an automobile and color TV (and work only a proportionate number of days)? It is possible that some persons find having a steady job is annoying, living in the same place more than a couple of years is boring, keeping up with all the "news" is tiring. Some persons may aspire to and be satisfied with being at the bottom of the pile. It is possible that seeing such a life style is frustrating, thwarting, and threatening for middle-class persons. Unfortunately, choices and commitments as to which life style will be pursued must sometimes be made long before the child is cognitively or experientially able to make the best decision for himself.

Assign Experts to Solve the Problem.   A society in which technology is highly developed tends to have a plentiful number of experts who are relied upon for getting and keeping the machinery moving. It is then to be anticipated that this same approach would be invoked to solve social problems. On the surface, this appears to be a highly appropriate method and one that should prove effective. Vocational training schools, employment counselors, early academic training, busing, urban renewal, each family having its own caseworker, are representative of the innovative productions of the experts. Although the plans looked good on the drawing board, they were not highly successful when put in practice. Consistent failure of these programs to do the job expected generated a certain amount of rebuttal. A frequently offered explanation was that the persons for whom the programs were planned were not involved and had no share in the planning. In his comprehensive review of the outcomes of forced busing to achieve integration, for example, Amor (1972) comments that the failure of the program might have been predicted since the families and children were not consulted regarding their views about busing.

Complaints from the recipients of these reform programs were acknowledged by assigning so-called "culturally different" persons to administer the programs on the basis that "it takes a poor man to understand a poor man." The core of "indigenous" experts has often had qualifications largely consisting of membership in a minority group. Although well intentioned in many instances, they have often added to rather than reduced the confusion. A prominent psychologist has made a strong recommendation that black children should be examined only by black psychologists using measuring scales expressly constructed for blacks. In a study carried out by Jacobs & DeGraaf (1973), in which the same black and white children were assessed by different black and white examiners, it was found that the psychologists consistently assigned lower evaluations to children with the same membership group as the psychologists.

A final observation entails an incident that occurred when one of the authors was serving on a team evaluating a special training program conducted by a large city school system. The program, then in its terminal stage, had solicited minority group members for training to serve as pupil personnel services workers in schools with large minority group enrollments. One of the trainees, giving a detailed picture of just how he performed his services, explained that a complete assessment of children referred for study was carried out, using Spanish editions of measuring scales where available. When pushed for more detail, particularly ways in which the trainee attempted to give the referring teacher specific information for helping the child being studied, the trainee responded, "I explained to the teacher that this girl is Mexican and that the Mexican girls don't like to go to school. This is the way it is for Mexican children." This is another example of a sincere and honest effort, but one that probably gave the teacher little if any new information on which an effective set of intervention strategies could be developed for helping the child. There have been reports of more dire consequences in which those given the assignment of assisting the culturally different took the opportunity to victimize their fellow group members. There are also instances in which minority group members, often serving in a nonpaid volunteer capacity, have performed outstanding services. These will be recounted in subsequent discussion.

It does not appear necessary to have "a poor man to understand a poor man." Words and communication styles may differ, but there is no incomprehensible gap so long as both persons want to communicate. It is advisable to consider that, although generally used to promote understanding, language can be used to distort and obscure, thus preventing rapprochement. The suggestion has been tendered that some of those persons designated as culturally different may be satisfied with their way of life. If this be the case, then it is conceivable that they could view language as a protection, insulating against nosey probes that infringe upon their individuality. The culturally different sometimes seem to have more than the usual amount of difficulty in communicating even with each other.

What Is Needed Is More Money.   At one level, this approach is illustrated by the request made to an agency by a client who said, "Don't send me another of those counselors. Just send me the money, that's what I need the most." It can be extended to "Don't educate me, don't train me for a job, or don't find me a new house, but I can use some money." Many, but not all, the culturally different seem to have a chronic shortage of cash. This can be so even when they receive a rather adequate salary. It leads to speculation about the management of the money. This is a very personal matter and one for which there may be no absolute answer, especially if the person has earned the money by his own efforts.

At another level, administrators of social welfare programs also seem to experience a chronic shortage of cash, judging from their continual requests to "give us a little more money" and we can implement this new service or provide assistance to that group. Unfortunately, there exist no guidelines or sets of standards for establishing how much money should be allocated to social reforms. Although money apportioned to social welfare programs in the United States exceeds all other expenditures, it may in fact be too small an investment.[1] On the other hand, what is accepted as the poverty level in the United States borders on the luxurious in other parts of the world.

Giving more money may be only another trap, the easy-way-out, "pie in the sky" kind of solution that we are often taken with. The root of the problem may rest in the fact that we simply do not know what is the most effective use to be made of the money that is available. Conventional psychotherapy is not accepted by the culturally different. It would be possible to embark upon an intensive vocational upgrading program, but there is the matter of who will be selected and how and for what they will be trained. The situation may be comparable to the dilemma faced by the culturally different individual with

---

1. *Note*: When the money allocated for defense and for welfare programs in the United States is examined in total, the following picture emerges: (1) Federal government—About $2/5$ for defense and military; about $1/3$ for social welfare programs. (2) State, county, and local governments—about $1/2$ for social welfare programs; none for defense and military (this is constitutionally a federal function). The combined money spent by all state, county, and local governments about equals the total budget of the federal government.

respect to how money is managed, but the magnitude of resources involved makes it urgent to seek more definite answers for the problem.

Educationally Oriented Programs

The fact that children are required to attend school, the belief that schools have a major part in preparation for life adjustment, and the availability of measuring devices yielding scores and predictions assure that schools and educational processes will have a priority in any effort to bring about changes in living patterns or conditions. The educational road, thus, has been the most heavily traveled route on the way to correcting the problems of cultural difference. There are two major lines of objectives that can be selected for attainment by education.

One is the familiar course of intensifying the acquisition of academic skills. The availability of materials, instructional methods, and personnel specialized in training for academic acquisition make it easy for the school to select such a vehicle as the first choice for bridging the cultural gap. Early school programs, training parents to act as teachers, compensating for identified academic deficits, busing to "higher quality" schools, and remedial teaching are some specific examples. These efforts were given substantial support by repeated "findings" of lower IQs, lower academic achievement scores, and measurable academic deficiencies among the culturally different. A lesser amount of strength was provided by sporadic reports of initial increases, albeit small, in measures of academic ability and achievement. The stage seemed set for eliminating the problem of inequality by transforming everyone into an equal academic achiever.

The other approach is one focusing on training in social development and human relations skills. Although probably the most defensible as products of education (not all of which has to take place in the formal setting of the school), training in tolerance, ways for getting along with all persons, fostering of self-esteem, social-problem solving, knowing how to make it in society, are all aspects of a path less well charted by the conventional educator. Along with the shortage of good maps, there has existed a minimum of instructional materials and methods, assessment devices, and skilled professional staffs. Even where parts of the road were discernible, there were unknown pitfalls and possible traps (how would parents react to training which was contrary to their values and threatened to alienate them from their children?). The net result has been that what might be a much more acceptable long-range solution to the problem of cultural difference, allowing each individual to achieve his full potential as a human being, has received secondary and slight attention in contrast to that given to building a kind of flawless academic machine.

Bicultural Education. For some time it has been evident that the blaze which heated up the old "melting pot" has died down. The many cultural groups identifiable in the United States today suggest that the fire never created more than a lukewarm temperature or that the cultural contents of the broth were highly resistant to combination by heat. New recipes, tested and proven by exemplary projects funded by the U.S. Department of Health, Education and Welfare (Title VII, Elementary and Secondary Education Act, Office of Child Development), have indicated ways that children from different cultural backgrounds can be successfully educated in almost any combination. Catalytic agents called for by the recipes are teachers and/or aides of bicultural backgrounds and the use of bicultural materials in instruction.

In contrast to early school programs like Head Start, these bicultural programs have proven highly effective in promoting substantially improved school achievement for the participants and the gains appear to be durable. The classroom activities have a bilingual focus, but all cultural differences are made use of in maintaining interest for learning. Reliance on the children to help each other master communication with two languages and continual use of presentations by parents (learning associated with constructing a piñata, or preparing a Chinese dinner to be eaten with chopsticks) has contributed to popular acceptance by students and the community. Whether it is the demonstrated success and acceptance of bicultural programs built about the specificity of bilingual training, or whether the impetus comes from legislative mandate for such programs (the first such legislation was passed in Massachusetts in 1971), the spread of bicultural programs of the bilingual prototype is limited only by the availability of bicultural persons for staffing. Thompson (1975) shares a vivid account illustrating that unless the teacher and/or aides are truly bicultural, they will not be effective, and in fact, they may widen the cultural gap when children react to a demeaning cultural "put down" handed out by a teacher of Spanish rather than a Mexican-American teacher.

Evaluation of Educational Approaches.   Results have been so consistent that there is little basis for questioning the fact that academically oriented educational programs have not proven adequate for resolving the problems of cultural difference. This is particularly true when the evaluation looks at goals of attaining equality by producing equal academic achievement. In a comprehensive review of the outcomes of compensatory education programs, Zigler (1973a, p. 3) conceded, "If Headstart is appraised in terms of its success in universally raising the IQs of poor children, and maintaining these IQs over time, one is tempted to write off Headstart as an abject failure." These are indeed strong pronouncements from the administrative father of the major federal effort and largest nationwide program for compensatory education. Evaluations of other aspects of educational programs are generally of the same tone. Amor (1972), for example, found that forced busing may even have contributed to such negative developments as increasing social distance between blacks and whites and a higher level of frustration but lower school grades for blacks who were often "on the spot" and faced with having to deal with an unfamiliar and vigorously competitive situation. Coleman (U. S. News & World Report, 1975) also regards busing in most large cities as futile and self-defeating. He further charges that "desegregation through the courts probably will have served in the long run to separate whites and blacks more

severely than before." More typical are the findings that early gains in measures of academic ability and achievement did not persist over two- or three-
year periods, and by the end of first or second grade culturally different children who had been in some compensatory type of program were indistinguishable from culturally different children who had not. A careful review by St.
John (1975) also failed to find any consistent academic gains accruing to
either blacks or whites attending desegregated schools and led her to question
why we should expect only one aspect of school experience—racial mix—to
have a pronounced effect on achievement.

A much brighter picture is available when success in promoting social competence is questioned. Improvements in adjustment to school, self-esteem,
getting along with other persons, and "the system" attest to the acquisition
of a set of skills that increase the individual's effectiveness in coping with life
problems. Zigler (1973a) emphasized that these changes were prevalent even
though the exact measurement of such skills is admittedly more complex than
that for measuring academic skills. Objective reports of strong, positive self-
concepts for minority group culturally different as found by Soares & Soares
(1969) and by Reece (1974) are supplemented by widespread observations of
improved capacity for students to work and learn together in an atmosphere
of acceptance and tolerance. In some of the data reviewed by Reece, black
students reported higher self-esteem and level of aspiration than did white
students. The increasing number of reports of gains in social competence
based on data collected in various situations cautions against attributing these
results to any particular program and may have special significance for the
educational approach.

Progress in Resolving Cultural Difference. There are no indices that
can be accepted as absolute indicators of change in cultural distance, especially since there is no agreement as to which one of several alternatives is to
be followed in remedying cultural difference. Poverty, an easily measured
condition frequently reported in association with cultural difference, is believed by many to be only a relative indicator. Complete and comprehensive
data are never immediately available. The rate of change in conditions of cultural difference has not been established to a degree that permits the acceptance or rejection of a 1% or 5% gain. The existence of these qualifying
conditions must be recognized in interpreting information relating to changes
in cultural difference.

Accumulating information suggests blacks have made spectacular progress
in moving upward in society (*Time,* June, 1974). The article presents impressive data to support the statement that increasing numbers of blacks are lifting themselves into the middle class, enjoying salaries, homes, and educational
levels paralleling those of whites. The data include these facts:

In 1961 only 13% of blacks earned annual salaries of $10,000 or more;
by 1971, 30% were in that category.

Between 1967 and 1972, the number of blacks attending college doubled

(727,000) ; 18% of all blacks aged 18 to 24 years were in college, compared with 26% of whites.

Between 1960 and 1971 the total number of professional technical jobs increased by 49%, but the number of blacks in the positions (lawyers, physicians, teachers, engineers, artists, writers, entertainers) increased by 128%.

Between 1960 and 1971 the number of managerial positions (officials, managers, proprietors) increased by 23% but the number of blacks in these jobs increased 200%.

Seventy-two blacks serve as board members of major corporations.

One hundred eight blacks are mayors of U.S. cities.

The ratio of blacks to whites in the lower income groups approximated the ratio of blacks to whites in the whole population.

The improved financial status of the blacks has touched off an argument as to whether or not a majority of the blacks are now "middle class." There tends to be general agreement that the social-interaction gap between blacks and whites remains, but the gap may actually be maintained by the new confidence of the blacks. Blacks seem to feel more at ease in being black, less dominated or "put down," and more the masters of their destiny. The rise of a strong black middle class has been accompanied by interesting developments. One sociologist noted "they are 105% Americans," convinced that all things are possible if you "hang in there" and work a little harder. Incidents such as the black who sent a stern letter to a well-known university admonishing action in which his son was discriminated against in favor of an applicant who came from a slum area are becoming common. A huge sign in a black affairs office that read, "Red and white are beautiful; black is proud," seems to capture the changed status of many blacks.

Somewhat sadly, a new conflict has opened as blacks who "made it" move away from blacks who remain in the poverty realm. Many middle-class blacks feel a deep sense of guilt for the seeming desertion of these individuals, often assuaged in typical middle-class fashion of contributing money for the aid of those less fortunate. Middle-class blacks also experience feelings of resentment toward lower-class blacks whose life styles are a source of annoyance and embarrassment.

It is impossible to assume that educational programs alone were able to effect these changes in status. Organized use of legal and economic procedures, the reestablishing of quota systems, providing education and vocational opportunities undoubtedly worked together to open up new and to widen existing channels. Those members of minority groups who move up in the society also make a great personal commitment. The first Cherokees who decided that attending Harvard University was preferable to hunting buffalo needed more than an extra warm blanket for the severe northern winters. The first blacks who moved into an all-white suburb had to have more than a tough skin. Those first to succeed were in a unique position for serving as models and advisors to others who wished to take the same route. It is in this capacity that many blacks, working as volunteers, have provided a vital service for members of their group. To "hear it like it is," they have added "see it like it is," in advising those who would like "a big piece of the system" to be smart by learning the rules and following them. To anyone who seeks a measure of revenge, the admonition is "Be successful. That's what really hurts."

Implications of Educational Programs for Cultural Difference.   The dismal results shown by initial efforts to deal with the problem of cultural difference by academically oriented programs, mainly compensatory in nature, have had a sobering effort on all educators (U.S. News & World Reports, 1975; Westinghouse, 1969). Some, for example Moore & Moore (1972), have openly advocated the abolishment of such programs, which they contend do more harm than good. Jencks (1972) has concluded that no amount of change in the schools would overcome the influence of luck and personality which he finds as the chief determinants of success. Other suggestions have been to change the emphasis or to eliminate certain aspects of current programs. Commenting on the academically oriented programs and the difficulties associated with failure to distinguish between careful and careless use of measuring scales, Kirp (1974, p. 33) stated, "Tests do not reveal, but merely remind, that non-middle class and minority children fare badly in schools as they presently are organized." If the educational system is to have a lasting impact on the problem of cultural difference, it would be well advised to focus efforts along lines that have had a demonstrated degree of success in fostering the acquisition of social competence. Admittedly there is a shortage of plans, materials, and methods for what, by any standards, looms as an enormous production job. A blueprint for the task is suggested by the review "Research Problems and Issues in the Area of Socialization" prepared by Sowder & Lazar (1972). Noting that they were unable to find evidence that any kind of family in the United States was doing an adequate job of preparing children to accept, tolerate, or mingle with people who hold values different from their own, Sowder and Lazar outlined a set of practices to promote tolerance and acceptance:

1. Create an atmosphere of freedom, flexibility, and approval
2. Limit conditions of frustration and thwarting
3. Deemphasize competitiveness
4. Train teachers for instruction of social competency
5. Recognize bigotry as the result of multiple rather than single variables

Specifications for putting such a design into classroom operation are detailed by Diggs (1974). Elaborating her belief that "Under the guidance of well-sensitized professional personnel, culturally different children can be given the background experiences necessary for them to grow at their own rate and in accordance with their own developmental and cultural characteristics" (p. 578), she proposes specific details of community-parent-school collaboration for the motivation, instructional methods, teacher and parent preparation, and instructional materials required for education across cultures. Illustrative of her practical approach is the description of how cultural diversity would need to be a characteristic of each classroom so as to provide the source materials for instruction in cultural differences.

Two prototype studies have provided preliminary support for expectations of a successful outcome for programs seeking to build social competency. The most intensive is that reported by Spivak & Shure (1974), who presented data collected over a four-year period of work with elementary-school-aged children. Spivak and Shure reported that there was no change in such measures as IQs, but children in their project showed consistent gains, which tended to be permanent, in social-problem-solving skills. The children's general school adjustment improved as their social-problem-solving skills increased. In a study carried out by Anderson & Johnson (1971), school achievement of Mexican-American students was found to be more related to the student's expectation of success, strength of self-concept, and amount of personal effort. Achievement was little, and less clearly, related to early difficulties with English language, differing socioeconomic status, and parental attitudes about school.

If the results from these investigations are general, a major role is identified for educational amelioration of the problem of cultural difference. Rather than seeking to deny and eliminate cultural differences, this approach capitalizes on these very characteristics of difference, focusing on aiding each child to achieve his full potential as a social being and in return to respect and assist every individual in the realization of that same right.

Summary

In the United States, a number of subcultures can be identified, each having unique values, standards, life styles, and communication modes.

Two large subcultures have been designated as "middle class" and "lower class," a differentiation made in the past on the basis of discernible differences in material possessions.

Members of the middle class tend to have a driving, work-to-get-ahead, achievement orientation.

Members of the lower class are more inclined to live on a day-to-day basis, content to take it easy, and not feeling pressured to "do better."

Life styles of the two groups have some inherent contradictions that are intensified as an individual is evaluated according to standards of his nonmembership group or when members of each group seek the same material gains.

Cultural difference may be confused with social deviancy, emotional disorder, and mental subnormality in superficial assessment.

Efforts to maintain the group structure result in members of both groups making use of such defensive techniques as stereotyping, prejudice, scapegoating, devaluing, and rationalization.

Persons in minority groups contribute disproportionately to the total number of lower-class persons who may, as a group, make up from one-third to two-fifths of the entire U.S. population.

Almost half the school-aged children may come from lower-class homes, a situation that concerns many professionals who feel that these children have fewer opportunities.

Broad social welfare programs to improve the lot and upgrade the living conditions of the lower class have included job training, medical care, nutritional supplements, improved housing, and compensatory education.

The increased availability of opportunities has resulted in measurable but small gains; the bulk of the problem remains.

Ultimate resolution of the nagging problem of cultural difference may hinge on affective educational efforts having the objective of increasing the acceptance of members of both groups for each other.

References

Amor, D. J. The evidence on busing. *The Public Interest*, 1972, **28,** 90–126.

Anderson, J. G., & Johnson, W. H. Stability and change among three generations of Mexican-Americans: factors affecting achievement. *American Educational Research Journal*, 1971, **8,** 285–309.

Ausubel, D., & Ausubel, P. Ego development among segregated Negro children. In A. H. Passow (Ed.), *Education in depressed areas.* New York: Teachers College Press, 1963, pp. 109–41.

Bernstein, B. Language and social class. *British Journal of Psychology*, 1960, **11,** 271–76.

Bloom, B. S. *Stability and change in human characteristics.* New York: Wiley, 1964.

Cloward, R. A., & Ohlin, L. E. *Delinquency and opportunity: a theory of delinquent gangs.* New York: Free Press, 1960.

Coleman, J. S. *Equality of educational opportunity.* Washington, D.C.: U.S. Government Printing Office, 1966.

Davis, A. *Social class and influence upon learning.* Cambridge: Harvard University Press, 1948.

Diggs, R. Education across cultures. *Exceptional Children*, 1974, **40,** 578–84.

Durkin, D. Children who read before grade one. *Reading Teacher*, 1961, **14,** 163–66.

Gerber, M. The psychomotor development of African children in the first year and the influence of maternal behavior. *Journal of Social Psychology*, 1958, **47,** 185–95.

Herzog, E., & Sudia, C. Fatherless homes—a review of research. *Children*, 1968, **15**, 177–82.

Jacobs, J. F., & DeGraaf, C. A. Expectancy and race: their influence on intelligence test scores. *Exceptional Children*, 1973, **40**, 108–9.

Jencks, C. *Inequality in America: a reassessment of the effect of family and schooling.* New York: Basic Books, 1972.

Jensen, A. R. Social class, race and genetics: implications for education. *American Educational Research Journal*, 1968, **5**, 1–42.

Kirp, D. Student classification, public policy and the courts. *Harvard Educational Review*, 1974, **44**, 7–52.

Labov, W., Cohen, P., Robbins, C., & Lewis, J. *A study of the non-standard English of Negro & Puerto Rican speakers in N.Y. City.* Final Report, U.S. Office of Education Cooperative Research Project No. 3288. Two volumes. New York: Columbia University, 1968.

Lewis, O. L. *La vida: a Puerto Rican family in the culture of poverty.* New York: Random House, 1966.

Lindgren, H. C. *Educational psychology in the classroom.* (4th ed.) New York: Wiley, 1972.

Miller, D. R., & Swanson, G. E. *Inner conflict and defense.* New York: Holt, Rinehart and Winston, 1960.

Minuchin, S., Montalvo, B., Guerney, B., Rosman, B.L., & Schumer, F. *Families of the slums.* New York: Basic Books, 1967.

Mnookin, R. Foster care: in whose best interest? *Harvard Educational Review*, 1973, **43**, 599–638.

Moore, R., & Moore, D. The dangers of early schooling. *Teachers College Record*, 1972, **74**, 55–79.

Pasamanick, B., & Knoblock, H. Epidemiological studies on the complications of pregnancy and the birth process. In G. S. Caplan (Ed.), *Prevention of mental disorders in children.* New York: Basic Books, 1961, pp. 74–94.

Reece, C. Black self-concept. *Children Today*, 1974, **3**, 24–26.

Riessman, F. *The culturally deprived child.* New York: Harper & Row, 1962.

Soares, A. T., & Soares, L. M. Self-perceptions of culturally disadvantaged children. *American Educational Research Journal*, 1969, **6**, 31–45.

Sowder, B., & Lazar, J. B. *Research problems and issues in the area of socialization.* Washington, D.C.: Social Research Group, 1972.

Spivak, G., & Shure, M. B. *Social adjustment of young children.* San Francisco: Jossey-Bass, 1974.

St. John, N. H. *School desegregation outcomes for children.* New York: Wiley Interscience, 1975.

Thompson, P. A case for bilingualism. *Instructor*, 1975, **84**, 50–55.

Time. America's rising black middle class, 1974, **103**, 19–28.

U.S. News & World Report. Busing: why tide is turning, 1975, **79**, 24–25.

Westinghouse. *The impact of Head Start: An evaluation of the effects of Head Start on children's cognitive and affective development.* Columbus, Ohio: Westinghouse Corporation and Ohio University, 1969.

Witmer, H. L. Children and poverty. *Children*, 1964, **11**, 68–72.

Zigler, E. Project Headstart: success or failure? *Children Today*, 1973, **2**, 2–7 (a).

Zigler, E. The trouble with our child care. *Day Care and Early Education*, 1973, **1**, 13–16 (b).

Suggested Readings

Minuchin, S., Montalvo, B., Guerney, B., Rosman, B. L., & Schumer, F. *Families of the slums.* New York: Basic Books, 1967.

A special issue: assessing minority group children. New York: Journal of School Psychology, 1973.

Special issue: disadvantaged children. Kent, Ohio: The School Psychology Digest, 1973.

Special issue: cultural diversity. Washington, D.C.: Exceptional Children, 1974.

8

Juvenile Delinquency

Delinquency remains one of the critical social problems in the United States. It is by no means a new problem in American society. Nor is it a problem confined to this country. It appears that delinquency is an intrinsic part of modern industrialized societies. In short, when we speak of delinquency, we are dealing with a historically chronic problem that has not yet yielded easily to preventive and treatment efforts.

Definition and Incidence

One difficulty that arises in discussing the concept of delinquency is a matter of definition. Delinquency is an imprecise term. Its meaning is vague not only from a legal viewpoint but psychologically and sociologically as well. Even among psychologists, there have been a variety of meanings attached to this term. For some psychologists, delinquency is viewed as a moral deficiency; for others, it is an underactivity of the central nervous system; and for still others, it is a score on a personality test (Wirt & Briggs, 1965). The diversity of meanings has been well illustrated by Carr (1950), who lists the following six terms as having been applied to the delinquent behavior of juveniles:

Term Applied	*Population*
Legal Delinquents	All youth committing antisocial acts as defined by law.
Detected Delinquents	All detected antisocial youth.
Agency Delinquents	All detected antisocial youth reaching any agency.
Alleged Delinquents	All apprehended antisocial youth brought to court.
Adjudged Delinquents	All antisocial youth legally "found" delinquent by court action.
Committed Delinquents	All adjudged delinquents committed to an institution.

Incidence figures vary with the definition used. The list is arranged hierarchically, with the highest-incidence figure associated with "legal" delinquents and the lowest-incidence figure associated with "committed" delinquents.

Before proceeding to the incidence figures for court cases, we must caution the reader against accepting these data at face value. National crime statistics are difficult to interpret (This is particularly true in the case of the FBI Uniform Crime Reports because they are based on the voluntary disclosure of local police reports, which tend to be unreliable and self-serving.) For one thing, the number of cases reported will be affected by differences between states as to whether a given activity is criminal. Second, states vary as to the type of case and ages of children over which the juvenile court has jurisdiction. Third, the number of court cases is significantly affected by the availability of other child-welfare agencies in the community. If these agencies are present, they may handle cases similar to those seen by juvenile courts in less well-to-do communities. The reader should bear in mind that juveniles brought before a court represent only about one-half of those juvenile offenders apprehended by the police (Federal Bureau of Investigation, 1963). Furthermore, a report by the President's Crime Commission (Phillips, 1967) concluded on the basis of a national survey covering 10,000 households that about half of those who had been victims of crime during the past year never

reported those crimes to the police. We will talk more about this problem—
that of "undetected" delinquency shortly. It is sufficient to note here that we
know a reasonable amount about the behavior and distribution of official
delinquents, but we know far less about the occurrence of actual delinquent
behavior and its distribution (Short, 1966).

The FBI Uniform Crime Reports indicate that the crime rate per 100,000
rose by 45% between 1965 and 1970. Between 1960 and 1970, the rate of
violent crime increased nearly three times as fast among persons under 18 as
among those in the over-18 group. Moreover, the growth rate for other types
of serious crime was approximately 6½ times as fast in the under-18 group
as in the over-18 group (113.7% versus 16.9%). In 1972, as in prior years,
juvenile referrals to court ranked from highest to lowest were for auto theft,
burglary, robbery, larceny, forcible rape, aggravated assault, and murder (FBI
Uniform Crime Reports, 1973).

Is delinquency really increasing in terms of the actual number of cases and
in terms of rate (per 1,000 juveniles, for example), or are the rising figures a
statistical artifact of better reporting procedures, greater public awareness,
and increased law enforcement and technology? It is difficult to answer this
question since no one really knows how many delinquents there are. The
factors mentioned above definitely have contributed to the rise observed in
incidence figures. Yet, by no stretch of the imagination can all of the increase
in delinquent activity be explained by these factors (Teeters & Matza, 1959).
Even the more hard-nosed researchers point out that there does seem to be
some real increase in delinquency in both the number of cases and the rate
(Wirt & Briggs, 1965). The emergence of new forms of delinquency among
new participants has also added to our concern (Freedman, 1966).

Factors Influencing Incidence

Age.   Delinquency is an age-bound phenomenon. It often starts relatively early in life. As Glueck & Glueck (1950) reported, almost 60% of
delinquents commit their first offense before age 10. Though delinquent conduct has an early onset, it is most common during the adolescent period.
Eaton & Polk (1961), for example, pointed out that adolescents accounted
for nearly 2 of every 3 referrals to the Los Angeles probation department.
Among the variables studied, age was found to be the most significant one
with respect to incidence. Similarly, Short (1966), quoting FBI statistics,
noted that 17-year-olds constituted the largest number of arrests. Then came
the 18-year-olds, followed by the 16-year-olds. For boys, the incidence doubled from age 11 to 12 and tripled between ages 12 and 17. For girls, the
incidence peaks at age 15 (Bell, Ross, & Simpson, 1964).

Kvaraceus (1966) speaks of a "delinquency curve"—a notion consistent
with the above data. He pointed out that delinquency reaches a high point
around age 17, then begins to level off. Kvaraceus also noted that the majority of juvenile delinquents become law-abiding citizens in adult life. Ausubel
(1965) noted that forty years of research unequivocally refuted the unin-

formed contention that juvenile delinquents eventually became adult criminals. A record of delinquency is by no means inevitably predictive of adult criminal behavior. In fact, the majority of delinquents eventually get along without serious difficulty. The problem of delinquency during adolescence remains, of course, an important one.

The more severely antisocial child might well, however, continue in his wayward manner. Robins (1966), for instance, on the basis of a follow-up study of gang-member delinquents, concluded that individuals who were persistent and dangerous adolescent offenders became even more serious adult offenders. This finding is consistent with other research, cited in Chapter 1, suggesting that serious acting-out behavior in children is predictive of adult maladjustment.

Sex. The sex of the offenders is also related to the frequency of arrest. Juvenile delinquency remains largely a male phenomenon. Youthful male offenders, for instance, outnumbered youthful female offenders by almost 6 to 1 in 1972, even though the number of males is slightly less than that of females in the general childhood population. The rate of delinquency is increasing among females, however. The five-year arrest trends for 1967–1972 revealed that arrests for females under age 18 increased 62% while arrests for young males under 18 rose 21%. The larger increase in girls' cases than in boys' occurred in urban, semiurban, and rural areas. The recent rise in girls' delinquency is at least partially attributable to the change in the female role. Whereas society had a protective attitude toward females and assigned them a passive role, girls are now becoming increasingly assertive and more independent in their day-to-day activities (Juvenile Court Statistics, 1972).

The type of crime for which the sexes are arrested also differs. FBI statistics indicate more than 40% of boys but only 25% of girls were arrested for offenses against property. Larceny was the most frequent single offense for both sexes. In cases of burglary and theft, however, offenses by males far exceeded those by females. Arrests for murder and manslaughter by negligence, though rare, were even more uncommon for girls than for boys. About an equal number of offenses were committed by the sexes with respect to liquor-law violations, drunk driving, disorderly conduct, gambling, and vagrancy. Sex offenses, excluding forcible rape, constituted the basis for arrest in 4% of offenses for girls but only 1.5% of arrests for boys. This latter finding can most likely be attributed to the double standard applied to sexual behavior in our society. Sexual offenses are perceived as being of a more serious nature when committed by girls than by boys, whereas stealing and aggressiveness are handled more sternly by authorities when committed by boys (Wirt & Briggs, 1965). In support of this hypothesis, it is interesting to note that more girls than boys are brought before the courts for sexual misbehavior despite the fact that more boys are involved in such violations. Moreover, girls are referred more than 50% of the time for misbehavior not ordinarily considered criminal—ungovernable behavior, curfew violations, running away, and truancy. Stealing and property destruction, on the other hand, constitute a primary basis of court referral for boys (U.S. Children's Bureau, 1966). Interestingly, girls are more frequently referred to courts by their mothers, whereas boys are more typically apprehended and referred by the police (Conger, Miller, Gaskill, & Walsmith, 1960).

Family Stability.   Rates of delinquent behavior have also been found to vary with the stability of the home situation. The research literature indicates that children from broken homes, as compared with those from intact homes, do contribute more than their share to delinquent activities. Eaton & Polk (1961) found that more than 50% of all delinquents came from homes broken by death or marital discord. Following a review of studies that used control groups and adjusted for age, ethnic, and neighborhood factors, Monahan (1957) concluded that children, especially girls, from intact homes have a distinct advantage over those from broken homes. The home of the delinquent was found to be much more "defective," "immoral," or "inadequate" than were homes in general. Nye (1958) asserts that the broken home fosters the type of delinquency broadly classified as "ungovernability." Truancy, running away from home, expulsion from school, and driving without a license are illustrative of offenses classified in this category.

Perhaps certain cautions are in order. First of all, Monahan (1957) warns against the danger of overgeneralization. We must not lose sight of the fact that only a small minority of youngsters growing up in broken homes become delinquents. Second, while no critical age has been established, it appears that older children are less adversely affected by broken homes than are younger children. Third, research indicates that delinquents are as likely to come from disorganized but structurally unbroken homes as they are from broken homes (Nye, 1958; Browning, 1960). In other words, the fact that the home is a happy one may be more important than the fact that it is structurally intact.

Turning to intact families, we find that family organization and relationship has a definite role in generating delinquency. Craig & Glick (1963, 1964) found three factors related to delinquency: (1) careless or inadequate supervision by mother or mother substitute; (2) erratic or overstrict discipline; and (3) cohesiveness of the family unit. Bandura & Walters (1959) obtained similar findings using 26 delinquents and 26 nondelinquents matched on social class and IQ range. According to these researchers, the parents of the delinquents were found to be more rejecting and less affectionate than those of the nondelinquents. The boys' relationships with their fathers were considered more important than their relationships with their mothers. Generally speaking, there was an aura of ill will between father and son. McCord, McCord, & Zola (1959), in their reevaluation of the Cambridge-Somerville youth study, found a higher incidence of delinquency among boys who experienced paternal rejection and neglect and little maternal affection. A higher incidence of convictions was found where the mother was rated as "nonloving" rather than "loving." The incidence was lowest where mothers were both "loving" and used consistent means of discipline. More recent work also indicates a very high correlation between the amount and severity of physical punishment endured by a child from 2 to 12 and the amount and severity of antisocial aggressiveness that he displays during adolescence (Button, 1973).

The current literature suggests that the relationship of the father to the son is an especially critical factor in the production of delinquent behavior. From a theoretical standpoint, Miller (1959a) argues that the lower-class child engages in gang delinquency in an attempt to establish his masculinity— something he cannot do within the confines of a female-based, father-absent household. Empirical support demonstrating the effect of impaired father-son relationships is reasonably abundant. For example, Siegman (1966) reported that father-absent boys were more delinquent than father-present boys. Like Miller, he hypothesized that father-absent boys rebel against a feminine identification by engaging in exaggerated masculine behavior. Likewise, Hurwitz, Kaplan, & Kaiser (1962), using a sample of 100 male delinquents, reported that boys who had been manhandled, especially by their fathers, tended to get into more difficulty than boys whose parents had more desirable coping patterns.

Theorists are now questioning the supremacy of maternal deprivation as a significant etiological factor in delinquent behavior (Andry, 1960) and are recognizing the importance of an adequate male model as a significant ingredient in the socialization process (Nash, 1965).

Socioeconomic Status. Viewed socioeconomically, delinquency appears to be a predominantly lower-class phenomenon. Reiss & Rhodes (1961), studying 9,238 white boys registered in the junior and senior high schools of Davidson County, Tennessee, reported that the largest proportion of delinquency tended to be in the lower-status areas. In 1963, Reiss and Rhodes expanded their findings to include the fact that official delinquency rates vary inversely with socioeconomic status. These investigators hypothesized that the lower-class adolescent compares his life unfavorably with that of the higher class. Eventually he experiences feelings of frustration and deprivation which, in turn, generate feelings of aggression and a higher rate of delinquent behavior. Perlman (1963) tried to explain this general relationship by use of several economic and social trends which, operating together or separately, could produce delinquency among the dissatisfied lower-class youths. Certain postwar conditions—the emphasis on success and false values, poor housing, the breakdown of the family, and violence—were social factors intrinsically involved. Socioeconomic trends, such as population growth, increased urbanization, unemployment, and automation, were also regarded as factors contributing to the frustration and inadequacy of lower-class youth.

Despite the above data, some workers are not convinced that delinquency is basically a lower-class phenomenon. First of all, the higher rates of delinquency among the lower classes are found only in large cities. Studies conducted in small cities and towns have not found greater delinquent involvement among the lower classes (Erickson & Empey, 1965; Nye, Short, & Olson, 1958). Clark & Wenninger (1962), using a total of 1,154 public-school students from four different types of communities, also noted that social-class differentiation is unrelated to the incidence of illegal behavior within small communities. These investigators advanced the notion that there are communitywide norms within these smaller towns that are related to illegal behavior irrespective of social class.

Second, studies of "undetected" delinquency also fail to substantiate the notion of greater delinquent involvement on the part of lower-class youth. Some investigators, concerned about the inadequacy of official court records as a criterion of illegal youthful behavior, have attempted to bridge the gap between official and unofficial delinquency rates by studying the extent of unrecorded delinquency. Short & Nye (1958), using student questionnaires on a 25% sample of all boys and girls in grades 9, 10, 11, and 12 in three medium-sized towns (10,000 to 30,000), found that there was no significant difference in the delinquent behavior of boys and girls in the different socio-economic strata. Differences that were found indicated greater delinquent involvement within the highest socioeconomic category than was previously considered. Other studies (Dentler & Monroe, 1961; Empey & Erickson, 1966), using the anonymous-questionnaire procedure, have also substantiated the finding that the number of violations differs little from one status level to another. Thus the traditional assumption of higher incidence of behavior problems in the lower socioeconomic stratum has been called into question. It must be noted, however, that these studies were carried out in small cities or towns, where communitywide norms rather than socioeconomic factors are related to delinquent pursuits. Clark & Wenninger (1962), who also used an anonymous self-report scale, found that although adolescents from various social strata had very similar overall delinquency rates, the more serious of-fenses were more likely to be committed by lower-class urban youth.

While we are unable to make any definitive statement as to the relationship of "undetected" delinquency to socioeconomic status, it is clear that the rela-tionship between social class and illegal behavior is by no means a simple one. In addition to further investigations on lower-class delinquents, we sorely need more research on the delinquent conduct of middle- and upper-class youth in order to clarify the role of socioeconomic factors in delinquency.

Racial and Ethnic Factors.   There is often considerable variation in reports of delinquency rates among various racial and ethnic groups. Jewish children, for example, contribute far less than their proportionate share of the delinquency statistics (Robison, 1957). Whereas in 1952, Jewish children comprised 15% of the general population in New York City, they accounted for only 3% of the juvenile-court cases. Japanese-Americans also have a very low rate of delinquency, perhaps because of their tradition of compliance, their emphasis on education, the intactness of their families, and the import-ance of family honor (Eisner & Tsuyemura, 1965).

On the other hand, several studies indicate high delinquency rates for blacks, Puerto Ricans, Mexicans, and American Indians. Black delinquency rates are two or three times as high as those of whites (Douglass, 1959). Differences in rate as to the type of offense have also been noted, with a higher proportion of black boys committing offenses against persons or property as contrasted to a higher proportion of white boys violating important social norms (Segal, 1966).

Studies point out a number of factors conducive to the production of antisocial behavior among black delinquents. These include a mother-centered family, the lack of a suitable male model, freer sexual behavior, illegitimacy, poverty, and an emphasis on physical combat. Delinquency-prone children, according to Cavan (1959), develop a concept of being deviant which is fostered by the parents. Clark (1959), analyzing the effects of minority status on personality patterns, concluded that the black child because of racial discrimination develops a self-concept that is negatively distorted, thus giving rise to hostile, aggressive, and antisocial responses. Hill (1959) expands this idea further, asserting that deviant behavior is a manner of adjusting to a segregated society in which many opportunities for recognition and accomplishment are unavailable.

Urban-Rural Differences.   The incidence of delinquency is about three times as high in urban as in rural areas. In fact, courts in urban areas handle more than two-thirds of all delinquency cases in the country. Clark & Wenninger (1962) found that rates for delinquent activity increase as one moves from rural farm to upper-class urban to industrial city and lower-class communities. This trend is especially true with regard to the more serious violations and to those involving a high degree of social organization. The greatest differences in rates of illegal activity occur between the lower-class urban and the upper-class communities. Upper-class urban youngsters are more prone to pass dirty pictures, gamble, and trespass, whereas their lower-class urban counterparts are more apt to steal major items, drink, carry weapons, and destroy property. There were no differences among the four communities with regard to the more minor misbehaviors. Consistent with the above findings, Ferdinand (1964) concluded that urban delinquents exhibited a much stronger preference for offenses against authority than did rural or village delinquents. Rural delinquents committed 1 offense against authority for every 13 property violations, whereas the urban offense ratio was 1 to 3.5.

Although juvenile delinquency remains largely an urban problem, juvenile-court statistics reveal that youth in rural areas show an even greater proportional increase than youth in the large urban areas. Thus, increases in delinquency are not limited to congested areas but are taking place in rural areas.

Intelligence.   Interest in the relationship between intelligence and juvenile crime has had a long and polemical history. While most of the early research indicated a 15-20 point difference in IQ score between delinquents and the general population, later research consistently reports a difference of only 8 IQ points. Moreover, when socioeconomic status is controlled, there seems to be even less difference in intellectual status between delinquents and nondelinquents (Caplan, 1965). Even if this 8-point difference were valid, such a difference would not warrant postulating low intelligence as a major cause of delinquency. Low intelligence, though in and of itself unrelated to delinquency, can predispose youngsters in certain instances by increasing suggestibility, the tendency to take imprudent risks, the probability of being caught, and the possibility of academic failure (Ausubel, 1965).

Constitutional Factors.   Interest in the area of constitutional factors has ranged from speculative discussion concerning hereditary factors to more rigorous studies on physiological factors. Early in this century, Lombroso (1918) advanced the notion that the criminal is biologically unable to behave in a responsible manner. He investigated the physical correlates associated with the presumed inborn antisocial traits. Later studies revealed that delinquents and nondelinquents did not differ with respect to recognizable physical stigmata. However, several studies continue to reveal a greater incidence of abnormal brain waves (EEG) among sociopathic delinquents, a group we will discuss shortly. There is further evidence to suggest that sociopaths, because of an inadequate constitution, are less able to respond with anticipatory anxiety to what are ordinarily tension-provoking stimuli. Without denying the possible etiological ramifications of these biological findings, especially in regard to certain delinquent subgroups, we must bear in mind the fact that many delinquents are free from such biological deviations and that similar abnormalities can be found in nondelinquent populations.

Much interest has also centered around the relationship between body build and delinquency. In their classic study comparing delinquent and nondelinquent youth, Glueck & Glueck (1956) reported a much higher proportion of muscular, big-boned, broad-shouldered boys (mesomorphs) among the delinquents. Conversely, the chunky, stocky boys (endomorphs) and the tall, thin boys (ectomorphs) were less apt to become delinquent. Has this relationship any causal significance? At this time, most authorities contend that physique most likely plays a predisposing role rather than a causal one. Given a mesomorphic build, a youngster with delinquent inclinations is better able to actualize his antisocial learnings through gang-type crimes. But this is not to say that his physique caused his delinquency. Possession of a brawny physique increases the probability that physically aggressive actions will prove effective. Also, physical characteristics can also indirectly affect aggressive behavior through their influence on choice of friends, which, in turn, determines to a large degree the types of models observed (Bandura, 1973). It must also be noted that 40% of the delinquents in the Gluecks' sample did not fit the mesomorphic category. Moreover, most husky youths are not juvenile delinquents. Certain select cases of delinquency might be accounted for by physical constitution.

More recently, there has been an expression of interest in the extra Y chromosome allegedly associated with violent crime against people (Jarvik, Klodin, & Matsuyama, 1973; Shah & Borgaonkar, 1974). In one study, we are told that mentally defective men institutionalized for various crimes showed a higher prevalence of the extra chromosome (2.9%) than would be expected among the general population (0.2%) (Jacobs, Brunton, & Melville, 1965). Because the XYY condition is associated with tallness, many studies used biased sampling procedures by selecting only tall criminals for chromosomal analysis. The control group should consist of tall noncriminals and not members of the general population. Although the XYY individuals who do run afoul of the law are not especially assaultive, they are arrested at an earlier age and more frequently. This differential arrest pattern, which might very well influence the course of future behavior regardless of genetic makeup, is conceivably related to physical stature.

In sum, though future research might prove otherwise, most authorities today find even the more modern versions of the "bad seed" hypothesis untenable and prefer to seek the roots of delinquent behavior in the environmental and psychological forces influencing behavior.

While man is endowed with the neurophysiological equipment to behave aggressively, the activation of this equipment depends upon appropriate stimulation and is subject to cortical control. Thus, the precise forms that aggressive behavior takes, the frequency with which it is expressed, the situations in which it occurs, and the specific targets selected for attack are largely determined by social experience (Bandura, 1973).

Psychological Dimensions

Despite the fact that delinquents and nondelinquents sometimes come from the same general family and socioeconomic backgrounds, have similar levels of intelligence, and are comparable in body build, they often differ with respect to personality characteristics. Studies using the Minnesota Multiphasic Personality Inventory indicate that such characteristics as impulsivity, aggressiveness, and irresponsibility are commonly found among those who engage in delinquent activities. On the other hand, people who score high on scales measuring social introversion, depression, and masculinity-femininity tend to have a lower-than-average rate of delinquency (Quay, 1965).

To the unsophisticated observer, the surface behavior of delinquent youth may appear very similar. Closer inspection reveals, however, the desirability of investigating differences in personality structures among subgroups within the general population. Indeed, the failure of earlier investigators to find meaningful personality differences between delinquents and nondelinquents (Schuessler & Cressey, 1950) can be attributed not only to the use of invalid psychological tests and unsophisticated research designs but also to the failure to seek differences in personality makeup within the subgroups of the total delinquent population (Quay, 1965).

Different investigators (Reiss, 1952; Quay, 1964, 1966), using a variety of research methodologies, have identified three broad personality dimensions among delinquents. The terminology varies but there is basic agreement among authorities as to the existence of these three categories: the psychopathic delinquent, the subcultural delinquent, and the neurotic delinquent.

The Psychopathic Delinquent.[1]   The first dimension represents a basic *deficiency in the socialization process.* Delinquent youngsters scoring high on this dimension have been given various labels: the psychopath, sociopath, unsocialized aggressive, defective-superego delinquent, and so forth. These youths are usually the products of rejecting homes. Professional workers generally regard this form of delinquency as the most severe and as having the poorest prognosis. Consequently, some form of residential treatment is apt to be employed. Clinicians are reluctant to diagnose a youngster as a sociopath since this label connotes incorrigibility. As mentioned in the earlier discussion on the stability of deviant behavior, Robins (1966), on the basis of a thirty-year follow-up study, reported that 2 out of 3 unsocialized aggressive youths persisted in their antisocial ways. What surprised most professional workers is the fact that 1 in 3 did show some improvement.

From the standpoint of clinical experience, those so labeled manifest many of the following behavioral characteristics:

1. Inadequate moral development is perhaps the most salient characteristic. While unsocialized aggressive children are intellectually able to distinguish between right and wrong, they frequently fail to observe such distinctions in their everyday behavior. Stealing, lying, drinking, and sexual misbehaviors are typical norm-violating activities on their part.

2. Associated with the deficiency in conscience development is the superficiality of guilt and anxiety. Though such youngsters often verbalize these feelings when in a tough situation, they seem incapable of experiencing such emotions to a degree typical of normal youth. Since they are generally not bothered by their misbehaviors, they have little motivation to change their ways. Consequently, they fail to learn from experience, continuing in their old acting-out ways. Being poorly motivated with respect to behavioral change, they make poor candidates for traditional forms of psychotherapy.

3. Rebelliousness and impulsivity are also commonly seen. Typically these youngsters will be in trouble both at home and at school. One way to detect such individuals is to check their case histories. A long history of frequent involvement with law-enforcement agencies and/or educational authorities is very much the rule. They have considerable difficulty in accepting any constituted form of authority and frequently try to escape from rather unpleasant situations by becoming truants or going AWOL.

4. Their egocentricity is also readily apparent. While they often appear outgoing, gregarious, and optimistic, they tend not to form close interpersonal ties with others. In general, their emotional ties and loyalties are extremely shallow even with their own families. Their sense of responsibility is quite poorly developed.

5. Their extrapunitiveness and inability to postpone pleasurable activities also lead them into difficulty. One delinquent boy told the author, when queried about why he was incarcerated at a youth camp, that he did not have any problems until he got "a damn social worker." Likewise, a sexually

---

1. Some workers prefer to use the term "sociopathic." The terms are synonymous.

provocative, blond high-school girl stated that she wanted to quit school and go to California "where things are happening." Striving toward long-range goals is usually out of the question. The smaller immediate pleasures of the present are perceived as better than the greater but more distant goods of the future. Such youths become easily bored, desire a frequent change of scenery, thrive on excitement, and want to be constantly on the go.

6. They often make a favorable impression on others and can, at times, be excellent manipulators. On one occasion a nice-looking, curly-haired delinquent adolescent escaped from a mental hospital at which one of the authors worked. As was customary in such cases, the sheriff was notified and a search was undertaken. When, after several hours, neither the sheriff nor the delinquent returned, another phone call was placed to the sheriff's office. It was then learned that the adolescent youth had "conned" the sheriff into writing a letter to the governor regarding his unjustified incarceration. Once this adolescent boy's long history of repeated criminal activity was revealed and his exploitation of others noted, the sheriff willingly returned him to the institutional setting.

A summary of typical behavior traits, life history characteristics, and questionnaire responses of the psychopathic delinquent are provided in Table 8–1.

Table 8–1.   The Psychopathic Delinquent[a]

Behavior Traits	Life History Characteristics
Disobedience	Assaultive
Disruptiveness	Defies authority
Fighting	Inadequate guilt feelings
Destructiveness	Irritable
Temper Tantrums	Quarrelsome
Irresponsibility	
Impertinence	
Jealousy	
(Shows signs of) Anger	
Bossiness	
Profanity	
Attention seeking	
Boisterousness	

Responses to Questionnaire
I do what I want to whether anybody likes it or not.
It's dumb to trust other people.
The only way to settle anything is to lick the guy.
I'm too tough a guy to get along with most kids.
If you don't have enough to live on, its okay to steal.
I go out of my way to meet trouble rather than try to escape it.

[a] Adapted from Quay, 1972.

The Subcultural Delinquent.   A second dimension that has been consistently uncovered represents a case of deviant socialization. But such an adjustment is deviant only in the sense that the antisocial values of the child's subculture are in conflict with those of the larger middle-class society. A delinquent youth scoring high on this dimension is referred to as a subcultural delinquent, socialized aggressive delinquent, sociologic delinquent, or integrated delinquent. Delinquent youngsters so designated typically come from a stable lower-class home in a deteriorated area of the community in which delinquent conduct constitutes an approved tradition. Their encounters with law-enforcement agencies stem from their prolonged daily exposure to behaviors that violate the legal norms of the larger society.

It should be noted that these youngsters are not emotionally disturbed. Aside from their delinquent pursuits, they are essentially normal youngsters. The prognosis is generally favorable, in that the vast majority grow up to be law-abiding citizens. They are not extremely anxious, as are neurotic children; nor do they experience a lack of personal identity, as do psychotic children. They differ from the sociopath in that they are able to experience guilt when they violate the standards of their own subculture and to form close emotional attachments and loyalties to others. Although able to identify with others, they usually select models that the larger community considers undesirable. For example, they are much more apt to identify with the "con" man or with an aggressive buddy than with the policeman or with conforming peers, since identifications of the former kind lead to prestigious behavior that offers status within their own peer group.

What are some of the central values cherished by this segment of the lower-class peer culture? A partial listing would include the ability to dupe or outsmart others, physical prowess (such as the ability to take it and dish it out), a rebelliousness toward any form of constituted authority (a chip on the shoulder attitude), a strong desire for excitement and thrill-seeking activities, and a strong belief in luck as a vital force in determining one's destiny (Miller, 1959a).

This type of delinquency represents more of a cultural than a psychological problem. Kvaraceus & Miller (1959) assert that 75% of delinquency is due to cultural factors and 25% to psychological factors. In other words, these investigators would view the overwhelming majority of delinquent activities as emanating from normal lower-class youngsters who reflect the patterned deviancy of their lower-class culture. Since many of their crimes are committed in groups, the preferred method of treatment involves placement of the offender in a group setting where he is given a chance to identify with the more appropriate models afforded him.

A summary of the life history characteristics and questionnaire responses of the subcultural delinquent is provided in Table 8-2.

The Neurotic Delinquent.   The third dimension along which delinquents might vary involves acting-out behavior that stems from personality disturbances. That is, beneath a facade of violence and aggression, certain

Table 8–2.   The Subcultural Delinquent[a]

Life History Characteristics

Has bad companions
Engages in gang activities
Engages in cooperative stealing
Habitually truant from school
Accepted by delinquent subgroups
Stays out late at nights
Strong allegiance to selected peers

Responses to Questionnaire

My folks usually blame bad company for the trouble I get into.
Before I do something, I try to consider how my friends will react to it.
Most boys stay in school because the law says they have to.
When a group of boys get together they are bound to get in trouble sooner or later.
It is very important to have enough friends and social life.
I have been expelled from school or nearly expelled.
Sometimes I have stolen things that I didn't really want.

[a] Adapted from Quay (1972). Empirical research on this dimension has come primarily from case history and questionnaire data.

Reflections by a Former Subcultural Delinquent

The first parking meter I ever ripped off was down on 7th Street. There was a cop just around the corner but that made it more exciting. I always had a daredevil spirit. I liked to take a dare. It gave me a thrill and it thrilled my buddies too. Nick told me to wait until he distracted the cop by asking for directions. Nick would pretend that he didn't understand and ask the cop to show him where some store was. So the cop and Nick would walk up the street away from me and the parking meter. And Nick would thank him for his help. Conning the cop was half of the excitement. When the cop was out of sight, I gave the meter a bunch of hard kicks. I used to wear those heavy shoes that were good for kicking. Some old dude went by and told me to stop. I told him to mind his own business before I kicked his ass. I ran with the whole damn parking meter under my arm as I went up the street. Later, Nick and I split the $2.40 that we got. Then we laughed about the whole thing with our buddies. We even reenacted it for them. We didn't get much loot but it wasn't a bad way to pass time.

delinquents are anxious, unhappy, and insecure. As Quay (1972) notes, "Fear, anxiety, and tension, when coupled with impulsiveness and cast into certain environmental circumstances, can result in overt behavioral acts defined as antisocial."

This youngster is commonly referred to as the solitary delinquent, the neurotic delinquent, the disturbed delinquent, or the weak-ego delinquent. There are at least five basic differences between the youngster scoring high on this dimension and those on the previously described dimensions:

1. Unlike the subcultural delinqeant in particular, in whom guilt tends not to be a component, the neurotic delinquent often experiences pangs of conscience and remorse over his transgressions.

2. The motivations underlying the antisocial behavior are presumed to be more unconsciously based in contrast to those of the subcultural delinquent, who more consciously opposes the larger social order. Among the possible factors involved in the learning and maintaining of this form of delinquent activity are the following:

   a. Some youngsters find it reinforcing to punish others (e.g., parents).
   b. Antisocial acts typically draw (negative) attention which may be reinforcing.
   c. Punishment is reinforcing to some children, perhaps because it is commonly associated with (negative) attention from others, or perhaps because punishment terminates the anxiety over one's misdeeds.
   d. Parents may receive a sense of vicarious reinforcement from their child's antisocial behavior.
   e. Parents may unwittingly model antisocial attitudes in subtle ways.

3. The neurotic delinquent tends to come from a middle-class home and neighborhood.

4. This delinquent is more inclined to engage in criminal activities by himself in contrast to the subcultural delinquent, who seems to prefer a gang type of delinquent activity.

The youngster scoring high on this dimension may engage in unlawful acts so that he will be caught and punished, presumably to satisfy deep-rooted feelings of guilt. Not uncommonly, his offenses seem purposeless and compulsive in nature. Lippman (1962) cites the case of an adolescent boy who obtained money by forging a check. As the adolescent was well known to the local merchant, the boy was easily apprehended by police. Shortly after being placed on probation, this boy committed the same offense in much the same manner on three more occasions. Again, he was quickly arrested. This boy's measured IQ was 170. Possible explanations for this kind of behavior were noted above in 2.

5. When institutionalized, the neurotic delinquent is less aggressive, more accepting of authority, more responsive to treatment efforts made in his behalf, and less likely to commit repeated delinquencies (Quay & Levinson, 1967). Although the neurotic delinquent's responsiveness to treatment is con-

sidered by clinicians to be more favorable than that of the psychopath, it is not considered to be as favorable as that of the subcultural delinquent.

A summary of the behavior traits, life history characteristics, and questionnaire responses of the neurotic delinquent are provided in Table 8–3.

Personality Insulators.   The preceding discussion pertained to personality factors associated with the production of delinquency. By now, the reader may well have asked himself, "Are there any personality factors that insulate children from delinquency?" We have already mentioned the Minnesota studies, which indicate that individuals with high scores on the depression, social-introversion, and masculinity-femininity scales are less apt to become involved with law-enforcement agencies. It was also found that subjects who had delinquency-prone personalities but resisted delinquency differed from those with similar personality dispositions who did become delinquent in coming from economically better homes, having better socially adjusted parents, and having better relationships within the family (Wirt & Briggs, 1959).

Perhaps the best-known studies in this regard have been conducted by Reckless, Dinitz, & Kay (1957) on nondelinquent boys living in high-delinquency areas. Using a group of 125 "good" boys (those thought to be insu-

Table 8–3.   The Neurotic Delinquent[a]

Behavior Traits	Life History Characteristics
Feelings of inferiority	Seclusive
Self-consciousness	Shy
Social withdrawal	Sensitive
Shyness	Worries
Anxiety	Timid
Crying	Has anxiety over own behavior
Shyness	
Hypersensitivity	
Seldom smiles	
Chews fingernails	
Depression, chronic sadness	

Response to Questionnaires
I don't think I'm quite as happy as others seem to be.
I often feel as though I have done something wrong or wicked.
I seem to do things I regret more often than most people do.
I just don't seem to get the breaks other people do.
People often talk about me behind my back.
I have more than my share of things to worry about.

[a] Adapted from Quay (1972).

lated against delinquency) and a group of 101 delinquency-prone boys, Reckless and his associates studied their personality differences from personal interviews, interviews with teachers and parents, the administration of a self-concept scale, and the California Personality Inventory. The results indicated that the good boys came from stable homes that kept them isolated from the delinquent patterns of the neighborhood. Close maternal supervision in the context of a harmonious family setting was thought to play a prominent role relative to the inhibition of delinquent activities. The good boys also scored significantly higher on the responsibility and socialization scales of the California Personality Inventory. They also seemed to have a more socialized self-concept in comparison to the delinquency-prone group. A follow-up study indicated that only 4% of the insulated group had become known to the police (Scarpitti, Murray, Dinitz, & Reckless, 1960) in contrast to almost 27% of the vulnerable group, who had been identified by teachers as potential delinquents (Dinitz, Scarpitti, & Reckless, 1962). A trend toward poorer socialization and a more impaired self-concept was also noted in the vulnerable group, whereas the good boys maintained favorable attitudes toward the law, school, their parents, and themselves. The authors concluded that one's self-concept can serve as either an inhibitor or an excitor relative to participation in unlawful activities. Later research by Scarpitti (1965) has confirmed the role played by a negative self-concept as a crucial predisposing factor toward delinquency.

Interaction of Psychological Variables.   Most of the research on characteristics has examined the relationship between delinquency and such variables as social class, IQ, and selected personality variables independently of one another. The interaction of the variables as antecedents of delinquent activities has for the most part been neglected. That the study of interactive effects among such variables as personality factors, neighborhood factors, IQ, and delinquency may well constitute a more valuable and true-to-life approach is seen in the research efforts of Conger, Miller, & Walsmith (1965). These authors caution that, though delinquents as a group show less acceptable behavior, experience more academic difficulties, and have more emotional problems, the extrapolation of these findings to delinquent subgroups was precluded by the marked variations in relationships of various personality traits to delinquency from one socioeconomic class–IQ group to another. In brief, these findings indicate that it is misleading to speak of personality differences between delinquents and nondelinquents on the basis of overall average differences. To convey the marked variation existing among the subgroups with respect to personality, it is necessary to take into account the intellectual and socioeconomic levels from which these youngsters derive. For example, within the "below-average IQ–nondeprived" subgroup, the nondelinquents earned higher mean scores on a delinquency scale than did the delinquents themselves.

Studies of this nature illustrate the complex interactions among variables related to delinquency and point out the dangers associated with research that considers these variables separately. Aside from their norm-violating behavior, delinquents are anything but a homogeneous group. The translation of this awareness into more complicated research designs represents a methodological advance in the field of delinquency, an advance that should assist in casting into sharper relief the factors contributing to delinquency.

Etiological Considerations

Like any complex and multidimensional problem, delinquency can be attacked on different levels. We can, for instance, approach it from a biological, sociological, or psychological vantage point. It is virtually impossible from a practical standpoint, however, to investigate all aspects of this problem simultaneously. Consequently, various disciplines have approached the problem, with each professional specialty stressing certain determinants of the problem.

Most theories of etiology can be subsumed under two broad categories. On the one hand, there are those that emphasize the importance of the attitudes and emotions of individual delinquents. This theoretical position is predicated on the assumption that delinquency results from the emotional problems of individual youngsters. The earliest child-guidance clinics working with delinquents received their theoretical support (rationale) from individual psychology and later from psychoanalytic or other psychiatric viewpoints (Wheeler, Cottrell, & Romasco, 1967). In brief, the clinical model focuses primarily on the pathology of the individual.

The other major approach views delinquency as sociogenic in nature. Advocates of this theoretical position stress the importance of the broader social environment as the source of delinquent conduct. The sociologist, accordingly, searches for causative factors in the social processes in the delinquent's environment. The treatment implications of these two major applications will be amplified later in the chapter.

Sociological Theories

Within the limits of our present discussion, we will consider only three of the current sociological theories that emphasize the origin and effects of delinquent subcultures. The first two theories view the rise of these subcultures as a consequence of socially induced frustrations sustained by the working class at the hands of the middle class.

Status Deprivation.   The first person to develop a theory of gang delinquency was Cohen (1955), who advanced the "status-deprivation theory." According to this position, the lower-class child is exposed to middle-class pressures for success through his contacts with teachers, playground directors, ministers, and so on. The lower-class child, though sensitive to the appraisals of various middle-class representatives, is experientially hindered in his ability to conform to middle-class standards. Postponement of gratification, for example, is less common among the working class than it is among the middle class. Cohen suggests that a loss of status results from social devaluation which, in turn, leads to rebellion. The lower-class child accordingly redefines the yardstick of status so that his own antisocial behavior constitutes the earmark of prestige. Thus, lower-class youth, confronted with a common loss of status, form a delinquent subculture that values the breaking of middle-class values. While lower-class delinquency is seen as an inability to compete successfully with the dominant and prestigious middle class, middle-class delinquency is viewed as an attempt to achieve masculinity.

Opportunity Structure.   A second major social theory that views gang delinquency as emanating from blockages in the attainment of highly valued middle-class success goals is Cloward & Ohlin's (1960) opportunity-structure theory. Whereas Cohen stressed the lower-class child's inability to measure up to middle-class standards, Cloward and Ohlin emphasize the unjust availability of opportunity among the lower classes. The lower-class child, in response to the limited opportunity afforded him, blames the social order. Alienation subsequently expresses itself in the development of various types of delinquent subcultures that offer illegal patterns of conduct as a source of status. This theory has had an important impact on action programs of prevention and treatment. Indeed, as we will discover later in the chapter, most treatment and prevention programs strive to offer delinquent and predelinquent youth an opportunity to develop skills that will enable them to participate meaningfully in adult society.

Focal Concerns.   Miller (1959a) has proposed an alternative theory challenging the two preceding formulations. Objecting to the reactive nature of gang culture, Miller views the life style of gang delinquency as a manifestation of lower-class culture. In other words, gang delinquency among lower-class youth is an expression of the values and thoughts pervading lower-class culture rather than a reaction against middle-class expectations and devaluations. What are the concerns around which lower-class life is patterned? The focal concerns Miller postulates are:

Trouble. Getting into trouble is one way in which the individual can gain status and recognition from his peers.

Toughness. Masculine behaviors such as bravery in the face of physical attack, an exploitative attitude toward women, and lack of sentimentality are all modeled and reinforced.

Smartness. The ability to dupe, con, or outsmart others is highly prized.

Excitement. Fighting, taking risks, using alcohol, gambling, and engaging in sex are all examples of the thrill-seeking behavior that is held in high esteem.

Fate. This refers to the belief that the locus of control over one's life is outside himself. If things go badly, lady luck or destiny was to blame.

Autonomy. The concern for independence finds expression in such assertions as "Nobody is gonna shove me around," or "I can take care of myself."

In brief, the lower-class delinquent becomes acculturated to a way of life that is consistent with these focal concerns but at odds with, or antithetical to, dominant norms and values.

Despite the fact that we have presented only skeletal outlines of these social theories, their relevance to the school's role in delinquency is readily evident. There are at least two major implications emanating from theoretical positions that view delinquency as a result of blocked goal success (Schafer & Polk, 1967). First, poor school performance might well constitute a *common* form of frustration, for example, poor grades and nonpromotion. Second, academic failure leads these lower-class youths to believe that desirable jobs might be unavailable to them. As a consequence of these thwartings, lower-class students are more prone to delinquent activities. As for the educational implications of Miller's views, Schafer and Polk suggest that the school itself may be contributing to a lack of acceptable commitment or at least may not seize the opportunity to establish such a commitment when it is lacking. To offset the above-mentioned consequences, many schools have modified educational programs for lower-class youth. We will talk about one such application —work-experience programs—later in the chapter.

Psychological Theories

Most sociological theories fail to account for the middle-class delinquent as well as the large majority of lower-class youth who lead law-abiding lives. As Bandura & Walters (1959) note, the sociological variables may not play a causative role but may simply provide conditions promoting the existence of psychological factors that produce antisocial conduct.

Emotional Disturbance.   As implied earlier, advocates of the psychological approach assume that antisocial acts have meaning to the individual delinquent in that his conduct represents either a reaction to frustrations within the family and/or peer group or an effort to meet unfulfilled needs, such as recognition. While the majority of delinquents are not emotionally disturbed, there remains a significant minority of delinquents for whom this designation is warranted. The psychological approach to delinquency is well illustrated by the classic study of Healy & Bronner (1936), in which case-study data were collected on 105 delinquents who had nondelinquent siblings near their own age. Despite similar environmental backgrounds, the delinquents differed markedly from their nondelinquent siblings in their personality traits, attitudes, and interpersonal relationships. The most noticeable difference between the two groups was in the area of family attitudes and emotional experiences. More than 90% of the delinquents were very unhappy with their life circumstances or extremely disturbed because of life experiences. In contrast, inner stresses were found in only 13% of the control subjects. Common emotional problems experienced by the delinquents included sharp feelings of rejection, inadequacy, insecurity, jealousy, and unhappiness.

Adult-Youth Alienation.   Ausubel (1965) has proposed a refreshing view, which, contrary to many of the psychological approaches, does not hold that the basic causal factor in juvenile delinquency resides in a pathological personality structure. It inheres, instead, in the developmental-cultural phenomenon of adult-youth alienation which adolescents experience. According to Ausubel, adolescents alienated from adult society become immersed in a peer culture that provides them with status-giving activities, norms of behavior, and distinctive training institutions of their own. At the same time, however, participation in the peer culture reinforces their feelings of alienation from adult society and promotes compensatory antisocial modes of conduct which sometimes take the form of juvenile delinquency. Adult-youth alienation varies in accordance with such contributing and precipitating factors as sex, social class, parental attitudes, temperament, personality characteristics, and intelligence. Alienation from adult society, for example, is greater among boys than among girls and more pronounced among adolescents in minority groups than in middle-class groups. Middle-class delinquency is viewed as the result of a serious deterioration in the moral values of middle-class adults since the end of World War II and their preoccupation with gaining material advantages at any cost.

Social Learning Theory.   Whereas sociological explanations commonly treat delinquents as persons who follow extralegal means to socially valued goals, psychological explanations commonly center around deficiencies within the individual (for example, the inability to delay gratification). The social learning theory view differs from traditional psychological theories in that the individual is seen neither as driven by inner psychological forces nor as buffeted helplessly by external circumstances. Rather, delinquent activity, like other forms of social behavior, is seen in terms of a continuous, reciprocal interplay between behavior and its controlling circumstances. Person-centered explanations and situation-centered explanations are both needed to account for and cope with the complex phenomena of delinquency. In brief, the environment does influence the person's behavior, but the person also influences the environment.

The following ideas are central to the social learning view (Bandura, 1973):

1. Delinquent behavior is learned through direct experience (rewarding and punishing consequences) and by observing the behavior of others.

2. Delinquent behavior is regulated and maintained by (a) environmental stimuli such as temporal, social, and situational factors (which indicate that conditions are ripe to break a law), verbal communications ("Let's rip this car off"), and the actions of others (committing crimes), or (b) feedback from the reinforcing consequences of one's actions. Three kinds of reinforcing consequences are particularly evident—peer reward ("Man, you really ripped him off good"), self-reward ("I felt good when I beat the shit

out of that big dude"), and vicarious reward ("I get a thrill out of seeing a guy mugged").

3. Cognitive control is also essential in controlling behavior. A delinquent's behavior is not always predictable from external sources of information (external inducements and reinforcing consequences). For man's cognitive abilities enable him to evaluate his experiences and thus partly determine how he will be affected by them. Because of man's planning ability, his behavior is probably more greatly influenced by *anticipated* consequences than by its actual consequences.

Because the treatment efforts we take depend largely upon what we regard as the causes of delinquency, it is not surprising to find that social learning theorists favor a wide variety of approaches in treating long-standing delinquent behavior. Prominent among the strategies are (1) reducing aversive social conditions that give rise to antisocial behavior, (2) developing skills that will provide new sources of reward, (3) modeling of alternate ways of coping (for example, exposure to others who behave in a restrained, nondelinquent way when tempted to break the law), (4) eliminating rewards for delinquent behavior while encouraging better solutions, (5) eliminating fantasies or beliefs that serve as instigators of illegal activity. In brief, social learning theory does not view delinquency as *caused* by forces within the individual nor by frustrating conditions within the society (as evidenced by the law abiding behavior of the vast majority of poor people). Instead, delinquency flourishes when norm-violating behaviors are valued, successful delinquent models are available, and delinquent actions are rewarded. Social learning theory is optimistic in that it views the social determinants of delinquent behavior as alterable.

Prediction

The problem of prediction is basic to any discussion of programs of prevention and treatment. There are now available a number of instruments designed to predict delinquency although few of these have been subjected to rigorous before-and-after tests of validation (Kvaraceus, 1966). The usual approach has been to administer a set of items to a group of delinquents and a group of nondelinquents. A comparison of their respective responses to these items is then conducted in an attempt to delineate the specific characteristics of the delinquent youth. Nondelinquent youth who possess the attributes characteristic of the delinquent sample are accordingly considered delinquency-prone. Finally the predictive value of the scores is ascertained through a follow-up study. While instruments for predicting delinquency have hardly received wide acclaim from either theorists or practitioners, few would deny the need for and value of a valid scale. What follows is a brief review of three of the more valid scales for predicting delinquency.

Glueck Prediction Tables

The first major effort to develop instruments for predicting delinquency was reported in 1950 by Sheldon and Eleanor Glueck (1950), who matched 500 delinquents and nondelinquents in the Boston area on the basis of age, ethnic origin, intelligence, and place of residence. Three tables were developed for distinguishing between these two groups. Table 1 dealt with five social factors: (1) discipline of the boy by the father, (2) affection of the mother for the boy, (3) affection of the father for the boy, (4) supervision of the boy by the mother, and (5) cohesiveness of the family. Table 2 dealt with personality traits as revealed by the Rorschach Psychodiagnostic Test. Table 3 dealt with personality characteristics as revealed through psychiatric interviewing. Of these three tables, only the social-factor table has been subjected to follow-up evaluation. The Gluecks recommend that delinquency prediction be made at the time the child enters school, around age 6.

To date, there has been only one major study that tested a group of youngsters at age 6 and then followed them up to determine the predictive validity of this instrument. In 1952-1953 the New York City Youth Board selected a sample of 224 first-grade boys from high-delinquency neighborhoods. Ratings on social factors were obtained through interviews conducted by social workers in the home setting. The investigators, in an effort to refine the social-factor table, devised a three-factor scale (supervision of the boy by the father, supervision of the boy by the mother, and family cohesiveness) and a two-factor scale (supervision of the boy by the mother, and family cohesiveness). After nine years of comprehensive follow-up, Craig & Glick (1964) concluded that the scale was a good differentiator between serious and persistent delinquents and nondelinquents. The results indicated, for example, that the three-factor scale predicted accurately 70% of delinquents and 85% of nondelinquents.

These findings seem encouraging, but objections raised by critics (Briggs & Wirt, 1965; Kvaraceus, 1966) cannot be lightly dismissed. The chief objections center around the subjectivity of the social workers' ratings, questionable statistical analysis, the nonapplicability of certain variables (for example, supervision by the father in fatherless homes), the cost in time and money of administering these scales, and the use of this scale with the general population. Glueck (1966b) has added two additional traits—nonsubmissiveness to authority, and destructiveness—in an effort to produce a more discriminative instrument. Although it is suggested (Glueck, 1966a) that these two new predictive instruments will be more accurate than the previously validated scales, the need for additional testing is also pointed out.

Minnesota Multiphasic Personality Inventory

The MMPI is perhaps the best known of the structured personality inventories. It consists of 550 true-false items and yields scores on 10 clinical scales. Over the years, a sample of more than 15,000 ninth-grade students in

Minnesota have been given this inventory in an effort to predict who will become delinquent. A follow-up study involving a search of police and juvenile-court records was made two years after the initial testing (Hathaway & Monachesi, 1953, 1957). Boys whose profiles on this inventory were most "normal" have the lowest delinquency rates. Elevations on certain scales, however, were found to be more closely related to the prediction of delinquency than others, with peaks on the psychopathic deviate and mania scales being most predictive of antisocial, acting-out forms of behavior. Those exhibiting a combination of characteristics associated with the psychopathic personality (such as impulsivity, rebelliousness, minimal guilt, and inability to learn from experience) and characteristics associated with mania (such as expansiveness, outgoingness, insufficient inhibitory capacity) were most likely to be known to the police and the juvenile courts. Certain neurotic indicators, on the other hand, such as a tendency to worry and to be anxious, were seen as favorable signs in that they seemed to have an inhibiting effect on potentially delinquent behavior. Wirt & Briggs (1959) found that delinquency could be more accurately predicted when social-agency contact was combined with the personality pattern than when either was used singly. These findings indicate the desirability of combining social factors and personality variables in the prediction of violative behavior.

This instrument has proved useful in differentiating between delinquent and nondelinquent groups but, despite what might be the most rigorous research to date on a predictive scale, it is generally inadequate for purposes of individual prediction. As far as school personnel are concerned, this inventory has additional limitations. It is not designed for use with elementary-school children, it uses language that may be objectionable and upsetting to many pupils and their parents (for example, "My sex life is satisfactory"), and it requires an experienced clinician for interpretation.

KD Scales

Kvaraceus (1953, 1956) has devised a scale consisting of 75 multiple-choice items designed to differentiate delinquents from nondelinquents. Differences in personality makeup, in home and family backgrounds, and in school experiences are explored. Kvaraceus has also developed a KD proneness scale and check list for use by teachers and other professional workers concerned with the prediction of delinquency. This list consists of 70 items concerning family, home, school, and personal factors.

There is also a nonverbal scale (Kvaraceus, 1961) which has received the most extensive validation of all the KD prediction scales (Kvaraceus, 1966). Administration of the scale consists in the presentation of 62 circles, each of which contains four pictures designed to differentiate delinquents from nondelinquents. The child is asked to select the picture that he likes the most and the one that he likes the least from each set. A three-year follow-up study conducted on almost 1,600 junior-high-school students indicated that there was a correspondence between the scores on this instrument and norm-violating behavior. The inconsistency in the findings suggested, however, that "the instrument should not be used for predictive purposes on a routine and perfunctory basis" (Kvaraceus, 1966). A check list for teacher use is provided in Table 8–4.

Shortcomings of Present Predictive Scales

Despite concerted efforts to predict delinquency, we have not as yet been successful in devising an instrument with high predictive power. Kvaraceus (1966) notes that we might well have to develop separate scales for middle-class and lower-class delinquent youth. He also points out that we might be more effective in identifying subcultural delinquents as opposed to emotionally disturbed delinquents. Briggs & Wirt (1965) assert that researchers must attend to a number of pragmatic concerns heretofore neglected if we are to know the actual value of a prediction system. To mention a few of the neglected concerns, we have to determine the cost of errors in prediction, for example, the cost of professional treatment for a child who probably would not have become delinquent anyway, the cost and availability of treatment facilities, and the cost of obtaining the predictive information. We must also specify what we consider acceptable rates of predictiveness success. Until we have dealt with such illustrative utilitarian matters, we will not be in a good position to know the real worth of any given predictive system. At present, it

Table 8–4.   Delinquency Proneness Check List for Teacher Use Based on School Factors Differentiating Delinquents from Nondelinquents in Five Major Studies[a]

Yes	No	?	Factor
( )	( )	( )	1. Shows marked dislike for school
( )	( )	( )	2. Resents school routine and restriction
( )	( )	( )	3. Uninterested in school program
( )	( )	( )	4. Is failing in a number of subjects
( )	( )	( )	5. Has repeated one or more grades
( )	( )	( )	6. Attends a special class for retarded pupils
( )	( )	( )	7. Has attended many different schools
( )	( )	( )	8. Intends to leave school as soon as the law allows
( )	( )	( )	9. Has only vague academic or vocational plans
( )	( )	( )	10. Has limited academic ability
( )	( )	( )	11. Is a seriously or persistently misbehaving child
( )	( )	( )	12. Destroys school materials or property
( )	( )	( )	13. Is cruel and bullying on the playground
( )	( )	( )	14. Has temper tantrums in the classroom
( )	( )	( )	15. Wants to stop schooling at once
( )	( )	( )	16. Truants from school

[a] From Kvaraceus (1966).

appears that teacher nominations provide as reliable a basis for the prediction of antisocial behavior as do the best psychometric instruments (Kvaraceus, 1966).

Prevention and Treatment

How one attempts to treat or prevent juvenile delinquency depends to a large extent on how he conceives the problem. Those who see this phenomenon as having a sociological base are much more inclined to influence social processes in the delinquent's surroundings. The sociological stance, as translated into treatment efforts, thus tends to focus on various types of environmental changes. Inherent in this approach is a concern over such sociological phenomena as family instability, social organization in the community, the role played by gang membership, and the difference in value systems among members of various socioeconomic strata. To implement their concerns, sociologists have traditionally relied on some form of social action. In some cases, the total environment is changed—for example, institutionalization. On other occasions, rehabilitation programs are attempted within the child's existing environment, for example, supervised youth organizations or settlement houses. In any event, treatment is centered around some kind of cultural or social alteration. Consistent with this orientation has been a corresponding emphasis on the development of either community programs or responsive group environments to facilitate the acquisition of socially appropriate behavior.

In the psychological approach, delinquent behavior is usually regarded as a symptom of some underlying personality problem. Though meaningless to the outside observer, the delinquent activity is presumed to be meaningful to the offender in that it represents an effort on his part to meet needs for status, security, acceptance, and so forth. The delinquent child, in response to thwarting and in an attempt to fulfill such unmet needs, thus resorts to illegal activities. In the implementation of this clinical orientation, treatment is generally focused on the individual, and reliance is accordingly placed on the skills of caseworkers or psychotherapists.

More recently, an instructional model of treatment has appeared on the scene. Whereas both the sociological and traditional psychological treatment programs derived from a search for underlying causative factors, the instructional model is more concerned with current factors and less concerned with remote causative factors. Instructional models of treatment are so named because of their systematic emphasis on teaching delinquents how to respond differently and to recognize the consequences of their behavior (Stephens, 1973). Behavior modification approaches and educational approaches are examples of the instructional model which has been gaining in popularity.

As we will see below, even though the treatment methods of the psychological and sociological approaches sometimes overlap or are used in combination, there remains a basic difference in viewpoints—a difference that is translated into noticeable differences in the objectives and methods of action programs.

Sociological Approaches

The sociological approaches attempt to change the individual through community or group programs. In this sense, sociological interventions generally have a more comprehensive base than do psychological interventions. In this section we will review some of the better-known studies and indicate recent trends in the treatment of delinquent youth.

Total-Community Approach.   Perhaps the best-known community-center program is the Chicago Area Project, which was initiated by Shaw and his associates (Kobrin, 1959). The first area project was developed in 1932, and by 1959 similar projects had arisen in twelve Chicago neighborhoods. These projects are predicated on the philosophy that the adults who live in these slum areas must become better motivated to accept greater responsibility in promoting socially acceptable behavior among the children in that area. The central aim is to involve local youngsters in various activities so that they will adopt conventional rather than delinquent modes of conduct.

Translating this philosophy into action was initiated by having a staff member identify leaders in the community and by enlisting their support for a strong local movement to combat delinquency. These natural leaders then formed organizations, directed the communities in establishing a program, and raised the funds necessary to support the program. In other words, the primary responsibility for the maintenance and effectiveness of the program lay with indigenous members of the low-income community. Outside professional direction, though given a definite role, was secondary. The area projects differed with respect to the specific contents of the programs, but all programs had three common elements: (1) the establishment of recreational programs, (2) the campaign for community improvement, and (3) direct work with gangs and individuals. The use of prestigious community leaders was to serve the dual purpose of attracting both other adults and youth members in the area as well as offering models for emulation.

As is the case with most projects of this nature, there has been little in the way of objective evaluation. It does appear, however, (1) that the residents of low-income areas can organize themselves effectively in developing welfare programs, (2) that these organizations are enduring, well administered, and adapted to the needs of the local situation, and (3) that such plans utilize leadership that would otherwise remain untapped (Witmer & Tufts, 1954). Whether or not these programs lower the incidence of delinquency is another question, however. Data based on the rate of delinquency between 1930 and 1942 in three of the four then existing project areas indicated a deceleration of delinquent activities, but whether such differences were a direct outcome of project efforts or due to other community factors is debatable. In any event, no spectacular claims have been made, and the subjective reactions have ranged from favorable to skeptical.

Group-Centered Approach. Another approach, which began in the 1920s and was given impetus by Thrasher's work with gangs, is becoming increasingly popular, especially in large urban areas. This is the use of the detached-worker approach. We have already noted that most delinquency occurs in the presence of other delinquents. Bearing this in mind, caseworkers evolved methods that reached beyond the child and his family and were extended to predelinquent or delinquent peer groups.

One of the most widely quoted group-work programs in Miller's Boston Delinquency Project (1962). This project, designed to counteract delinquency in a lower-class Boston area, ran for a period of three years (1954–1957). Unlike some group projects that simply encourage the child to become a member of an organized club (for example, a baseball team), this program attempted to influence the value systems of lower-class street gangs which lead them into conflict with law-enforcement agents. (Miller, as noted earlier, views lower-class delinquency as emanating in the mores of lower-class culture.) This project also differed from others in that all workers were professionally trained, each worker except one was assigned to a single group, and regular psychiatric consultation was available.

During the three-year treatment span, 205 youngsters in seven corner groups were given intensive service. By "intensive" we mean approximately 18 to 21 hours of actual contact per week, with contacts ranging over a period of 10 to 34 months. Of the seven groups, four were white males (mostly Irish), one was black male, one was black female, and one was white female. The control subjects consisted of seven groups that had received only superficial assistance. The ages of the subjects ranged from 12 to 18 at the start of the program. There were three major phases to the project. Specifically, the professional staff sought (1) to establish personal relationships; (2) to modify behavior through organized group activities, through direct influence, and through serving as intermediaries between the youth and the adult institutions, for example, setting up job interviews; and (3) to terminate the relationship in a therapeutic manner.

Did the project succeed in reducing violative behavior? To answer this question, three separate measures of change were used: (1) the incidence of disapproved forms of customary behavior (immoral behavior); (2) illegal behavior (unofficial crime); and (3) court appearances. While two earlier reports (Miller, 1957, 1959b) might lead us to believe that a "limited but definite" diminution in delinquent activities had occurred, later statistics based on all three of these criteria indicated that the project had a "negligible impact" on the incidence of violative behavior. This negative-impact finding seems most applicable to those treatment methods which were most extensively employed and hence most fully tested in the study. These included the use of organized recreational activities, the establishment of local citizens' councils, the identification and contacting of adolescent corner gangs, the establishment of relationships with gang members, the provision of access to adult institutions, and the availability of more socially acceptable adult models. The authors concluded that the incentives provided for engaging in anti-social behavior were more powerful than any counterpressures the project could bring to bear.

Institutional Approach.   The Highfields Project (Weeks, 1958) illustrates a short-term community-therapy approach for youthful first offenders aged 16–17. Highfields, a specialized facility where not more than 21 boys reside at any one time, uses an open approach to treatment. For example, there are no guards and the boys are allowed to visit local villages to pursue activities of interest to them. A serious attempt is made to let the adolescents lead as "normal" lives as possible. There is no formal schooling, but supervised work experiences are provided. Group sessions designed to help the youngsters understand the motivations underlying their behavior and to modify certain undesirable attitudes are also conducted five nights a week.

What were the results of this study? First of all, there was little evidence that the Highfields boys modified their attitudes toward law and order, toward life, or toward their families. Second, there appeared to be little change in basic personality structure as a consequence of treatment. Finally, follow-up data gathered over a 12-month period after release indicated a significantly lower recidivism rate among 229 Highfields boys when compared with boys from a more traditional type of reform school. Further analysis of the data indicated that the better parole record was accounted for by a greater number of black boys in the Highfields facility than in the control group; that is, black boys from Highfields responded more favorably following release. White boys from both institutions had similar rates of recidivism, however. Also of interest is the cost of this short-term treatment, which was approximately one-third that of the more traditional program. In large measure, the differences in cost can be attributed to the fact that boys in the more traditional school had been incarcerated for a longer period of time. Though research of this particular type is certainly needed and has merit, it is unfortunate that the research design was not a particularly tight one. Replication using more rigorous control is indicated (for example, random assignment to experimental and control conditions).

Institutional treatment has generally produced little positive effect (Caditz, 1959). In fact, there is substantial evidence indicating that the longer the youngster spends in a "correctional" setting, the more apt he is to fail when released on parole (Weeks, 1958). Several factors most likely are operative in the production of such results: the size of the patient population in the institution, the staff-inmate ratio, the shortage of professionally trained personnel, the inappropriateness of treatment efforts, and the return to an unhealthy environment upon release. A report on three studies (Buehler, Patterson, & Furniss, 1966) has documented what might be an even more important factor, namely, the reward system of the institution itself. According to the results, the social living system of a correctional institution tends to reinforce delinquent behavior (often through nonverbal communications) and to punish socially conforming behaviors. Such findings, if representative, constitute a severe attack on institutional treatment and call for an overhaul in the scheduling of reinforcers within this type of social system.

Evaluation of Sociological Approaches. We have accumulated over the years a vast body of findings about the control of delinquent behavior. The conclusions to be drawn have been aptly stated as follows:

> Indeed, as of now, there are no demonstrable and proven methods for reducing the incidence of serious delinquent acts through preventive or rehabilitative procedures. Either the descriptive knowledge has not been translated into feasible action programs, or the programs have not been successfully implemented; or if implemented, they have lacked evaluation; or if evaluated, the results have usually been negative; and in the few cases of reported positive results, replications have been lacking.
>
> At the same time, there are systematic and plausible sets of ideas about delinquency that find at least partial support and that may be converted into systematic action strategies. These ideas deserve careful development and refinement, for in the absence of hard evidence they remain our best guide to action, and it sometimes takes years of planning and effort before programs can be successfully launched [Wheeler, Cottrell, & Romasco, 1967].

Others have been less kind in their appraisal of sociological explanations in light of certain points that are at odds with those sociological theories that view delinquency as an aggressive response to frustrations imposed by the middle class. First of all, it should be noted that while pervasive discontent may be a facilitative condition of collective aggression, it is not a necessary or a sufficient condition (Bandura, 1973). The vast majority of disadvantaged people (80–85%) do not engage in aggressively disruptive behavior. In fact, informal observation suggests that dissatisfaction produces greater aggression in those whose violent efforts have been reinforced with social and economic gains than in those who have lost hope. Relative frustration may be a better predictor of violence than absolute discontent. Conceptual and operational ambiguity have hindered evaluation of this hypothesis. For example, different results may be obtained depending on whether poor people use their present aspirations, their past gratifications, or the life conditions of others selected for comparison purposes to evaluate their life circumstances. We must also bear in mind that student activists come in disproportionate numbers from advantaged homes. Discontent stemming from crowding as an explanatory factor is also called into question as a result of cross-cultural studies. New York City, for instance, is much more densely populated than Los Angeles (26,000 people per square mile in New York City compared to 5,500 in Los Angeles), yet Los Angeles has a higher crime rate (Johnson, 1972).

Psychological Approaches

Few delinquents are enthusiastic about psychotherapy. To most delinquents, the therapist is an outsider—an enemy not to be trusted. Delinquents are typically suspicious, fearing that the therapist has ulterior motives. More-over, this population is not a particularly introspective group. They do not see themselves as having problems, but tend to put blame on factors external to themselves. When we recall the characteristics of the unsocialized and socialized aggressive delinquents, we have some idea of their lack of readi-ness for conventional treatment procedures. Consequently, delinquents are extremely difficult to get into treatment and if they are coerced, they have difficulty forming a positive relationship with the therapist.

Employer-Employee Approach.   To circumvent many of the difficulties associated with the "doctor-patient" relationship in the treatment of unreach-able lower-class delinquents, Slack (1960) cleverly substituted an "experi-menter-subject" or "employer-employee" relationship. In this approach the delinquents were asked if they would be willing to work an hour or two a day. The prospective employer explained that the work was not hard and that they could quit any time they wanted. During their first visits to the labora-tory, the subjects were told that the employer's job was "to learn about the kids in the neighborhood" and that he was willing to pay them if they were willing to talk about themselves and to take psychological tests. Material rewards such as food, cigarettes, and candy were made available to the sub-jects. Periodic bonuses were also given. Provided with this nurturant atmos-phere, the subjects eventually came to have confidence in the therapist and to develop a therapeutic relationship with him. Once the youngster realized that he no longer was coming only for the sake of the material gains but because of the relationship itself, he was involved in a more conventional form of treatment.

The results of this study were positive in terms of initiating a positive rela-tionship with unreachable delinquents. The small number of subjects (seven), the absence of a control group, and the presentation of only qualitative re-sults are some of the more obvious shortcomings of the study. All in all, it would appear, however, that Slack did achieve his objective of devising a technique for introducing hard-core cases to treatment. Though a successful introduction to therapy is not a sufficient condition in itself, its accomplish-ment nonetheless represents considerable movement, as anyone who has worked with such cases will testify.

Schwitzgebel & Kolb (1964) continued Slack's employer-employee method. These investigators used 20 boys between the ages of 15 and 21 in the experi-mental group. All had been imprisoned at one time. A control group matched in type of offense, age of first offense, nationality, time imprisoned, and place of residence was used for comparison purposes. The subjects received $1.00 an hour for interview sessions. The approach was a problem-oriented one as opposed to a theory oriented one. The subjects were seen approximately three times a week for about nine months with a store being used as a meeting place. After fifteen appointments, attendance became dependable for 90% of the subjects.

A follow-up study three years later showed that the number of arrests and the length of incarceration of the experimental group was approximately one-half that of the control group. There were no statistically significant differences in recidivism rates, although the trend was in the expected direction. This latter negative finding may be due to the different definitions of crime employed by the two groups, however. Unofficial crime rates were used as a criterion for the experimental group, whereas official crime rates—a less rigorous criterion—was used for the control group. Schwitzgebel concluded that the modification of delinquent behavior is more effectively achieved by the development of competing socially acceptable behaviors through operant-conditioning techniques (giving of money, cigarettes, food, and the like) than by direct attacks on delinquent behaviors per se. In accordance with this interpretation, Schwitzgebel's (1967) later research has been based primarily on an operant-conditioning paradigm.

A Learning Theory Approach. Schwitzgebel's later work provides a nice introduction to the present topic, namely, behavior modification or learning theory approaches to the treatment of delinquent behavior. For most learning theorists, antisocial behavior is learned, maintained, and modified by the same learning theory principles as are other learned behaviors. Given this assumption, Burchard (1967) created an experimental residential environment where consequences for one's behavior were programed according to learning theory principles. The program was a standardized one that involved mostly nonprofessionals.

As is characteristic of behavior modification approaches, specific target behaviors were selected for modification. These included maintaining a job, staying in school, buying food and meals, cooperating with peers and adults, budgeting money, and buying and caring for clothes—behaviors that would facilitate adjustment in the community. Tokens that could be exchanged for such things as an hour of recreation with female residents and a trip to town were used as rewards for desirable behavior. Conversely, undesirable target behaviors (fighting, lying, stealing, property damage, and so on) were punished. Punishment took the form of time-outs and seclusion, during which time tokens could not be earned. Moreover, when a staff member said "Time out," it cost the delinquent four tokens. When a staff member had to say "Seclusion," a charge of fifteen tokens was assessed. Within this context, Burchard completed a series of illustrative experiments with quite favorable results.

Psychoanalytically Oriented Approach. The behavior modification approach has utilized as subjects what we have termed the sociological or subcultural delinquent. The late Adelaide Johnson (1959), who is known for her work with individual or neurotic delinquents, took a quite different tack, emphasizing the need to involve parents in treatment since the child's delinquent activities are presumably initiated and maintained by the parents. In her psychoanalytically oriented therapy sessions with parents, she stressed the need for frankness, making very clear their involvement in the child's problems.

There were two main drawbacks to this approach. First, intensive treatment efforts require involving the family; this approach is impractical for most child-guidance clinics, since parents are typically not available for more than one visit per week. Second, the danger of intensifying an already emotionally upset parent through direct confrontation must be also weighed. This circumstance could be especially unfortunate in those instances where we wrongly ascribe the child's acting-out to deficiencies in the parent's conscience.

Evaluation of Psychological Approaches.   Much remains to be learned about the treatment and prevention of delinquency. As indicated above, intervention outcomes are far from wholly satisfactory. We have no sure-fire techniques that will reduce delinquency appreciably. Commonly employed approaches such as casework, counseling, psychiatric therapy, and recreational programs most likely have an ameliorative effect in certain cases, but they have not kept the rate of delinquent activity from climbing. Yet, despite the rather disappointing findings, it behooves workers to continue to evaluate the effectiveness of their endeavors. Though some clinicians and theorists still appear to think otherwise, it is encouraging to note that we are becoming more and more appreciative of the necessity for objective appraisal of our intervention efforts. We can no longer afford to assume romantically that our attempts and idealistic desires to reduce delinquent activities are being magically fulfilled.

Bearing in mind the limited results of achievement efforts and the transitory nature of most delinquent activity, Miller (Kvaraceus, 1966) questions whether the huge expenditures for treatment are worthwhile. But although this questioning attitude deserves more consideration than most workers are apt to give it, it seems quite clear that treatment efforts will not be deterred by the negligible results reported in evaluative studies. We will continue to train more psychiatrists, psychologists, social workers, and school counselors to fulfill their established roles. Since this is the case, it behooves us to ask why our results have been so limited and to inquire as to what we must do to better our therapeutic record. First of all, we must face the possibility regarding the inappropriateness of traditional treatment strategies. Empirical support for this hypothesis is seen in a study by Gottesfeld (1965), in which a list of 65 different treatment methods were sent in questionnaire form to 235 professional workers and 332 gang-member delinquents. The professionals were instructed to rate the usefulness of these methods, and the delinquents were asked to indicate their preferences among the various methods. The results indicated some very basic differences in orientation between the two groups. Whereas the professionals believed that the worker should be nonjudgmental and nonauthoritative in his role, the delinquents seemed to express a need for a mature parent substitute who would teach them how to relate better socially and help them to find a place in adult society.

Many authorities now recognize that we have used psychotherapy on many delinquents who were not in need of this type of treatment. This is especially true of the sociological delinquent, who is a basically sound youngster from the standpoint of mental health. Furthermore, we have not geared our treatment methodologies, by and large, to those who externalize their problems. Instead, we have focused most of our energies on the development of treatment strategies suited to those who internalize their problems. We expect delinquents, whose adjustive behaviors are already suspect, to adapt to our treatment methodologies, whereas we—as rigorously trained professionals—seem to feel little need or obligation to gear our treatment techniques to their level of readiness. Can you imagine a medical doctor expecting a patient to adapt his biochemistry so that it will respond more readily to the prescribed drug? Just as we have hard-core delinquents, it also appears that we have hard-core professionals. Researchers who use the employer-employee model and behavior modification procedures deserve recognition for their more functional, straightforward, and down-to-earth approaches. They have devised rewards and incentives that are sociologically consistent with the delinquent's subculture and are apparently sufficiently powerful to lead or entice these youngsters to establish more legal modes of meeting their needs.

One of the more divergent approaches involves the use of former delinquents as nonprofessional workers. Since peers can inhibit the norm-violating activities of others, it might well be that the ex-delinquent peer has certain advantages as a therapist. For one thing, there is less social distance between him and the client than usually exists between the middle-class professional and the lower-class patient. Moreover, the indigenous nonprofessional is typically seen as "one of us." He is also able to give help with present reality crises, and he can offer this help within the confines of the client's daily surroundings. In other words, the client does not have to go to the therapist's office or to the community agency. The nonprofessional is thus able to give help in an informal manner. Anyone who has had experience with lower-class delinquents readily recognizes their aversion to the formal, futuristic atmosphere that is characteristic of conventional forms of therapy. While it is still too early to evaluate the effectiveness of such approaches, it does appear on a priori grounds that they have considerable merit. Conceivably, the use of indigenous nonprofessionals could not only lead to more effective intervention approaches, but also help to alleviate the existing manpower shortage in the mental-health fields. Let us hope that the professionally trained workers will not become too threatened if these paraprofessionals achieve results which have thus far eluded us.

We must also devote greater consideration to gearing our intervention approaches to the child's sex, developmental level, socioeconomic status, and "type" of delinquency. Thus, for example, an employer-employee type of therapy might fit well with the older adolescent offenders but would be inappropriate for younger delinquents. It might well prove that the type of intervention is a more important determinant of effectiveness than the earliness of intervention. For example, finding a delinquent a job that offers him adult status and recognition and thus removes him from his poor environment might be more effective than doing intensive casework with a much younger child who is living in the slums with his parents. Or, with respect to the various dimensions of delinquent activity, we might do well to concentrate treatment efforts to those who are most apt to continue in their wayward manner. Unfortunately, those with the most unfavorable prognoses are the very youngsters who are least apt to receive help since they do not fit our traditional treatment model. Hopefully, however, the emergence of more innovative approaches will serve to remedy this state of affairs.

Educational Approaches

As authorities have become increasingly concerned about the close relationship between academic failure and delinquency, schools today have been given appreciably more responsibility for socially maladjusted youth. This association between antisocial behavior and difficulty in school continues to be supported by current research. Burke & Simons (1965), for instance, find that among institutionalized delinquents, 90% were reported as truants or had made poor adjustments to school, about 75% had repeated two or more grades or had dropped out of school before the legal age, and 67% were reading below the sixth-grade level. Similarly, noting that low academic achievement, absenteeism, and impulsivity differentiate delinquents from non-delinquents in both white and black populations, Miller (1959a) optimistically hypothesized that the incidence of delinquency would decrease as educational achievements increase.

The growing conviction that juvenile delinquency is partly heightened by certain other widespread conditions in American education is reflected in a report prepared by the Task Force on Juvenile Delinquency (1967). According to Schafer & Polk (1967), there are four basic ways in which school experiences can contribute to delinquency:

1. By stressing the need for educational success and yet simultaneously insuring educational failure, the schools block legitimate means of entering the mainstream of American life.

2. Educational activities often seem meaningless in relation to the students' needs. Hence, because school tasks and rewards are perceived as unrelated to the students' future role in life, education becomes a rather empty activity. Consequently, illegitimate alternatives assume greater attractiveness.

3. The school is often unable to elicit a strong degree of commitment to conformity and legitimate achievement from students. A sense of alienation results which renders students more susceptible to delinquent pursuits.

4. The manner in which the school handles student misconduct is also relevant in this connection. For example, overly punitive sanctions of a degrading nature can serve to push the student toward illegitimate forms of commitment.

Since the conditions that give rise to these unfortunate debilitating effects are deeply rooted in existing notions and organizations of our educational system, Schafer and Polk argue that education must do more than adopt stop-gap measures that deal solely with surface problems. Adding more counselors and social workers, for example, constitutes a rather myopic viewpoint which ignores broader dimensions of the school's role in delinquency. These authors stress the need for such things as fostering a belief in the educability of all pupils, expanding preschool educational facilities, developing meaningful and relevant instruction, innovating more appropriate teaching strategies, using flexible grouping, continuing reeducation of teachers, providing alternate career-oriented programs, increasing the accessibility to higher education, reintegrating dropouts, and so forth. Unless fundamental and radical educational changes are made in the schools, these authors declare, schools will continue to contribute significantly to delinquency.

Despite the relationship of such factors as educational retardation, truancy, and school adjustment to delinquent pursuits, teachers receive little training in the area of delinquency (Eichorn, 1965). A survey of 260 educators in graduate courses revealed that about half of them had no more than one or two class hours devoted to this topic. The same criticism might well be leveled with respect to the management of aggressive students in general, namely, that teachers are given only minimal instruction in how to cope with acting-out youth, despite the fact that these youngsters are the very ones who are most disruptive to effective classroom functioning. In this section, we will focus primarily on special classes, work-experience programs, and behavior modification techniques, although passing reference will be made to other modifications in educational strategies for delinquent youth. The classroom management of aggressive students is treated in Chapters 2 and 12.

Educational Provisions.   In view of the educational retardation of delinquents, there have been numerous attempts to modify the educational provisions provided socially maladjusted youth. Kvaraceus and Ulrich (1959) have done an admirable job of surveying the various ways in which school districts throughout the country have tried to meet the educational needs of these youths. The approaches included identification procedures, provisions within the classroom, curricular adaptations, special classes, and closer relationships with families, law-enforcement agencies, and community agencies. Their work, though nonevaluative, nonetheless provides a valuable resource for educational practitioners in that it delineates general principles and examples of specific action programs.

Special Classes.   Evidence that the schools can occupy a strategic position in coping with juvenile delinquency is seen in the results of a study conducted in Quincy, Illinois (Bowman, 1959). Several traditional approaches were initially utilized with semidelinquent and delinquent adolescents in an effort to mobilize the talents of youngsters in the community. Foster-home placement was used but found to be unsuccessful, especially with the children between the ages of 12 and 14. Intensive casework was also attempted but proved to be too time-consuming. No community agency was sufficiently staffed to undertake such an intensive program on any sort of extensive basis. Recreational programs were also tried but found to be wanting. These programs, it was concluded, provided an excellent means for contact between children and the community but could not be relied upon to effect any significant changes in acting-out children.

Finally, an approach was tried that would permit intensive contact with target groups and yet be available to the typical community, namely, school intervention. Sixty youngsters who were doing poorly in their eighth-grade schoolwork were selected for intensive study. Of these subjects, nearly all were discipline problems and 41% had police or court records. The subjects were randomly assigned to three groups of 20 each. Thus, there were two experimental groups and one control group. Teachers were assigned on the basis of their interest in working with acting-out pupils. As such, these teachers had no special training in handling delinquent youths. Pupils in the experimental programs spent from one-half to three-fourths of their school day with one teacher who was sympathetic toward them. Instructional methods and materials were adjusted to the child's interests and level of functioning in order to make school activities pleasanter. Practical materials were stressed more than textbooks, and the pace of instruction was slowed. During the first two periods of the morning the focus was on academic subjects with the third period being devoted to discussion and films on general and social problems. For some subjects the afternoon session consisted of study periods, small-group discussions, handwork, and special projects. For others, outside employment constituted the main activity during the afternoon.

Written reactions to the special classes by the students were favorable. As might be expected from the slowed pace, differences in academic performance between the experimental and control subjects were only slight. There were also no significant differences between the two groups in the number of school dropouts. It appears, however, that youngsters in the experimental group achieved a greater job success as reflected by employer ratings and job stability. The experimental subjects also seemed to have a greater interest in school as inferred from their better attendance records. Of most significance, however, were their respective delinquency rates. Whereas the rate for the control subjects more than tripled, the rate for the experimental subjects decreased by more than one-third. Furthermore, there were fewer serious offenses among the students in the special classes. While the number of subjects is too small to permit widespread generalization, the findings do suggest the benefits that can accrue from the use of special classes, where the pupils are provided with interested teachers, a revised curriculum, and freedom from competition with more advanced students.

Work-Experience Program.   Work-experience programs are becoming increasingly popular as a form of educational therapy for delinquent youth. Recognizing that treatment of delinquents in the usual clinic setting had not been highly successful, Massimo & Shore (1963) sought to determine the effectiveness of a comprehensive vocationally oriented treatment program. This experiment included 20 adolescent boys of normal intellectual ability. All had histories of antisocial behavior and were out of school at the time of the study. They either had been suspended by school authorities or had voluntarily withdrawn. The subjects were randomly assigned to either an experimental or a control group. Those adolescents in the experimental group received the services of a detached worker who provided, over a 10-month period, three types of services: intensive psychotherapy, remedial education, and employment. It was hypothesized that this treatment program would lead to positive changes in ego functioning as evidenced by changes in academic skills, personality attitudes, and overt behavior.

All three hypotheses were confirmed. Educational-achievement test scores favored the experimental group at a statistically significant level. Three dimensions of personality in terms of attitudes—toward the control of aggression, toward the self, and toward authority—all improved for the experimental subjects. Overt behavior as reflected in the work-history records also favored the experimental group. At the end of the 10-month period, seven members of the experimental group were still on the job, with the other three members having returned to school. On the other hand, three of the control group were unemployed throughout the 10-month period, and a fourth was unemployed at the end of this period. Further, only one of the control group returned to school. Probation officers, who did not know whether a child belonged to the experimental or the control group, also rated members of the treatment group as improved in overt behavior. A 10-year follow-up study indicated that those who did well during the program had been able to maintain their gains while the adjustment of control subjects continued to deteriorate over time (Shore & Massimo, 1973). In general, eight of ten of the treated group seemed to have made an adequate adjustment in contrast to only two of the ten control-group subjects. The treated group had a more stable job history and continued to show fewer arrests than the untreated group. There seemed to be minimal change in direction of overall adjustment in either group over the intervening decade.

Though the number of subjects was quite small and the therapeutic variables difficult to disentangle because of the comprehensive nature of this program, the results are sufficiently promising to encourage further investigation along these lines. It should certainly be cautioned, contrary to the belief of some educators, that school programs of this nature are probably not suitable for all deviant youth. The psychotic youngster and the hostile sociopath are examples of those who might be too disturbed to profit from interventions of this kind. The interested reader can find additional descriptions of work-experience programs for delinquent youth by consulting Schreiber (1966).

National interest in the role of employment has increased over the last ten years (for example, the National Job Corps) but many of the programs were poorly planned with meager evaluation and almost nonexistent follow-up (Shore & Massimo, 1973). Hence, for the present the findings must be regarded as tentative. Nevertheless, it would appear, as Schreiber (1966) declares, that school-based work-study programs do provide a second chance for alienated youth to join the achievement-based mainstream of American life. These programs, while differing considerably from one another, do possess common therapeutic elements that have been succinctly stated by Schreiber as follows:

> [These programs] (1) encourage and permit alienated youth to improve their self-images and self-concepts; (2) enable them to learn and exercise self-discipline and to develop proper work habits and work attitudes; (3) enable them to maintain at least minimum levels of education and work skills which are marketable; (4) offer alienated youth opportunities to relate themselves with and to other persons and encourage them to do so; and (5) give direct and indirect satisfaction to the individual in knowing that he can both undertake and complete a job satisfactorily.

Behavior Modification-Remediation Approaches.   A fascinating investigation of remedial reading by Staats & Butterfield (1965) combined the use of two emerging approaches to the mental-health problems of children, namely, behavior modification principles and the use of nonprofessionals. The subject for this study was a 14-year-old culturally deprived juvenile delinquent who had a long history of delinquency and maladjustment. His difficulties in school were, in part, attributable to his lack of academic skills and to his failure to respond to traditional classroom reinforcers. He had a full-scale IQ of 90 on the Wechsler Intelligence Scale for Children. His Verbal Scale IQ was 77, however, which would indicate a slow rate of school-learning ability. The method of treatment relied on an extrinsic token reinforcement system, with three types of tokens being used: a blue token was worth one-tenth of one cent; a white token was worth one-third of one cent; and a red token was worth one-half of a cent. Correct responses on the first trial yielded a token of high value, whereas correct responses made following errors yielded tokens of lower reinforcement value. The tokens could be used to purchase a variety of items; that is, the child could choose his own reward. Materials from the Science Research Associates reading kits were adapted for use in the study. Vocabulary words were typed on separate 3×5 cards. Oral reading materials of paragraph length were typed on separate 5×8 cards, so that each story could be presented individually. Comprehension questions were typed on $8\frac{1}{2} \times 13$ sheets of paper for use in promoting the understanding or silent-reading materials. The objective was to develop remedial reading procedures that could be applied in a standard manner by nonprofessionals trained in this procedure. The tutor in the study was a probation officer.

Forty hours of remedial reading spread over a $4\frac{1}{2}$-month interval yielded considerable success. For example, the boy's reading ability rose from a beginning second-grade level to a fourth-grade level. This gain might not seem impressive except for the fact that this boy accomplished more in reading during this $4\frac{1}{2}$-month period than he had in all of his previous $8\frac{1}{2}$ years of schooling. Moreover, he passed all of his courses in school for the first time, his misbehavior became less frequent, and his general attitude toward school improved. Some other points of interest include the fact that the subject received only $20.31 worth of tokens and that reading itself became reinforcing, so that more reading responses were made per reinforcer as time went on. The most important educational implication stemming from this case study is that standard reading materials can be adapted to a relatively uniform type of presentation by training nonprofessionals in the context of reinforcement principles. Later research (Staats, Minke, Goodwin, & Landeen, 1967) based on mentally retarded, culturally disadvantaged, and emotionally disturbed subjects of junior-high-school age provided a more general test of these procedures and, by and large, confirmed their practical value. High-school students and adult volunteers served as the tutors in this later research project.

CASE. Another impressive illustration of the behavior modification approach has been carried out with delinquents at the National Training School for Boys by Cohen (1966). The project was entitled CASE (Contingencies Applicable for Special Education). The specific target behavior in this study—academic performance—was shaped through the use of programed instruction. Once a student successfully completed 90% of a unit, he was eligible to take an examination on which he could earn points worth one cent each. These points could then be spent for Cokes, potato chips, items from Sears Roebuck, entrance into the lounge to visit with friends, book rentals, time in the library, and so forth.

Cohen reported that the systematic contingent application of reinforcement yielded best results when it took place in a highly structured environment that increased the likelihood of prosocial behavior and decreased the likelihood of antisocial behavior. To this end, a special environment was prepared, consisting of classrooms, study booths, control rooms, a library, a store, and a lounge. The results reflected a gradual shifting away from material reinforcers, like Cokes, toward more educationally relevant rewards, like new programs. Aside from the enormous surge in educational activities, there were also favorable changes in the social behavior of the subjects. In fact, there were no discipline problems or property destruction during a 4½-month period.

The academic gains are very impressive. In Table 8–5 it can be seen that the percentage of students achieving on the lower half of the traditional twelve grades of school at the time of their entrance, shifted in the direction of achievement levels appropriate to the upper half of the twelve grades. In English, for example, all of the students were functioning at an elementary-school level when they entered the program. By the time of their departure, 59% of them were functioning somewhere between an eighth- and a twelfth-grade level. The average rate of academic growth was twice the average for American public school students. Perhaps even more important, there were attitudinal changes, and their recidivist rates during the first year after release was two-thirds lower than the norm for the National Training School for Boys. The recidivist rate approached this norm by the end of their third year following release (Cohen, 1973). This latter finding stresses the need to program for transfer of gains achieved in the correctional setting to the community setting. The study highlights another point often overlooked, namely,

Table 8–5.   Academic Achievement Levels of CASE Students in Various Curriculum Areas at Times of Entry and Exit

Curriculum Area	Entrance Placement in Curriculum Level				Terminal Achievement in Curriculum Level			
	F # %	*S* # %	*JR* # %	*SR* # %	*F* # %	*S* # %	*JR* # %	*SR* # %
Reading	8–26	13–37	14–37	1–0	1– 6	10–28	14–40	11–26
English	35–97	1– 3	0– 0	0–0	3– 8	12–33	9–26	12–33
Science	8–18	28–82	0– 0	0–0	5– 9	10–29	16–44	5–18
Mathematics	26–75	10–25	0– 0	0–0	5–17	3– 8	19–50	9–25
Social Studies	12–33	24–67	0– 0	0–0	2– 6	13–36	7–19	14–39

F = Freshman = grades 1–4   JR = Juniors = grades 8–10.5
S = Sophomores = grades 5–7   SR = Seniors = grades 10.6–12

that the school practices are just one of many sources that can, for better or for worse, influence the course of delinquent behavior. Lest we succumb to simplistic explanations, we must pay heed to the interrelationship between problem behavior in the schools and numerous out-of-school factors (for example, mass media, the peer group, the family, the religious group) that have an impact on the child's progress.

PICA.   Cohen and his colleagues (1971) have also devised a learning model for public schools called PICA—Programming Interpersonal Curricula for Adolescents. This is an educational model to be administered by teachers and not a therapeutic model for use by therapists. As was true in the CASE model, contingency management is central to the PICA model. Students can earn rewards for achievement in language and mathematics, and for appropriate behavior in the school, home, and community. This program consists of 180 class lessons spread out over seven courses, which include Teen-Agers' Rights and Responsibilities, Prevention of Abuse of Drugs, sex education, operant behavior, problem solving in the family, the contemporary scene, and "how to" skills for both academic and daily life.

The results for the last year of this project, which was carried out in the laboratory school with extremely disruptive, unmanageable, predelinquents before moving into public schools, are presented in Figure 8–1 and Figure 8–2. The students not only made dramatic improvement in the academic area but also posed fewer discipline problems than formerly.

The findings of these two studies bear considerable significance in light of the shortage of mental-health specialists and remedial teachers. The authors know of no school district that has a sufficient number of remedial reading specialists or, for that matter, the enabling funds to employ them in the needed quantities. The tendency for gains to spread beyond the cognitive and academic areas into the social and emotional realms also merits close atten-

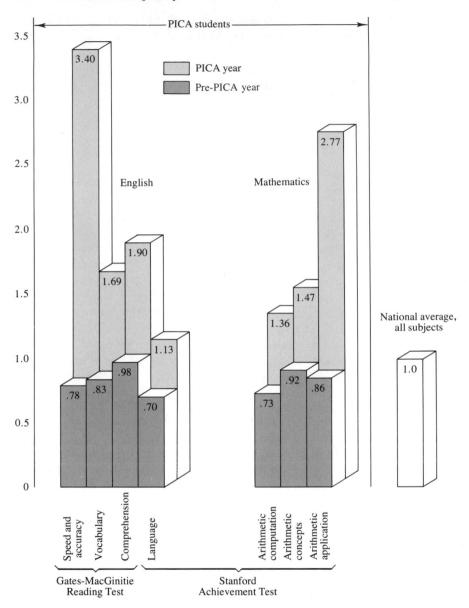

Figure 8–1. Comparison of student grade-level increases: PICA year and pre-PICA years.

tion, for it speaks to one role that the school can legitimately and apparently successfully assume relative to mental health. Like work-study programs, remedial programs offer students a reality-based therapy that is not typically achieved during the insulated "talk-therapy" sessions in the clinician's office.

Community-Based Approaches. An increasing number of professionals are becoming opposed to institutionalization for the vast majority of juvenile

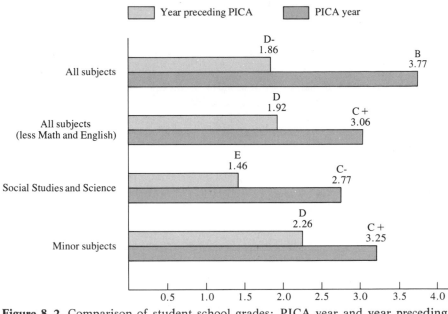

Figure 8–2. Comparison of student school grades: PICA year and year preceding PICA.

offenders. Institutionalization is not only inhumane but it is also expensive. Jerome Miller (1972), a foremost leader in the abolishment of reform schools, states, "At a cost of $9,000 per child annually to maintain a child in a training school, the boys could instead be sent to the finest prep school in America, on a world cruise during the summer, and be given year round psychiatric, medical, and dental services."[2] As delinquency rates continue to climb, we must seek alternative modes of help. The following report on experiments at Achievement Place are included because they combine many of the current treatment trends, namely community-based treatment, innovation coupled with evaluation, the use of peers, increased self-government, and the use of behavior modification procedures.

Achievement Place is a community-based, family-style treatment program designed to teach delinquent youth social, academic, self-help, and pre-vocational skills that will help them out of trouble (Phillips, Phillips, Fixsen, & Wolf, 1973). The youngsters at Achievement Place range in age from 12 to 16, are in junior high school, and are about three to four years below grade level academically. Each boy receives a point card to record his behavior. At first, the child can exchange his points for privileges (snacks, use of telephone, television time, home time, and so on) on a daily basis. Later on, he exchanges points on a weekly basis. Finally, he goes on a merit system, the last step each boy must progress through before going home. The boys con-

2. Cost estimates given here would apply to purchase of such a program only prior to 1966.

tinue to attend the same school from which they came but teachers fill out a report each day. Performance at school (for example, following the teacher's rules and making good use of class time) can earn him points at Achievement Place. The youngsters hold a family conference during or just after dinner to discuss the days events, to conduct a "trial," to decide on consequences for rule violations, and to establish new rules or modify old ones. The teaching-parents at Achievement Place also attend the home's semi-self-governing meeting. Data gathered on a series of adjustment measures yielded the following findings:

1. Achievement Place youth had far fewer police and court contacts following treatment in comparison with two other delinquent groups (see Figure 8–3). This finding is of considerable interest because it challenges the notion that community-based programs expose the community to continuing law violators.

2. Only 19% of Achievement Place boys were institutionalized either during or after treatment, whereas over 50% of Boys School youth and probation youth had committed a delinquent act resulting in institutionalization within two years after treatment.

3. Among those who attended school following treatment, 90% of Achievement Place youth were passing their courses with a D minus or better in contrast to 40 to 50% of Boys Schools and probation yuth.

4. By one-and-a-half years following treatment, 90% of Achievement Place youth were attending school while only 9% of Boys School youth and 37% of probation youth were still in school.

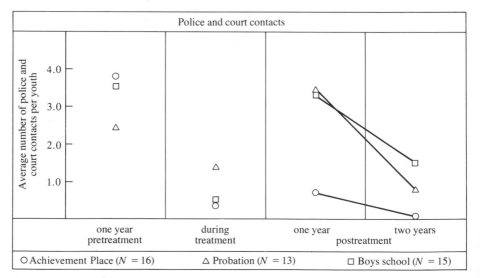

Figure 8–3

5. Achievement Place cost about one-fourth as much as building a state institution.

While the groups used in the above comparisons were not randomly assigned, the preliminary results are encouraging. Research using random selection and placement procedures is currently under way. Even if subsequent research fails to demonstrate the superiority of community-based treatment over traditional correctional schools (and we have no reason at this time to believe that this will be the case), the humaneness and expense factors favor the use of group homes and halfway houses in the community. The use of small, homelike facilities staffed with trained and concerned people should go far in realizing the 1970 White House Conference goal of eliminating all large institutions except perhaps for the most hard-core delinquents. (Bear in mind we will always need some institutions for that volatile, hard-core group who will slit someone's throat and then laugh about it.) We may, however, in the next few years, witness a trend similar to that in Denmark and Sweden, where nearly all deviant children are treated in their own communities.

Summary

Delinquency remains a critical social problem in American society.

Delinquency is an imprecise term not only from a legal viewpoint but from psychological and sociological viewpoints as well.

Granted that crime statistics are difficult to interpret, most authorities contend that delinquency is on the rise.

Delinquency is an age-bound phenomenon which reaches a peak around age 17 before leveling off.

The majority of delinquents eventually get along without serious difficulty once they reach adulthood. This finding in no way minimizes the significance of the delinquency problem during childhood and adolescence, however.

Delinquency is predominantly a male phenomenon although the incidence of female arrests is on the increase.

A child's relationship with his parents seems critical with respect to delinquent activity. Lax, erratic, or overly strict disciplinary techniques, broken homes, inadequate supervision, lack of cohesiveness as a family unit, and few close ties with the father are among the factors commonly found to be related to norm violation.

Delinquency appears to be predominantly a lower-class phenomenon although the relationship between illegal activity and socioeconomic status is not a simple one.

The incidence of delinquent activity also differs among various racial and ethnic groups.

Delinquency is primarily an urban problem but prevalence figures indicate an increase in rural and suburban areas.

While constitutional factors can sometimes play a role in delinquent pursuits, most authorities favor sociological and/or psychological explanations of delinquency.

Psychological research has consistently unearthed three dimensions of delinquency: the psychopathic delinquent, the subcultural delinquent, and the neurotic delinquent. Psychopathic delinquency is regarded as the most severe and as having the poorest prognosis. Subcultural delinquency probably has the most favorable prognosis of the three "varieties."

There are two broad theories as to the causes of delinquent activity. Sociological theories emphasize broad aspects of the social environment—for example, community disorganization. Psychological theories of delinquency, on the other hand, tend to stress the pathology of the individual —for example, feelings of rejection.

While a few predictive scales appear to be more valid than others, none of the predictive procedures available meets the requirements of a well-validated and practical predictive system. At present, teacher nominations appear to be as useful for forecasting delinquent behavior as are the best psychological measures.

Treatment approaches based on a sociological model of causation tend to focus on such phenomena as social organization in the community, the role played by gang membership, and the differences in values among members of different social classes.

Whereas sociological approaches search for underlying causative factors in society, psychologically based treatment approaches have, on the other hand, traditionally relied upon clinical procedures aimed at the discovery of causes within the delinquent's personality makeup.

Whereas both the traditional sociological and psychological treatment methods are based on a "medical model" in that they search for underlying, deep-rooted causative factors, a more recent psychological approach based on an instructional model has been gaining in popularity. According to this method, correctional work is an educational process designed to facilitate the learning of appropriate behaviors and attitudes.

Of the various treatment approaches discussed, the instructional model seems to hold the most promise.

The use of peers, self-government, behavior modification procedures, community-based help, and innovation coupled with evaluation all reflect current treatment trends.

References

Andry, R. G. *Delinquency and parental pathology*. London: Methuen, 1960.

Ausubel, D. Psychological factors in juvenile delinquency. Paper read at seminar on juvenile delinquency, Marylhurst College, Oregon, October 1965.

Bandura, A. *Aggression: a social learning analysis*. Englewood Cliffs, N.J.: Prentice-Hall, 1973.

Bandura, A., & Walters, R. H. *Adolescent aggression*. New York: Ronald Press, 1959.

Bell, J. C., Ross, A., & Simpson, A. Incidence and estimated prevalence of recorded delinquency in a metropolitan area. *American Sociological Review*, 1964, **29**, 90–92.

Bowman, P. H. Effects of a revised school program on potential delinquents. *Annals of the American Academy of Political Social Science*, 1959, **322**, 53–61.

Briggs, P. F., & Wirt, R. D. Prediction. In H. C. Quay (Ed.), *Juvenile delinquency*. Princeton, N.J.: Van Nostrand, 1965, pp. 170–208.

Browning, C. J. Differential impact of family disorganization on male adolescents. *Social Problems*, 1960, **8**, 37–44.

Buehler, E., Patterson, G., & Furniss, J. The reinforcement of behavior in institutional settings. *Behavioral Research and Therapy*, 1966, **4**, 157–67.

Burchard, J. D. Systematic socialization: a programmed environment for the rehabilitation of antisocial retardates. *Psychological Record*, 1967, **17**, 461–76.

Burke, N. S., & Simons, A. E. Factors which precipitate dropouts and delinquency. *Federal Probation*, 1965, **29**, 28–32.

Button, A. Some antecedents of felonious and delinquent behavior. *Journal of Child Clinical Psychology*, 1973, **2 (3)**, 35–37.

Caditz, S. Effect of a training school experience on the personality of delinquent boys. *Journal of Consulting Psychology*, 1959, **23**, 501–9.

Caplan, N. S. Intellectual functioning. In H. C. Quay (Ed.), *Juvenile delinquency*. Princeton, N.J.: Van Nostrand, 1965, pp. 100–38.

Carr, L. *Delinquency control*. New York: Harper & Row, 1950.

Cavan, R. Negro family disorganization and juvenile delinquency. *Journal of Negro Education*, 1959, **28**, 230–39.

Clark, J., & Wenninger, E. Socio-economic class and area as correlates of illegal behavior among juveniles. *American Sociological Review*, 1962, **27**, 826–34.

Clark, K. B. Color, class, personality and juvenile delinquency. *Journal of Negro Education*, 1959, **28**, 240–51.

Cloward, R. A., & Ohlin, L. E. *Delinquency and opportunity: a theory of delinquent gangs*. New York: Free Press, 1960.

Cohen, A. *Delinquent boys*. Glencoe, Ill.: Free Press, 1955.

Cohen, A. *Deviance and control*. Englewood Cliffs, N.J.: Prentice-Hall, 1966.

Cohen, A., Filipczak, J., Slavin, J., & Boren, J. *Programming interpersonal curricula for adolescents*. Silver Spring, Md.: Institute for Behavioral Research, Inc., 1971.

Cohen, A. Behavior modification and socially deviant youth. In C. Thoresen (Ed.), *Behavior modification in education*. Yearbook of the National Society for the Study of Education, 1973, **72,** Part 1, pp. 291–314.

Conger, J., Miller, W., Gaskill, H., & Walsmith, C. *Progress report*. NIMH Grant No. M-3040. Washington, D.C.: Public Health Service, 1960.

Conger, J., Miller, W., & Walsmith, C. Antecedents of delinquency: personality, social class and intelligence. In P. H. Mussen, J. J. Conger, & J. Kagan (Eds.), *Readings in child development and personality.* New York: Harper & Row, 1965, pp. 442–68.

Craig, M. M., & Glick, S. J. Ten years' experience with the Glueck Social Prediction Table. *Crime & Delinquency,* 1963, **9,** 249–61.

Craig, M. M., & Glick, S. J. *A manual of procedures for application of the Glueck Prediction Table.* New York City Youth Board, 1964.

Dentler, R., & Monroe, L. Early adolescent theft. *American Sociological Review,* 1961, **26,** 733–43.

Dinitz, S., Scarpitti, F., & Reckless, W. Delinquency vulnerability: a cross group and longitudinal analysis. *American Sociological Review,* 1962, **27,** 515–17.

Douglass, J. H. The extent and characteristics of juvenile delinquency among Negroes in the United States. *Journal of Negro Education,* 1959, **28,** 214–29.

Eaton, J., & Polk, K. *Measuring delinquency.* Pittsburgh: University of Pittsburgh Press, 1961.

Eichorn, J. R. Delinquency and the educational system. In H. C. Quay (Ed.), *Juvenile delinquency.* Princeton, N.J.: Van Nostrand, 1965, pp. 298–337.

Eisner, V., & Tsuyemura, H. Interaction of juveniles with the law. *Public Health Report,* 1965, **80,** 689–91.

Empey, L. T., & Erickson, M. L. Hidden delinquency and social status. *Social Forces,* 1966, **44,** 546–54.

Erickson, M., & Empey, L. Class position, peers, and delinquency. *Sociology and Social Research,* 1965, **49,** 268–82.

Federal Bureau of Investigation. *Uniform Crime Report,* 1963. Washington, D.C.: U.S. Department of Justice, 1963.

Federal Bureau of Investigation. *Uniform Crime Reports,* 1973. Washington, D.C.: U.S. Department of Justice, 1972.

Ferdinand, T. N. The offense patterns and family structures of urban, village and rural delinquents. *Journal of Criminal Law, Criminology and Police Science,* 1964, **55,** 86–93.

Freedman, M. Background of deviancy. In W. W. Wattenberg (Ed.), Social deviancy among youth. *Yearbook of the National Society for the Study of Education,* 1966, **65,** Part I, pp. 28–58.

Glueck, E. T. Distinguishing delinquents from pseudodelinquents. *Harvard Educational Review,* 1966, **36,** 119–30. (a)

Glueck, E. T. A more discriminative instrument for the identification of potential delinquents at school entrance. *Journal of Criminal Law, Criminology, and Police Science,* 1966, **57,** 27–30. (b)

Glueck, S., & Glueck, E. *Unraveling juvenile delinquency.* New York: Commonwealth Fund, 1950.

Glueck, S., & Glueck, E. *Physique and deliniquency.* New York: Harper & Row, 1956.

Gottesfeld, H. Professionals and delinquents evaluate professional methods with delinquents. *Social Problems,* 1965, **13,** 45–59.

Hathaway, S. R., & Monachesi, E. D. *Analyzing and predicting juvenile delinquency with the MMPI.* Minneapolis: University of Minnesota Press, 1953.

Hathaway, S. R., & Monachesi, E. D. The personalities of predelinquent boys. *Journal of Criminal Law, Criminology and Police Science,* 1957, **48,** 149–63.

Healy, W., & Bronner, A. F. *New light on delinquency and its treatment.* New Haven: Yale University Press, 1936.

Hill, M. The metropolis and juvenile delinquency among Negroes. *Journal of Negro Education*, 1959, **28**, 277–85.

Hurwitz, J. I., Kaplan, D., & Kaiser, E. Parental coping patterns and delinquency. *Journal of Offender Therapy*, 1962, **6**, 2–4.

Jacobs, P., Brunton, M., & Melville, M. Aggressive behavior, mental subnormality, and the XYY male. *Nature*, 1965, **208**, 1351–52.

Jarvik, L., Klodin, V., & Matsuyama, S. Human aggression and the extra Y chromosone. *American Psychologist*, 1973, **28**, 674–82.

Johnson, A. Juvenile delinquency. In S. Arieti (Ed.), *American handbook of psychiatry*. New York: Basic Books, 1959, pp. 840–56.

Johnson, R. *Aggression in man and animals*. Philadelphia: W. B. Saunders, 1972.

Juvenile court statistics 1970. Washington, D.C.: National Center for Social Statistics, U.S. Department of Health, Education and Welfare, 1972.

Kobrin, S. The Chicago area project—a 25-year assessment. *Annals of the American Academy of Political and Social Science*, 1959, **322**, 19–29.

Kvaraceus, W. C. *KD proneness scale and check list*. New York: World Book, 1953.

Kvaraceus, W. C. *Forecasting juvenile delinquency*. New York: World Book, 1956.

Kvaraceus, W. C. Forecasting delinquency: a three-year experiment. *Exceptional Children*, 1961, **27**, 429–35.

Kvaraceus, W. C. Problems of early identification and prevention of delinquency. In W. W. Wattenberg (Ed.), Social deviancy among youth. *Yearbook of the National Society for the Study of Education*, 1966, **65**, Part I, 189–220.

Kvaraceus, W. C., & Miller, W. B. *Delinquent behavior*. Vol. 1, *Culture and the individual*. Washington, D.C.: National Education Association, 1959.

Kvaraceus, W. C., & Ulrich, W. E. *Delinquent behavior*. Vol. 2, *Principles and practice*. Washington, D.C.: National Education Association, 1959.

Lippman, H. S. *Treatment of the child in emotional conflict*. (2nd ed.) New York: McGraw-Hill, 1962.

Lombroso, C. *Crime: its causes and remedies*. (English trans. Henry P. Horton) Boston: Little, Brown, 1918.

McCord, W., McCord, J., & Zola, I. *Origins of crime: a new evaluation of the Cambridge-Somerville youth study*. New York: Columbia University Press, 1959.

Massimo, J. L., & Shore, M. F. The effectiveness of a comprehensive vocationally oriented psychotherapeutic program for adolescent delinquent boys. *American Journal of Orthopsychiatry*, 1963, **33**, 634–42.

Miller, J. *A strategy for youth in trouble*. Boston: Massachusetts Department of Youth Services, 1972.

Miller, W. The impact of a community group work program on delinquent corner groups. *Social Science Review*, 1957, **31**, 390–406.

Miller, W. Lower class culture as a generating milieu of gang delinquency. *Journal of Social Issues*, 1959, **14**, 5–19. (a)

Miller, W. Preventive work with street-corner groups: Boston Delinquency Project. *Annals of the American Academy of Political and Social Science*, 1959, **322**, 97–106. (b)

Miller, W. The impact of a "total-community" delinquency control project. *Social Problems*, 1962, **10**, 168–91.

Monahan, T. P. Family status and the delinquent child: a reappraisal and some new findings. *Social Forces*, 1957, **35**, 250–58.

Nash, J. The father in contemporary culture and current psychological literature. *Child Development*, 1965, **36**, 261–97.

Nye, F. I. *Family relationships and delinquent behavior*. New York: Wiley, 1958.

Nye, I., Short, J., & Olson, V. Socio-economic status and delinquent behavior. *American Journal of Sociology*, 1958, **63**, 381–89.

Perlman, R. Juvenile delinquency and some social and economic trends. *Welfare Review*, 1963, **1**, 12–20.

Phillips, E. Crime, victims, and the police. *Trans-action*, 1967, **4**, 36–44.

Phillips, E., Phillips, E., Fixsen, D., & Wolf, M. Achievement place. Behavior-shaping work for delinquents. *Psychology Today*, 1973, **7**, 75–79.

Quay, H. C. Dimensions of personality in delinquent boys as inferred from the factor analysis of case history data. *Child Development*, 1964, **35**, 479–84.

Quay, H. C. Personality and delinquency. In H. C. Quay (Ed.), *Juvenile delinquency*. Princeton, N.J.: Van Nostrand, 1965, pp. 139–66.

Quay, H. C. Personality dimensions in preadolescent delinquent boys. *Educational and Psychological Measurement*, 1966, **26**, 99–110.

Quay, H. Patterns of aggression, withdrawal and immaturity. In H. Quay and J. Werry (Eds.), *Psychopathological disorders of childhood*. New York: Wiley, 1972.

Quay, H. & Levinson, R. The prediction of institutional adjustment of four subgroups of delinquent boys. Unpublished manuscript, 1967.

Reckless, W., Dinitz, S., & Kay, B. The self-component in potential delinquency and potential nondelinquency. *American Sociological Review*, 1957, **22**, 566–70.

Reiss, A. J. Social correlates of psychological types of delinquency. *American Sociological Review*, 1952, **17**, 710–18.

Reiss, A. J., & Rhodes, A. The distribution of juvenile delinquency in the social class structure. *American Sociological Review*, 1961, **26**, 720–32.

Reiss, H., Jr., & Rhodes, A. Status deprivation and delinquent behavior. *Sociological Quarterly*, 1963, **4**, 135–49.

Robins, L. N. *Deviant children grown up*. Baltimore: Williams & Wilkins, 1966.

Robison, S. A study of delinquency among Jewish children in New York City. In M. Sklare (Ed.). *The Jews: social patterns of an American group*. Glencoe, Ill.: Free Press, 1957, pp. 535–50.

Scarpitti, F. Delinquent and nondelinquent perceptions of self, values, and opportunity. *Mental Hygiene*, 1965, **49**, 399–400.

Scarpitti, F., Murray, E., Dinitz, S., & Reckless, W. The "good" boy in a high delinquency area: four years later. *American Sociological Review*, 1960, **25**, 555–58.

Schafer, W. E., & Polk, K. Delinquency and the schools. In Task Force on Juvenile Delinquency. *Juvenile delinquency and youth crime*. Washington, D.C.: Government Printing Office, 1967, pp. 222–77.

Schreiber, D. Work-experience programs. In W. W. Wattenberg (Ed.), Social deviancy among youth. *Yearbook of the National Society for the Study of Education*, 1966, **65**, Part I, pp. 280–314.

Schuessler, K., & Cressey, D. Personality characteristics of criminals. *American Journal of Sociology*, 1950, **55**, 476–84.

Schwitzgebel, R. Short-term operant conditioning of adolescent offenders on socially relevant variables. *Journal of Abnormal Psychology*, 1967, **72**, 134–42.

Schwitzgebel, R., & Kolb, D. Inducing behavior change in adolescent delinquents. *Behavior Research and Theory*, 1964, **1**, 297–304.

Segal, B. E. Racial perspectives and attitudes among Negro and white delinquent boys: an empirical examination. *Phylon*, 1966, **27**, 27–39.

Shah, S., & Borgaonkar, D. The XYY chromosone abnormality. Some "facts" and some "fantasies"? *American Psychologist*, 1974, **29**, 357–59.

Shore, M., & Massimo, J. After ten years: a follow-up study of comprehensive vocationally oriented psychotherapy. *American Journal of Orthopsychiatry*, 1973, **43(1)**, 128–32.

Short, F. J., Jr. Juvenile delinquency: the sociocultural context. In M. L. Hoffman & L. W. Hoffman (Eds.), *Review of child development research*. Vol. II. New York: Russell Sage Foundation, 1966, pp. 423–68.

Short, J. F., & Nye, F. I. Extent of unrecorded delinquency; tentative conclusions. *Journal of Criminal Law, Criminology, and Police Science*, 1958, **49**, 296–302.

Siegman, A. Father absence during early childhood and antisocial behavior. *Journal of Abnormal Psychology*, 1966, **71**, 71–74.

Slack, C. W. Experimenter-subject psychotherapy: a new method of introducing intensive office treatment for unreasonable cases. *Mental Hygiene*, 1960, **44**, 238–56.

Staats, A. W., & Butterfield, W. Treatment of nonreading in a culturally deprived juvenile delinquent: an application of reinforcement principles. *Child Development*, 1965, **36**, 925–42.

Staats, A. W., Minke, K. A., Goodwin, W., & Landeen, J. Cognitive behavior modification: "motivated learning" reading treatment with subprofessional therapy-technicians. *Behavior Research and Therapy*, 1967, **5**, 283–99.

Stephens, T. Modeling and delinquent youth. *Review of Educational Research*. 1973, **43** (3), 323–40.

Task Force on Juvenile Delinquency. *Juvenile delinquency and youth crime*. Washington, D.C.: Government Printing Office, 1967.

Teeters, N., & Matza, D. The extent of delinquency in the United States. *Journal of Negro Education*, 1959, **28**, 200–13.

U.S. Children's Bureau. *Juvenile court statistics*. Statistical Series No. 85. Washington, D.C.: Government Printing Office, 1966.

Weeks, H. *Youthful offenders at Highfields: an evaluation of the effects of short-term treatment of delinquent boys*. Ann Arbor: University of Michigan Press, 1958.

Wheeler, S., Cottrell, L. S., Jr., & Romasco, A. Juvenile delinquency: its prevention and control. In Task Force on Juvenile Delinquency, *Juvenile delinquency and youth crime*. Washington, D.C.: Government Printing Office, 1967, pp. 409–28.

Wirt, R. D., & Briggs, P. F. Personality and environmental factors in the development of delinquency. *Psychological Monographs*, 1959, **73** (485).

Wirt, R. D., & Briggs, P. F. The meaning of delinquency. In H. C. Quay (Ed.), *Juvenile delinquency*. Princeton, N.J.: Van Nostrand, 1965, pp. 1–26.

Witmer, H., & Tufts, E. *The effectiveness of delinquency prevention programs*. U.S. Children's Bureau Publication No. 350. Washington, D.C.: Government Printing Office, 1954.

Suggested Readings

Community-based correctional programs; models and practices. Bethesda, Md.: National Institute of Mental Health, 1971.

Kvaraceus, W. *Prevention and control of delinquency: the school counselor's role.* Geneva, Illinois: Houghton Mifflin, 1971.

Polk, K., & Schafer, W. (Eds.) *Schools and delinquency.* Englewood Cliffs, N.J.: *of Experimental Analysis of Behavior,* 1959, **2,** 323–34.

Silberberg, N., & Silberberg, M. School achievement and delinquency. *Review of Educational Research,* 1971, **41,** 1, 17–33.

Stephens, T. Using reinforcement and social modeling with delinquent youth. *Review of Educational Research,* 1973, **43,** (3), 323–40.

9

Childhood Psychoses

Childhood psychoses have probably attracted more attention than have any other childhood disorder because of their spectacular and bizarre nature. Indeed, the history of emotionally disturbed children has centered predominantly around these baffling disturbances (Kanner, 1962). Yet, despite the aroused concern and voluminous literature available on the subject, very little of a definitive nature is known regarding the etiology or treatment of psychoses in children. We are not even sure whether psychotic conditions in children are a manifestation of the same basic disorder seen in adults or whether they are a special type of ego malfunction. While there are a number of theories on childhood psychoses, the present state of knowledge is fragmented and confused.

Definition

Contributing to this confusion has been the lack of agreement among authorities in the field concerning the term to be used in describing or labeling this condition. By 1900, professional workers were willing to recognize and accept the existence of psychotic disturbances in children. Yet, it was not until the 1930s that systematic efforts were put forth to investigate seriously debilitating childhood emotional disorders with respect to diagnosis, etiology, course, and treatment (Kanner, 1962). While it was Bleuler who in 1911 introduced the term "schizophrenia," it was Potter (1933) who, some twenty years later, was apparently the first to employ the term with reference to children.

Kanner (1962) observed that in the 1940s two opposing trends emerged relative to terminology. On the one hand, there was a tendency toward inexplicitness. Beata Rank (1949), for example, coined the term "atypical child" to encompass a wide variety of serious disorders manifesting themselves in early childhood. The inexactness or vagueness inherent in this term is reflected, for instance, in the lack of differentiation between such conditions as childhood psychosis and mental deficiency. In a similar vein, Blau (1962) wrote:

> Much confusion arises from indecision and evasion regarding the name of the syndrome. To my mind the following designations are more or less synonymous: atypical, prepsychosis, ego deviant, seriously deviant child, infantile anaclitic depression, preschizophrenia, autistic, symbiotic, brain injured, incipient schizophrenia, pseudo psychoses, pseudo neurotic psychoses, abnormal child, schizoid personality, impulse ridden character, and oligophrenia. All conditions are of serious ego disturbance.

On the other hand, Kanner and others have stressed the need for more precise terminology rather than clumping an assortment or variety of "heterogeneous clinical entities" under a common rubric. In keeping with this philosophy, Kanner (1943) delineated early infantile autism as a distinct clinical entity. Mahler (1952) discussed symbiosis as a form of childhood schizophrenia, and Bender (1954) analyzed childhood schizophrenia into three basic subtypes: the pseudo-defective, the pseudo-neurotic, and the pseudo-psychopathic.

Kessler (1966) notes that general terms for childhood psychosis included schizophrenia (used by Bender and by Goldfarb), atypical child (Rank and

Putnam's preferred term), and infantile psychosis. Among the more specific terms used to describe subcategories are autism (Kanner) and symbiosis (Mahler). The loose terminology continues to pose an obstacle to the undertaking of careful research in this field; some kind of terminological consensus is mandatory if the frontiers of knowledge are to be advanced. For purposes of discussion, this childhood disorder will be defined as a severe deviation in ego functioning which manifests itself in disordered thinking, affect, speech, perception, motility, and individuation (Committee on Child Psychiatry, 1966). In this chapter, we will restrict discussion to three forms of psychotic manifestation in children: childhood schizophrenia, infantile autism, and symbiotic psychosis.

Incidence

As is true of most behavior disorders in children, it is extremely difficult to know the frequency of psychotic conditions in children. Estimates will be influenced by the definition used, the biases of the diagnostician, and the policies of the reporting agency. Despite the tremendous difficulties involved in obtaining epidemiological data, certain trends can be gleaned from available statistics. First, childhood psychoses appear to be relatively uncommon disorders. Based on studies of the general population, it appears that there is a rate of 4 or 4.5 cases per 10,000 children (Hermelin & O'Connor, 1970; Lotter 1966). Data based on outpatient clinics in the United States for 1961 indicate that the rate is about 8 or 9 per 100,000 boys and just 3 per 100,000 girls in the age range 5 to 14 (Rosen, Bahn, & Kramer, 1964). Data based on first admissions to 284 state and county hospitals in the United States also reveal that childhood psychotics under 15 years of age constitute less than one-half of 1 per cent of all hospitalized patients (U.S. Dept. of HEW, 1964). Second, reported psychotic conditions in youth are most common during the 15–17 age range (23.6 per 100,000 males and 17.6 per 100,000 females) and least common in the category under 5 years of age (1.6 per 100,000 males and .7 per 100,000 females) (Rosen et al., 1964). This increase during the stressful adolescent years is also reflected in data based on hospitalized patients (U.S. Dept. of HEW, 1964). For example, in 1964 there were fewer than 700 psychotic patients under 15 years of age in state and county hospitals, compared to more than 6,400 psychotic patients in the 15–24 age range. To some extent such increases may reflect a reduced parental tolerance as well as an inability to deal with serious overt pathology in older children, rather than an actual increase in incidence. It is doubtful, however, if such factors could account for the large differences reported above. Third, as the age trend implies, the frequency of psychotic conditions appears to be far higher in adults than in children. Finally, there are some interesting sex differences occurring with age. According to data based on state and county hospitals (U.S. Dept. of HEW, 1964) there were 2 females to every 3 male patients under 15 years of age, whereas there were 4 female patients to every 5 male patients in the 15–24 age range. Similarly, reports from community clinics (Rosen et al., 1964) indicate that whereas the rates for psychotic youth under 18 years of age indicated a sex ratio of 3 boys to 1 girl, the rates in adulthood become equalized.

Characteristics

Childhood Schizophrenia

Childhood schizophrenia, a term generally reserved for psychotic disorders making their appearance after the first four or five years of life, manifests itself in many ways. The wide variety of symptomatology among children classified as schizophrenic has been very adequately described by Boatman & Szurek (1960), who list more than 100 different abnormal symptoms. The symptomatology apparently varies with the child's developmental level, the age of onset, the nature of early childhood experiences, and the type of defense mechanisms used (Rabinovitch, 1954). Despite the marked heterogeneity of symptomatology, there is a basic core disturbance, namely, the child's lack of contact with reality and his subsequent development of his own world. In addition to the central core disturbance, there are additional secondary characteristics, the major ones being represented in Kaufman's list of "clinical manifestations" (Kaufman, Herrick, Willer, Frank, & Heims, 1959):

1. Bizarre body movements, such as robotlike walking or fluid, graceful gyrations.

2. Repetitive, stereotyped motions, such as twirling objects and arm flapping.

3. Distorted use of body or body parts, such as the use of a body fragment to represent a totality or the use of the total body to represent a body part.

4. Conveying a nonhuman identity by posture, movement, or sound, for example, barking or rocking or calling oneself a windshield wiper.

5. Disturbances in speech structure and content, such as speaking in fragments of sentences; displaying asynchronism of affect, verbal content, and tone of voice; parroting; or expressing distorted identification by misuse of the personal pronouns.

6. Apparent denial of the human quality of people near one, such as attempting to use a nearby person as a stepladder when reaching for an object.

7. Inappropriate affect, ranging from flatness to explosiveness.

8. Special interest in, or knowledge of, some particular subject related to the child's pathology, such as detailed information of the city's transportation system.

9. Distorted time orientation, with a blending of past, present, and future; for example, the child may relate events which happened years ago

such as his fantasied fears in a manner suggesting that they are part of his current existence.

In brief, it appears that a wide number of areas of development—cognition, perception, emotion, language, and physical motor—are impaired as a result of the child's basic disability. Since so many of these features are seen developmentally in children, it would be advisable to caution that probably no *one* of them is sufficient, in and of itself, to justify the label *psychosis*. Yet, since three of these characteristics—language disturbances, impaired interpersonal relationships, and inappropriate affect—appear so commonly in childhood schizophrenia, we will discuss them in greater detail. Moreover, in keeping with the psychoeducational nature of this text, attention is focused on the classroom achievements of these atypical students.

Disturbed Language and Speech.   One of the most widely noticed disturbances in childhood schizophrenia centers around the use of language and speech. Though there is a miscellany of linguistic distortions rather than a single pattern, the fact remains that many childhood schizophrenics do show peculiarities in this area. The language and speech disturbances are most likely symptomatic of fragmented and disintegrated thought processes. Consistent with this hypothesis is the finding that the presence of meaningful speech by age 5 is predictive of a more favorable later outcome. In an effort to uncover factors related to aberrant speech, Goldfarb, Goldfarb, & Scholl (1966) matched 23 schizophrenic children and their mothers with 23 normal children and their mothers. Comparisons of the speech and communicative abilities of the two groups supported the contention that mothers of schizophrenic children, as objects for emulation and as sources of reinforcement, constituted one factor in the production of aberrant language patterns in their offspring.

Some schizophrenic youngsters are mute or will only utter single words on rare occasions. For example, one schizophrenic boy in a state hospital would never say a word to anyone, although he would infrequently say an isolated word or two (*dog* or *blue*) when the teacher had her back turned. Those who do have speech often do not use it for communicative purposes. On the contrary, their idiosyncratic use of language commonly interferes with effective communication as much as it facilitates it. In fact, Kanner (1946) contends that their metaphorical language is designed to safeguard their personal seclusion. Hence, language, instead of serving to maintain the child's contact with reality, enables him to become more detached.

Repetition of words in a parrotlike fashion is not uncommon. Obsessively focusing on certain events and evidencing this preoccupation verbally are another impressive feature often witnessed. Then again, language distortions sometimes manifest themselves in the development of a private language, with old words being given different meanings or with unusual word sequences being devised. Confusion in pronoun use, reflective of ego-identity problems, has also been noted. These youngsters not uncommonly refer to themselves as "you" and tend to avoid the use of "I." Play with words and sounds is seen in rhyming and alliterative speech.

In addition to an inability to use language as a means of effective interpersonal communication, speech disorders are often present. Goldfarb, Braunstein, & Lorgo (1956) reported on a study of speech disorders found in 12 schizophrenic children, based on clinicians' judgments after one year's observation of these children. Most characteristic of the speech problems noted was an absence of inflections, which resulted in a dull or wooden voice quality. Thus, whereas normal youngsters can effectively convey mood or emotion by means of their voices, many schizophrenic ones cannot. Nasality, denasality, breathiness, throatiness, and glottalization were also common. As has been noted by other clinicians, some schizophrenic children are characterized by very high-pitched voices. The authors recall one schizophrenic adolescent in a public-school class for the mentally retarded who would frequently talk in a high-pitched, squeaky voice, but who would return to a more normal pitch once he was instructed to "fix" his voice. Goldfarb and his associates (1956) also found that emphasis is placed on the syllables and words not essential to the meaning of the message. Further, there is little relationship between facial and body gestures on the one hand and spoken words on the other hand. In short, the individualized and sometimes bizarre patterns of language and speech result in an inability to use language for normal purposes of communication.

Impaired Interpersonal Relations.   Impaired interpersonal relationships are also highly characteristic of the schizophrenic youngster. Whether this disability expresses itself in the form of an empty, symbiotic clinging or an estranged aloofness, a severe and enduring impairment of emotional interactions with other people is clearly evident. The symbiotic child, while attaching himself tenaciously to the mother, nonetheless manifests an absence of normal emotional relationships with others. Autistic youngsters, on the other hand, often give the impression that others are not around, reacting toward others as though they were inanimate parts of the surroundings. People seem to have little meaning for them. Their highly impersonal relations and aloneness have been described as "a noninvolvement" because of their nonresponsiveness to people.

In addition to the indifference and withdrawal that typify the schizophrenics' relations with adults as well as peers, their discomfort in the presence of others is seen in their inability to maintain eye contact. In marked contrast to their interpersonal isolation is their relationship with inanimate objects. One autistic child with whom the authors worked would invariably avoid contacts with others, remaining emotionally neutral in their presence. Furthermore, he would not associate with any agemates or adults in his cottage or classroom. Yet, when provided with tops or other objects to spin, he would immediately smile and show considerable fascination with the objects. Once the objects were put away, however, he quickly reverted to his characteristic state of detachment, manifesting no apparent positive affect. Selective reactions to surroundings, as illustrated above, have led many clinicians to suspect that schizophrenic children, though conveying the impression of being oblivious to the environment, are actually aware—perhaps painfully so—of what is happening around them.

Distorted Affect.   Distortions of affect, while expressing themselves in a variety of ways, constitute another major symptom. The schizophrenic child may be extremely withdrawn or submissive at times and uncontrollably and viciously assaultive toward others and himself on other occasions. Seemingly insignificant changes in the routine or environment, which interfere with his rigid need for sameness, can precipitate excessive anxiety or rage. For example, certain schizophrenic youngsters sometimes become quite upset when they have a substitute teacher or when the classroom is rearranged.

Emotional expression, often described as flattened or wooden, becomes acutely heightened during the temper outbursts. The severely withdrawn child may show delight while watching a spinning object or spinning himself, but be emotionally neutral and noninvolved when approached by adults or peers. Teachers and parents often complain that they cannot reach these youngsters and that the children wall themselves off with their blank and unresponsive behavior.

Retarded Educational Performance.   Another characteristic, one of central concern to teachers, has to do with the educational progress of such atypical pupils. That a large majority of schizophrenic children, whose contact with reality is markedly impaired, should experience difficulty in learning is not unexpected. Success in academic subjects, such as reading and arithmetic, requires concentration, assertiveness, and an interest in the external environment. Marked withdrawal, individualized or idiosyncratic language patterns, and personal nonaccessibility—characteristics seen in varying degrees among most schizophrenic youngsters—obviously are not conducive to the effective utilization of a child's intellectual potential. Educational retardation is therefore a common finding in studies on schizophrenic children. From the standpoint of classroom performance, these atypical children often function much as educable mentally handicapped children do.

In certain instances, the teacher or psychologist may underestimate the academic accomplishments of a schizophrenic youngster because of his nonparticipation in classroom activities. Surprisingly, some schizophrenic pupils —despite their apparent unawareness of, noninvolvement in, or personal detachment from, the classroom environment—have mastered academic skills at their expected levels of achievement, as revealed by their performance on standardized achievement tests. This result often surprises teachers in that, although the child has mastered appropriate academic skills, he has not displayed any evidence of these accomplishments in his classroom performance. In other words, even though the pupil may have acquired skills at a level commensurate with his current level of mental ability, he fails to translate these learnings into meaningful classroom activities.

Schizophrenic youngsters sometimes mask their school learnings through the use of negativism. One 10-year-old schizophrenic girl, who was enrolled in a public-school class for the trainable mentally handicapped, would cooperate with the examining psychologist until she noticed that she was complying with his desires. At that point, she would become silent, pout, and sometimes lie on the floor, emitting guttural sounds. If coaxed or humored, she would read selections on a third-grade level during the testing, but in the special-class setting she gave no indication whatsoever of ability to read.

As is characteristic of their performance on psychological tests, the school performance of schizophrenic children is frequently erratic. They may on occasion successfully complete a complex academic assignment, only to fail simpler assignments. It is this kind of inconsistency that, in addition to frustrating or bewildering the teacher, also signifies that the child has more intellectual capacity than can be mobilized on any consistent basis.

While the majority of schizophrenic pupils are difficult for the teacher to reach, there are some who communicate verbally and who are more accessible. For this type of schizophrenic pupil, intellectual processes may be reasonably intact and academic accomplishment may well be commensurate with the expected level of achievement. In fact, some schizophrenic children may be precocious and mentally astute, excelling in abstract thinking and displaying special talents in language, graphic arts, and dancing. Hence, though the vast majority of schizophrenic children can be expected to encounter difficulty in school-learning activities, we should guard against the danger of overgeneralization and realize that some of these youngsters do learn despite their severe personality impairments.

Jerry: A Schizophrenic Child

Although of normal pregnancy and delivery, Jerry did not walk until 17 months of age and he was not toilet trained when he entered Linwood Children's Hospital at age 5 years and 5 months. The mother is described as an extremely rigid woman who looks as though she is always close to tears. Jerry's father appears easygoing on the surface but he will not let anything interfere with his own narrow world, which consists primarily of his job and his car. He believes that Jerry will never improve. The following observations were made of Jerry when he was 8½ years old, some three years after he entered Linwood Children's Center:

When brought in by Miss Simons, Jerry responded to my request to shake hands, offering the left hand. A little later, when playing with toys, he used the right hand predominantly. When invited, he sat down on my lap, at first a bit uncomfortable in the chair when I tried to place him in an embracive position. It did not take a long while for Jerry to adjust, whereupon he was not only quite comfortable but even seemed to enjoy the contact. During the interview, he accepted some cuddling from me and, of course, from Miss Simons. This he did in a passive way but willingly, never showing any signs of fear or shrinking. He could be induced to play at a primitive level, such as running after him. This he enjoyed considerably, exhibiting rather good locomotor ability. Jerry performed the cylinder block test and the pyramid consisting of rings of different sizes. Again, he skillfully put the blocks in accordance with size, immediately noticing one mistake and correcting it. After some hesitation, he handed several objects to other people. On one occasion, when I placed a book of matches on the table and asked him to hand me a match, he literally took a match out of the book and handed one to me. There was no verbalization or vocal sounds during the entire performance, except that sometimes, when chased, there was audible laughter.

At this time, I could find no evidence of any kind of compulsiveness. Jerry does not present even one of the principal elements of autism; there is no ritualism, no repetitiousness, no insistence on the preservation of sameness. Also, he accepted closeness to people much more readily than an autistic child. There is quite a bit of passivity in his behavior, a facile acceptance of an approach that he enjoys, but with no reciprocity during the period of our interview. Any contribution on his part had to be guided manually. To this, he also conformed in the past.

From time to time, he looked away in a manner which would impress an observer of an adult with possible hallucinations. As he is now, I cannot possibly view this child as either inherently mentally defective or as atypically autistic. If I were pushed into a corner to make a diagnostic pronouncement, I would consider this boy as rather globally schizophrenic, without any kind of specific categorization (Kanner, 1973).

Infantile Autism

While various workers differ in their classification of psychotic disturbances among children, two subcategories have received particular attention, namely, infantile autism and symbiotic psychosis. Early infantile autism was first described by Leo Kanner, when he reported the case histories of 11 youngsters whose behavioral abnormalities constituted a syndrome previously unknown (Kanner, 1944). The six characteristic features of this disturbance are (1) profound withdrawal of contact with other people, (2) an intense need to preserve the status quo, (3) skillful relationships with objects, as opposed to (4) an inability to deal with people, (5) an intelligent, pensive expression despite the extremely low level of intellectual functioning, and (6) severe disturbance of language functioning.

Because a primitive state of autism arises during the first three months of life, this disorder often goes unrecognized by the infant's parents. In fact, the infant is often viewed as quite healthy and alert in appearance. However, those experienced with babies may begin to notice signs of difficulty as early as the fourth month. From this point on, the severe symptomatology becomes more apparent. In addition to some of the characteristics mentioned above, there are persistent rocking motions and head banging. By the time the baby is 2 years old, the parents are typically quite concerned over the child's pattern of development, especially his self-insulation.

While Kanner views infantile autism as a variation of childhood schizophrenia, Rimland (1964) cogently argues that infantile autism is a unique disorder. He contends that the controversy surrounding these two disorders stems from (1) the infrequent incidence of autism so that many professional workers and writers have never encountered an authentic case, (2) the prevailing belief that childhood behavioral disturbances are psychological in origin, a belief somewhat incompatible with the specificity of this disorder (the more specific a given syndrome, the more some workers believe that it is physical in nature), and (3) the general inadequacy of current classification systems.

After analyzing available evidence, Rimland postulated 15 points of contrast to discredit the view that infantile autism is simply one of the schizophrenias.

1. *Onset and Course.* The diagnosis of childhood schizophrenia involves symptoms occurring after a period of normal development, whereas symptoms of autism are present from the beginning of life. Evidence suggests that the autistic child remains unchanged in his early detachment, whereas a schizophrenic child eventually develops symptomatology (delusions and hallucinations) of the adult schizophrenic.

2. *Health and Appearance.* Autistic children are routinely characterized by outstanding health, whereas schizophrenic children are typically characterized by "poor health from birth."

3. *Electroencephalography.* Research indicates that more than 4 out of 5 schizophrenic youngsters have abnormal EEG recordings. Austistic children, on the other hand, tend to have normal EEG recordings.

4. *Physical Responsiveness.* Autistic children are generally physically unresponsive to adults, but schizophrenic children tend to mold themselves to adults.

5. *Autistic Aloneness.* The autistic child is known for his inability to adjust emotionally to adults. The schizophrenic child, however, is often far from being emotionally unresponsive and can elicit adult empathy.

6. *Preservation of Sameness.* This characteristic constitutes a cardinal

symptom among autistic youngsters, but is uncommon among schizophrenic youngsters.

7. *Hallucinations.* There is an apparent absence of hallucinatory activities in autistic children, whereas both visual and auditory hallucinations and delusional systems have been elicited among schizophrenic children.

8. *Mode of Performance.* Autistic children appear to be much more skillful in gross and fine motor coordination than are schizophrenic children.

9. *Language.* While tending to have no or minimal language, characteristic of autistic children, but not of schizophrenic children, are the language patterns of affirmation by repetition, pronominal reversal, delayed echolalia, metaphoric language, and part-whole confusion.

10. *Idiot/Savant Performance.* Unusual abilities, such as phenomenal memories and musical and mechanical abilities, are frequently found in autistic children but only rarely in schizophrenics.

11. *Personal Orientation.* The autistic child seems to be more detached from, and indifferent to, his surroundings. Conversely, the schizophrenic seems more anxious and confused about his relationships to his surroundings. Whereas "frantic withdrawal and rejection" appear to describe the schizophrenic child's personal orientation, "aloneness and nonparticipation" seem to describe the autistic child's orientation.

12. *Conditionability.* Schizophrenic children appear to condition much more rapidly than do autistic children.

13. *Twins.* Autism seems to be disproportionately more common in twins than is childhood schizophrenia. Furthermore, when schizophrenia does occur in twins, these sets usually assume the typical ratio of two or more dizygotic pairs for each monozygotic pair. Conversely, the preponderance of autistic twins are monozygotic.

14. *Family Background.* Parents of autistic youngsters are typically intellectual and highly educated, while parents of many schizophrenic children are generally less advantaged.

15. *Family Mental Disorder.* The families of autistic children (parents, grandparents, and siblings) appear to have a lower incidence of mental illness. The converse appears to be true of families of schizophrenics.

Ken, an Autistic Child

Ken had been in treatment for more than 4 years at the Linwood Children's Center. He had posed problems from a very early age to the extent that his parents sought professional help when Ken was in his third year of life. He seemed content to stay in his playpen. He showed fears of strangers, drinking glasses, and leaving the house. He had a small vocabulary but he did not use words to communicate. His mother committed suicide in the basement when he was four years old. Since then he has had a fear of basements. Since the father's remarriage, Ken has developed good sphincter control. The following observations were made of Ken when he was 9½ years old:

Ken, when seen today, appeared to be in good physical condition. He is sturdily built and has a somewhat large cranium and rather high forehead. He has gained speech to the extent that there is considerable echolalia. His voice is high pitched; for want of a better term, I would say that it resembles somewhat the voice of "Donald Duck." Much is not intelligible, but his echolalic expressions are pronounced more clearly than naming of things. Obviously most of Ken's speech is not intended for communication. Echolalia assumes the inflections of the way the sentence has been presented to him. In between, he interjects frequently something that sounds like "da-da-da-de-da," again in a high-pitched tone. All the while, the boy seems reasonably comfortable in the situation. There is no evidence of the self-destruction, often such as choking himself and others, which existed at the time when he came here.

Ken does simple jigsaw puzzles adequately, and erected a tower at least 12 blocks in height before it collapsed. He put the blocks down, making sure that the upper side matched the rest. The boy allowed changes to be made in the order but then rearranged all blocks in the same manner, returning two that I deliberately handed to him with the wrong side up.

Ken's responses seem more directed to the testing materials than to me. He typically placed testing materials (blocks) to his lips and made rocking motions while sucking on the objects and humming. There was not obvious objection to my taking the objects from him, despite their apparent pleasure for him.

His behavior today makes me feel that this is a typical autistic child who is just beginning to show signs of emergence. He has learned to sing "Jingle Bells" with a reasonably good reproduction of the tune, and to draw a Christmas tree. Ken even made a primitive attempt to draw a person, named some of the elementary colors, and responded to Miss Simons' correction of some not too well pronounced words. The child is now ready for more intensive instruction and I strongly recommend that he remain at the Linwood Children's Center. There has been definite progress since his arrival at the Center and more can be anticipated (Kanner, 1973).

Symbiotic Psychosis

Another commonly cited subcategory is that of symbiotic psychosis. This condition seems to have a later onset than autism, with symbiotic psychosis usually appearing between the ages of 2½ and 5. Kessler (1966) notes that symbiotic psychotics seem less strange than do autistic youngsters and they are frequently diagnosed as being borderline between neurosis and psychosis. An intensive case study will often reveal a normal accomplishment of developmental tasks followed by a regression at the time of a traumatic incident. The symptomatology associated with this disorder typically becomes apparent about the time the child gives up the normal dependent relationship with his mother. With the advent of increased neuromuscular maturation, the normal child is able to separate himself from his mother and to distinguish between self and nonself. The symbiotic child's sense of differentiation remains in an infantile state, and he cannot function independently of the mother.

In psychoanalytic parlance, the child is unable to distinguish himself from his mother and he is living on a borrowed ego. Whereas the autistic child quickly avoids contact with people, the symbiotic child has an intense attachment to his mother from whom he cannot tolerate emotional separation. Mahler (1952), who first defined the syndrome, notes that intense anxiety is elicited by threatened separation from the mother. The child, through his symbiotic alignment with the mother, attempts to defend against the anxiety and insecurity associated with psychological differentiation. It is impossible, however, for the child to maintain an unthreatened relationship with his mother, for such events as the mother becoming ill or the birth of a sibling normally arise. The child is unable to fend against such traumas, however, and psychosis ensues. While acknowledging that symbiotic psychoses seem to afflict only constitutionally vulnerable infants, the core deficiency impairing the child's ability to function adequately is the lack or loss of the ability to participate in the dependency relationship with the mother.

Mahler, Furer, and Settlage (1959) list six primary symptoms of this disorder:

1. Panic reactions with violent rage.
2. Unpredictable outbursts of excitement and apparent pleasure, alternating with violence and destructiveness.
3. Confusion between inner and outer reality, a consequence of the fusion of self and nonself.
4. Inability to differentiate between animate and inanimate reality, and use of magical control over external stimuli.
5. A strong, but spurious, clinging attachment to adults.
6. Conspicuous presence of inappropriate thinking, feeling, and acting.

Secondary symptoms develop as the psychosis lingers. These include panic in new situations, bizarre communication, and difficulties in habit-training areas. After a period of time, the symbiotic youngster often becomes indistinguishable from his autistic counterpart because of the similarity in symptomatology.

Differential Diagnostic Considerations

As a general rule, a clinician relies on four sources of data in rendering a diagnosis of childhood psychosis: (1) case-history materials, (2) clinical observation, (3) medical findings, and (4) psychological test results. Differential diagnosis can be very difficult because the symptoms of psychotic conditions in children are sometimes similar to those of other aberrant conditions. It is extremely difficult and sometimes impossible to distinguish, for example, between a young mentally retarded child and an emotionally disturbed child who displays minimal speech and unresponsiveness to the environment. Another complex diagnostic problem is sometimes posed with respect to assessing the child's reality-testing. It is frequently no easy matter to distinguish between the active fantasy life characteristic of many young children with vivid imaginations and the blurring of reality characteristic of seriously impaired children. In such cases, there are no firm guidelines to follow. Rather, all of the adjustment characteristics, test data, and the history must be considered carefully. With somewhat older youth, the diagnosis of schizophrenia can frequently be made on the basis of pathological behavior which is more openly bizarre (White & Watt, 1973).

In essence, the diagnostic process is a sifting procedure in which the attempt is to rule out systematically those disorders with overlapping symptomatology. The disorders that most commonly require differentiation include mental retardation, brain damage, and severe personality disturbances. The problem of differentiation among the various classes of psychoses in children has been handled earlier in the chapter and, hence, will not be repeated here. In sorting out childhood psychoses, diagnosticians would do well to bear in mind the axiom that it is the entire diagnostic picture rather than a single pathological feature that differentiates the psychotic condition from other conditions.

Mental Retardation

Mental retardation is one condition for which childhood psychosis is sometimes mistaken. As noted earlier in the chapter, the severely disturbed child often functions below grade level, as does the mentally retarded child. In terms of their everyday academic performance, many disturbed children operate on a level much like that of a mentally retarded child. Such poor academic performance often raises questions in the teacher's and psychologist's minds as to the child's intellectual adequacy.

Since many psychotic children do score in the defective range on intelligence tests, it sometimes happens that they are hospitalized and mistaken for mental retardates. One youngster, for example, spent eight years in a state hospital before it was realized that he was not mentally retarded. He was admitted at age 4 with a reported IQ score of 35 on the Stanford-Binet. Later measures, taken when he was more experienced in responding, revealed that he was essentially of normal intelligence.

What clinicians regard as more revealing than intelligence quotients are the intratest variations and the quality of the subject's responses. For diagnostic purposes, it is sometimes helpful to distinguish between inconsistent and consistent patterns of performance. On the other hand, clues as to hidden intellectual potential will often be suggested by inconsistent performance on a test of intelligence. The child may, for example, miss the answer to a simple question only to answer a much more difficult question of a similar nature. Such inconsistency would lead the teacher or clinician to suspect that the child might not be mentally retarded, as his overall IQ score suggested. Consistently low performance, on the other hand, might lead one to suspect that a child is not emotionally disturbed, since emotionally based disturbances in thinking might occur randomly on any type of test at any time rather than being specific for given functions (Des Lauriers & Halpern, 1947). In other words, consistent patterns of deviation and performance may lead one to suspect conditions like brain damage and mental retardation. Piotrowski (1937) found, for example, that schizophrenic children (aged 5 to 16), in contrast to high-grade congenitally defective children, consistently obtained higher scores on verbal tests than on nonverbal tests. Analysis of the answers given to specific items is also warranted because the nature of some responses not uncommonly conveys the bizarre thought disorders associated with psychotic conditions in children.

For purposes of differential diagnosis, clinicians generally regard personality assessment more useful than intellectual assessment. Techniques of personality assessment must be carefully chosen on the basis of appropriateness for the response capability of the child. Perceptual difficulties, poor reality-testing, lack of stable self-concept, and absence of meaningful identifications are significant responses for schizophrenic children (Halpern, 1960).

Case-history materials and clinical observations are also helpful in distinguishing a mentally deficient child from a psychotic youngster. Children with infantile autism can be distinguished from mental retardates by virtue of their good intellectual potential—excellent memories and musical abilities—and certain physical characteristics—graceful movements and the absence of a dull appearance (Rimland, 1964). Moreover, the isolation, aloneness, and detachment typical of the autistic child stand in contrast to the stable and unimaginative activities of the retarded child (Kanner, 1949).

Though we have stressed how childhood psychoses can be mistaken for mental retardation, the reverse situation can also obtain, especially in those mentally retarded children who have met with severe sensory and social isolation and intense parental rejection. It must also be noted that some children can be both mentally retarded and psychotic.

Brain Damage

Organic impairments constitute another set of conditions that sometimes simulate psychoses in children, especially young children with organically based language disorders. Isolated from others by their lack of communicative ability, these youngsters may develop an autisticlike existence of their own and thereby pose a particularly difficult diagnostic puzzle. Again, four kinds of evidence are helpful in rendering a differential diagnosis:

1. *Psychological tests,* especially those designed to measure specific mental functions, such as visual-motor coordination, can be informative, particularly when integrated with case-history material and clinical observation. One of the best-known tests for organic brain damage is the Bender Gestalt Test, which samples the child's ability to reproduce geometric figures. Intelligence tests like the Wechsler Intelligence Scale for Children and projective techniques like the Rorschach Psychodiagnostic Test have also been used to detect organic brain damage. Though sometimes helpful in individual cases, these tests certainly cannot be regarded as an open sesame to differential diagnosis.

2. *Medical tests* can be helpful in individual cases. By and large, however, their validity is probably overestimated by nonmedical people. For example, Shaw & Lucas (1970) note that the electroencephalograph, which is one of the most common medical tools, is of "little or no value" in the diagnosis of brain damage in children.

3. *Case-history materials* often supply evidence suggestive of organic involvement. Obstetrical complications, aftereffects of childhood illnesses, head injuries, and prolonged high fevers are typical of information gleaned from a case history that can be relevant to differential diagnosis. Again, however, such evidence is rarely conclusive.

4. *Clinical observation* is quite revealing, generally speaking. Both the brain-injured child and the psychotic child may be hyperactive and distractible, but of diagnostic significance is the marked difference in how youngsters with these two conditions relate to others and organize their worlds of experience.

Etiological Considerations

Questions pertaining to the issue of etiology have met with a diversity of professional opinions. Although workers no longer view the causes of psychoses in children as strictly dichotomous, we will for purposes of discussion represent viewpoints as falling into two categories: the psychogenic and the somatogenic. Incidentally, it is interesting to note that even though many of the early workers were reluctant to admit the possibility of insanity in children, most of the probable causes of psychoses in children had already been discussed by 1900.

The Psychogenic View

Parent-Child Relations. In the early part of this century, emphasis was placed on the role played by congenital factors in the production of childhood schizophrenia. However, the advent of Freud's psychodynamic position ushered in a new era, stressing the role of parental attitudes as determinants of childhood psychopathology (Gianascol, 1963). Early workers, including Jung, Sullivan, Brill, and Klein, also implicated parental relationships as having a causal role. In recent years, mothers have been indicted to such an extent that a new term was coined—the schizophrenic mother—to indicate their causal role.

Two workers who are particularly well known for their descriptions of the parents of autistic children are Kanner and Eisenberg. The parents of autistic youngsters, according to these authors, are cold, distant, intelligent, sophisticated, obsessional, and highly impersonal and mechanistic in their life adjustments. Lacking in emotional warmth, they are said to rear their children in "emotional iceboxes." On the basis of their clinical experience and research with such youngsters, these authors concluded that autism stems from an innate inability to relate to people which is adversely influenced by the attributes of their parents.

In one particular study of 100 fathers of autistic youngsters, Eisenberg (1957) found that in 85 there were serious personality difficulties which adversely influenced the fulfillment of a normal father-child relationship. This study suggests that consideration must be given to paternal as well as maternal inadequacies and also lends support to a psychodynamic explanation of schizophrenia.

We must remember however, that there are many frigid parents who do not produce schizophrenic children. Indeed, there seems to be a mounting body of contradictory evidence against the "cherchez la mère" school of thought. Rutter & Sussenwein (1971) found that parents of autistic children did not differ from parents of other children who had language disorders in terms of obsessionality, detachment, or warmth. Numerous other studies of parental attitudes, characteristics, and practices have failed to show any pattern toward involvement as a significant etiological factor (Friedman, 1974). Leo Kanner, himself, declared: "Herewith I especially acquit you people as parents. I have been misquoted many times. From the very first publication to the last I spoke of this condition in no uncertain terms as 'innate' " (Rimland, 1972). In brief, many investigators have found a wide diversity of personalities among parents of such atypical youngsters.

A revealing study by Klebanoff (1959), investigating the relationship between parental attitudes and childhood schizophrenia, indicates the need for a more cautious and careful appraisal of cause-effect relationships. Hypothesizing that parental attitudes might be the result rather than the cause of childhood schizophrenia, the investigator administered a parental-attitude questionnaire to 15 mothers of hospitalized schizophrenics, 15 mothers of hospitalized mentally deficient and brain-injured children, and 26 mothers of normal youngsters. Although there were differences in educational level among the mothers, the three groups were matched on age, religion, and socioeconomic status. The results showed that the mothers of schizophrenic children had less deviant attributes than did the mothers of the brain-injured and retarded children. This finding suggested that parents who have children with severe clinical conditions developed faulty child-rearing attitudes and practices as a consequence of their having to manage and care for difficult children and that their faulty attitudes did not cause the disability. The finding illustrates the complexities and the pitfalls involved in a search for causes.

Family Relations. In recent years, attention has shifted from the schizophrenic mother to the schizophrenic family as a unit of study. While there have been many investigations contributing to the analysis of family interaction patterns and their relationships to schizophrenia, three groups have been particularly influential in shaping the course of current opinion and research (Mischler & Waxler, 1965).

1. Lidz & Fleck (1960) contend that it is not the individual characteristics of the parents that create conditions conducive to schizophrenia, but the conditions of strife characterizing the family. According to these theorists, there is a blurring of the age-sex structures in the family that prevents the child from learning appropriate forms of behavior. In other words, the child does not learn to behave appropriately because the parents themselves behave inappropriately for their age and sex with regard to each other and to the child. This theory depicts two types of family pathology patterns: the skewed and the schism. In the marital schism pattern there is chronic strife, discord, and threat of separation. Neither problems nor satisfactions are shared. The work of one partner is frequently devalued to the child by the other partner, and there is competition for the child's loyalty. This pattern has been found to be related empirically to the development of schizophrenia in male children. In the marital skewed pattern, the conflict is less open. While the marital relationship is not threatened, family life is dominated by the psychopathology of one partner over the other. This latter type of deviant family interaction has been found to be associated empirically with schizophrenia in female children. In brief, both types of environments expose the child to a family irrationality that hinders the growth of a healthy ego.

2. The double-bind theory has been developed by Bateson, Weakland, and Haley. The basic ingredients of the double-bind situation are (1) an intense interpersonal relationship, (2) conflicting communications, and (3) an individual who is unable to comment on the message so as to clarify its meaning (Weakland, 1960). The child, dependent on the parent, has to try to make reasonable responses to the confused communications he receives. The child's situation is rendered more difficult in that he is not allowed to question a message or show that he perceives the inadequacy of the communications. With repeated exposures to such irrationality, the child either fails to develop or loses his hold on a rational existence. An experiment by Berger (1965) found that a 30-item scale designed to reveal inconsistency of the sort described by the double-bind hypothesis did differentiate between normals and schizophrenics. However, only 5 of the 30 items discriminated between schizophrenics and a maladjusted, nonschizophrenic group. These data would seem to suggest that the double-bind situation can lead to other forms of maladjustment besides schizophrenia.

3. The last of the family-interaction theories is Wynne's, which stresses the role of ego functioning as a link between the individual and the culture. The prerequisite for the formation of a healthy ego and adequate identification, according to Wynne & Singer (1963), is a stable and coherent environment that provides opportunities to reality-test a variety of roles during the course of development. Families of schizophrenics, however, lack both of these attributes: stability and coherency. The instabilities at home, together with the too loose or too rigid or too ambiguous role relationships, hinder the development of a stable personal identity. In brief, the thought disturbances typically associated with schizophrenia are believed to be the consequence of disordered patterns of family interaction.

While it certainly seems reasonable that early experiences, especially those in the home, lead to the development of learned behavior patterns, normal as well as abnormal, a critical review of the research literature conducted over the past forty years has failed to uncover factors in family interaction parent-child relationships that can be identified as unique to the parents of psychotic children (Frank, 1965; Jacob, 1975). Whether this finding is due to the absence of specific patterns or of inadequate research remains to be seen, but all of the theories of family interaction discussed above have yet to explain why some children who are exposed to the postulated pathological conditions fail to become schizophrenics. Moreover, we may ask why some children exposed to these particularly deviant family situations do not become neurotic delinquents instead of psychotics. Many questions remain to be answered; yet, in all fairness, it should be noted that these theories have served to alert us to what might be significant phenomena in family life which had been neglected by other theorists and researchers (Mischler & Waxler, 1965).

Learning Theory.   Ferster (1961), using learning concepts, has offered a clear conceptualization of infantile autism. He attributes the two major and related characteristics of this disorder—limited responsiveness to social control and deficient linguistic facility—to parent-child interactions. In developing his theory, Ferster advances the notion of a critical age period, 1½ to 4, in the development of this severe ego disturbance. He reasons that parents, as the primary socialization agents, can readily extinguish the development of normal behaviors and positively reinforce the development of deviant behaviors by virtue of the amount of control they have over the child at this stage of life.

In an effort to answer the question as to what specific circumstances promote autism, Ferster examined parental behaviors which might be instrumental in this respect. He hypothesized that the inadequate speech development so characteristic of the autistic child has its origins in the absence of a positively reinforcing environment. The parents are described by Ferster as concerned with their own interests (for example, telephone conversations) and problems (for example, somatic complaints) to a degree that interference by the child in their daily affairs rapidly acquires an aversive quality. The parents, in an effort to minimize the child's nuisance value, ignore him whenever possible. The parent may respond to the child's verbal demands (for example. "Give me an apple"), but pay little attention to the child's other uses of language, such as description (for example, "Here comes the milkman"). If valid, this formulation helps to explain why language, when used by the autistic child, often takes the form of requests related to some deprivation (for example, "Candy"). Under such conditions, the child never learns to respond to the more verbal social reinforcers (for example, "Good boy"). Instead, he continues to respond to the more concrete rewards associated with the satisfaction (reduction) of his own primary needs, such as hunger and thirst. This hypothesis might well explain an observation based on therapeutic experience with psychotic children, namely, that the therapist must be directly useful to the child by providing immediate and material satisfactions (Kessler, 1966).

Since the child living under these conditions has no socially acceptable means of gaining attention, he resorts to temper tantrums, self-destructive activities, and other primitive forms of behavior which the parent then, in turn, positively reinforces with personal attention. As a consequence of such child-rearing conditions, the child develops a narrow behavioral repertoire, meager linguistic facility, and only a limited responsiveness to social control; that is, he develops a syndrome called autism.

Ironically, psychoanalytically oriented environmentalists and the classical behaviorists joined in the witchhunt that placed the blame on early mother-child interactions. Later applications of learning theory made no commitment to a particular etiology of autism. Instead of posing etiological questions to which answers are currently unavilable, there is an attempt to ameliorate certain immediate problems on the basis of what is known today (Lovaas & Koegel, 1973).

The Somatogenic View

Organic Causes. Evidence supporting the psychogenic viewpoint is not so conclusive as to rule out the possibility of a biological basis for psychotic conditions in children. In fact, despite the absence of crucial research data, most experienced workers seem to favor a constitutional viewpoint of etiology. As Shaw and Lucas (1970) note, many psychotic youngsters come from reasonably healthy and normal environments which could not have conceivably produced such severe disturbances. They also question whether such "total absence of the integrative function of the nervous system" could be a learned phenomenon. In a similar vein, Rimland (1964) has advanced a neurological theory of infantile autism in which the basic disorder is related to the reticular formation of the brain stem.

One of the strongest proponents of the constitutional viewpoint is Loretta Bender (1968). She regards childhood schizophrenia as a maturational lag that begins during the embryonic period. Maturational regularities are upset with precocious development in some areas and obvious retardation in other areas. Because of the organic involvement of the central nervous system, the child is unable to organize his experiences in an orderly fashion. Although Bender regards the predisposition toward childhood schizophrenia as hereditary in nature, she views the schizophrenic reaction itself as being precipitated by a physiological crisis, such as a trauma in the prenatal period, at birth, or during infancy. Studies on schizophrenic children do reveal deficiencies in activities related to nervous-system functioning, for example, visual-motor perception.

In the last decade, there have been a number of major studies demonstrating an organic base of a central cognitive or sensory disorder as the major causative factor in autism (White, 1974). Wing (1974), for example, makes an excellent case for a broad diffusion of organically based disturbances, including cognitive, language, and perceptual integration and function.

Genetic Causes. Kallmann's (1956) findings are among the most commonly cited evidence supporting a genetic basis for schizophrenia. Studying the blood kin of all schizophrenics admitted to a Berlin hospital between 1893 to 1902, with follow-up to 1929, he found that:

1. Schizophrenia occurs in less than 1% of the general population. If one parent is schizophrenic, however, the same disorder develops in about one-sixth of the offspring. If both parents are schizophrenic, more than two-thirds of the offspring are similarly affected.
2. Similar results were obtained for siblings of the patients. Schizophrenia was found in 85% of the cases where the sibling was an identical twin of the patient, in about 15% of fraternal twins and full siblings, and in about 7% of half-siblings.

More recent data, based on 57 pairs of twins, one of whom was diagnosed as schizophrenic, likewise indicated a strong genetic basis. When an identical twin was schizophrenic, the other twin was found to be 42 times as likely to become schizophrenic as was an individual from the general population. With fraternal twins of the same sex, if one was schizophrenic, the other was at least 9 times as likely to develop schizophrenia as was someone from the general population (Gottesman & Shields, 1972).

Many psychologists and geneticists do not view schizophrenia as directly inherited in the same sense that eye color is inherited. Rather, they assume that some predisposing factor is inherited that renders the individual susceptible to environmental insult and to the subsequent development of particular sets of reactions. According to this view, the person would not develop the disorder unless exposed to damaging experiences. Most workers, including those who question the extent of genetic involvement, as implied by the studies discussed above, do concede that there is an inherited predisposition to this disorder. The method of inheritance is not understood, although it seems likely that several genes are involved. Whether this predisposition takes the form of an innate, unresponsive passivity or a heightened sensitivity to fear and pain is still a moot issue.

Those who favor a more environmental viewpoint argue, with some validity, that the finding of schizophrenia among other family members does not constitute conclusive evidence for a genetically based disorder, since twins, especially identical twins, have very similar learning environments. Unfortunately there have been very few recorded cases of schizophrenic twins who have been reared apart. Consequently, we lack studies that might provide more crucial evidence on this point. A further theoretical difficulty inheres in the fact that no one has yet identified the physical anomaly that is presumably inherited and which accounts for the genetic effects. Until such evidence is forthcoming, the genetic explanation of schizophrenia will remain a supposition, albeit a potentially fruitful one for future research.

Biochemical Causes. A recent and highly favored view is that child schizophrenia might turn out to be a specific metabolic disorder (Benda, 1968). The importance of serotonin as an etiological agent has been investigated in a number of studies. Ritvo et al. (1970) found significantly higher whole blood serotonin levels in preschool-age autistic youngsters than in age-matched normal children. The state of the knowledge regarding brain chemistry has been succinctly stated by Mandell, Segal, Kuczenski, & Knapp (1972) as follows:

> It has become gnawingly apparent that major mental illnesses such as schizophrenia or manic-depressive disease are complex psychobiological phenomena made up of genetic, developmental and psychosocial parameters. They are no more likely to have a single cause than do such traits as height, weight, personality or intelligence. For this reason, claims that some laboratory has found a "cause" or a "cure" for these mental diseases are highly suspect and at times may even damage the serious work by the thousands of researchers who are taking the myriad, small steps that are necessary before we can understand these illnesses. The new sophistication of neurobiological and biochemical research will continue to add pieces of understanding to the puzzle of brain and behavior. Few of us, however, expect the discovery of a single cause or cure—now or ever. The periodic claims that emerge from time to time seem to result from the desperation that these diseases evoke in patients, in their families, and in physician researchers.

While there are no firm answers in the search for biochemical causes and while the "cure" via medication has not materialized in research to date (Ornitz, 1973), there is no question but that this field will continue to be a hotbed of research activity.

The Multiple-Causation View

Some authorities do not conceive of childhood schizophrenia as a single entity attributable to a single cause. Goldfarb (1961), rather than postulating a single cause, proposes a continuum of causal factors ranging from the purely somatic to the purely psychogenic. Thus, this worker, who prefers to classify childhood schizophrenia on the basis of etiology as well as on overt symptomatology, believes that such profound ego impairments can arise from organic inadequacies in the child or from psychosocial inadequacies in family relations.

Goldfarb's research with 26 schizophrenic children admitted for residential treatment lends support to his contention that organic and nonorganic subgroups do exist. Reasoning analogously, he argues that childhood schizophrenia, like mental retardation, can be the result of either hereditary or environmental factors or varied combinations thereof. It would certainly be premature at this time to accept his notions on etiology. Yet, his reasoning carries considerable appeal as it seems to reflect the complex realities of clinical experiences. Other theorists, while giving lip service to the role of dual etiological factors, tend to place greater emphasis on either one or the other in explaining all cases of childhood schizophrenia.

Treatment Approaches

The numerous approaches to the treatment of psychotic children have run the gamut from psychotherapy to physical therapy. By and large, the particular treatment approach is related to the clinician's view of etiology. Generally speaking, if the condition is regarded as psychogenic in nature, then psychological interventions will be prescribed. Conversely, if the condition is regarded as somatogenic in nature, then a variety of physical interventions may be attempted. Treatment plans, of necessity, are always contingent upon the facilities accessible. The available care plans may vary from weekly outpatient sessions to day-care centers to residential treatment centers, depending on the severity of the condition, the nature of the home environment, and the philosophy of treatment facilities. In the next section we discuss philosophies of and attempts at psychotherapeutic interventions with psychotic children. In the following sections, behavioristic approaches, educational therapies, residential treatment, and physiological interventions are reviewed.

Psychotherapeutic Approaches

Individual Therapy. By way of introduction, it may be instructive to see what happens to troubled youngsters when they are referred to community agencies. In a study conducted by Bahn, Chandler, & Eisenberg (1962), data from 50 mental-health centers in Maryland were used to assess the degree to which psychiatric classification was a significant variable in determining the course of community clinic services for 5,000 child patients seen during an 18-month period (July 1958 through December 1959). The following findings pertain to child services afforded psychotic children by psychiatric clinics in the community:

1. Of four psychiatric classifications—neuroses, transient situational disorders, psychoses, and personality disorders—children with psychotic conditions (the most severe of emotional disorders) had the second-shortest

clinic stay. Only those children with personality disorders were seen for a shorter period of treatment.

2. Psychotic children were the least likely of these four groups to receive outpatient treatment. Only 1 in 5 such youngsters was given outpatient treatment. Since these children had such a guarded prognosis, many community agencies (which can offer only limited help) declined to accept them. Typically, this diagnosis led to hospital referral. In fact, more than 1 in 2 were referred to mental hospitals. There were no immediate plans made for the future in 7% of the cases.

3. This diagnosis was associated with the poorest rate of improvement. Despite the fact that only 1 of 5 was chosen for outpatient treatment, there were two unimproved patients for each improved patient. Such data convey the severity or seriously incapacitating nature of this disorder.

Mahler, Furer, & Settlage (1959) are quite specific with regard to therapeutic goals with psychotic children: (1) to establish greater body integrity and a sense of identity, (2) to develop object relationships, and (3) to restore missing or distorted maturational and developmental ego functions. These goals are accomplished by having the child go through the stages of normal development he has missed. The therapist provides the child with a substitute ego, thus helping the child to progress through the autistic, symbiotic, and separation-individuation phases. The therapist helps to shelter the child from realities that may be too harsh. Yet, he assists the child in understanding various aspects of reality, such as body functions and social relationships. He also sets firm limits on destructive behaviors.

Individual treatment is seen by Mahler as a preferred method of treatment with autistic children. The detached autistic child who shies away from personal contacts must be drawn out and helped to test reality through the provision of satisfying, pleasurable forms of stimulation. Caution must be exercised against hastening reality contacts, however, lest the child be thrown into a state of panic and further withdrawal.

The symbiotic child, on the other hand, can benefit from the educational therapy afforded by the residential treatment school. Since he needs diversified parent substitutes to counteract his pathological attachment to the mother, the symbiotic child is given support by the numerous adults with whom he interacts in the residential treatment center. Only through living on the borrowed ego strength of other adults can he eventually develop sufficient ego strength of his own. Although the child may come to function on a higher level, Mahler is quite pessimistic regarding the prospects for attaining a normal adjustment.

Bender, an advocate of the genetic viewpoint, suggests psychotherapy as an aid in adjusting to internal and external pressures. The child is helped to develop a tolerance for disturbance stemming from his basic disorder (Bender & Guerevitz, 1955). The formation of active defense mechanisms is supported, clearer conceptions of his body image and identity are attempted, and more effective relations to people and objects are sought (Bender, 1960). In brief, psychotherapy is designed to enable the child to live more effectively with the results of his genetically based disturbance by relieving anxiety, supporting ego defense mechanisms, and stimulating maturational processes (Bender, 1947).

Group Therapy.   Group therapy has been used not only with parents of schizophrenic children to help them overcome such feelings as guilt, despair, and resentment, but also with schizophrenic children themselves. In one study (Speers & Lansing, 1964), group-therapy procedures were used with preschool autistic youngsters and their parents. The early results indicated that the children became more withdrawn as a consequence of their association with other atypical children. Panic reactions were evident and biting would sometimes occur. One interesting technique involved giving mirrors to individual children so that they might watch others in the group by turning the mirror at an angle and also alleviate anxiety over their own self-images by looking at themselves in the mirror occasionally. The investigators noted that the addition of a new child to the group often served as a catalyst for group formation, for the original group members then had a common enemy against whom they could unite. Gradually, with the passage of time, structured play activities became possible, speech became more communicative, children became capable of following directions, and established group members helped control the panic reactions of new members. In addition to the group-therapy sessions, considerable attention was given to these youngsters by staff nurses, psychologists, and occupational and recreational therapists. Prior to this experiment it was commonly believed that the treatment of young psychotic children must be restricted to individual treatment sessions.

Another study (Lifton & Smolen, 1966) also suggested the feasibility of group therapy with child schizophrenics. Basing treatment on the premise that childhood schizophrenia is a severe, multiply caused ego disturbance, the therapist assisted the children by explaining the children's behavior to them and by preventing self-destructive activities as well as activities harmful to others. Praise was given for improvements in social behavior. Warmth and personal support were available when needed. Higher levels of ego integration were achieved, withdrawal and isolation tendencies lessened, and bizarre behavior and irrational thought processes decreased. The authors were careful to point out, however, that the greatest behavioral changes occurred in children whose egos were most intact prior to treatment. Treatment was least successful with the very young severely disturbed children.

Parental Involvement.   We again encounter divergent viewpoints when we broach the topic of parental involvement. Some therapists insist that the parents become involved in therapy on either an individual or a group basis before the child will be accepted for treatment. Mahler (1965), who stresses the importance of the child's symbiotic relationship to the mother, for instance, tries to treat mother and child simultaneously. Even Bender, who sees childhood schizophrenia as an essentially biological disorder, stresses the need for group-therapy sessions with parents to help them become more effective in dealing with their children's problems. In contrast, Bettelheim (1950) prefers not to deal with parents. He states that he has had little luck working with these parents and advocates that the child be separated from the home situation.

General Effectiveness and Prognosis.   Of all the behavior disorders that children manifest, perhaps none has a more uniformly unfavorable prognosis than that of childhood psychosis. The only other severe disorder rivaling childhood psychosis in this regard is that of the sociopathic personality. Even the educable mentally retarded child seems to fare far better in adult life than does the childhood schizophrenic. Though some improvements in behavior are noted over time, the outlook for the schizophrenic child remains a gloomy one. The large majority of such youngsters will never live full, normal lives. In general, the research indicates that the probabilities of remission are at best 1 in 4.

A major longitudinal study was conducted by Bender & Freedman (1952) on 120 schizophrenic children seen at the Children's Psychiatric Service at Bellevue. Only a small segment of these youngsters, whose ages ranged from 3 to 11 at the time of initial diagnosis and from 17 to 26 at the time of follow-up, were found to be making an adequate adjustment to early adulthood. More than three-fourths were hospitalized in state institutions for the mentally ill or mentally defective. Less than one-fourth were living in the community, and even among these more than half were probably still schizophrenic.

Bennett & Klein (1966), who conducted one of the longest follow-up studies, examined 14 cases of childhood schizophrenia 30 years later; 4 of the subjects could not be located for additional study. These workers found that in adult life only 1 of the 10 was able to maintain himself outside of a hospital setting and 9 were in institutions. Of the institutionalized cases, 2 were at the same level of dysfunction and 7 had severely regressed.

Eisenberg (1956) followed the later adjustment of 80 autistic children seen at Johns Hopkins Children's Psychiatric Service. Of the 63 who were traced, he classified 46 of these youngsters as achieving a poor adjustment, 14 as having a fairly adequate adjustment, and only 3 as achieving a good adjustment. By combining these last two categories, we see that only 1 in 4 achieved a reasonably normal adjustment. Rimland (1964) states that no form of psychiatric treatment has been known to alter the course of autism.

Bettelheim (1967) is certainly one of the most optimistic authorities when it comes to the treatability of autistic youngsters. His views, which stand in sharp contrast to those of other experts on this topic, are based on the outcomes of 40 autistic youngsters treated at his Orthogenic School in Chicago. Applying Eisenberg's categories, 17 (42%) were rated as having achieved a good adjustment, 15 (37%) as having a fair adjustment, and only 8 (20%) as having a poor adjustment. Differences between these findings and those of other studies were attributed by Bettelheim to the intensity of treatment given. He argues that infantile autism can be influenced by therapy if treatment efforts are sufficiently intense. Bettelheim stresses that it takes the schizophrenic child about as many years to recover as it requires for the average child to develop his personality, that is, some two to four years of uninterrupted living in an environment conducive to autonomous personality development.

Kanner (1973) also reports more positive outcomes from residential treatment. There are also a number of recent reports expressing guarded enthusiasm for multidimensional approaches that entail combinations of parental involvement and training, play therapy, psychoeducational approaches, and sensory exercises (Rutter & Sussenwein, 1971; Schloper & Reichler, 1971; Goldfarb, Mintz, & Strook, 1969; Des Lauriers & Carlson, 1969; Ayres & Heskett, 1972). Yet, most authorities who have worked with psychotic children contend that psychotherapeutic treatment efforts have not cured the disordered thought processes that constitute the chief disturbance in these atypical children. While the child remains psychotic, much can be done to improve his adjustment, however. Ego disturbances that so seriously impair several aspects of functioning with their early onset in life appear to be longlasting and severe in nature.

Certain specific behaviors, especially language, seem to be related to prognosis. Eisenberg (1956), for example, noted that the presence or absence of speech by age 5 was the most critical factor in forecasting the child's status in later life. Of those who had useful speech by age 5, half achieved a reasonably normal adjustment in adolescence. Conversely, of those 31 schizophrenic youngsters characterized by mutism at age 5, only 1 achieved a fair or good adjustment. In a later study, Brown (1963) also cited severe language impairments among schizophrenic children as predictive of poor later adjustment. Her data, however, suggested a cutoff age of 3 instead of 5, as suggested by Eisenberg's data.

While the findings differ as to the age of demarcation, perhaps because of differences in severity among the samples studied, it appears that adequate language usage during the preschool period is highly predictive of adequate social adjustment in cases of childhood schizophrenia. In addition to basic language disturbances, Brown also found that inability to use objects for their intended purposes or functions, repetitive motor play, and severe autism were associated with later adjustment difficulties. On the other hand, an expression of interest in one's surroundings, effective communication, and directed aggression were disclosed to be signs associated with a more favorable outcome.

Psychotherapy is a particularly slow and difficult process with psychotic children. Frequently they have difficulty in forming a close tie with the therapist because of their severe disturbances in ego functioning. Progress is often discouraging, and the dividends in improvement minimal in contrast to the patience, effort, and time invested. Nearly all studies and reviews of psychoanalytically oriented therapy emphasize the lack of positive results. Davids (1972) notes that there appears to be little relationship between specific aspects of treatment and the outcome observed at follow-up. Instead the best predictors of therapeutic outcomes are the kinds of behaviors the child shows before treatment (for example, adequacy of speech and level of intellectual functioning) (Rutter, 1966).

Behavior Modification Approaches

As is evident from the foregoing, psychotic conditions in children have not proved amenable to traditional forms of psychotherapeutic interventions. A recent and radically different treatment approach which has stimulated interest, especially among psychologists, is that of behavior therapy. Rooted in Pavlovian classical conditioning and in various schools of learning theory that have since emerged, behavioristic therapy involves the application of learning theory principles to the modification of behavior. The term *behavior therapy*, as such, refers more to an approach than to any particular technique. As a part of experimental psychology, behavioristic treatment has been applied to the alteration of extremely inappropriate behaviors, including those typically found in child psychotics.

The Use of Reinforcement. It was Skinner (1953) who provided the impetus for treating schizophrenic children by reinforcement techniques devoid of verbal instruction. Ferster (1961) later offered a conceptual analysis of childhood schizophrenia couched in a learning theory framework. Ferster, in collaboration with his colleague DeMyer (Ferster & DeMyer, 1962), was successful in managing and expanding the behavioral repertoire of autistic youngsters in a controlled laboratory setting.

Additional research by Hingtgen, Sanders, & DeMyer (1963) indicated that social responses in a schizophrenic child can be shaped by making reinforcement contingent upon interpersonal associations. These investigators used 6 childhood schizophrenics, aged 3 through 8, who had not previously interacted socially with their peers. They were trained to operate a lever that released coins which could then be spent in vending machines for treats such as candy and food. Subjects were paired and given 30-minute training sessions daily. After an average of 23 training sessions, the results indicated that it was possible to establish social interactions between psychotic children by using the method of successive approximations—a procedure whereby approximations of the desired response are shaped gradually. The frequency of physical contacts between children (though not directly reinforced) increased, and both vocal responses and facial expressions directed toward partners were noted. This study and a later one (Hingtgen & Trost, 1966) suggested the feasibility of positive reinforcement as a therapeutic intervention technique designed to increase the social and vocal behavior repertoire of young schizophrenic children.

We would be remiss in our duties if we failed to report the experimental studies done by Ivar Lovaas and his associates on childhood schizophrenia. One of the studies (Lovaas, Freitag, Gold, & Kassorla, 1963) dealt with the effects of presenting and withdrawing social reinforcers on the deeply ingrained self-destructive tendencies of a 9-year-old schizophrenic child. In addition to the self-destructive behaviors, self-stimulatory activities and stereotypic interactions with inanimate objects also constituted a major part of this child's behavior patterns. To minimize external distractions, therapy sessions were conducted in a room containing only tables and objects. Through the use of social reinforcements such as smiling and verbal approval, this 9-year-old girl was taught over a two-month interval certain physical responses, such as dancing and clapping her hands to music. During the period that followed, the acquired behaviors were extinguished by withdrawing reinforcement. Following this extinction period, successive acquisitions and withdrawal procedures were repeated. The researchers noted that self-injurious activities occurred when approval for physical responses was withdrawn. Similarly, musical behavior response was minimal when the self-injurious behaviors were at a peak.

The Use of Punishment.   The use of mild punishment in conjunction with the use of positive reinforcement is also receiving considerable attention in the literature. Whereas punishment as a behavioral technique has been traditionally conceived as applicable primarily to acting-out behavior, this therapeutic technique has also been extended to extremely withdrawn youngsters, as is exemplified in the research by Lovaas, Freitag, Gold, & Kassorla (1965) on a schizophrenic girl who was administered mild electric shocks when she became uncontrollable.[1] Being barefooted, she was given mild shocks through the floor when she began to stare bizarrely at her hand instead of attending to her reading assignment. After the shock, the teacher would then insist that the girl continue with her reading. After a while, the girl would again become unmanageable, and another mild jolt of electricity was administered. The verbal response "No" was paired with the presentation of the punishment in the hope that she would eventually be able to respond to the verbal stimulus alone. Lovaas, Berberich, Perloff, & Schaeffer (1966) have also conditioned autistic children to approach adults in order to avoid a painful electric shock.

The use of electric shock seems particularly effective in drastically reducing vicious attacks on others and self-destructive behaviors such as head banging and the biting of one's own flesh. This technique, usually employed only when all else has failed, seems unequally effective in reducing or eliminating dangerous behaviors among severely impaired youngsters. The evi-

---

1. Popular usage tends to equate electric shock and electroconvulsive therapy. This is unfortunate for, technically speaking, electric shock as used by Lovaas involves the presentation of a painful stimulus without corresponding loss of consciousness, while electroconvulsive shock therapy, which is discussed later in this chapter in conjunction with Loretta Bender's work, induces a seizure resulting in the loss of consciousness. Whereas electric shock seems uniquely suited to the alleviation of dangerous behaviors in severely impaired youngsters, electroconvulsive shock treatment is generally regarded as indicated where depression is prominent in the syndrome. While many psychologists might have reservations about both types of treatment, most regard electroconvulsive therapy as the more severe of the two.

dence thus far has not indicated undesirable side effects and has, in fact, opened the way for new modes of interacting with the environment, particularly when combined with positive reinforcement.

As noted above, punishment has been most commonly used to combat hostile, antisocial behavior. In the first systematic and successful study of behavioristic treatment of an antistic child, Wolf, Risley, & Mees (1964) found a combination of mild punishment and extinction effective in alleviating certain annoying behaviors. Among the target behaviors selected for modification were his bedtime difficulties, eating problems, and the throwing of his corrective lenses. His resistance at bedtime was handled by leaving the bedroom door open as long as he would remain in bed. When he got out of bed, however, he was instructed to return to his bed or told that the door would be closed. If he did not comply, the mild aversive consequence, namely, closing the door, was enforced. After the sixth night of such treatment, the boy seldom posed bedtime difficulties during the rest of his stay in the hospital or at home following his discharge.

This same boy's eating habits also posed problems for the staff. He would take food from other children's plates, refuse to use silverware, and commonly throw his food around the dining room. These problems were handled by removing his plate for a few minutes whenever he ate with his fingers and by removing him from the room whenever he snatched food from others or tossed his food about. After a few warnings and actual removal from the dining room, the boy's food-stealing and food-throwing behaviors were completely eliminated. He also learned to use eating utensils after his plate had been removed several times during one meal.

This boy's series of eye operations early in life necessitated the wearing of glasses. His glasses-throwing behavior, therefore, obviously, had to be controlled, especially since it proved to be moderately expensive. Consequently, he was isolated in a room for ten minutes following each glasses-throwing episode. When a temper tantrum developed in the course of the correction, he had to remain in isolation until it had ceased. Within five days, the boy stopped throwing his glasses.

The mother reported, some six months after her son's discharge, that he was still wearing his glasses, posed no sleep problems, and engaged in no more temper tantrums. In summary, by the removal of reinforcements for obnoxious behaviors and by the administration of mild aversive stimulation, this boy became a much more manageable and acceptable child. A ten-year follow-up study indicated the benefits of early behavioral intervention and systematic follow through in this severely disturbed child (Nedelman & Sulzbacker, 1972). It is interesting to note that the concept of punishment which had earlier fallen into disrepute as a shaper of human behavior is now being reassessed by psychologists. More will be said about this concept in the chapter on classroom management.

Parental Involvement.   One of the most encouraging aspects of behavior therapy has been the ability to train significant others in the child's life so that they can play a therapeutic part in the child's rehabilitation program. To date, undergraduate college students (Davidson, 1965), psychiatric nurses (Ayllon & Michael, 1959), teachers (Zimmerman & Zimmerman, 1962), and parents (Risley & Wolf, 1964) have been trained as behavioral technicians.

Risley and Wolf, realizing that the parents must be involved if the child's newly acquired behavior patterns are to persist, trained parents in the techniques of behavioral modification. In such cases, the parents generally observe the techniques used by the behavior therapist in establishing and maintaining the child's more desirable behaviors. Sometimes the therapist will also go into the home to observe the parents in action. Of the seven sets of parents so trained, all, according to Risley and Wolf, are assuming a major role in the rehabilitation of their disturbed children. This type of parental training serves to ensure gains made during therapy by facilitating the continuity of treatment efforts.

General Effectiveness and Prognosis.   Lest the reader be misled by the encouraging results discussed above, it should be noted that behavioristic treatment has not to date transformed schizophrenic children into normal youngsters (Leff, 1968).

In an important and fascinating study, Lovaas, Koegel, Simmons, & Long (1973) examined the results of behavior therapy on 20 autistic children. They found that:

1. Inappropriate behaviors such as self-stimulation and echolalia decreased during treatment while desired behavior such as appropriate speech, appropriate play, and social nonverbal behaviors increased.

2. Following some eight months of treatment, spontaneous social interactions and the spontaneous use of language occurred in some of the youngsters.

3. IQs and social quotients increased during treatment.

4. While all improved, there were vast individual differences with respect to the degree of improvement. What one child learned in one hour, another child took one year to learn. Lovaas likens the improvement to making from 10 to 20 steps on a 100-step ladder. One child might start at step 80 and gain an additional 20 steps—a dramatic change resulting in normality—whereas another child might start at step 10 and move to step 20 following treatment—a rather minimal change leaving the child still seriously impaired. The investigators were particularly successful at suppressing self-destructive behaviors. In minutes, they were sometimes able to stop the self-destructive behavior of children who had been mutilating themselves for years. The investigators' most significant disappointment centered around their failure to isolate a "pivotal" response, that is, one behavior that when altered would have produced a profound personality change. For instance, in one case it was hoped that a child's learning of his name would help establish his awareness of himself.

5. Follow-up measures taken 1 to 4 years after treatment uncovered

large differences between groups of children. To a large extent, these differences appeared to result from differences in the posttreatment environments. Children "discharged" to their trained parents who continued the treatment program at home fared better than those in institutions. Unfortunately, the children were not randomly assigned to parent-trained and hospitalized groups. Consequently, a number of variables were left uncontrolled (for example, age of the child, amount and type of play at intake, testability on standardized scales); thus it is difficult to associate child characteristics with prognosis.

6. Brief reinstatement of behavior therapy could temporarily reestablish some of the initial treatment gains made by children who were subsequently hospitalized.

The improvements noted, though minute relative to the gains needed for a satisfactory adjustment, do represent substantial progress, considering the extreme inaccessibility of schizophrenic youngsters. Some critics complain that these youngsters are still psychotic following the treatment of specific target behaviors. While the criticism is valid, and readily admitted by the behavior therapist, such critics often fail to remember how disruptive and annoying these target behaviors were to those living with the seriously disturbed youngsters in question. The basic personality structures have not been reconstructed, true enough, but life has become more meaningful for them and a closer linking to reality has been established as consequences of such treatment. Further, these youngsters become more acceptable to their parents and their caretakers.

Bettelheim (1967) opines that conditioning therapies are too mechanistic and that behavioristic treatment intensifies the regarding of psychotic children as objects instead of as individuals capable of making their own choices. It may well be that we need mechanistic approaches to deal with these mechanical children, at least until such time as people can become social reinforcers for them. Moreover, it would seem that implicit in behavioristic treatment is the therapist's respect for the child's capacity to change. On the assumption that the therapist's attitude is conveyed to the child, behavior therapy therefore need not be the dehumanizing experience many critics claim. While it would be rash to abandon traditional forms of psychotherapeutic intervention, it would be equally imprudent to overlook what appears to be a promising fresh approach to what has heretofore been an untreatable problem.

Educational Approaches

Psychotic youngsters are usually not encountered by teachers in the public-school regular classroom. When they are found in the regular class, they are most typically at the kindergarten or first-grade level or at preadolescence. Even public-school teachers of special education classes for the disturbed do not encounter large numbers of psychotic pupils. According to the landmark survey of public-school classes for the disturbed, conducted by Morse, Cutler,

& Fink (1964), only 1 in 10 pupils enrolled in these classes is considered psychotic. The large majority of such youngsters are in residential institutions or, having been excluded from school, at home. One of the serious draw-backs in caring for schizophrenic children at home is the shortage of community day schools that will accept them. Some of the more forward-looking organizations and states in the nation are currently putting forth efforts to provide such facilities.

Surprisingly little has been done in the area of educating severely disturbed pupils. By and large, educational programs have taken the form of "holding actions" or of quasi-therapy. In the former, the educational goal is to help the child maintain his earlier academic learnings rather than to stress the acquisition of new skills and concepts. In other words, the child is "marking time" until he is given some form of treatment or is released from the institution. The fact of the matter is that many such pupils are sent to residential schools that do not have sound educational or therapeutic programs. In other words, the "problem" is simply shifted from the public school to the residential school without the child's being afforded any greater opportunity for rehabilitation. Conditions in the regular classroom might well improve, but at the child's expense. Altogether too common is the practice whereby a seriously disturbed child is declared uneducable and removed from school without any adequate consideration of those circumstances in which the child might be educated or treated therapeutically. The child simply does not "fit" what the school has to offer, so he has to go. This practice seems even more common with senior-high-school students than with elementary-school pupils.

Strangely enough, many residential institutions regard holding actions as a legitimate goal. The education of these youngsters has also been retarded by quasi-therapeutic philosophies that view educational programs as secondary to the treatment of the child's emotional problems. It is still widely believed, at least as reflected in the literature, that once the child achieves a more satisfactory personal adjustment, it will be relatively easy for him to catch up academically. Because adherents to this philosophy have emphasized the therapeutic aspects of the educative process, there has been a dearth of material forthcoming on curricula and teaching methods for seriously disturbed children. True, there are some rather broad philosophies regarding the education of emotionally disturbed children, such as those advanced by Bruno Bettelheim, Fritz Redl, Virginia Axline, and Clark Moustakas. But there is scarcely anything in the literature that deals with specific factors that enhance or interfere with academic achievement in schizophrenic youngsters. Fortunately, we are now witnessing a shift toward an educational philosophy that lays greater stress on the academic aspects of the school programs for the disturbed.

It is still too early to tell if it is a wise investment of the professional skills of teachers to continue to teach children who, as a group, seem to benefit so little from teaching. There is a definite need for teachers to share their experiences relative to teaching techniques and programs for severely disturbed youngsters (Johnson & Juul, 1960). Relatively controlled observations and measurements of improvement in learning are also badly needed. At present, descriptions of characteristic learning patterns of schizophrenic pupils are nonexistent. Research in this area is complicated by the fact that current psychiatric classification systems have, at best, only minimal educational significance. It has not been possible to establish anything approximating a one-to-one correspondence between the degree or type of personality maladjustment and the extent of educational attainment. More approximate taxonomies are essential if the mental-hygiene fields are to aid the teacher for the role of therapeutic educator.

While the answer to this question as to educational benefits must, of necessity, remain indefinite at this time, some developments indicate that the situation is not altogether hopeless. Goldberg (1952), for example, conducted an experiment at Bellevue Hospital with schizophrenic children who had reading disabilities. One group was given only psychotherapy, and the other group was given psychotherapy plus individual tutoring in reading. This experiment demonstrated that an individualized remedial reading program was a valuable adjunct with schizophrenic children, not only for the reading gains involved, but also as an effective form of therapy. Goldberg believes that the approach to teaching emotionally disturbed children should vary somewhat from the conventional approach. She notes that schizophrenic children need a very concrete approach to the task. In teaching the mechanics of reading, Goldberg found clay to be a very helpful tool. Raised letters were formed with clay. Of all the teaching tools employed, clay was found to produce the least amount of anxiety. Emotionally neutral reading materials also seemed to work best with these youngsters. Through the use of such materials, the instructor is able to deal with conflict-free or safe areas of the child's makeup. To increase the feelings of achievement, books with few pages and short chapters were used. Of the utmost importance is the establishment of a positive relationship between the tutor and the child. Hirschberg (1953) has also cited the ego-building potential of education. An educational orientation toward reality, together with a focus on the development of skill and mastery, can go far in providing a source of self-esteem.

Classroom programs using behavior modification procedures can be both feasible and productive. Koegel & Rincover (1974), for example, showed that certain elementary-classroom skills such as speech, attending to the teacher, imitation, etc., could be taught to autistic children through the use of behavior modification procedures in one-to-one sessions (see Table 9–1). Moreover, these skills could then be evoked in successively larger group sizes. Simultaneously the frequency of reinforcement was systematically decreased so that the teacher was able to provide sufficient reinforcers in the group setting. Once this was achieved, academic progress followed. By the end of this study, the children were able to tell time, read first-grade books, print letters of the alphabet, and solve simple arithmetic problems. Note, however, that it was necessary to program for the transfer of appropriate responding in the one-to-one sessions to the group setting, which involved up to eight youngsters.

The use of the "teacher-mom" to teach childhood schizophrenics and those with organic impairments represents an innovative educational approach that relies on volunteer services (Donahue, 1967). In the Elmont program, mothers characterized by empathy, warmth, and dedication were recruited to work in a day-care program. Two mothers who worked every other day were assigned to each child. Professional services were, for the most part, limited to a consultative basis. A primary-grade teacher, for instance, instructed mothers on teaching methods and on individualizing instructional programs. While there was an emphasis on individualized education, there was also a core of group activities such as the "good morning" exercises and a 15- to 20-minute group activity period consisting of arts, crafts, music, play, and snack. While evaluation of this project remains at the impressionistic level, the low operating costs and the fact that 11 of the first 21 children were returned successfully to class is quite impressive.

Bettelheim's Psychoanalytic Approach.   One of the better-known approaches to the treatment and education of severely disturbed children is that developed by Bettelheim at the Orthogenic School for emotionally disturbed children. The school's basic aim is to satisfy the emotional needs of the children. To this end, extensive use is made of environmental or milieu therapy, which implies that treatment occurs throughout the child's day. Milieu therapy demands an ordered, controlled environment. Yet the permissiveness of the institution is also stressed, for assertive action on the child's part is needed to circumvent the danger of a passive, automatonlike adjustment to institutional regulations (Bettelheim & Sylvester, 1948). The atmosphere may well be termed one of "structured permissiveness." As a child-centered institution, the Orthogenic School stresses a pleasant atmosphere so that the child will feel welcome. Ample gratification is afforded the child; for example, food is always available because it is regarded as symbolic of security and of all other gratifications.

In the milieu therapy, formal schooling is considered an integral part of institutional life (Bettelheim, 1950). A great deal of attention is directed to the child's emotional problems, whether or not they are associated with academic matters. Considerably less attention is devoted to the child's academic accomplishments, and competition with oneself is substituted for competition with classmates. The criterion of teaching success rests more on the teacher's ability to foster a relaxed atmosphere in a tense classroom than on her students' scholastic gains. Further, of the 3½ hours spent in a classroom on a typical school day, considerable time is given over to nonacademic activities, such as drawing and caring for classroom animals (fish, turtles). Educational progress, it is reasoned, will come readily once the emotional problems have been resolved. In fact, the problem, according to Bettelheim, is not a student's slow rate of progress but a too rapid rate, which might

Table 9–1. Examples of One-to-One Teaching Sessions[a]

One-to-One Training of Basic Classroom Skills	Acquisition of New Behaviors in the Classroom
General Class of Stimuli	*General Class of Stimuli*
I. Attending to the teacher	I. Discrimination training: body parts, colors, people, animals, clothing, household and classroom objects and activities, *etc.*
Examples	*Examples*
A. "Look at me"	A. "Touch your ___" (pants, finger, *etc.*)
B. "Sit down"	B. "What color is this?" (red, blue, green, *etc.*)
C. "Hands on the table"	C. "Who is that?" (Mommy, Polly, Lynn, *etc.*)
	D. "What does the bird do?" (fly, *etc.*)
	E. "What do you eat with?" (fork, knife, *etc.*)
	F. "What clothes are you wearing? (shirt, pants, shoes, *etc.*)
II. Imitation	II. Basic writing skills
A. "Do this"—teacher touches nose, feet, elbow, head, *etc.*	A. "Pick up the pencil"
B. "Do this"—teacher stands up, jumps, claps hands, picks up pencil, stacks blocks, hangs up coat, *etc.*	B. "Draw a___," (A, B, *etc.*)
	C. "Trace the lines" (cat, elephant, *etc.*)
	D. "Write your name" (Eddie, *etc.*)
III. Speech	III. Basic reading skills: *Distar Reading series*
A. "Say m," "b," "c," *etc.*	A. "This is___; say___," (mm, aa, *etc.*)
B. "Do this"—teacher holds lips in position to say "mm"	B. "When I point to the sound, tell me what it says," (d, i, r, *etc.*)
C. "Say car," "mama," *etc.*	C. "What is this (*e.g.,* th), "and

this" (a), "and this" (t)
"Say it fast" (that)

D. "What word is this?" (feed, sock, etc.)

IV. Basic arithmetic skills: *Distar Arithmetic series*

A. "What number is this?" (1, 2, 3, etc.)

B. "Count to___" (10, 20, 50, etc.)

C. "How many balls do you see?" (1, 5, 10, etc.)

[a] From Koegel & Rincover (1974). Reproduced with permission of the publisher.

pose problems of adjustment once the youngster returns to a regular class in the community. Though classes are scheduled daily, the child is not kept in school against his will; he is free to leave if he so desires. Class size is small to facilitate individualized instruction, and the teacher is given considerable latitude in developing a program in the child's best interest. Whenever possible, the pupils are encouraged to set their own tasks. Teacher-parent contacts are generally discouraged since they are viewed as more harmful than beneficial. A parent, for example, may ask why his child has not progressed academically, with the result that the teacher may be made unnecessarily defensive.

Hewett's Learning Theory Approach. An approach to the education of seriously disturbed youngsters, which is quite different from Bettelheim's psychoanalytic philosophy, comes from recent developments in learning theory. The use of operant-conditioning techniques is illustrated in a study that represents one of the few explicit attempts to teach reading to a 13-year-old autistic child who had not developed speech. Hewett (1964), noting the boy's interest in jigsaw puzzles, letters, and gumdrops, took advantage of these interests in setting up a simple operant-conditioning model. The six stages used in this boy's educational programming were:

1. Associating picture cards with concrete objects.
2. Matching picture and word symbols.
3. Building a 55-word sight vocabulary.
4. Classifying words and pictures.

(These four stages took up most of the first year of the educational programming. By then, the boy was interested in learning per se, and the teacher had taken on secondary reinforcement value.)

5. Learning the alphabet. (This task was to promote his communication skills, although he still did not talk.)
6. Writing simple phrases. (He would hold up the phrase cards to make his needs known.)

Hewett states that the acquisition of rudimentary reading and writing skills increased the boy's interest in his surroundings and rendered him more susceptible to control. Given ordinary instructional techniques, this youngster would have been considered unteachable—a backward case unfit for school even in a residential setting.

Autistic youngsters have also acquired speech through the use of conditioning models (Hewett, 1965; Lovaas et al., 1966). Although the acquisition of reading skills and speech does not constitute a cure for these severe disabilities, it does afford a significant means of social interaction and reality contacts.

Another recent development that bears on such germane issues as classroom discipline, educational sequencing, and pupil motivation is Hewett's engineered classroom. Based on a behavior modification model, the engineered classroom is designed to implement Hewett's hierarchy of educational tasks, a hierarchy that takes into account the normal stages of psychoeducational development in which disturbed children are often deficient (Hewett & Forness, 1974, Hewett, 1967a, 1967b). This theoretical framework for teacher-pupil interaction allows the teacher to adopt a developmental viewpoint and to set realistic educational goals for emotionally disturbed children with learning disabilities.

Each of the seven levels in this hierarchy (see Table 9–2) is concerned with the reciprocal tasks of the student and the teacher in the development of a working educational relationship. Whereas the average child has successfully mastered the first five levels in this hierarchy prior to school entrance, the majority of emotionally disturbed pupils have not. As Hewett (1967a) notes, many disturbed youngsters lack the readiness necessary for a successful school adjustment because they have difficulty in paying attention, following directions, getting along with others, and so forth. Hewett does more than simply enumerate the levels in the educational hierarchy through which disturbed pupils should progress. He goes on to describe the educational tasks, types of rewards, and degrees of teacher structure that correspond to the level at which the child is currently functioning.

Perhaps the main merit of Hewett's hierarchy is that it allows the teacher to assess the child's specific liabilities and to establish an educational program for a particular child on the basis of this assessment. For example, with a child at a primitive level of development, it would be necessary for the teacher to secure the child's attention through the use of concrete rewards before advancing to the response level, where the basic concern is to get the child involved in learning. Or, for an unruly pupil, it may be necessary to focus on the social level, in which social appropriateness is basic, before advancing to the mastery or achievement level.

Note that the nature of the rewards varies with the developmental readiness of the child. The diversity of rewards (concrete, social attention, task completion, sensory stimulation, task accuracy, and task success) used in this approach takes into consideration the complexity of human motivation and learning. It is certainly more than a narrowly conceived behavior modification paradigm based on candy as the primary reinforcement. Note also that the degree of teacher structure varies with the developmental level of the child. In line with this learning theory approach, the child is assisted along the educational hierarchy through the use of the principle of "shaping." Hence, rather than unrealistically demanding that the disturbed pupil perform the ultimate in desired classroom behavior—namely, the mastery level, which is characterized by self-motivation and successful achievement—the teacher guides the pupil toward that goal through a series of successive approximations. The child achieves some degree of mastery at one level before proceeding to the next level until ultimately he reaches the mastery level.

In implementing his hierarchical approach to the education of disturbed children, Hewett advocates that the physical environment of the classroom be divided into three sections that parallel the levels in the hierarchy. Thus, there are (1) a mastery-achievement center, where academic lessons are undertaken; (2) an exploratory social center, which is further subdivided

Table 9–2. The Hierarchy of Educational Tasks with Emotionally Disturbed Children

Hierarchy Level	Attention	Response	Order	Exploratory	Social	Mastery	Achievement
Child's problem	Inattention due to withdrawal or resistance.	Lack of involvement and unwillingness to respond in learning.	Inability to follow directions.	Incomplete or inaccurate knowledge of environment.	Failure to value social approval or disapproval.	Deficits in basic adaptive and school skills not in keeping with IQ.	Lack of self-motivation for learning.
Educational task	Get child to pay attention to teacher and task.	Get child to respond to tasks he likes and which offer promise of success.	Get child to complete tasks with specific starting points and steps leading to a conclusion.	Increase child's efficiency as an explorer and get him involved in multisensory exploration of his environment.	Get child to work for teacher and peer-group approval and to avoid their disapproval.	Remediation of basic skill deficiencies.	Development of interest in acquiring knowledge.
Learner reward	Provided by tangible rewards (e.g., food, money, tokens).	Provided by gaining social attention.	Provided through task completion.	Provided by sensory stimulation.	Provided by social approval.	Provided through task accuracy.	Provided through intellectual task success.
Teacher structure	Minimal.	Still limited.	Emphasized.	Emphasized.	Based on standards of appropriateness.	Based on curriculum assignments.	Minimal.

SOURCE: F. Hewett. Educational engineering with emotionally disturbed children. *Exceptional Children*, 1967, **33**, 459–67. Reprinted by permission.

into science, art, and communications areas; and (3) an order center, in which skills at the first three levels of the hierarchy are developed. Check marks are also given to the students in accordance with very specific stand ards. Thus, for example, two check marks are given for starting an assign-ment (a task that falls at the attention level of the hierarchy), and three check marks are given for completing the assignment (a task that falls at the response level). When maladaptive behavior occurs—for example, day-dreaming—assignments are quickly altered.

Although Hewett provides a list of student interventions that correspond to the levels of the hierarchy, the teacher is allowed considerable latitude in the choice of intervention techniques when undesirable behavior occurs. For instance, a child who has become bored and restless at the mastery level might be given a pass to the exploratory center, where he can engage in an art, science, or communication activity. The teacher thereby offers the stud-ent an opportunity for motor release of his tensions while minimizing the need for disciplinary action. Further, the pupil learns that certain types of behaviors are appropriate and specific to each of the designated areas of the classroom.

Hewett believes that, given a well-organized classroom, an aide to assist the teacher, and the use of concrete rewards at times, this design can be functional for the education of disturbed children in both institutional and public-school settings. Psychotic youngsters, when included in a public-school setting, would be working for the most part on the first five tasks in the hierarchy, although not always so.

How effective is this approach? Hewett, Taylor, & Artuso (1968) re-ported that emotionally handicapped children in engineered classrooms main-tained a task-attention advantage of 5–20% over pupils in control class-rooms. Gains in arithmetic fundamentals were significantly associated with the use of the engineered design, but reading and spelling gains were not significantly different between the experimental and control conditions.

Residential Treatment Approaches

As was indicated earlier in the discussion of the study conducted by Bahn et al. (1962), the majority of psychotic children are referred for residential treatment. Although the schizophrenic child might be best treated at home (Bakwin & Bakwin, 1966), environmental change is necessary to treat cer-tain psychotic children. Environmental change, which might entail sending the child to a residential treatment center or boarding school, affords the child new experiences with other adults and other children in a hopefully therapeutic milieu.

One experiment studying the differential treatment of day-school versus residential treatment centers was reported by Goldfarb, Goldfarb, & Pollack (1966). This study, extended over a three-year period, involved 13 well-matched pairs from structurally intact homes. All subjects showed early signs of schizophrenia. In general, children from both treatment groups who showed a minimal degree of adaptive capacity at the start of treatment showed no improvement in ego status and remained unscorable on the Wechsler Intelligence Scale for Children. Among those children who were initially scorable on the Wechsler scale, the organically impaired schizophrenic children receiving day-care treatment showed progress that was not appreciably different from those receiving residential care. The nonorganically deficient schizophrenic child in the residential treatment center, on the other hand, showed greater improvement, especially in the third year of treatment, than did the matched children in the day-care centers. The authors concluded that day-care facilities might well receive increasing usage for organically defective schizophrenic youngsters, whereas residential centers might be advised for maximum benefit to the nonorganically impaired schizophrenic children.

Physiological Interventions

Convulsive Therapy.   Since the clinical manifestations of childhood schizophrenia run the gamut from the psychological to the biological, it is not surprising that a variety of types of treatments has evolved. This section will focus on two of the physical methods of treatment: electroconvulsive therapy and drugs. Electroconvulsive treatment is used in some centers, particularly where large numbers of youngsters must be treated and processed quickly (Ekstein, Bryant, & Friedman, 1958). Bender (1947), who views the disorder chiefly as a biological phenomenon, has used both drugs and electroconvulsive treatments with severely disturbed children. She has concluded that the treatments do lessen the child's anxiety and increase his manageability. Moreover, according to Bender, convulsive therapy is better tolerated by children than by adults, and there is no discernible intellectual impairment in the children. The ultimate prognosis, however, is not improved. Because of its controversial nature, convulsive therapy is much less widely used today than in the past.

Psychoactive Drugs.   Clinicians now seem to favor the use of psychoactive drugs in coping with conditions that were previously treated by convulsive therapy. Psychopharmacologic treatment is considered not only safer but also more successful than convulsive therapy (Shaw & Lucas, 1970). Bender (1960) notes that the psychoactive drugs seem to reduce anxiety, impulsivity, and disorganized behavior patterns while promoting more harmonious interpersonal relationships. While clinicians do not view these drugs as curative, they do regard them as a useful adjunct to other therapeutic interventions such as group therapy or play therapy.

Drugs used in the treatment of schizophrenic children fall basically into two categories: the tranquilizers and the antidepressants. Whether or not psychoactive drugs will be beneficial to a specific child is difficult to determine in advance. The drug's effectiveness depends on the child in question, the therapist's attitude when dispensing the drug (for example, enthusiasm or suggestion), and the child's environment (Shaw & Lucas, 1970). Although tranquilizers and antidepressant drugs are now accorded a definite place in the treatment plan, particularly in residential treatment centers, there have been few well-controlled studies evaluating their effectiveness. In general, these studies have suffered from personal bias, the absence of adequate control groups, and the limited use of statistical techniques of evaluation (Rosenblum, 1962). We still do not understand the chemistry of these drugs nor their loci of operation within the central nervous system (Mariner, 1967). All we know is that when dosages within specific ranges are administered, desirable changes in behavior occur in some children. Why they occur we do not understand at this time.

Aims and Methods of Treatment Approaches

To summarize this section on treatment, therapeutic efforts have generally centered about one or more of the following aims and methods:

1. To supply the missing basic needs—psychotherapy.
2. To remove stresses operating on the child—residential placement.
3. To assist in the development of more appropriate skills—behavior therapy or therapeutic education.
4. To compensate for organic deficits—medications.
5. To rehabilitate the child so that he is better able to accept and live with his disability—supportive counseling.

The approach or combination of approaches selected will vary with the amenability of the child's disturbance; the personality, training, and philosophy of the particular mental-health specialist; the facilities available, and so forth. Since there are as yet no surefire treatment approaches, a diversity of approaches ranging from the physiological to the psychological might well be regarded as essential.

Summary

Despite the voluminous literature on psychosis in children, our fragmented knowledge suggests a need for caution and humility regarding such issues as diagnosis, etiology, and treatment.

Although there is controversy as to definition, most authorities agree that childhood psychoses are a relatively rare condition. It is not known at this time whether childhood schizophrenia is directly related to adult schizophrenia, which differs in its manifestations and is much more common.

The fundamental impairment in these disorders centers around the child's lack of contact with reality. Disturbances in language and speech, impaired interpersonal relationships, inappropriate emotion, and retardation in educational performance are among the other symptoms commonly noted.

Rimland regards infantile autism as a separate disorder from childhood schizophrenia, and he has delineated some fifteen points on which the two disorders differ.

Symbiotic psychosis is another commonly cited subcategory of childhood psychoses. According to Mahler, psychosis results when the child's intense relationship with the mother is severely threatened or severed.

Diagnosticians rely upon four sources of data (case-history materials, clinical observations, medical findings, and psychological test results) in rendering a diagnosis of childhood psychosis. It is necessary to differentiate childhood psychoses from such disorders as mental retardation, brain damage, and other severe personality and language disturbances.

Theories of etiology can be divided into the psychogenic and the somatogenic. Psychogenic explanations focus on faulty child-parent relationships, family interaction patterns, and reinforcement conditions in the environment. Somatogenic explanations focus on possible biological deficits in the constitutional genetic or biochemical makeup of the individual. At present, most experts seem to favor the somatogenic explanations although it should be recognized that there may well be different types of childhood psychoses, each of which has a different weighting of biological and psychological factors.

In light of the divergent etiological stances, it is hardly surprising to find a multitude of treatment positions. Follow-up studies of psychotic youngsters who have received psychotherapeutic treatment indicate that, at best, only 1 in 4 achieves a reasonably adequate adjustment. Nearly all of the research on psychoanalytically oriented treatment stresses the lack of positive results. Behavioristic treatment efforts have been successful in facilitating the development of desired behavior and in reducing undesired behavior, particularly self-destructive and self-stimulating acts. Behavior therapy has not, however, provided a cure for autism.

The education of psychotic youngsters remains a neglected topic. Whether these children can benefit sufficiently to justify the expenditure of time and money is a moot issue. Bettelheim's psychoanalytic approach and Hewett's learning theory approach were presented as two of the better-known examples of educational programs for severely disturbed youth.

The use of tranquilizing and antidepressant drugs has largely replaced the use of electroconvulsive therapy in the treatment of psychotic children.

References

Ayers, A., & Heskett, W. Sensory integrative dysfunction in a young schizophrenic girl. *Journal of Autism and Childhood Schizophrenia*, 1972, **2**, 2, 174–81.

Ayllon, T., & Michael, J. The psychiatric nurse as a behavioral engineer. *Journal of Experimental Analysis of Behavior*, 1959, **2**, 323–34.

Bahn, A., Chandler, C., & Eisenberg, L. Diagnostic characteristics related to services in psychiatric clinics for children. *Milbank Memorial Fund Quarterly*, 1962, **15**, 289–318.

Bakwin, H., & Bakwin, R. *Clinical management of behavior disorders in children.* (3rd ed.) Philadelphia: Saunders, 1966.

Benda, C. A distinctive metabolic disorder. *International Journal of Psychiatry*, 1968, **5**, 3, 220–21.

Bender, L. Childhood schizophrenia: clinical study of one hundred schizophrenic children. *American Journal of Orthopsychiatry*, 1947, **17**, 40–56.

Bender, L. Current research in childhood schizophrenia. *American Journal of Psychiatry*, 1954, **110**, 855–56.

Bender, L. Treatment in early schizophrenia. *Progress in Psychotherapy*, 1960, **5**, 177–84.

Bender, L. Childhood schizophrenia: a review. *International Journal of Psychiatry*, 1968, **5**, 3, 211–30.

Bender, L., & Freedman, A. M. A study of the first three years in the maturation of schizophrenic children. *Quarterly Journal of Child Behavior*, 1952, **4**, 245.

Bender, L., & Guerevitz, S. Results of psychotherapy with young schizophrenic children. *American Journal of Orthopsychiatry*, 1955, **25**, 162–70.

Bennett, S., & Klein, H. R. Childhood schizophrenia: 30 years later. *American Journal of Psychiatry*, 1966, **122**, 1121–24.

Berger, A. A test of the double-bind hypothesis of schizophrenia. *Family Process*, 1965, **4**, 198–205.

Bettelheim, B. *Love is not enough.* Glencoe, Ill.: Free Press, 1950.

Bettelheim, B. *The empty fortress.* Glencoe, Ill.: Free Press, 1967.

Bettelheim, B., & Sylvester, E. A therapeutic milieu. *American Journal of Orthopsychiatry*, 1948, **18**, 191–206.

Blau, A. The nature of childhood schizophrenia. *Journal of the American Academy of Child Psychiatry*, 1962, **2**, 225–35.

Boatman, J. J., & Szurek, S. A. A clinical study of childhood schizophrenia. In D. Jackson (Ed.), *The etiology of schizophrenia.* New York: Basic Books, 1960, pp. 388–440.

Brown, J. L. Follow-up study of preschool children of atypical development (infantile psychosis): later personality patterns in adaptation to maturational stress. *American Journal of Orthopsychiatry*, 1963, **33**, 336–38.

Committee on Child Psychiatry. *Psychopathological disorders in childhood: theoretical considerations and a proposed classification.* New York: Group for the Advancement of Psychiatry, 1966.

Conners, K. Pharmacotherapy of psychopathology in children. In H. Quay & J. Werry (Eds.) *Psychopathological disorders in childhood.* New York: Wiley, 1972, pp. 316–47.

Davids, A. *Abnormal children and youth: therapy and research.* New York: Wiley, 1972.

Davidson, G. The training of undergraduates as social reinforcers for autistic children. In L. P. Ullman & L. Krasner (Eds.), *Case studies in behavior modification.* New York: Holt, Rinehart, and Winston, 1965, pp. 146–48.

Des Lauriers, A., & Carlson, C. *Your child is asleep: early infantile autism.* Homewood, Ill.: Dorsey Press, 1969.

Des Lauriers, A., & Halpern, F. Psychological tests in childhood schizophrenia. *American Journal of Orthopsychiatry*, 1947, **17**, 56–57.

Donahue, G. A school district program for schizophrenic, organic and seriously disturbed children. In E. Cowen, A. Gardner, & M. Zax (Eds.) *Emergent approaches to mental health problems*. New York: Appleton-Century-Crofts, 1967, pp. 369–86.

Eisenberg, L. The autistic child in adolescence. *American Journal of Psychiatry*, 1956, **112**, 607–12.

Eisenberg, L. Fathers of autistic children. *American Journal of Orthopsychiatry*, 1957, **27**, 715–24.

Ekstein, R., Bryant, K., & Friedman, S. Childhood schizophrenia and allied conditions. In L. Bellak (Ed.), *Schizophrenia: a review of the syndrome*. New York: Logos Press, 1958, pp. 555–693.

Ferster, C. B. Positive reinforcement and behavioral deficits of autistic children. *Child Development*, 1961, **32**, 437–56.

Ferster, C. B., & DeMyer, M. K. A method for the experimental analysis of the behavior of autistic children. *American Journal of Orthopsychiatry*, 1962, **32**, 89–98.

Frank, G. H. The role of the family in the development of psychopathology. *Psychological Bulletin*, 1965, **64**, 191–203.

Friedman, E. Early infantile autism. *Journal of Child Clinical Psychology*, 1974, **3**, 1, 4–10.

Gianascol, A. Psychodynamic approaches to childhood schizophrenia: a review. *Journal of Nervous and Mental Disorders*, 1963, **137**, 336–48.

Goldberg, I. Tutoring as a method of psychotherapy in schizophrenic children with reading disabilities. *Quarterly Journal of Child Behavior*, 1952, **4**, 273–80.

Goldfarb, W. *Childhood schizophrenia*. Cambridge: Harvard University Press, 1961.

Goldfarb, W., Braunstein, P., & Lorgo, I. A study of speech patterns in a group of schizophrenic children. *American Journal of Orthopsychiatry*, 1956, **26**, 544–55.

Goldfarb, W., Goldfarb, N., & Pollack, R. Treatment of childhood schizophrenia: a three-year comparison of day and residential treatment. *Archives of General Psychiatry*, 1966, **14**, 119–28.

Goldfarb, W., Goldfarb, N., & Scholl, H. The speech of mothers of schizophrenic children. *American Journal of Psychiatry*, 1966, **122**, 1220–27.

Goldfarb, W., Mintz, I., & Strook, K. *Time to heal corrective socialization: a treatment approach to childhood schizophrenia*. New York: International Universities Press, 1969.

Gottesman, I., & Shields, J. *Schizophrenia and genetics: a twin study vantage point*. New York: Academic Press, 1972.

Halpern, F. The Rorschach test with children. In A. Rabin & M. Haworth (Eds.), *Projective techniques with children*. New York: Grune & Stratton, 1960, pp. 14–28.

Hermelin, B., & O'Connor, N. *Psychological experiments with autistic children*. Oxford, England: Pergamon Press, 1970.

Hewett, F. Teaching reading to an autistic boy through operant conditioning. *Reading Teacher*, 1964, **17**, 613–18.

Hewett, F. Teaching speech to an autistic child through operant conditioning. *American Journal of Orthopsychiatry*, 1965, **35**, 927–36.

Hewett, F. Educational engineering with emotionally disturbed children. *Exceptional Children*, 1967, **33,** 459–67. (a)

Hewett, F. A school in a psychiatric hospital. *Mental Hygiene*, 1967, **51,** 75–83. (b)

Hewett, F., & Forness, S. R., *Education of exceptional learners.* Boston: Allyn & Bacon, 1974.

Hewett, F., Taylor, F., & Artuso, A. The Santa Monica Project. *Exceptional Children*, 1968, **34,** 387.

Hingtgen, J., Sanders, B., & DeMyer, M. Shaping cooperative responses in early childhood schizophrenics. Paper read at meeting of American Psychological Association, Philadelphia, August, 1963.

Hingtgen, J. N., & Trost, F. C., Jr. Shaping cooperative responses in early childhood schizophrenics: II. Reinforcement of mutual contact and vocal responses. In R. Ulrich, T. Stachnik, & J. Mabry (Eds.), *Control of human behavior.* Glenview, Ill.: Scott, Foresman, 1966, pp. 110–13.

Hirschberg, C. The role of education in the treatment of emotionally disturbed children through planned ego development. *American Journal of Orthopsychiatry*, 1953, **23,** 684–90.

Jacob, T. Family interaction in disturbed and normal families: A methodological and substantive review. *Psychological Bulletin*, 1975, **82,** 33–65.

Johnson, J., & Juul, K. Learning characteristics in a schizophrenic boy. *Exceptional Children*, 1960, **26,** 135–38.

Kallmann, F. J. The genetics of human behavior. *American Journal of Psychiatry*, 1956, **113,** 496–501.

Kanner, L. Autistic disturbances of affective contact. *Nervous Child*, 1943, **2,** 217–50.

Kanner, L. Early infantile autism. *Journal of Pediatrics*, 1944, **25,** 211–17.

Kanner, L. Irrelevant and metaphorical language in early infantile autism. *American Journal of Psychiatry*, 1946, **103,** 242–46.

Kanner, L. Problems of nosology and psychodynamics. *American Journal of Orthopsychiatry*, 1949, **19,** 416–76.

Kanner, L. Emotionally disturbed children: a historical review. *Child Development*, 1962, **33,** 97–102.

Kanner, L. *Childhood psychosis: initial studies and new insight.* Washington, D.C.: Winston & Sons, 1973.

Kaufman, I., Herrick, J. Willer, L., Frank T., & Heims, L. Four types of defenses in mothers and fathers of schizophrenic children. *American Journal of Orthopsychiatry*, 1959, **29,** 460–72.

Kessler, J. W. *Psychopathology of childhood.* Englewood Cliffs, N.J.: Prentice-Hall, 1966.

Klebanoff, L. Parental attitudes of mothers of schizophrenic, brain-injured and retarded and normal children. *American Journal of Orthopsychiatry*, 1959, **29,** 445–54.

Koegel, R., & Rincover, A. Treatment of psychotic children in a classroom environment: 1. Learning in a large group. *Journal of Applied Behavior Analysis*, 1974, **7,** 1, 45–60.

Leff, R. Behavior modification and the psychoses of childhood: a review. *Psychological Bulletin*, 1968, **69,** 396–409.

Lidz, T., & Fleck, S. Schizophrenia, human interaction, and the role of the family. In D. Jackson (Ed.), *The etiology of schizophrenia.* New York: Basic Books, 1960, pp. 323–45.

Lifton, N., & Smolen, E. Group psychotherapy with schizophrenic children. *International Journal of Psychotherapy*, 1966, **16**, 23–41.

Lotter, V. Epidemiology of autistic conditions in young children: 1: Prevalence. *Social Psychiatry*, 1966, **1**, 124–37.

Lovaas, O. I., Freitag, G., Gold, V., & Kassorla, I. Experimental studies in childhood schizophrenia. *Journal of Experimental Psychology*, 1963, **66**, 67–73.

Lovaas, O. I., Freitag, G., Gold, V., & Kassorla, I. Experimental studies in childhood schizophrenia: analysis of self-destructive behavior. *Journal of Experimental Child Psychology*, 1965, **2**, 67–84.

Lovaas, I., Berberich, J., Perloff, B., & Schaeffer, B. Acquisition of imitative speech by schizophrenic children. *Science*, 1966, **151**, 705–7.

Lovaas, I. & Koegel, R. Behavior therapy with autistic children. In C. Thoresen (Ed.), Behavior modification in education. *Yearbook of the National Society for the Study of Education*, 1973, Part 1, pp. 230–58.

Lovaas, I., Koegel, R., Simmons, J., & Long, J. Some generalization and follow-up measures on autistic children in behavior therapy. *Journal of Applied Behavior Analysis*, 1973, **6**, 1, 131–65.

Mahler, M. S. On child psychosis and schizophrenia: autistic and symbiotic infantile psychoses. In R. S. Eissler, A. Freud, H. Hartmann, & E. Kris (Eds.), *The psychoanalytic study of the child*. Vol. 7. New York: International Universities Press, 1952, pp. 286–305.

Mahler, M. S. On early infantile psychosis. *Journal of the American Academy of Child Psychiatry*, 1965, **4**, 554–68.

Mahler, M. The self-limitations of Loretta Bender's biological theory. *International Journal of Psychiatry*, 1968, **5**, 3, 230–36.

Mahler, M. S., Furer, M., & Settlage, C. F. Severe emotional disturbances in childhood: psychosis. In S. Arieti (Ed.), *American handbook of psychiatry*. New York: Basic Books, 1959, pp. 816–39.

Mandell, A., Segal, D., Kuczenski, R., & Knapp, S. The search for the schizococcus. *Psychology Today*, 1972, **6**, 68–72.

Mariner, A. A critical look at professional education in the mental health field. *American Psychologist*, 1967, **22**, 271–81.

Mischler, E., & Waxler, N. Family interaction processes and schizophrenia: a review of current theories. *Merrill-Palmer Quarterly*, 1965, **11**, 269–315.

Morse, W. C., Cutler, R. L., & Fink, A. H. *Public school classes for the emotionally handicapped: a research analysis*. Washington, D.C.: Council for Exceptional Children, 1964.

Nedelman, D., & Sulzbacher, S. Dicky at thirteen years of age: A long-term success following early application of operant conditioning procedures. In G. Semb (Ed.), *Behavior analysis and education*. Lawrence, Kansas: University of Kansas Press, 1972, pp. 3–10.

Ornitz, E. Childhood autism: a review of the clinical and experimental literature. *California Medicine*, 1973, **118**, 21–47.

Piotrowski, Z. A comparison of congenitally defective children with schizophrenic children with respect to personality structure and intellectual type. *Proceedings of the American Association on Mental Deficiency*, 1937, **42**, 78–90.

Potter, H. W. Schizophrenia in children. *American Journal of Psychiatry*, 1933, **12**, 1253.

Rabinovitch, R. An evaluation of present trends in psychotherapy of children. *Journal of Psychiatric Social Work*, 1954, **24,** 11–19.

Rank, B. Adaptation of the psychoanalytic technique for the treatment of young children with atypical development. *American Journal of Orthopsychiatry*, 1949, **19,** 130–39.

Rimland, B. *Infantile autism: the syndrome and its implications for a neural theory of behavior.* New York: Appleton-Century-Crofts, 1964.

Rimland, B. Comment on Ward's "Early Infantile Autism." *Psychological Bulletin*, 1972, **77,** 1, 52–53.

Risley, T., & Wolf, M. Experimental manipulation of autistic behaviors and generalization into the home. Paper read at meeting of American Psychological Association, Los Angeles, September, 1964.

Ritvo, E., Yuwiler, A., Geller, E., Ornitz, E., Saeger, K., & Plotkin, S. Increased blood serotonin and platelets in early infantile autism. *Archives of General Psychiatry*, 1970, **23,** 566–72.

Rosen, B. M., Bahn, A. K., & Kramer, M. Demographic and diagnostic characteristics of psychiatric clinic outpatients in the U.S.A., 1961. *American Journal of Orthopsychiatry*, 1964, **34,** 455–68.

Rosenblum, S. Practices and problems in the use of tranquilizers with exceptional children. In E. Trapp & P. Himelstein (Eds.), *Readings on the exceptional child.* New York: Appleton-Century-Crofts, 1962, pp. 639–57.

Rutter, M. Prognosis: Psychotic children in adolescence and early life. In J. Wing (Ed.), *Early Childhood autism: clinical, educational, and social aspects.* London: Pergamon Press, 1966.

Rutter, M., & Sussenwein, F. A developmental and behavioral approach to the treatment of preschool autistic children. *Journal of Autism and Childhood Schizophrenia*, 1971, **1,** 4, 376–97.

Schloper, E., & Reichler, R. Parents as co-therapists in the treatment of psychotic children. *Journal of Autism and Childhood Schizophrenia*, 1971, **1,** 1, 87–102.

Shaw, C. R. & Lucas, A. *The psychiatric disorders of childhood.* (2nd ed.) New York: Appleton-Century-Crofts, 1970.

Skinner, B. F. Some contributions of an experimental analysis of behavior to psychology as a whole. *American Psychologist*, 1953, **8,** 69–78.

Speers, R., & Lansing, C. Group psychotherapy with preschool children and collateral group therapy of their parents: a preliminary report of the first two years. *American Journal of Orthopsychiatry*, 1964, **34,** 659–66.

U.S. Department of Health, Education and Welfare. *Patients in mental institutions, 1963.* Washington, D.C.: Government Printing Office, 1964.

Weakland, J. The double-bind hypothesis of schizophrenia and the three party interaction. In D. Jackson (Ed.), *The etiology of schizophrenia.* New York: Basic Books, 1960, pp. 373–88.

White, L. Organic factors and psychophysiology in childhood schizophrenia. *Psychological Bulletin*, 1974, **81,** 238–55.

White, R. W., & Watt, N. *The abnormal personality.* (4th ed.) New York: Ronald Press, 1973.

Wing, J. *Early childhood autism.* (2nd ed.) London: Pergamon Press, 1974.

Wolf, M. M., Risley, T., & Mees, H. L. Application of operant conditioning procedures to the behavior problems of an autistic child. *Behavior Research Therapy*, 1964, **1,** 305–12.

Wynne, L., & Singer, M. Thought disorder and the family relations of schizophrenics. I: a research strategy. *Archives of General Psychiatry*, 1963, **9**, 191–98.

Zimmerman, E., & Zimmerman, J. The alteration of behavior in a special classroom situation. *Journal of Experimental Analysis of Behavior*, 1962, **5**, 59–60.

Suggested Readings

Axline, V. *Dibs in search of self.* New York: Ballantine Books, 1964.

Bettelheim, B. *The empty fortress.* Glencoe, Ill. Free Press, 1967.

Gottesman, I., & Shields, J. *Schizophrenia and genetics: a twin study vantage point.* New York: Academic Press, 1972.

Kanner, L. *Childhood psychosis: initial studies and new insights.* Washington, D.C.: Winston & Sons, 1973.

Lovaas, I. Some generalization and follow-up measures on autistic children in behavior therapy. *Journal of Applied Behavior Analysis.* 1973, **6**, 131–66.

Wing, J. *Early childhood autism.* (2nd ed.) London: Pergamon Press, 1974.

PART III

Intervention
and
Prevention
Strategies

Approaches to Treatment of Children

In contrast to the discussions of treatment in the earlier chapters of this book, which dealt with the treatment of specific disorders, the discussion in this chapter deals with various general approaches to therapy with children. The plan is to consider first the differences between therapeutic approaches for children and those for adults. Then we turn to play therapy and an assessment of the effectiveness of various traditional treatment approaches. Finally, the chapter concludes with a presentation of a group of innovations in treatment approaches that are receiving attention from psychologists.

Differences between Adult and Child Psychotherapy

The basic principles of psychotherapy with children are not essentially different from those of psychotherapy with adults, but the immaturity and dependent status of the child necessitate certain modifications in the emphasis and application of these principles (White & Watt, 1973). Hence it seems appropriate to examine certain differences that exist between children and adults so that we may better understand the bases for therapeutic methods with children. The reader should keep these differences in mind when considering the treatment approaches discussed later in the chapter.

Motivation for Treatment

As Table 10–1 shows, one important difference occurs in the approach to the therapy situation. The adult typically comes to treatment recognizing that he has a personal problem. Although he may need the support of others to reach this decision, the ultimate responsibility for seeking help is his. Few children, however, request psychotherapeutic help. Rather, they are usually placed into therapy by an adult, with little or no explanation as to why. The child may be experiencing strong anxiety or suffering from emotional deprivation, but it is doubtful that these states can be utilized to motivate him to look forward to therapy. Not only do children lack motivation in the usual adult sense to work on their own problems, but they not uncommonly have fears regarding what the therapist will do to them. Some children readily adjust to the playroom without the assistance of the therapist. In these instances, therapy can proceed without specifically designed attempts to establish a therapeutic relationship.

But there are children who question their presence at the clinic, who are angry and defiant, who become passive, or who are indifferent. With these children, an explanation that reflects the therapist's respect for the child is indicated. Care must be exercised lest the child feel that the therapist is "taking sides" with the parents or the teacher. A reality-based explanation geared to the child's developmental level is recommended in such instances. In brief, the child's anxieties, suspicions, and low level of motivation frequently require demonstration to him that the therapist is an empathic, benign, and helpful companion as the first step in establishing a therapeutic relationship. Some therapists, like Anna Freud (1946) and Pearson (1949), advocate an initial orientation and "getting-acquainted" approach in the beginning sessions to prepare the child for more intensive treatment later.

Insight into Treatment Objectives

A related barrier to therapy is centered about the fact that the therapist and child lack the commonality of purpose more characteristic of adult therapy. Whereas the adult client is likely to be cognizant of certain common goals of treatment that he shares with the therapist and is somewhat more accepting of the impending personality reorganization, the child (because of his more limited cognitive and experiential background) may well lack insight both as to the roles that he and the therapist are to assume and as to the purposes of treatment. He may appreciate neither the desirability nor the possibility of behavioral change. Given this lack of common goals, much of the child's desire to remain in treatment must come from satisfactions inherent in the treatment setting itself.

Linguistic Development

Another fundamental difference is the child's relative lack of verbal development. True enough, he can communicate verbally with adults, but he is apt to find the formal sort of psychiatric interview too stilted to permit a comfortable feeling in the situation. The child's limited experience may be reflected in an uncertainty as to how or what to label his feelings, whereas the use of concrete materials of play renders the child more secure since he is able to manipulate and control these tangibles with more assurance than he can the abstractions of words. Evidence from developmental studies in cognition would also indicate, especially for children below junior-high-school age, the suitability of concrete materials as opposed to verbal abstractions as a means of expression (Piaget, 1960). Lippman (1962) observes that children often show greater anxiety in direct interviews than in play. Limited verbal facility may engender feelings of inadequacy and failure on the part of the child, thus adding to the difficulty in establishing a trusting relationship with the therapist. As Watson (1951) notes, suspicion and hostility are likely to be encountered particularly with young or intellectually dull children as well as with delinquents.

Many of these problems can be alleviated through the medium of play therapy because play is something these children can comprehend and use as a means of communication. Since play therapy entails substantially less speech-mediated interaction than does psychotherapy with adults, nonverbal aspects are accorded a more important position. According to Watson (1951), this is a two-way proposition. The therapist must be especially alert to the child's facial expressions, postural adjustments, and expressive movements, realizing that these may well be the child's primary means of expression. In turn, the child reacts to similar nonverbal behavior on the therapist's part. Many therapists believe that how the therapist feels is more important than what he says and does.

The above remarks are not intended to deny the fact that some prepubescents communicate very well through language. In such instances the necessity of nonverbal forms of communication may well be markedly reduced.

Table 10–1.　A Summary of Differences between Adults and Children with Implications for Child Therapy

Factor	*Adult*	*Child*	*Treatment Implication for Child*
Motivation for treatment	Often self-referred; better motivated to work on his difficulties.	Referred by others; lacks motivation to work on own problems.	Some therapists feel the need for initial sessions to develop a therapeutic relationship upon which to base later, more intensive therapy.
Insight into treatment objectives	More likely to share common goals with therapist and to be aware of his own role in therapy.	More apt to lack common goals with therapist.	The child must find therapy intrinsically interesting; his needs for exploration and manipulation should be utilized.
Linguistic development	Satisfactory verbal facility.	Limited verbal facility; greater use of nonverbal communication.	Speech-mediated interactions are minimized, with more emphasis on nonverbal communication and experiencing of consequences.
Dependence on environmental forces	More independent of environment.	Very dependent on environment and significant others.	Treatment must accord more attention to dealing with significant others in the child's life and to external reality pressures.
Plasticity of personality	More "set" in his ways; defenses are better established.	More pliable and open to therapeutic influence; less integration and internal consistency in personality.	Intervention procedures should be undertaken before personality becomes stabilized; less need for depth-therapy techniques, as the child is more susceptible to environmental influences.

In many cases, extended conversations, whether they delve into the child's past or focus upon current maladaptive behavior, may be unnecessary and at times even detrimental to the child's progress. What may be as significant or perhaps more so than treatment by talk is that the child experiences pleasant or reinforcing consequences for appropriate action and neutral or unpleasant consequences for inappropriate actions. As you will see, most of the approaches in this chapter require relatively little in the way of linguistic facility on the child's part.

Dependence on Environmental Forces

The child's dependency on the adults in his life also has implications for treatment. Whereas the adult is relatively independent of the significant others in his environment, the child is still very much at their mercy. The adult can quit his job, change his residence, and replace companions much more readily than the child can quit school, change homes, and substitute peer groups. As a consequence of his immature and dependent status, the young child is more subject to environmental stresses and strains. Since the child in treatment is typically still living in the situation that caused or contributed to his difficulties, emphasis must be devoted to the child's current reality conditions.

Since it is commonly accepted that the child's disturbance is often inextricably bound up with problems of the significant others in his surroundings, many therapists do not advocate psychotherapy with children younger than 14 years of age unless the parents are also willing to become involved in the treatment process (White & Watt, 1973). Parental involvement necessitated by the child's dependency status poses challenges, however, which demand skillful management in the therapy program; for example, there may be parental rivalry with the therapist for the child's affection. More will be said about working with parents in the chapter on environmental intervention.

Plasticity of Personality

Another difference centers around the lack of crystallization in the child's personality. Because the child's personality is relatively undeveloped, unformed, and changing rapidly, it tends to be more pliable than the enduring adult personality. Hence, the potentiality for change should be greater prior to the establishment of a more consistent and more stable personality structure. Defense mechanisms are apt to be less deeply rooted and therefore more amenable to the types of relearning experiences offered in the therapy setting. Because of the greater fluidity and more elastic nature of the personality, greater liability and inconsistency of behavior as well as an intermingling of reality and fantasy in the child can be anticipated (Slavson, 1952; Watson, 1951). Consequently, the course of child therapy is likely to be characterized by greater discontinuity than is adult therapy, as exemplified by shifts from one activity to another, from reality to fantasy, and from deeper to more surface aspects of the difficulty. The greater fluidity and inconsistency that characterize the child's personality may also require that less effort be directed toward the "uncovering" aspects of therapy and more toward the "covering-up" aspects. Further, these characteristics of child personality underscore the need for the therapist's ability to distinguish between more permanent or repetitive problems and those of a transitory character.

Differences Related to Play Therapy

Slavson (1947) has cited other differences that further highlight the potential value of play techniques. Illustratively, the child is considerably more impulsive than the adult; he is less subject to repressive forces and more willing to act out and speak about matters that are embarrassing to an older person; his fantasy life is closer to the surface; his attention span is shorter; he is more concerned with locomotion and expression, so that physical activity is of greater importance to him. The implications of these differences are reflected in Slavson's group-therapy approach, which is discussed later in the chapter.

Play Therapy

The child has a rich fantasy life which in early years he can express in a spontaneous and vivid manner, and unless strong repressive forces are at work, his fantasies can be utilized for uncovering and alleviating conflicts. Daily observation reveals that small children have a remarkable facility for switching back and forth between reality and fantasy—from their own subjective inner world to the objective outside world of reality. They also use toys and play to express externally their inner fantasies. In doing so, they build up a world as important and meaningful to them as reality. It is this expressive capacity and fascination on the child's part that is utilized by the therapist during treatment. Thus, play therapy is based upon the fact that play is the child's natural medium of self-expression. The therapeutic use of play provides an opportunity for the child to formulate his feelings and problems, in much the same manner that the more linguistically facile adult talks out his difficulties in certain types of adult therapy.

All proponents of expressive or evocative play therapy view the establishment of a therapeutic relationship as a prerequisite for successful treatment. If this relationship is lacking, there may be play but not play therapy in any genuine sense. As Watson notes (1951):

> Psychotherapy with children requires that the child be given an opportunity to interact with an adult (the therapist) who takes a different attitude toward his problem from that he has previously experienced. This the therapeutic attitude supplies, no matter how it is expressed. Of course, merely making it available is not enough; the child must experience it. Although play may share in the development of this interaction, the attitude may be maintained in its absence. Play is merely one way of allowing the therapist to interact with a child patient.

Thus, play becomes a medium of therapy, and as such it must occur within the framework of a relationship that is established through the participation of two people. It is the uniqueness of this relationship and of the circumstances that produces the special meaning to what the child does, whether it be playing or talking or just sitting. Froebel (quoted in Jackson & Todd, 1950) commented several decades ago:

> Child's play is not mere sport. It is full of meaning and serious impact. Cherish it and encourage it. For to one who has insight into human nature, the trend of the whole future life of the child is revealed in his freely chosen play.

Historical Background

The study of the treatment of emotional disturbance in children is a relatively recent development compared to the attention given emotional disturbance in adults. Contributions to child treatment have come from psychoanalysis, psychology, genetic psychology, and social work, among other sources. All have increased our knowledge of the child, but the greatest contributions to the treatment of problem behavior in children have come from those directly concerned with psychopathology. Outstanding is the work by Freud and his students.

One of Freud's major concerns was the development of a treatment for adults having neurotic symptoms. In his investigations he concluded that the problems of the neurotic adult derived from sexual conflicts in early childhood. From his clinical experience with adult patients, he inferred that young children have an active sexual life and vivid fantasies. In 1906 he presented a case entitled "Analysis of a Phobia in a Five-Year-Old Boy"—the celebrated "Case of Little Hans"—to support his contentions (1909). Freud did not conduct the analysis; it was carried out by the boy's father, himself an analyst. Although the interpretations of some of the findings might be questioned, this report did, nevertheless, represent the first application of psychoanalysis to the problems of children and hence gave impetus to a lively interest in child analysis.

About 1920 Hermine Hug-Hellmuth, a psychoanalytically oriented educator, began to treat maladjusted children within the framework of Freudian theory. She used play as a basic part of her procedures with children under 7 years of age and as an aid to communication at later ages. When dealing with children aged 7 or 8, she believed that the analyst could often facilitate the therapeutic process by sharing in the play activities. In essence, her approach, which combined Freudian theory and educational methods, consisted in observing the child at play and in translating each pattern of behavior into the analyst's set of symbols.

It was not until some ten years later, however, when Anna Freud and Melanie Klein reported their observations and theoretical discussions of the therapeutic process with children that child psychoanalysis began to be practiced on a sizable scale. Although both adhered to general psychoanalytic theories of child therapy, each formulated treatment procedures differing in many significant respects.

The pioneer efforts of these women greatly influenced the thinking of mental-health specialists in this country. Perhaps of more direct consequence was the establishment of the child-guidance movement. While many individuals figured in this movement, it was Lightner Witmer who in 1896 founded the first child-guidance clinic as a consequence of his interest in the school-aged child with problems. Shortly thereafter, other clinics were founded, with practices based on an integration of psychoanalytic and psychobiological principles as exemplified by Sigmund Freud and Adolf Meyer. By 1921, a large number of clinics attached to mental hospitals, schools, courts, colleges, and social agencies were employing a case-study and team approach to the disorders of children. The National Committee for Mental Hygiene and the Commonwealth Fund supported the developments of these clinics, and as they expanded, advances were made in the techniques of child therapy. By 1930, there were more than 500 such clinics.

Characteristicallly, child psychoanalysis and child therapy have differed in that the latter represents a less intense approach and is more apt to use environmental interventions. Accordingly, in child therapy the child is seen less frequently, and work with the parents may be undertaken. As Wattenberg (1966) notes, therapists today are realizing that the child's reality conditions are as important as how the child feels.

Anna Freud's Psychoanalytic Approach

Anna Freud (1946) advocates a psychoanalytic orientation but maintains that the classical techniques of adult psychoanalysis require certain modification for applicability to children because the young are unable to develop a transference neurosis and because their ego ideal is still relatively weak. Although she has since modified her views regarding the possibility of a transference neurosis occurring in treatment, she continues to believe that it cannot equal that of the adult variety (A. Freud, 1965).

Seeing toys more for assessing the child's growth, she finds them useful in establishing a close relationship in the preanalytic phase of treatment which she regards as a necessary preparation for effective analytic interpretation. Free play, however, is not regarded as a substitute for free association. During the stage of analysis proper, various techniques are used as avenues to the unconscious. These include the taking of a case history from the child and the mother, the analyzing of drawings, and the interpreting of dreams. The technique of interpretation constitutes a cornerstone of psychoanalytic practice and is designed to promote insight on the child's part. Basically, interpretations center around connections between the past and the present, sometimes between a fantasy and a feeling, but most commonly between a defense and a feeling (Kessler, 1966).

Freud highlights the need to work with parents, realizing that the initiation, continuance, and termination of treatment are contingent upon their insight and motivations. Moreover, Anna Freud is careful to note that psychoanalytic treatment is not suitable for all types of children. It may be contraindicated for the psychotic and for those who have a marked difficulty in establishing a relationship due to severe emotional deprivations in early life. The existence of severe infantile neurosis and verbal facility are regarded as two prerequisites for analytic treatment.

Axline's Client-Centered Approach

Virginia Axline (1947), following closely the therapeutic approach of Carl Rogers, regards play as therapeutic because of the freedom of expression given the child within the atmosphere of a secure relationship with the therapist. Treatment begins in the first session. The child is taken as he is, accepted without censure from the therapist, given ample opportunity to express his feelings in as permissive a climate as the situation will permit, and helped to recognize and clarify his feelings. The notion of respect for the individual and his potential for self-discrimination is central to this viewpoint. Consistent with the idea of man as a self-autonomous individual, no attempt at interpretation or manipulation is consciously made. Rather, the therapist, sensitive to the feelings of the child, reflects attitudes back to him so the child may achieve a better understanding of himself. Responsibility for growth is placed with the child, as it is assumed that he possesses not only the ability to handle his problems successfully but also an inner drive toward self-actualization and maturity as well. Thus, there is a basic trust that the client will make the best decision. The function of therapy is to create an atmosphere conducive to the release of these positive internal growth forces.

Although the role of the client is stressed, the therapist is by no means a passive agent, for it is his sensitive participation that helps the child to clarify his feelings and revise his self-concept. The therapist establishes a relationship that enables the child to reveal his real self and thereby facilitates the development of his personality.

Axline, who has worked mostly with children aged 4 to 8, believes that a favorable outcome in therapy can be expected even though the parents are not involved in treatment. Nevertheless, she feels that work with parents can expedite the therapeutic process, especially in cases involving handicapped children.[1]

Axline (1964) has given a succinct statement of her position in the following basic principles, which serve as guidelines for the nondirective therapist:

1. The therapist must develop a warm, friendly relationship with the child, in which good rapport is established as soon as possible.

---

1. For an excellent description of Axline's approach to play therapy, see her exciting and informative book, *Dibs in Search of Self*. New York: Ballantine Books, 1964.

2. The therapist accepts the child exactly as he is.

3. The therapist establishes a feeling of permissiveness in the relationship so that the child feels free to express his feelings completely.

4. The therapist is alert to recognize the feelings the child is expressing and reflects those feelings back to him in such a manner that he gains insight into his behavior.

5. The therapist maintains a deep respect for the child's ability to solve his own problems if given an opportunity to do so. The responsibility to make choices and to institute change is the child's.

6. The therapist does not attempt to direct the child's actions or conversation in any manner. The child leads the way; the therapist follows.

7. The therapist does not attempt to hurry the therapy along. It is a gradual process and is recognized as such by the therapist.

8. The therapist establishes only those limitations that are necessary to anchor the therapy to the world of reality and to make the child aware of his responsibility in the relationship.

Slavson's Activity Group Psychotherapy

Slavson is best known for his *activity group psychotherapy*, which represents an adaptation of group therapy to children. In this approach, the group is regarded as a substitute family, with the therapist assuming the role of an impartial and calm parent substitute. Activity (for example, a group project) is substituted for the usual verbal interaction characteristic of adult group psychotherapy. Conversations do occur in the weekly meetings but in conjunction with the activities in which the youngsters are participating. Permissiveness, while a basic element in this approach, is carried out in a specifically structured setting. Through "passive restraint," the therapist conveys to the child and the group that he does not approve of certain behavior. Another therapeutic element is that of social imitation. Slavson, through personal example, displays socially acceptable behavior and by so doing offers the disturbed child modeling cues for more desirable behavior. For example, at the end of the session, the therapist begins to clean up the room and the children gradually do likewise. Such therapeutic factors as emotional release, relationship, and insight are also considered operative although insight is not accorded a role of importance. The use of interpretation is accordingly deemphasized.[2]

The goals of Slavson's approach are to provide a spontaneous discharge of drives and a lowering of tension through emotional and physical activity in a group setting that allows unimpeded acting-out within the limits of personal safety. Tensions are discharged, emotions expressed, ego strength established, self-esteem enhanced, and limitations discovered.

With respect to age, activity group psychotherapy is seen as suitable for use

---

2. For additional discussion of expressive therapies with children, see Hammer & Kaplan (1967) and Haworth (1964).

with youngsters between ages 7 and 14. With respect to disturbance, it is indicated for a wide variety of disturbed children—the acting-out child, the child with character disorders, and the child with neurotic disturbances.

After a period of from six to eight months, the child's social adjustment to the group has progressed to the extent that a return to the neighborhood group is possible. The permissive atmosphere of the group setting does, however, contraindicate the presence of the extremely hostile and uncontrolled child. The psychotic child would also not be considered for this type of treatment.

Evaluation of Psychotherapy

Empirical Studies

Parents and educators often turn to mental-health specialists when attempting to resolve the problems their children or pupils present. Today there are approximately 2,000 outpatient clinics and more than 400 hospitals with psychiatric units offering mental-health services (Bower, 1970). The question naturally arises, How effective is the treatment provided by these facilities? The authors can recall numerous occasions when they sat in on case conferences with mental-health specialists and school personnel and heard a sigh of relief from the participants once the child was recommended for psychotherapy.

How realistic is it to feel such a sense of relief? Generally speaking, results at termination of treatment indicate that from two-thirds to three-fourths of children seen at child-guidance centers show improvement. Typical of such findings was a large-scale national investigation of outpatient psychiatric clinics in 1959, conducted by Norman, Rosen, & Bahn (1962), who discovered an improvement rate of 72%. Follow-up studies, moreover, indicate that children treated on an outpatient basis maintain their improved status (Levitt, 1957). The results of psychotherapy with residential treatment cases yield similarly high improvement rates both at the time of termination of treatment (Reid & Hagen, 1952) and at the time of follow-up (Rubin, 1962). Hence, data obtained on outpatients and inpatients at the close of therapy and at the time of follow-up seemingly suggest that the grounds for the sigh of relief alluded to earlier are realistically based.

There are, however, two disquieting aspects regarding the outcomes of psychotherapeutic treatment of children. First, of approximately 200,000 children seen in outpatient psychiatric clinics in 1959, only one-fourth were accepted for direct treatment of some kind, another fourth were clinic-terminated as unsuitable for treatment, and half were clinic-terminated with the majority of such cases being referred to the originating agency (Norman et al., 1962). As Redl (1966) notes, the model of "the holy trinity" (psychiatrist, psychologist, and social worker) is obsolescent, and the need for new modes of treatment to cope with the new mixtures of childhood disturbances is apparent. Schofield (1964), in a somewhat similar vein, points out that psychotherapists have not been trained to deal with some of the more common types of problems being referred to them, namely, difficulties symptomatic of social distress and discomfort.

Second, professional rejoicing over the high improvement rates for those accepted for treatment would have to be predicated upon the proposition that untreated disturbed youngsters do not improve. But an examination of the base rates for improvement without psychotherapy yields little support for such a proposition. The best-known studies on psychotherapeutic outcomes with children have been conducted by Eugene Levitt, and these will be discussed in some detail because of their significance and the controversy they have engendered.

In attempting to take an objective look at the outcomes of traditional psychotherapy with children, Levitt (1957) reviewed 18 reports of evaluations at the close of treatment and 17 reports at the time of follow-up. The studies reviewed were conducted between 1929 and 1955 and involved more than 7,500 clients who might be crudely labeled as having neurotic disturbances. About two-thirds of these children were classified as either much improved or partly improved at termination of treatment, and more than three-fourths of these children were so classified upon follow-up some five years later on the average. However, using "defectors" from therapy as a control group, that is, children who had been accepted for treatment but who had withdrawn from the waiting list before treatment began, Levitt obtained comparable improvement rates (72.5%).

In his latest review, Levitt (1963) reported on studies that appeared between 1957 and 1963. Like his earlier findings, the more recent ones offer little comfort to the proponents of traditional therapeutic approaches in that they failed to offer any satisfactory evidence that traditional psychotherapy increases the likelihood of relief accorded to emotionally disturbed children. Levitt went one step further in his latest report by analyzing the results for various diagnostic groups. As shown in Table 10–2, the data tentatively suggest that the lowest therapeutic rates occurred for cases of delinquent and acting-out behaviors and that the highest improvement rates were for specific maladaptive symptoms like enuresis and school phobia.

In still another study, Levitt, Beiser, & Robertson (1959) reported on 192 clients who had had ten or more therapy sessions at the Institute for Juvenile Research in Chicago, one of the largest child-guidance centers in the country. The treated group and the defector controls were compared on 26 variables through psychological tests, objective facts about adjustment, parental ratings, self-ratings, and the clinical judgment of interviewers. There were no significant differences found between the two groups on any of these outcome variables. On the average, five years had elapsed since treatment, and the average age at the time of follow-up was 16. Thus, the findings of this long-range follow-up study support those of Levitt's other reviews, which dealt a serious blow to the contention that therapy facilitates recovery from neurotic and emotional disturbances in children.

Table 10–2.   A Summary of Studies on Selected Psychiatric Disorders of Children

Type of Disorder	Number of Studies	Much Improved		Partly Improved		Unimproved		Total	Overall (%) Improved
		(N)	(%)	(N)	(%)	(N)	(%)	(N)	
Neurosis	3	34	15	107	46	89	39	230	61
Acting-out	5	108	31	84	24	157	45	349	55
Special Symptoms	5	114	54	49	23	50	23	213	77
Psychosis	5	62	25	102	40	88	35	252	65
Mixed	6	138	20	337	48	222	32	697	68
Total	24[a]	456	26.2	679	39.0	606	34.8	1741	65.2

[a] The study of P. Annesley, Psychiatric illness in adolescence: presentation and prognosis. *Journal of Mental Science*, 1961, **107**, 268–78, contributed data to three classifications.

Source: E. Levitt. Psychotherapy with children: a further review. *Behavior Research Therapy*, 1963, **1**, 45–61. Reprinted with permission of Pergamon Press.

As might be expected, Levitt's findings have not gone unnoticed. The major objections to his studies have centered around the use of defectors as a control group and the use of inexperienced therapists. Critics (Eisenberg & Gruenberg, 1961; Heinicke, 1960; Hood-Williams, 1960; Ross & Lacey, 1961) contend that defectors are inappropriate as control baselines, because they may be less seriously disturbed youngsters who are able to respond in a therapeutically favorable way to the diagnostic assessment alone. Levitt (1963) readily admits the possibility of a "therapeutic diagnosis" issue; yet his findings were that interim improvement between diagnostic assessment and the offer of therapy was the sole explanation for termination of treatment in only 12% of the cases. Thus, it seems unlikely that the interim improvement in symptoms can adequately account for the overall improvement rate. Besides, the interim-improvement phenomenon should also have presumably existed in the case of the treated group, thereby balancing this factor in the defector group. Despite having compared the defector group and treated cases on 61 factors, including two clinical estimates relative to severity of disturbance, Levitt found few differences. Hence, although it can be said that the use of those who had been accepted for treatment but who dropped off the waiting list prior to actual treatment may result in the selection of a biased group, Levitt's study does not show this to be the case. Even if the two groups did differ in severity, this factor may not have been crucial. For, interestingly, Shepherd, Oppenheim, and Mitchell (1971) in their Buckinghamshire study found that treated children with the most severe initial problems showed the greatest rate of improvement in comparison with children treated for problems initially regarded as mild or moderate. The rate of improvement for troubled nontreated children was fairly constant at each level of severity. They also reported that about two-thirds of their troubled children showed improvement whether professionally treated or not.

As to the second major objection to Levitt's studies, Kessler (1966) noted that almost half the children in the 1959 study were seen by student therapists with less than one year's experience, and only one-third of the child patients were treated by therapists who had more than three years' experience. Granted that many inexperienced therapists use clinics to gain experience before entering private practice, it does not follow that the use of inexperienced therapists minimizes the prospect for a favorable therapeutic outcome. In fact, there is some evidence to suggest that inexperienced therapists achieve better results than do their more experienced colleagues, perhaps because of the greater enthusiasm of the former. Moreover, it may be that non-professional therapists can perform as well as professional therapists (Rioch, Elkes, Flint, Udansky, Newman, & Silber, 1963; Poser, 1966; Truax & Carkhuff, 1967). Besides, the use of relatively inexperienced therapists is typical of most other clinics.

There is still another problem that must be considered in evaluating the results of psychotherapy: the placebo effect, which in medicine refers to the observation that patients respond favorably when administered either sugar pills or a saline solution instead of an appropriate medication. Since the placebo effect is of a psychological nature, its role cannot be ignored in evaluating the outcomes of psychotherapy. This effect is regarded by some authorities as a nonspecific result of psychotherapy and as playing a possible role in the consistently high rates of psychotherapeutic improvement (Rosenthal & Frank, 1956). It is interesting to note, in this connection, that the majority of disturbed children improve regardless of age, sex, treatment setting, affiliation of the therapist, length of time spent in treatment, and whether or not they complete the treatment.

Others would argue that the efficacy of psychotherapy with children is limited to the placebo effect since the two-thirds improvement rate in therapy is about the same as the improvement rate resulting from the placebo effect in illnesses with emotional components. Basically, the placebo effect can take two forms: the use of suggestion or authority by the therapist and/or the attention, interest, and concern shown the child (Patterson, 1959). A genuinely rigorous experiment, as Ginott (1961) notes, requires a comparison of three groups to which subjects have been randomly assigned: (1) a therapy group, (2) a no-therapy group, and (3) a placebo group who have play sessions at the clinic but without a therapist. As Ginott (1961) contends, "Thus far, there is no evidence to indicate the superiority of play therapy over dancing lessons in the treatment of shyness nor its superiority over boxing lessons in the treatment of aggressiveness."

Spontaneous Remissions

Granted that the issue is still a hotly debated one, the evidence bearing on psychotherapeutic outcomes indicates that the effectiveness of expressive treatment procedures has not lived up to expectations. Yet, it is comforting to note that the majority of neurotic-seeming children do achieve a reasonably adequate adjustment regardless of whether or not they receive professional treatment. Thus, despite the child's defenses having failed and his having reached a low ebb, the odds are that he will not stick at this low point (White & Watt, 1973).

What factors are responsible for the spontaneous reduction of deviant behavior? Certainly, one factor that cannot be discounted is the placebo effect, mentioned above, for the child's behavior, especially as it reaches a low ebb, is apt to elicit attention, concern, and authoritative reassurance that the behavior will improve. Also, parents, teachers, and other agents in the child's environment often intervene by changing their own behavior, reducing stress on the child when they realize that the child is in a crisis state.

Alternative explanations employing learning theory constructs—such as aversive stimulation, extinction, positive reinforcement, and so forth—also enable us to account for spontaneous remissions in children. Aversive stimulation is most likely operative in cases where the untreated neurosis becomes so painful that the child himself actively seeks to improve his lot in life. Secondary gains no doubt play a reinforcing role in certain cases of neurosis, but "secondary pains" are also operative. As White & Watt (1973) assert, the neurotic adjustment is apt to be an unpleasant one that motivates the child to seek "a new balance of forces toward remission." The authors can readily recall school-phobic youngsters who, suffering from the unpleasant state of having nothing to do at home, willingly attempted a return to school despite their initial anxieties.

According to Eysenck (1963a, 1963b), spontaneous remissions can also be expected simply on the basis of extinction, since the presentation in everyday life of the conditioned stimulus that produces the troublesome behavior without the presentation of the reinforcing stimuli is likely to eliminate the maladaptive responses. Positive reinforcement for adaptive behavior following extinction, discrimination learning based on expectations related to cultural conceptions regarding appropriate behavior for one's developmental level, and nonsystematic desensitization also probably account for the elimination of maladaptive behaviors in untreated cases.

In addition to explanations based on the placebo effect and learning theory, evidence bearing on this issue of spontaneous recovery is forthcoming from the study of personality development in children. Such study has indicated the child's substantial ability to withstand environmental insult. The notion of the child as a delicate individual who must be protected from stresses, strains, and traumas and who must have exceptional amounts of "tender, loving care" is obviously distorted. The child not only possesses a substantial capacity for compensation and adjustment but also a remarkable capability for self repair when damage is inflicted (Anderson, 1948). Fortunately, the child is a durable creature. The authors, like many other teachers and clinicians recalling their experiences with children from seriously disturbed homes, have wondered why the children were as well adjusted as they were, in light of the environmental insult. This observation is not intended to deny the role of parental and social pathology in childhood disorders but is mentioned simply to illustrate the resiliency of the child's personality.

The findings presented on intervention efforts lend support to Redl's (1966) contention that we need new modes of treatment to cope with the new types of disturbances that have arisen. In large measure, youngsters have been referred to the psychiatric clinic even though they did not fit the classical model provided by the trinity of psychiatrist, psychologist, and social worker. It is little wonder that half of the clients come back, like the proverbial bad penny, to the agency initiating the referral. As those in charge of the daily management of disturbed children stress, we need services that are closer to the real-life situation of the children than the clinic model permits. Furthermore, we need new team members—the educational therapist, the public-health nurse, the pediatrician, the teacher—in addition to the traditional mental health specialists if we are to implement a more realistic approach to the problems presented by today's disturbed youth.

Conclusion

Because of the difficult methodological problems associated with research in this area (for example, using adequate control groups, equating therapies and therapists, increasing the sensitivity of the measuring instruments, locating former clients for follow-up study, estimating how much time should elapse between treatment and follow-up, controlling for placebo effect, and spontaneous cures), conclusive findings are hard to come by. Levitt in his reviews of traditional or psychoanalytically flavored treatment is quick to point out that his findings do not prove that psychotherapy with children is ineffective or useless. It is conceivable that the measuring procedures were not sensitive enough to detect changes stemming from treatment. Moreover, it should be remembered that some diagnostic groups (for example, children with specific problems) benefited more than other groups. It is also quite possible that some therapists are much more helpful than other therapists, as Ricks (1974) notes in his discussion of "supershrink."

Nonetheless, Levitt's large-scale studies clearly indicate that we cannot live on our laurels. We must seek alternatives to traditional treatment approaches for children's problems. We will now present a sampling of approaches that are drawing interest from mental-health specialists. Some of the approaches focus largely on individuals or small groups, while others emphasize more of a social systems approach. Then again, some approaches are medically oriented while others stress the importance of learning and environmental impacts. Many of these approaches take place in the natural environment of the child. There is an increasing belief that change is best effected by working through adults who are in position to deal with the child's problem when and where it occurs. With the exception of the behavior modification approach, and to some extent drug treatment, the outcomes of the approaches to be presented in the next section have not been carefully researched.

Recent Innovations

Behavior Therapy

Since modern psychology has been largely dominated by theories of learning, it is understandable that the most distinctive contribution made by psychologists to treatment efforts has come in the area of learning theory. In large measure the application of learning theory concepts to the modification of deviant behavior can be attributed to the increasing number of clinical psychologists since World War II, the emphasis on more sophisticated training in research methodology at the doctoral level, the questioning of the traditional methods of psychotherapy, and the growing dissatisfaction with the appropriateness of the medical model for extension to behavior disorders (Ullmann & Krasner, 1965). Through the efforts of Dollard & Miller (1950), Shoben (1949), and Mowrer (1950), psychodynamic views were recast in learning theory terms but, as Ullmann & Krasner (1965) assert, a new approach to *doing* therapy was not forthcoming, simply a new way of *talking about therapy*. Of the various learning theory approaches to therapy, behavior therapy is attracting the most attention today and is probably the most relevant to the treatment of childhood disorders.

Basically, behavior therapy refers to the systematic application of learning theory principles to the rational modification of deviant behavior (Franks, 1965). The term *behavior therapy* embraces not a specific technique but a variety of methods stemming from learning theory and focusing on the modification of deviant behavior. As such, it represents a meeting point for experimental and clinical psychology, fields that traditionally have been apart from each other.

While the roots of modifying behavior date back to the early Greeks, systematic attempts to produce changes as a consequence of manipulated environmental contingencies are a relatively recent phenomenon. Watson's classic study in 1920 on the development of a phobia in a very young child played a key role by demonstrating that the emotional response of the human infant can be conditioned to previously innocuous objects. Thus, although 11-month-old Albert originally showed no fear in response to the sight of a white rat, he displayed a conditioned fear response soon after the simultaneous pairing of a white rat and the striking of a steel bar. Moreover, this fear spread to other furry animals and to furry objects, such as beards and cotton wool. This conditioned fear response also tended to persist throughout the months that Albert was available for study (Watson & Raynor, 1920).

Four years later, another experiment demonstrated that it was possible to eliminate a child's phobia. Jones (1924), using 3-year-old Peter, showed that a fear response that had generalized could also be eliminated through the use of a conditioning process. After conducting research on several other pre schoolers, Jones concluded that direct conditioning and social imitation were effective means for eliminating fears. In that same year, Burnham (1924) published *The Normal Mind*, a book that anticipated techniques to be used by later behavior therapists.

Additional work in the treatment of tics, nailbiting, and stuttering (Dunlap, 1932) and fears (Jersild & Holmes, 1935) also contributed to both theory and practice. Mowrer & Mowrer's (1938) work on the conditioning of enuretics also represented a significant advance in the application of learning theory to children's disorders. But it was not until twenty years later that the next important step was made, when Wolpe (1958) formulated a systematic theory of neurosis and psychotherapy based on the principle of reciprocal inhibition (techniques designed to inhibit anxiety responses). Finally, in 1963, the journal *Behavior Research and Therapy* was established for those interested in behavior modification (Rachman, 1963).

Contrasts with Expressive Therapies. CURRENT VERSUS REMOTE CAUSES.   While both groups seek causes of behavior, the behaviorists search for the determinants of current maladaptive behavior by examining the child's present environmental circumstances whereas the psychoanalytically oriented delve into past events in the child's life. The behavorists are less concerned with the question, "How did he get that way?" than with the issue "What can we do to help him?" (Ross, 1974). Thus, one of the first areas of disagreement between expressive therapies and behavior therapies centers around the issue of current behavior or symptomatic treatment versus treatment of the underlying pathology. Psychoanalytically oriented therapists have traditionally shied away from the treatment of symptoms or current maladaptive behavior in accordance with the "symptom-underlying-disease medical model" discussed in Chapter 3. Accordingly, the psychoanalytically oriented view the behavior therapist as naïvely pragmatic. Relying on a hydraulic-energy analogy, the Freudians view the symptom as an outlet for a highly charged pent-up energy that must find relief in one form or another. Neurotic symptoms thus represent the manifestation of the central conflict. Hence the Freudians maintain that if one simply removes the current maladaptive behavior (for example, a reading disability) and not the underlying motivational forces, substitute symptoms can be expected. Moreover, according to the Freudian exposition, the therapist, by his attempts at symptomatic treatment, actually runs the risk of doing some further psychological damage to the patient by blocking energy release. It is not surprising, in light of this model, that the expression of feeling is considered a basic therapeutic ingredient in traditional forms of psychotherapy for both children and adults. In both Freudian and Rogerian therapies, the therapist is permissive since the tendencies toward self-realization or the biological urges will out inevitably, once provided with an accepting atmosphere which permits expression.

The learning theorists, on the other hand, view symptoms very differently. For Eysenck (1960), there is no neurosis underlying the symptom; there is just the symptom. As he boldly asserts, "Get rid of the symptom and you have eliminated the neurosis." In a similar, but somewhat milder vein, Franks (1965) adds:

> Even if we assume that the present symptom owes its origin to some past trauma, it need follow neither that the trauma is of direct concern to the

subject in the present nor that focusing attention upon the original traumatic situation inevitably must bring about the elimination of the present symptom. There is thus justification for concentrating on what is of concern, namely the symptom. It may be that it is not the original and long-past trauma which is still causing the present persisting symptom which is bringing about the emotional disturbance.

It is interesting to note that psychoanalytically oriented therapists do not conjecture as to the psychic damage that might ensue as a consequence of not treating symptoms, for example, enuresis. In the behavior therapy approach, there is thus no search for relatively autonomous internal agents and processes in the form of dammed-up energy, complexes, unconscious psychic forces, free-floating libidos, or other hypothetical entities (Bandura & Walters, 1963). The learning theorist objects that such hypothetical conflicts are not directly subject to manipulation and, therefore, cannot play a major role in behavior modification. According to learning theory, there is little justifiable basis for the notion of symptom substitution from either a theoretical or an experimental standpoint. The behaviorist views the symptom as a dominant response that has been learned in relation to a specific stimulus situation. If this response or symptom is removed, the next most dominant response in the hierarchy is apt to occur. The behaviorist admits that the response obtained after behavioristic treatment may on occasion be a maladaptive one, but he does not regard the production of another undesirable behavior as inevitable or as symptom substitution in the Freudian sense of the term.

What would the behavior therapist do in the event that another maladaptive behavior occurred after treatment? He would continue to eliminate such responses from the behavior repertoire until adaptive behaviors occur. Contrary to widespread opinion, there is little if any evidence to substantiate the notion of symptom substitution (Baker, 1969; Hampe, Noble, Miller, & Barrett, 1973; O'Leary & Wilson, 1975). It seems more reasonable to speak of behavior substitution than symptom substitution.

It is evident from the above that the behavior therapist makes an explicit attempt to produce new behavior in his client. Indeed, the modification of behavior is the central target of treatment. The nondirective therapist, on the other hand, never explicitly encourages his client toward certain courses of new behavior; he assumes that the individual will choose the right behavior or make the best decision once his internal growth forces have been released. Psychoanalytically oriented therapists are likewise reluctant to steer the client toward new modes of behavior.

CONTROL VERSUS SELF-DIRECTION.   This brings us to another difference between the two approaches. In comparison with traditional approaches, behavior therapy represents a directive and manipulative approach. Expressive therapies, conversely, seek to treat the client without influencing him, by merely relieving the disabling psychic impairment (such as anxiety) and allowing him to find his own solution.

Certain points should be noted as being germane to the manipulation versus the understanding issue. First, all therapists, regardless of orientation, most likely exert some influence on the client and his future actions. Thus, differences in the degree of manipulation between these two approaches may not be as great as initially suspected. There is, indeed, sufficient evidence to document the subtle influence of therapist manipulation in dynamic treatment approaches (Bandura, 1961; Greenspoon, 1962). Hence, if objection is to be voiced, it must not be focused on the issue of manipulation per se. The basic moral question is not whether the behavior of others will be controlled but by whom, by what means, and for what ends (for example, conformity versus self-direction). Moreover, it would seem that some control, especially as it is oriented toward the well-being of both the individual and society, is necessary and desirable. The use of manipulation, ironically enough, enables the client to assume more flexible behaviors and thereby achieve greater individual self-determination by freeing him from present rigid and maladaptive behaviors. Common to contrary belief, behavior modification can not only support a humanistic philosophy, but do a better job of accomplishing humanistic goals. Secondly, it is the psychologist's and counselor's job to change students. If students are unchanged following treatment, then the therapist has failed. If the specialist's job is to change behavior, then he should use the most effective means to accomplish the objectives of treatment. In many cases, the student can be involved in setting the goals, means, and techniques. Third, while the behavioristic approach may be designed as manipulative, it is basically in keeping with the American tradition of achieving results in the most direct way. Ruesch & Bateson (1951) note that things typically have to be done fast in America and that therapy is no exception to the rule.

RELATIONSHIP, EMOTIONAL RELEASE, AND INSIGHT. Another point of disagreement involves the role of the therapeutic relationship and transference. The evocative therapies, which tend to sanctify the therapist-client relationship, customarily devote considerable attention to such factors as rapport, understanding, acceptance, permissiveness, insight, emphasis on feelings, and at times the transference relationship. The procedures and objectives of behavior therapy, on the other hand, are such that these factors are given less attention, primarily because they are not regarded as essential prerequisites for successful therapy (Franks, 1965). The induction of cognitive contingencies may well be beneficial in behavioristic treatment (Peterson & London, 1965), but insight per se is not seen as a basic ingredient. It may be, as Bandura & Walters (1963) suggest, that insight is an outcome of the therapeutic process rather than an essential cause of successful treatment. As a consequence of its deemphasis on insight as a therapeutic ingredient, behavior therapy may be better suited to a wider child clientele than are the more conventional therapies. As Franks (1965) writes:

> Unlike much of psychoanalytically oriented therapy, a behavior therapy program need not be restricted to the more sophisticated members of the

society. It usually can be adapted to those who are intellectually, emotionally, or culturally at a disadvantage or whose knowledge of the therapist's language is limited.

Other evocative therapies would likewise seem inappropriate to children of low intelligence and/or of lower cultural standing in that the emphasis on permissiveness and/or the achievement of insight are too sociologically foreign to the culturally disadvantaged and to those of less than normal intelligence. Whereas the expressive therapies, with their emphasis on insight and self-knowledge, appeal to a more privileged and educated population, they are not appealing to most deprived people (Riessman, 1962). The mechanical and gadgetry aspects, together with the more directive atmosphere of behavior treatment, may lead to a more substantial initial gratification and therefore to greater motivation for therapy on the deprived youngster's part.

RESEARCH ORIENTATION.   A fourth difference lies in the evaluation of treatment outcomes. The behaviorists tend to emphasize evaluative strategies (data gathering, reliable observation, establishment of baselines, etc.) that publicly validate the effectiveness of intervention procedures. Traditional or evocative therapists have, on the other hand, spent less time evaluating outcomes of their work, with the result that they are in a less advantageous position to change their procedures if the intervention is unsuccessful. To a large degree, the criterion used by traditional therapists seems to be a subjective one of inner certitude.

Evaluation.   To date, there has been little experimental validation of the use of behavior therapy with children. The case-study approach, in which each child serves as his own control, has constituted the main avenue of exploration and assessment. Because there is no untreated control group, no one knows for certain whether the problem would disappear or improve without treatment. Then again, there is the problem of the placebo effect. Moreover, as Ross (1974) notes, the effectiveness of any treatment approach cannot be established until systematic follow-up studies establish the stability of improvements. The few follow-up studies available do indicate that treatment effects may be maintained up to a year later (Baker, 1969: Nolan, Mattis, & Holliday, 1970). In one of the largest follow-up studies, Lovaas, Koegel, Simmons, & Long (1973) studied autistic youngsters two years after treatment. While all benefited in varying degrees during treatment, large differences were evident upon follow-up depending upon the contingencies in the child's environment. If the child went to an institution where the contingencies were different following behavior therapy, the constructive behavior deteriorated. On the other hand, children who remained at home where their parents continued in the use of contingency management continued to improve. The problem of generalization over time, across situations, and across behaviors has proved a difficult one. Indeed, most investigators in the field of behavior modification have failed to find generalization when they assess the behavior of children in treatment and nontreatment settings (Russell, 1974). The lack of transfer strongly indicates the need for greater attention to the problem of transfer. Generalization cannot be left to chance. Rarely are we content to restrict behavioral changes to the treatment setting. Instead we want the desirable changes to carry over from one classroom to another, from the correctional school to life in the community, or from the therapist's office to the home. Therapists, educators, and parents must program for generalization or transfer.[3] In one project, the authors were able to achieve transfer of socially appropriate behaviors learned in a resource room to the regular classroom through the use of a passport—a form of educational or behavior contract—that called for the reinforcement of target behaviors in both settings. Children were not accepted for resource room help unless the regular class teacher agreed to reinforce desired behaviors and weaken undesired behaviors in her classroom. Unfortunately, the criterion of generalization has received low priority in research efforts and the issue of long-term effectiveness has only begun to receive the attention it deserves (Hanley, 1970; Kazdin & Bootzin, 1973).

In addition to the relative absence of data on generalization, there is the lack of any definitive experimental research comparing the effectiveness of behavior therapy with other psychotherapeutic approaches involving children with different kinds of problems. Thus, at this time we cannot state with any degree of appreciable certitude that behavior therapy is superior to other approaches for children with varying conditions.

Finally, there is reason to be concerned about the nonspecific placebo effect as a factor in behavior therapy's power. A recent review by Russell (1974) indicates that much of the success of behavior therapy arises from the placebo effect ("suggestion," "hope," "faith," "concern," and "expectation"). The placebo problem is not restricted to behavior therapy. As noted earlier, it may be a potent factor in all intervention procedures when a client is in trouble and seeks relief from a difficult problem. What is distinctive about behavior therapy is its open and willing attempt to measure and control for its effects. Thus, more definitive rigorous experimentation concerning the role played by placebo effects will have to be carried out before the power of specific behavior modifications is clearly known.

While many problems remain with regard to implementation in natural settings (Reppucci & Saunders, 1974), the authors suspect that behavior therapy will register its greatest success in disorders due primarily to faulty learning and in disorders that involve specific symptomatology to be overcome. Although conclusive judgments would be premature, the results to date have been sufficiently encouraging to warrant continued investigations and practice in this area. The absence of demonstrated effectiveness of the evocative therapies, coupled with the shortage of trained mental-health specialists, would seem to leave us little other choice. Indeed, we can ill afford to ignore what appears to be a promising intervention approach. Increased

---

3. For suggestions on the programming of transfer, see Kazdin, 1975.

Table 10–3.   A Behavioral Contract

Privileges	*Responsibilities*
General In exchange for the privilege of remaining together and preserving some semblance of family integrity, Mr. and Mrs. Bremer and Candy all agree to	
	concentrate on positively reinforcing each other's behavior while diminishing the present overemphasis upon the faults of the others.
Specific In exchange for the privilege of riding the bus directly from school into town after school on school days	Candy agrees to phone her father by 4:00 P.M. to tell him that she is all right and to return home by 5:15 P.M.
In exchange for the privilege of going out at 7:00 P.M. on one weekend evening without having to account for her whereabouts	Candy must maintain a weekly average of "B" in the academic ratings of all of her classes and must return home by 11:30 P.M.
In exchange for the privilege of going out a second weekend night	Candy must tell her parents by 6:00 P.M. of her destination and her companion, and must return home by 11:30 P.M.
In exchange for the privilege of going out between 11:00 A.M. and 5:15 P.M. Saturdays, Sundays, and holidays	Candy agrees to have completed all household chores *before* leaving and to telephone her parents once during the time she is out to tell them that she is all right.
In exchange for the privilege of having Candy complete household chores and maintain her curfew	Mr. and Mrs. Bremer agree to pay Candy $1.50 on the morning following days on which the money is earned.
Bonuses and Sanctions If Candy is 1–10 minutes late	she must come in the same amount of time earlier the following day, but she does not forfeit her money for the day.
If Candy is 11–30 minutes late	she must come in 22–60 minutes earlier the following day and does forfeit her money for the day.

Table 10–3 continued

Privileges	Responsibilities
Bonuses and Sanctions	
If Candy is 31–60 minutes late	she loses the privilege of going out the following day and does forfeit her money for the day.
For each half hour of tardiness over one hour, Candy	loses her privilege of going out and her money for one additional day.
Candy may go out on Sunday evenings from 7:00 to 9:30 P.M. and either Monday or Thursday evening	if she abides by all the terms of this contract from Sunday through Saturday with a total tardiness not exceeding 30 minutes, which must have been made up as above.
Candy may add a total of two hours divided among one to three curfews	if she abides by all the terms of this contract for two weeks with a total tardiness not exceeding 30 minutes, which must have been made up as above, and if she requests permission to use this additional time by 9:00 P.M.

Monitoring

Mr. and Mrs. Bremer agree to keep written records of the hours of Candy's leaving and coming home and of the completion of her chores.
Candy agrees to furnish her parents with a school monitoring card each Friday at dinner.

extension of this approach to groups and the development of a core of psychotechnicians could prove productive means of tackling the nation's foremost health problem on a larger scale by providing more treatment services in close proximity to the child's life setting.

Many mental-health workers are unwilling to substitute the modification of behavior for personality reorganization as a goal of treatment. Controversy regarding the goals of therapy will probably rage for some time to come. Behavior modification is a less ambitious objective than that of other therapy approaches, which seem to undertake a total rebuilding of the individual. Yet, as Lewis (1965) asserts:

> If we cannot aspire to reconstruction of personality that will have long range beneficial effects, we can modify disturbing behavior in specific ways in present social contexts. This more modest aspiration may not only be

more realistic, but it may be all that is required of the child-helping professions in a society that is relatively open and provides a variety of opportunity systems in which a child can reconcile his personal needs with society's expectations of him.

Extensions of Behavior Modification.   Among the more interesting extensions of behavior modification are the use of group approaches (Rose, 1972), behavioral contracting (Stuart, 1971), modeling and role playing (Sarason & Sarason, 1974), self-management (Lovitt, 1973), and punishment (Lovaas et al., 1973). The technique of behavioral contracting with a delinquent girl is illustrated in Table 10–3 (Stuart, 1971). The use of role playing, a form of modeling which permits observation of the details and subtleties of social roles, is illustrated in the transcript on avoiding fights.

The Avoidance of a Fight

Introduction. All of you guys have a sense of honor and pride. There are times in everybody's lives when your honor is at stake, and you have to take some action to protect it. For example, you might fight, or quit a job, or make a protest. Some people, however, seem to get into situations where they feel their honor is at stake more often than others. A number of guys here seem to do this—they keep getting themselves into situations where they feel they have to fight or do something else (a dare) to protect their honor. Most people learn ways to avoid getting into such situations when it really isn't necessary. For example, most adults know how to argue with each other without having it lead to a fight. If an argument does lead to a fight, it's usually because the two people start criticizing or insulting each other more and more, until they feel their honor is at stake, then it's too late to back out of it so they fight. The way adults avoid this is by thinking ahead, and controlling themselves. They are willing to accept some criticism and to ease off on their criticism of the other person when they see things getting hot. This is sometimes difficult to learn, but it is important, and through practice you can do it.

Scene a. We'll do two scenes today. In each case we will first show you the wrong way to handle the situation, and then show you a better way. We'll then have you guys do it the right way. The first scene takes place Friday afternoon as two guys are walking home from school.

BILL: What're you doing, George, trying to make it through the easy way?

GEORGE: (a little angry) What do you mean?

BILL: Trying to convince the teacher you're not as stupid as you look, huh?

GEORGE: Just what the hell are you getting at?

BILL: Now don't start playing innocent. We all saw you brown-nosing the teacher after class.

GEORGE: I don't kiss up to nobody. I was just trying to get something clear.

BILL: Sure you were. That's the third time this week. Man, have you turned into a fink.

GEORGE: What the hell's bugging you? Did Sheila turn you down again?

BILL: Nothing's bugging me and leave Sheila out of it. I just wanted to tell you you look like a real ass running up to the teacher like that. And we don't need any punks like you trying to cut our throats.

GEORGE: Talking about asses, you sure made a fool out of yourself in class today. We haven't had such a good laugh in a long time. You're almost as stupid as your fat sister.

BILL: Shut up.

GEORGE: That was the dumbest comment I ever heard.

BILL: Just one more word out of you, and . . .

GEORGE: The teacher says, "What's an equilateral triangle?" and you said—

BILL: You bastard. (hits him)

Discussion points. 1. Note how Bill starts out with a chip on his shoulder and tries to get George mad. 2 George then tries to get even until they both get so mad they have it out.

Scene b. The scene takes place on Friday afternoon as two guys are walking home from school.

BILL: What're you doing, George, trying to make it through the easy way?

GEORGE: What do you mean?

BILL: Trying to convince the teacher you're not as stupid as you look, huh?

GEORGE: What's bothering you? So far, you aren't getting through.

BILL: Now don't play innocent. Today was the third time this week you talked to the teacher after class. If that isn't brown-nosing, I don't know what is.

GEORGE: Oh that. Well, you know, I've been having a lot of trouble in geometry. So I went up and asked the teacher a couple questions about last night's assignments.

BILL: And at the same time you were trying to get a little pull with him.

GEORGE: You know damn well I don't brown-nose anyone. As it is, I'll be lucky to make a C in that class. Look, if you were having trouble in that class, wouldn't you do the same thing?

BILL: Are you nuts? I'd never do anything like that.

GEORGE: Well, it's better than flunking the course. And if people don't like it, that's just tough.

BILL: I still think it looks real funny.

GEORGE: Yeah, but what can you do?

BILL: I don't know but I don't think I'd do that.

GEORGE: Well, maybe you don't mind flunking. I gotta get home. See you.

BILL: Yeah, see you around.

Discussion points. 1. What is wrong with scene a? What are things that *might* happen? 2. Generalize to other areas of possible confrontation (Sarason & Ganzer, 1971).

Family Therapy

Advocates of family therapy involve the family along with the child in the context of treatment in the daily natural environment. There are at least two assumptions behind this approach—the belief that noxious family relationships cause emotional problems in children and the belief that the emotional problems of any one family member are determined and kept alive by the problems of the relationships within the family. Hence, the mother, father, and children must be treated as a total unit. In the majority of cases, the child is presumed to be reacting to problems in the family. In brief, for those who ascribe to faulty family relationships a primary causal role in the emotional problems of children, family therapy would be the treatment of first choice. This treatment would seek to alter the underlying conflicts in the family.

The job of the family therapist is to discern how the family functions, how it communicates, how it resolves conflicts, and how, if at all, it forms suballiances (Engel, 1972). To achieve these ends, the therapist (or therapists) takes on the role of a participant observer in the family. In addition to observing and articulating what is going on, the therapist may also serve as a model. Filming the family in action and viewing through one-way mirrors might be among the approaches used to help family members to see how central themes in the family (such as scapegoating a delinquent or underachieving son) affect one another and impede healthy communication in the group. Minuchin and his colleagues' classic (1967) work with slum families, Ackerman's psychoanalytic approach (1958), Bell's emphasis on family roles (1961), and Haley's reliance upon communication networks reflect the great variability among some of the better-known family therapists.

As interest in the use of nonprofessionals as a resource in dealing with mental-health problems of children began to flourish many family therapists sought to use parents as therapists. Since parents are the most important individuals in a child's life, excluding them wastes a valuable resource (Schreibman & Koegel, 1975). Not only can parents learn to be therapists, but in many cases their participation is essential. As psychology moved out of the therapist's office into the child's natural environment, working through parents became inevitable. In this section, we sample three popular approaches to providing a significant role for parents as therapists.

Filial Therapy: A Reflective Approach. Filial therapy is a variant of client-centered or nondirective play therapy developed by Bernard Guerney (1964). Parents are taught client-centered play therapy in much the same way that might occur in the training of psychologists. For example, if a child came home from school upset and said that the teacher had spanked him, the parents might make any of the following reflective comments (Ginott, 1965).

It must have been terribly embarrassing.

It must have made you furious.

You must have hated your teacher at that moment.

It must have hurt your feelings terribly.

Parent training takes place with the children in the home and in the clinic under the supervision of a psychologist. From six to eight mothers are trained in groups to develop reflective empathic skills during weekly half-hour play therapy sessions with their own children. After the training sessions, parents are given corrective feedback in group meetings by a therapist. For example, some parents simply restate the content of the child's statement rather than clarify the child's feelings. Besides benefiting the child directly, filial therapy attempts to bring to light parental problems with their children so that these can be worked on during the group discussions. Preliminary research indicates that mothers receiving this training exhibit more reflective statements, fewer directive statements, and increased empathy and greater involvement in their play sessions (Stover & Guerney, 1967; Stover, Guerney, & O'Connell, 1971). The research thus suggests that parents' behavior became more like that of the client-centered therapist. In addition, children of trained parents increased their verbalization of negative feelings toward their parents, while control children did not.

At this time we do not know whether this approach is suitable for parents of varying personality and socioeconomic makeups, or for children with different kinds of problems. There is also the realistic concern of generalizability —namely, do the gains made in therapy sessions carry over to the parents' daily interactions with their children. It might well be that some reflective techniques are too vaguely defined or applied to have much practical importance. Parents may have to focus on a particular problem in order to change it (Tavormina, 1974). Finally, assuming that parental behaviors do carry over, we must ask whether the *child's* mental health is improved as a consequence.

Behavioral Approaches. Training parents in behavior modification is a young but active field. Behavior modification techniques held promise partly because they could be learned in a relatively short period of time. Parents have used behavior modification techniques to modify specific behavior of children who were diagnosed as brain damaged (Salzinger, Feldman, & Portnoy, 1970), autistic (Schreibman & Koegel, 1975; Nordquist & Wahler, 1973), school phobic (Patterson, 1965), predelinquent (Kifer, Lewis, Green, & Phillips, 1974), and retarded (Neisworth & Smith, 1973). Parents have also served as therapists in treating aggressive behaviors (Patterson, 1973), sibling fighting (O'Leary, O'Leary, & Becker, 1967), tantrum behavior (Williams, 1959), withdrawal behavior (Allen, Hart, Buell, Harris, & Wolfe, 1965), enuresis (Bucher, 1972) as well as other everyday home problems (Hall, Axelrod, Tyler, Grief, Jones, & Robertson, 1972). Training has been given to a wide variety of parents and usually follows one or more of three approaches—educational group settings, individual consultations, or controlled learning environments.

The study by Hawkins, Peterson, Schweid, & Bijou (1966) illustrates how individual guidance can be given in the home. The focus of this study was on the hyperactive behavior of a preschool child of borderline intelligence. There were five phases:

1. A baseline period during which observations were made of mother-child interactions.

2. A first experimental period, during which the mother was given training in certain behavior modification techniques.

3. A second baseline period, during which the mother was told to behave toward the child as she had previously.

4. A second experimental period similar to the first experimental period.

5. A follow-up, 24 days after the last experimental period.

One of the first steps in the behavior therapy approach is the delineation of the specific disruptive target behaviors. In this case, the child's objectionable activities consisted in (1) biting his shirt or arm, (2) sticking out his tongue, (3) kicking or hitting himself, others, or objects, (4) using derogatory language, (5) removing or threatening to remove his clothes, (6) saying "No!" to requests made of him, (7) threatening to damage persons or objects, (8) throwing objects, and (9) pushing his sister.

After observing and recording the mother and child during the 16 baseline sessions (Phase 1), the investigators told the mother the nine objectionable target behaviors. She was shown three signals that were to be used by the experimenter to indicate how she should behave toward the boy (Phase 2). Upon Signal A, she was to tell him to stop whatever obnoxious behavior he happened to be engaging in at the time. Upon Signal B, she was to isolate him by placing him in his room and locking the door. Upon Signal C, she was to reward his behavior immediately through the use of praise, attention, and physical affection.

During this second phase, Signal A was given every time the child manifested one of the nine target behaviors. If he persisted, Signal B was given.

When placed in the time-out room, he had to remain there for a minimum of five minutes and quiet down for a short period of time before being let out. The room was devoid of toys and other stimulating objects, so that placement there would not constitute a reward for misbehavior. Signal C was used whenever he showed desirable behaviors.

After 6 experimental sessions, the child's objectionable behaviors decreased to a stable level (see Figure 10–1). At this time, the mother was told to interact with him as she had prior to the training sessions (Phase 3). The experimenter observed the mother but did not cue her. After this second baseline period of 14 sessions, the second experimental period of 6 sessions was begun. Finally, 24 days later, during which time the mother could use any techniques she chose, three posttreatment checks were made. As shown in Figure 10–1, the rate of objectionable behavior following parent training was about one-sixth of what it had been previously.

Training parents or potential therapists in behavior modification principles seems to have several advantages (O'Dell, 1974):

1. Many parents can learn the principles of behavior modification and carry out treatment programs.

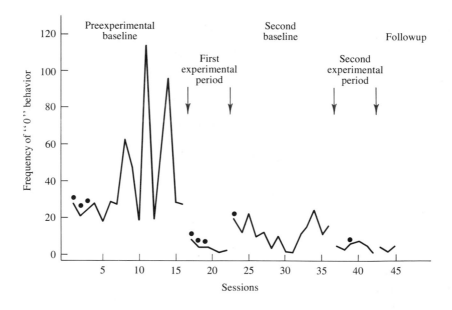

Figure 10–1. Number of 10-second intervals, per 1-hour session, in which O (objectionable) behavior occurred. (*Source*: R. Hawkins, R. Peterson, E. Schweid, & S. Bijou. Behavior therapy in the home: amelioration of problem parent-child relations with the parent in a therapeutic role. *Journal of Experimental Child Psychology*, 1966, **4,** 99–107.)

2. Many people can be trained at one time.

3. Only a short period of training is required.

4. A minimum of professional staff can have a broader impact on mental health than is true in one-to-one treatment models.

5. The behavior modification model appeals to parents because it does not assume "sick" behavior like the medical model.

6. Many childhood problems consist of rather well-defined behaviors that lend themselves to behavior modification techniques.

7. These techniques are based on empirically derived theory.

8. These techniques can be used to deal with problems in the child's natural setting.

Dreikurs's Family Council.   Dreikurs, a proponent of democratic family practices, recommends a family council at which parents sit down with their children as equal partners to arrive at solutions to family problems. Dreikurs believes that the family council is the best way to resolve everyday problems. Family meetings are to be characterized by mutual respect, trust, equality, and cooperation. Each member of the family old enough to voice an opinion should be included and permitted to vote. Each meeting has a chairman and a secretary. Officers rotate so that each member will share the privileges and responsibilities of office. A specific time should be set aside for the council to meet each week.

The family meeting seeks to find solutions to family problems rather than to express gripes. Whoever complains is expected to present a suggested solution. The family council's primary purpose is to provide a forum where every member is given the chance to present his views with respect to any household matter. Initially, the meetings could involve such things as planning for family fun, evening snacks, TV viewing, household chores, respect for privacy, use of the telephone, and so forth. Certain topics such as financial matters can be reserved for parental discussion.

Agreement on issues will not always be reached and a decision may be postponed until the next meeting. Putting a decision off is not necessarily undesirable, for a delayed decision can give family members time to sort out their feelings and ideas. Once a decision is reached, any changes have to wait until the next session. Children should be allowed to accept the responsibility for their decisions. For instance, one 9 year old decided to grow a tomato garden as a money-making venture. Because the parents knew that the area selected for the garden was ill-suited for growing purposes, they easily could have squelched the idea. Instead, the child's suggestion was treated with dignified consideration. Although the entire crop was lost to tomato bugs, the experience did provide the youngster with an opportunity to analyze and to evaluate his thinking about real life concerns (Dreikurs, Grunwald, & Pepper, 1971).

If the child fails to live up to his responsibilities, the parent may do likewise. Thus, if the child does not wash the dishes, then the mother does not prepare the next meal. Before long, the child soon learns that everyone has responsibilities that must be met and that their own well-being is enhanced by what they contribute as well as by what they receive (Dreikurs & Grey, 1970).

In sum, the family council offers an atmosphere for democratic living in which the child is given practice in making decisions, taking responsibility, being a constructive family member. A well-functioning household demands cooperation from others. No one person should have to shoulder full responsibility.

While there has been no research-based evaluation of this approach, it does seem a useful tool for those parents who value the democratic process and who are reasonably well educated, intact emotionally.

Many parents, however, will be apprehensive about having open and free discussions, especially if there are enough children so that the parents can be outvoted. The family council is probably less well suited to more autocratically run homes and to lower-class families. Finally, this approach is also apt to be ignored by solicitous parents who are too frightened to permit their children to experience the consequences of their decisions. For those families who can feel comfortable with this approach, it does seem to provide an effective means of teaching children how to assess and cope with the problems of family life.

Evaluation of Treatment by Parents.   Using parents as therapists with their own children can have several advantages. (1) If the training is carried out in the home, the problem of transferring the gains made in the therapist's office to the child's natural setting is diminished. (2) Once trained, parents can provide treatment throughout the day. (3) The rest of the family can benefit. For example, the delinquency rate of the rest of the family may decrease (Horn, 1975). (4) The number of available therapists is automatically increased by recruiting the services of parents. (5) Treatment costs incurred by the family are decreased.

Certain problems still have to be resolved if the potential of parents as therapists is to be realized. (1) There is a need to compare reflective and behavioral approaches with regard to both cost and effectiveness for different parent populations and child problems (Tavormina, 1974). (2) The majority of parent training models are inefficient in terms of the need for services. Modeling procedures coupled with educational television may have more potential than current one-to-one or small-group models. (3) We must devise ways to increase the probability that the gains made during treatment carry over to other settings. (4) Parent variability remains a major problem. Further study is needed to confirm preliminary findings that approaches emphasizing direct teaching are more effective with a wider clientele than approaches emphasizing verbal learning (O'Dell, 1974). (5) Many parents are either unable or unwilling to commit themselves to the extent needed to resolve their children's problems.

Reality Therapy

One approach to therapy that has attracted wide attention from practitioners in the schools is that of William Glasser's reality therapy. Reality therapy derives its name from its emphasis on behavior in the real world rather than a client's subjective interpretation of his feelings and his thoughts (Barr, 1974).

Basic Concepts.   Responsibility is a central concept in reality therapy. Responsible behavior leads to happiness. And a person is happy or unhappy because of his own decisions, not because of the conditions in which he finds himself. No one forced him to steal money, to curse his teacher, to take drugs, or to neglect class assignments. He chose these actions and only he can and must assume responsibility for those choices. Man is accountable for his actions.

For Glasser, responsible behavior means that man meets his two fundamental needs—a sense of involvement and a feeling of self worth—in a way that does not hurt others. If a person feels involved, he feels that others care, that he matters to others, and that he, in turn, cares about others. The individual, in short, is able to love and be loved. A person must do more than become involved with others, however. He must regard himself as successful or he will experience unbearable pain. He must feel worthwhile to himself and to others.

The following notions are central to the implementation of reality therapy as it relates to classroom practice:

1. The teacher becomes involved with the student. Glasser asks the teacher to spend 30 seconds a day relating to the difficult student at a time when the student is engaging in acceptable behavior.

2. The child is asked, "What are you doing?"

3. The child is asked, "Is what you're doing helping you, me, or the class?" In essence, the child is asked to make a value judgment about his own behavior. If the child believes that his behavior is all right, there is little hope of changing the child at that time. The child will then have to suffer the natural consequences of his refusal to change his behavior.

4. If the student says, "No, what I am doing is not helping," then the teacher assists the child in formulating a plan aimed at some desired goal. Making plans is frequently the most time-consuming part of reality therapy. To insure success, the contract usually calls for small steps at a time. To try to accomplish too much too quickly increases the probability of failure. The experienced teacher will not agree to an unrealistic plan. The plan is written down and both copies are signed. The client keeps one and the teacher keeps the other.

5. Once the plan is formulated, the student is asked to commit himself to that plan. "Are you willing to contend with the hassle that this plan might cause?" "Are you going to follow through?" If the student's answer is affirm-

ative, a second contract stating his commitment is then prepared, photo-copied, and signed.

6. If the plan succeeds, there will be a change in behavior. If the plan fails, the student is asked not to make excuses. Excuses are not accepted, for they only promote irresponsible behavior. If the plan fails, a new one is drawn up. The teacher simply falls back on the basic axiom of reality therapy, namely, that an individual is capable of making conscious decisions regarding his behavior, and starts anew.

7. The teacher never punishes the child, for punishment disrupts the warm personal relationship between them and produces a sense of failure on the child's part.

8. The question "why" is never asked. There is no attempt to provide insight. The focus is on behavior—the "what," "when," "where," and "how." Exploring the "why" tends to elicit excuses for irresponsible behavior.

9. The focus is on the present and not on the past. The past is over and unchangeable (Barr, 1974). History cannot be rewritten. Identifying the origins of one's problems, according to this theory, is not only unnecessary, it can be harmful. The more one dwells upon the past (e.g., "My mother never really loved me"; "I grew up in a ghetto"), the sorrier one feels for himself. Spending one's energies in self-pity detracts from constructive solutions to one's problems. Nurturing one's wounded pride is too expensive a luxury.

Class Meetings.   Among the most innovative approaches advocated by Glasser is the use of class meetings led by the teacher to solve behavioral and educational problems (Glasser, 1969). The students sit in a circle and each youngster has a turn to speak. If the student has nothing he wants to say, he has the right to pass. If a student does not want to take part in the meetings, he can sit apart from the circle.

There are three types of meetings, all of which are designed to provide the student with a feeling of involvement and success. In the *open-ended meetings,* the children discuss thought-provoking questions related to their lives or the curriculum. These meetings are designed to promote educational relevance by dealing with intellectually important topics. Factual answers are not sought; instead the teacher attempts to stimulate the children to think. The open-ended meetings are the easiest ones to conduct and should be held daily if possible. A second type of meeting is the *social-problem-solving meeting,* which attempts to solve social problems of the school itself. While school often encourages students to apply their intelligence to the solution of mathematical problems, for example, it rarely provides students with opportunities to apply their intelligence to the solution of personal and social problems confronting them. Given little help, students tend to evade problems, to lie their way out of various predicaments, to rely on others for solutions, or to give up. None of these courses of action prepares a person for dealing with present or later difficulties in life. The social-problem-solving meeting can help children to learn more effective ways of coping with dilemmas. Glasser offers the following guidelines for this kind of meeting: (1) Either students or teacher may bring up problems for discussion. (2) The discussion is always to be directed toward solving the problem. The solution should not include punishment or assessment of blame. The purpose is always positive, to wit, to find better ways to behave. (3) Meetings should be held in a circle and led by the teacher. These meetings should not be held nearly as often as open-ended meetings and they will last from 10 to 30 minutes for children in the lower grades and from 30 to 45 minutes for older students. Pertinence of the problems and regularity of the meetings are more important than duration of the meetings, however. Sample topics might include truancy, use of drugs, loneliness, extortion, stealing, streaking, class bullies, and respect for others. It should be explained that the purpose of the meeting is to find solutions and not who is at fault. Because it generally takes about 30 class meetings before teachers feel comfortable and become effective as discussion leaders, they should not become discouraged if the early meetings do not always live up to expectations. It is also a good idea for teachers who are friends to team up during the early stages of group meetings.

The *educational diagnostic meetings* help teachers to achieve a quick evaluation of whether or not they have reached their educational objectives. These meetings are closely related to topics that the class is currently studying. Because it is difficult for teachers, given their own blind spots, to see clearly what their classes know, it can be helpful for teachers to exchange classes.

All three of the meetings discussed above can help to bridge the gap between school and everyday life. Moreover, children gain the important belief that they can shape their own destinies and that they are a vital part of their world. Also, the child develops confidence as a result of stating his opinion before a group.

Evaluation of Reality Therapy.   Reality therapy is a straightforward approach that has considerable appeal. Its stress on the development of personal responsibility, its concern with the child's problems in the real world, its teaching children to use their brains in the solution of social problems, and its reliance on logic and behavior rather than insight will earn this approach high marks from practitioners. Like any approach, it is not without its limitations, however. Glasser's insistence on a firm commitment, for example, would seemingly limit the number of students with whom this approach can be used. Many of the troublesome students find their misbehavior very rewarding and are, therefore, not inclined to make a commitment to change their ways. Others have already "tuned out" because of early failure experiences. Commitment does not come easily for such youngsters, for they have reached the point where they no longer care.

As valuable as class meetings can be, many teachers feel uncomfortable in conducting class meetings. Some teachers are too authoritarian to use this approach effectively. Others simply lack the skills required in getting meetings underway and in keeping them going in meaningful ways. Still others are afraid that class meetings will give the student too much power and that they will then "take over" the class. Thus, for a variety of reasons, teachers will need training and encouragement if they are to use class meetings to best advantage, if at all.

Reality Therapy and Behavior Therapy Compared. The reader has probably noticed some similarities between Glasser's reality therapy and behavior modification. Features common to both approaches include an emphasis on (1) behavior (the what, where, when, and how but not the why); (2) the current functioning of the child rather than his past history; (3) the development of greater responsibility in the child; (4) the use of teacher or therapist directiveness; (5) the use of small steps in facilitating growth; (6) teacher encouragement of appropriate student behavior (the "catch them being good" slogan); and (7) the use of plans or contracts. There are certain differences between the two schools of thought, however. Among the more salient differences are Glasser's (1) stated categorical opposition to the use of punishment (there is a greater divergence of views among behavior modification people regarding the use of punishment, with some categorically opposed to it while others favor it under certain conditions); (2) reliance on social encouragement from teachers and peers as well as intrinsic satisfactions of self-worth and self-accomplishment (this is in contrast to behavior modification, which uses tangible and activity rewards in addition to people and intrinsic rewards); (3) reliance on motivation and commitment to improve (while the behaviorists recognize that these factors should ideally be present at the outset, they often attempt to deal with cases wherein motivation and commitment may initially be limited or absent. By rearranging environmental contingencies, the behaviorists attempt to instill a desire to change); (4) neglect of systematic evaluation (the behavior modifiers stress the importance of outcome research in validating intervention procedures).

Drug Therapy

The use of drugs for improving the behavior and learning of children dates back to 1937, when Charles Bradley observed that Benzedrine, a central nervous system stimulant, produced "spectacular" effects in school children suffering from behavioral disturbances. In recent years, there has been an increased interest in the medical use of drugs to control behavior disorders in children. Despite the mounting body of research, this topic continues to be emotionally charged and surrounded by controversy. Some view drug therapy as the passport to a brave new world while others perceive it as the gateway to the inferno. For better or for worse, depending on the individual case, the administration of drugs has become established as one of the preferred forms of treatment in many school situations. While no one knows for sure the extent to which drug therapy is being practiced, one authority estimated that some 150,000 to 200,000 children are now being treated with stimulant drugs and that the trend was expected to increase in the future. Moreover, an NIMH estimate reports that there are up to four million "hyperactive" children who could benefit from stimulant drugs.

In this section, we devote most of our attention to the use of stimulant drugs in the treatment of behavior disorders in children for the following reasons: the current interest on the part of educators, parents, and the federal government regarding the use of stimulant drugs to manage problem children; the increasing amount of well-controlled research conducted on stimulant drugs as compared with other drugs (e.g., tranquilizers); the findings of beneficial therapeutic outcomes in a field wherein positive gains are not commonly achieved; and the fact that stimulant drugs are used more commonly than other drugs to manage behavior in school. Less attention is directed to other forms of psychopharmacological treatment. Table 10–4 provides an overview of the major forms of drug therapy and their effects on behavior.

Stimulant Drugs.   In large measure, the stimulant drugs have been prescribed for children characterized by minimal brain dysfunction, a syn-

Table 10–4.   Major Drug Effects of Therapeutic Relevance

Psychomotor Stimulants *(Amphetamine-like)*	*Antidepressants* *(Imipramine-like)*
Greatly increase	Slightly reduce
arousal—excitability	arousal—excitability
wakefulness	discouragement, apathy
activity drive	Slightly increase
responses to stimuli	responses to stimuli
active avoidance—escape	struggle—escape
fighting behavior	defensive fighting
inhibitory control	*Narcotics*
Major Tranquilizers	*(Morphine-like)*
(Chlorpromazine-like)	Greatly reduce
Greatly reduce	arousal—excitability
arousal—excitability	activity drive
activity drive	biosocial drives
responses to stimuli	responses to stimuli (pain)
active avoidance—escape	active avoidance—escape
fighting behavior	fighting behavior
Minor Tranquilizers	discouragement, apathy
(Chlordiazepoxide-like)	*Hallucinogens*
Slightly reduce	*(LSD-like)*
arousal—excitability	Greatly increase
inhibitory control	arousal—excitability
passive avoidance behavior	activity drive
fighting behavior	responses to stimuli
Slightly increase	Greatly impair
responses to stimuli	inhibitory control
social approach	perception
errors of commission	information processing

Source: Irwin (1968). (Reprinted from the *American Journal of Psychiatry*, vol. 124 [February Suppl.], pp 1–20, 1968. Copyright 1968, the American Psychiatric Association.)

drome that has proved difficult to diagnose. Paradoxically, the stimulant drugs have a calming effect on hyperactive children.

Much of the early research pointed to the benefits stemming from the use of stimulant drugs. In one summary of research reflecting over a decade of observations with the use of amphetamines—Benzedrine and Dexedrine—we are told that 60 to 75% of children were clinically improved, 15 to 25% showed no change, and that 10 to 15% showed unfavorable results (Bradley, 1950). Improvements were reported in such diverse areas as school adjustment, academic performance, readiness for testing, enuresis, increased striving for achievement, and increased attention spans. These early findings are in basic agreement with later research conducted in different settings and carried out under different methods. In general, stimulant medications have proven beneficial in about one-half to two-thirds of children for whom it was deemed appropriate treatment (Office of Child Development, 1971).

In the same year as Bradley's follow-up report (1950), Ritalin (methylphenidate hydrochloride) was patented by CIBA Pharmaceutical House. Ritalin is a substance chemically related to the amphetamines; however, it has a calming rather than a stimulating effect. It is probably the safest of the available stimulants (Irwin, 1974). Among other disorders, it is suggested for use as an aid to the general management of children suffering from minimal brain dysfunction. Ritalin is most commonly administered orally 2 or 3 times daily, preferably 30 to 45 minutes before meals. Ideally, the desired effects of the drug should last long enough to cover the homework time period without having a prebedtime rebound. Because many amphetamines are now available in long-acting tablet form, it is possible to achieve this with a single morning dose, though some youngsters will require another dosage around 3–4 P.M. Unfortunately, Ritalin has a shorter span of action, so that more frequent administration may be required (Laufer, 1971). Ritalin is not recommended for children under 6 years of age because safety standards and efficacy in this age range have not been established. It is usually no longer needed once the hyperactive child reaches puberty (Shaw & Lucas, 1970).

Effects of Stimulant Drugs on Behavior. The findings regarding the specific impact of stimulant drugs on children may be summarized as follows:

1. *Complex Intellectual Functioning.* Several studies indicate that stimulant drugs may increase the child's capacity to pay attention and to utilize cognitive abilities more effectively. Although stimulants enhance intellectual performance (for example, reading, arithmetic, performance IQ), there is no agreement as to why these changes occur. For example, are higher thought processes directly affected or is the ability to attend altered? The process of attending is a complex process and there is no conclusive evidence indicating what specific components of attending behavior (such as arousal, orienting reaction, the stoppage of distracting motor movements), if any, are involved.

Conners (1972) believes that in large measure the changes seen in many intellectual and performance tests are most likely a function of the enhanced capacity to attend and/or to control responsivity.

2. *Motor Activity.* Research studies have yielded inconclusive results regarding the impact of stimulant drugs on student activity level. The contradictory findings regarding the amount of motor activity may in large measure be a function of the various scales and objective instruments used to measure very different aspects of activity level. Despite the mixed findings, teachers do report improvement in such aspects of student performance as classroom behavior, attitude toward authority, and attitude toward peers. While the activity level may or may not be altered, it does appear that stimulant drugs do allow the hyperactive student to engage in more organized, goal-directed behavior patterns which more closely comply with classroom standards of conduct and performance. In brief, the channeling of energy into more organized, socially acceptable behaviors may result in the child's being perceived as less hyperactive. The subdued activity level may very well be an artifact of observation which does not reflect gross body movement and activity level so much as it does the child's better integrated or more controlled response to the social and academic demands of the school situation. The child may expend as much energy as he did prior to medication, but he now channels his vigor into more acceptable and goal-directed activities (Grinspoon & Singer, 1973).

3. *Inhibitory Control.* There is a substantial body of evidence indicating that stimulant drugs may facilitate the child's ability to delay, to plan, and to respond in a more controlled, integrated way. Many authorities regard this general "inhibitory" quality of drugs as perhaps the single most important effect on student behavior. We do know that stimulants enhance performance, but we do not know whether these changes in performance are due to increased attention to the task, increased motivation, a more reflective approach, a lowered activity level, or a greater selectivity in response to incoming stimulation. These remain matters to be clarified by further inquiry (Conners, 1971).

4. *Mood and Personality.* The effects of stimulant drugs on mood and personality are still not well understood. While some authorities maintain that stimulant drugs do not produce a euphoric effect in children, other investigators do report a more zestful, vigorous, and energetic approach to tasks. Still other researchers have found increased signs of happiness, friendliness, and cooperativeness as a result of drug therapy. Occasionally, however, there have been reports of sadness and depression (crying, withdrawn and motionless behavior), particularly among hyperactive children with epilepsy. These mixed responses may well be due to the use of heterogeneous populations who differ in their clinical diagnosis, reasons for referral for treatment, and the types of learning difficulties. Research controlling the above variables will be needed before any firm conclusion can be reached regarding the effects of stimulant drugs on personality and mood (Conners, 1972).

Guidelines in the Use of Drug Treatment

1. With respect to milder learning behavior disorders, it is probably advisable to consider an initial use of a placebo. Neurotic, anxious youngsters are more likely to respond positively to a placebo than are hyperactive problem children (Conners, 1971). Virtually every study reveals the potency of the placebo effect, and the benefits arising from this effect should not be overlooked. The placebo effect will probably be greater in "drug taking" families than in non-drug-taking families.

2. No drug should be used (a) without firm indication for its use, (b) without careful supervision of the child treated, and (c) without caution regarding toxicity (Eisenberg, 1971). Regrettably, drugs are often prescribed without a clear indication for their use. There is no simple homogeneous diagnostic category backed up by clear-cut, validated procedures of assessment that unequivocally lead to a prescription for drug treatment. Although drugs are widely used to treat children suffering from hyperkinesis or minimal brain dysfunction, this syndrome is little understood and is difficult to diagnose validly.

Because of the current enthusiasm regarding the use of drugs, many medical doctors prescribe them primarily at the request of teachers and parents even though the doctors remain unsure as to the nature and etiology of the hyperactivity or the adults' threshold for annoyance. Because approximately 50% of both parents and teachers perceive their youngsters as overactive, the physician must distinguish between the normal active ebullience of children on the one hand, and central nervous system impairment or excessive hyperactivity of physiological origin on the other hand. The physician must not allow himself to become the agent of disturbed parents, anxious teachers, or uninformed judges (Eisenberg, 1971). Many doctors believe that stimulant drugs should be used only with children whose hyperactivity stems from central nervous system disorders. Yet the diagnosis of minimal brain dysfunction is no easy matter. Moreover, there appears to be no conclusive evidence that organically impaired students with behavior problems respond any more favorably than apparently nonorganically impaired youngsters with similar behavior problems.

It is important that the physician receive feedback from several sources regarding the child's progress while under medication. The sources of feedback should include the child's self-report, parental observations, teacher's perceptions as well as those of other school personnel such as the school nurse, counselor, social worker, or school psychologist. Information deriving from multiple sources can be of invaluable assistance to the physician with respect to adjustment in the child's medication. Because stimulant drugs are prescribed by physicians, it is often the educational and psychological components that tend to be the most neglected aspects of planning. Lack of closer communication between parent, teacher, and physician is the commonest basis for mismanagement in drug treatment programs. Table 10–5 is a check list for teacher rating that has proven useful for disclosing change in the behavior of children receiving medication.

Contraindications. As noted earlier, not all children improve on stimulant medications. In a small percentage of cases, increased agitation, "tension," and anxiety may occur. Even among those who are behaviorally benefited, unwanted side effects often occur. The more common include an amphetamine look (a pale, pinched, serious facial expression, with dark hollows under the eyes), loss of appetite, insomnia, headache and abdominal pain, dizziness, fine tremor, and coldness of the extremities. These side effects are generally reported as mild enough so that medication need not be discontinued. Most of the above side effects occur within the first week or two of treatment and gradually diminish or disappear as treatment is continued. In general, Ritalin seems to have fewer toxic effects than other stimulants. While the immediate short-term toxic effects are generally known, there are far fewer relevant data available on long-term toxic effects. In light of this paucity of data regarding long-term toxic effects, various authorities have urged caution regarding the use of medication over long periods of time.

Our discussion thus far has looked at possible toxic effects. How about the possibility of drug addiction? The limited research available on this topic does not support the dire prediction as to the outcome of long-term use of medication for hyperkinetic children (Laufer, 1971). Thirty years of *clinical* experience and a small number of scientific studies have failed to uncover any association between the medical use of stimulants during the preadolescent years and later drug abuse. In a similar vein, epileptics treated with barbiturates from infancy to adulthood do not develop problems of drug dependency or abuse. Likewise, no evidence exists that individuals treated for diabetes, hypothyroidism, or other conditions requiring prolonged drug use are more likely to become subject to drug abuse. While the concern over the use of stimulants among adolescents is certainly real and understandable, there is no evidence at this time to assume that the pleasurable subjective state experienced by adolescents who, for example, smoke marijuana is in any way comparable to that of preadolescents. In fact, clinical experience indicates that most preadolescents are quite willing to stop drug treatment so that they no longer have to take their "medicine."

3. An old and familiar drug is to be preferred to a new drug unless there is clear evidence to support the superiority of the latter. This form of pharmacological conservatism is employed to guard against possible unknown toxic effects of newer drugs that have had but brief clinical and scientific trial. Stimulant drugs (Benzedrine, dextroamphetamine, and methylphenidate) have the longest histories and are among the safest drugs for children. Certain of the minor tranquilizers (for example, diphenylmethane derivatives and substituted propanediols) which are anti-anxiety drugs rank next in terms of relative safety. Of the major tranquilizers, the phenothiazine derivatives (for example, thoridazine and chlorpromazine) appear to be the most commonly used to manage severely psychotic behavior in children. Drugs in this latter category can produce more serious effects and children receiving them should be under close medical supervision. Most evidence

suggests that tranquilizing drugs tend to impair learning performance in disturbed children.

4. Drugs should be used no longer than is absolutely necessary. It is often desirable to interrupt medication (for example, on weekends, school

Table 10–5.   Teacher Questionnaire

I. Identifying Information
   Child's Name: School:
   Grade: How long have you known this child?
II. In your own words briefly describe the child's main problem.
III. Standardized Test Results
   1. Intelligence tests
      Name of Test   *Date*   *C.A.*   *M.A.*   *IQ*

   2. Most recent achievement tests
                        Grade When Tested   *Achievement Grade Level*

      Reading
      Spelling
      Arithmetic
IV. Achievement in School Subjects (list subjects)
      Subject   *Very Good*   *Average*   *Barely Passing*   *Failing*

   What special placement or help has he had? (Underline below)
   Ungraded, sight-saving, special class, remedial reading, speech correction, tutoring
   Other (specify) ————————————————————————
   Please check for *every* item the one that is most true of this child.

	Not at All	Just a Little	Pretty Much	Very Much
V. Behavior of Child				
1. Sits fiddling with small objects	—	—	—	—
2. Hums and makes other odd noises	—	—	—	—
3. Falls apart under stress of examination	—	—	—	—
4. Coordination poor	—	—	—	—
5. Restless or overactive	—	—	—	—
6. Excitable	—	—	—	—
7. Inattentive	—	—	—	—
8. Difficulty in concentrating	—	—	—	—
9. Oversensitive	—	—	—	—
10. Overly serious or sad	—	—	—	—
11. Daydreams	—	—	—	—
12. Sullen or sulky	—	—	—	—
13. Selfish	—	—	—	—
14. Disturbs other children	—	—	—	—
15. Quarrelsome	—	—	—	—
16. Tattles	—	—	—	—
17. Acts "smart"	—	—	—	—
18. Destructive	—	—	—	—
19. Steals	—	—	—	—
20. Lies	—	—	—	—
21. Temper outbursts	—	—	—	—

Table 10–5. continued

	Not at All	Just a Little	Pretty Much	Very Much
VI. Group Participation				
1. Isolates himself from other children	—	—	—	—
2. Appears to be unaccepted by group	—	—	—	—
3. Appears to be easily led	—	—	—	—
4. No sense of fair play	—	—	—	—
5. Appears to lack leadership	—	—	—	—
6. Does not get along with opposite sex	—	—	—	—
7. Does not get along with same sex	—	—	—	—
8. Teases other children or interferes with their activities	—	—	—	—
VII. Attitude toward Authority				
1. Submissive	—	—	—	—
2. Defiant	—	—	—	—
3. Impudent	—	—	—	—
4. Shy	—	—	—	—
5. Fearful	—	—	—	—
6. Excessive demands for teacher's attention	—	—	—	—
7. Stubborn	—	—	—	—
8. Overly anxious	—	—	—	—
9. Uncooperative	—	—	—	—
10. Attendance problem	—	—	—	—
VIII. Family				

1. Do other children in the family attending your school present problems? (Amplify)
2. Please add information about this child's home or family relationships which might have bearing on his attitudes and behavior, and add any suggestions for improvement of his behavior and adjustment.

Signature:
Title:
Date:

Name of Principal:
Name of school:
Address of school:

Source: C. K. Conners. A teacher rating scale for use in drug studies with children. *American Journal of Psychiatry*, 1969, **126**, pp. 884–888.

vacations) to see if the symptoms diminish or disappear without continuance of the medication. "Drug holidays" can be a useful way of evaluating the effects of treatment.

5. Drug treatment constitutes only one part of the total treatment program. Drugs should be used as a means to an end and not as an end in and of themselves. Any drug treatment program must be accompanied by other

appropriate interventions such as remedial instruction. If warranted, behavior modification techniques, parent counseling, recreational programs, and other measures to encourage personal and academic development ought to be incorporated into the treatment program. Drugs by themselves teach a child nothing. What they can do is to make children more amenable to other intervention efforts that will enable them to become more mature. Because of the relative ease of giving children pills to overcome overactive and impulsive behavior, we must be constantly on guard against the danger of using drugs as the only or primary means of treating problem children. While a coordinated treatment program may cost more in terms of time and energy, it is essential for the child's realization of his potential. Drug treatment is both a powerful and dangerous tool. It should not be used by itself; rather it should be integrated with a variety of other services and disciplines.

Summary

All intervention programs must take into account certain differences between adults and children. Foremost among the differences are such factors as motivation for treatment, amount of insight into treatment objectives, linguistic facility, dependence on environmental forces, and developmental plasticity.

Studies investigating the outcomes of traditional psychotherapeutic approaches with children have failed to substantiate their effectiveness. Fortunately, about two-thirds of youngsters seen at child-guidance clinics improve whether or not they are treated professionally.

There are several promising recent approaches which vary in their focus and scope. Future research and practice will determine their true value.

Behavior therapy represents the application of learning theory principles to the modification of behavior.

Behavior modification differs from other therapies in its focus on current causes of maladaptive behavior, its use of relatively directive procedures, its relative deemphasis on insight, emotional release, and intense therapist-client relationships, and finally, in its concern with evaluating the outcomes of intervention efforts.

Studies comparing effectiveness of behavior modification procedures with other therapeutic approaches remain to be undertaken. Moreover, research dealing with the issue of generalization of treatment results over time, across settings, and across behaviors needs to be explored further.

Group approaches, behavioral contracting, modeling, self-management, and scheduled punishment are examples of the more interesting extensions of behavior modification applications.

Family therapy approaches vary quite widely in their theoretical orientations. One aspect of family therapy that has attracted attention is the use of parents as therapists.

Filial therapy is a form of client-centered play therapy in which the parents are to interact in a reflective, empathic, and involved manner with their children.

Parents have also been trained to use behavior modification techniques with their children. While additional research will be needed to determine whether the promise of behavior modification approaches will become fact, preliminary findings have been encouraging.

Dreikurs's family council advocates a procedure in which family members sit down and democratically arrive at solutions to family problems. There has been no research regarding the effectiveness of this approach, but it may be well suited to reasonably intelligent, intact parents who espouse democratic values.

Reality therapy focuses on the client's behavior in the real world rather than the client's subjective interpretation of feelings and thoughts.

According to reality therapy, man must act responsibly in meeting his needs for love and accomplishment.

When dealing with the individual child, Glasser concentrates on the child's behavior ("What are you doing?"), the making of a value judgment ("Is what you're doing helping . . .?"), and the development of a plan for change.

The strengths and weaknesses of reality therapy were presented. It was also contrasted with behavior modification as an intervention approach.

Drug therapy dates back some forty years but only recently has it receive widespread attention as a means for dealing with behavior disturbances in children.

Discussion was limited primarily to the use of stimulant drugs since these have been the most carefully researched and the most widely used with public-school children.

Stimulant drugs facilitate the child's ability (a) to attend and to apply his intelligence, (b) to inhibit behavior, (c) to engage in goal-directed pursuits, (d) and to improve mood.

Initially, the use of a placebo might be considered. No drug should be prescribed without a firm indication for its use, without careful supervision, and without care regarding toxicity. Older, more carefully studied drugs are generally preferable to new drugs. Drugs should be used no longer than is necessary. Finally, remember that drug treatment is only one part of the treatment program.

References

Ackerman, N. W. *The psychodynamics of family life.* New York: Basic Books, 1958.

Allen, K. E., Hart, B., Buell, J. S., Harris, F. R., & Wolfe, M. M. Effects of social reinforcement on isolate behavior of a nursery school child. In L. P. Ullmann & L. Krasner (Eds.), *Case studies in behavior modification.* New York: Holt, Rinehart, and Winston, 1965.

Anderson, J. Personality organization in children. *American Psychologist,* 1948, **3**, 409–16.

Axline, V. *Play therapy.* Boston: Houghton Mifflin, 1947.

Axline, V. The eight basic principles. In M. Haworth (Ed.), *Child psychotherapy.* New York: Basic Books, 1964.

Baker, B. Symptom treatment and symptom substitution in enuresis. *Journal of Abnormal Psychology,* 1969, **74,** 42–49.

Bandura, A. Psychotherapy as a learning process. *Psychological Bulletin,* 1961, **58,** 143–57.

Bandura, A., & Walters, R. H. *Social learning and personality development.* New York: Holt, Rinehart, and Winston, 1963.

Barr, N. The responsible world of reality therapy. *Psychology Today,* 1974, **65,** 67–68.

Bell, J. E. Family group therapy. *Public Health Monograph,* U.S. Dept. of Health, Education and Welfare, 1961, No. 64.

Bower, E. M. Mental health. In R. Ebel (Ed.), *Encyclopedia of educational research.* (4th ed.) New York: Macmillan, 1970, pp. 811–28.

Bradley, C. Benzedrine and dexedrine in the treatment of children's behavior disorders. *Pediatrics,* 1950, **5,** 24–36.

Bucher, B. D. Learning theory. In B. B. Wolman (Ed.), *Manual of child psychopathology.* New York: McGraw-Hill, 1972.

Burnham, W. H. *The normal mind.* New York: Appleton-Century-Crofts, 1924.

Conners, C. K. A teacher rating scale for use in drug studies with children. *American Journal of Psychiatry,* 1969, **126**(6), 152–56.

Conners, C. K. Drugs in the management of children with learning disabilities. In L. Tarnopol (Ed.), *Learning disorders in children: diagnosis medication, education.* Boston: Little, Brown, 1971, pp. 253–301.

Conners, C. K. Pharmacotherapy of psychopathology in children. In H. Quay & J. Werry (Eds.), *Psychopathological disorders of childhood.* New York: Wiley, 1972, pp. 316–47.

Dollard, J., & Miller, N. E. *Personality and psychotherapy.* New York: McGraw-Hill, 1950.

Dreikurs, R., & Grey, L. *A parent's guide to child discipline.* New York: Hawthorne Books, 1970.

Dreikurs, R., Grunwald, B., & Pepper, F. *Maintaining sanity in the classroom: illustrated teaching techniques.* New York: Harper & Row, 1971.

Dunlap, K. *Habits: their making and unmaking.* New York: Liveright, 1932.

Eisenberg, L. Principles of drug therapy in child psychiatry with special reference to stimulant drugs. *American Journal of Orthopsychiatry,* 1971, **41**(3), 371–79.

Eisenberg, L., & Gruenberg, E. The current status of secondary prevention in child psychiatry. *American Journal of Orthopsychiatry,* 1961, **81,** 355–67.

Engel, M. *Psychopathology in childhood.* New York: Harcourt Brace Jovanovich, 1972.

Eysenck, H. Learning theory and behavior therapy. In H. Eysenck, *Behavior therapy and the neuroses.* London: Pergamon Press, 1960, pp. 4–21.

Eysenck, H. Behavior therapy extinction and relapse in neurosis. *British Journal of Psychiatry,* 1963, **109,** 12–18. (a)

Eysenck, H. Behavior therapy, spontaneous remission and transference in neurotics. *American Journal of Psychiatry,* 1963, **119,** 867–71. (b)

Franks, C. Behavior therapy, psychology and the psychiatrist: contributions, evalution and overview. *American Journal of Orthopsychiatry,* 1965, **85,** 145–51.

Freud, A. *Psychoanalytic treatment of children.* London: Imago, 1946.

Freud, A. *Normality and pathology in childhood.* New York: International Universities Press, 1965.

Freud, S. Analysis of a phobia in a five-year-old boy. *Standard edition of the complete psychological works of Sigmund Freud,* 1909, Vol. 10 (edited and translated by James Strachey). London: The Hogarth Press Ltd., 1955.

Ginott, H. *Group psychotherapy with children.* New York: McGraw-Hill, 1961.

Ginott, H. *Between parent and child.* New York: Macmillan, 1965.

Glasser, W. *Schools without failure.* New York: Harper & Row, 1969.

Greenspoon, J. Verbal conditioning and clinical psychology. In A. J. Bachrach (Ed.), *Experimental foundations of clinical psychology.* New York: Basic Books, 1962, pp. 510–53.

Grinspoon, L., & Singer, S. Amphetamines in the treatment of hyper-kinetic children. *Harvard Educational Review,* 1973, **43**(4), 515–55.

Guerney, B. Filial therapy: description and rationale. *Journal of Consulting Psychology,* 1964, **28,** 304–10.

Hall, R., Axelrod, S., Tyler, L., Grief, E., Jones, F., & Robertson, R. Modification of behavior problems in the home with a parent as observer and experimenter. *Journal of Applied Behavior Analysis,* 1972, **5,** 53–64.

Hammer, M., & Kaplan, A. M. *The practice of psychotherapy with children.* Homewood, Ill.: Dorsey Press, 1967.

Hampe, E., Noble, H., Miller, L., & Barrett, C. Phobic children one and two years posttreatment. *Journal of Abnormal Psychology,* 1973, **82,** 446–53.

Hanley, E. Review of research involving applied behavior analysis in the classroom. *Review of Educational Research,* 1970, **40,** 5, 597–625.

Hawkins, R. P. It's time we taught the young how to be good parents (and don't we wish we'd started a long time ago?). *Psychology Today,* 1972, **6,** 28.

Hawkins, R., Peterson, R., Schweid, E., & Bijou, S. Behavior therapy in the home: amelioration of problem parent-child relations with the parent in a therapeutic role. *Journal of Experimental Child Psychology,* 1966, **4,** 99–107.

Haworth, M. *Child psychotherapy.* New York: Basic Books, 1964.

Heinicke, C. Research on psychotherapy with children: a review and suggestions for further study. *American Journal of Orthopsychiatry,* 1960, **30,** 483–93.

Hood-Williams, J. The results of psychotherapy with children: a revolution. *Journal of Consulting Psychology,* 1960, **24,** 84–88.

Horn, P. Fighting delinquency with family therapy. *Psychology Today,* March 1975, **8,** 79.

Irwin, S. Major drug effects of therapeutic relevance. *American Journal of Psychiatry,* 1968, **124,** 1–19.

Irwin, S. The uses and relative hazard potential of psychoactive drugs. *Bulletin of the Menninger Clinic*, 1974, **38** (1), 14–18.

Jackson, L., & Todd, K. *Child treatment and the therapy of play*. (2nd ed.) New York: Ronald Press, 1950.

Jersild, F., & Holmes, F. Methods of overcoming children's fears. *Journal of Psychology*, 1935, **1**, 75–104.

Jones, M. C. A laboratory study of fear: the case of Peter. *Journal of Genetic Psychology*, 1924, **31**, 308–15.

Kazdin, A. *Behavior modification in applied settings*. Homewood, Ill.: Dorsey Press, 1975.

Kazdin, A., & Bootzin, R. The token economy: an examination of issues. In R. Rubin, J. Bradley, & J. Henderson (Eds.), *Advances in behavior therapy*, Vol. 4. New York: Academic Press, 1973.

Kessler, J. W. *Psychopathology of childhood*. Englewood Cliffs, N.J.: Prentice-Hall, 1966.

Kifer, R. E., Lewis, M. A., Green, D. R., & Phillips, E. L. Training predelinquent youths and their parents to negotiate conflict situations. *Journal of Applied Behavior Analysis*, 1974, **7** (3), 357–64.

Laufer, M. Long-term management and some follow-up findings on the use of drugs with minimal cerebral dysfunctions. *Journal of Learning Disabilities*, 1971, **4**, 518–22.

Levitt, E. Results of psychotherapy with children: an evaluation. *Journal of Consulting Psychology*, 1957, **21**, 189–96.

Levitt, E. Psychotherapy with children: a further review. *Behavior Research and Therapy*, 1963, **1**, 45–51.

Levitt, E., Beiser, H., & Robertson, R. A follow-up evaluation of cases treated at a community child guidance clinic. *American Journal of Orthopsychiatry*, 1959, **29**, 337–47.

Lewis, W. Continuity and intervention in emotional disturbance; a review. *Exceptional Children*, 1965, **32**, 465–75.

Lippman, H. S. *Treatment of the child in emotional conflict*. (2nd ed.) New York: McGraw-Hill, 1962.

Lovaas, I., Koegel R., Simmons, J., & Long, J. Some generalization and follow-up measures on autistic children in behavior therapy. *Journal of Applied Behavior Analysis*, 1973, **6**, 131–66.

Lovitt, T. Self-management projects with children with behavioral disorders. *Journal of Learning Disabilities*, 1973, **6**, 138–50.

Minuchin, S., Montalvo, B., Guerney, B., Rosman, B., & Schumer, F. *Families of the slums*. New York: Basic Books, 1967.

Mowrer, O. H. *Learning theory and personality dynamics*. New York: Ronald Press, 1950.

Mowrer, O., & Mowrer, W. Enuresis: a method for its study and treatment. *American Journal of Orthopsychiatry*, 1938, **8**, 436–59.

Neisworth, J., & Smith, R. *Modifying retarded behavior*. Geneva, Ill.: Houghton Mifflin, 1973.

Nolan, J., Mattis, P., & Holliday, W. Long term effects of behavior therapy: a 12 month follow-up. *Journal of Abnormal Psychology*, 1970, **76**, 88–92.

Nordquist, V. M., & Wahler, R. G. Naturalistic treatment of an autistic child. *Journal of Applied Behavior Analysis,* 1973, **6** (1), 79–88.

Norman, V., Rosen, B., & Bahn, A. Psychiatric clinic out-patients in the United States, 1959. *Mental Hygiene*, 1962, **46**, 321–43.

O'Dell, S. Training parents in behavior modification. *Psychological Bulletin*, 1974, **81**, 418–33.

Office of Child Development. *Report on the conference on the use of stimulant drugs with behaviorally disturbed young school children.* Department of Health, Education and Welfare, 1971.

O'Leary, K., & Wilson, G. *Behavior therapy.* Englewood Cliffs, N.J.: Prentice-Hall, 1975.

O'Leary, K., O'Leary, S., & Becker, W. Modification of deviant sibling interaction pattern in the home. *Behavior Research and Therapy*, 1967, **5**, 113–20.

Patterson, G. R. A learning theory approach to the school phobic child. In L. P. Ullmann & L. Krasner (Eds.), *Case studies in behavior modification.* New York: Holt, Rinehart, and Winston, 1965.

Patterson, G. R. Reprogramming the families of aggressive boys. In C. Thoresen (Ed.) *Behavior modification in education,* 72nd Yearbook for the National Society for the Study of Education. Chicago: University of Chicago Press, 1973, pp. 154–92.

Pearson, G. H. J. *Emotional disorders of children.* New York: Norton, 1949.

Peterson, D., & London, P. A role for cognition in the behavioral treatment of a child's eliminative disturbance. In L. P. Ullman & L. Krasner (Eds.), *Case studies in behavior modification.* New York: Holt, Rinehart, and Winston, 1965, pp. 289–94.

Piaget, J. *Psychology of intelligence.* Paterson, N.J.: Littlefield, Adams, 1960.

Poser, E. G. The effect of therapist training on group therapeutic outcome. *Journal of Consulting Psychology*, 1966, **30**, 283–89.

Rachman, S. Introduction to behavior therapy. *Behavior Research and Therapy*, 1963, **1**, 3–15.

Redl, F. *When we deal with children.* New York: Free Press, 1966.

Reid, J. H., & Hagen, H. *Residential treatment of emotionally disturbed children.* New York: Child Welfare League of America, 1952.

Reppucci, N., & Saunders, J. Social psychology of behavior modification. *American Psychologist*, 1974, **29**, 649–60.

Ricks, D. Supershrink: Methods of a therapist judged successful on the basis of adult outcomes of adolescent patients. In D. Ricks, A. Thomas, and M. Roff (Eds.), *Life history research in psychopathology,* Vol. 3. Minneapolis, Minn.: The University of Minnesota Press, 1974.

Riessman, F. *The culturally deprived child.* New York: Harper & Row, 1962.

Rioch, M. J., Elkes, C., Flint, A. A., Udansky, B. S., Newman, R. G., & Silber, E. National Institute of Mental Health pilot study in training of mental health counselors. *American Journal of Orthopsychiatry*, 1963, **33**, 678–89.

Rose, S. *Treating children in groups.* San Francisco; Jossey-Bass, 1972.

Rosenthal, D., & Frank, J. Psychotherapy and the placebo effect. *Psychological Bulletin*, 1956, **53**, 294–302.

Ross, A. *Psychological disorders of children: a behavioral approach to theory, research, and therapy.* New York: McGraw-Hill, 1974.

Ross, A. O., & Lacey, H. M. Characteristics of terminators and remainers in child guidance treatment. *Journal of Consulting Psychology*, 1961, **25**, 420–24.

Rubin, E. Special education in a psychiatric hospital. *Exceptional Children*, 1962, **29**, 184–90.

Ruesch, J., & Bateson, G. *Communication: the social matrix of psychiatry.* New York: Norton, 1951.

Russell, E. The power of behavior control: a critique of behavior modification methods. *Journal of Clinical Psychology,* Special Monograph Supplement 1974, **30**(2), 111–36.

Salzinger, K., Feldman, R., & Portnoy, S. Training parents of brain injured children in the use of operant conditioning procedures. *Behavior Therapy,* 1970, **1**, 4–32.

Sarason, I., & Ganzer, V. *Modeling: An approach to the rehabilitation of juvenile offenders.* Final report to social and rehabilitation service of the Department of Health, Education and Welfare. 1971 Grant #15-P-55303.

Sarason, I., & Sarason, B. *Constructive classroom behavior: a teacher's guide to modeling and role playing techniques.* New York: Behavioral Publications, 1974.

Schofield, W. *Psychotherapy: The purchase of friendship.* Englewood Cliffs, N.J.: Prentice-Hall, 1964.

Schreibman, L., & Koegel, R. Autism: a defeatable horror. *Psychology Today,* March 1975, 61–67.

Shaw, C. R., & Lucas, A. *The psychiatric disorders of childhood* (2nd ed.). New York: Appleton-Century-Crofts, 1970.

Shepherd, M., Oppenheim, B., & Mitchell, S. *Childhood behavior and mental health.* New York: Grune & Stratton, 1971.

Shoben, E. Psychotherapy as a problem in learning theory. *Psychological Bulletin,* 1949, **46**, 366–92.

Slavson, S. General principles and dynamics. In S. Slavson (Ed.) *The practice of group therapy.* New York: International Universities Press, 1947, pp. 13–39.

Slavson, S. *Child psychotherapy.* New York: Columbia University Press, 1952.

Stover, L., & Guerney, B. The efficacy of training procedures for mothers in filial therapy. *Psychotherapy,* 1967, **4**, 110–15.

Stover, L., Guerney, B., & O'Connell, M. Measurements of acceptance following self-direction, involvement and empathy in adult-child interaction. *Journal of Psychology,* 1971, **77**, 261–69.

Stuart, R. Behavioral contracting with the families of delinquents. *Journal of Behavioral Therapy and Experimental Psychiatry.* 1971, **2**, 1–11.

Tavormina, J. Basic models of parent counseling: a critical review. *Psychological Bulletin,* 1974, **81**, 827–35.

Truax, C. B., & Carkhuff, R. R. *Toward effective counseling and psychotherapy training and practice.* Chicago: Aldine, 1967.

Ullmann, L. P., & Krasner, L. *Case studies in behavior modification.* New York: Holt, Rinehart & Winston, 1965.

Watson, J., & Raynor, R. Conditioned emotional reactions. *Journal of Experimental Psychology,* 1920, **3**, 1–14.

Watson, R. I. *The clinical method in psychology.* New York: Harper & Row, 1951.

Wattenberg, W. Review of Trends. In W. W. Wattenberg (Ed.), *Social Deviancy Among Youth. Yearbook of the National Society for the Study of Education,* 1966, **65**, Part I, pp. 4–27.

White, R. W., & Watt, N. *The abnormal personality.* (4th ed.) New York: Ronald Press, 1973.

Williams, C. G. The elimination of tantrum behavior by extinction procedures. *Journal of Abnormal and Social Psychology,* 1959, **59**, 269.

Wolpe, J. *Psychotherapy by reciprocal inhibition.* Stanford, Calif.: Stanford University Press, 1958.

Suggested Readings

Davids, A. *Abnormal children and youth: therapy and youth.* New York: Wiley, 1972.

Gazda, G. *Group counseling: a developmental approach.* Boston: Allyn & Bacon, 1971.

Glasser, W. *Schools without failure.* New York: Harper & Row, 1969.

Levitt, E. Research on psychotherapy with children. In A. Bergin & S. Garfield (Eds.), *Handbook of psychotherapy and behavior change.* New York: Wiley, 1971, pp. 474–94.

Ohlsen, M. *Counseling children in groups.* New York: Holt, Rinehart, and Winston, 1973.

11

Community Resources for Intervention

Although it is generally recognized that behavioral outcome is influenced, for better or worse, by situational factors, the possibilities for correcting adjustment difficulties by making changes in the environment are often over-looked. Several factors seem to contribute to this reluctance:

1. The prevailing revered status attached to the home and family as the irreplaceable center for human development.

2. The view that behavior disorders are the outcome of internal (psychic) conflicts.

3. The contention that psychotherapy is the only method for the permanent correction of behavior disorders.

4. The unwillingness of any sector of society to accept the financial obligations required to provide a total treatment center.

The weight of these influences can be observed in such rationalizations as, (1) "any home is better than no home," (2) the "rule" many mental-health clinics have against classifying a subteen-aged child as psychotic, (3) the citing of the "failures" of inadequately funded residential treatment centers, and (4) the frank puzzlement that gives rise to a "wait and see" attitude rather than one of active intervention.

Overview

The Development of Community Services

Knowledge about behavior disorders obviously dictates the efforts made to correct them. The facilities established and the focus of treatment mirror theories as to the causes of behavior disorders and the consequent beliefs as to the proper methods for alleviating the disabilities. At first, it was felt that little could be done to change disordered behavior, which was viewed as a consequence of unfortunate hereditary agents. Treatment consisted of diagnosis and custodial care. Gradually, there was recognition that experiences, particularly those of home and family, had a profound influence on the child's personality. This finding justified correction of impaired interpersonal relationships by psychotherapy provided directly to the child and indirectly through the parents. It became increasingly evident that children left to fend for themselves—provided with inadequate supervision, stimulation, and attention of all kinds—faced a future filled with grave risks to their physical health, safety, and emotional well-being.

The failure to produce the needed supply of specific professional workers (psychiatrists, psychologists, and social workers) and the admission of the improbability of meeting this demand forced the consideration of alternative feasible procedures for the delivery of essential corrective services. For example, at the Mid-Decade Conference on Children and Youth in Washington, D.C., is was reported that there were only 14,000 pediatricians in the United States in 1966, and few of these had resourceful psychiatric backgrounds. At that time, there were approximately 61.8 million children under age 14 in the United States. Surveys carried out by the National Association of School Psychologists in 1970 revealed that there were fewer than 8,000 psychologists employed in schools and approximately the same number of psychologists were on the staffs of hospitals and clinics. Kadushin (1970) reported there were approximately 56,000 MSW-trained social workers in the United States but only about one-half of these were employed. The sobering realization of this manpower problem forced the reconsideration of methods for changing behavior.

Signposts pointed to several promising approaches. Environmental forces of all types are particularly effective in shaping the organization of the child's personality. Inducing "change" in behavior by creating situations to accommodate certain kinds of behavior has a potential equal to that of an approach that molds behavior to fit a particular situation. The frequent failure of the child to continue to make it in the community following release from a hospital or clinic also points to the necessity for correcting environmental sources of stress as a routine part of all treatment.

Preliminary Diagnostic Evaluation

Obtaining adequate care for the child is the compelling objective. Needed services may be available in a home, family, specialized community agency, or residential unit. Ideally the services should be in an arrangement that permits the child to move from one dispensing agency or site with a minimum of difficulty. In practice, this ideal centralized organization is not found, and marshaling the services required by a child is frequently a challenge for even the most experienced professional worker.

Planning the treatment program begins with the recognition that behavior is the outcome of many factors, internal and external. This makes it necessary to carry out a detailed appraisal of the adjustment problem as a preliminary step in correction. Not only are personal and situational variables interacting to produce behavior, but even when the arrangement giving rise to the behavior contains the same factors, the force contributed by the same factor can be different. The child who kicks his parents' shins may do so as an impulsive release of rage triggered by a temporary thwarting, as a well-established habit for releasing his aggressive self-assertion tendencies, or as a way of demanding attention. Allowance must also be made for the fact that thwarting, habit patterns, and seeking attention can and do find expression in numerous responses other than that of kicking parents' shins.

All this is to say that behavior and adjustment are individual matters. They can be changed, but not until the child's capacity for coping with stress, the types of pressures impinging upon him, and the tolerance limits and outlets available in his surroundings have been ascertained. Diagnostic appraisal is the process of carrying out this total assessment.

Assessment of the Problem

An adjustment problem is usually indicated by the child's failure to achieve some developmental standard. Children are everywhere grouped with others of the same chronological age: play groups, church schools, nursery schools, public schools. In a culture that tends to be preoccupied with the welfare of its children, this grouping makes it easy to compare the performance of children. Persons charged with supervising these groups typically give parents "progress reports" which indicate how the child is doing. Acting on information from these sources, many parents seek additional assistance for the child. They may consult their friends, ministers, or the child's teacher. Frequently, a physician is consulted about the problem.

In other instances, parents may be busily occupied in providing economic necessities or managing a large family with many children. Some persons may find all their abilities absorbed in trying to keep their own personal balance and sanity. In any event, the children in such homes receive minimal care, even though the parents may be well intentioned. Children experiencing adjustment problems in such situations are dependent upon outsiders—caseworkers from community agencies, probation officials, ministers, recreation workers, or interested neighbors—for spotting their adjustment problems.

Whoever becomes involved in dealing with the difficulty begins by making a study of the total situation. This may be carried out formally or informally, briefly or over an extended time. Although each professional person (caseworker, minister, teacher, psychologist, physician) may see the child from a slightly different perspective, the intent is to identify the stresses and possible danger to the child. Even though severely incapacitating at the time, a temporary developmental lag is to be treated in a different way than is a moderately impairing chronic problem. The social acceptability of the problem must also be considered. For whatever reasons it may be manifested, behavior that is not easily tolerated by society (overt aggressive acts) becomes the object of urgent efforts for change.

Included in the assessment preliminary to applying corrective procedures is an approximation of the child's capacities for coping with his problem. Foremost is a consideration of the child's general physical health. Formal measures of intellectual ability, social development, and emotional maturity, though desirable, are not always available, and assessment proceeds in a kind of all-or-none fashion. A younger child is usually regarded as having very limited personal resources, so that he must be protected from being overwhelmed by pressures on him. An older child has comparably greater personal assets for coping with pressures, so that he may require support rather than shielding. The study must carefully differentiate defects in personality organization from deficiencies in the skills incorporated in the child's personality structure.

Parents as a Potential Resource

Sizing up the parents is an essential step in formulating corrective action. It is helpful to know the details of the parents' own personality makeup and adjustment. Parental hostility, dependency, persistence, or antisocial orientations exert an influence on children, directly or indirectly. Such specific information is seldom available, but effective planning can be implemented on the basis of more easily acquired information. The amount of time the parent is actually available to spend with the child is, after all, a more real problem than the parent's wish or ideal. A parent may have the best intentions, but be absent from the home 90% of the time because of the nature of his work (for example, employment necessitating traveling). Even when home all of the time, a parent who has many children will have proportionately little time to give to any one individual child.

Parental capacity to be of assistance to the child must also be ascertained. If the parent is taxed in maintaining his own day-to-day living, there is not likely to be much resource left over to give to the child. If the parent is of limited ability, there is a concomitant limitation in the extent to which the parent can profit from training in how to be a more adequate parent. Even if the parent is of average ability and willing to become actively involved in helping the child, it is well to keep in mind that changes in adult behavior are not easily effected. Some individuals, otherwise competent, may have deeply ingrained personality traits that render them ineffectual in fulfilling a total parental role. The adequacy of the parent may ultimately best be determined by extended observation of the parent's success in fulfilling his role in the correction program. The hateful, blocking, thwarting parent is undoubtedly the most likely to hinder any steps for alleviation of the problem. Nevertheless, recent programs for special groups of children of migrant workers and of the socially disadvantaged have reported considerable success in training parents formerly thought to be of questionable adequacy to help their children learn to read and have better attitudes about school or work.

Other Situational Resources

In addition to the parents, there are generally other important persons (adults or older children) within the child's circle. These persons represent an important influence as helpful or obstructive contributors to the changing of disordered behavior. Scoutmasters, church workers, recreational workers, and teachers are present in varying numbers in the community. Other relatives or older siblings in the home should not be omitted in the assessment of resourceful persons.

Besides the backing represented by the persons in contact with the child, there are important, sometimes even essential, supports to be found in facilities available in the community. One of the most important of these community resources is the recreational program available. Chances to develop new skills in crafts programs, to play ball, to swim, and the like hold opportunities to experience successes, earn status, learn rules of the game, and acquire responsibilities as part of a team. Community child-guidance and family-service clinics offer counseling and other kinds of psychotherapy to children and families. Sheltered workshops, job-training schools, day schools, residential schools, summer camps, church- or YMCA-sponsored recreational programs all increase the number of chances for the child to find success.

Child Advocates

A number of movements with nationwide scope have recently organized to act as spokesman and representative for an individual child to ensure the child's having access to needed services. One of the best known is the Child Advocacy program, sponsored by a consortium of federal agencies involved in children's services. Another such national group is the voluntary association of persons and private organizations known as the Children's Lobby. At the state level, there may be appointed public officials termed "ombudsmen" who have the duty of investigating and protecting infringements on children's rights. Concomitant with such offices is legislation defining a specific status (orphan, dependent child, emotionally disturbed child) and prescribing certain "rights" that must be granted to specified children. Where legislation stipulates that the child is entitled to certain benefits, the task of the ombudsman or "enabler" is made very clear. Persons in the role of children's advocates, ombudsmen, or enablers are increasingly to be found in local communities and promise a powerful ally for assisting the child.

Totaling Up the Assessment

The greatest skill is required in integrating information about the factors contributing to the child's adjustment difficulty. A child may be doing poorly at home and at school because of a chronic health problem that drains his vitality. The parents may emerge as a potent resource, welcoming and putting into practice newly offered advice about child care. Or the parent, for various reasons, may have to be omitted as a source of support and assistance for resolving the child's problem. There may be other persons—playground supervisors, caseworkers, or teachers—whose influence on the child can be marshaled. Where a chronically handicapping condition is identified, such as mental retardation or deafness, for example, treatment should be oriented to building the child's capacity for coping with the demands of the environment rather than to remedying the defect. The community may be an isolated and impoverished one with no planned recreational outlets or program and only meager church, school, or interest-group offerings. In some communities a range of facilities offering medical, psychological, recreational, vocational, psychiatric, and remedial services may be available.

In any event, the treatment program must take into account the child's individual assets for meeting adjustment demands. In some instances, the child will be able to deal with his situation if he can be provided with temporary reassurance, support, or specific training. Teaching the child to swim, to play a musical instrument, to control aggressive impulses, or to read can then strengthen an already sound personality organization. Proceeding along this path is contingent upon the availability of the facilities and professional specialists for carrying out the particular training. In other instances, it may be all too apparent that the undeveloped personality organization of the child is beset by formidable pressures. Placement in a totally new situation ("repotting") is necessary before the child can blossom forth to his full potential. There are no fixed rules for making the decision, and there is frequently considerable urgency associated with the process of developing a corrective procedure. Where the child's personal resources permit, a treatment strategy seeking to straighten the bent twig is preferable to the more drastic approach of transplantation.

The Implementation of Diagnostic Findings

The appraisal of an adjustment problem can entail a lengthy and involved set of procedures, including examination of the child, study of the home and family, evaluation of the parents' capacity to cooperate, and determination of available community resources. The carrying-out of a treatment program is often infinitely more complex. There is no central supervisory person or agency in many instances. Coordinating a treatment program is more cumbersome when agencies and professionals are reluctant to impinge upon one another's domain.

The responsibility for implementing a program is usually given to the parents. Otherwise, the child's guaradian becomes the responsible person. The guardian may be a caseworker, an institutional superintendent, or a court judge. In a hospital it is the physician. If designated interventionists such as advocates, ombudsmen, or enablers are available to intercede for the child, the rigors of coordinating a treatment program can be greatly reduced. The follow-up is seldom without problems, and workers typically must distinguish the ideal from the practical treatment regimen.

The Role of Children's Courts

Special courts for handling legal proceedings involving children appeared with the turn of the century. Collectively referred to as juvenile courts, they are also known as children's courts and family courts. In addition to the presiding judge, the juvenile-court staff includes probation officers and caseworkers. In larger metropolitan centers, the staff may be augmented by psychologists and psychiatrists. Children's-court proceedings tend to be very informal, with the court operating from a broadly liberal orientation, and in an advisory capacity. Initial functions of the juvenile courts were mainly attempts to rehabilitate and protect the child with minimal concern for the levying of punishment or enforcing legal penalties for infractions committed. So long as corrective and rehabilitative actions predominated, common safeguards for constitutional rights were not deemed important for work that was essentially humanitarian in nature. The success of the juvenile courts in these matters resulted in the assignment of additional responsibilities, some of which could be construed as placing the court in an adversary position when dealing with children. As a corollary to this expanded role, juvenile court procedures have tended to become more fixed to ensure full protection of the child's constitutional rights, including right to counsel, open hearings, limitations on use of hearsay evidence, right to bail, proof beyond a reasonable doubt, and guards against self-incrimination.

The jurisdictional domain of juvenile courts now includes (1) situations in which the child's actions may endanger himself or the community, (2) instances wherein the quality of the care the child receives is questionable, and (3) actions involving the child's legal status and his rights. The court enters the picture when the child is deemed dependent, delinquent, neglected, abused, or in need of supervision within the confines of legal definitions of these terms. Slight variations in the definitions may be noted when statutes of one state are compared with those of another state.

Guardianship Services

The courts have been most effective when they have assumed the role of guardianship for children. Guardianship is continued for an indefinite period of time and can be an effective control measure. Although children's courts usually only see that recommendations or changes suggested by caseworkers or other agencies are carried out, the courts have considerable resources to implement corrective procedures. Courts may stipulate attendance in a vocational or trade school, treatment by psychotherapy, the assignment of a caseworker to work with parents, placement in a foster home or children's residential home, or commitment to a correctional institution. Parents may contest decisions, but the courts usually have the support of other legal agencies and often hold in abeyance more stringent consequences which may be invoked in any review of proceedings.

Recognizing that they are often forced to deal with problem behavior in terminal stages, juvenile officials have pushed for and obtained in approximately 40 states an important set of responsibilities. These are referred to as "protective services" and pertain to cases involving the neglect and abuse of children. This is a controversial but undeniably necessary extension of the state's authority. The state has two concerns at stake. On the one hand, neglected and abused children frequently wind up as wards of the state in one or another way. From another point of view, the child has certain rights and privileges the state must guarantee. To complicate the matter, protective services can entail the deprivation of the rights and liberties of parents. The parent has a right to live as he pleases within broad limits; that is, he doesn't have to have a job, be married to the person he lives with, or spend his money on his family. Courts have decreed the rights of each citizen include the freedom to marry, establish a home, bring up children, and enjoy privacy. The implementation of protective services thus brings into the arena a three-way conflict between society's rights, the child's rights, and the parent's rights.

Protective Services

Protective services can do much to correct the past trend of too little, too late. They offer a clear and direct procedure for intervention on behalf of children. Requests for protective service are made to a designated social agency working in close cooperation with juvenile courts. Referrals come from schools, police, neighbors, physicians, other social agencies, and other courts. Upon receipt of the referral, a caseworker makes a call to the home, where the parents are advised of the complaint and are given an explanation of the routine of relevant legal procedures (which vary slightly from state to state). The caseworker carries out an investigation and offers assistance (counseling, day care, or the like) to the parents. The caseworker's findings are reported to the court. If the parent accepts the plan outlined by the caseworker, no court action is taken. If the parent refuses to cooperate, the court can pursue a sequence of actions. A probation officer or caseworker may be assigned to work with the parents and supervise the child. Continued lack of cooperation can result in the child's being removed from the home and legal proceedings being initiated against the parent. The entire plan places much dependence upon the wisdom of the judge in interpreting such vague conditions as "proper care" and situations "prejudicial to the child's well-being." Protective services represent a significant intervention step and will undoubtedly be greatly extended in future applications. Recent decisions to the effect that a child must be represented by legal counsel in any court action may intensify the entire issue of "protection" versus "rights" of children.

Child Abuse and Right to Treatment

In response to increasing complaints of abuse of children, legislation was passed in 1974 on the national level. Public Law 93-247 (Child Abuse and Treatment Act) defined "child abuse and neglect" to mean physical or mental injury, sexual abuse, negligent treatment, or maltreatment of a child under the age of 18 by a person who is responsible for the child's welfare under circumstances indicating that the child's health or welfare is harmed or threatened thereby. As states have moved to implement the law, the definition of abuse has sometimes been expanded to cover nutritional neglect. As enacted by the states, provisions include designation of agencies for receiving and acting on reports, the specification of persons especially charged with reporting (teachers, physicians, etc.), and the procedures for reporting and follow-up investigation. Persons who are charged with reporting are immune from all legal recourse by persons named as possible child abusers even when the report is found to be unsubstantiated.

Court decisions growing out of a series of actions (*Morales* v. *Turman, Willowbrook, Wyatt*) have held that a diagnosis must be made on the basis of enabling the child to have access to treatment appropriate for the condition over and beyond mere institutionalization for protective custody, and that comprehensive treatment and rehabilitation services must be provided each individual child. If extended to all treatment programs, these interpretations could have the most profound impact on children's services. Other changes include the growing requirements for including the child in the decision-making processes that plan any treatment program for the child.

As a result of his experiences in evaluating treatment programs for children in state institutions, Dr. George Thomas (1974) has proposed a set of "Children's Rights," guidelines to ensure individual children's having direct input regarding participation in any treatment program, including their placement in or removal from institutions.

Modification Approaches

Environmental modification assists the child by varying some aspect or component of his surroundings. Environmental modification techniques are the most frequently used intervention procedures. The child is not removed from his home, and the emphasis is on reducing the press of forces that impinge upon the child or on strengthening the child's capacity for dealing with the elements making up his environment. In a sense, the environment is changed, but the change is in the nature of a rearrangement of the situation. The relationships among the various parts of the child's situation are redefined and readjusted. For example, the child's contacts with well-intentioned but interfering grandparents may be stopped. Parents may be advised of the importance for assigning jobs as a way of instilling a sense of responsibility in the child. Physical health may be improved by specific medical or surgical procedures. The child's ability to meet demands from his surroundings successfully may be bolstered by specific training such as remedial instruction or the teaching of particular skills.

Environmental modification can be viewed as a kind of psychological first aid administered after it has been ascertained what capacity the child has for responding and what response is expected of him. The decision must indicate that the adjustment balance can be restored by modifying specific disturbing influences or by adding new experiences. The focus is on the control of external forces so as to promote the continuation of optimal development of the child. The assumption is made that the child has skills and abilities to profit from the new opportunities. The general objectives are those of providing structured socialization contacts, training in specific skills, retraining of specific habitual outlets for aggressive or destructive behaviors, encouraging socially acceptable outlets for fantasies, bringing new opportunities for status and identification, or continuing supervisory care on a temporary basis.

Briefly summarized, the goals of environmental modification are the same as for all therapeutic intervention efforts:

1. Guiding mental attitudes into socially acceptable channels.
2. Restoration of self-confidence and personal security.
3. Replacement of discouragement with encouragement.
4. Establishment and promotion of good work habits.
5. Increasing opportunities for socialization.
6. Learning of specific skills needed for work or school.

In the course of achieving these goals, the entire environment is searched and advantage is taken of all opportunities. Community resources are usually to be found in some one of the following groupings of services. The availability of facilities is a function of the size of the community—large communities tend to have more of a variety of all resources. The discussion at this point makes only brief reference to educational resources and programs for the maladjusted child since educational intervention facilities were treated in conjunction with the specific disabilities discussed in Chapters 4 through 9.

Recreational Community Programs

Park and Playground Facilities.   Most cities of any size offer organized recreational activities on some type of regular schedule. These include playground equipment; areas for playing baseball, football, basketball, volleyball, and tennis; swimming pools; and other sports activities. In some communities there are regular special classes with instructions available in arts and crafts, dancing, tumbling, trampoline, or baton twirling. There is usually some supervision, and the instructional staff is augmented during school vacation periods. In the summer, daycamping activities and nature study may be offered. Fees are usually minimal, but transportation can be a problem in some instances. Organized recreational programs can offer a wholesome use of leisure time, new friendships, chances for success in athletics, and opportunities in learning how to function as a member of a socially approved group.

Summer Camps.   Summer camps are sometimes a part of community recreation programs but are more likely to be sponsored by churches, the YMCA, or the YWCA. There are numerous private camps, but the fees for private camps limit their availability. Fees and transportation are less costly for the semiprivate camps. Summer-camp experiences emphasize the fostering of independence and self-reliance. There are also excellent opportunities for contacts and training in the give and take of group social relationships. Training in arts and crafts, archery, fishing, canoeing, or horseback riding can be a unique experience and give the child a sense of being "expert" in a prestigious skill area. This "expertise" can be a solid contribution to ideas of personal competence and positive self-concept. The story of Jodi illustrates many of the values of summer camp for a troubled child.

After-School Programs.   Schools in large cities have had recreational programs or after-school "study" centers for many years. These programs are usually offered in areas where other recreational opportunities are limited and where there is a high percentage of homes without parental supervision during the working day. An example is New York City's All-Day Neighborhood School, where an extra teacher is assigned for each grade level from kindergarten through grade six. These teachers work from 11:00 A.M. to 5:00 P.M. From 11:00 A.M. to 3:30 P.M., the teachers are engaged in remedial work with individuals and small groups. From 3:00 to 5:00 P.M., they conduct an "activity" program composed of homework study, interest clubs, individual hobbies, field trips, organized games, and individualized recreational reading. The program appears to be an exemplary model that merits general emulation. It would be difficult to provide such a comprehensive and pertinent set of opportunities, ranging from remediation through planned use of leisure time, in any other single program.

Jodi

Jodi sat silently beside her mother on their way to keep an appointment at the Family Services Agency. She found it confusing and, in a way, sort of funny that she and her mother should be going to a "family" service agency. This really capped a long list of strange and difficult to understand things that were happening. It was obvious to her that they were no longer a family . . . her mother and father had gotten a divorce and her older brothers lived far away in Cleveland with her father. Jodi guessed he was still her father . . . so many things seemed uncertain and all mixed up now that she and her mother had moved to Akron, away from her former friends and school. Just when Jodi was beginning to get on to reading . . . something that had been difficult for her and had caused lots of embarrassment in the third grade. Now it was really bad. No one wanted to be her friend. Kids at the new school seemed to think she was just real dumb and unable to do anything. They all had their own friends. It seemed a good idea just to run away . . . far away even from her mother. Only Jodi wasn't exactly sure of how to run away, which direction to go. As they pulled into the parking lot, Jodi decided to ask Mr. Williams, the man with whom she had her "appointments" at the agency, about running away. Wasn't he always urging her to ask him questions?

Jodi sat dangling her toes in the water of the lake that surrounded Camp Perrin, liking the late afternoon sun and waiting for her friends, Beth and Patty, to come along. They were going for a canoe ride and maybe a swim. This was the next to the last day of summer camp, and Jodi could hardly believe it had gone so quickly! School would be starting again in less than two weeks. She smiled a little as her thoughts flashed back to the beginning of summer. Mr. Williams had not been at all surprised about her wanting to run away; in fact he had suggested a way for Jodi to try out running away by going to summer camp to see if she liked being away. Jodi had agreed mostly because she had planned to leave camp. But it had been busy from the start, when every one of the girls had to find as many persons with the same numbered tag as her own . . . what a fun way to make new friends! And all the cool things to do. . . . Who would ever believe that Ms. Schmidt was a reading teacher? (Who would believe that Jodi had made such rapid progress in reading and now read newspapers and big books all by herself?) . . . And learning to play the guitar had been easy. . . . Jodi was glad she had not run away. She looked forward to going back to school. Wouldn't the kids be surprised to find that she could play a guitar (and even more surprised about her reading)? Beth was also her good friend, and Beth was in the *sixth* grade at Jodi's school. What more could any fourth-grade girl want. . . .

Other Recreational Centers. Other recreational activities are made available by churches, the YMCA-YWCA, scouting organizations, business-men's organizations (Kiwanis, Rotary, Optimists), and civic groups. Included are a variety of youth centers, where dancing and informal get-togethers are scheduled under supervision. The YMCA-YWCA and scouting organizations offer individual and group activities from weight lifting to team sports. They also have instruction in hobbies and crafts. Churches are increasingly entering the field of providing recreational programs, usually directed toward the adolescent. These community programs can be excellent opportunities for social contacts. They are able to supply both male and female identification models. The hobby and craft programs may develop long-standing recreational interests along socially approved lines.

Specialized Community Programs

General Hospitals, Medical Clinics, and Crippled Children's Clinics. Adequate medical and surgical treatment is basic to ensuring that the child is maximally prepared to cope with life's demands. Physical health can make the difference in all-important initial success or failure experiences. Repeated failures associated with a physical disability or the inability to participate fully in normal play activities may foster a nucleus of self-doubt and a diminished zest for persistence. Despite tremendous advances in treatment methods made in the field of medicine, these services remain difficult to obtain for many children. While it is true that medical services are costly, some of the difficulty in delivery of services has been associated with lack of communications systems for dissemination of information, the chronic shortage of persons trained in newest techniques, and the burdensome but necessary record keeping for indicating the present status of a child's health. Rapid application of communications technology, from "walkie-talkie" radios to helicopters and elaborate computer machines, has vastly extended medical services. Some of the innovations and increases in services include:

1. Creation of a coordinated network of crisis centers that provide specified services (such as cardiac surgery, treatment for burns) for designated geographic areas.

2. Greater use of paraprofessionals at all levels; the most dramatic example may be the medically trained rescue squad worker.

3. Use of computers to study treatment outcomes and thus refine and improve treatment probabilities.

4. More direct involvement of the family and patient as resources in the treatment processes.

New programs reflecting the expansion of medical services include the Medicheck program as set out in Section 49, Title XIX of the 1972 Revised Social Security Act, and the fully equipped mobile medical service centers that some state health departments have especially designed to reach groups such as children of migrant workers. The Medicheck program provides for each child a computerized record showing vaccinations, essential checkups, results of routine screenings, and other such pertinent health information.

Large general hospitals are organizing clinics to provide a complete range of medical, surgical, psychiatric, educational, physical therapy, and speech correction services. Such elaborate children's clinics were formerly found only in association with medical schools. The cost of medical services is a formidable barrier for children from less economically advantaged families. Public facilities, such as crippled children's services, are frequently limited in the kinds of conditions or children they can accept. Privately sponsored facilities, such as Shriners hospitals for crippled children, have limited capacities. Nevertheless, adequate medical care is paramount in the prevention of later adjustment problems; physicians, clinics, or hospitals providing these services must be searched out.

Mental-Health, Guidance, and Counseling Clinics.   The support of federal financing has made it possible for community mental-health or child-guidance clinics to become established in most cities of more than 50,000 population. Typically, mental-health clinics are staffed by psychiatrists, social workers, and psychologists. These specialists carry out diagnostic evaluations and provide various types of psychotherapy. A major part of the treatment offered by mental-health clinics consists of counseling for parents and play therapy for children. Costs are generally minimal, but the demands for services are great. Most mental health clinics have extensive waiting lists, even though treatment is on a voluntary basis. Clients are selected on the basis of being able to participate as outpatients, that is, persons who are not so incapacitated as to require hospitalization (inpatients). The parent must contact the clinic, but suggestions as to the advisability of this self-referral may come from schools, courts, physicians, ministers, or other social agencies. Unfortunately, it is difficult for many persons to find immediate rewards in psychotherapy, as attested by the large number of clients—estimated as high as 50%—who are seen for only one or two contacts.

Family service agencies, which closely resemble the organization and staff complement of the mental-health clinic, have had rapid national growth. These agencies are found in most large urban centers, although they are more numerous in the northeastern quarter of the United States. Historically, family service agencies were a practical answer to the predicament expressed as "I need money, not counseling." These agencies are distinguished by their organization around the function of providing practical, on-the-spot casework, rather than psychiatric service. Consistent with this orientation, they perform a minimum of diagnostic functions. The staff consists mostly of trained caseworkers who make use of many techniques in dealing with families in crises. Counseling services are available, often in the form of patching up and improving relationships between parents, but the caseworker is willing and expects actively to assist the family in finding a more suitable house or better jobs or in living on a planned budget. The caseworker frequently contacts the family in home visits rather than waiting for the family to come to the agency's offices. Family service agencies work with clients on a voluntary basis. They can usually be counted upon to provide rapid service, but they may elect to refer "difficult" cases, such as those requiring hospitalization or involving a psychotic disorder, to other facilities. Their practical approach often brings quick results, and they are likely to be in close working contact with all other community agencies.

Vocational Counseling and Training Agencies. Vocational training and job preparation are based on the recognized economic necessity of gainful employment and on the alarming number of youths who are unprepared for it. For a number of years, the Division of Vocational Rehabilitation (DVR) has marshaled powerful resources in preparing and assisting handicapped persons to find employment. The DVR is possibly the most important single resource that can be brought to bear in assisting qualified persons. DVR will pay the costs of medical and surgical treatment, educational or specific vocational instruction, and psychotherapy. Because of the success the DVR has demonstrated in work with the handicapped, these programs have been copied by public schools as a regular service in job training and preparation to be made available to students not eligible for DVR programs.

Representing an ultimate development in dealing with adjustment problems, the "sheltered workshop" offers a daywork situation arranged to accommodate the individual. It can be viewed as a permanent employment situation for persons with very limited resources, such as the severely mentally retarded, or as a temporary training experience for assisting individuals to overcome a specific disability, such as the impulsive emotionally disturbed. Sheltered workshops have small staff complements and emphasize vocational activities. They may be associated with other community agencies, such as churches, schools, or parent groups. As yet, sheltered workshops are not widespread, but they are increasing in number and community support. They accept clients on referral from other community agencies, from public schools, and from residential schools. Clients are often paid a small wage, money left over from defraying the operating expenses of the workshop.

Special day schools that give training in specific marketable skills, such as welding, automobile repair, building maintenance, or packing products, have become a part of most large school systems. These facilities are limited to older youth, but they are an essential resource. Adolescents who have dropped out of school or who are not academically oriented often distinguish themselves in trade schools. The success of these training schools is so generally recognized in contributing to youth adjustment that they have been incorporated as central components in recent programs initiated by the President's Commission on Juvenile Delinquency.

Programs of Temporary Shelter

Nursery Schools.   Nursery schools are predominantly privately operated centers for children who are close to the usual school-entrance age. They originally appeared on the scene as a kind of supplement to the home experiences of children of working parents, the mother often working only part-time. Since most nursery schools are privately operated, they vary widely as to physical facilities, staff competency, and quality of program. In some, the emphasis is on educational rather than mothering activities, and the program often closely resembles that of public-school kindergarten. Children generally attend for a relatively short period of time. Unfortunately, there have been occasional reports of glaring inadequacies, bordering on neglect, so that many states have instituted licensing standards for approved nursery schools. Nursery schools can provide programs excellent in every respect, but the cost is generally prohibitive for those children who may be most in need of this help.

Day-Care Centers. Day-care centers are intended to provide substitute maternal care for the young child during a major part of the day and in the absence of parents. The emphasis is on meeting basic physical, emotional, intellectual, and social needs in a homelike setting. Publicly supported centers are usually conveniently located in neighborhoods where both parents are likely to be working, family incomes are low, and recreational facilities are minimal. Some large industrial companies are establishing day-care centers for the children of mothers employed by the company. Many of these centers have a well-trained staff of specialists and planned programs of social, motor, and language-stimulating activities. Attention is given to rest and nutritional requirements of the child and transportation may be provided in some instances.

Unfortunately, laxity in local regulation and/or funding support results in approximately 80% of the children being served in inadequate conditions, according to Zigler (1973). Surveys reported to the Office of Child Development show that about 40% of the children receiving day care are in neighborhood homes where the supervising adult may be senile, alcoholic, or emotionally disturbed to the point of being unable to tend to the child's requirements for basic physical safety, much less to satisfy normal socio-psychological and nutritional needs. Since day-care service was given number one priority by the 1970 White House Conference on Children and Youth, such programs are assured of top funding support. A program for training persons to work in day-care centers is funded by the Office of Child Development, and states are being encouraged to set up standards for program regulation. Although some centers are expanding the services they offer to include temporary residential care, the high costs of adequate day care seriously restrict the expansion of this type of service.

Operation Outreach.   Even though Head Start programs did not accomplish original expectations for eliminating certain problems associated with cultural difference, early school programs can usually be found as a part of community school systems. Since the general conditions for promoting optimal physical, social, and intellectual development in the early childhood period are similar for the handicapped and nonhandicapped, early school programs of the Head Start type seemed especially suited for serving handicapped children (Klein & Randolph, 1974). Advocates for handicapped children were successful in securing legislative mandate (Public Law 92-424, 1972) for including handicapped children in early school programs.

Consequently, an intensive search was conducted by health departments, schools, and other community agencies, going out into the neighborhoods to locate and diagnose handicapped children. The success of "Operation Outreach" in identifying and placing handicapped children in early school programs is illustrated by Figure 11–1. Expectations for successful later school integration ("mainstreaming") on the basis of advantages gained from individualized instruction, attention to the total development of the child, and concern for securing parental involvement must await verification. Favorable outcomes for many of the handicapped children may be anticipated, but Cohen (1975) has cautioned against expecting complete success, since she believes that many handicapped children will require more specialized services than are available in the usual early school program.

Services for Runaways.   Reliable statistics on the exact number of children who run away from home are difficult to obtain, but estimates range from approximately 300,000 upward annually. Data maintained by the John Howard Society indicate that more than a half million children under 16 years of age ran away from home in 1974. Formerly a behavior almost exclusively of boys, 53% of these runaways were girls. About two-thirds of the children reported they were running to something and the other one-third were running away from something. Even the more conservative estimates suggest a problem of considerable magnitude, and law enforcement officials and agencies have been taxed to cope with these children who are not really criminal (but are violating a law).

Intensive work by juvenile authorities in one midwestern county turned up some surprising findings. About one-half of the runaways were repeaters, children who were running for at least the second time. Runaways soon learn skills for avoiding being apprehended. Nationwide, there are networks of homes, forming a kind of underground railway for runaways, where chil-

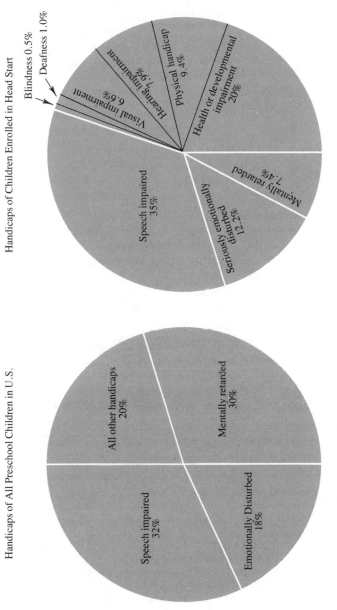

Handicaps of All Preschool Children in U.S.

Handicaps of Children Enrolled in Head Start

Blindness 0.5%
Deafness 1.0%
Visual impairment 6.6%
Hearing impairment 7.9%
Physical handicap 9.4%
Health or developmental impairment 20%
Mentally retarded 7.4%
Seriously emotionally disturbed 12.2%
Speech impaired 35%

All other handicaps 20%
Mentally retarded 30%
Emotionally Disturbed 18%
Speech impaired 32%

Figure 11–1. Comparative incidence of handicapping conditions among preschool children, 1974. (From *Children Today*, 1974, **3**, 9. U.S. Government Printing Office.)

dren can obtain lodging and maintenance at any time for as long as they choose (or sometimes for only as long as the adults in these homes choose). Names and addresses of these homes are shared so that a youth can plan a journey accordingly. Characteristics of the adults who maintain such homes, all extralegally, vary greatly. Some are benevolent and sincerely try to assist the runaways, protecting them from harm and working to effect a reconciliation with the parents. In other instances, the adults seem to be somewhat nonconforming and encourage the "doing of your own thing," but do not victimize or otherwise take any advantage of the youths they shelter. Yet another group of adults are in active conflict with society and expect the runaways to participate actively in various antisocial and delinquent enterprises. In these instances, the price exacted for shelter is costly. Once entangled in a web of organized stealing, prostitution, sexual abuse, or drug addiction, the youth is reduced to a helpless dependency from which escape is difficult.

In an effort to keep children who run away from compounding adjustment difficulties, officials working with juveniles have established reception centers in many areas. These are often located close to major highway intersections, a favored travel mode, and are open all the time. Help, especially in the form of food, small amounts of money, and transportation is available. Youths are not pressured and need not give any information in order to receive help. The only two questions they may be asked are, What do you need, and Is there any message we can deliver for you? During 1974, the Office of Youth Development (HEW) awarded $2.1 million in a comprehensive effort to identify techniques and programs for serving runaways. One funded program termed "Hotline" enables a youth anywhere in the United States to call a toll-free number (800-621-4000) and with complete anonymity request aid or delivery of a message.

The Role of the Parent

It should be apparent that environmental modification relies heavily upon working with the parent. The child is regarded as having the capacity to cope with his environment with only slight rearrangements or temporary supporting measures. Environmental modification approaches focus upon elimination, replacement, addition, or improvement of the existing surroundings. To accomplish those objectives, use is made of community resources, medical clinics, clubs, social groups, children's agencies, recreational programs, and vocational-training centers. It is essential to know what experiences, opportunities, or services each such facility can present. Ideally, the referring person is acquainted with the caliber of the caseworker, group leader, or supervisor of each facility.

Even though new thrusts and different approaches to child-care services appear, the parent continues to hold a central position. In one attempt to solve the often difficult matter of getting parents to take full advantage of services offered, planners of the Comprehensive Pediatric Care Center, designed to service low-income families in a sector of Baltimore, Maryland, deliberately promoted a volunteer parent group from the target population. In addition to being assigned real jobs on the clinic staff, these parents were given the task of publicizing the services that were available. Thus involved, the parents' enthusiastic support assured success for the center. Other promising approaches have concentrated on helping parents by supplying information that will assist them to make decisions as to the need for assistance, identifying the locations where services are available, detailing the specific services offered by specific agencies, explaining the implications of diagnoses or services given to the child, closely supporting parents' efforts to obtain needed services, and making "watch dog" follow-up contacts to encourage parents to pursue getting complete services. It has long been recognized that the stability a child may attain at a service agency is often destroyed by stresses incurred as the child returns to his home. A possibility for closing this gap by actively involving parents simultaneously in the treatment given the child is reported by Heiting (1971). It was found that maintaining close ties with the parents throughout the entire period of the child's treatment provided these advantages:

1. Presence of the parents acted to offset the child's fear of being abandoned and sent away from home.

2. Direct observation of interactions between the parent and child aided the staff in identifying specific behaviors as the focus for corrective attention.

3. Continued parent contact kept alive the fact that there was a problem and encouraged the parent to find some alternative ways for interacting with the child.

4. Making the parent part of the treatment program forced the detached or neglectful parent to accept his responsibilities to the child for either learning to get along with the child or giving up the child to a more favorable substitute family.

Generally, the parent must make the request for service, and so remains a key aspect of the treatment program. Whenever possible, work with the parent should center on help for the child and should avoid the parent's personal problems. Until other evidence is accumulated, it must be assumed that the parent has made an honest request for assistance and is able and willing to follow through with suggestions. Diagnostic-evaluative impressions must be shared with the parent in meaningful terms, and the parent apprised of the treatment objectives and plan. The following steps outline a guide for working with parents:

1. Allow for parental participation in dealing with the problem.

2. Involve the parent to the extent of his capacity and willingness.

3. Do not waver or become lost in a search for specific causes.

4. Be reassuring by taking charge of the problem and making specific recommendations that can be carried out.

Alteration Approaches

The procedures to be used in alleviating an adjustment problem are dependent upon the findings gained in diagnostic appraisal. As a general rule, the less the total life organization can be disrupted, the better the possibilities of the child's being able to profit from the treatment. (A poor home is better than no home.) When there are indications that moderate rearrangements of the existing environment will not be adequate for correcting the problem, more drastic measures must be considered. Less frequently used than environmental modification, environmental alteration has the objective of bringing about a total change in the child's surroundings. Alteration is dictated by the assumption that the child, for one reason or another, cannot continue in his present situation.

Because such a rearrangement of the child's life must be embarked upon only after the most careful appraisal, it is essential to ascertain that the child is able to profit from, rather than merely to tolerate, the new situation. To place a severely mentally retarded child in a highly stimulating, enriched, and achievement-demanding home may be the beginning of a change for the worse. Not only the potential for adjustment but the plasticity of the child must be considered. Age, then, becomes an important variable. Havighurst (1960) has found that foster homes are of limited value in effecting personality changes in children after they reach preadolescence.

A total incapacitation is seldom encountered, and partial changes may render the child socially competent. In such instances, a new family with a different set of parents may be sufficient for the continuation of normal development. This setup is especially true for the child who is young and possesses at least average physical and psychological resources. In other cases, it is apparent that the child has only the most tenuous relationship with his present surroundings and has no choice but to develop highly maladjustive strategies for maintaining himself in that situation. When even placement in a new family would not change behavior, and psychotherapy seems futile, it may then be necessary for a time to provide a completely controlled environment. Institutional placement becomes a necessity for the preservation of the child and the only hope for eventually building his capacity for tolerating a noninstitutional situation.

Jon's Reactions to Institutionalization

Jon stared out the window of his room . . . was it really a room? There were heavy iron bars on the window. Maybe this was really a space ship and he was all alone on a journey to Neptune. When had he

left? . . . Today . . . Thursday . . . Monday . . . Where was Wednesday?
. . . Who was Wednesday . . . Monday was Wednesday, or was
Wednesday Monday? Jon had noted that things often had two meanings,
two names . . . one that lots of people used and a special private one
that only he (and probably a few other spacemen) knew about. He had
talked about this with the school counselor, the one who had then had a
conference with his parents right before they went to see that doctor that
gave Jon those pills to take. Jon had not continued to take them because
they didn't taste like pills and he wasn't sure what they were. . . . As he
grasped the bars on the window, Jon noted the deep cuts on his wrists.
Had he been captured and tortured? Who were his enemies—where
were they now? He had told them only that he was a pupil in seventh
grade at Roosevelt Junior High, who never bothered anyone (he didn't
want them to know he spent all his time studying in the library and
reading about science and philosophy. Lots of people couldn't even spell
"astrophysics"). Maybe now he was being held a prisoner at the
Children's County Psychiatric Hospital. . . . Who would look for a
spaceman in a children's hospital . . . very good trick. Why did his
mother cry . . . was she just pretending, or did she not know that
spacemen may be captured and tortured? That was a long time ago . . .
or was she still his mother then? Jon couldn't figure it all out. . . . His
father worked in the bank. . . . His father might have been a spaceman
because no one could talk with him either , , , at least Jon had never
been able to find anything they could talk about. . . .

Jon had that funny feeling again that he was somehow two people
. . . was he twins, or did he have a twin? . . . When he was in third
grade, there were twins—girls that no one could tell apart. They
sometimes made a game of fooling people. . . . Was something or
somebody making Jon play that kind of game too? . . . He didn't want
to hurt anyone, he loved his mother. . . . Why did his mother bring him
here, away from his own home? . . . Didn't his family understand about
spacemen . . . didn't they love him? Did his own family not want him
anymore? . . . Didn't anybody want him? Dr. Baker at the hospital (if
this really was a hospital), who came by to talk with Jon, said she cared
about him. Maybe she did . . . she knew that Jon was a spaceman and
it didn't seem to bother her. . . . Sometimes Dr. Baker seemed like his
mother. Was this another trick being played on him? . . . Jon began to
shout for Dr. Baker. He had to find out just who she was and what was
going on about all these double people. . . .

There are no hard-and-fast rules to be followed in every case. Watson
(1951) has suggested a list of criteria that may be helpful in deciding
whether or not to transplant a child to a new environment:

1. The parents reject the child and are inaccessible for change by existing resources.

2. The parents' own needs cause them to be so deeply involved with the child as to prevent the child profiting from any environmental modifications and yet the parents are unable to accept treatment for themselves.

3. The child is delinquent and lives in a family group that contributes to his delinquency.

4. The mother is absent from the home, and there is no adequate mother substitute.

5. The care of the child places a disproportionate drain on the resources of the parental home (parents or child are extremely limited, severely retarded, and the like).

6. The child has not been able to profit from help supplied by other procedures and facilities.

7. Diagnostic study indicates that a totally new environment is the only likely way to help the child.

8. The type of situation in which the child can succeed has been ascertained and such a situation has been located.

Facilities available for placement of the child vary from a completely new family to a controlled and structured residential institution.

Placement Alternatives

Foster-Home Placement.   Finding a new family for the child is a procedure that has long been made use of in providing for children's needs. It is in many ways a "natural" approach—it attempts to continue the customary developmental situation found in our society, the family unit. The human infant is totally unable to provide for himself. The dependency upon adults tapers off as the child's maturing capacities permit him to assume more self-reliance, but full independence is not achieved until late in the adolescent period. Foster-home placement is a necessity for the infant even when there are no indications of adjustment problems. Sudden loss of both parents, for example, requires some provision for replacing the parents. In other instances, the parent—for example, a young unmarried mother—may decide to give up a child. These placements are generally made through a process of adoption, a legal procedure usually arranged by a caseworker and entailing court action.

Of greater relevance to intervention as a way of correcting a child's adjustment problems is action that takes him from his parents. This is a drastic step in which the recognized rights of the parent are superseded in the interest of protecting the rights of the child and/or society. Removal of the child from his original home is carried out by some interested agency acting with court sanction. The actual process is generally supervised by a caseworker. Removal of the child is undertaken only after detailed diagnostic study has established the child's basic potential for adequate adjustment and the inadequacy of the current home situation.

Upon being taken from his parents by court action, a child may be deemed suitable for adoption and placed in a permanent new home. Because it is difficult to obtain the legally required evidence of abuse, neglect, or condition detrimental to the child's psychological well-being, many children, especially older ones, are more likely to be adjudicated to the custody of the court than taken outright from parents. This motion gives the court and cooperating social agency necessary legal authority for controlling the child's placement. It has the advantage of permitting the court to act quickly and makes it more likely that the child will be placed in another home, since foster care is easier to secure than adoption. Prospective adoptive parents frequently are reluctant to commit themselves quickly to the binding responsibility of formal adoption. The placement of the child in a home by the court, with the court retaining custody of the child, may also permit the court to allocate money for the support of the child, thus lessening the financial obligation of the foster parents. The court has legitimate reasons for maintaining an evaluative relationship with the child in the foster home. Court control can be an effective bargaining device for insisting upon certain minimal conditions and standards within the home. If the child and the foster-home parents do not hit it off well, it is a relatively easy matter to place the child in another home.

The popularity of foster homes is suggested by statistics maintained by the Children's Bureau (HEW), which show that the total number of children in residential (institutional) care has decreased each year since 1933 even though opinion varies as to the preferred placement. More than twice as many children are in foster homes as are in residential placement. Agencies have overcome what were once considered impossible barriers to adoption such as ethnic and color differences and physical and mental handicaps. It is difficult to document outcomes of placement since whether a given situation is a source of happiness or distress for a particular individual is a subjective judgment. Continued exposure to conditions of relative happiness or distress also appears to have differential and unpredictable consequences for various persons. In the absence of any proven set of criteria or principles indicating which is the preferred choice, decisions about placement tend to be dictated by the hunches of an individual caseworker, agency policy, and the fact that residential care costs three to four times as much as foster home care. Standards for residential care have steadily risen but money allocated for such services has declined far below the level for purchasing quality residential care. In contrast, money allocated for support of foster-home care has annually increased and standards for acceptable foster parents and homes have declined. Changes in legal processes for placement have tended to make residential placement more difficult while making foster-home placements easier to accomplish.

Since the most obvious advantage of foster-home placement is the opportunity to supply the child with a family situation in which he can continue normal growth and development, the nature of the home and the characteristics of the new parents should be carefully considered. In their comprehensive review of foster-care services, Dinnage & Pringle (1967) came to the conclusion that the physical features of the home were generally of less important than the personal characteristics of the foster parents. They suggested characteristics for the successful foster parent:

1. Age over 40 years
2. No children of own living in the home
3. Wife not employed outside the home
4. Middle socioeconomic status
5. Average in education and ambition
6. Stable, confident, and satisfied with life
7. "Home and family" oriented

Although admitting that some of the most satisfactory foster home placements were those in which there was a fortuitous matching of a proper parental excess (mothering) with a child's deficit (rejection), they also listed some reasons why half of all foster-home placements fail:

1. Inadequate study of the home and the child
2. Placements with young parents who have their own children living in the home
3. Parents whose lives are organized about "causes"
4. Parents of a marked inclination to experiment and venture
5. Persons seeking only the status of parents
6. Parents who themselves have a pattern of being unable to cope with life demands
7. The presence of wide differences in religious, educational, or moral beliefs held by the parent and the child
8. Children who are ten years of age or older, and especially those who have failed in a series of previous foster placements

Child candidates for foster-home placement are referred by social agencies, probation and juvenile officials, and children's institutions. As can be gathered from the preceding discussion, there are many advantages to the courts' retaining custody of the child and purchasing the necessary services of a family and home for the child. Many children are able to profit from the new home and family, extinguishing old and maladjustive behavior patterns and acquiring new and socially acceptable responses. Other children, particularly young ones, are not able to profit from a new home or family; such children require a more structured and controlled environment.

Institutional Placement

For those children who have limited capicity for dealing with life-adjustment demands, a situation is required in which there is scheduling, regulation, control of demands, and the supplying of highly particular training and procedures. These services are usually available in the continual-care programs of an institutional setting. For children having the most limited potentials for life adjustment, such as the severely mentally retarded, permanent institutional placement may be necessary. Other children can benefit from the services provided by an institution to the extent that they may be able to move out into a regular place in society and function adequately.

Specific Treatment: Short- or Long-Term Agencies

Included here are institutions that offer specific services. The service may be surgical or medical care to correct a physical defect (deformed leg or foot) or to diagnose and treat a medical problem, such as epilepsy or a metabolic dysfunction (diabetes). During the time the child is hospitalized, as for a lengthy series of surgical operations, he will require other services, such as psychotherapy or educational tutoring. Other problems that necessitate residential facilities for treatment are those requiring specific and prolonged therapy and special education and training. The deaf, blind, language-disabled, socially deviant, and emotionally disturbed are examples. Residential schools for the cerebral-palsied, blind, or deaf are to be found in most states. The emphasis is on providing particular training, and the staff is made up largely of teachers trained in the special educational problems of these exceptional children. Children are in these schools only for the usual school year, going home in the summers. After a few years, a majority have had enough special help to be able to keep up in regular schools.

Another type of residential school where children may be admitted for up to several years for special service is the institution dealing with social and emotional problems. Schools concerned with social deviants are more numerous, and several may be found in even less populous states. More popularly known as "training schools," "reformatories," or "detention homes," these institutions were originally designed to take the place of jails and adult reformatories. The emphasis was on control and supervision of the children committed to the institution by court decree. Gradually, improvements have been made to include education and casework-counseling services to the children. Institutions for the socially deviant are among the most overcrowded facilities to be found. They have all too often served more as crime schools for the children committed, so that most workers are reluctant to make this type of placement.

Residential facilities for emotionally disturbed children have always been in critically short supply. Privately operated institutions, generally bearing the title of "school," are so costly as to be prohibitive for all but a few children. In some states, schools for the emotionally disturbed are being opened under state auspices. These are frequently in association with existing state mental hospitals. Those in conjunction with medical schools tend to have the most complete staff complement and a favorably low staff-patient ratio. Residential institutions for the emotionally disturbed have as their special service various types of treatment for emotional disorders. Psychotherapy, chemotherapy, education, and an emphasis on family living units are typical. The Sonja Heinkman Orthogenic School, associated with the University of Chicago, is an excellent example of the milieu approach to treatment. Some larger cities have semiprivate residential schools for the emotionally disturbed. In general, there is a long waiting list even for the expensive private schools. Admission to state-operated schools is usually by court-ordered commitment. Parents or guardians must arrange the admission for either a public or a private institution.

Complete Home: Long Term or Permanent

A second major group of residential institutions is organized to provide a home for children on a permanent basis. These institutions, sometimes referred to as "orphanages" or simply as "homes," are also designated as "group homes" in the current technical literature. They are frequently privately operated, especially by church groups, but most counties and large cities also have such facilities for dependent or abandoned children. A number of children are adopted or placed in regular homes from these institutions. But, for a significant number of children, the institution becomes their permanent home and they reside there until they are "graduated" or reach the release age, often about 18 or 19 years of age. The emphasis is on providing the routine as well as the physical and emotional needs of family home life. There are institutional "parent" persons and frequently casework service. Larger institutions (more than 30 children) are often organized on the "cottage" plan. Children are assigned to small groups for living in one of several residence buildings, like a large house, on the institution's grounds. Necessary special services—medical, dental, or educational—are generally purchased or arranged for the children from sources in the surrounding community. Developmental institutions have the advantages of stability and consistency, but children in residence can fall into a pattern of isolation unless frequent contacts with the community are included in the total program.

Placement Objectives and Outcomes

Objectives.   The removal of a child from his home is likely to arouse a number of controversial feelings. In some ways, such a step seems to threaten the very existence of society by breaking up the basic societal unit, the family. Nevertheless, some form of placement is vital for some children; for example, there is obvious justification in hospitalizing a child for a series of bone-graft operations that will require months to complete. The child whose parents are suddenly removed or absented from the home must have a continuation of care and supervision. But there are other reasons for which placements are made. The practice is to remove the child from a home environment judged to be one in which the child can never learn to adjust or to attain stability. If the decision is that the child must have a neutral, highly structured environment that makes minimal demands on him in order to protect and then strengthen his capacity for adjustment, then placement in an institution is made.

Demands and Conditions of Placement.   The intention of placement as a method for permitting the child to continue the pattern of normal development is not debatable. There are many successful outcomes providing tangible evidence of the effectiveness of placement. Placement as a technique for intervention has, in fact, become widespread and gives every indication of gaining even more general use and acceptance.

Workers dealing with children have often been intrigued with a technique that looks good on paper but in practice proves disappointing. Some techniques for changing behavior, including some that require the greatest skill in diagnostic evaluation or training and time from the worker, appear to have little observable benefit for the child or may even make him worse. For example, a carefully made diagnostic study may indicate that a severely rejected child should be placed in an orphanage. As a consequence, the child may interpret the action as tangible evidence that he is rejected. To add to the problem, he may view his being taken from his home as severe punishment. In discussing this possibility, Fine (1966) cautioned that movement of a child to a foster home "even one especially selected to meet the anticipated needs of the . . . youngsters, is . . . a calculated risk." It is a shock for some children to find that having another person interested in them demands interpersonal responsibilities they have not acquired. The child may resist intensively and actively these new responsibilities, negating any possible benefit from the change. Fine concludes by suggesting that placements be made only reluctantly and with generous support for the new parents and for the child.

A study carried out by Jenkins & Sauber (1964) listed the reasons given for placement of children in New York City from May through August of 1963. A total of 891 children (all over 6 months old) from 425 families were placed, for these reasons:

29%—physical illness of an adult in the family
11%—mother had mental illness
17%—child had severe emotional problems
10%—severe parental neglect or abuse
33%—miscellaneous, including parental incompatibility, parental incompetence, drug addiction, alcoholism, arrest, child abandonment, and unwillingness of caretakers other than parents to continue care in the home

It was found that the majority of the families from which these children were removed lived in conditions of poverty and lacked supportive community services. The problems confronting the families seem to be directly related to pressures associated with limited finances. Of the 425 families, 44% were one-parent families, mostly headed by the mother. Only 38% of the families were receiving public assistance at the time of the placement. Follow-up study of the children placed revealed the surprising information that 49% spent no more than 3 months in placement; 16% were in placement for less than one week. Emotionally disturbed children were in foster care for the longest period of time, and there seems little reason to question a residential setting as the preferred placement for the emotionally disturbed child.

The findings obtained by Jenkins and Sauber imply that greater use of existing community resources, such as casework services, mental-health clinics, and day-care centers, could assist these families under stress. Financial supports also seem to have the same potential for the alleviation of pressures. The most surprising data concern the follow-up on the length of time spent in placement. It seems obvious that homemaker service, employment of a caretaker, or temporary shelters could easily avoid the necessity of making from one-fourth to one-half of the placements reported in this study.

Outcomes as Gauged by Children's Reactions. Intervention has the objective of improving the child's chances for realizing his potential for adjustment. However, the pressures for action have often been so great that there has been limited opportunity to follow the outcome of intervention. Yet the question must be raised: How effective is such intervention as placement in another home or in an institution? The question may best be answered by the children themselves.

A study conducted by DeFries, Jenkins, & Williams (1964) compared the responses of two groups of children matched on sex, age, IQ, and socioeconomic background. At the start of the study, all of the children were emotionally disturbed wards of the New York City Department of Welfare. One group remained under treatment in a residential institution. Children in the other group were placed in foster homes where they and the foster parents were also supplied psychotherapy. Surprisingly, children in the foster-home placement did less well than did those who continued to live in the institution. Foster-home placement seemed to have the adverse effect of accentuating the children's feelings of being different. Most unexpected were these children's reports that their needs for satisfying affectional relationships were not fulfilled in the foster homes. Older children seemed to encounter somewhat more adjustment stress in foster-home placement than did younger children. In a review that questioned the adequacy of "the good old foster home" for dealing with disturbed children, Redl (1966) came to this conclusion:

> As an institution for the safeguarding of the mental health of vulnerable children, the foster home of yesterday is either extinct or not sufficient anymore. It is an obsolete answer to a current problem of huge proportions.

Redl made a strong plea for well-staffed residential treatment centers to care for disturbed children.

Recounting his experiences in dealing with long-term institutionally placed children, Moss (1966) reported that most institutionalized children have little idea of how and why they came into placement and of what is planned for their future. They may harbor bitter feelings of having been victimized or experience chronic pain at having been rejected by parents or society in general. An orientation of inadequacy, helplessness, and accompanying hopelessness may develop if the child's predicament is not realized and dealt with. Moss recommends including the child in discussions about his future as a way of instilling a healthier outlook. The essential ingredient influencing successful outcomes in placement may be that of "adequate parental care," the quality of the interaction between the child and parent substitutes. A parental figure and child can be together constantly in the same room, a room filled with stimulating objects (toys), sounds (music, language), and activities, and yet the child can be subject to deprivation with profound consequences. What is necessary for adequate parental care is not objective stimulation nor an emotional feeling but rather a complex relationship in which there is mutual interaction between the child and parent substitute, a reciprocal interchange of give-and-take out of which the child can develop adaptive skills. A permanent staff in the ratio of one worker for each two children during waking hours is basic for assuring adequate parental care. Children may be most in need of this aspect of treatment between the ages of 2 and 5 years.

It is apparent that intervention can be highly effective by way of making it possible for children to overcome adjustment difficulties. While many children who are given selected assistance will be able to continue patterns of normal development, the same procedures may compound and prolong adjustment problems for other children. Placement is most likely to aggravate adjustment and must be sparingly used and closely observed for signs of unfavorable consequences. The objectives of intervention involving placement must be made explicit to the child and to the parents. Foster-home placement appears to be especially hazardous for older children.

Problems in Integrating Services

Overlap

Even when services to children are well defined and services to dependent families are clear-cut, there remains a large gray area in which the services overlap. The problem is made more difficult by the fact that these services are seldom defined or definable with specificity. Jenkins & Sauber (1964) found that the families of children given placement services typically were living on the edges of poverty and lacked the support of existing community services. Parents were sometimes bogged down by more demands for being parents than they could muster, but family problems were also frequently related to inadequate economic resources.

Buell (1952) found that 6% of the families in one area were receiving 68% of the available community services. He describes the "multiple agency contacting" family, which often adds to the pressures impinging on it by being involved with four or five agencies. Each agency must make a diagnostic intake study preparatory to assisting the family. These diagnostic studies are often remarkably similar. The recommendations may depend on the agency's particular service. One worker tells the family to clean up the living quarters, another wants the children taken to school immediately, another tells a parent to enter the hospital tomorrow, yet another wants the parent to take the job the worker has found or financial aid will be terminated, and a juvenile officer comes by to take a child for questioning. Such an array of demands is enough to disrupt even the most stable of families. Puzzled as to which "boss" should be heeded, the parents may believe the safest course of action is to do nothing. A smoldering resentment at all the pressure may find expression in passive, uncooperative attitudes which are exceedingly difficult to deal with.

The Need for Centralization

It becomes apparent that some organization and coordination of services is essential, for multiple agency contacts obviously increase the pressures on an already disabled family unit. There is also the matter of tying up the services of personnel already in short supply in duplications of intake interviews, home visits, and related diagnostic study. Not only is there misuse of specialist personnel, but the actual delivery of available services is impaired when there is no central coordination. Any one community agency should be able to deliver services directly (casework, financial aid) or indirectly (surgical care, temporary placement). Ways are being found to circumvent artificially drawn but real barriers based on professional areas of competence. But these must presently be approached indirectly and thus are time-consuming. A direct approach would be more efficient and possibly more effective. In addition to actually increasing services available by cutting duplications, central coordination has the potential for supplying answers to urgent questions. Solutions to these problems are essential for effective allocations and planning for future service-delivery systems:

1. Why do some families seem to fall apart, becoming totally disorganized and chaotic, even in the absence of discernible stresses?
2. What types of temporary crisis care should be developed and how can they be integrated as elements of a continuing treatment program?
3. How can the return of children to the mainstream be speeded up?
4. Which manpower and technological components are basic to an effective centralized total child care services agency?

The gray areas in the delivery of children's services are in parent-child relationships, protective services, and supervisory care. It is here that details of planning and coordination must be carefully worked out as is illustrated by Braginsky & Braginsky's (1974) findings that "retarded" children were institutionalized because of family disintegration and rejection and not because of being mentally retarded. One of many possibilities is for the school to be designated as the center for coordination, in recognition of the major influence of the school upon the child. New York and Idaho have made significant advances in facilitating court action on behalf of children. Physicians, who are frequently the first to be consulted regarding the need for services, are likely to be the least knowledgeable about community resources unless they are among the few who have had specific training in community services (Olshansky & Sternfeld, 1962). A study of children in residential treatment identified complex problems in referral-admission-release policies, follow-up services, and parent participation and resulted in Rhode Island's creating a central state office for coordinating these services (Maluccio, 1974).

In discussing untangling the barriers impeding delivery of services to children, Hobbs (1975) identified two major difficulties:

1. Agencies like to coordinate but object to being coordinated.
2. Agencies tend to give first priority to agency survival and second priority to the services they are charged with providing.

The entire matter is complex, demanding integration of children's, parent's, and society's rights. In view of the many legal aspects, the solutions may eventually be worked out through court actions.

Emerging Trends

A continuing expansion in intervention services is to be expected. Despite the admitted limitation, some type of intervention stands as the most effective procedure for influencing the welfare of maladjusted children. Information collected by the U.S. Children's Bureau (1965) indicated that only one-fourth to one-half of those children known or estimated to be in need of services were receiving them in 1964. In a discussion of children's problems, Witmer (1964) reported that one-fourth of all children were in homes where the family income was inadequate to provide basic needs. Out of the practice of providing services, ideas and beliefs initially having only theoretical existence have become solid and effective intervention techniques. Foster-home placement is currently the major child service, but there has been a reappraisal of institutional placement. Formerly regarded as punitive and ineffectual, institutions can contribute far more than mere custodial care for the child if they are provided with adequate staffs. The capacity for positive contribution is greatly strengthened when education is recognized as an important kind of therapy and when it is realized that many parents cannot be changed so that treatment directed to them may be wasted. The following sections review some of the major new developments in children's services.

Project Re-Ed

A grant from the federal government in 1961 launched a promising special study project to investigate facilities for the emotionally disturbed child of school age. The state mental-health departments of Tennessee and South Carolina are cooperatively involved in administering two residential schools that form the nucleus of the project. Each school enrolls 40 children aged 6 to 12 years. The children are subdivided into 5 working groups of 8 children each. For each of these groups a team of staff members is continuously assigned; the team includes teacher-counselors, teacher-counselor trainees, teacher aides, and resource persons from the special areas of art, music, and physical education. The staff team is assisted by volunteer workers. The schools have psychiatric, educational, social-work, and psychological-consultative services, but these are for diagnostic evaluation of the child and consultation for the staff members. The program now serves all of Tennessee and one center has been opened in Kentucky.

Treatment centers about the educational program provided by or under the supervision of the teacher-counselor. Children are referred by local area schools and are informed that they will return there. From Sunday evening through Friday afternoon the children are in residence at the project school. Weekends are spent at home with the family, thus enforcing the parents' rights vis-à-vis the child. Outstanding innovations are the teacher-counselor as a mental-health specialist and the concept of coordination and control remaining with the local community school, along with reduced costs, intensive short-term intervention, mobilization of community resources, and a focus on behavioral and personal competence.

Project Re-Ed has had a promising debut and seems to have much to commend it as a facility for the emotionally disturbed. It is not intended to take the place of psychiatric institutions for severely disturbed children, but it appears to have the capacity to prevent such severe personality disorganization. Evaluations of Re-Ed (Weinstein, 1971) have found it to be a generally effective program with approximately 80% of its graduates maintaining improvement for at least 6 months following discharge. Moreover, the cost was only one-third that of in-patient care in a state psychiatric facility.

Illinois Zone Centers

The need for some type of residential facility for emotionally disturbed children remains the most critical deficit of all services for children. The Illinois Department of Mental Health has put into operation a model plan for speeding up services to children. The state is divided into eight geographic regions, termed "zones." Centrally located in each zone is a center staffed and equipped to carry out extensive diagnostic evaluations. Added to the usual diagnostic team of psychiatrist, social worker, and psychologist is an educational specialist. The center has a limited number of residential spaces, which can be assigned either on an extended diagnostic-observation basis or on a temporary (or emergency) treatment basis. The staff of the center maintains contacts with all other possible treatment agencies in the zone area, and referrals may be made back to these agencies, as well as being received from them. A service most recently inaugurated sends staff members skilled in behavior modification techniques into the homes of children having severe adjustment problems. The staff member remains to do on-the-spot training of parents in procedures appropriate for the disturbed child.

The zone centers have the advantages of being part of the community, being easily accessible, holding accommodations for short-term intensive care, and having a representative staff complement. They concentrate treatment by focusing on the specific symptom or disability that is preventing the child from getting along in school or the community.

Halfway Houses

The necessity for some type of mediating step to bridge the suddenly incurred changes from institutional life to community life has long been recognized. Very few institutions make a provision for this transition. The Division of Vocational Rehabilitation (DVR) is keenly aware of the problem and frequently has purchased this type of service for its clients. The problem is most severe for older adolescents and youths who have lived in an institution for several years. The Illinois Department of Mental Health has established a halfway house unit made up of several residences in a large city. Youths released from state institutions may live in the halfway house for as long as two years while locating work, completing training, or simply getting used to "the grind." Counseling, financial assistance, and technical advice are available.

Day-Care Centers as Diagnostic-Observation and Parent-Training Stations

A portion of the greatly increased funding support of day-care programs has been allocated for the operation of day-care centers located so as to serve children of ADC (Aid for Dependent Children) and working mothers. Day-care centers have recognized the value of including training to help parents of children served to be more effective in the parental role. The demand for day-care service is growing rapidly. Professional workers have become aware of the potential of this service, which is primarily for preschool children. A pattern is evolving in which the staff of day-care centers is greatly strengthened and the centers become continuous observation stations. In this way potential behavior problems can be detected early, and prompt treatment can prevent more serious or chronic problems.

New Personnel Categories

It is generally recognized that needed professional workers may never be trained in sufficient quantity. Some of the most imaginative developments have been concerned with solving the manpower shortage. Leaders in the field have urged trying out what are sometimes referred to as "auxiliary" or "subprofessional" personnel. In describing the effectiveness of such persons, Brieland (1965) lists three possible types of subprofessional workers who can make important contributions in children's services:

1. Case aide—a caseworker trained at the bachelor's-degree level
2. Preprofessional—a college graduate trained in a field related to casework

3. Volunteer—an assistant who may or may not have had college training, but who enjoys working with children and is willing to tutor, take children on trips, supervise games, and so on

There are enthusiastic reports of the successful use of such subprofessional workers. In Chicago, college students organized and manned a volunteer program called Helping Hands, in which tutoring, recreational, and enrichment activities were provided after school for disadvantaged children. In New York City, Philadelphia, and Los Angeles there has been success in using "the poor to help the poor." Persons are employed as aides to work in subprofessional activities with the disadvantaged. This arrangement can provide needed employment in addition to speeding up the acceptance of offered services when local persons man neighborhood "information" centers.

It has been suggested that the only way to attack the vexing problem of getting services to migrant worker families may be that of employing individuals from these same migrant groups to carry out activities of tutoring, counseling, and supervisory care for children. The success of such an effort remains to be verified, but the idea is illustrative of the innovative approaches that are evolving in a sincere effort to make it feasible for each child to have a maximum opportunity for realizing his potential.

Delivery of Services to Sparsely Populated Areas

At several points, we have mentioned that large communities have more of the resources customarily utilized in intervention approaches. This has been a description, not a criticism. Acute shortages in trained mental-health manpower are perhaps nowhere more evident than in sparsely populated areas. The provision of mental-health and welfare services to communities of fewer than 50,000 persons is indeed an urgent and challenging problem.

That there is no shortage in these areas of what is perhaps the most important of all resources—human ingenuity—is attested to by the number of communities that have met the problem. In some instances, counties are banding together to form a single service unit. In a centrally located center, mental-health clinics, vocational-rehabilitation offices, general hospitals, and other welfare service facilities are situated. In another plan, a group of specialists may have a regular schedule of working in several medium-sized towns for one or two days a week. Mental-health specialists have sometimes worked out schedules that allow them to work in a regular consultative capacity with local-community paraprofessionals (ministers, teachers, public-health nurses, physicians) who are apt to have the most direct day-to-day contacts with persons needing help.

The involvement of interested citizens of the community in planning programs for the delivery of services to the populace is in its own right an essential service. Participants in such community-action projects may find helpful the recommendations for improving services to children compiled by Jenkins & Sauber (1964):

1. Round-the-clock intake services
2. Greater interagency coordination
3. Provision of funds to pay relatives and family friends to care for the children
4. Expansion of family and group day-care facilities
5. More shelter-care resources
6. Increased supply of long-term placement resources for emotionally disturbed children
7. Expansion of and more flexibility in homemaker services
8. Expansion of community psychiatric services
9. Improved means for reporting child abuse and neglect
10. Increased services aimed at strengthening family life

Marshaling Volunteer Workers

One of the most satisfactory approaches for expanding services has been that of organizing volunteer workers, who can be recruited in every community. Acknowledging that some of the most effective services have been delivered by volunteer and nonprofessional organizations, of which Alcoholics Anonymous is an outstanding example, most community-based agencies are finding ways for tapping this rich resource as a way of supplementing an overburdened staff. Volunteer workers have proven immensely resourceful, even when not directly attached to a specific agency. In some communities, volunteers man twenty-four-hour crisis services in the form of telephone centers such as "PATH" (Personal Assistance Telephone Help), where anyone can call at any time for information about any problem or concern, revealing only as much and pursuing the concern only to the extent desired. Other innovative volunteer services include parents who serve as "uncles and aunts," taking children for weekend visits from residential centers or families under stress. An unexpected added value of the work of volunteers is the fact that volunteers generally become ardent spokesmen and supporters of the agency or service to which they relate.

Humanitarian Emphases

Many professional workers are convinced that new concerns in the delivery of existing services is more urgent than is the discovery of new services. They cite the extreme objectivity, mechanization, and professional lingo characteristic of the setting in which many services are delivered. Such aloofness, distance, and unintelligibility may be interpreted as disregard, neglect, or belittlement and can quickly alienate the person seeking reassurance and concerned understanding. As a consequence, uncooperativeness, resignation, and an increasing feeling of helplessness may easily override any beneficial aspect of the treatment. Many professional workers have found that treatment does not work when the child is dealt with as an IBM number and that fads and shortcuts may compound more than cure. Possibly of the greatest significance are those resources inherent in having the complete cooperation and trust of the client. Dealing with the client in an open, unhurried, and friendly manner to ensure his complete understanding of the treatment processes and possible outcomes, although not new, is proving more effective than many therapy fads. A particularly common problem has been the tendency of a client to feel rebuffed or "dumb" when he asks for a service not offered by some agency. As a way of preventing such a treatment barrier, the newly opening Monroe Development Center, a facility designed to serve a wide spectrum of severely impaired children in the Rochester area of New York, has established close contacts with 18 other child-care service agencies in the community. The center is thus able to assure all clients that something can and will be done for the client's problem. Another evidence of a spreading humanitarian concern is to be observed in the follow-up services that many agencies now include as a routine part of all treatment.

Issues in Child-Care Services

The discussion of community child-care services has tended to follow an approach of emphasizing the positive features in the belief that practitioners can be of greater assistance to a child than can a critic. The intent has not been to suggest that all services described are perfect or that persons engaged in delivery of services should not be expected to change. Methods for intervention evolve slowly and are proven over time. Generally several treatment approaches may have approximately equal effectiveness. The decision to invoke one or another treatment method is largely a subjective one, growing out of the professional worker's appraisal of the situation and his perceived personal competencies. An awareness of these issues by each therapist can help to reduce unwanted consequences.

Idealized Image of the Family

In a provoking analysis of the family unit as found in the United States, Whistell (1970) points out that a stylized concept of the family (father, mother, children, in perfect harmony) is accepted as typical and general. Self-sufficiency, mutual concern for members, healthy stimulation, individual respect and freedom, and uniquely satisfying opportunities are qualities blatantly ascribed to the family by the communications media, the arts, and the behavioral sciences. This stereotyped model is invoked as the yardstick for measuring the adequacy of adulthood, social competency, and general success and happiness in life. Used as the base for evaluation by legal, social, medical, behavioral, and religious professionals, it has serious implications for the assignment of services and selection of treatment objectives. Whistell suggests that the popular picture is far from the truth in that most families are overburdened with responsibilities and struggle for unobtainable goals, a situation that guarantees significant amounts of frustration, defeat, and failure for parents and children. Additional misconceptions include the family's being the unduplicable center devoted to the exclusive serving of children's interests.

This misconception makes it difficult for many persons to understand why a child would be dissatisfied and unappreciative of his home and parents. The strength of the idolization afforded the family unit makes it difficult for everyone, including professional workers, to accept the fact that children may be less than the center of attention. They may in fact be unwanted, abused, neglected, or have an existence only in that they make the status of parents for some persons.

Unanticipated Consequences of Placement

Placement of the child in a foster home or a residential setting has come to be accepted as the ultimate in providing services for the child. Once the child is accepted in placement, the professional worker has typically breathed a sigh of relief and chalked up another "success." So complete is the faith that the child's problems are now assured correction that there is seldom any follow-up of placement. Information provided by workers on residential staffs indicates that the picture is not so simply resolved. At the start, the child's adjustment may worsen as the child senses placement as evidence that no one, including his parents, wants him. The apparent rejection can be a severe blow, jarring an already weak self-esteem. Placement invariably results in a reduction if not a frank elimination of forces that normally support and maintain the child. Parents may believe the child no longer needs their attention or that they will only be interfering with efforts of the institutional staff.

In some instances, the gap between parent and child may be unintentionally widened by well-meaning staff persons who are attempting to develop a close relationship with the child. Yet another undesirable consequence of placement can occur when a child is accepted or forced into a residential or other setting that is really not prepared to offer the specific service required by the child. Even parents and workers may find a measure of relief in the belief that "something is at last being done," when, in actuality, the move may prevent the development of the special services the child really needs. The child's problem is thus only aggravated and prolonged.

Slowness of Legal and Other Procedures

Reference has been made to the basic role of legal proceedings in the sanctioning and apportionment of many intervention efforts. The motion of legal machinery is notoriously slow, if for no other reason than the necessity for meeting all requirements for safeguarding the child's rights. The delay may assure protection of legal rights and allow for a desired complete study of the problem, but when treatment is finally made available, the child may have difficulty connecting the treatment to his problems "of long ago." This is especially likely to be true when the behavior problem entails a pattern of social maladjustment.

In other instances, the painfully slow preliminary procedures may prevent the child from receiving treatment when most critically needed. By the time the hearing, investigation, home study, diagnosis, and selection of a treatment program have all been put together, a child's condition can easily have changed. When the change is for the better, improvement can be interpreted as indicating the child no longer needs help. Although the acute signs of disorder may have subsided, the chronic features may remain and go untreated. An outcome less directly damaging to the child, but of unknown jeopardy for children's services, occurs if the child has actually recovered from his difficulty during the time his case is being "worked on." When the child finally appears for treatment, examination reveals treatment is no longer needed, thus capping a waste of resources and creating a confusion that leaves the treatment agency and the child wondering what it is all about.

Implications of Treatment Innovations

An important set of considerations rests almost exclusively with the therapist who must select methods and allocate resources of treatment. All available information considered, many conditions seem to respond about equally well to a number of different approaches. There are at the same time some conditions for which no treatment seems to be effective. The sincere professional worker, wanting to be of all possible help, is faced with excessive demands for services, must acknowledge a training in therapy that is at best limited, and is well aware of the uncertainties regarding etiologies and treatment outcomes. A situation is thus set in which the therapist himself may experience feelings of frustration, helplessness, and anxiety.

In the effort to cope with these demands, therapists, like all people, make some good and some bad moves. A common practice is to "try something else," and the field of therapy has witnessed a plethora of fads and new fashions, some standing largely on a foundation of "innovation." In a thoughtful review of these developments, Mishne (1972) points out that "fad adherents as a group seem to have little capacity to tolerate the human condition of anxiety" (p. 303). Recounting that just as social forces and technological developments are viewed as major dehumanizing aspects of society, so treatment programs based on panaceas, mechanical constructs, or a molding of the client to fit the services offered are equally lacking in respect for humanism and individuality. The use of paraprofessional workers, on the increase in child-care services, can be viewed as a clever way for generating more service or as a slighting of the child who cannot afford to pay for the fully qualified professional worker. Charting a treatment program without information supplied by a careful diagnostic study is a special variety of therapeutic "forked tongue," which can avoid duplications in services but can also be demeaning to the child whose problems are thus judged as not worthy of study.

Summary

The community holds potent resources for facilitating and promoting a satisfactory adjustment for every child.

An in-depth study of the problem and the objectives and methods to be used in correcting it are essential as preliminary steps in community intervention.

Environmental modification approaches for helping the child permit him to remain in the home and may entail counseling for the family, surgical or medical services, special help from the school, recreational, or vocational services, or temporary shelter care.

Environmental alteration procedures center about moving the child to a new setting and include foster-home placement, change in guardianship for the child, and residential placement.

To be effective, all community child welfare specialists and resources must collaborate in the intervention effort.

Courts and child advocacy agents have assumed an increasing role in the delivery of community services to children.

Community intervention efforts appear to be more effective when parental involvement is obtained.

Promising new approaches for providing needed services include administrative centralization, use of volunteers, and unique organization to allocate services in short supply.

Associated with the increase in services are certain issues such as child-parent-society rights, degrading of service quality, dependency, and adequacy of any given home for any given child.

References

Braginsky B. M., & Braginsky, D. D. The mentally retarded: Society's Hansels and Gretels. *Psychology Today*, 1974, **7**, 18–30.

Brieland, D. The efficient use of child welfare personnel. *Children*, 1965, **12**, 91–96.

Buell, B. *Community planning for human services*. New York: Columbia University Press, 1952.

Cohen, S. Integrating children with handicaps into early childhood education programs. *Children Today*, 1975, **4**, 15–17.

DeFries, Z., Jenkins, S., & Williams, E. E. Treatment of disturbed children in foster care. *American Journal of Orthopsychiatry*, 1964, **34**, 126–39.

Dinnage, R., & Pringle, M. W. K. *Foster home care facts and fallacies*. New York: Humanities Press, 1967.

Fine, R. Moving emotionally disturbed children from institution to foster families. *Children*, 1966, **13**, 221–26.

Havighurst, R. J. *Education in metropolitan areas*. Boston: Allyn & Bacon, 1960.

Heiting, K. H. Involving parents in residential treatment of children. *Children*, 1971, **18**, 162–67.

Hobbs, N. *The futures of children*. San Francisco, Calif.: Jossey-Bass, 1975.

Jenkins, S., & Sauber, M. *Paths to child placement: family situations prior to foster care*. New York: Community Council of Greater New York, 1964.

Kadushin, A. *Child welfare services: a source book*. New York: Macmillan, 1970.

Klein, J. W., & Randolph, L. A. Placing handicapped children in Head Start programs. *Children Today*, 1974, **4**, 7–9.

Maluccio, A. Residential treatment of disturbed children: a study of service delivery. *Child Welfare*, 1974. **54**, 225–35.

Mid-Decade Conference on Children and Youth Report. Washington, D.C.: National Committee for Children and Youth, 1966.

Mishne, J. Traditional knowledge reaffirmed. *Social Caseworker*, 1972, **53**, 300–6.

Moss, S. Z. How children feel about being placed away from home. *Children*, 1966, **13**, 153–57.

Olshansky, S., & Sternfeld, L. Attitudes of some pediatricians toward the institutionalization of mentally retarded children. *Training School Bulletin*, 1962, **59**, 67–73.

Redl, F. *When we deal with children*. New York: Free Press, 1966.

Thomas, G. Children in institutions. *Children Today*, 1974, **3**, 34–35.

U.S. Children's Bureau: child welfare statistics, 1964. Washington, D.C.: Government Printing Office, 1965.

Watson, R. I. *The clinical method in psychology*. New York: Harper & Row, 1951.

Weinstein, L. The evaluation research: the effectiveness of the Re-Ed intervention. Unpublished manuscript. George Peabody College for Teachers, 1971.

Whistell, R. L. B. The idealized model of the American family. *Social Caseworker*, 1970, **51**, 195–98.

Witmer, H. L. Children and poverty. *Children*, 1964, **11**, 207–13.

Zigler, E. The trouble with our child care. *Day Care & Early Education*, 1973, **1**, 13–16.

Suggested Readings

Bower, E. M., & Hollister, W. G. (Eds.) *Behavioral science frontiers in education*. New York: Wiley, 1967.

Costin, L. B. *Child welfare: policies and practices*. New York: McGraw-Hill, 1972.

Glasscote, R. M., Raybin, J. B. Reifler, C. B., & Kane, A. W. *The alternative services: their role in mental health*. Washington, D.C.: American Psychiatric Association, 1975.

Shore, M. F., & Mannino, F. V. (Eds.) *Mental health and the community: problems, programs, and strategies*. New York: Behavioral Publications, 1969.

Zax, M., & Specter, G. *An introduction to community psychology*. New York: Wiley, 1974.

Classroom Management of Behavior Problems

In keeping with the new outlook in school mental hygiene, teachers have been assigned a central role in promoting the mental health of their pupils. By and large, however, while teachers have been given this added responsibility, they have not been adequately equipped with the tools needed to fulfill their new role. One important aspect of classroom mental health of substantial concern to teachers centers around the problem of classroom discipline, and it is to this topic that this chapter addresses itself. There are times in every teacher's day when he must interfere with the pupils' behavior in order to safeguard the classroom program of instruction as well as the psychological and physical safety of the pupils.

After a discussion of the inadequacy of professional technical assistance offered teachers in the past, we focus on two current approaches that have much to offer regarding daily classroom management. The basic concern is with the control of surface behavior rather than with the underlying attitudes, although some consideration is also given to the latter. The specific thesis of this chapter is that teachers *can* cope with problem behavior and do this as well as psychiatrists, psychologists, and social workers. While a "hands-off" policy prevailed in the past, it is becoming increasingly evident that teachers who are successful in managing the behavior of nondisturbed children are also relatively successful with emotionally disturbed children (Kounin, Friesen, & Norton, 1966).

Statement of the Problem

Many schoolteachers, males as well as females, are concerned about matters of classroom discipline. A survey by the National Education Association (1973), for example, noted that discipline was a frequently reported problem among teachers. This same study also revealed that educational leaders regarded the maintenance of discipline as an even greater problem of teachers. Whereas 54% of teachers listed the management of disruptive students as a problem, 88% of educational leaders listed this problem as affecting a teacher's work. Even experienced teachers are often at a loss on how best to proceed in coping with deviant behavior. Many teachers still use outdated and psychologically unsound disciplinary measures with physical force and corporal punishment of various sorts being used more than the situation warrants (Maurer, 1974).

Teachers seem especially concerned about the child with disorderly conduct, although less so than their counterparts did forty years ago. Back in 1928, Wickman (1928) asked teachers and mental-hygiene specialists to rate the severity of various behavior problems and discovered that the two groups rated the problems quite differently. Teachers, in general, were more concerned about acting-out behaviors, such as stealing and disobedience; whereas the clinicians were most concerned about the withdrawn child.

In keeping with the mental-hygiene spirit of the times, the conclusion was that teachers should be taught more about the nature of problem behavior so that their value judgments would be more in line with those of clinicians. More recent replication of Wickman's research (Stouffer, 1959) indicates that teachers' judgments as to the seriousness of withdrawn behavior are, by and large, more consistent with those of professional clinicians. As shown in Table 12–1, however, teachers and parents are most concerned with behavior

Table 12–1.   The Twenty Most Serious Behavior Problems of School-Aged Children Ranked According to Their Seriousness

Mental Hygienists	Teachers	Parents
1. Unsocial, withdrawing	1. Unreliableness	1. Stealing
2. Unhappy, depressed	2. Stealing	2. Untruthfulness
3. Fearfulness	3. Unhappy, depressed	3. Heterosexual activity
4. Suspiciousness	4. Cruelty, bullying	4. Destroying school materials
5. Cruelty, bullying	5. Untruthfulness	5. Cheating
6. Shyness	6. Unsocial, withdrawing	6. Cruelty, bullying
7. Enuresis (bedwetting)	7. Truancy	7. Unreliableness
8. Resentfulness	8. Impertinence, defiance	8. Truancy
9. Stealing	9. Cheating	9. Disobedience
10. Sensitiveness	10. Easily discouraged	10. Impertinence, defiance
11. Dreaminess	11. Resentfulness	11. Obscene notes, talk
12. Nervousness	12. Destroying school materials	12. Impudence
13. Suggestible	13. Suggestible	13. Selfishness
14. Overcritical of others	14. Heterosexual activity	14. Unhappy, depressed
15. Easily discouraged	15. Domineering	15. Masturbation
16. Temper tantrums	16. Temper tantrums	16. Suggestible
17. Dominating	17. Selfishness	17. Domineering
18. Truancy	18. Nervousness	18. Easily discouraged
19. Physical coward	19. Disobedience	19. Profanity
20. Untruthfulness	20. Laziness	20. Lack of interest in work

Source: Adapted by permission of the author and publisher from two tables in G. A. W. Stouffer, Jr., The attitudes of parents toward certain behavior problems of children. *Teachers College Bulletin*, 1959. **5**, 173–74.

that defies authority and moral dictates. Overall, parents tended to have attitudes similar to those of teachers in the late 1920s.

Are teachers mistaken in their greater concern with antisocial behavior than with introverted behavior? Perhaps not. As was mentioned in the earlier discussion on the stability of deviant behavior, it is the shy child whose behavior tends to be nonpersistent over time, whereas the behavior of the seriously aggressive child signifies the more serious psychological implications for later adjustment. Curiously, despite longitudinal data on the stability of aberrant behavior in children, it still seems today that many clinicians and educators accept the implications of the Wickman-type studies, which chastise teachers in varying degrees for their emphasis on the acting-out child.

Some teachers, feeling that it is not their responsibility to deal with emotionally disturbed children, wash their hands of the whole disciplinary affair. Realistically, however, it appears that they have little choice in this matter, at least for the foreseeable future. Bower (1970) contends that, in the average classroom, there are 3 youngsters who warrant the emotionally handicapped label. There are about 9 disturbed children in the average classroom if we include students with mild and moderate problems (Glidewell & Swallow, 1968). Hence, even though some teachers would prefer not to concern themselves with the management of problem behavior, this is not likely to be their fate. While it is true that schools refer more youngsters than does any other agency to professionally trained workers, it is equally evident that the teacher, nonetheless, remains the person who has primary responsibility for the classroom management of the disturbed child. One hour of therapy per week often does little to lessen the need for coping with the child's disturbing behavior during the remaining hours that he is in school.

Rather than decreasing the role of the teacher as it relates to the mental health of children, there is a definite movement in the direction of greater teacher involvement in such matters. Expansion of the teacher's role has stemmed largely from the following factors:

1. The shortage of mental-health workers has served to force expansion of mental-health forces to include school personnel, even though the role the latter are to play in this respect has not been clearly conceptualized or delineated. Authorities like Fritz Redl point to a need for additional mental-health professionals to supplement the traditional clinical team. Some speak of the need for "invisible" therapists.

2. The inadequacy of the clinic model to deal with the varieties of disturbed children that our society is producing is another factor. In one large urban area, almost 3 out of every 5 patients in child psychiatric clinics did not complete treatment (Frumkin, 1955). The abrupt termination of clinic treatment has been ascribed by some authors (Overall & Aronson, 1963) to a discrepancy between the expectations of the lower-socioeconomic patients and their middle-class therapists. Nationally, the fact that only 1 in 4 child psychiatric patients receive direct treatment of some kind also highlights the obsolescence of the psychiatric model (Norman, Rosen, & Bahn, 1962). While we have traditionally modeled intervention after the clinic concept of treatment, the need for a more realistic mental-health approach is becoming increasingly recognized. Just as the mounting dissatisfaction with the clinic concept of treatment has led to the development of community psychiatry, so has it led to a new look in school mental hygiene. The current realization that the child's life conditions—for example, the school—are as important as his feelings must obviously involve teachers to a greater extent than in the past.

3. Evaluations of therapy with children have also forced us to try other methods. Even with cases for whom the clinic model is supposedly appropriate, for example, middle-class neurotic youngsters, the effectiveness of treatment remains to be demonstrated (Bahn, Chandler, & Eisenberg, 1962).

4. The rising popularity of behavior modification has also resulted in a more central role for teachers in the quest for better mental health for our children. When the psychodynamic model was the preferred method, the teacher was accorded at best a second-string status on the clinical team. Today

it may well be the mental-health specialist who will assume a supportive role (Gallagher & Chalfant, 1966).

The Psychiatric versus the Educational Model

The values advocated by educators and those favoring a psychiatric model often clash, and the clash has led to a role conflict on the part of teachers. The divergence in values espoused by these two groups has been summarized by White (1965):

> It would be fair to say that the mental health movement has revered warmth of feeling; spontaneity; insight; a high interest in others, particularly peers; the ability to communicate, especially one's feelings; warm teachers, and democratic classrooms. The same movement has been against: being compulsive; competitive striving; intellectualism; being either thing- or achievement-oriented; being emotionally unresponsive, as well as being angry or passionate; being a loner; not confiding in others; teachers who are curriculum-oriented; the regimentation of school life; group tests; red tape; and vice-principals in charge of discipline. Many of these are precisely the values revered by educators committed to the "cognitive" cause.

Because mental-hygiene specialists have not fully understood the teacher's role, they have made little available to teachers by way of specific and concrete practical suggestions pertaining to the management of the child's daily behavior. It is the sad truth that mental-health concepts advanced by psycho-dynamically oriented clinicians have proved of little value to teachers on the front lines. Teachers have asked for practical and concrete suggestions, says Morse (1961), only to be given general platitudes. Teachers have, therefore, been forced to rely on their own common sense and ingenuity. Admonitions to be accepting, nonthreatening, and understanding of the child's needs have not helped teachers very much in coping with aberrant behavior. Ausubel (1961) opines that permissiveness was perhaps overdone between 1935 and 1955 and that there has been a shift away from permissiveness in recent years. In giving advice to educators, mental-health professionals seem to forget about the following aspects of the teacher's role which makes it difficult for him to heed the advice given:

1. The teacher is a group worker; and therefore cannot usually work with just one child.

2. The teacher's primary goal is not to increase the child's personal insights but to achieve certain academic objectives.

3. The teacher must reflect cultural values; and therefore cannot be permissively accepting.

4. The teacher deals primarily with conscious or preconscious processes; and is not prepared to handle unconscious processes and materials.

5. The teacher must focus on the reality problems as they exist in the situational present.

Because of these basic differences in outlook, the folklore of mental-hygiene concepts disseminated in teacher-training courses has most likely promoted the mental health neither of children nor of their teachers. In fact, personal adjustment and academic achievement were seen as incompatible objectives. Teachers, being asked to do what they cannot, have consequently been made to feel anxious, inadequate, helpless, and guilty. The result has been that they are less well prepared to fulfill their mental-health roles.

There are certain theoretical models, we believe, that yield more specific and practical aids for classroom management than the psychiatric model permits. Furthermore, these intervention models, namely, Redl's psychodynamic approach and the behavioral approach, are more consistent with the teacher's role than is the traditional psychiatric model.

Redl's Psychodynamic Approach

In this section we will consider management techniques stemming from a psychodynamic model developed by Redl for use with severely antisocial children. Unlike other psychodynamic management models, Redl's approach offers specific and practical techniques consistent with the teacher's role. The methods he advocates can be useful not only in the immediate control of classroom discipline problems but also in the long-range working-through of mental-health goals for the child. Moreover, the techniques are useful for group as well as individual management.

Group Management

Cognizant that no pattern of teacher-pupil interaction alone is sufficient to establish and maintain discipline, Redl (1966) underscores the importance of group psychological factors in the production of classroom difficulties. Rather than viewing discipline cases as a consequence of a given child's particular disturbance, he argues that the large majority of such cases involve a mixture of individual disturbances and factors peculiar to the group atmosphere surrounding the incident in question. It is necessary, therefore, to conduct an analysis of the individual and group factors together with their respective importance in the production of misbehavior in a given situation. The teacher, who is first and foremost a group leader, consequently needs skill not only in child-study techniques but also in group analysis, for the one-to-one teacher-pupil relationship is an ideal rarely obtained in reality. Even in special-education classes for emotionally handicapped children, where class size averages from 8 to 10 pupils, the teacher must be well versed in group-management skills.

Common Group Malfunctions. In analyzing some of the more typical things that go wrong in group settings, Redl cites the following six categories:

1. *Dissatisfaction in Work Process.* Basic dissatisfaction sometimes stems

from curricula and teaching approaches which are inconsistent with the children's needs. Assignments that are too easy or too difficult for the pupil, verbal instruction that is too abstract or distant from the child's social background, tasks that are unfairly assessed, and faulty scheduling or sequencing of classroom activities are just some of the problems found in this category. Some educators would go so far as to attribute most discipline problems to this complex factor, but Redl warns that to do so is as mistaken as assuming that all disciplinary cases are produced solely by personality factors. That frustrations do result from a discrepancy between situational demands and the child's ability to cope with them is well established, but to state this as the primary cause of disciplinary issues is an overstatement.

2. *Emotional Unrest in Interpersonal Relations.* Tensions stemming from strained interpersonal relations can also produce classroom discipline problems. Though not usually the intended recipient of such outcropping tensions, the teacher must nonetheless cope with the forthcoming disturbances. Typical of such difficulties are conflicts between cliques, between personal friendships and academic interests, and over the distribution of roles within the group. Such tensions can pose substantial trouble for the teacher, especially if the unrest becomes widespread and disrupts group harmony.

3. *Disturbances in Group Climate.* A punitive classroom climate is one of the most common causes of group disorders. Predicated upon a lack of respect for the individual and characterized by an atmosphere of fear, this climate has particularly deleterious effects on group order and morale. Resistance to teacher standards might well be, in this case, a sign of a healthy personality rather than an unhealthy one. The emotional-blackmail climate is based upon the teacher's withdrawal of love resulting in guilt feelings on the pupil's part if the teacher's code is violated. Climates characterized by vicious competition among students or a snobbish sense of group pride also represent unhealthy group tones.

4. *Mistakes in Organization and Group Leadership.* Though a teacher may be knowledgeable in terms of his subject-matter area and equitable in terms of his relationship with the class, he may encounter difficulties when it comes to the mechanics of group leadership. Being ill-prepared for group leadership, teachers are prone to problems arising from too much or too little group structure, a lack of sensitivity to student feelings, and a nonjudicious imposition of their own values on the pupils.

5. *Emotional Strain and Sudden Change.* Chronic anxiety, boredom, and resistance to classroom change on the pupil's part are well known, but often overlooked, enemies of classroom order.

6. *Composition of the Group.* No one has the solution to the problem of achieving the most effective grouping, although any teacher will readily admit that the makeup of his class is a factor of vital importance in the establishment and maintenance of discipline. Since variability in group composition is always present and can sometimes be very healthy, the issue, says Redl, is not one of heterogeneity versus homogeneity, but one of grouping on relevant variables. It is of prime importance that, though grouped according to rele-

vant criteria, the extremes be avoided on criteria nonessential to the group's *raison d'être*. When analyzing the sources of misbehavior, the teacher would do well to consider such criteria as the socioeconomic level of his pupils, their independence-dependence level, their approach-withdrawal tendencies, as well as their self-governing abilities and interest levels. (Administrators would be advised to seek teacher input in grouping arrangements; teachers typically have no input in making up a class.)

Three Issues concerning Discipline.   There are three basic problems regarding group discipline with which the teacher must come to grips, according to Redl. First, he must consider the effects of a given disciplinary action upon the individual and upon the group. Since discipline affects both the individual and the group, difficulty sometimes arises. For example, being very harsh and threatening may be good for a particular group at a particular time, but this technique may be harmful to the shy children in the group who do not respond therapeutically to this kind of atmosphere. Redl offers a guideline for individual-group decisions, namely, the law of "marginal antisepsis." This law states that a given technique that is appropriate for the individual must be at least harmless to the growth of the group and vice versa. Redl stresses the need for a "double-orientation" if teachers are to have hygienic discipline.

A second consideration hinges around the objective of group discipline. Does the teacher want to modify surface behavior or to seek a more deep-rooted change in attitude? Usually, both types of changes are sought, but complications arise since some techniques are more appropriate to one objective than the other. Again the law of marginal antisepsis applies. Any technique devised to alter disruptive momentary behavior should be at least harmless to the accomplishment of longer-range objectives of a basic attitudinal change and vice versa.

Third, the teacher must ask whether or not his disciplinary techniques are effective. Unfortunately, the yardsticks used are often misleading. For example, the teacher may, through a show of force, suppress certain aggressive behaviors in the classroom and feel that this technique works; yet he may not realize that his pupils are now more aggressive in the bus on the way home from school. Anyone who has ever sat in the teachers' lounge of a school is aware of how freely advice is given about disciplinary techniques that work. To determine whether they really work or not, Redl argues that one must consider the disciplinary techniques in light of the individuals in question, the effects on the group as well as on the individual, the influence on surface behavior versus attitudinal change, and finally, the subsurface effects. Only after examination of these circumstances will one be prepared to answer the question of whether a technique works or not.

Influence Techniques

The influence techniques can be divided for purposes of discussion into four basic categories: (1) techniques supporting self-control; (2) techniques involving task assistance; (3) techniques of reality and value appraisals; and

(4) techniques working the pleasure-pain principle (Redl & Wattenberg, 1959). We will confine our discussion to those methods of Redl's that have most relevance to the classroom. It should be borne in mind that these techniques are regarded by Redl and his associates as tools for helping the teachers through difficult or rough moments. They are not intended to replace a well-thought-out classroom program, in the broadest sense of the term.[1]

Support of Self-Control. The first group of techniques yields most effective dividends when used with children whose behavioral controls, though generally adequate, need strengthening at times. Basically these children are reasonably well motivated to do what is expected of them, but they have momentary lapses because of overexcitement, forgetfulness, and so forth. Once assisted by the teacher, these children are able to get back on the right track without much ado. The following techniques seem to work well with such youngsters:

1. *Signal Interference.* Most teachers realize the value of preventing misbehavior before it spreads. Cues from the teacher, such as giving a cool stare, pointing a finger, tapping the chalk, quietly mentioning the child's name, and so forth, are often sufficient to help many children regain control.

2. *Planned Ignoring.* Behaviors will sometimes disappear or diminish in frequency if not rewarded. A given misbehavior may thus cease of its own accord once the teacher intentionally ignores it. As is true of all techniques to be discussed, the teacher must decide when it is appropriate to use this approach. Although the technique works well with certain pupils and certain behaviors, it is subject to many of the same limitations that extinction has (see pp. 505-506).

3. *Interest Boosting.* A technique long used by teachers in drawing a pupil's wandering attention back to the work at hand is to convey interest in the child's work. This procedure serves to renew the child's interest in the task; the underlying assumption is that he has the skills necessary for successful completion.

4. *Humor.* Humor can also be used in handling behavior problems, that is, the friendly use of humor that elicits responses incompatible with anxiety and aggression. Sarcasm predicated upon teacher hostility is likely to elicit great covert or overt aggression and hostility. The use of humor shows a pupil that the teacher is human and that he is secure enough in his role to be able to joke. The authors recall one bright lower-class pupil who habitually defied direct orders. Through good-natured kidding and interest boosting on the teacher's part, the pupil was able to complete assignments. The fact that he was quite aware of the teacher's strategy did not seem to limit the effectiveness of the "humorous" approach.

---

1. While we have not discussed educational programming in any detail, we heartily recommend Redl & Wineman's (1952) discussion of programming for ego support for a fuller treatment of this neglected topic.

5. *Diversion.* Another technique widely employed by both teachers and parents is that of diversion. It consists in distracting the child from his objectionable pursuits by directing his attention toward more desirable activities. Frequently, the asking of a simple question may suffice. The question serves to interrupt the undesirable activity and simultaneously to channel energies along more acceptable lines.

One of the main advantages of these techniques is that they prevent small incidents from blossoming into more difficult situations. Such incidents nipped in the bud are less painful to both the teacher and the pupil. Another advantage of these techniques centers around the cardinal rule for discipline: never intervene any further than is necessary to handle the situation. Stated otherwise, the use of intervention procedures should be parsimonious. While these techniques are based on common sense, many beginning teachers overreact to mild forms of student misbehavior, with the consequence that they use drastic forms of intervention when subtle interventions would do. It is imprudent to use physical restraint when a quiet glance in the offender's direction will suffice. Since the supportive techniques entail minimal interference, they are less apt to arouse counterhostility on the student's part. Moreover, once applied, the supportive techniques enable the student to regulate his own behavior in an acceptable manner once again.

It should be mentioned, however, that these techniques are less effective with children whose control systems are not intact. Further, these low-pressure methods are of limited value once misbehavior has advanced beyond the beginning stage and emotional contagion has spread. The teacher must know when to intervene, for the timing of disciplinary actions often determines their outcomes.

Situational Assistance.   Some youngsters misbehave because the situational demands, social as well as academic, exceed the students' skills and abilities. Though students may have reasonably adequate behavior controls, misbehavior can sometimes be expected when goals are blocked and frustration ensues. The teacher can assist in such situations by manipulating the outside barriers that thwart the pupil. Such assistance may not solve long-range problems, but it does permit the energies of both the student and the teacher to be directed to the task at hand. The following list is not exhaustive:

1. *Hurdle Help.* The child sometimes misbehaves because he cannot understand or execute the required assignment. Rather than lose face in the eyes of his peers, he prefers not to ask for help. His sense of frustration and anxiety, resulting from his inability in this situation, is further heightened by his seeing that his classmates are working diligently on the task. Thus, he is prone to pester others. In such situations, a wise teacher offers the child the help needed to grasp the concept or skills involved rather than focusing on misbehavior.

2. *Restructuring the Class Setting.* Students, like most other human beings,

become bored or overly excited on occasions. In certain instances, it may be more profitable to alter the situation than to call attention to the restlessness. For example, instead of oral book reports in the traditional manner, tension due to restlessness could be relieved by having the students role-play the reports. If the teacher feels that restructuring classroom activities will benefit the learning process, he should be flexible enough to make the necessary changes. In their study of certain dimensions of teacher behaviors as they relate to the behavior of emotionally disturbed children in regular class-rooms, Kounin, Friesen, & Norton (1966) noted that programing to reduce pupil satiation was one concrete teaching technique that influenced the amount of classroom deviancy. It is easy to become a slave to a standardized program, which no doubt affords a sense of security for both teacher and pupil. However, at some point, this security can lead to stagnation and inhibit further development of one's capacities for development and change. Some persons, teachers and pupils alike, may be able to tolerate less change than others, but probably all persons should have training in coping with change and variety.

3. *Routines.* Although some classrooms are too regimented and, therefore, subject to trouble, other classroom programs lead to trouble for exactly the opposite reason. Both acting-out and withdrawn students need and benefit from structure. The environmental predictability stemming from routine offers students guidelines for their actions and a sense of security. Routinizing classroom activities, such as the start of the school day, pencil sharpening, trips to the lavatory, and so forth, should help to minimize classroom behavior problems.

4. *Removing Seductive Objects.*   Almost every parent recalls removing from the scene objects that result in his child's misbehaving. Beginning teachers soon realize that some objects hold an irresistible appeal to pupils, especially to those with inadequate behavioral controls. Some objects and children just do not mix well. Leaving science equipment, shop tools, athletic gear, and valuables about only invites trouble. Once a teacher becomes aware of what triggers certain students, he is wise to avoid these situations or objects. It serves no constructive purpose to expose youngsters with inadequate personal controls to temptations they cannot resist.

5. *Antiseptic Bouncing.* Times arise when it is necessary to remove or restrain a child. The possibilities of physical danger and emotional contagion offer two examples of when such action is necessary. Unfortunately, there are few places in the typical school building to which a pupil may be nonpunitively exiled. In one well-staffed school system, a buzzer system was installed in the classroom so that the teacher could signal the social worker or school counselor when a child had to be ousted. Sending the child on errands to the office with a sealed note explaining the situation is also a technique permitting hygienic removal in cases of emergency. The authors know of cases in which volatile children were taught to signal the teacher once they felt an outburst coming on so that he could head off the trouble by sending them out of the

room to cool off and regain self-control before returning to class. Antiseptic bouncing not only enables the child to save face with his classmates but spares his teacher the problem of having to cope with temper flareups.

6. *Physical Restraint.* Sometimes a child erupts aggressively in the class-room and physical restraint is the only course of action open to the teacher. The authors remember one occasion during which a fifth-grade pupil felled his teacher, cursing and kicking her as she lay on the floor. Another teacher, quickly summoned, held the boy until he had calmed down. In such situations, it is important that the teacher's approach be protective and not counteraggressive. It is well to tell the explosive youngster gently that he is not going to be hurt, but simply that he is going to be restrained until he gets over his attack.

Reality and Value Appraisal.   Another set of devices involves various kinds of appeals to values held by the youngsters. Illustrative of the variety of appeals that can be made are:

1. An appeal to a personal relationship between the teacher and the child; for example, "Jim, that noise bothers me."

2. An appeal to reality implications; for example, "You can get hurt by doing that."

3. An appeal to conscience; for example, "You're not that kind of child."

4. An appeal to group codes; for example, "I don't think the other fellows would like that."

5. Appeal to pride in personal improvement; for example, "You'd feel better if you got your assignments done right."

6. Appeal to hierarchial limitations; for example, "I can't always stop you from fighting, but I do have to notify the principal."

To use these appeals effectively, the teacher must be well aware of the child's value system. This technique requires sensitivity and empathy on the teacher's part.

Research by Kounin, Gump, & Ryan (1961) found that *task* appeals for example, "We can't get the job done if you're going to make all that noise") elicited more favorable student reactions than did *personal* appeals (for example, "I don't like boys who make that kind of noise") . Students witnessing task-appeal techniques also rated their teachers as more skillful in handling children and expressed greater interest in the subject matter being taught than did students experiencing personal appeals. Centering on the immediate task thus seems to result in less classroom deviancy than does reliance on teacher relationship.

As with any other influence technique, the use of appeals can be overworked. If used sparingly, the seriousness of the incident or situation is impressed on the class. On the other hand, if it is overused, and there is a tendency to misuse this approach since the use of appeals makes teachers feel good, the technique loses much of its effectiveness. Another limitation arises when the teacher encounters a child who is markedly deficient in the values to which teachers commonly address their appeals. On the positive side, this technique can help to develop or strengthen the very values that will permit self-control.

The Pleasure-Pain Principle.   Much of Redl's discussion of these topics might be subsumed under the learning theory concepts of positive reinforcement and punishment. The basic rationale underlying the use of the pleasure-pain technique is that behavior which leads to unpleasant experiences for the child will be avoided. While acknowledging that such techniques as rewards, promises, threats, praise, blame, and punishment can have a constructive effect in modifying undesirable behavior, Redl is apparently more impressed with their limitations or misuses. For example, he considers that rewards and promises work well in the achievement of long-range goals with children whose egos are intact, but that these techniques are limited to the achievement of short-term goals with youngsters whose egos are impaired.

Let us examine Redl's discussion of punishment since there is current controversy surrounding the use of this technique. Redl & Wattenberg (1959) specify exact prerequisite conditions for the constructive use of this method:

1. There should be some concern by the child over his misdeed; that is, there should be a conflict between his control system and his impulses.

2. The child must know that the teacher basically likes and accepts him even though he has to punish him on this occasion.

3. The punishment meted out should, in the child's eyes, be a reasonable and preferably a natural consequence of his action.

Though, at first glance, these criteria do not seem too stringent, Redl believes that in reality these conditions are less commonly met than might be presumed. For example, some youngsters may not be upset by their behavior. Then again, teachers are probably more inclined to punish youngsters with whom they have a poor relationship.

In addition to the cautions cited in our earlier discussion of punishment, Redl notes:

1. The timing of the punishment is highly critical. If it occurs too soon, when the child is still in an irrational state, or too long after the incident, he is less able to see the relationship between his actions and the imposed consequences.

2. The teacher can be easily led to believe that he has achieved results he has not. For example, the child may overtly conform to his teacher's demands, but he may be even more aggressive with his peers on the playground.

3. The length or nature of the punishment should fit the offense and the child's developmental level. If the primary-school child is deprived of pleasant activities for prolonged periods of time, he comes to see the teacher as mean and the desired educational benefit intended is consequently nullified.

Life-Space Interviewing

A most important skill for teachers is the ability to talk effectively with children, especially for purposes of managing problem behavior. To this end, life-space interviewing (LSI), or reality-interviewing as it is sometimes called, was developed. The main goal of this technique is to achieve some degree of behavioral conformity on the child's part. It can be used apart from or in conjunction with the influence techniques discussed earlier. It is not a moralistic approach but a dynamic one based in large measure on the teacher's empathic relationship with the child.[2]

In contrast to counseling and psychotherapy, which generally take place in the interview room, LSI occurs in the more natural context of the child's daily environment. As far as teachers are concerned, what are most often needed are on-the-scene impromptu talks about specific troublesome incidents. To have a child discuss an incident with his counselor or therapist next week is of little assistance to the teacher who must somehow cope with the child's behavior here and now. Reality-interviewing thus affords a kind of needed instant therapy. The potency of LSI accrues from the fact that since the child's disequilibrium is greatest during times of crisis, the teacher is especially able through minimal assistance to influence outcomes that are hanging in a state of delicate balance. Stated otherwise, in crisis situations people are better motivated to seek and use the help afforded them. It would, therefore, seem that critical incidents afford an excellent teaching opportunity for teachers.

Objectives. In essence, there are two broad goals of LSI: (1) clinical exploitation of life events, and (2) emotional first aid (Redl, 1959). At times, the purpose of the interview may be to help the youngster over momentary difficulties and back to his normal self. On other occasions, the teacher may attempt to work through some long-range goals with the child. A given incident may offer the teacher a long-awaited or golden opportunity to attack an issue that needs further explanation. In everyday practice, it is often difficult to know in advance of the interview which of the two broad objectives one will seek. Many times, both processes may be combined in a single interview.

CLINICAL EXPLOITATION OF LIFE EVENTS.   Attempts at clinical exploitation aimed at long-range clinical goals may involve:

1. Giving a reality "rub-in" to youngsters who habitually misinterpret interpersonal situations (for example, youngsters who think the teacher is "against" them) or who fail to derive meaning from social situations.

2. Demonstrating that the maladaptive style of life really involves more secondary pains than secondary gains.

---

2. Extended treatment of this method is beyond the scope of this chapter, but we will attempt to present a general description of this type of interviewing. The student who wants to learn more is referred to Redl & Wineman (1952) and Newman (1963).

3. Stimulating numb value areas by appealing to potential or dormant values of the child or his peer group.

4. Convincing the child through word and action that there are other ways of behaving (defenses) that are satisfying.

5. Expanding the child's own psychological boundaries to include other adults and teachers or to permit acceptance of formerly unacceptable aspects of himself.

EMOTIONAL FIRST AID.   Like the clinical exploitation of life events, emotional first aid is accomplished through the process of empathic communication between the child and the teacher. The following goals are ilustrative:

1. To drain off hostilities of daily frustrations so as to prevent an intolerable accumulation.

2. To provide emotional support when children are overwhelmed by feelings of panic or guilt.

3. To maintain a relationship with the child so that he does not retreat into his own world as a consequence of emotional upheaval.

4. To govern social traffic so as to remind wayward pupils of "house" policies and regulations.

5. To serve as an umpire in disputes, fights, and other "loaded transactions."

Guidelines for the Interview.   Bernstein (1963) offers the following guidelines as being useful and supportive in school-oriented reality-interviewing:

1. Be polite. Offer the child a chair. Produce a tissue if it is needed. While teachers and other adults demand good manners from children, they are occasionally guilty of excessive rudeness toward the children.

2. Don't tower over a little child. Kneel or bend down to him. Have a small chair or stool in the office for really little children and another one for you to sit on. Be wary about lifting a kindergartner or first-grader onto a desk or table. Although a well-meant action, it may push a frightened child into a screaming panic because he feels trapped in midair and can't get down.

3. When you are sure of your ground, it can be a good approach to confront a child with your knowledge of his misdeed, and not give an inch. This can be a tremendous relief to the child who otherwise would have to clam up or spend twenty minutes denying the facts. Confrontation, however, is not likely to be successful with the child who feels that everybody is his enemy.

4. Be sparing with your use of "Why?" It is very difficult to explore reasons and all but impossible for a child to lay his motivations out on the principal's desk for dissection. It is much better to say, "We can't have this art on the lavatory walls. I'm not going to let you continue. We have to talk about this a little."

5. Get conversation going about the actual situation. Obtain a description of what happened. *Listen* to what the child says.

6. If you think a child is overwhelmed with guilt or shame, begin by minimizing the weightiness of the problem at hand, for example, by saying, "This action doesn't bother me too much, but we had better look into it, for it can cause *you* trouble."

7. Say what you know the child wants to say but can't put into words. "You were very disappointed, weren't you? You had been counting on this talk for a long time and couldn't stand to have to wait any longer."

8. Be aware of the kinds of thinking demanded by the particular situation. Bright children frequently become involved in relationships beyond their grasp in terms of emotional and personal maturity.

9. Help the child with plans for specific steps to improve the situation.

10. At some point in the interview, give the child an opportunity to ask *you* questions, or say, "Is there anything you want to tell me?" or, "Is there something you would like me to try to do for you?" Be prepared for some remarkable questions and disclosures, but after you've done this a few times you'll be convinced of how helpless and frightened the misbehavers are and you'll be moved by the depth and intensity of their desire to be "in" and to be good.

What Happens in the Interview?

In any exchange between teachers and children the comments and questions of the teacher—or principal—are useful if they help the child out of his difficulty. They are of no avail if they dig deeper the hole he is in. Too often we says things like:

—You apologize this minute.
—Your mind is in the gutter.
—Why did you throw the ball across the room?
—Why did you hit the little girl? She's half your size.
—Why did you write this fresh note to Mary Jane? And I want the truth!
—What makes you think you can use that kind of language to me? Is that the way you talk to your mother?

(The suggestion here is that the principal thinks it probably *is* the way Margaret talks to her mother and that lets Margaret know that he thinks that the whole family is beneath contempt.)

—A boy who doesn't have a father certainly should be more responsible.
—I'm ashamed of you. You're a big boy now.

The teacher or principal may deliver a long lecture. A lecture is not an interview. Often our remarks are moralizing, shaming, or belittling. We push and probe and insist that a child tell us why he did something when he couldn't possible tell why even if he wanted to. Then, in our effort to "close the case" with some kind of overt action, we require a public apology from the child.

It is, of course, much faster to list the foregoing useless if not damaging gambits than to describe interview behavior that is likely to be useful to the child. The interview that follows is presented not necessarily as a model but as case material that may be useful for discussion.

Lee's mother had phoned to tell the principal that Lee was uneasy about coming to school. Bill was demanding money from him. Lee wanted to pay to avoid trouble with Bill.

PRINCIPAL: Hello, Bill. Sit down. Do you know why I sent for you?

BILL: No.

PRINCIPAL: Strange business—requiring kids to give you money or comic books or you beat them up. Did somebody ever do this to you?

B.: No. We made a bet. He lost. I said: "You owe me Cokes."

P.: You *both* made a bet?—or you said, "I bet you such and such"?

B.: Well, I really set it up.

P.: And you decided what he owed you *after* he lost the bet?

B.: Yes.

P.: What about that?

B.: Guess I shouldn't.

P.: What should you?

B.: Agree first.

P.: This beating up. Now what about that?

B.: (Tears) I told him he didn't have to pay up.

P.: He doesn't think so. Do you wish you had more money for Cokes or comic books?

B.: Yes.

P.: Most kids do want more money.

B.: But I have money. I go to a skating club and I pay for it from my own money.

P.: Good. How do you get your own money?

B.: I shovel snow, cut grass, do jobs.

P.: Good.

(Bill—tears dry now, Kleenex operation.)

P.: How are you going to handle this from now on? Are you feeling sore at Lee because I got hold of this?

B.: No.

P.: Well, you could be. But his mother got it out of him and she told me. Think you can be friends with him?

B.: Yes.

P.: You're a nice kid and I'm sure you're sorry. (Eyes tearful again.) Sometimes kids see TV or grownups act a certain way and try to imitate it.

(Bill smiling, clearly thinking about something he had seen or heard.)

P.: Was there some of that in this?

B.: Yes.

P.: Well, trying things out is one way to find out what won't work —that's what growing up is. Have you gotten this one out of your system?

B.: Yes.

P.: Do I need to call your mother?

B.: No.

P.: Okay—just between us, then. Come back if you need help getting things straightened out with Lee. Do you have any of his money?

B.: No—just comic books. I'll return them.

P.: You feel better now?

B.: Yes.

P.: Anything else you want to say—or ask?

B.: Is Lee's mother going to call my mother?

P.: I really don't know. I doubt it. She wasn't angry. Just wanted this stopped.

(Bill still worried and not making a move to go.)

P.: Still worried about your mother?

B.: Yes.

P.: Have you changed your mind? Want me to tell her for you?

B.: No.

P.: So?

B.: I don't know. I'll see.

P.: Let me know what you decide or if you want help.

Interview behavior has a heavy nonverbal component. The attitude, gesture, tone of the teacher or principal are of critical importance. Silence, too, is part of the communication. Timing is significant. To say to a child "I know you're sorry about this" at the right time is extremely valuable. To say it at the wrong time may push him further into the sullen silence that got him into trouble in the first place. Certainly, meaningful communication is going on if the principal puts his hand on a boy's shoulder to give him time to recover.

Life-space interviews inevitably involve many unknowns. Therefore it is good to try to recognize what can be known, to recognize what is happening before our eyes, to grasp the significance of the child's interview behavior. Is he trying to tell us something or to keep from telling us?

A silent partner in an interview is frustrating indeed. Is the youngster tongue-tied by embarrassment? He may be embarrassed about the reason for the interview or he may be embarrassed about having to talk to us about it. Is he keeping quiet because he knows it's a good idea not to trust adults or is he afraid he will get other kids in trouble? Are echoes of another situation interfering with his ability to hear what you are saying in this one? Is he silent because he is too upset, too angry to talk, and needs all his energies just to hold himself together? None of this necessarily means that he is unmindful of the trouble he is in. It helps to acknowledge to a child that we realize that he is too upset to talk, or that we know that some things are hard to talk about. A brief postponement may help. An older girl will appreciate the opportunity to go to the restroom, wash her face with cold water, comb her hair. A young child may need more time to finish sobbing and may be able to use a cookie or cold milk to advantage.

A child may retreat to obdurate silence to keep from crying. When a child is afraid of his own feelings, toughness is a ready armor against the kindness of a fond teacher—a kindness that if acknowledged will make him fall apart.

Source: From Bernstein (1963)

Pluses and Minuses.   There is no question but that LSI can be a powerful tool for the hygienic management of classroom behavior problems. Outstanding features of this approach are its (1) not blaming the child but presenting the problem in an open, honest way, (2) clarifying the problem so that the child cannot get away with blaming others, and (3) putting responsibility on the child for helping to resolve the problem. Like other approaches, LSI is subject to limitations, three of which are particularly prominent:

1. LSI is a highly complex and sophisticated clinical technique which requires more extensive supervised training in the form of seminars and practicum experiences (for example, the Fresh Air Camp at the University of Michigan) than most teacher-training institutions are willing or able to muster. The method requires considerable teacher sensitivity as well as an awareness of individual and group dynamics. The teacher must know what issues to select for clinical exploitation, which materials to interpret and which to leave untouched, what the influences of the setting imply, and so forth. Moreover, since reality-interviewing is more art than science, it is difficult to communicate to others.

2. Teachers with 25–30 pupils often do not have time to conduct individual interviews. Advocates of this approach are well aware of this limitation and advise the use of a "crisis teacher" to circumvent this difficulty (Morse, 1962).

3. Since LSI is most effectively implemented in a totally hygienic milieu, it demands satisfactory cooperation among all members of the school staff, especially between the teacher and the principal, as well as an awareness of the psychosocial totality of the school setting. Initially, it might seem that securing the necessary cooperation would not be difficult among professional people, but a study by Long (1963) suggests otherwise. In his follow-up study of teachers trained in life-space interviewing, Long reported that many of the teachers stated that their fellow teachers were critical of and unsympathetic toward this approach. Consequently, most of the teachers gradually gave up on this approach. Long concludes that if universities are to teach LSI methods, then they should maintain contact with or train psychologists and counselors already in the public schools so that the necessary support for this approach can be provided. These findings also highlight the need for in-service training of administrators as well as teachers.

Behavioral Approaches

Rationale

The behavioral approach is essentially interested in the modification of behavior. Little attention is devoted to the etiology of the troublesome behavior. The inner dynamics or the underlying phenomena are definitely relegated to a secondary status.

Before explorating of the techniques emanating from his approach, it is appropriate to ask why teachers should focus primarily on maladaptive *symptoms* or behaviors rather than on remote *causes* of the maladaptive behavior. There are several reasons for this emphasis on symptoms:

1. Teachers, by virtue of their orientation, are not trained to probe the inner dynamics of behavior. They cannot deal with transference neuroses, interpret free associations, or explore dammed-up psychic processes. Indeed, mental-hygiene specialists themselves have large gaps in their knowledge relative to the causes of behavior even after extensive diagnostic workups have been made. The search for nonobservable causes is further complicated by the fact that, typically, behavior is multiply caused; rarely is the etiology singular in nature. Not only are there multiple causes, but the causes interact, so that specific delineation of the causative factors becomes even more difficult. In certain cases, any one of the component etiological factors may not be sufficient, in and of itself, to produce deviant behavior. Yet, taken together, these factors are capable of producing such behavior. The difficulties associated with diagnosis in cases of multiple causes are illustrated in a study by Lambert & Grossman (1964), in which two teams of psychologists, neurologists, pediatricians, and educators were to determine independently if the learning and behavior difficulties of a given group of students had an organic basis. The results indicated that there was little agreement between the two teams as to the cause of the difficulty for individual students.

2. Even when teachers are able to identify or infer the underlying causes of deviant behavior, they are rarely in a position where they can directly manipulate the causes so as to modify their influences on the child's classroom adjustment. For example, if the problem lies in the parent-child relationship or in a brain lesion, there are seldom few, if any, constructive intervention techniques a teacher can employ. Yet, the child's troublesome behavior persists and must be handled as constructively as possible.

3. Even in those select cases in which the causes can be identified and manipulated directly, the maladaptive behaviors may persist. Consider the pupil whose reading disability is caused by a combination of faulty, limited language practices and poor vision. If and when these etiological factors are identified and cleared up, attention still must be focused on this inadequate reading behavior in order for the child to be successful in reality. Until such efforts are undertaken, his mental health will most likely continue to suffer.

4. In certain cases, the behaviors or symptoms may, in and of themselves, become quite incapacitating and therefore warrant attention. This point is most dramatically illustrated in certain cases of reading disability where the relationships between education and emotional maladjustment are closely intertwined.

5. There is no reason to believe that when the teacher assists the child in modifying a given behavior, another undesirable behavior will inevitably take its place. The available evidence indicates that there is little support for this Freudian theory of symptom substitution (Grossberg, 1964). Symptom treatment can permit the breaking of a vicious circle of maladaptive behavior in which disabling symptoms either intensify the primary problem or become causes of other maladaptive behaviors. This latter possibility is illustrated in cases of learning disabilities which, though originally symptomatic of a more basic disturbance, come to produce additional anxiety, discomfort, and failure. By modification of the behavior, however, it is sometimes possible to reverse this downward spiral. For example, as the symptomatic behavior (for example, a reading disability) begins to clear up, the child is perceived and treated by others in a more favorable light. The parents view him as more worthwhile, as do his peers. Consequently, the child comes to view himself differently and to set new expectations for his own behavior.

6. Finally, as already implied, it is important to note that the teacher most commonly has no recourse other than to deal with behavior directly. However, if he can do this effectively, he will have gone far in meeting his mental-health responsibilities to his pupils. He should by no means disparage his accomplishments since he has restricted his assistance to a behavioral level. The science of psychology has not yet advanced to the stage that permits complete personality reorganization.

Four Steps in Behavior Modification

Target Selection.   The first step involves the selection of specific target behaviors to change. In many cases, there are several target behaviors that the teacher might like to change. In these instances, it is necessary to establish priorities by deciding which behaviors are most important to the child's academic and social functioning.

Targets must be specific, observable, countable, and measurable. By selecting targets with these characteristics, we can tell whether the strategies being used are having the intended effect.

Be sure not to bite off too much. Altogether too frequently we choose goals that are too broad and ambitious. Rather than attempting to correct a global personality defect, we recommend an analytic approach, which takes small steps at a time. It will accomplish more in the long run. It is more productive to try to reduce refusals to complete assigned tasks in biology class than it is to try to correct a rebellious attitude toward authority.

Finally, identify behaviors to be increased as well as those to be decreased. When possible, choose behaviors that are incompatible (for example, paying attention and unnecessary noisemaking).

Examining the Antecedents and Consequences. It is frequently helpful to see under what conditions the target behaviors are most apt to occur. For instance, once the teacher notes that Jim completes structured assignments accurately but whines and dawdles when given unstructured assignments, he is in a position to modify Jim's behavior by providing more concrete and specific directions for the completion of assignments. *Gradually,* Jim can be helped to map out the steps necessary for completion of unstructured tasks.

To illustrate the value in identifying the consequences of a behavior, consider the case of Sam, the class clown. When Sam's teacher stopped to remember what happened after Sam acted up, it became apparent that the clowning was being kept alive by peer group laughter and teacher scolding. Armed with this knowledge, the teacher was able to decrease the frequency of clowning by getting the peer group and himself to ignore such unacceptable behavior. Remember, looking to see what happens *before* and *after* behavior can be invaluable in decreasing undesired behavior and increasing desired behavior.

Choosing Strategies. Now it is time to select the techniques you will use to encourage acceptable performance and to discourage unacceptable performance. For the learning and maintaining of appropriate behaviors, positive reinforcement and modeling techniques are indicated. We will refer to these two techniques as *behavior formation* techniques. With regard to discouraging behavior, extinction and punishment techniques are commonly used. These are referred to as *behavior elimination* techniques.

Recording Results. It is essential that both teacher and student have feedback on what is happening to the target behavior. The data let both of them know whether the procedures are taking effect. Only the data on the behavior can tell whether the program was effective.

Three Significant Questions

If a positive approach to classroom discipline is to be realized, we must ask the following questions regarding the disorderly student when we plan our strategies for modifying his behavior.

1. Does he know what is expected of him—that is, does he clearly understand what the rules are? Directions can appear crystal clear to the teacher but the information they provide students may well be incomplete, inaccurate, or conflicting. If there is some confusion about the ground rules, then it is necessary to make them as explicit as possible. Listing the rules on the board, having the student explain in his own words what the rules mean, minimizing distractions while giving directions, and keeping rules short are all ways in which the student can be helped to understand the rules. The teacher should also be careful to relate the student's behavior to the rule so that he knows exactly what he is being rewarded or punished for (e.g., "Now, you're *paying attention*").

2. If the student knows the rules but still misbehaves, then you should consider the second question: Does he have the skills and abilities to do what I asked him to accomplish? Much misbehavior probably occurs as a result of demands that exceed the student's current level of readiness. When behavior problems stem from skill deficits and are secondary to the learning problem, it is necessary to teach the academic and social skills needed to assume the role of a student. The four techniques discussed in this chapter should help teachers to overcome deficits in the skill area. Providing greater freedom regarding choice in the curriculum also deserves serious consideration in such cases. One high school, for instance, listed more than fifty different English and social studies courses from which the students could choose. In short, one can change the student and/or change his environment.

3. When the student knows what the rules are and when he has the competencies to perform in an acceptable way, and yet continues to misbehave, then we must ask a third question: Is he motivated to do what is expected of him? On many occasions the disruptive student finds his deviant ways more satisfying than conventional ways. In such cases, we need to increase the reward value of the school setting so that students move toward it instead of away from it or by striking out at it. Again, the techniques to be presented should prove relevant to the solution of motivational problems. Let us at this point turn to the various techniques that can be used in a positive approach to classroom discipline.

Behavior Formation Techniques

Positive Reinforcement. If a behavior has the effect we want, then we are inclined to repeat it. Behavior, in other words, is determined in large measure by its consequences. For instance, if a student can attract attention by blurting out answers in class, he will probably not raise his hand and wait his turn. All behaviors must have a payoff of some kind or we discontinue them. Among the most common payoffs for misbehavior are attracting attention, gaining power, getting revenge, and being left alone.

The giving of rewards constitutes one of the most valuable tools teachers have at their disposal. Teachers have long recognized the importance of rewards and often use them to change behavior. Thus, the teacher who says, "I see that Johnny is ready to begin his math now that recess is over" is rewarding Johnny by giving him recognition for his attentiveness and studiousness.

One of the merits of this approach stems from its applicability to all students. It is not for just the antisocial student or just for the educationally disadvantaged or for the brain-injured or for the emotionally disturbed or for the normal child. Every student, regardless of the label we attach to him, needs ample rewards if he is to behave and achieve in school. To be effective, the teacher must answer questions relating to the frequency of reward, the timing of reward, and type of reward to be used.

HOW OFTEN SHOULD I BE REWARDING?   With respect to the frequency of rewards, a distinction must be made between the acquisition (i.e., learning or building) of a behavior and its maintenance. When the teacher wants a student to behave differently, he should ideally reward the student *every time* the given behavior occurs. (In actual practice, it is not always possible to reward a behavior every time it occurs. The student's action should be rewarded as often as possible however. Remember, the greater the frequency and amount of the reward, the faster the learning.) Thus, for example, the habitually hostile child who makes a friendly or cooperative or nonaggressive response toward a classmate should be rewarded *every time* he does so. Rewarding him once or twice is not enough. We must do it again and again on a *regular* basis until his cooperative behavior toward others has been securely acquired. Then, it is no longer necessary to give frequent rewards. In fact, it would then be best that the teacher reinforce such behavior every now and then (intermittent reinforcement) rather than 100% of the time, since intermittent reinforcement renders the behavior less subject to forgetting. Once the new behavior has been acquired, the problem centers around the maintenance of behavior—i.e., with how long the student will remember to behave this way once you are occupied with other students or activities and cannot reward him regularly. After all, to get along in the classroom, the student has to behave appropriately without the teacher's paying attention to him all the time. Having established the desirable behavior, we should reward the student every now and then for appropriate behavior.

WHEN SHOULD I BE REWARDING?   Timing is especially critical in our giving of rewards. Sometimes teachers give rewards before the child has complied with demands. This is a mistake, for there is little incentive to put forth effort once the payoff has been received. This is why we customarily pay people *after* they do the job.

How much time should elapse between performance of the desired behavior and giving of the reward? Initially, the delay factor may have to be quite short when dealing with acting-out youngsters because they typically have difficulty postponing gratification. Step by step, however, the interval can be lengthened as the child acquires more adequate behavioral controls. Hence, the teacher may initially have to reward the conduct-disordered child immediately after his good behavior at recess time or in the laboratory. Eventually, if all proceeds well the student will develop greater ability to postpone gratification. One teacher was able to lengthen the time interval by asking the student if he would mind waiting until tomorrow to get his lifesaver. Another teacher, who had been using art activities for some time as a potent reward, asked the student if it would be all right if they skipped art this afternoon since other class activities had in fact run behind schedule.

The delay interval may also have to be short with youngsters whose self-esteem and self-confidence are severely impaired. A seriously disabled reader may, for example, need a reward such as the teacher's praise or encouragement immediately after he has sounded out a single word. Later, as he gains in reading skills and personal confidence, he may not need to be rewarded until he has completed a whole page or story. In fact, once the student's frustration tolerance increases, the reward need not even be given during the school day or in the school setting. The accumulations of so many points may be used to earn him a fishing trip with his dad on the weekend or entitle him to the school picnic coming up next month or to watch his favorite TV program that night or to go horseback riding.

WHAT TYPE OF REWARD SHOULD I USE? The third question teachers should ask has to do with the wide variety of rewards that teachers can use. For purposes of exposition, the rewards listed in Table 12–2 are arbitrarily divided into four categories—tangible rewards, people rewards, activity rewards, and intrinsic rewards. Though listed separately, the effective classroom teacher will use different kinds of rewards rather than overworking a single reward. Even mature adults require the kinds of rewards presented. See the case on rowdy behavior in the study hall for an example of the use of positive reinforcement.

One problem that crops up is the student's failure to display rewardable behavior. In this case, the teacher can do one of two things. He can reward small improvements (the method of successive approximations) or use modeling procedures.

Modeling. Positive reward can sometimes be an exceedingly slow method for the learning of *new* complex behaviors. Effective as positive rewards are for strengthening old behaviors, they often demand arduous and ingenious changes in classroom procedures to produce appropriate *new* behaviors which can then be rewarded. As we noted earlier, the new behavior or some approximation thereof must first occur before appropriate rewards can be applied. In addition to being time-consuming, the rewarding of trial-and-error learning can prove hazardous in many natural settings. For example,

Table 12–2. **Examples of Different Types of Rewards**

Tangible Rewards	People Rewards	Activity Rewards	Intrinsic Rewards
Candy	Praise	Going on field trip	Overcoming a problem or handicap
Popcorn	A smile	Choosing your own seat	Success experiences
Whistles	A wink	Reading a favorite story	A sense of pride in accomplishment
Stars	Expressing interest	Putting head down and	Allowing student to plot his progress
Trinkets	Physical nearness	resting	Using content that is humorous, dramatic,
Points	Approval	Doing crossword puzzle	or surprising
Money	Picking teacher as a playmate	Drawing	Letting the student catch teacher mistakes
Comics	Showing respect	Cleaning erasers	Providing for repetition by converting
Baseball cards	Having parents sign note of	Tutoring	drills into games
Athletic passes	good behavior	Having a "rap" session	Allowing student to explore his curiosity
	Membership in "Who's Who	Getting extra recess	about a topic
	Club"		Developing a sense of mastery
			Allowing student to vary methods by which
			he learns—e.g., use of slides
			Writing creative short stories

Rowdy Behavior in Study Hall

One beginning teacher used the novel reward of killing flies to maintain quiet in a normally rowdy study hall composed of 36 students (29 boys and 16 of them on the ninth-grade football team!). The use of fly killing was a natural reward, since the room was infested with flies and a solution was needed. The entire football squad armed with books, magazines, and construction paper came up with an answer. After stopping the confusion, the teacher announced that the students who studied and were quiet during the hour would have the last five minutes free to participate in the war on the flies or to remain seated as rooting spectators. This novel reward worked effectively as the students learned to come into the room, sit down, and open their books, waiting and watching the clock until fly-killing time arrived.

When the fly population dropped off, the students continued the desirable study hall behavior for "a free time" period the last five minutes of each study hall session.

Comment: Who would have ever thought of fly killing as an activity reward to be earned for acceptable behavior? The answer is, of course, an observant teacher with practical ingenuity. Note that behavior modification techniques can be applied to the class as a whole.

if we waited for an individual learning to swim to exhibit spontaneously a proper stroke or an approximation thereof and then rewarded him, few of us would live long enough to become adept swimmers.[3] Modeling procedures (which refer to such processes as imitation, observational learning, role-playing, vicarious experience, and emotional contagion) can circumvent these difficulties, thereby offering a shortcut to the learning of complex tasks. The importance of learning by watching has been stressed by Bandura (1969), who notes, "It would be difficult to imagine a culture in which the language,

3. Reward procedures can be used alone to evoke new patterns of behavior when (1) the individual already has the available component skills, (2) environmental conditions exist that are capable of arousing actions that are similar to the desired behaviors, and (3) the student and teacher possess sufficient endurance to employ such time-consuming methods (Bandura, 1969).

mores, vocational and avocational patterns, familial customs, and educational, social and political practices were shaped in each new member through a gradual process of differential reinforcement without the response guidance of models who exemplify the accumulated cultural repertories in their own behavior." Under most natural learning conditions, social behaviors are typically learned through imitation in large segments or in toto rather than acquired in a piecemeal, trial-and-error manner. The sheer simplicity of learning through imitation justifies its use in preference to or in combination with positive reward. There is no question but that modeling procedures are an economical means of transmitting new appropriate behaviors, especially when telling the student what to do (verbal modeling) is combined with demonstrations. In actual classroom situations these two ways of encouraging behavior—positive reward and modeling—are typically combined, with the student obtaining a reward when he imitates an act performed by the model. Once acquired, the behavior can often be maintained without external support, since human beings learn to reward themselves for behaving appropriately. The combination of modeling and reward procedures is probably the most effective method of transmitting, eliciting, and maintaining social behavior.

Teachers who are aware of the importance of observational learning realize that we often teach by example. Since the learning and regulation of human behavior can be strongly influenced through examples of socially acceptable behavior, teachers are often able to influence student behavior through the use of modeling. Though much remains to be learned about modeling procedures, these techniques are well suited for use by educators with withdrawn students, antisocial youngsters, and those who simply are lacking in adequate social and scholastic skills.

Despite having distinct practical value, these techniques have been neglected in helping students to behave more constructively. Training institutions have long recognized the importance of modeling procedures in the preparation of future teachers, and therefore have attempted to provide adequate models in the form of critic teachers; however, less attention has been devoted by training institutions to using the modeling procedures as a means of influencing the behavior of the pupils with whom the teachers will have to work.

EFFECTS OF MODELING. There are three main effects of exposure to models: (1) Students can acquire *new* behaviors. (2) Inhibitory responses already learned by the student can be strengthened or weakened. For example, children who see an agemate punished or rewarded for aggressive behavior tend to decrease or increase their aggressive behavior accordingly. (3) Modeling can trigger or elicit behaviors the student has already acquired. This eliciting effect is distinguished from the above two effects in that the behavior imitated is neither new nor previously punished. That is, the eliciting effect refers to the triggering of previously acquired behaviors that are either socially neutral or approved. For instance, the example set by the teacher or a classmate might prompt the student to volunteer to clean up the blackboards, to help another student who is having trouble with an assignment, or to settle down and finish an assignment.

FACTORS INFLUENCING MODELING. Mere exposure to a model is obviously no guarantee that the student will imitate what the teacher wants him to. Susceptibility to social modeling influence is largely determined by three factors—characteristics of the model, characteristics of the observer, and the consequences (pleasant and unpleasant) associated with modeling behaviors.

1. The first set of factors relating to characteristics of the model include such things as the model's perceived expertise or competence, his status or prestige, his firmness, his personal warmth, his age, his sex, ethnic status, and organizational affiliations. Thus, for example, students readily identify with nurturant teacher celebrities and with older students.

2. Characteristics of the observer that influence imitative behavior include such factors as the student's sex, race, socioeconomic level, and personality characteristics (dependency needs, achievement motivation, hostility level, cooperativeness, etc.). Thus, we find that boys imitate aggressive behavior more readily than girls, dependent youngsters and those with a cooperative set (as opposed to a competitive orientation) are more susceptible to imitative influences, and angry and authoritarian students respond readily to aggressive models (Flanders, 1968).

3. Outcomes of the modeled behavior are extremely important in determining the extent of imitation. In fact, the use of appealing incentives can, in the majority of instances, override the effects of model and observer characteristics (Bandura, 1969). For example, a teacher having only average social power and status in the eyes of his students can still promote imitative behavior simply by telling them that they will be handsomely rewarded for later reproducing what he teaches them (that is, for modeling his behavior). In brief, the student will perform more of what he has learned if he has heard of or seen someone being rewarded for that performance. On the other hand, as noted earlier, the student will not be as likely to engage in the kind of behavior for which he has seen others punished.

Behavior Elimination Techniques

Extinction. Just as there is a substantial body of research demonstrating that the presentation of rewards can facilitate the learning and maintenance of given behaviors, there is a growing body of literature demonstrating that extinction—which refers to a process of discouraging certain specific behaviors by not rewarding them—can reduce or eliminate troublesome behaviors. For if a behavior is learned through the giving of rewards, then it can be unlearned by taking the rewards away. If a given behavior no longer has its intended effect, its frequency tends to diminish.

As Hunter (1967) points out, "We don't keep on doing something that doesn't work." If the troublesome student acts out and nothing happens, he soon gets the message and abandons the particular maladaptive way. In short, simply removing the rewarding consequences of an act constitutes an effective way of discouraging it. This technique has been found effective with a wide variety of behavior.

Despite the simplicity and potency of this principle, teachers often fail to use it to its best advantage. A fuller understanding of the cautions and guidelines regarding the use of this technique should enable us to apply it to better advantage.

1. Combine extinction and positive reinforcement. Extinction removes the payoff for unacceptable behaviors, whereas positive reinforcement increases the probability that an acceptable behavior will replace the extinguished behavior.

2. If old habits recur, remain calm and lay the unwanted behavior to rest once again by undertaking another series of extinction trials. Fortunately, the unwanted behavior can be more readily extinguished on the second series of extinction trials.

3. Ignoring behavior leads to extinction when the payoff is attention. Being aware of the value of ignoring is one matter, and practicing to ignore is quite another. Ignoring requires rigorous self-control.

4. Just as peer group reinforcement can serve as a powerful strengthener of behavior, group extinction procedures can also serve as powerful weakeners of behavior. Enlisting peer group support can be very beneficial. For example, at a class meeting, the group might make a rule to the effect that all clowning behavior will be ignored by them.

5. When reinforcement for maladaptive behavior comes from the act itself (for example, fighting and seeing a look of pain on the victim's face), other tactics such as punishment are necessary.

6. When the dangers of physical injury and emotional contagion are distinct possibilities, some form of punishment (isolation or physical restraint) is the method of choice.

7. In applying extinction procedures, expect misbehavior to remain at a high level or actually increase during the initial stages. Don't let this discourage you. Be consistent and the frequency of behavior will taper off.

8. New misbehaviors sometimes emerge (for example, verbal impersonations of the teacher after pantomiming has been extinguished). The problems associated with extinguishing a long succession of inappropriate behaviors can be eliminated by combining extinction with positive reinforcement and/or modeling.

Because teachers have not always taken the above guidelines into account, they have sometimes become discouraged in their use of this technique. The writers have seen many teachers disheartened in trying to implement the school counselor's advice not to reward maladaptive behavior. What commonly happens, unless the above precautions are noted, is that the teachers'

efforts to extinguish unacceptable student behavior themselves undergo extinction. Extinction procedures can be a valuable aid to the teacher when
used wisely, however.

Punishment. OBJECTIONS TO THE USE OF PUNISHMENT. Punishment
is as old as human history. It is an inevitable part of everyone's learning experiences. Indications are that punishment is here to stay. And by the usual
standards of scientific merit—efficiency and effectiveness—the research findings on the use of punishment as a means of modifying troublesome behavior
ought to evoke admiration (Baer, 1971). The use of negative consequences
has been disavowed, however, on both moral and scientific grounds.

From a moral viewpoint, the word punishment connotes inhumane treatment, negative attitudes, and hostile acts. Even if successful, punishment
forces the person to do something against his will. Baer suggests that much
of our revulsion regarding punishment is based on our reactions against the
snake-pit-like conditions found many years ago in our state hospitals and
prisons. Advocating the use of punishment is in the minds of many people
tantamount to asking them to forgo years of progress in human reform. In
actuality, however, it is probably much more humane to subject people to a
small number of brief painful experiences in exchange for the interminable
pain of a lifelong maladjustment. Society has to ask itself a basic question,
namely which punishment is tougher on the individual and which one lasts
longer (Baer, 1971).

Traditionally, certain specific objections have been raised on scientific
grounds against the use of punishment as a behavior modification technique.
And the cautions to be discussed suggest that if punishment is to be used as a
means of changing behavior, it should be judiciously applied. As Bandura (1969) notes, "Because of the varied and complex effects of punishment
particularly when socially mediated, it must be employed with care and skill
in programs of behavioral change." Let us at this point consider five of the
most common scientific criticisms leveled against punishment.

1. *Short-Term Effects.* Laboratory studies that have been conducted on
animals suggest that punishment does not eliminate the maladaptive response.
Instead, it merely slows down the rate at which the troublesome behaviors
are exhibited. How many times have you scolded a student, kept him in from
recess, retained him after school, put him out in the hall, threatened to lower
his grade, or sent him to the principal's office, only to find that he engages in
the very same misbehavior after a short while?

2. *Lack of Direction.* Punishment simply serves notice to stop inappropriate behaviors. It does not indicate to the student what behaviors are appropriate in the situation. How often do we catch ourselves saying things like:
"George, stop that and do what you're suppose to be doing." "Sally, quit
that fooling around and do it right." "Pete, do you have to do that? Settle
down!" "Don, get with it!" Our verbal reprimands make it painfully clear to

the student that we want him to stop misbehaving but rarely make explicit what we want him to do. Consequently, the student may frequently not know exactly how he is to remedy the situation.

3. *Escape and Avoidance Behaviors.* Foremost among the unfavorable side effects of punishment is the development of avoidance behaviors. It is common knowledge that we have a strong tendency to avoid contact with individuals and situations that we find unpleasant. In many instances, these resulting escape and avoidance behaviors (truancy, lying, cheating, etc.) may be more unwholesome than the behavior that the original punishment was designed to eliminate. Moreover, once these escape behaviors become established, they can be difficult to eliminate. One especially unfortunate consequence of escape behaviors is an avoidance of teachers and/or other change agents. This can prove a particularly serious hindrance in that it deprives the student of the opportunity to learn both attitudes and behaviors normally acquired through unforced modeling.

4. *Constricted Behavior.* There are two other consequences that can stem from the use of punishment: namely, the inhibition of socially desirable behaviors and the development of personal rigidity. The effects of punishment are not always confined to the behaviors that we want eliminated. Harsh punishments, especially those applied over lengthy periods of time, can also lead to the inhibition of socially desirable behaviors and to a loss of spontaneity. In other words, the punished student may come to suppress socially acceptable patterns of behavior that are not in need of censure. As a consequence of overgeneralization to other aspects of behavior, the student may also become less flexible in his adjustment.

5. *Setting a Bad Example.* On many occasions, the teacher's words or direct teachings say one thing to the student while his actions or indirect teachings say something contradictory. Unwittingly, parents and teachers provide a clear-cut model of the very kind of behavior from which they want their children or students to refrain.

Despite the limitations associated with this technique, many psychologists now contend that certain negative sanctions, if properly applied, can assist in eliminating detrimental patterns of adjustment. As we shall see shortly, the undesirable byproducts are not necessarily inherent in punishment but stem from the faulty fashion in which it is applied. Indeed, considerable human behavior is changed and maintained by natural aversive consequences without any ill effects. To avoid painful consequences, we put on warm clothes to protect against the cold, we walk along the side of the road, we run from falling objects, we try not to fall down, we drive properly so that we do not lose our driver's license, we guard ourselves in various ways so that we do not get jilted by girl friends, we try to be careful in our business transactions so that we do not lose money, we work industriously and get along with our superiors to avoid the unpleasant consequences of losing our jobs, and so forth. We engage in a great deal of behavior simply to avoid pain, and our personalities do not become warped as a result. Few would criticize the use of punishment in teaching young children to stay out of busy streets, to keep their hands off hot stoves, or to refrain from inserting metal objects in electric wall sockets (Bandura, 1969).

The use of punishment as an intervention technique is most likely necessary in that it is impossible to guide children effectively through the use of only positive reinforcement and extinction. Ausubel (1961), among others, rejects the idea that only "positive" forms of discipline are beneficial. He points out that a child does not come to regard rudeness as an undesirable form of behavior simply by reinforcing respect for others. As Ausubel (1961) asserts, "It is impossible for children to learn what is not approved and tolerated simply by generalizing in reverse from the approval they receive for the behavior that is acceptable."

GUIDELINES TOWARD A MORE EFFECTIVE USE OF PUNISHMENT

1. Punishment should be used in a corrective way. It is designed to help the student improve now and in the future. It is not to retaliate for wrongdoing in the past. Punishment prompted by teacher mood has no place in the classroom. Moral indignation may make the teacher feel better but it will not change student behavior. Punishment is to be used in a rational, systematic way designed to improve student behavior, not to provide a cathartic effect for the punishment agent.

2. Ideally, punishment should be inherent in the situation rather than an expression of the power of one person over another. In other words, punishment should express the reality of the social or physical situation. The idea is to let the child experience the unpleasant but natural or logical result of his own actions. Used in this way, we can minimize or avoid the dangers associated with one human being's delivering punishment to another.

3. The role of the teacher is to be that of a friendly bystander who is interested and objective. Note that it is the tone of the teacher's voice that provides a true barometer of the teacher's attitudes toward the child.

4. On those occasions when it is necessary for one human being (for example, teacher, principal, peer group) to punish another human being (for example, student), it should be done in an impersonal, matter-of-fact way. The punishing agent must guard against the tendency to yell or scold, for this indicates that his attitude is one of revenge and often reinforces unacceptable behavior.

5. Once a good rule has been agreed upon, the youngster who violates it should experience the unpleasant consequences of his misbehavior. Excuses and promises are not accepted. There is to be no escape from the unpleasant consequences of the actions. Acceptance of rationalizations only serves to promote social and personal irresponsibility. Insist on performance.

6. A youngster should be given one warning or signal before punishment is delivered. The warning may eliminate the need for punishment. Even when the warning proves ineffective, it adds an element of fairness to what follows. On those occasions when the warning fails to deter unacceptable behavior,

extended discussion or "reasoning" is contraindicated since teacher attention tends to strengthen unacceptable behavior.

7. The nature of the punishment and the manner of presenting it should avoid the arousal of strong emotional responses in the person punished. The use of a behavioral contract in which the student has a choice of consequences (as well as goals) can prove helpful in this regard.

8. The teacher must be consistent in his use of punishment. Ideally, the target behavior should be punished each time it occurs. Once the student has learned the habit of not responding in a particular way, intermittent punishment should be used.

9. When used contingently and immediately, mild punishment can produce enduring positive change in cases where severe punishment alone fails.

10. Avoid extended periods of punishment, especially where low-intensity punishments are used. Letting the youngster experience the maximum intensity of the punishment is more humane and effective than exposing him to a prolonged series of lesser punishments. A firmly presented time-out period is more effective than several "no's" of increasing loudness.

11. One strategy that is designed to promote a durable elimination involves the combined use of punishment and reward. Various research studies indicate that this combination is much more effective and efficient than the use of punishment alone. Punishment reminds the student what not to do. The reward of appropriate alternative behavior tells the student what he should do.

12. Timing plays an important role in determining the effectiveness of punishment. Available evidence indicates rather consistently that children who are punished early in a given sequence of misbehavior develop greater resistance to temptation than those who are punished only after completion of the misdeed. Punishing a child after he has stolen something leaves the initial phases of interest, intention, and approach relatively unaffected.

13. To guard against behavioral constriction we must reward acceptable behaviors that are related or similar in nature to the ones being punished. For instance, hitting others may be punished but desirable assertiveness may be rewarded. This sort of selective reinforcement greatly assists the student to discriminate what behaviors are acceptable for a given situation.

14. Remove or reduce the *magnitude* and *frequency* of the rewards that are maintaining misbehavior. Punishment works much more effectively and efficiently once the rewards that maintain misbehavior are eliminated or decreased.

15. Be certain that the delivery of punishment is not associated with the giving of reinforcement. For example, if removal from the group is a rewarding experience, then it will not be effective in modifying the target behavior.

16. Punishment should be used in a way that fosters self-direction. The use of behavior contracts is helpful in that it promotes self-direction by having the student assume responsibility for his own behavior. The basic rationale is to provide opportunities for some degree of choice in determining one's goals and to let him experience the consequences of his actions. Allowing

the student to end the punishment when his behavior improves also facilitates self-direction.

17. It is important that the use of punishment require little of the teacher's time and energy. If delivery of the punishment is punishing to the teacher, he is apt to stop it because he is inconvenienced by the punishment rather than because the misbehavior has improved. For example, keeping the child after school may involve as much hardship for the teacher as it does for the student.

Summary

Classroom discipline continues to be a source of concern for school personnel. Effective yet humanitarian discipline is necessary for children's socialization as well as their educability.

While today's teachers are better able to identify withdrawn children than their counterparts over forty years ago, they are still concerned—and appropriately so—with the aggressive child.

Because of a variety of factors (shortage of mental-health professionals, shortcomings inherent in the clinic model, questionable outcomes of child therapy, and the rise of behavior modification procedures), teachers will become increasingly involved in the management of difficult students.

Because mental-health workers and teachers frequently have fundamentally different perspectives and objectives, they often have difficulty formulating coordinated plans for children in need of help.

Two promising approaches to classroom discipline were discussed—a psychodynamic approach and a behavioral approach.

Teachers must be effective group workers. Among other things, this means that teachers need to be adept in handling a host of common group problems such an irrelevant curriculum, clique formation, emotional-blackmail climates, automatic imposition of values on others, boredom, anxiety, and the makeup of the class.

Redl notes that group leaders must consider (a) the effects of a given disciplinary action on both the individual and the group, (b) whether to try to modify surface behavior or more deep-seated changes in attitude, and (c) a variety of factors in judging the effectiveness of a given technique.

Signal interference, planned ignoring, interest boosting, humor, and diversion can all be useful ways to cope with problems posed by reasonably well-intentioned students.

Hurdle help, situational alterations, thoughtful routines, removal of seductive objects, antiseptic bouncing, and physical restraint are ways in which the teachers can help students who are frustrated by situational barriers in the school setting.

In an effort to modify the child's behavior, the sensitive and empathic teacher will also appeal to various values held by the child.

Although rewards, promises, threats, and blame can have beneficial outcomes, Redl believes that these techniques have more shortcomings than advantages.

Training in life-space interviewing is designed to provide teachers with skills for effective communication with problem students. The two broad objectives of life-space interviewing are clinical exploitation of life events and emotional first aid.

Specific guidelines for the life-space interview were discussed together with its limitations.

Behavioral approaches are based on learning theory concepts.

Behavioral approaches deal more with current behavior than with the remote causes of the behavior. Several reasons were advanced as to why behavioral approaches are particularly suitable for use by classroom teachers.

The four steps in behavior modification entail the selection of a target behavior, analysis of the antecedents and consequences of the behavior in question, selection of strategies to change the behavior, and recording of results.

The teacher must ask if the students have a clear understanding of the rules, if they have the abilities to comply with the rules, and if the students are motivated to meet expectations.

Positive reinforcement is perhaps the most powerful of the behavior modification techniques for encouraging behavior. Attention must be paid to the timing, frequency, and nature of rewards.

Modeling procedures can also be extremely helpful in encouraging behavior. Unfortunately, they are not used as often by teachers as they might be. Discussion focused on the three main effects of exposure to modeling as well as the three sets of factors that influence modeling.

Extinction is one technique that can weaken behavior. Several guidelines were presented so that this might be used to the fullest advantage.

Although the use of punishment has been subjected to considerable criticism, it appears that the limitations of this approach are not inherent in the technique itself but instead stems from its misuse. Because it is a complex technique, however, it should be used as a last resort and the cautions and guidelines noted should be observed.

References

Ausubel, D. A new look at classroom discipline. *Phi Delta Kappan*, 1961, **43,** 25–30.

Baer, D. Let's take another look at punishment. *Psychology Today*, 1971, **4,** 32–37, 111.

Bahn, A., Chandler, C., & Eisenberg, L. Diagnostic characteristics related to services in psychiatric clinics for children. *Milbank Memorial Fund Quarterly*, 1962, **40,** 289 318.

Bandura, A. *Principles of behavior modification*. New York: Holt, Rinehart, and Winston, 1969.

Bernstein, M. Life space interview in the school setting. In R. G. Newman & M. M. Keith (Eds.), *The school-centered life space interview*. Washington, D.C.: Washington School of Psychiatry, 1963, pp. 35–44.

Bower, E. M. Mental health. In R. Ebel (Ed.), *Encyclopedia of educational research* (4th ed.) New York: Macmillan, 1970, pp. 811–28.

Flanders, J. A review of research on imitative behavior. *Psychological Bulletin*, 1968, **69** (5), 316–37.

Frumkin, R. M. Occupation and major mental disorders. In A. M. Rose (Ed.), *Mental health and mental disorder*. New York: Norton, 1955, pp. 136–60.

Gallagher, J. J., & Chalfant, J. C. The training of educational specialists for emotionally disturbed and socially maladjusted children. In W. W. Wattenberg (Ed.), Social deviancy among youth. *Yearbook of the National Society for the Study of Education, 1966, 65, Part I*, pp. 398–422.

Glidewell, J., & Swallow, C. *The prevalence of maladjustment in elementary schools*. Chicago, Ill.: University of Chicago Press, 1968.

Grossberg, J. Behavior therapy: a review. *Psychological Bulletin*, 1964, **62,** 73–88.

Hunter, M. *Reinforcement*. El Segrendo, Calif.: TIP Publications, 1967.

Kounin, J., Friesen, W., & Norton, A. Managing emotionally disturbed children in regular classrooms. *Journal of Educational Psychology*, 1966, **57,** 1–13.

Kounin, J., Gump, P., & Ryan, J. Explorations in classroom management. *Journal of Teacher Education*, 1961, **12,** 235–46.

Lambert, N., & Grossman, H. *Problems in determining the etiology of learning and behavior problems*. Sacramento: California State Department of Education, 1964.

Long, N. Some problems in teaching life space interviewing techniques to graduate students in education in a large class at Indiana University. In R .G. Newman & M. M. Keith (Eds.), *The school-centered life space interview*. Washington, D.C.: Washington School of Psychiatry, 1963, pp. 51–56.

Maurer, A. Corporal punishment. *American Psychologist*, 1974, **29** (8), 614–26.

Morse, W. The mental hygiene dilemma in public education. *American Journal of Orthopsychiatry*, 1961, **31,** 332–38.

Morse, W. The crisis teacher: public school provision for the disturbed pupil. *University of Michigan School of Education Bulletin*, 1962, **37,** 10–14.

National Education Association. *A comparison of teacher and educational leader assessments of teacher needs*. Washington, D.C.: 1973.

Newman, R. G. The school-centered life space interview. In R. G. Newman & M. M. Keith (Eds.), *The school-centered life space interview*. Washington, D.C.: Washington School of Psychiatry, 1963, pp. 13–34.

Norman, V., Rosen, B., & Bahn, A. Psychiatric clinic out-patients in the United States, 1959. *Mental Hygiene*, 1962, **46**, 321–43.

Overall, B., & Aronson, H. Expectations of psychotherapy in patients of lower socioeconomic class. *American Journal of Orthopsychiatry*, 1963, **33**, 421–30.

Redl, F. The concept of the life space interview. *American Journal of Orthopsychiatry*, 1959, **29**, 1–18.

Redl, F. *When we deal with children.* New York: Free Press, 1966.

Redl, F., & Wattenberg, W. *Mental hygiene in teaching.* New York: Harcourt, Brace & World, 1959.

Redl, F., & Wineman, D. *Controls from within.* New York: Free Press, 1952.

Stouffer, G. A. W., Jr. The attitudes of parents toward certain behavior problems of children. *Teachers College Bulletin*, 1959, **5**, 173–74.

White, M. Little red schoolhouse and little white clinic. *Teachers College Record*, 1965, **67**, 188–200.

Wickman, E. *Children's behavior and teachers' attitudes.* New York: Commonwealth Fund, 1928.

Suggested Readings

Clarizio, H. *Toward positive classroom discipline.* (2nd ed.) New York: Wiley, 1976.

De Risi, W., & Butz, G. *Writing behavioral contracts.* Champaign, Ill.: Research Press, 1975.

Kazdin, A. *Behavior modification in applied settings.* Homewood, Ill.: Dorsey Press, 1975.

Mager, R., & Piper, P. *Analyzing performance problems or you really oughta wanna.* Belmont, Calif.: Fearon Publishers, 1970.

Newman, R., & Keith, M. *The school-centered life space interview.* Washington, D.C.: Washington School of Psychiatry, 1963.

13

The Prevention
of
Behavior
Disorders

It is customary to distinguish among three kinds or levels of prevention: primary, secondary, and tertiary. *Primary prevention* has as its objective the reduction of behavioral disorders; it aims to prevent various disorders from arising initially. Early identification of emotional disturbance represents one such strategy. In addition, this type of prevention involves the promotion of psychological robustness; that is, it attempts to strengthen personality development, for emotional well-being is more than the mere absence of pathology. Current curriculum approaches that strive to provide ego-enhancing experiences are illustrative of this phase of primary prevention. *Secondary prevention* involves the identification of vulnerable groups and is akin to the concept of treatment in that it aims to shorten the duration and diminish the impact of a given disorder through therapeutic interventions. Head Start programs constitute an example of attempts at secondary prevention. *Tertiary prevention* is similar to the concept of rehabilitation. The aim here is to assist the individual to live as useful a life as possible despite some degree of chronic impairment.

The ensuing discussion focuses for the most part on primary prevention. The chapter opens by establishing the need for preventive actions. Next, attention turns to some of the reasons why preventive programs have remained more at the conceptual than at the action level. Discussion then centers around programs dealing with the biological, sociological, and psychological aspects of prevention. Finally, the chapter closes with a discussion of the role played by the school in primary prevention.

The Need for Preventive Strategies

Three basic factors suggest the need for preventive action: (1) the scope of the mental health problem; (2) the shortage of professional health specialists, generated in part by the clinic model of treatment; and (3) the dubious value of the majority of treatment approaches.

The Scope of the Problem

First, let us briefly review the incidence of maladjustment in youth. Bower (1970) indicated that 10% of the children in public schools have mental health problems. Using this figure, Bower estimated that there are now 5.5 million youth, from kindergarten through college, with moderate to severe mental health problems. As a conservative estimate, 300,000 youth under 18 years of age are seen annually in outpatient clinics for relatively less severe emotional disturbances, and an estimated additional 500,000 might be classified as manifesting psychotic or borderline behavior (National Association for Mental Health, 1966). More recently, it has been estimated that almost 1½ million youth under age 18 need immediate help and that less than 30% is receiving it (Cowen, 1973).

Second, let us examine the need for preventive programs with normal children. The fact that the majority of disturbed adults were normal children clearly highlights the need for preventive actions with this population. Despite the finding that a higher percentage of disturbed children as compared to the percentage of normal children (about 30% versus 8%) eventually wind up in the population of disturbed adults, the population of normal children contributes more actual bodies to the population of disturbed adults than does the population of disturbed children.[1] To illustrate, 3.6 million (about 8%) of 45 million normal youth will become disturbed as adults in contrast to 1.5 million (30%) of 5 million troubled youth. Thus, based on a ratio of 3.6 to 1.5, we see that about 70% of disturbed adults come from the population of normal children.

The Shortage of Manpower

The number of mental health specialists has not kept pace with the rising number of cases. George Albee (1967), an authority on manpower needs in the mental health fields, declares that the mental health professionals are not going to be able to provide the services promised. He feels that practitioners have made irresponsible promises—to union workers, to the aged, to the poor, and to Congress. For example, if only 1% of the United Auto Workers sought psychiatric service, there would be another 20,000 cases to treat annually. The Medicare bill promises such help not only to the elderly, but for all persons adjudged "medically indigent" and for their children.

The number of trained mental health professionals has increased dramatically in recent years. Yet even conservative estimates of population in need of service by 1985 indicate a growing disparity between supply and demand (Report of the Joint Commission, 1973). It is little wonder that Albee sees a day of reckoning before long.

Note that the discussion pertains to *demand*—the number of professionals required to handle actual cases—and not *need*—the number required to perform an adequate job in the mental health field. No one knows how many are *needed*, but is known that the number is certainly much larger than the number of professionals *demanded*.

The Expense and Inadequacy of Treatment

Not only have services been promised that cannot be delivered, but the services delivered are both expensive and inadequate. With respect to outpatient services, the lack of a centralized administration has resulted in the duplication of diagnostic and treatment services, with people being shunted from one community agency to another. The need for an administrative

---

1. These figures are based on studies showing a persistence rate of 30% for troubled children, a 90% rate of normality and 10% abnormality rate among both children and adults, and a solving for the unknown (the rate at which the normal child eventually contributes to the population of adult disturbance). The mathematical calculations are as follows:

$$x90 + \left(\frac{3}{10}\right)10 - 10$$
$$90x + 3 = 10$$
$$90x = 10 - 3$$
$$x = \frac{7}{90}$$
$$x = 7.7\% \text{ or about } 8\%$$

reorganization that meets the needs of the people rather than the needs of an antiquated organization is becoming increasingly apparent (Gardner, 1967). The costs incurred in the course of inpatient treatment are even higher in comparison to those associated with outpatient treatment. The cost of maintaining a single delinquent in a public training school is, for instance, $3,000 a year[2] (Polk & Schafer, 1967), and private care units consisting of from 20 to 60 disturbed youngsters cost about $10,000 per child per year (Bower, 1970). The latest therapeutic bandwagon, the community mental health center, is also tremendously expensive. In 1963, the Community Mental Health Act provided $150 million in grants from 1963 to 1967 for the construction of these centers. The projected operating costs of a given center for the first year is $500,000 (Bower, 1970). These costs are merely illustrative and do not speak to the cost of state and county mental hospitals, of outpatient treatment, and, most seriously, of wasted human resources.

The expense created by treatment of maladjusted youth might be tolerable —provided the services rendered were adequate. But this is not the case. Despite the existence of more than 2,000 outpatient clinics and 400 psychiatric units in general hospitals, the rates of mental disorders have remained unchanged or, perhaps, have increased. Just as the advent of the child-guidance movement in the early 1900s was hailed as a boon, so now the far-reaching benefits of the community health center are perhaps exaggerated. While a shift from the therapist's office to the community is needed, little benefit can be expected by simply transplanting present policies and practices to a new setting. As Cowen, Gardner, & Zax (1967) note:

> Function, not locus, is the critical element, and the potential shift of our mental health operations to a community base should be a means rather than an end. Inherent in such a shift are the opportunities to study more relevant and meaningful questions, to extend the reach of mental health operations, to look at resources rather than deficits, and to develop specific mental health programs with greater social utility. Without recognition of the salience of these functions, there is the danger that the community approach will, in the final reckoning, offer little more than the oft-maligned "old wine in new bottles."

To be genuinely innovative, the workers in community mental health centers must have knowledge of social processes and social organization (Reiff, 1966). Unfortunately, these centers are manned by the "old guard," who lack such knowhow. Since the old guard were trained primarily in therapy, the expectation may well be for "old wine in new bottles."

---

2. Acknowledgment is made of the differing costs for children's services given in various sections of this text. The figures are correct in the context cited. Costs vary according to (1) type of service (day or residential school, public or private facility), (2) kind of placement (temporary shelter, foster home, institutional), and (3) the inflationary spiral (1970 costs are greater than those for 1969, etc.). An excellent discussion of costs of child care services is presented in Fanshel & Shinn (1972).

It should be apparent that unwarranted reliance has been on treatment approaches, especially on psychotherapy. As noted in the section on the evaluation of therapy, the results have been disappointing despite the selection of the most suitable patients for treatment. Clearly, though there will always be a need for treatment interventions, there is no scientific basis for the assumption that traditional forms of treatment will provide an adequate solution to the nation's mental health problems. Many workers now feel that the ounce of prevention could not conceivably be less effective than the pound of cure.

Medical science has accomplished much along the lines of mass prevention. Vaccines for polio, measles, and mumps are currently available. Yet, the behavioral sciences seem quite content to provide treatment on a one-to-one basis for psychological disturbances. The futility of this approach is well exemplified in Bower's (1964) relating an old Cornish custom for determining a man's sanity. According to this method, the suspect was given a scoop and asked to empty the water from a bucket placed under an open tap. If the man turned off the faucet, he was deemed rational and sane. If, on the other hand, he continued to scoop while letting the water run, he was deemed insane. Reasoning analogously, it would appear that most mental health workers might also be deemed irrational. Ingenuity has provided various curricula in bucket-scooping. It takes a psychiatrist approximately 12 years to become a fully trained bucket scooper; a Ph.D. psychologist, about 8 years; and a social worker, about 6 years. As Bower queries, Is it not time to offer at least a 4-year curriculum in tap turning?

Deterrents to Implementation

The concept of prevention, as it receives increasing attention from certain mental health professions, has, as Bower (1964) points out, taken on an air of magic. It has become a high-status term "that has had little action implementation in the field of mental and emotional disorders." Why has this concept not been more actively translated into action programs? What are the principal obstructions responsible for its remaining largely a theoretical construct? In addition to the general lack of useful knowledge about human behavior, deterrents to preventive programs have typically assumed one or more of the following forms (Bower, 1964; Zax & Specter, 1974; Broskowski & Baker, 1974).

1. The size and complexity of the problem have overwhelmed lay groups and behavioral scientists alike. Since maladjustment arises from such varied sources as faulty parent-child relations, poverty, racial discrimination, constitutional factors, and school failure, many workers believe that anything short of a major societal overhaul would prove inconsequential. The problem is so vast that few know where to begin. The ensuing emotional response to the frustrations associated with prevention is one of despair. Consequently, few are inclined to make any full-hearted effort along this line.

2. A second resistance centers around the invasion-of-privacy issue. Always a cherished right, the freedom to live one's own life continues to be publicly reinforced. In certain states, for example, the schools need permission to administer personality tests to students. To prevent maladjustment is to meddle in people affairs. The crux of the difficulty lies in finding a way of intervention acceptable to the public. Traffic regulations and medical inoculations are accepted without much protest. Schools as a primary institution in society have an advantage in that they do have certain rights to interfere in the lives of their students. Moreover, there is a receptiveness on the part of most parents to such interventions. The schools must be careful, however, to restrict interference to their sanctioned function: the education of youth. Thus, schools must demonstrate that ancillary services (psychological evaluation, counseling, and the like) are necessary to the child's educational progress.

3. Another deterrent involves certain cultural values. Notable among these is the belief that by working hard, controlling impulses, and using intellect, a person will be successful and achieve virtue. Conversely, if he is not conscientious, follows the pleasure principle, and lets emotions override his better judgment, he will be unsuccessful, a failure, and regarded as evil. In short, the individual derives from life what he deserves.

4. Still another barrier to the development of prevention programs resides within the professional community itself. Unfortunately, the majority of mental health professionals view their primary task as one of treatment, not of prevention. The preoccupation is more with mental *illness* than with mental *health*. Witness the fact that, until recently, there was no word in our language to describe an ego-enhancing experience (*stren*). But there has long been a term (*trauma*) to indicate an ego-debilitating experience. An ever-expanding segment of mental health workers is becoming more prevention-oriented, but it remains difficult to enlist the full-fledged support of those doing therapy on a one-to-one relationship. Preventive work is regarded as less concrete, less exciting, and less urgent than therapy, which is geared toward the immediate, the tangible, and the already overt disturbance (Cruickshank, 1963).

5. A final problem involves specifying and evaluating the goals of prevention. Is the goal that of promoting emotional robustness? Or is it that of reducing pathology—for example, delinquency? As Bower (1964) states:

> If our prime intention is the promotion of emotional robustness and of the ability to cope with life rather than to defend against it, the goal needs to be given a base of health objectives that are specific, positive and (hopefully) measurable.

Difficult as the talks may be, it is essential to establish both operational definitions of objectives and evaluative baselines if any programs are to be implemented and assessed. The day of the "soft sell" may well be on the way out for the mental health fields; they will have to demonstrate their worth as helpers of humanity.

The Foci of Attack

Since it is often impractical to deal with all of the complexities of the problem of prevention, various workers have concentrated their energies and competencies on more delimited aspects of the problem. For purposes of discussion, these efforts can be subsumed under three main headings: biological approaches, sociological approaches, and psychological approaches.

Biological Approaches

General Physical Robustness. Many authorities have emphasized the importance of an adequate physical constitution as a basis for sound mental health. Perhaps the first and most important influence is that of pregnancy and childbirth. Notable among the studies in this area are those of Pasamanick & Knobloch (1966; see also Knobloch & Pasamanick, 1966). These investigators, fully aware that many factors in addition to abnormalities of pregnancy and childbirth cause behavior disturbances, reported that inspection of the medical histories of children with behavior problems revealed more complications of pregnancy and more incidence of prematurity than existed in the matched control. Such complications, especially evident for hyperactive, confused, and disorganized youngsters, also occurred more frequently in children having hearing defects, strabismus, school accidents, infantile autism, and delinquent symptoms.

One disconcerting fact concerning youngsters who suffer injury before or during birth is that a large proportion of them are born to mothers in the low socioeconomic strata. These mothers, in contrast to those who are more affluent, are more apt to have poor diets and to receive less careful medical care during pregnancy. That the diet factor can be critical is attested to by Knobloch & Pasamanick's (1966) finding that pregnancy abnormalities occur more often in mothers who are underweight at the beginning of pregnancy and who remain so during pregnancy. They also report that supplementing the mother's diet with vitamins and proteins can reduce the incidence of pregnancy problems. While this country as a whole enjoys the highest standard of living in the world, the nation is far from achieving the best record with respect to complications of pregnancy and birth. It may be necessary for health-department personnel to rent and operate buildings adjacent to laundromats so as to provide ready access to medical assistance for lower-class mothers. There seems little question that promoting greater use of public health services would reduce the amount of organically based pathology via either prevention or early identification and treatment. Prenatal care must be given a high priority in preventive efforts (Report of the Joint Commission, 1973). Other approaches to meeting physical needs include campaigns to provide food, adequate shelter, opportunities to exercise the body, and sensory stimulation. Elimination of physical hazards (for example, the eating of paint containing lead) is also illustrative of social action programs undertaken to enhance physical well-being.

Genetic Aspects. In addition to the biological preventive measures of promoting physical health, attempts have been made to manipulate heredity in order to produce sound people from sound genes. Because some disorders are presumed or known to have a genetic basis, it is not unexpected to find that some workers have advocated eugenic measures. Foremost among these techniques have been sterilization, birth control, and therapeutic abortions. Certainly, few would question the need or desirability of a sound genetic base. Nevertheless, it would be premature and extremely questionable to apply genetic regulations or approaches on a wholesale basis in light of the present state of knowledge concerning the role of genetics in such disorders as schizophrenia, mental retardation, antisocial personalities, and neuroses. This caution is not to deny the value of genetic counseling in certain cases, however.

Sociological Approaches

To a significant extent, modern mental health concerns are intimately related to urbanization, technology, and contemporary civilization (Arnhoff, 1968). Indeed, as the mental health fields become increasingly aware of the relationship between social structure and such social problems as violence, delinquency, poverty, and traditional mental disorder, the need for sociological intervention also becomes increasingly evident. Primary prevention cannot be limited to biological or psychological efforts, for over and over again studies suggest the importance of problems of housing, jobs, money, prejudice, and the struggle for security and status. The learned discussions on such problems as guilt, shame, low self-esteem, discrimination, aggression, alcoholism, suicide, psychosis, and delinquency dissolve into the inescapable facts of everyday living (Kraft, 1964).

Social Engineering. In light of the potential for the shaping of human behavior as a function of environmental forces, it is not surprising that attempts have been made to restructure the social and physical environment. Lazarus (1969) has labeled this solution a "social engineering" approach to mental health. Social planning embraces such questions as what resources are available to members of the community for jobs, for continued education of a functional nature, for social interaction facilitating self-respect, for harmonious racial and ethnic relations, and so on. If the above social concerns can be corrected, then the child has a better chance to grow into a socially healthy and competent individual.

Social action approaches have also attempted to increase youth's eventual access to the good life through improvements in the educational system. With respect to social engineering and the schools, Zax & Cowen (1972) explain:

> Perhaps the most important role that the future school mental health professional can play is as a social engineer or social systems consultant, rather than simply as a person who renders direct service to already bleeding

psyches. The challenge and potential of schools should be seen in terms of how they can promote effective education and health, rather than how they can combat pathology.

Deterrents.   Though sociological intervention is not yet a strong approach, resistance to such a movement is already evident. Many lay people fear that social engineering implies a costly welfare state. Support is also not strong among traditional mental-health professionals, who tend to feel threatened by the social-engineering approach. As Lazarus (1969) notes, community uncertainty and ignorance about the effects of proposed changes hinder the implementation of the social-engineering approach. Any plan is bound to affect the lives of many people, and one cannot be sure whether the desired effects or other more undesirable effects would be produced. Moreover, people in the community often fail to agree as to what constitutes a desirable effect (for example, school integration). Also, it is difficult to tell whether mental health is a cause or a result of social conditions (Wagenfield, 1972).

Sarason (1971), a prominent consultant to schools, is also well aware of resistances to change, noting that, "The more things change, the more they remain the same." To illustrate, children do not seem to enjoy the world of numbers any more under the new math program than under the old math. Students seem to find it as dull and as chorelike as ever. Moreover, because of certain unique organizational characteristics (for example, having a monopoly on formal education, rewarding staff on the basis of seniority and amount of formal education rather than for quality of job performance), the school may well be one of the most difficult institutions to modify. The problem of school change is a complex one that does not yield to simple solutions.

Psychological Approaches

Parent Education. Numerous studies have documented the need for healthy parent-child relationships. Because authorities have long recognized the significance of a family milieu that fosters growth, the psychological aspects of prevention have emphasized parent education as a preventive tool. The fundamental premise of parent education is based on the notion that childhood pathology is related to parental pathology and that alteration of undesirable parent influences can be beneficial to the child's emotional well-being. Parent education is by no means a recent intervention strategy, for man has been giving his fellow man advice on child rearing for hundreds of years. Today, the Child Study Association of America and the National Congress of Parents and Teachers represent the two major organizations concerned with parent education.

Parent educators come from diverse professional fields, such as child development, education, home economics, psychology, social work, pediatrics, and public nursing. Other caretakers include family physicians, clergymen, probation and parole officers, and public-school teachers. Most of these workers, unfortunately, receive very limited training in parent education, despite the fact that they are presumed to have competence in this field.

The basic aims of parent-education programs are to provide normative information about children, to offer recommendations on child-rearing practices, and to change parents' attitudes toward their children if indicated. The ultimate goal is not designed to modify parental attitudes and behaviors per se, but to promote the overall development of children.

Three basic approaches to parent education were identified by Brim (1959): (1) mass media, (2) group discussion, and (3) individual guidance.

MASS MEDIA.   The first approach relies heavily on the printed word. More than ten years ago, Brim estimated that about 25 million pamphlets were distributed annually. Brim also included a single-lecture technique in the category of mass media, for example, a meeting of the local Parent Teachers Association. There seems little doubt that this approach does succeed in reaching a large segment of the population. It may well be, however, that those parents most in need of such exposure do not receive it, while those who do not need it eagerly seek it. This situation may well be analogous to the Sunday sermon: that is, those who need it most are at home, not at church.

Educational television shows such as "Sesame Street" and "The Electric Company," with their generous use of entertaining cartoons, music, electronic effects, and professional actors, constitute another potentially valuable approach to upgrading the intellectual achievements of poor children (Bogatz & Ball, 1974). Other television programs such as the "Inside-Outside" series, "Echoes of Childhood," and "Misterogers" deal with problems associated with emotional growth. Because of the widespread availability of television sets in our country and the large amount of time spent in viewing, educational television would seemingly hold considerable potential for primary prevention—a potential that we are just now beginning to tap.

GROUP DISCUSSION.   The group discussion approach varies with the nature of the group and the qualifications of the leader. At the extreme, these meetings sometimes border on group psychotherapy. Expectant mothers and parents of preschool children are perhaps the most common participants in group discussions. It is becoming increasingly popular, however, to offer group guidance to parents of handicapped youth. By sharing their joys and frustrations, by offering one another emotional support through discovering that their situation is not unique, and by relating practical ways of helping their children, the parents (under the direction of an experienced professional) find renewed strength to cope with the daily demands of life with a handicapped child. Only those who have lived with an emotionally disturbed or mentally retarded or orthopedically handicapped child can fully appreciate the parental strains associated with rearing such a child. Disbelief, bitterness, ambivalence, and uncertainty are common to all parents of handicapped youth (Kessler, 1966). Because people are more receptive to advice at the time of an emotionally upsetting incident, "crisis counseling" can be an effective technique.[3]

PARENT EFFECTIVENESS TRAINING.   One approach that has received widespread attention since its initiation in 1962 is Parent Effectiveness Training (PET), which consists of 24 hours of classroom instruction involving lectures, general group discussions, and role playing. The instructors are recruited from two main sources—parents who, after having taken the course, want to teach others and various professionals, such as clergymen, teachers, and mental health specialists. Parent effectiveness training is advanced as an alternative to the authoritarian approach in which case the children lose, and to permissiveness, in which case parents lose. PET offers a "no-lose" method, whereby the child and parents mutually work out a solution acceptable to both parties, thereby eliminating the need for the parent to use power to force the child into submission. PET also stresses the importance of active listening, effective communication, and methods for determining whether the parent or the child should "own" (assume responsibility for solving) a given problem (Gordon, 1970). Careful evaluation of this approach must be undertaken before the value of this approach will be known but it does have advantages, such as dealing with problems before parent-child relations deteriorate, attracting parents who would not go to a psychologist, keeping intervention costs low, involving fathers as well as mothers, relying on the group as a medium for attitudinal and behavioral change, and providing a model that can be readily implemented in a community.

AN APPLIED HIGH SCHOOL COURSE.   Because PET relies on parents to volunteer themselves for training, this approach may well miss those who need it the most. To circumvent this possibility, Robert Hawkins (1972) has proposed a one-year compulsory parent-training course as part of the school curriculum. This course, as proposed by Hawkins, would differ from related existing courses (for example, homemaking) in that it would involve both sexes, actual practice in a realistic setting (for example, a day-care center or nursery school), and instructor observation of and feedback on the student's live performance. Although the laboratory experience would constitute the major portion of the course work, this would be accompanied by class discussion, readings, field trips, role playing, and films. For instance, the group, by viewing a film on how a troubled child interacts with his parents, could observe and discuss how parents inadvertently encourage undesired behaviors (for example, temper tantrums). A program such as this would also help them learn not to overreact to the problems of childhood (for example, negativism in 2 year olds). This course is not designed to teach a fixed set of universal behaviors. Instead of telling prospective parents *what* to teach, it would teach them *how* to teach according to learning theory principles.

---

3. For further reading, the student is referred to Gildea, Glidewell, & Kanter (1967); Hereford (1963); and Karnes & Zehrbach (1972).

Whether the training would generalize to the home setting at a later date remains an issue to be investigated. But this is a promising approach. We know that parents and students can master learning theory principles. Certainly, as Hawkins argues, if we feel that a practical course in driver's training is important for future drivers, is not a required practical course in order for future parents? The need for such training is underscored by the finding that fewer than one-third of teenagers know that lack of love and affection during the first year of life is psychologically damaging (Horn, 1975).

INDIVIDUAL GUIDANCE; THE FLORIDA PARENT EDUCATION PROGRAM. One of the best known models for parent involvement combining individual guidance group meetings is the Florida Parent Education Program developed in 1970 by Ira Gordon. Project goals were twofold: (1) to increase the likelihood that the young child will reach a higher level of intellectual and personal development and (2) to simultaneously foster the parents' competence and feelings of self-worth. From the time of the child's infancy through age two, paraprofessional disadvantaged women who are trained parent educators make home visits about once a week. The primary purpose of the home visit is to teach specific mother-infant activities designed to promote cognitive and affective development. To a large degree, the cognitive activities are centered around Piagetian principles and tasks.

The parents of the two and three year olds were also visited on a weekly basis. In addition, these youngsters attended a new home-oriented setting—a "backyard" center. These centers were located in the homes of mothers whose children were in the program. A group of about five preschoolers were transported to these specially equipped home centers twice a week for two-hour sessions. Although the curriculum materials were the same, each center used the toys and materials in their own somewhat individualistic ways. The particular characteristics of each center varied according to the personality, attitudes, and characteristics of its director. Average weekly attendance of students was 70%, a very respectable attendance rate for young disadvantaged children.

When the child was in the backyard center, the parent educator worked with the mother on a once-a-week basis. The mother was only not instructed in the mechanics of the tasks but also in general attitudes toward use of them together with some explanation of the underlying rationale. The parent educator demonstrated and the mother followed her example. Materials not ordinarily present in the home (clay, books, blocks) were made available on either a permanent or loan basis. The work with the mother and the tasks in the center are integrated so that home and center activities complement and supplement each other. For instance, if center activities focus on experiences designed to lead to conservation of quantity, the mother might be taught how to play a water game with her child in which the size or shape of the container change but the amount of water remain the same.

The paraprofessional parent educator also worked with children in kindergarten through grade three, spending part of the day in actual classroom activity and part of the day in home visits with the mother teaching her specific ideas and activities that will reinforce school learnings. The parent educator's assumption of a strong liaison role for home-school communication is a distinguishing characteristic of the Florida model (Evans, 1975). Parents are also encouraged to participate in (a) designing learning activities, (b) serving as volunteers in the classroom (c) representing project parents as members of a policy advisory committee, and (d) becoming trained as parent educators.

Data from the infant stimulation project have been positive. The use of paraprofessionals on a once-a-week basis combined with a small group setting for four hours a week lead to the improved cognitive performance of the children and positive attitudes and behaviors on the mother's part toward their children. The viability of such a program is certainly a major finding. The fact that paraprofessionals can operate such programs, that parents will voluntarily send their children to attend such a program, and that the parents will participate through home visits represents no small accomplishment. The development of materials that will stimulate cognitive and personality development among children this young is also significant (Gordon, 1975).

EVALUATION.   One problem facing parent educators is the fact that the professional advice to parents on child-rearing practices changes with the times. Stendler (1950), for instance, after reviewing the articles on child rearing in three women's magazines between 1890 and 1950, described the period between 1890 and 1910 as one of "sweet permissiveness," during which "mother knew best." Between 1910 and 1930, rigid habit training was stressed; youngsters were not to be picked up when they cried for fear they would become spoiled. In 1948, feeding the baby on demand was in vogue, just the opposite of the 1920s, when rigid feeding schedules were in fashion. Today, mothers are encouraged to pick up their children, coo at them, cuddle them, and so on, to provide the stimulation necessary for proper development. Behavioral scientists do not have absolute truths; they merely establish temporary findings.

Frank's (1965) conclusion to his review of forty years of research also sounds a somber note:

> No factors were found in the parent-child interaction of schizophrenics, neurotics, or those with behavior disorders which could be identified as unique to them or which could distinguish one group from the other, or any of the groups from the families of the controls.

While such differences might exist, data (Frank, 1965; Jacob, 1975) certainly raise a question that proponents of parent programs must seriously consider.

Brim (1959) notes that evaluating the outcomes of parent education is not an easy process. Most research in this area has looked at the effects that such programs have had on the parents. Even with this relatively modest criterion, the results of parent programs must be regarded as inconclusive in light of the absence of reliable and valid measuring instruments and the lack of adequate control groups. It is recognized that the results of such programs should be assessed in terms of their effects on the children, but the methodological problems in such an assessment prove even more formidable. Take, for example, the matter of incidence. It is conceivable that an educational program for parents could reduce the actual incidence of emotional disturbance but produce an increase in recorded incidence because of such factors as the expanding definition of emotional disturbance, the increasing treatment facilities, and the growing concern about disturbed children. Brim also notes that parent programs could be improving the mental health of normal children; that is, healthy children might become psychologically more mature. Yet, such improvements might well go unnoticed.

Community Mental Health. SERVICES TO BE RENDERED. There is much discussion of *community mental health* today, but there is little agreement as to the precise meaning of the term. It is different things to different people. The myriad of meanings is not surprising in light of the varied and sundry activities subsumed under this umbrella term. Basic to all definitions of this concept is the fact that it points to a declining role of the traditional state hospital and the rise of the community mental health center with all of the attendant auxiliary services essential for the treatment of the mentally ill.

Hume (1964) has delineated nine functions of community psychiatry:

1. *Community organization work,* that is, assessment of community resources for psychiatric patients, evaluation of their use, measurement of unmet needs (i.e., community self-surveys), plus participation with other agency representatives and community leaders.

2. *Program administration* (including planning, evaluation, management, staffing, and financing) of either direct or indirect, partial or comprehensive, community mental health services for the whole population.

3. *Supervision,* not only as an administrative adjunct, but also as a method of improving the professional performance of all the staff of a community mental health service or program.

4. *The training of lay leaders,* health educators, or specialists in the use of mass media, in order that they may disseminate information and general education to the public on mental health matters.

5. *In-service training,* that is, organized programs of mental health education for the nonpsychiatric professions such as medicine, nursing, and the law, and for the staffs of nonpsychiatric agencies such as schools, welfare, public health, and probation departments.

6. *Consultation* to nonpsychiatric agencies and professions in connection with a wide variety of mental health problems encountered within such agencies in their work with people.

7. *Research* in community psychiatry, such as case studies, program evaluation, biostatistical and epidemiological studies, mental health surveys, and studies of psychiatric institutions as social systems.

8. *Utilization* of the laws touching upon community psychiatry—for example, enabling acts and welfare, family, and commitment laws.

9. *Development of leadership,* participation in committee work and other group endeavors, and promotion of communication.

Bower (1970) notes that community health centers are being established not in the large, metropolitan areas (where mental health professionals have already congregated), but in middle-size cities with populations of approximately 65,000. He views this trend as desirable in that the community-center idea is better suited to the needs of moderate-size communities than it is to the needs of large urban areas. Although psychiatrists and psychologists will be on the staff, they will be heavily outnumbered by social workers.

PROBLEMS TO BE SOLVED.   Since community mental health programs are of relatively recent vintage and assume a diversity of functions, it would be premature to pass judgment on them. Nevertheless, some concerns have already been expressed. Foremost among these is the definition of community mental health. Granted that the field is still young and given the potential danger of premature narrowing, "some defining and crystallizing of core elements is needed," if only to permit effective communication between professionals (Cowen, 1973). For some mental health workers, community mental health has the same aim as traditional treatment approaches with its focus on individual pathology except that the individual's problems are considered within the framework of community influences. At the other extreme, community mental health connotes not only the alleviation of suffering but the promotion of the healthy development of an entire population. Its agents are not just mental-health specialists, but are community care givers capable of contributing to one's optimal development (Zax & Specter, 1974). A second concern centers around the type of training being given community mental health specialists. It is apparent that current training programs in psychology and psychiatry have to be radically revised if the many functions listed above are to be performed. Currently, there appear to be few commonly accepted standards with regard to training requirements for community mental health consultants beyond clinical training and experience (Haylett & Rapoport, 1964). Another problem centers around the danger that the change may be merely of the *locus* of function and not the *type* of treatment rendered.

Other serious questions that must eventually be answered have been raised by Dunham (1965):

What are the possible techniques that can be developed to treat the "collectivity"? Why do psychiatrists think that it is possible to treat the "collectivity" when there still exists a marked uncertainty with respect to the treatment and cure of the individual case? What causes the psychiatrist to think that if he advances certain techniques for treating the "collectivity," they will have community acceptance? If he begins to "treat" a group through discussions in order to develop personal insights, what assurances does he have that the results will be psychologically beneficial to the persons? Does the psychiatrist know how to organize a community along mentally hygienic lines and if he does, what evidence does he have that such an organization will be an improvement over the existing organization? In what institutional setting or in what cultural milieu would the psychiatrist expect to begin in order to move toward more healthy social relationships in the community? These are serious questions and I raise them with reference to the notion that the community is the patient.

To this list of difficulties, we add Bower's (1970) belief that the major obstacle to the community mental health approach centers in the danger of fragmentation of services stemming from the autonomy and isolation that exist in various community agencies.

In sum, the idea of mental health professionals going into the life situations of people in a community at key points where adjustment difficulties are apt to arise—for example, the schools—is an intriguing one. Only evaluation over time will determine how viable this idea is. We now shift our discussion to one aspect of the community mental health movement that is receiving special attention—mental health consultation in the schools.

Primary Prevention in the Schools

Though no single institution appears to be adequate to the task of development and socialization, the school does have some advantages over other institutions. Briefly summarized, the school has access to large numbers of youths over long periods of time during the formative years. In addition, it has a culturally sanctioned right to "interfere" in other people's business, at least to the extent that the interference pertains to the child's educability. As psychology has become penetrated by public health concepts and has advanced into community-action settings, mental health specialists have become increasingly aware of the schools as a base of operation. Though there are many ways in which the educational process and mental health are interrelated, the current discussion will be limited to four aspects of the school's involvement in preventive efforts: (1) consultation, (2) early identification, (3) curriculum approaches, and (4) the role of stress.[4]

Consultation

Consultation is an activity that goes on between mental health specialists and care-giving professionals. Although consultation is sometimes seen as an innovation, it is not a new activity. As Caplan (1970) notes, we are now attempting to formalize and professionalize the consultation process, which has till now been largely informal.

---

4. For an extended discussion of the school's role in mental health, see Allinsmith & Goethals (1962), Bower & Hollister (1967), Clarizio (1969), Rhodes (1968), Kaplan (1971), and Tanner & Lindgren (1971).

Mental health specialists have become increasingly aware of and concerned about the fact that they are seeing only a minority of the children with behavioral disturbances. The vast remainder are for better or worse being dealt with by other community caregivers—teachers, pediatricians, public health nurses, clergymen, lawyers, and policemen. Because the large number of children with disorders in behavior precludes direct intervention from a mental health specialist, the obvious alternative is to try to help children in need indirectly by influencing community caregivers. In some communities, caregivers may be the only ones available to help. Even when professional mental health workers are available, only a small percentage of help seekers with psychological problems go to society's designated specialists in this area. Instead the vast majority of help seekers search out front-line workers with whom they often have a relationship of trust. Thus, in many cases, consultation may be the only available vehicle through which the specialist can influence the lives of those who need help (Cowen, 1973). We are confining our discussion to consultation with one community caregiver, namely, the teacher.

What is consultation? Many use the term to refer to practically any form of service. Gallessich (1973) has, for example, pointed out the unfortunate trend toward using the term so loosely that it could mean testing and diagnosing, in-service education, working with school personnel regarding matters of school mental health, assisting with research activities, or discussing problems with the school principal. If we are to formalize and professionalize consultative services, however, we must use the term in a way that refers to a fairly distinctive method of providing services. The characteristics of mental health consultation have been most clearly outlined by Caplan (1970) as follows:

1. It is a method between two professionals in respect to a client or a program for clients.

2. The consultants must have expertise in the areas in which they are to consult. Because consultation has become a prestigious professional activity in which many people want to engage, it is imperative that we do more than pay lip service to this guideline requiring professional competence.

3. Consultants bear no administrative responsibility for the consultee's work.

4. The consultee does not have to accept the consultant's ideas or suggestions.

5. The consultant and consultee function as coequals who respect each other's area of expertise.

6. This coordinate relationship is fostered by the fact that the consultant is usually a member of a different profession.

7. Consultation is usually given as a short series of interviews—two or three on the average.

8. Consultation will continue as long as unusual work problems are encountered by the consultee.

9. A consultant has no set, predetermined body of information to teach.

10. There are two basic goals of consultation—to help the consultee improve his handling or understanding of a current work problem and to increase the consultee's ability to master future problems of a similar nature.

11. The objective of consultation is to improve the consultee's job performance (for example, to make a teacher more effective.) While successful consultation may have a secondary therapeutic effect, the primary goal of consultation is not to improve the consultee's sense of well-being or personal worth.

12. The consultant does not invade the consultee's privacy. In fact, discussion of the consultee's personal problems is not allowed.

13. The consultant must be sensitive to the feelings of the consultee, but the consultant deals with the personal problems of the consultee in a special way, to wit, as these problems influence effectiveness[5] in the work setting.

14. Consultation usually is only one of the professional services of a specialist, namely, to render indirect service to someone who is in direct contact with the child via a series of short interviews characterized by a coordinate relationship. For instance, if it becomes apparent that consultation is not the method of choice, the consultant may put aside his consultative role and provide in-service education or psychotherapy. Although assuming another role often destroys the coordinate relationship characteristic of the consultative model, using methods other than consultation may be the most realistic thing to do in a given situation.

Types of Consultation. Caplan (1970) has identified four "types" of consultation—client-centered case consultation, consultee-centered case consultation, program-centered administrative consultation, consultee-centered administrative consultation. In practice consultation activities will typically cut across categories rather than fall neatly into one. For convenience of presentation, we will discuss each type separately, however.

CLIENT-CENTERED CASE CONSULTATION. In this kind of consultation the consultant brings his expertise to bear on the consultee's work difficulty, which relates to the management of a particular case or group of cases. The primary objective is to communicate to the consultee how his client can be helped. This type of consultation is the most familiar type practiced by mental health professionals. Usually the specialist examines the child, renders a diagnosis, and makes recommendations for disposition and management. For example, a school psychologist after testing and interviewing a troublesome fifth-grade boy might suggest that a behavioral contract be developed whereby the student could earn the privilege of being an office helper over the noon hour by staying out of fights.

.5. Note that increased effectiveness might result in lowering as well as raising one's productivity.

CONSULTEE-CENTERED CASE CONSULTATION.   The goal of this type of consultation is to improve the consultee's ability to function effectively in relation to a given kind of case so that future as well as current clients may benefit from the consultee's increased cognitive grasp and emotional mastery of the issues. There is a strong educational emphasis so that future professional functioning is enhanced. The consultant focuses on certain aspects of the case rather than making a complete diagnosis. The client is not seen directly by the consultant. Instead the consultant increases the proportion of his consulting time spent with the consultee. Most of the information about the client is gathered from the consultee, although the consultant may sometimes consult others (for example, other teachers who have the same student) or observe the child in action. Through consultation of this kind, the consultant can increase one or more of the following: the consultee's knowledge regarding a particular type of case; the consultee's skill; the consultee's confidence; and the consultee's professional objectivity. Because consultee-centered consultation is expensive in terms of the consultant's time, consideration should be given to group educational methods, which appear to be as effective and which are cheaper. For instance, the school psychologist or counselor may conduct workshops to help teachers deal with the dilemma posed by the shy, withdrawn student.

PROGRAM-CENTERED ADMINISTRATIVE CONSULTATION.   This variety of consultation has to do with the improvement of existing programs or the development of new ones. While it is hoped that the consultees will learn enough from the consultant's analysis and prescriptions to deal independently with future problems of a similar nature, this aspiration remains secondary to a main goal of providing solutions to current administrative concerns. In many ways this type of consultation resembles client-centered case consultation. In both kinds of consultation, the consultant is personally responsible for assessing the problem and precribing a course of action. One main difference is that now the consultant focuses on the problems of an organization instead of the problems of a client (for example, a student). Secondly, recommendations entail a plan for administrative action instead of a plan for management of the client. Still another difference has to do with the kind of expertise demanded. In program-centered consultation, the nature of the program or policy problem demands that the consultant draw upon his knowledge and experience in the field of organizational theory, planning, and fiscal and personnel management, in addition to his clinical expertise. Client-centered consultation is relatively easier for the consultant in light of his clinical training because he draws primarily from his background in psychology, counseling, social work, or psychiatry.

CONSULTEE-CENTERED ADMINISTRATIVE CONSULTATION.   In many ways this type of consultation is analogous to consultee-centered case consultation except that the emphasis here is on the problem of programming and organization and not on helping the consultee to deal with a particular client. The consultant may be invited to help a single administrator or group of central staff. Unlike program-centered administrative consultation, which tends to be more of a "one-shot" affair, this kind of consultation will continue over a substantial period of time—months or years.

As in consultee-centered case consultation, consultees may suffer from a lack of knowledge, skills, self-confidence, or objectivity in consultee-centered administrative consultation. But the consultee can suffer as a result of group problems—faulty leadership, lack of role clarity, communication blocks, and the like. The consultant must help the consultee to understand and to cope with these so that the mission of the organization can be carried out now and in the future.

ADVOCACY CONSULTATION.   In addition to the kinds of consultation listed by Caplan, there is a fifth type of consultation that seeks to promote the rights of children. Nearly a century after the first child labor laws, social reformers are now making a concentrated effort to safeguard the rights of children. In school systems, child advocates are working to change discriminatory policies and practices. Among the advocacy-related activities practiced by school psychologists are testifying in family court on behalf of disadvantaged families, supporting parents who legitimately question the school's assessment results on interpretations, conferring with lawyers regarding actions for children with special needs, finding teacher aides so that a child may remain in the regular classroom, helping to form a county child advocacy group, and trying to convince administrators about provisions for children with special needs (Mearig, 1974).

Unlike most consultants, the advocacy consultant often initiates the helping relationship. At times, he works without organizational sanction, a condition that can result in intensification of conflict with administrators. The client is not the established institution but the community. Advocacy consultation also differs in the assumption that power equalization via overt political negotiation and direct action is necessary to produce social change (Gallessich, 1974).

Guidelines to Consultation.   The discussion that follows touches only on some major guidelines of mental health consultation, as extended discussion of these is beyond the scope of the present text. The reader should also bear in mind that these guidelines have evolved from the experiences of consultants and are not yet grounded in research.

1. ESTABLISHING CONTACT WITH THOSE IN AUTHORITY.   The experienced consultant recognizes the importance of making personal contact with those in authority as soon as possible after his initial entry into the system. The purpose of this contact is to obtain sanction for his consultative operations in the institution. This contact is particularly important if the consultant has been brought in by a staff member who is seen as marginal or deviant by the central staff. While the marginal staff member may serve a useful function by introducing the consultant into the system, the consultant must be careful not to become too closely associated with the marginal staff

member who seeks support and assistance in dealing with his work problems. The writers recall one case in which a project director brought them in to serve as consultants in a behavior modification program with predelinquents and delinquent youngsters from the inner city. The project director was not trusted by the superintendent of schools nor by his central staff because the project director had remained politically neutral during the intense power struggle in which the superintendent and his staff had risen to their administrative posts. In this circumstance, it was necessary to maintain relationships characterized by mutual trust and respect with the project director, while seeking similar contacts with the superintendent and certain other influential members of the central staff to insure the kinds of communications and coordination necessary to implement the program.

2. DEVELOPING A CONSULTATION CONTRACT.   During his initial contacts, the consultant develops a joint plan or consultation contract as a result of discussions with representatives of the institution. First of all, he must obtain sanction for the services to be rendered. For example, in the behavior modification project mentioned above, it was necessary to clarify what we would be doing not only with the superintendent of schools but also with the assistant superintendent in charge of special projects, the director of special education, the director of research, the project director, building principals, vice-principals, and social workers. All of these individuals were in a position to exert a great deal of influence on the line workers—the teachers of the resource rooms and regular class teachers.

Once sanction has been obtained for one's consultative activities in general, it is time to consider the specific content of the contract. In the early stages of the consultant's work in a given setting, neither party may be very clear about terms of the contract. After formulating a tentative contract through preliminary discussions, attention is focused on other matters, such as the following (Gallessich, 1973):

a. *Accessibility to staff.* Both parties have to reach agreement regarding issues such as, Who is to have priority in consultation time? Will the specialist work with individuals or groups? Will the consultant work with only higher echelon staff or with personnel in all hierarchical layers? These and related issues are best resolved before the initiation of actual services.

b. *Definition of services.* What tasks is the consultant to perform? Is the consultant expected to engage in extraconsultative services? For example, in the behavior modification project in which the authors were involved, we were responsible for selection of teachers and secretaries for the project, collection of research data, and leadership at the in-service workshop for resource and regular teachers associated with the project. In addition to stating what the consultant will do, the contract should specify what the consultant will *not* do.

c. *Inclusiveness of consultant in the system.* The degree of inclusiveness achieved within a given organizational family by the consultant varies greatly. In some circumstances, the consultant is genuinely external to the system and is brought in frequently as a tangential resource. The consultant who is brought in from the outside may experience difficulty because of insufficient availability, lack of continuity, lack of deep commitment, and lack of in-depth knowledge about the school. The outside consultant may, on the other hand, be more detached, be in a better position to have perspective, and have greater freedom.

At the other extreme is the inside or in-house consultant. This person has an advantage in that he knows the system (that is, where the power is, the strategic leverage points, and so on), identifies with the system's needs and aspirations, speaks the language, understands the institutional norms, and is a familiar figure. The inside change agent can be at a disadvantage, however, because he may lack perspective, may lack the special skill needed for change, may have an inadequate power base, may have to live down past failures, may not have independence of movement, may be a "yes man" because his salary is paid by the system, and typically faces the difficult task of redefining his ongoing relationships with other members of the system (Havelock, 1973).

Regardless of whether one is an internal or external consultant, he must guard against the possible loss of objectivity. Conferences with fellow consultants who work in other settings and/or the use of a consultant team are helpful in maintaining or restoring the consultant's objectivity.

d. *Confidentiality.* If a consultant is to be trusted and respected, he must be allowed confidentiality. If the consultant is perceived as the boss's spy, then his effectiveness is seriously undermined, if not destroyed. If, on the other hand, he models discretion and withholds information in an ethical fashion, his services to the organization are greatly enhanced.

e. *Revision.* The nature of the consultation contract changes as conditions in the consultee's institution and in the consultant's life change. A clause should always be written in calling for systematic review and revision of the contract. The consultant and institutional representatives must always work for the contract of "best fit."

3. DEVELOPING AN ORGANIZATIONAL PERSPECTIVE.   A crucial factor in determining the consultant's success is his skill in assessing the organization in which he is working. Without a careful diagnosis of institutional makeup, it is difficult to predict which services and changes are most likely to prove successful. Gallessich (1973) notes four domains the consultant probes in his effort to achieve an organizational perspective.

a. *External forces.* A school does not exist by itself. Instead, it is affected by a number of factors external to its physical boundaries. Most important among these are the central administration with its value orientation, the school board, the community with its parent groups, neighborhood problems, teachers' unions, and state departments of education (e.g., the accountability movement). The consultant's awareness of the impact of external factors enables him to decide whether or not to become involved with the school system at this point in time as well as to provide information as to what services may be needed. For instance, based upon his analysis, he may decide to focus on improved school-community relations, clarify the degree of latitude given by the central administration, and strengthen the leadership role of the principal. A consultant who lacks organizational sensitivity can be headed for disaster.

b. *Internal factors.* Although more apparent than external factors, internal organizational factors—formal structure, roles, and norms—can also prove difficult to clarify and modify. Answers are sought for such questions as, Are the arrangements for leadership and division of responsibilities clear? Are the various roles clear? Are the relationships and communication across grade levels adequate? What topics are avoided during faculty meetings? What behaviors does the principal reward or punish? What role does the secretary play in school functioning? Who are the natural leaders among the faculty? What are the attitudes, problems, and strengths of the student body? What norms are prevalant? These and other questions can be answered through contact with various members of the school staff. Because a lack of understanding of the school's culture is a common cause of failure in our change efforts, careful assessment of internal forces is essential to effective consultation.

c. *The school's trajectory.* Looking at the history or movement of the school over time is one way of learning about its trajectory. What are the trends on such dimensions as the faculty morale and stability, student composition and achievements, educational philosophy, and acceptance of the school by the community? Knowing to what extent the school's trajectory has been and is being influenced by internal and external factors can be helpful in providing realistic analysis and prediction of organizational change.

d. *Staff perceptions of the consultant's role.* To be most effective, a consultant must understand how others view his role. The consultant will want to know the answers to questions such as, Who was responsible for his entry into the system and how is this person or faction seen by the consultees? Is he expected to perform a miracle or are expectations realistic? What timetable for change do the consultees have in mind? Does the administrator want a consultant to share blame for some impending disaster? Do the teachers want the consultant to confirm the fact that the situation is hopeless? Do they see him as someone who will suggest the removal of difficult children from the classroom? Is the consultant seen primarily as a status symbol? Is the consultant employed because the funding agency insisted on his presence? Or is the consultant seen as someone who will help the administrator "clean house"? Because staff members will vary in their perceptions of the consultant's role, he may well spend some time clarifying his role with the entire staff. In any event, he would do well to take into account others' perceptions of his role when he spells out what he will and what he will not do in the consultation contract.

4. ESTABLISHING PROXIMITY. The consultant must be available to the consultee while at the same time not fostering an overdependence upon

his services. Consultation can and often is carried out in formal settings (for example, the case conference), but it can perhaps be conducted more successfully in informal settings. For example, the lounge, if properly used, can be one of the most appropriate places in the school for consultation with teachers who genuinely enjoy dealing with issues in a more relaxed atmosphere. There are times, however, when teachers may not want certain problems aired in the presence of colleagues. This is particularly true if the problem reflects on the teacher's competence or might elicit disapproval from the principal. In such instances, it is best to find a more private setting. By and large, however, the consultant will find it advantageous to establish proximity through the use of casual contacts. This means that the consultant does things such as eating with teachers, hanging around after meetings to talk, visiting classrooms, and attending assemblies.

While it is important for the consultant to gain access to consultees and to develop a coordinate relationship, care should be taken to avoid the development of a psychotherapeutic relationship with the consultee. The primary purpose of consultation is to help the consultee to improve his handling of children and not to work on his personal problems. Private matters are not to be dealt with on "company time." The development of a hierarchical psychotherapeutic relationship can be avoided by restricting conversation to the client's difficulties, by quickly but tactfully interrupting long dialogues on the consultee's part, and by asking how consultee generalizations, say for example, about culturally different children, relate to the case under consideration (Caplan, 1970).

5. DEALING WITH RESISTANCES TO CONSULTATION.   A fellow consultant once remarked that teachers will sometimes act toward the consultant much like a negative or passive aggressive child acts toward the teacher. Why is it that teachers resist? One reason is that many teachers view the need for consultation as a publicly visible sign of professional inadequacy (Caplan, 1970). Sarason (1971) points out that teachers are often bothered by the upsetting realization that part of the child's problem resides in their own lack of knowledge, understanding, and techniques. Resistance stemming from this source has been dealt with in the following ways (Caplan, 1970): (a) Emphasize that consultation deals with cases in which the *problems of clients* are complicated, unclear, and bewildering, rather than stressing the formulation that the consultant tries to help *consultees* who are confused. (b) Foster the consultees' self-respect by making it clear to them that their cases are just as intellectually taxing to you as they are to them. (c) The effective consultant will show respect for the consultee by demonstrating a dependence on the consultee not only for essential information but also for successful implementation of the plan they evolve together. The coequal approach is demanded by the realities of the situation—it is not just an idealistic technical strategy. (d) The consultant is advised to accept the teacher's current state of knowledge about the situation, to express appreciation for the teacher's powers of

observation, and to avoid questions that the teacher is probably not able to answer. (e) Using "one-downsmanship" is often necessary to achieve a coequal relationship that helps to restore a teacher's sense of adequacy and worth. For example, if the teacher agrees to meet at a time convenient to the consultant, the consultant should make it clear that he recognizes how busy the teacher is and set a meeting time convenient to the teacher. (f) Arranging to consult with teachers who are perceived as outstanding by faculty can help to avoid any stigma that may be associated with asking for consultative help. The consultee may feel less loss of face when he realizes that respected experienced teachers also need help at times.

Teachers can also be resistant because they often see consultants as nonunderstanding, unhelpful, and unsympathetic. For example, why else, the teacher reasons, would a consultant ask him to give more individual attention to a student when he (the teacher) has to cover X amount of material in X amount of time with thirty other students who vary widely in intellectual ability, interpersonal skill, knowledge of subject matter, and motivation? Consultants can become more positively perceived by demonstrating an awareness of the school's culture and the teacher's dilemma. For instance, if the consultant and teacher work out a behavior modification program for a particular child, the consultant might show respect for the teacher's busy day by arranging for an aide, tutor, or fellow student to assume responsibility for recording the target child's progress.

Anxiety about the consultant can lead teachers to resist the consultation process. One common concern is that the consultant will discover their innermost thoughts, attack their defenses, possibly blame and expose their work deficiencies to others in the school, or leave them "in the lurch" when a case proves difficult. As the consultant becomes known in the system and develops a reputation for being an approachable, trustworthy, and competent specialist, anxieties about him will be reduced. Old-timers on the staff can often reassure new staff about the consultant's safeness and dependability.

Not all teacher resistance is motivated by threats to their professional competence or self-esteem. Uncooperativeness on the teacher's part can at times have a realistic basis. Regrettably, many of the plans evolved by specialists are not practical or realistic in light of the teacher's role, the district or school's orientation, and the realities of the classroom. For instance, to suggest a more accepting and permissive classroom handling of a disturbed child might well ignore how a teacher's management skills are evaluated by his supervisors and fellow teachers. This "advice" might also not pay sufficient heed to the modeling effect; that is, other students might become more unruly if the disturbed child is allowed to behave aggressively.

Teacher uncooperativeness may also stem from undesirable attitudes on the consultant's part. Feelings of condescension, for example, can interfere with effective consultation. Because consultees are very sensitive to the consultant's feelings and attitudes toward them and their profession, consultants must "take stock" of their own prejudices or steoreotypes and strive to overcome them.

Early Identification

Bower (1974) suggests that screening locations are best situated at points of transition between one institution and the next (for example, between the family and the school). The kindergarten or first-grade level is a strategic time to identify problems for parents are anxious to get their children off to a good start on a journey of 10 to 20 years. Furthermore, entrance into school is a natural, positively perceived rendezvous for the two major caretakers of children: parents and teachers.

The Preschool Period.   Retrospective studies suggest the feasibility of identifying emotional disturbances at the preschool level. In one study, the investigators examined the histories of 60 youngsters seen at a child-guidance clinic and found that more than half of them had noticeable problems prior to school entrance (Oppenheimer & Mandel, 1959). Similarly, Bolton (1955) noted that 75 of 100 children seen at a clinic had manifested observable symptoms prior to kindergarten entrance. The difficulty of retrospective studies with respect to early identification and prediction is that they do not reveal how many youngsters in the general population had shown similar symptoms and yet later made an adequate adjustment to school (false positives) or how many who had not displayed observable symptoms grew up to be maladjusted (false negatives).

In another preschool study (Lindemann & Ross, 1955), which was a follow-up investigation, an attempt was made to predict kindergarten adjustment of 50 youngsters on the basis of parent interviews, systematic observation of the child, teacher ratings, teacher interviews, sociometric data, and the use of a standardized type of doll play. The play information was analyzed on the basis of four criteria: (1) the ease with which the child left the mother; (2) the extent to which the child controlled his emotions; (3) the amount of unusual behavior; and (4) the number of special demands made on the clinician. The investigators concluded that observation of the doll-play situation provided a relatively objective, economical, and valid indication of success in kindergarten.

THE SUMTER CHILD STUDY PROJECT   (Newton & Brown, 1967). One of the better-known examples of primary prevention at the preschool level, this project was carried out in Sumter, North Carolina. The purposes of the project were twofold—to develop a psychological screening procedure to predict how the child would adjust to school entry and future school stress, and to develop appropriate interventions to augment the child's coping skills. Screening procedures six months prior to school entrance consisted of structured observations and testing of the child by a psychologist together with an interview by a social worker. Each child was then given a rating by the team. When the youngsters were divided into two groups—the adjusted and the maladjusted—and compared against later performance criteria (number of reading requirements completed, absenteeism, initiative, curiosity, self-concept), it was found that there were significant differences between the two groups. The investigators also report on the basis of their clinical observations that intervention efforts have contributed to the children's adjustment but hard data on this point will be needed to objectify the stated gains.

The Elementary-School Period. EMOTIONAL PROBLEMS. Earlier discussion has already pointed out that elementary-school teachers are able to render reasonably reliable appraisals of a child's current personal adjustment. For instance, with respect to emotional disturbance, Lambert & Bower (1961) reported that 90% of elementary-school pupils so labeled by teachers were also adjudged disturbed by experienced clinicians following individual assessment. Teacher ratings are also as reliable a technique as any available for the prediction of juvenile delinquency.

One of the best-known programs for early identification is the Primary Mental Health Project, which has been in existence for over a dozen years in the city of Rochester, New York. During that time, it has gone through several phases. One of the original objectives of this program was the early identification and prevention of emotional disorders. To achieve this end, the school social worker interviewed the mothers of all first graders, classroom observations were made of all children, and some psychological testing was done with first graders. A clinical judgment was made on each child on the basis of this information. Those already showing problems or apparently having great potential for future disturbance were called the Red-Tag (RT) group. About 30% of entering first graders were given this label. Those adjusting well and thought likely to continue this way were called the Non-Red Tag (NRT) group. The overall quality of family life seemed to be the most significant factor in determining whether a child fell into the RT or NRT group. The RT children differed from the NRT group on a variety of school record measures (nurse referrals, attendance, grade-point average, achievement test scores) as well as on several adjustment measures (teachers' ratings, clinicians' ratings, anxiety measures, self-report, and peer perceptions).

The treatment part of the program was directed primarily toward school personnel and parents. The informal school luncheons attended by the school principal, nurse, teachers, and special teachers provided a vehicle for discussing children who were causing concern. Evening meetings for parents were devoted to the topic of social and emotional development of children. The children were given direct service in an after-school program. These one-hour sessions led by teachers who had a facility for working with maladjusted students ran for a period of 20 weeks. The mental health specialists' role was that of a consultant and resource person rather than that of a direct service-giver. A follow-up study of the RT and NRT some six years later when they were in the seventh grade yielded no definitive conclusions. The two groups differed on 14 of the 46 comparisons but the pattern of differences was not clear-cut. The RT children were found to have lower grades, were more apt to be underachievers, and had poorer attendance records than NRT children. On the other hand, they were less anxious and scored better on standard achievement tests, as a group than NRT children.

At that time, it was decided to provide more direct service to children. Because this required additional manpower, housewives who had demonstrated their success as mothers were recruited as teacher aides. At first, these aides were assigned to a particular classroom but this arrangement produced conflict between the teacher aides and the regular classroom teachers over their respective educational responsibilities. Subsequently, the teacher aides operated outside the classroom. In concert, a team consisting of the teacher aide, teacher, and mental health consultant would establish a set of objectives for each child who would generally be seen by the teacher aide for several one-half-hour periods a week. On occasion, small groups of youngsters were seen by the aide.

Another concept of the revised program entailed an after-school day-care program staffed by another paraprofessional—an undergraduate college volunteer—who worked with small groups of acting out, undersocialized, or underachieving students.

Detailed evaluation of the revised form of the Rochester Primary Mental Health Program is not yet available but measures that do bear on its effectiveness suggest its promise. To wit, four of the original six aides are still with the program, referrals to aides have grown substantially, and the school system is now committed to hiring aides for several inner city schools out of its own funds (Zax & Specter, 1974). The program also appears most appropriately suited to shy-anxious children but less well suited to the needs of acting-out and learning-problem students (Lorion, Cowen, & Caldwell, 1974). These investigators deserve credit for being one of the few groups willing to undertake evaluation of their school-based treatment program and to make changes on the basis of their findings.

LEARNING DISABILITY.   In recent years there has been an increasing interest in the early identification of children who will later become learning disability cases. Haring & Ridgeway (1967) screened 1,200 youngsters from 48 kindergarten classes in Kansas. In their search for distinctive psychometric patterns, the investigators administered a battery of tests measuring language perception and motor skills to all high-risk children. No specific test patterns worthy of note were found. This negative finding is not surprising because of the heterogeneous nature of their group.

Ferinden & Jacobson (1970) sought to determine which tests were most effective in accurately predicting later reading difficulties. Four diagnostic scales—the Wide Range Achievement Test, the Evanston Early Identification Scale, the Bender Gestalt Visual Motor Test, and the Metropolitan Reading Readiness Test—were used to select kindergartners from 10 classrooms. The authors concluded that teachers were about 80% effective in identifying children with learning problems using merely their own subjective judgment.

The scale that added the most to teacher judgment was the Metropolitan Readiness Test, which is nationally the most commonly used screening measure (Maitland, Nadeau, & Nadeau, 1974). The combination of teacher judgment and this brief readiness test reportedly resulted in 90% accuracy in screening.

DeHirsch, Jansky, & Langford (1966) reported a successful attempt in predicting failure in reading by the end of the second grade. Giving a battery of 37 tests to 53 kindergartners who had average ability and no obvious problems, these investigators claimed a 91% success in prediction.

One team of investigators (Feshbach, Adelman, & Fuller, 1974) compared two alternate models (the de Hirsch Predictive Index of Reading Failure and teachers' ratings) used to identify kindergarten children with a high risk of reading failure. They found that both approaches were about 75% accurate in their predictions but that they differed markedly in the types of errors made. With the de Hirsch scales, there were almost twice as many false positives (youngsters predicted to become reading failures but who did achieve satisfactorily) as in the teachers' ratings. Whether the de Hirsch approach or teachers' ratings are differentially valuable in developing an intervention program is, of course, a separate issue. It is heartening to note that a kindergarten teacher's ratings can predict first grade achievement at least as well as a psychometric battery designed for this purpose.[6]

Some Unresolved Problems. Educators and mental health specialists have often expressed a desire for earlier identification of problems in children as a preventive step. Moreover, the research literature suggests that through a combination of approachs utilizing teacher judgment, peer perception, and self-rating, deviant youth can be identified during the early school years. Yet several factors militate against the identification of problems in the early years of childhood (Bower, 1969):

1. Screening and diagnosing emotional and learning disability problems during the preschool years and in kindergarten pose more difficulties than when attempted with somewhat older children. Even experienced professionals, when dealing with individual children, have no reliable means for distinguishing between problems of a transitory nature and those indicative of later, more serious pathology. An extensive study involving more than 2,400 children in a southwest farming county in Minnesota demonstrated the difficulty associated with prediction of later individual adjustment (Anderson, 1959). In 1950, the subjects (who were in grades 4 through 12) were given a series of inventories dealing with such factors as family attitudes, social responsibility, and psychoneurotic symptoms. Teacher ratings on 20 personality characteristics were also obtained. Follow-up study conducted from 1954 to 1957 utilized personality inventories and teacher ratings. The major

---

6. For additional research on this topic the reader is referred Wissink, Kass, & Ferrell (1975); Mardell & Goldenberg (1975); Koppitz (1975); and Lesiak & Wait (1974).

finding pertaining to prediction of individual behavior over a span of 5–7 years was essentially a negative one. In other words, it cannot be stated with certainty that a youngster who does poorly as measured by the available tests and rating scales will make a poor adjustment some years later. Changes within the person and changes in the demands made on him over time were regarded as two factors rendering prediction difficult. Curiously, it was easier to predict outstanding adjustment than poor adjustment. The present screening devices are not sufficiently discriminating to identify who will be emotionally disturbed in later life. As noted early in this book, it is not yet fully understood what kinds of disturbed youngsters grow up to be disturbed adults (with the exceptions of severe delinquents and grossly disturbed children).

2. It is difficult to arouse parental concern when the child is young since the pathology is apt to express itself in a mild form. Likewise, teachers are often inclined to give the young pupil additional time in which to rally before requesting professional help. By the primary grades or early elementary-school years, however, teachers and parents become increasingly concerned about the child's maladjusted behavior and therefore seek assistance at that time.

3. It is often not until the middle elementary years that latent pathology becomes overt under the stresses and pressures for adjustment to the academic and behavioral demands of the classroom. Torrance (1962) points to a number of cultural discontinuities that typically occur in the lives of middle-class pupils in the fourth grade. Classroom activities become more formal and organized, children are expected to sit in orderly rows in the classroom and are given less motor freedom, and they are supposed to "get down to business."

4. Teachers and parents are quite able to tolerate the mild forms of overt pathology characteristic of young children, whereas they are less well equipped or prepared to cope with the acting-out behavior of older children.

5. As Bower (1969) notes, it is not known "how early is early" in the detection of childhood disorders. How soon must intervention procedures be implemented after the onset of a problem in order for the intervention to be economical and effective? For example, is identification at the third-grade level early enough for neurotic youth? for delinquent youth? for learning-disability cases? At present, the notion that early detection leads to efficient and effective treatment, though seemingly logical, remains an assumption rather than a fact. This idea raises a related point. If large numbers of maladjusted youngsters are identified, what is going to be done about them? Current treatment services are already overloaded. Few school administrators would care to have a large identifiable group of students whose educational and personal needs cannot be met. At the present time, there is no definite answer to such dilemmas.

6. Many youngsters appear to "outgrow" their childhood disorders and enter successfully the mainstream of American adult life. What impact would the identification and labeling of such youngsters as "emotionally disturbed"

have upon their later adjustment? Would the identification of these youngsters result in a self-fulfilling prophecy? Again, this is a difficult question to which there is no conclusive reply.

7. Few if any of the studies on identification of emotional disturbance or learning disability have explored the usefulness of various cutoff points. In selecting a cutoff point, say between emotionally disturbed and normal children, one must balance between two kinds of errors. If the cutoff point is set too high, then one will label as emotionally disturbed many youngsters who, in reality, are normal. These cases are called false positives. On the other hand, if the cutoff point is set too low, then an increased number of emotionally disturbed children will be considered normal when in fact they are troubled youth. These cases are called false negatives.

One cannot change the cutoff point without changing the number of both false positives and false negatives. This issue has to be recognized as part of the problem of any screening effort (Gallagher & Bradley, 1972). Regrettably, few if any studies on early identification of emotional disturbances or learning disability report data on the percentage of diagnostic misses, namely, those labeled as having the condition who, in fact, do not have it (false positives), and those labeled as free from the condition but who, in fact, have it (false negatives). It is usually the diagnostic "hits" or general accuracy that is reported and the reader is left in the dark as to the diagnostic misses. Information on both the diagnostic hits and misses is needed to evaluate the effectiveness of identification procedures.

In summary, while the principle of early identification may in theory be a desirable one, it remains a very difficult practice to implement effectively and economically. The comments of Briggs & Wirt (1965) on the prediction of delinquent behavior also realistically depict some of the down-to-earth problems associated with prediction of deviant behavior in general:

> Prediction involves attention to many factors that are largely utilitarian or functional. Examples of these points are the criterion of socially unacceptable delinquent behavior to be predicted, the cost of information relating to prediction, the use to be made of the prediction, acceptable rates of success, the cost of error in the prediction of a delinquent, and, finally, the costs of treatment and the availability of slots into which prospective treatment cases may be fitted. All prediction systems have left these factors unspecified, which leaves completely untold the value of such a system.

It is to be hoped future research will provide answers to these pragmatic concerns.

Curriculum Approaches

Some workers believe that one of the most effective ways to promote the mental health of students entails the incorporation of psychological concepts into the curriculum. Such incorporation would not only insure a definite place for mental health instruction, but also accomplish this instruction in a systematic manner. Curriculum approaches fall into one of three basic types (Kaplan, 1971): (1) incidental instruction, (2) separate courses, and (3) units. Each approach has advantages and disadvantages. Following discussion of these three specific approaches, we will discuss the role of broader curriculum intervention in the form of progressive education.

Teachable Moments.   Incidental instruction refers to instruction that occurs when problems are immediate and real, when motivation and interest are maximal. For example, the class and teacher might discuss the impending death of a hospitalized classmate who is in fact terminally ill. Drawbacks to this approach center around the need for teacher sensitivity and teacher sophistication in child developmental and mental health.

Separate Courses.   Separate courses have also been used. Outstanding among these are the Bullis Project and Roen's behavioral-science curriculum. In the Bullis Project (described in Kaplan, 1971), the teacher is provided with a basic textbook containing lesson plans and stimulus stories. These stories, which center around emotional problems similar to those preadolescents and early adolescents might be experiencing, are read to the class. After a discussion of the stories, the teacher summarizes the mental health principles involved and the students record the conclusions in a daily log. Sample topics include "How Emotions Are Aroused," "Overcoming Personal Handicaps," and "Submitting to Authority." Kaplan contends that this approach is too didactic and moralistic. To the authors' knowledge, there has been no research evaluation of this approach.

Roen (1965, 1967) developed a behavioral-sciences course he taught to fourth graders. The class met for 40 minutes once a week over the school year. Roen reports that it was not difficult to recast concepts into terms the students could comprehend. A seminar entitled "Teaching the Behavioral Sciences to Children" was used to assist teachers. The course content included such topics as the influences of heredity and environment on development, Erikson's psychosocial stages of development, the self concept, various learning theory concepts, the concept of intelligence, institutional influences on development, and sociological analysis of the classroom. At the end of the course, each student was asked to write an autobiography discussing his uniqueness as a person and the particular forces producing that uniqueness. It is still too early to determine the effectiveness of this behavioral-science teaching program. Preliminary evaluation indicates, however, that these elementary-school students mastered the course content satisfactorily. Further, the children reportedly responded enthusiastically to the course, and there were no complaints from adults in the community. Evidence on the benefits to mental health is minimal, however. Other efforts in this direction are represented in the works of Sugarman (1965) and Limbacher (1967).

Units.   The third approach, the use of mental health units, is viewed by Kaplan as a compromise between the other two approaches. These units, which are built around problems at various stages of development, become an integral part of courses already in the curriculum and provide consistent and systematic mental health instruction. The Ojemann Projects, which used special units in addition to revised basic text material, serve as an example of this approach.

Since 1941, Ojemann and his associates have developed and evaluated a curriculum approach to mental health that emphasizes a causal orientation to the social environment. By incorporating behavioral-science concepts into a curriculum that focuses on the causes or motivations of human behavior—as opposed to the surface or behavioral aspects—Ojemann hopes that the student will be better prepared to solve problems confronting him now and in the future. The basic rationale is that a person who becomes more fully aware and appreciative of the dynamics of human behavior in general and of his own in particular is better able to cope with personal and social crises.

A dynamic approach involves an awareness of the probabilistic nature of human behavior, an attitude of flexibility and tolerance, and an ability to view a given situation from another's perspective. The approach, in short, seeks to foster a greater sensitivity to interpersonal relationships so that more effective interaction with the environment is facilitated (see Table 13–1). Many adults are capable of solving impersonal problems but fail to "use their heads" in coping with personal and social anxieties. Ojemann (1967) contends, and we are inclined to concur, that a sensible arrangement would be to lay a foundation in the causal or motivational approach to behavior in children starting in kindergarten. Then, as the child passes into adulthood, he can add to this foundation and apply such a base to the study of marriage and family relationships, employer-employee interactions, and so forth. This approach not only enables the child to surmount current crises but establishes a foundation for the solution of crises in later development.

How does Ojemann hope to establish a causal approach? For one thing, he stresses the need to educate the teacher "to live a causal approach in the classroom." As a modeling procedure, daily associations with a teacher who handles situations in an understanding way can go far in developing a causal approach to life.

One teaching strategy used during the primary grades consists of narratives in which the surface and causal approaches are contrasted. In kindergarten and first grade, the teacher reads the narratives. In the later grades, the child reads them by himself. Each narrative depicts a situation in which a character in the story responds in a surface way initially, but in a causal way after he has thought through the situation again. Realistic stories are used. To promote a more generalized approach, stories involve children both older and younger than those in the class, as well as children from different environments. Discussion focusing on the meaning and causes of the behavior in question follows each narrative.

At the elementary and secondary levels, the social sciences and English literature offer numerous opportunities to study the forces influencing the behavior of people. Even in areas such as math and science, the teacher can serve as a model for this type of approach.

**Table 13–1.   The Surface versus the Causal Approach of the Teacher
to Child Behavior**

Surface	*Causal*
1. The teacher responds to the "what" of the situation in an emotional way.	1. The teacher responds to the "why" of the situation objectively.
2. The teacher does not appear to think of the causes of behavior when he:	2. The teacher appears to be thinking of the causes of behavior when he:
a. Responds to the action rather than to the reason for the action.	a. Runs over in his mind possible reasons for the action.
b. Labels behavior as "good," "bad," etc.	b. Seeks the meaning of the behavior and avoids snap judgments or hasty interpretations.
c. Makes generalizations to apply to every situation, e.g., "all boys are like that."	c. Searches for specific and concrete clues derived from details of the behavior.
d. Responds with a stock solution or rule-of-thumb procedure, e.g., lateness is punished by staying in after school.	d. Varies the method; uses a tentative approach, i.e., will try other ways of dealing with a situation if one does not work. In seeking a solution, takes into account motivating forces and particular method used.
3. The teacher does not take account of the multiplicity and complexity of causes.	3. The teacher thinks of alternative explanations for the behavior. The proposition that behavior has many causes may be elaborated as follows:
	a. The same cause may result in a variety of behaviors.
	b. A variety of causes may result in similar behavior.
4. The teacher fails to take into account the later effects of the techniques employed and assumes the effects.	4. The teacher checks for the effects of the method he employs and considers its effects before using it.
5. The "surface" approach is characterized by a rigidity of techniques—essentially static.	5. The "causal" approach is characterized by a flexibility, a tentativeness, a trying-out technique, which accommodates new information as it is accumulated—essentially dynamic.

Source: J. D. Lafferty, D. Dennerll, & P. Rettich. A creative school mental health program. *National Elementary Principal*, 1964, **43**, 28–35. Copyright 1964. National Association of Elementary School Principals. All rights reserved.

Evaluations of this approach to date have been promising. The results of more than a dozen research studies indicate that an "appreciation of the dynamics of behavior is accompanied by significant changes in such dimensions as manifest anxiety, tendency to immediate arbitrary punitiveness, antidemocratic tendencies, conception of the teacher and tolerance of ambiguity" (Ojemann, 1967). There is some evidence, then, that education in the behavioral sciences can produce youngsters who are less anxiety-ridden, less arbitrary, and less authoritarian in handling personal problems.

Certain cautions must be noted, however. (1) For the most part, paper-and-pencil tests were used to assess program effects. It is conceivable that through prolonged exposure to the teacher, children in the experimental classes may have been inadvertently influenced to select the socially desirable or "healthy" answer. No observations were made to indicate whether the experimental groups behaved differently in ways other than their test-taking behavior. (2) Because a variety of procedures were used in training the teachers, it is not clear that the causal curriculum orientation was the most critical factor in producing changes. (3) The program has not had a wide impact on schools, in part because the training procedure is difficult to master and the training is not offered in universities. If the essential elements of the program could be precisely identified, training might then become an easier matter.

Perhaps as we have moved out of the "Sputnik era" into an era that places greater stress on the interrelationship between cognitive and affective development, we are witnessing a trend toward viewing mental health as an integral part of the basic curriculum. As ego psychologists like Bower continue to point out the importance of ego or cognitive processes as basic to successful coping, it is to be hoped that this trend will persist.

Traditional versus Progressive Education.   The mental health movement and progressive education were contemporaneous phases of the same wave of humanistic reform. Both movements aimed at correcting certain deplorable conditions and a better way of life. In many respects, the progressivists' goals for education were almost indistinguishable from the objectives advanced by mental health specialists (Tanner & Lindgren, 1971).

What is the psychological impact of school experience in traditional versus progressive education? In what might well represent the most extensive and careful work yet done on traditional versus modern education, Minuchin, Biber, Shapiro, & Zimiles (1969) studied the effects of two progressive and two traditional public schools on the cognitive and social functioning and the self-views of fourth graders attending the schools. The traditional schools saw their basic task as fostering the students' mastery of an established body of knowledge and skills. Accordingly, "teaching was directed to a body of knowledge, as organized in textbooks and curriculum syllabi, to be mastered at a level that would make it available to recall and replication in its original form and meanings" (p. 36f.). The modern schools viewed their task as that of promoting the children's curiosity, exploration, spontaneity, and self-direction and had in common a preference for instructional methods involving discovery, discussion, experimentation, and activity. The basic findings were that: (1) there is little evidence that modern schools make for superior or even for systematically different cognitive functioning in comparison with traditional schools. The students of the two types of schools were much alike with regard to problem-solving processes and expressions of degree of imaginativeness in non-problem-solving settings. Qualitative reports also suggested that the modern school pupils were more unified and effective in a group problem-solving task, in comparison with traditional school students. This finding may be due to the smaller class sizes in the modern schools, however. (2) With respect to social attitudes, it was found that children from modern schools tended to be more clearly identified with their schools than children from traditional schools. That is, peer group affiliation is fostered somewhat more strongly at the modern than at the traditional schools. There were few consistent differences, however, between the two types of schooling in terms of the students' ideas of right and wrong and in terms of whether students perceived adults as accepting-benevolent or as controlling-disapproving. (3) The third area of investigation entailed the child's self-views. Specifically, it was hypothesized that children from modern schools would have greater self-knowledge. Results for only one of the six measures designed to test this hypothesis supported it. In two other aspects of self-views, it was predicted that (a) children from modern schools would show less sex-role stereotyping and therefore less allegiance to their own sex role and (b) there would be differences between the two groups in terms of how they envisioned their futures and in their preferences for different stages of life. Although the investigators write as if their data support the distinction between modern and traditional schools, inspection of the results by and large suggests that the type of school attended made for little difference in the child's self-view. Thus despite the investigators' contention that the outcomes of this study were broadly consistent with their expectations, the actual data appear more largely to support the conclusion that the type of school environment, as implemented and evaluated in this study, had minimal impact upon the child's cognitive processes, social attitudes, or views of himself (Wallach, 1971).

This study raises a number of questions. Is the type of school attended really unimportant? Or are the measuring instruments not sufficiently sensitive to uncover these differences? Are these two constructs too complex and heterogeneous to be viable? Are there certain commonalities in both traditional and progressive schools that offset any differences between them? Does good, high-quality teaching within either educational philosophy facilitate personal competence? Does the influence of the community and of child-rearing practices in the home override any impact that the different types of schools might have? These and other issues must be settled before we will know the psychological impact of various kinds of school experiences.

The Role of Stress: Harmful or Helpful?

There are two divergent conceptions regarding the impact of stress on mental health. One, the traditional notion, views stress as something noxious and therefore to be avoided. The other regards stress as a force that can be used productively to build immunity to anxiety.

According to the traditional Freudian hypothesis, traumatic events during early life render the individual more susceptible to anxiety in adulthood.

Proponents of the view that conceives of stress as undesirable typically oppose such practices as early reading, the use of grading in assessment, and the emphasis on academic excellence. They express concern over the price of competition, the frantic pace in education, and the emotional risks associated with increased demands for scholastic accomplishment. They raise such questions as: Does exposure to anxiety-producing situations endanger pupil mental health? What happens to students when they are prized more for academic achievement than for any other reason? What are the consequences of prolonged exposure to moderate stress?

What are some of the more common stresses in the educational setting? One common source of stress centers around the curriculum. Subsumed under the general heading of stress-inducing curricular experiences are grouping policies, promotional policies, and evaluation policies (Ringness, 1968). Inadequate provision for individual differences also constitutes a major shortcoming. For students exposed to a curriculum that does not match their abilities, interests, and cultural backgrounds, school soon becomes like a prison. Less obvious but nonetheless quite real and pervasive sources of frustration have been identified by Jackson (1968) from his observations of life in the classroom. He discusses four unpublicized features of school that can irritate students—delay, denial, interruption, and social distraction. Students seem to spend a surprising amount of time waiting—to sharpen pencils, to empty full bladders, to go to recess, to have teachers check papers, and so on. Denial is experienced when questions are ignored and requests refused. Classroom discontinuity stems from student misbehavior, outside visitors, bells ending classes, and other petty distractions and interruptions. It is difficult to determine the impact of these four hidden aspects of the school life. While the episodes, in and of themselves, appear trivial enough, their significance increases when they are considered cumulatively over a 12-year period.

Activities for Reducing Stress.   Stress-reducing activities fall into three basic categories: (1) modification or elimination, (2) isolation of vulnerable children from stress that cannot be modified, and (3) interception of problems at an early stage (Lambert, 1964).

There are several ways in which the school can modify or reduce stress. Some examples are:

1. Shorten the pupil's school day.

2. Place him in a smaller group within the classroom or in another class.

3. Have a home-school conference to elicit parental understanding and help.

4. Use new teaching techniques in areas where a child has previously failed. For example, the use of counters in building arithmetic concepts, kinesthetic (tracing-sounding) approaches in spelling, and/or programmed learning materials may offer the child new opportunities for success.

5. Have a morning nutrition period to forestall hunger pangs that interfere with concentration in schoolwork.

In many cases it is difficult to reduce the cause of stress. Under such circumstances the following kinds of activities have proven helpful:

1. Assign the child to a resource room for part of the day.
2. See if medication is needed.
3. Use cubicles or "offices."
4. Excuse the student from stress-producing activities.
5. Eliminate grading for the time being, substituting charts of the child's progress.

Schools can also do much to intercept problems early in an attempt to prevent further difficulty. Some activities involving early identification and treatment of stress are listed below:

1. Provide screening programs for locating children with potential physical, emotional, and social difficulties. Follow up with diagnosis and recommendations for specific interventions.
2. Have an orientation program for parents and children when the children are beginning a new grade sequence or a new school.
3. Check pupil progress regularly for students who may fail or have difficulty.
4. Use remedial education as soon as the help is indicated.
5. Refer the pupil to other professional workers to obtain additional assistance.

Activities to Strengthen Personality.   While massive stress can be harmful and lead to unhealthy patterns of behavior, stress, when properly managed, can also stimulate growth and maturity. Here are some examples of ways in which the school can help build personality strength in students who experience stress:

1. Help students through minor traumas by role playing.
2. Get youngsters together in some type of nonacademic activity such as crafts, music, and field trips to emphasize mutual interests and development of special skills and talents.
3. Assist the child in his ability to relate to others by establishing a "mother," "father," or "big-brother" bank in the school.
4. Increase the youngster's motivation to cope actively with his shortcomings by finding areas of interest. For example, help adolescents learn to read in order to pass the examination for a driver's license.
5. Hold group problem-solving meetings in order to teach students to apply their intelligence to personal and social dilemmas.

Summary

Specialists recognize three kinds of prevention. Primary prevention seeks to keep problems from arising in the first place. Secondary prevention is analogous to treatment. Tertiary prevention is analogous to rehabilitation.

The need for preventive action is dictated by the scope of mental health problems, the lack of well-trained professionals, and the doubtful outcomes of treatment efforts.

Although the notion of prevention has become increasingly popular, it has not proved an easy concept to implement. Among the deterrents to action programs are such factors as the size and complexity of the mental health problem, the invasion-of-privacy issue, certain cultural values, and professional resistance.

Because it is impractical to work on all aspects of prevention simultaneously, workers have taken more limited actions. In general, these actions have centered around biological, sociological, or psychological approaches.

Parent education was discussed in conjunction with psychological approaches. The basic approaches to parent education center around mass media, group discussion, and individual guidance. Examples of the better-known programs were discussed.

The community mental health movement, which enables an individual to be treated within the community and in his natural environment, entails traditional treatment approaches as well as consultation, education, training and research, and child advocacy. There are difficulties in achieving full implementation of this concept but no one denies its appreciable potential as a reality based intervention strategy.

Four aspects of primary prevention efforts in the schools were presented: consultation efforts, early identification, curriculum approaches, and the role of stress.

Consultation refers to a process wherein two professionals (consultant and consultee) function as coequals in the solution of a work-related problem.

There are four types of consultation: client-centered case consultation, consultee-centered case consultation, program-centered administrative consultation, and consultee-centered administrative consultation. Differences and similarities among the four kinds of consultation were noted.

Experienced consultants offer the following guidelines: establish contact with those in power positions; develop a consultation contract; assess the organizational makeup; establish a sufficient degree of contact with consultees; and develop ways to minimize or reduce resistances to consultation.

The early identification of emotional and learning disability cases is receiving a great deal of attention, but a number of crucial concerns remain to be answered before screening procedures will become practical.

Curriculum approaches incorporating psychological concepts fall into one of three basic types—incidental instruction, separate courses, and units. Each approach has its advantages and disadvantages. Broader curriculum approaches have appeared in the form of progressive education.

Divergent views on the role of stress have been presented. Stressful experiences (the natural shocks of life) can serve the purpose of growth and health provided the individual is not overwhelmed. Strategies for dealing with students suffering from stress were presented.

References

Albee, G. The relation of conceptual models to manpower needs. In E. L. Cowen, E. A. Gardner, & M. Zax (Eds.), *Emergent approaches to mental health problems.* New York: Appleton-Century-Crofts, 1967, pp. 63–73.

Allinsmith, W., & Goethals, G. *The role of the schools in mental health.* New York: Basic Books, 1962.

Anderson, J. *A survey of children's adjustment over time: a report to the people people of Nobles County.* Minneapolis: Institute of Child Development and Welfare, University of Minnesota, 1959.

Arnhoff, F. N. Realities and mental health manpower. *Mental Hygiene,* 1968, **52,** 181–89.

Bogatz, G., & Ball, S. A summary of the major findings in the second year of Sesame Street: a continuing evaluation. In H. Clarizio, R. Craig, & W. Mehrens (Eds.), *Contemporary Issues In Educational Psychology.* (2nd ed.) Boston: Allyn & Bacon, 1974.

Bolton, A. A prophylactic approach to child psychiatry. *Journal of Mental Science,* 1955, **101,** 696–703.

Bower, E. M. The modification, mediation and utilization of stress during the school years. *American Journal of Orthopsychiatry,* 1964, **34,** 667–74.

Bower, E. M. *The early identification of emotionally handicapped children in school.* (2nd ed.) Springfield, Ill.: Thomas, 1969.

Bower, E. M. Mental health. In R. Ebel (Ed.), *Encyclopedia of educational research.* (4th ed.) New York: Macmillan, 1970, pp. 811–28.

Bower, E. M. The primacy of primary prevention. *The School Psychology Digest,* 1974, **3,** 4–11.

Bower, E. M., & Hollister, W. G. (Eds.). *Behavioral science frontiers in education.* New York: Wiley, 1967.

Briggs, P. F., & Wirt, R. D. Prediction. In H. C. Quay (Ed.). *Juvenile delinquency.* Princeton, N.J.: Van Nostrand, 1965, pp. 170–208.

Brim, O. *Education for child rearing.* New York: Russell Sage Foundation, 1959.

Broskowski, A., & Baker, F. Professional, organizational, and social barriers to primary prevention. *American Journal of Orthopsychiatry,* 1974, **44,** 707–19.

Caplan, G. *The theory and practice of mental health consultation.* New York: Basic Books, 1970.

Clarizio, H. F. *Mental health and the educative process.* Chicago: Rand McNally, 1969.

Cowen, E. Social and community interventions. *Annual Review of Psychology,* 1973, **24,** 423–71.

Cowen, E. L., Gardner, E. A., & Zax, M. (Eds.). *Emergent approaches to mental health problems.* New York: Appleton-Century-Crofts, 1967.

Cruickshank, W. *Psychology of exceptional children and youth.* (2nd ed.) Englewood Cliffs, N.J.: Prentice-Hall, 1963.

DeHirsch, K., Jansky, J., & Langford, W. *Predicting reading failure.* New York: Harper & Row, 1966.

Dunham, H. W. Community psychiatry: the newest therapeutic bandwagon. *Archives of General Psychiatry*, 1965, **12**, 303–13.

Evans, E. *Contemporary influences in early childhood education* (2nd ed.). New York: Holt, Rinehart, and Winston, 1975.

Fanshel, D., & Shinn, E. *Dollars and sense in the care of children.* New York: Child Welfare League of America, 1972.

Ferinden, W. E., & Jacobson, S. Early identification of learning disabilities. *Journal of Learning Disabilities*, 1970, **3**, 589–93.

Feshbach, S., Adelman, H., & Fuller, W. Early identification of children with high risk of failure. *Journal of Learning Disabilities*, 1974, **7**, 49–54.

Frank, G. H. The role of the family in the development of psychopathology. *Psychological Bulletin*, 1965, **64**, 191–203.

Gallagher, J., & Bradley, R. Early identification of developmental difficulties. In I. J. Gordon (Ed.), Early childhood education. *Yearbook of the National Society for the Study of Eduction*, 1972, Part II, **71**, 87–122.

Gallessich, J. Organizational factors influencing consultation in the school. *Journal of School Psychology*, 1973, **11**(1), 57–65.

Gallessich, J. Training the schol psychologist for consultation. *Journal of School Psychology*, 1974, **12**(2), 138–49.

Gardner, E. Psychological care for the poor: the need for new service patterns with a proposal for meeting this need. In E. L. Cowen, E. A. Gardner, & M. Zax (Eds.), *Emergent approaches to mental health problems.* New York: Appleton-Century-Crofts, 1967, pp. 185–213.

Gildea, M., Glidewell, J., & Kanter, M. The St. Louis school mental health project: history and evaluation. In E. Cowen, E. Gardner, & M. Zax (Eds.), *Emergent approaches to mental health problems.* New York: Appleton-Century-Crofts, 1967, pp. 290–306.

Gordon, I. *Human development, a transactional perspective.* New York: Harper & Row, 1975.

Gordon, I. *Parent effectiveness training.* New York: Wyden Press, 1970.

Haring, N. G., & Ridgeway, R. Early identification of children with learning disabilities. *Exceptional Children*, 1967, **33**, 387–95.

Havelock, R. *The change agent's guide to innovation in education.* Englewood Cliffs, N.J.: Educational Technology Publications, 1973.

Hawkins, R. It's time we taught the young how to be good parents (and don't you wish we'd started a long time ago?). *Psychology Today*, 1972, **6**, 6 28–40.

Haylett, C. H., & Rapoport, L. Mental health consultation. In L. Bellak (Ed.), *Handbook of community psychiatry and community mental health.* New York: Grune & Stratton, 1964, pp. 319–39.

Hereford, C. *Changing parent attitudes through group discussion.* Austin, Texas: University of Texas Press, 1963.

Horn, J. A new teenage course: learning to be parents. *Psychology Today*, 1975, **8**, 79–80.

Hume, P. B. Principles and practices of community psychiatry: the role and training of the specialist in community psychiatry. In L. Bellak (Ed.), *Handbook of community psychiatry and community mental health.* New York: Grune & Stratton, 1964, pp. 65–81.

Jackson, P. *Life in classrooms.* New York: Holt, Rinehart, and Winston, 1968.

Jacob, T. Family interaction in disturbed and normal families: a methodological and substantive review: *Psychological Bulletin*, 1975, **82**, 33–65.

Kaplan, L. *Mental health and human relations in education*. (2nd ed.) New York: Harper & Row, 1971.

Karnes, M., & Zehrbach, R. Flexibility in getting parents involved in the school. *Teaching Exceptional Children*, 1972, **5**, 1, 16–19.

Kessler, J. W. *Psychopathology of childhood*. Englewood Cliffs, N.J.: Prentice-Hall, 1966.

Knobloch, H., & Pasamanick, B. Prospective studies on the epidemiology of reproductive casualty: Methods, findings and some implications. *Merrill-Palmer Quarterly*, 1966, **12**, 27–42.

Koppitz, E. Bender Gestalt Test, Visual Aural Digit Span Test and reading achievement. *Journal of Learning Disabilities*, 1975, **8**, 154–57.

Kraft, I. Preventing mental ill health in early childhood. *Mental Hygiene*, 1964, **48**, 413–23.

Lafferty, J. D., Dennerll, D., & Rettich, P. A creative school mental health program. *National Elementary Principal*, 1964, **43**, 28–35.

Lambert, N. *The protection and promotion of mental health in schools*. Washington, D.C.: United States Government Printing Office, 1964.

Lambert, N., & Bower, E. *Technical report on in-school screening of emotionally handicapped children*. Princeton, N.J.: Educational Testing Service, 1961.

Lazarus, R. S. *Patterns of adjustments and human effectiveness*. New York: McGraw-Hill, 1969.

Lesiak, W., & Wait, J. The diagnostic kindergarten. *Psychology in the Schools*, 1974, **11**, 282–90.

Limbacher, W. An approach to elementary training in mental health. *Journal of School Psychology*, 1967, **5**, 225–35.

Lindemann, E., & Ross, A. A follow-up study of a predictive test of social adaptation in preschool children. In G. Caplan (Ed.), *Emotional problems of early childhood*. New York: Basic Books, 1955, pp. 79–93.

Lorion, R., Cowen, E., & Caldwell, R. Problem types of children referred to a school-based mental health prorgam: identification and outcome. *Journal of Consulting and Clinical Psychology*, 1974, **42**, 491–96.

Maitland, S., Nadeau, J., & Nadeau, G. Early screening practices. *Journal of Learning Disabilities*, 1974, **7**, 55–59.

Mardell, C., & Goldenberg, D. For prekindergarten screening information: DIAL. *Journal of Learning Disabilities*, 1975, **8**, 140–47.

Mearig, J. On becoming a child advocate in school psychology. *Journal of School Psychology*, 1974, **12**, 121–29.

Minuchin, P., Biber, B., Shapiro, E., & Zimiles, E. *The psychological impact of school experience*. New York: Basic Books, 1969.

National Association for Mental Health. *Facts about mental illness*. New York: National Association for Mental Health, 1966.

Newton, R., & Brown, R. A preventive approach to developmental problems in school children. In E. M. Bower & W. G. Hollister (Eds.), *Behavioral science frontiers in education*. New York: Wiley, 1967, pp. 499–528.

Ojemann, R. Incorporating psychological concepts in the school curriculum. *Journal of School Psychology*, 1967, **5**, 195–204.

Oppenheimer, E., & Mandel, M. Behavior disturbances of school children in relation to the preschool period. *American Journal of Public Health*, 1959, **49**, 1537–42.

Pasamanick, B., & Knobloch, H. Retrospective studies on the epidemiology of reproductive casualty: old and new. *Merrill-Palmer Quarterly*, 1966, **12**, 7–23.

Polk, K., & Schafer, W. Delinquency and the school. In Task Force on Juvenile Delinquency, *Juvenile delinquency and youth crime*. Washington, D.C.: Government Printing Office, 1967, pp. 222–27.

Reiff, R. Mental health manpower and institutional change. *American Psychologist*, 1966, **21**, 540–48.

Report of the Joint Commission. *The mental health of children: services, research and manpower*. New York: Harper & Row, 1973.

Rhodes, W. Utilization of mental health professionals in the school. In American Educational Research Association, mental and physical health. *Review of Educational Research*, 1968, **38**, (5).

Ringness, T. *Mental health in the school*. New York: Random House, 1968.

Roen, S. The behavioral sciences in the primary grades. *American Psychologist*, 1965, **20**, 450–52.

Roen, S. Primary prevention in the classroom through a teaching program in the behavioral sciences. In E. L. Cowen, E. A. Gardner, & M. Zax (Eds.), *Emergent approaches to mental health problems*. New York: Appleton-Century-Crofts, 1967, pp. 252–70.

Sarason, S. B. *The culture of the school and the problem of change*. Boston: Allyn & Bacon, 1971.

Stendler, C. Sixty years of child training practices: revolution in the nursery. *Journal of Pediatrics*, 1950, **36**, 122–34.

Sugarman, D. *Seven stories for growth: a tool for emotional education*. New York: Pittman Publishing Corp., 1965.

Tanner, L., & Lindgren, A. *Classroom teaching and learning: a mental health approach*. New York: Holt, Rinehart, and Winston, 1971.

Torrance, E. *Guiding creative talent*. Englewood Cliffs, N.J.: Prentice-Hall, 1962.

Wagenfield, M. The primary prevention of mental illness: A sociological perspective. *Journal of Health and Social Behavior*, 1972, **13**, 195–203.

Wallach, M. Essay review on the psychological impact of school experience. *Harvard Educational Review*, 1971, **41**, 2, 230–39.

Wissink, J., Kass, C., & Ferrell, W. A Bayesian approach to the identification of children with learning disabilities. *Journal of Learning Disabilities*, 1975, **8**, 158–66.

Zax, M., & Cowen, E. *Abnormal psychology: changing conceptions*. New York: Holt, Rinehart, and Winston, 1972.

Zax, M., & Specter, G. *An introduction to community psychology*. New York: Wiley, 1974.

Suggested Readings

Beiser, A., & Green, R. *Mental health consultation and education*. Palo Alto, Calif.: National Press Books, 1972.

Bessell, H., & Palomares, U. *Methods in human development*. San Diego: Human Development Training Institute, 1967.

Jones, R. *Fantasy and feeling in education*. New York: New York University Press, 1968.

Lesser, G. *Children and television: Lessons from Sesame Street*. New York: Vintage Press, 1975.

Todd, K. *Promoting mental health in the classroom—a handbook for teachers*. Washington, D.C.: National Institute of Mental Health, 1973.

Appendix

A Summary of Studies on General Maladjustment of Children in Grades K-12

Investigator(s)	School Location	Grade Levels	Race and/or Class	Method	Population at Risk	School Maladjustment	Clinical Maladjustment	Referral
Haggerty (1925)[a]	Minneapolis, Minnesota	1–8	Children from one of the "better industrial districts."	Teachers rated children on 16 "undesirable" behaviors.	801	51.0		
Wickman (1929)	Cleveland, Ohio	1–6	"Representative public school."	Teachers rated children on 51 behaviors.	874	53.0[b]		
				A scale of overall adjustment.			7.0	
Hildreth (1929)	Lincoln School, New York City	1–12	Unknown.	Teachers used 7 criteria to identify "problem pupils."	500		8.0	
McClure (1929)	Toledo, Ohio	1–8	All children in elementary schools in the city.	Teachers were asked to identify children who "should be referred to the Juvenile Adjustment Agency."	26,364			2.0
Yourman (1932)	New York City, New York	K–8	Children from highest, average, and lowest socio-economic levels of city; ethnically diverse.	Teachers rated children on a scale of overall adjustment in school.	13,761		11.0	
Snyder (1934)	Jersey City, New Jersey	K–8	Schools representative of city's population; included children of "native-born," "Polish-born," and "Italian-born" parents; also blacks.	Teachers identified pupils they considered to be "problems" and gave reasons for their choices.	13,632		6.9	
Young-Masten (1938)	New Haven, Connecticut	K–8	All children in elementary schools in the city.	Teachers were asked to identify children most seriously maladjusted and to give reasons for choice.	11,150		10.0	

Study	Location	Grade	Sample	N	%	%	Method
(1942b)	Ohio	4–6		1,52?	12.0	12.0	modified H-O-W[c] schedule; 9 other criteria, including peer and observer ratings, used.
Mangus (1949)	Miami County, Ohio	3 & 6	Children, village and rural. County "fairly typical of counties in western Ohio."	1,229	28.0	28.1[d] / 18.8[e]	Teachers rated children on 7-point scale of adjustment. Combined score from teachers' ratings and from sociometric and personality tests.
Glidewell et al. (1959)	St. Louis County, Missouri	3	Children, white; all social classes included.	830	28.0	8.2	Teachers' ratings on overall adjustment of the children; 4 categories.
Bower et al. (1958)	California	4–6	All social classes; distribution of occupations of parents representative of state as a whole.	5,587	23.9	*[f]	Teachers' ratings on overall adjustment, 3 categories.
Glidewell (1961)	St. Louis County, Missouri	3	Children, white; all social classes included.	530		2.0	Teachers referred children for professional help.
Morse (1961)	Communities in Michigan, excluding Detroit	K–12	Unknown.		3.0 to 12.0		Unknown.
Turner (1962)	St. Louis, Missouri	3 & 4	Blacks and whites; middle and lower classes.	2,017	32.8		Teachers were asked to assess adjustment and give reason for judgment.

[a] For bibliographical citations, see Glidewell & Swallow (1968).

[b] Wickman's 53% and Haggerty's 51% refer to rates for children who gave evidence of one or more of the "undesirable" behaviors rated.

[c] For an explanation of this schedule, no longer in use, see Rogers (1942b) in Glidewell & Swallow (1968).

[d] Teachers were urged to put 10% of their students in the lowest place on scale.

[e] Had Mangus used "6" as a cut-off on his composite instead of "7," 11.1% of the children would have been judged clinically maladjusted....

[f] Bower et al. suggested that at least 3 children in an average classroom are "emotionally disturbed." Their estimate of clinical maladjustment seems to be about 10%, but which data provide the bases for their estimate are not clear.

Source: Adapted from J. Glidewell & C. Swallow. The prevalence of maladjustment in elementary schools. Chicago: University of Chicago Press, 1968.

Investigator(s)	School Location	Grade Levels	Race and/or Class	Method	Population at Risk	School Maladjustment	Clinical Maladjustment	Referral
Gordon[g] (1962)	Middlesex County, New Jersey	K–6	Entire range of social classes; about 15% black.	Teachers rated children on 5-point scale of adjustment.	53,995		11.3	
Cowen et al. (1963)	Rochester, New York	1–3	Upper lower-class, ethnically representative except for substantial underweighting of Jews and blacks.	Teachers' ratings of ability and their discussions with mental health team entered into assessment of adjustment based on many criteria.	108	37.0		
Gordon (1963)	Key School, Philadelphia	K–6	Working class; about 40% black.	Teachers rated children on 5-point scale of adjustment.	553		18.6	
				Bower Lambert screening device.[h]			10.6	
Gordon (1963)	Jamesburg, New Jersey	K–6	Lower middle-class; about 10% black.	Teachers rated children on 5-point scale of adjustment.	455		11.8	
				Bower Lambert screening device.			20.2	
Lichtenstein (1963)	Baltimore, Maryland	1–6	Unknown, some variation.	Teachers identified pupils according to 4 criteria of adjustment.	16,748		9.9	
Woolf (1964)	Hunterdon County, New Jersey	K–8	Sample mostly white.	Teachers used Gordon's 5-point scale of adjustment.	9,618		13.3	
Mental Health Research Unit (1964)	Onondaga County, New York	2–4	Unknown, nonurban, some variation.	Teachers identified "problem" and "emotionally disturbed" children.	6,788	15.3	7.6	

Study	Location	Grades	Sample	Criteria	N	%	%	%
Springfield Services Department (1965)	Springfield, New Jersey	K–8	Sample mostly white.	Teachers used Gordon's 5-point scale of adjustment.	2,182		12.7	
Cowen et al. (1966)	Rochester, New York	1–3	Upper lower-class, ethnically representative except for substantial underweighting of Jews and blacks.	Teachers' ratings of ability and their discussion with mental health team entered into assessment of adjustment based on many criteria.	103	30.0		
Stennett (1966)	Rural northern Minnesota	4–6	Rural, white.	Modified version of Bower screening instrument.	333		22.0	
Maes[i] (1966)	Lansing, Michigan	4–6	Unknown.	Mental health specialists in child-guidance clinic identified children in need of therapy.	588			6.9
White & Charry[j] (1966)	Westchester County, New York	K–12	"Representative of the higher-income, outer rings which encircle many of our large cities."	Children referred to school psychologists by teachers parents, and others.	49,918			4.8
Kellam & Schiff (1967)	Woodlawn area of Chicago, Illinois	1	Black, lower-class, "deprived."	Teachers rated children on scale of "global adaptation."	2,010	69.3		
Approximations (weighted means):						30.2	10.5	3.8

[a] Gordon, in a personal communication, supplied race and social-class data for his three studies; he also supplied information about race for the Hunterdon County, New Jersey, and Springfield, New Jersey, studies.

[h] This device consists of teacher, peer, and self-report tests.

[i] Because the "referral" children were identified first and then studied with their classmates in this study, this rate is likely to be an overestimate.

[j] In this study, each participating school had a school psychologist on the staff. This degree of availability of school psychologists is unusual and presented an optimum for referral.

Glossary

a—prefix denoting without or absence (alexia means inability to read)

achievement motivation—the need to do something well that is influenced by an expectancy of success or a fear of failure.

adaptive behavior—the degree to which an individual meets standards for independence and responsibility for his age and social group.

aggression—behavior designed to hurt other people or to destroy some aspect of the environment.

agraphia—inability to write.

anomaly—growth, development, or formation that differs from the usual.

anoxia—decreased amount of oxygen carried by the bloodstream.

antecedents—conditions or events that precede a response and are observed to be associated with its occurrence.

anthropologist—a specialist in the study of physical, cultural, and social characteristics of mankind.

antidepressants—psychoactive drugs that reduce anxiety and discouragement while increasing struggle, defensive fighting, and responses to stimuli.

anxiety—apprehensiveness or uneasiness with physiological correlates, the source of which may be largely unrecognized.

aphasia—inability to understand or formulate words in speech or writing, presumably as a consequence of central nervous system injury.

assertion training—techniques used with passive individuals to promote confident and constructively aggressive behavior.

astereognosis—inability to identify objects by touch.

ataxia—inability to make purposeful motor responses.

audiometry—the measurement of sound, especially that in the human speech range.

aversion—an intense dislike or repugnance.

barbiturates—psychoactive drugs having a general sedative effect.

behavioral analysis—the diagnostic methodolgy used in conjunction with behavior modification.

behavioral constriction—a potential by-product of the use of punishment involving inhibition of socially desirable behaviors and development of personal rigidity.

behavior formation techniques—strategies designed to promote learning and maintaining of new behaviors.

behavior modification—use of learning theory principles to bring about changes in specified target behaviors.

Benzedrine—a central nervous system stimulant.

bicultural—referring to the blending of two cultures representatively.

brain-injured child—child who before, during, or after birth has received an injury to or suffered an infection of the brain. As a result of such organic impairment, there may be disturbances that prevent or impede the normal learning process.

brain syndromes—a generic term for a system of acute and chronic conditions, variously reversible and irreversible, resulting from physiological impairment and intoxication of the brain.

caseworker—one engaged in the amelioration of personal or family maladjustments; a social worker.

catharsis—giving expression to painful experiences and emotions, especially in the psychotherapeutic process.

child advocate—one who actively pursues and seeks support for a child's rights and entitlements.

choreiform movements—involuntary irregular and jerking movements.

client-centered case consultation—consultation in which the consultant attends directly to the particular problem of the consultee.

CNS (or C.N.S.)—the central nervous system.

community mental health—a variety of approaches designed to meet mental health needs within the community.

compulsion—irresistible impulse to perform an act.

conditioning—a type of learning in which there is a pairing based on repeated simultaneous association in time or place or other similarity of objects, persons, or situations.

consultation contract—a joint plan outlining the objectives of consultation and the means by which they will be achieved.

consultee-centered administrative consultation—consultation in which the emphasis is on problems of programming and organization.

consultee-centered case consultation—consultation designed to improve the consultee's ability to deal with a particular kind of case.

conventional morality—a stage of moral development at which standards of morality are external but motivation to comply is internalized.

cretinism—a congenital deficiency of thyroid secretion resulting in generalized underdevelopment.

critical periods—periods of time in an individual's development when he is most susceptible to a specific environmental influence.

"culture fair" scale—a measuring technique constructed so as to minimize biasing influences of a cultural nature.

dependency—the social tie that develops between the mother and infant which may later be expressed in either instrumental (task-oriented) or emotional (person-oriented) forms; also termed *attachment*.

desensitization—a behavior therapy technique in which the individual is exposed gradually and systematically to frightening events, objects, or situations.

developmental deviation—a generic term referring to expressions of adjustment or coping problems beyond the normal range of difficulty.

diagnosis—the act of finding out what problem a person has, i.e., the symptoms, causes, prognosis, and treatment.

disjunctive—irregular, erratic, and uneven; appearing disconnected.

distorted affect—a generic term for a variety of conditions in which one's emotional responses is not stable or consistent with one's ideation or setting.

dominance—tendency for one side of the body and related organ systems to assume direction and control over those of the other side; for many persons, the right side (hand, eye, foot) dominates the left side.

double-bind theory—a concept of family relations in which the child is expected to make reasonable responses to confused or contradictory communications; responding to either set of conditions is painful for the child.

dys-—prefix denoting impaired or incomplete functioning or ability (dyslexia means impaired reading skill)

dyscalculia—impaired ability to calculate, to manipulate number symbols, or to do simple arithmetic.

dyslalia—impaired speech ability.

dyslexia—severely impaired reading ability presumed to stem from central nervous system dysfunction.

echolalia—parrot-like repetition of everything said to a person.

educational contracts—written agreements between the adult and child, specifying target behavior and contingencies of reinforcement; also termed behavior contracts.

EEG (or E.E.G.)—electroencephalograph, a tracing showing the pattern of electrical activity in the cortical areas of the brain.

ego—the self, or individual, which exists apart from others; organization of attitudes about the self.

ego psychology—a generic term for a class of theories emphasizing the role of the ego or cognitive processes in successful coping.

ego strength—one's ability to adjust and to cope with stresses of living.

electroconvulsive therapy—a biological treatment in which an electric current is conducted through the brain and results in convulsions.

emotionally disturbed—a term that refers to a child's unexplained *inability* (a) to learn, (b) to act as mature as his peers, (c) to achieve adequate social relationships, (d) to display confidence, and (e) to cope with stress; also termed emotionally handicapped.

encephalitis—inflammation of the brain caused by injury, infection, or poison.

environmental alteration—an approach in which the child is removed from his present family or environment and placed in a totally new situation, such as a residential school.

environmental modification—an approach in which the child continues to live with his family but there is some rearrangement of the surroundings.

etiology—the study of causes or origins of a behavior disorder.

eugenics—the science of improving the human race by a careful selection of mating partners.

expressive therapy—a generic term for a class of psychotherapies intended to evoke and treat the underlying causes of disordered behaviors; also termed evocative therapy; the emphasis is on talking things out.

extended family—social organization in which several adult persons, males and females, act as parents.

extinction—the weakening of a response by withholding the reinforcement associated with it.

extrapunitiveness—blaming others or expressing one's anger toward others.

factor analysis—a statistical method used to identify the minimum number of factors responsible for the relationships among characteristics.

familial—tending to manifest itself in family lines; thus, hereditary.

family therapy—a generic term for a class of therapies based on the proposition that disordered behavior is a function of the entire family rather than only one of its members.

filial therapy—a variant of nondirective play therapy in which parents are taught to conduct client-centered play therapy as it would be conducted by a professional therapist.

focal concern—a sociological theory of delinquency that ascribes delinquent behavior to the child's normal responses to lower-class norms of behavior, such as toughness, smartness, and high need for excitement.

follow-up study—a reevaluation of deviant individuals after a period of time has elapsed.

free association—a therapeutic technique in which the patient is asked to relax and verbalize every passing thought.

frustration-aggression hypothesis—the concept that aggression is a necessary and inevitable consequence of one's frustration.

galactosemia—a congenital condition resulting in incomplete metabolism of galactose with consequent mental retardation, cataracts, and liver damage.

generalization—the occurrence of a response under conditions different from those with which the response was originally associated.

genetic counseling—advice as to possible outcomes for children of parents whose familial history has been expertly appraised and studied.

genetic psychology—developmental psychology.

group psychotherapy—a generic name for a variety of techniques in which a number of patients are treated at the same time.

guardian—a person legally placed in charge of the affairs of a minor.

hallucinogens—psychoactive drugs that increase arousal and activity while impairing inhibitory control, perception, and information processing.

Hawthorne effect—an improvement in performance due to the increased recognition that one receives as a participant in a special project.

hyperactivity—a pattern of behavior characterized by a high degree of mobility and motor restlessness.

hydrocephaly—a condition in which fluids accumulate in areas about the brain resulting in enlargement of the head.

id—in psychoanalytic theory, a reservoir of all primitive emotional forces or instincts.

idealistic normality—normality defined according to the patterns of behavior considered most desirable.

infantile autism—a form of childhood psychosis involving mutism, indifference, repetitive acts, and general detachment.

juvenile delinquency—a legal term referring to antisocial acts committed by children.

lability—tendency to show rapidly changing emotional states; emotional instability.

laterality—tendency to use either the right or the left side of the body in tasks that require only one hand, foot, or eye.

life-space interviewing—the technique of holding on-the-scene, impromptu talks with the individual about troublesome incidents.

machismo—a life pattern in which masculine behaviors are dominantly emphasized.

matrifocal—describing a form of social organization in which the mother holds a dominant position or central authority.

maturational lag—delay in attaining a recognized stage or point in developmental sequence, such as ability to walk alone.

medical model—the conceptual system in which abnormal behavior is analyzed as if it were similar to the physical disease process; also termed disease model.

milieu therapy—a method of therapy based on consideration of the total environment in which a child lives.

minimal brain dysfunction (MBD)—mild neurological abnormality sometimes thought to be implicated in specific learning disabilities.

modeling—learning through imitation and observation of the behavior of others (imitation).

moral development—the domain of development involving changes in moral judgment, moral feeling, and moral conduct.

narcotics—psychoactive drugs that reduce arousal, activity, biosocial drives, and responses to stimuli.

negativism—a pattern of adjustment consisting of uncooperative and disagreeable behavior.

neurosis—an emotional disorder usually characterized by anxiety, guilt, and moderately severe incapacitation.

neurotic delinquent—one whose antisocial behavior is attributable to anxiety, unhappiness, and insecurity; also termed disturbed or individual delinquent.

neurotic paradox—term suggested for behavior in which there is a self-defeating element, such as the person who wishes to have more friends but feels too ill to attend a party or social function.

neurotogenic—contributing to the onset or development of a neurosis.

neurotropic—having a selective affinity for tissues of the nervous system.

obsession—recurring ideas that preoccupy an individual's thinking.

ombudsman—an official appointed to investigate citizen's complaints that governmental agencies may be infringing on the rights of individuals.

operant conditioning—management of the consequences of behavior in order to increase or decrease the frequency of a response.

opportunity structure theory—sociological theory of delinquency that characterizes delinquent behavior as the child's response when he is blocked from access to middle-class goals and material goods.

paraprofessional—one with less technical training who works along with and under the direct supervision of a fully trained professional to perform specific tasks.

parent effectiveness training (PET)—a course of training consisting of lectures, discussions, and role playing intended to offer a democratic "no lose" alternative to authoritarian and permissive child rearing.

passive aggression—aggression expressed as uncooperative, inefficient, obstructionist behavior.

patriarchal—description a social organization, as a family, in which authority is centered with a male adult, usually the father.

perception—the interpretation of sensory information, association of stimulus with meaning.

perseveration—tendency to continue with a task or activity without the ability to shift or change easily to another task.

personality disorders—conditions resulting from developmental defects or pathological patterns in the structure of the personality, involving little or no anxiety or stress for the individual.

phenylketonuria—a genetic disorder with associated impaired metabolism which, if untreated, results in mental deficiency.

phobia—a fear, especially one illogical and exaggerated.

placebo—an inactive treatment not designed specifically to bring about changes in behavior.

play therapy—a technique for analysis and treatment of children's behavior disorders that allows children to express conflicts through the use of playthings.

pleasure-pain principle—the concept that man is motivated by the avoidance of pain and the search for pleasure.

positive reinforcement—a stimulus that, if made contingent upon a response, increases the frequency of the response.

postconventional morality—a stage of moral development at which the standards and the motivation for compliance are internalized.

pragmatic—practical.

preconventional morality—a stage of moral development at which both the moral standards and the motivation to comply are external.

primary prevention—attempts to keep emotional problems from arising in the first place.

problems in living—a term associated with Thomas Szasz and intended to replace the designation   mental illness'' by presenting a conceptual alternative.

prognosis—the projected outcome or course for a given condition.

program-centered administrative consultation—consultation intended to improve existing programs or to develop new programs.

protective services—the assuming of temporary or partial guardianship for the purpose of making changes to assure the safety of a minor.

psychiatrist—a physician specializing in the treatment of mental illnesses.

psychoactive drugs—drugs capable of manipulating psychological and behavioral characteristics.

psychoanalysis—the Freudian theory of personality and technique for treating personality disturbances.

psychodynamic—pertaining to motivational processes.

psychoeducational approach—application of psychological and psychodynamic approaches in the school by school staff.

psychogenic—originating in psychological phenomena, i.e., in the individual's past experience.

psycholinguistics—field of study that blends aspects of two disciplines—psychology and linguistics—to examine the total picture of the language process.

psychopathic delinquent—a delinquent who manifests severe antisocial behavior; also termed sociopath.

psychophysiological disorders—conditions indicated by the presence of structural organic impairments associated with psychological origins.

psychosis—a severe behavior disorder characterized by disrupted thinking, inappropriate affect, and a loss of contact with reality.

psychotherapy—use of psychological methods in the treatment of emotional and behavior disorders.

punishment decrease—a decrement in the probability of occurrence of a response resulting from presentation of a stimulus contingent upon the response or from contingent removal of rewards.

reactive disorder—a condition consisting of responses to external stressful events; also termed *transient situational disorder*.

reality therapy—a method of therapy that emphasizes behavior in the real world and the client's responsibility for his behavior.

receptive language—language spoken or written by others and received by the individual. The receptive language skills are listening and reading.

recidivism—falling back into a life of crime.

residential treatment—a general term referring to treatment approaches carried out in an institutional setting.

retrospective study—a research technique involving selection of subjects on the basis of certain deviant characteristics and the subsequent reconstruction of their childhoods.

Ritalin—a drug, chemically related to the stimulants, that has a calming effect.

role playing—a technique used in therapy in which the client takes on the attributes and behaviors of others.

schizophrenia—a form of psychotic reaction involving disorientation, cognitive and affective disturbances, and withdrawal.

schizophrenogenic family—a family with an organization and set of characteristics likely to produce schizophrenia in its members.

secondary gains—advantages in addition to anxiety reduction that accrue to an individual through his use of neurotic symptoms.

secondary prevention—measures to shorten the duration and diminish the impact of a disorder; also termed *treatment.*

self-esteem—a positive and favorable concept of oneself.

serotonin—a hormonelike substance in the brain, blood, and smooth tissues. Abnormal serotonin metabolism may cause some psychoses.

sheltered workshop—a facility where light manufacturing is performed under the close supervision of a staff of specialists such as teachers, psychologists, and vocational counselors.

social engineering—a generic term for a variety of techniques involving manipulation of the social and physical environment for the purpose of fostering mental health.

social learning theory—a theoretical position that stresses the importance of reinforcement and modeling as determinants of interpersonal behavior.

social reinforcements—rewards rooted in interpersonal relations such as warmth and praise.

somatogenic—originating in bodily phenomena.

spontaneous remission—the disappearance of a behavior disorder without therapeutic intervention.

Stanford-Binet Intelligence Scale (Binet Scale)—a widely used scale for assessing school learning ability in individual examination of persons aged 2 through approximately 16 years.

statistical normality—a definition of normality based on what the average or typical person does.

status deprivation theory—sociological theory of delinquency that attributes delinquency to a child's inability to perform in accordance with middle-class expectations and pressures.

stereotype—a fixed and unvarying notion or conception of an individual or group of persons.

stimulant drugs—psychoactive drugs that increase arousal, activity, inhibitory control, and wakefulness.

stren—an ego-enhancing or growth-producing experience.

stress—physical and psychological pressures that can enhance or impair personality development.

subcultural delinquent—one whose antisocial behavior is attributable to deviant socialization, in contradiction to the values of the middle class; also termed *gang delinquent.*

successive approximations—a method of shaping a complicated response by successively reinforcing the individual for responses that progressively approach the target response.

superego—in psychoanalytic theory, the constellation of one's conscience and the moral values of society.

survival reading—reading that concentrates on being able to read essential-for-living materials such as driver's license examinations, job application blanks, income tax forms.

symbiotic psychosis—an early childhood psychotic reaction in which the child neither differentiates himself from the mother nor is able to function independently of her.

symptom substitution—the concept that when a maladaptive behavior is treated without also treating its causes, other maladaptive behaviors will inevitably replace them as expressions of the same causes.

target behavior—the specific behavior to be changed in conjunction with a behavior modification program.

taxonomy—a scheme or a system used to categorize behavior disorders; classification.

teacher-mom—a volunteer mother engaged in a day-care program.

temperament—an individual's customary mood or disposition.

tertiary prevention—rehabilitative efforts aimed at assisting the individual to live a useful life despite a degree of chronic impairment.

tic—involuntary contraction and twitching of an isolated small muscle group.

tranquilizers—psychoactive drugs, classified into major and minor varieties, that generally reduce arousal, inhibitory control, responses to stimuli, fighting behavior, and passive avoidance to varying degrees.

transference—the unconscious tendency to attribute to the therapist attitudes and feelings associated with one's parents.

transient situational disorder—a condition of temporary pathological responses to external stressful conditions observed in basically healthy personalities; also termed *reactive disorder*.

trauma—an ego-debilitating experience involving severe stress.

trisomy 21—a condition of generalized physical and mental underdevelopment, with recognizable physical traits (formerly known as "mongolism").

Wechsler Intelligence Scale for Children (WISC), Revised—a widely used scale for individual assessment of learning ability of persons aged 6 through 16 years.

XYY—a male genotype with extra Y chromosome that is allegedly associated with criminal and aggressive behavior in certain instances.

Author Index

Subject Index

Printer and Binder: Halliday Lithograph Corporation

80 81 7 6